Studies in Jāhiliyya and Early Islam

M. J. Kister

Studies in Jāhiliyya and Early Islam

VARIORUM REPRINTS
London 1980

British Library CIP data

Kister, M.J.
Studies on Jāhiliyya and early Islam.
– (Collected studies series; CS123).
1. Arabia – History
I. Title
939'.4 DS231

ISBN 0-86078-068-6

Published in Great Britain by Variorum Reprints
20 Pembridge Mews London W11 3EQ

Printed in Great Britain by Kingprint Ltd
Richmond Surrey TW9 4PD

VARIORUM REPRINT CS123

CONTENTS

This volume contains a total of 360 pages

PREFACE

The studies collected in this volume represent an effort to evaluate material that had been overlooked or not fully exploited in previously published research. They are based in part on unpublished sources, and touch upon social, political, cultural and religious aspects of the life of the tribal groups in the Arabian peninsula during the period of transition from Jāhiliyya to Islām. The relations between some of these groupings and Mecca are reviewed, and their attitude towards the kingdom of al-Ḥīra is examined. Attention is given to certain events recorded in the *Sīra* literature and some developments in early Islām are elucidated.

It is hoped that the discussion of these subjects may shed some light on the developments of the period, and will encourage further research.

I should like to express my gratitude to the editors and publishers of the journals and books in which these studies originally appeared for their generous agreement to this reprint. I am also indebted to Mr Amiqam Elad for the preparation of the index.

M. J. KISTER

Jerusalem

March 1980

I

MECCA AND TAMĪM

(ASPECTS OF THEIR RELATIONS)

The history of Tamīm in the times of the Jāhiliyya is of special importance. Information about Tamīm in Arabian sources point clearly to the close relations of the leaders of Tamīm with the kings of al-Ḥīra. But there was another centre as well, with which Tamīm was closely connected: it was Mecca. It may be ventured to say that Tamīm played a considerable role in the history of Mecca in the times of the Jāhiliyya and were quite helpful in the establishment of the dominant position of this city in the tribal society of the Arabian peninsula.

The examination of the contacts between Mecca and Tamīm may shed some light on the origin of the "tribal commonwealth" under the leadership of Mecca and on the ways of Meccan diplomacy in its tribal environment. A scrutiny of these data may lead to a revision of some opinions about the relations between Mecca and the tribes and to an elucidation of some events during the period of the struggle between the Prophet and Mecca.

The discussion of the relations between Mecca and Tamīm may be preceded by some remarks about the relations between the Arab tribes and al-Ḥīra at the end of the sixth century.

The second half of the 6th century was a period of fundamental changes in the relations between the tribes of North-East Arabia and al-Ḥīra. The defeat of the forces of al-Ḥīra, who took part in the raids against tribes and fought in the inter-tribal encounters—undermined the prestige of the rulers in the opinion of the tribes. Privileges of guarding of caravans granted to some chiefs caused jealousy and conflict between the tribes and led to clashes between them. Discontented tribes rose in rebellion against al-Ḥīra. Raids on caravans of the rulers occurred frequently and roads of commerce became unsafe; the rulers of al-Ḥīra began to lose control of the commercial roads and their prestige dwindled. The weakness of the rulers of al-Ḥīra and their Persian masters was apparent; troops of the Persian garrisons who took part in some battles on the side of the loyal tribes were defeated. A case of this kind is recorded by al-Balādhurī.

Wa-aghārat Bakru bnu Wā'ilin 'alā Banī 'Amri bni Tamīmin yauma l-Ṣalībi wa-ma'ahum nāsun min al-Asāwirati, fa-hazamathum Banū 'Amrin, wa-qatala Ṭarīfun ra'sa 'l-Asāwirati, fa-qāla:

Wa-laulā 'ṭṭirādi bi-l-Ṣalībi lasuwwiqat: nisā'u unāsin bayna Durnā wa-Bāriqi

"And the Bakr b. Wā'il attacked the Banū 'Amr (of Tamīm) at the "Day of al-Ṣalīb". With them were men from the Asāwira. The Banū 'Amr defeated them and Ṭarīf killed the chief of the Asāwira and said:

Were it not my drive at al-Ṣalīb—there would have been driven women of men between Durnā and Bāriq" [1]).

Equipment supplied by the Persians to loyal tribes was taken as booty by the victorious hostile tribes [2]).

Meanwhile the disintegration of the Persian Empire at the end of the 6th century must have been felt at al-Ḥīra. Al-Nu'mān, the last ruler of al-Ḥīra, seems to have sympathised with the Arabs and it is plausible that he might have come in touch with some leaders of tribes, attempting to make common cause with the strong tribes. In an apocryphal story the following saying is attributed to al-Nu'mān: *innamā anā rajulun min-kum, wa-innamā malaktu wa-'azaztu bi-makānikum wa-mā yutakhawwafu min nāḥiyatikum ... li-ya'lama anna 'l-'Araba 'alā ghayri mā ẓanna au ḥaddatha nafsahu ...* [3]). Nöldeke rightly stressed the fact that the dynasty of Lakhm

1) al-Balādhurī: *Ansāb*, ms. f. 105b.

2) See *Naqā'iḍ*, p. 581: *wa-kānat Bakrun taḥta yadi Kisrā wa-Fārisa. Qāla: fa-kānū yuqawwimūnahum wa-yujahhizūnahum. Fa-aqbalū min 'indi 'āmili 'Ayni 'l-Tamri*...etc. ("Bakr were under the control of Kisrā and the Perisans. They used to strengthen them and to equip them. They came from the governor (of Kisrā) of 'Ayn al-Tamr...").

3) Ibn 'Abd Rabbihi: *al-'Iqd al-farīd* I, 169.

seems to have become too independent in their attitude for Kisrā [1]). Rothstein quotes a passage from al-Dīnawarī in which Kisrā is said to have argued that he killed al-Nu'mān because al-Nu'mān and his family made common cause with the Arabs [2]). According to a tradition, recorded by Abu 'l-Baqā', Kisrā intended after the death of al-Mundhir to send a Persian governor with 12,000 Asāwira to al-Ḥīra. He changed his mind and decided to appoint one of the children of al-Mundhir after a talk with 'Adiyy b. Zayd [3]). Poetry of the Jāhiliyya fairly reflects the resistance of the tribes to foreign rule; poets praise their clans that they fought the kings [4]) and killed them [5]). Al-Nu'mānn must have been aware of chaos in the Persian Empire and of the rise of the power of the Arab tribes and might have planned a new line in his policy which did not accord with Persian interests. There must be a grain of truth in the suspicions of Kisrā. It seems that the dynasty of Lakhm was abolished because it could not be trusted. The Lakhmids became unable to secure the ways of commerce. They failed to prevent the Arab tribes to raid the territories of the Persian Empire.

Nöldeke suggests that the abolition of the dynasty of Lakhm facilitated the raids of the territory of al-Ḥīra by the Arab tribes [6]). Brockelmann considers the defeat of the Persian forces at Dhū Qār as a consequence of the abolition of this dynasty [7]). Levi della Vida assumes that "with the fall of this buffer state the door was opened to Arabians for invasion" [8]). But the door was in fact opened to Arab invasion because of the decline of the Persian Empire and of the rise of power of the Arab

---

1) T. Nöldeke: *Geschichte der Perser u. Araber*, p. 332, n. 1.
2) Rothstein: *Die Dynastie der Laḫmiden*, pp. 116-117.
3) Abū 'l-Baqā': *Manāqib*, ms. f. 106a.
4) See Levi della Vida: *Pre-Islamic Arabia (The Arab Heritage)*, p. 50.
5) See al-Zubayr b. Bakkār: *Nasab Quraysh* I, 26:
Al-qātilīna min al-Manādhiri sab'atan
fī 'l-kahfi fauqa wasā'idi l-rayḥāni
(said in praise of the Banū Ḥarmala. The *al-Manādhira* are explained as "al-Nu'mān b. al-Mundhir and his kin").
6) T. Nöldeke, *op. cit.*, *ib.*
7) C. Brockelmann: *History of the Islamic Peoples*, p. 8.
8) Levi della Vida, *op. cit.*, p. 51.

tribes. Persian garrisons were not able to prevent the raids of the tribes and Persian troops were defeated by troops of Arab tribes.

The Arab tribes, disappointed by the policy of al-Ḥīra and Persia, and aware of the weakness of the client kingdom began to look for a body politic of their own with a competent leadership. This was created by the emergence of a new idea of an eqalitarian association, based on common interest: "The Commonwealth of Mecca".

The traditions about this period of the establishment of the power of Mecca, although scanty, give us a rough idea of the stages of this development.

A concise account of Muḥammad b. Sallām [1]) furnishes an introduction to the problem. The Quraysh were merchants. Their trade did not, however, exceed the boundaries of Mecca. The foreign merchants brought their merchandise and the merchants of Mecca sold the wares to the inhabitants of Mecca and the neighbouring tribes. Such was their trade till Hāshim b. ʿAbd Manāf went to Syria and alighted (in the territory) of the Emperor (Qayṣar). He slaughtered every day a sheep and prepared a broth with crumbled bread for the neighbouring people. Thus he gained his nickname "Hāshim", "the crumbler of the bread in the broth" [2]). (His name was in fact ʿAmr.) He was invited by the Emperor and used to visit him. When he realised that he had gained his favour, he asked him to give the merchants of Mecca a letter of safe conduct for themselves and their merchandise. They would bring leathers and clothes from the Ḥijāz to Syria, which would be cheaper for the inhabitants of Syria. The Emperor granted him the requested letter of safe conduct for the merchants from Mecca, visiting Syria. On his way back he met the chiefs of the tribes he passed, and secured from them the *īlāf*, the pact of security in their tribal areas, yet without concluding an

---

1) al-Qālī: *Dhayl al-amālī*, p. 200; al-Kalāʿī: *al-Iktifāʾ* I, 207-209; Muhammad Hamidullah: *Al-īlāf* ou les rapports economic—diplomatiques de la Mecque pre Islamique (*Mélanges Louis Massignon*, II, 293 seq.); idem: *Muslim Conduct of State*, 102; Ẓāfir al-Qāsimī: *al-Īlaf wa-l-maʿūnāt ghayru ʾl-mashrūṭa*, RAAD, XXXIV, pp. 243-255.

2) For another explanation of this nickname see Caetani: *Annali* I, 109-110 (90).

alliance. The merchants of Quraysh would carry the goods to Syria, paying the Bedouins their capital and their profit (scil. for their goods) [1]). Hāshim himself went out with the merchants of Mecca in order to carry out the provisions of the treaties concluded with the tribes. He led the Meccan merchants to Syria and settled them in Syrian towns. He died on this journey at Ghazza. Al-Muṭṭalib b. ʿAbd Manāf went to al-Yaman and gained a similar charter for the merchants of Quraysh from the rulers of al-Yaman and *īlāf* from the chiefs. He died in Radmān. ʿAbd Shams b. ʿAbd Manāf went to Abyssinia and on his way gained the *īlāf*. Naufal, the youngest of the brothers, got the charter from the Persian Emperor (Kisrā) and *īlāf* from the tribal chiefs (on the way to Persia). He then went back to ʿIrāq and died in Salmān. Quraysh afterwards developed their trade. Quraysh developed their trade in the period of the Jāhiliyya and their wealth increased. It was the Banū ʿAbd Manāf to whom Quraysh in Jāhiliyya were mostly indebted (for their deed).

Ibn Saʿd records the story of Hāshim who got the *īlāf* and the charters of the rulers [2]). The charters of the rulers are rendered by al-Qālī *ʿahd* or *amān*. Ibn Saʿd uses the term *ḥilf*. Muḥ. b. Ḥabīb uses (in the chapter of the *īlāf*) the word *īlāf* for the charters and the agreements with the chiefs of the tribes [3]).

Al-Balādhurī uses in his report about the *īlāf* the expression *ʿiṣam* for

---

1) Muh. Hamidullah translates *wa-ʿalā anna Qurayshan taḥmilu lahum* (so in the text of *al-Munammaq*; the text of al-Qālī has *ilayhim*) *baḍāʾiʿa fa-yakfūnahum ḥumlānahā wa-yuʾaddūna ilayhim ruʾūsa amwālihim wa-ribḥahum* as follows:

> „et leur remettraient la prix réalisée, sans pour autant les charger des pais ou déduire des commisions . ."; he renders the passage into English as follows: ". . promised . . to carry their goods as agents without commission for commercial purposes or otherwise concluded treaties of friendship . ."

This translation seems to be inaccurate.

2) Ibn Saʿd: *Ṭabaqāt* I, 75-80 (ed. Beirut); a tradition told on the authority of ʿAbdallah b. Naufal b. al-Ḥārith (see Ibn Ḥajar: *al-Iṣāba*, No. 4994) states that Hāshim wrote to al-Najāshī (the king of Abyssinia) asking him to grant a charter for the merchants of Mecca. The economic base of the *īlāf* is here recorded as follows: . . . *ʿalā an taḥmila Qurayshun baḍaʾiʿahum wa-lā kirāʾa ʿalā ahli l-ṭarīqi* (p. 78). This helps to understand the passage discussed in the preceding note.

3) Muḥ. b. Ḥabīb: *al-Muḥabbar*, p. 162 seq.

the charters of the rulers. Naufal b. ʿAbd Manāf is said to have got the *ʿiṣam* from the kings of al-ʿIrāq [1]).

Al-Ṭabarī uses the words *ʿiṣām* and *ḥabl* to denote the charter. Naufal got the *ḥabl* from the Chosroes (al-Akāsira) and they (i.e. the merchants of Quraysh) frequented al-ʿIrāq and Persia [2]).

Al-Thaʿālibī records that Hāshim took the *īlāf* from the enemies [3]).

This phrase about the *īlāf* taken from the enemies is recorded by al-Thaʿālibī in another report, which essentially deviates from the narratives about the *īlāf* mentioned above [4]). Quraysh—reports al-Thaʿālibī—used to trade only with merchants who frequented the markets of Dhū Majāz and ʿUkāẓ during the sacred months and came to Mecca. The reason for this was, that Quraysh were devoted to their *dīn* and loved their *ḥaram* and their *bayt* and used to serve the visitors of Mecca to their advantage. The first, who went out to Syria and visited kings and made far journeys and passed by enemies (i.e. hostile tribes) and took from them the *īlāf* mentioned by Allah (in the Qurʾān) was Hāshim. Al-Thaʿālibī mentions his two trips (to the ʿAbāhila in al-Yaman and al-Yaksūm in Abyssinia in winter; to Syria and Byzantium in summer) and says about the *īlāf*: he took the *īlāf* from the heads of the tribes and the chieftains for two reasons: because the people of the *ḥaram* and others were not safe (of the attacks) of the "wolves of the Arabs" and the Bedouin brigands and men of raids and people involved

---

1) al-Balādhurī: *Ansāb*, I, 59; for the word *ʿuṣum* see al-Aʿshā: *Dīwān*, p. 29.
2) al-Ṭabarī: *Taʾrīkh* II, 12.
3) al-Thaʿālibī: *Laṭāʾif al-maʿārif*, p. 5 (ed. de Jong, 1867).
4) al-Ṭhaʿālibī: *Thimār al-qulūb*, p. 89 seq. The exclusiveness of the *īlāf* for Quraysh is attested in the report by the verses of Musāwir b. Hind:

Zaʿamtum anna ikhwatakum Qurayshun
lahum ilfun wa-laysa lakum ilāfū.
Ulāʾika ūminū jūʿan wa-khaufan
wa-qad jāʾat Banū Asadin wa-khāfū.

See *Ḥamāsa* (Sharḥ al-Marzūqī - ed. A. S. Hārūn), p. 1449, No. 605; comp. al-Balādhurī: *Ansāb* I, 89 (Nutayla about her son Ḍirār b. ʿAbd al-Muṭṭalib):

sanna li-Fihrin sunnata ʾl-īlāfi

and see al-Hamdānī *al-Iklīl* I/II, ms. f. 26a:

Fa-lā tuqṣū Maʿaddan, inna fīhā
ilāfa ʾllāhi wa-l-amru ʾl-samīnu.

in long-lasting actions of revenge and because there were tribes that like the tribes of Ṭayy, Khathʿam and Quḍāʿa, did not respect the sanctity of the *ḥaram*, and the sacred months whilst the other tribes performed the pilgrimage to the Kaʿba and respected the House. The *īlāf*, records al-Thaʿālibī, meant a sum that was granted by Hāshim to the heads of the tribes as profit while he undertook the transport of their wares together with his own and drove for them camels along with his camels, in order to relieve them of the hardships of the journey and to relieve Quraysh from the fear of the enemies. That was an advantage for both sides; the staying (scil. the Bedouins) were profiting, the journeying (Qurashites-scil.) were safe (guarded). Conditions of Quraysh improved.

Ibn Abī ʾl-Ḥadīd records two accounts:[1]) the account given by al-Qālī and an account of al-Jāḥiẓ recorded in his *Faḍl Hāshim ʿalā ʿAbd Shams*[2]). This account of al-Jāḥiẓ is explicit about the shares of profit given the chiefs of the tribes by Hāshim. (. .*wa-sharika fī tijāratihi ruʾasāʾa ʾl-qabāʾili min al-ʿArabi* . . . *wa-jaʿala lahum maʿahu ribḥan* . . .)

Al-Jāḥiẓ records another version about the *īlāf*: Hāshim imposed taxes on the heads of the chiefs of the tribes. These sums collected by Hāshim enabled him to organise the defence for the people of Mecca from brigands and tribes who did not respect the sanctity of Mecca[3]).

The account of al-Yaʿqūbī[4]) gives the already mentioned version about the four brothers who gained the *īlāf*. The account contains, however, a sentence, which gives a clue for the assessment of the validity of these agreements of the *īlāf*, concluded by Hāshim: After the death of Hāshim—says al-Yaʿqūbī—Quraysh were afraid that the Bedouin tribes might get the upper hand. This sentence indicates that the *īlāf* agreements had not been actually carried out. Quraysh feared that some tribes might refrain from carrying out the terms of the pacts. It was the energetic action of the sons of ʿAbd Manāf and the profits granted the chiefs which caused that the chiefs kept their obligations in connection with the *īlāf*.

---

1) Ibn Abī ʾl-Ḥadīd: *Sharḥ nahj al-balāgha* III, 454, 458.
2) al-Jāḥiẓ: *Rasāʾil*, p. 70 (ed. Sandūbī). 3) *ib.*
4) al-Yaʿqūbī: *Taʾrīkh* I, 278 (ed. Najaf I, 200).

Lexical explanations of the word *īlāf* examined by Birkeland render the word as "protection", "a pact providing security" etc. [1]) Birkeland states that the meaning of the word "protection" is not given in the commentaries of the Qur'ān, except Alūsī. This explanation is, however, given by Abū Ḥayyān [2]). Abū Ḥayyān quotes the opinion of al-Naqqāsh, that there were 4 journeys (i.e. they sent 4 caravans: to Syria, Abyssinia, al-Yaman and Persia). Abū Ḥayyān does not agree with the refutation of Ibn ʿAṭiyya and quotes for his argument the story of the 4 sons of ʿAbd Manāf, who got the *īlāf*. Abū Ḥayyān quotes the explanation of al-Azharī of the word *īlāf*, and the verses of Maṭrūd b. Kaʿb. (translated by Birkeland) [3]). The explanation of al-Azharī is given as well in the commentary of the *Maʿāhid al-tanṣīṣ* to the verses of Musāwir b. Hind. [4]): "a kind of protection by means of guarding (*Shibhu'l-ijārati bi-l-khafāra*)".

It may be said that the accounts about the *īlāf* outline the essential phenomena of the changes in Mecca. Mecca, a small centre for distribution of goods for the Bedouin tribes in the vicinity of the city, rose to the position of an important centre of transit trade. It was the merchants of Mecca, who carried the wares to Syria, Abyssinia, al-ʿIraq and al-Yaman. The family who laid the foundations for the revolutionary change was that of ʿAbd Manāf. The trade based on the pacts of *īlāf* was a joint enterprise of the clans of Quraysh headed by the family of ʿAbd Manāf. The pacts concluded with the tribes were based on a hitherto unknown principle of trade interest. It was not an alliance (*ḥilf*) with obligations of mutual help and protection. It was not an obligation of the tribes to guard the caravans of Quraysh against payment practised by the tribes in their relations with the caravans of al-Ḥīra. The *īlāf* agreements were set up on a base of share in profit for the heads of the tribes and apparently employment of the men of the tribes as escort of the caravans.

---

1) H. Birkeland: *The Lord Guideth*, p. 106-107; comp. al-Zamakhsharī: *al-Fā'iq* I, 40 (ed. Muḥ. Abū 'l-Faḍl Ibrāhīm-Bijāwi).

2) Abū Ḥayyān: *al-Baḥr al-muḥīṭ* VIII, 515 (Sūrat li-īlāfi Qurayshin).

3) Birkeland, *op. cit.*, p. 119; see al-Qālī: *Amālī* I, 241; al-Bakrī: *Simṭ*, p. 547-50; al-Sharīf al-Murtaḍā: *Amālī* IV, 178-79.

4) al-ʿAbbāsī: *Maʿāhid al-tanṣīṣ* I, 95 (Cairo 1316 AH).

One may assume that the *īlāf* must have contained a paragraph concerning the observation of the sacred months, namely the keeping of peace during these months and respecting the sanctity of Mecca (or rather the inviolability of Mecca). The *īlāf* meant in fact the acceptance of the "Pax Meccana" by the tribes, the acknowledgment of the position of the Meccans and the Meccan trade and the setting up of an economic co-operation based on common interest. That explains the peculiar passage in the account of al-Thaʿālibī about the pacts with the (hitherto) hostile tribes.

Birkeland, discussing the historical background of the verses 1-2 of Sūra 106, stresses the importance of the *īlāf* pacts and states that "their (i.e. Quraysh) financial skill and their possession of the sacred territory had made them the economic masters of Western Arabia about a hundred years before the Prophet [1])". But the statement of Birkeland may be extended to Eastern Arabia as well. The dimensions of the trade of Quraysh were very large [2]).

It is conceivable, that the tribal chiefs might have preferred to collaborate with the merchants of Mecca. In their co-operation with Quraysh their profits were more stable, they could establish closer relations with them and actually did so. They were welcomed in Mecca and could enter it without fear. In al-Ḥīra they were submissive and servile, in Mecca they could negotiate as equals.

The impression made by the enterprise of Mecca is vividly described in a story recorded by al-Yaʿqūbī [3]): A Kalbī tribesman in the service of a Kalbī woman (a merchant) on the Syrian border witnessed the arrival of a Meccan caravan in Syria. He gives details about the personality of Hāshim and his dignity, about the respect shown to him by the chiefs of Mecca, about his generosity and remarks: "By God, that is the true splendour, not the splendour of the Banū Jafna". It is a sentence which is remarkable: the glory of the Qurashī leader, his manners and

---

1) Birkeland, *op. cit.*, p. 122 seq.

2) See E. R. Wolf: The social organization of Mecca and the origins of Islam, *Southwestern Journal of Anthropology*, 1951, pp. 330-337.

3) al-Yaʿqūbī: *Taʾrīkh* I, 280 (201 ed. Najaf).

behaviour were much more akin to the Kalbī Bedouin than the aloofness of the Jafnī ruler. It is a sentence forming a prelude for the future.

A peculiar tradition, which seems to throw some light on the situation in Mecca in the times of Hāshim deserves to be examined. This tradition, quoted by al-Suyūṭī from the *Muwaffaqiyyāt* of al-Zubayr b. Bakkār [1]) is told on the authority of ʿUmar b. ʿAbd al-ʿAzīz. According to this tradition the nobles of Quraysh used to practice in the Jāhiliya the *iʿtifād* [2]). *Iʿtifād*—records al-Suyūṭī—meant that when they lost their property they used to leave for the deserts, where they pitched tents and patiently awaited death "one after another" (*tanāwabū*) till they died, before people might know about their plight. So things went on till Hāshim grew up and became a man of influence among his people. He summoned Quraysh and said: "O Quraysh, might goes with abundance, and you became the richest of the Arabs and the mightiest and the *iʿtifād* ruined many of you". He put forward his proposition which was accepted by Quraysh, to attach to every rich Qurashī a poor man. The poor would help the rich in his journeys with the caravans and "live in his shade by the redundance of his property". That would be the means to stop the custom of *iʿtifād*. They agreed and Hāshim brought the people together (i.e. the rich and the poor). When the event of Elephant occurred (that was the key of the Prophecy and the commencement of the splendour of Quraysh, so that all people respect them; in this year the Prophet was born) and when later revelations were revealed to the Prophet—God revealed to the Prophet ordering him to inform his people what he did for them and how He helped them against the people of the Elephant. "Hast thou not seen how thy Lord dealt with the owners of the Elephant?" [3]). Then He said: "And why did I do it, O Muḥammad, for your people, whilst they were at that time worshippers of idols? So He said to them: *Li-īlāfi Qurayshin* [4]). It means: Because of their mutual feeling of mercy and

---

1) al-Suyūṭī: *al-Durr al-manthūr* VI, 397 (Sūra 106).
2) in text *iḥtifād*, which must be a mistake.
3) Sūra CV.
4) Sūra CVI.

their mutual help. They were pagans. He freed them from the fear of the Elephant. "He fed them against hunger" means the hunger of *iʿtifād*.

The tendency of the tradition is to render the word *li-īlāfi Quraysh* as denoting *li-tarāḥumi Qurayshin wa-tawāṣulihim*. But the story itself, rather loosely connected with the interpretation of the *āya*, seems in fact, to reflect the situation before the *īlāf*. Al-Zubayr b. Bakkār had an outstanding knowledge of the social and economic situation of Mecca in the times of Jāhiliyya and this story may contain a good deal of truth. The tradition points to the fact, that before the action of Hāshim the caravans were sent by individuals. Before the *īlāf* were concluded the sending of caravans seems to have been very risky and in case of an attack of brigands or of a hostile tribe the tradesman, who invested all his capital, lost everything. It was the *īlāf* which made the journeys secure.

The proposition of Hāshim to include the poor in the enterprise of the caravans was a bold one. It meant to give the poor some shares in the profits as payment for their work or, probably, against investment of small sums by poor relatives.

This trend seems to be echoed in one of the verses of Maṭrūd b. Kaʿb: [1])

> *Wa-l-khāliṭūna ghaniyyahum bi-faqīrihim*
> *ḥattā yakūna faqīruhum ka-l-kāfi*
>
> "And who mix their rich with their poor
> till their poor becomes like an able (man to bestow his favour on needy)".

This idea of "mixing of the poor" (or inferior people) with rich and wealthy was an ideal of the Jāhilī society and is attested by verses [2]).

---

1) See above p. 120 n. 3; and see these verses as well: Ibn al-ʿArabī: *Muḥāḍarat al-abrār* II, 119; al-Ṭabarsī: *Majmaʿ al-bayān* (Sūra 106); al-Balādhurī: *Ansāb* I, 58; al-Yaʿqūbī: *Taʾrīkh* I, 202 (ed. Najaf); al-Diyārbakrī: *Taʾrīkh al-Khamīs* I, 156.

2) Comp. al-Qālī: *Amālī* II, 158; al-Bakrī: *Simṭ* p. 548; Ibn Sharaf: *Rasāʾil al-intiqād* (*Rasāʾil al-bulaghāʾ* p. 334) (Khirniq):

It is a significant tradition in which the ideal of the Jāhiliyya is reflected in care for the needy of the clan, whereas the embracing of Islam is considered as deviation from this ideal.

Nu'aym b. 'Abdallah [1]) of the 'Uwayj (of the 'Adiyy Quraysh) embraced Islam. His father used to feed the poor of the 'Adiyy. After Nu'aym had embraced Islam he was met by al-Walīd b. al-Mughīra al-Makhzūmī who said to him: "O son of 'Abdallah, you pulled down what your father built and you cut what he linked (by his favours), when you followed Muḥammad" [2]).

The account of al-Balādhurī about the *Ḥilf al-Fuḍūl* mentions a special obligation to help the needy arriving at Mecca with the surplus of the property of the people who entered the alliance (...*Ta'āqadū 'alā ... wa-muwāsāti ahli 'l-fāqati mimman warada Makkata bi-fuḍūli amwālihim*") [3]).

An Anṣārī poet, al-Nu'mān b. 'Ajlān while boasting of the deeds of the Anṣār for the Muhājirūn, says:

Wa-qulnā li-qaumin hājarū: marḥaban bikum
wa-ahlan wa-sahlan, qad amintum min al-faqri

Wa-l-khāliṭīna naḥītahum bi-nuḍārihim
wa-dhawī 'l-ghinā minhum bi-dhī 'l-faqri

and see Ibn al-Shajarī: *al-Ḥamāsa*, p. 56 ('Amr b. Iṭnāba):
Wa-l-khāliṭīna ḥalīfahum bi ṣarīḥihim
wa-l-bādhilīna 'aṭā'ahum li-l-sā'ili

and see al-Khālidiyyāni: *al-Ashbāh* I, 20; Ḥassān: *Dīwān* p. 308:
Wa-l-khāliṭīna ghaniyyahum bi-faqīrihim
wa-l-mun'imīna 'alā 'l-faqīri l-murmili

and comp. al-A'shā: *Dīwān* III, 35:
Wa-ahāna ṣāliḥa mālihi li-faqīrihā
wa-asā, wa-aṣlaḥa baynahā, wa-sā'a lahā

and see Ibn 'Abd al-Barr: *al-Istī'āb*, p. 300 (al-Nu'mān b. Bashīr):
Fa-lā ta'dudi 'l-maulā sharīkaka fī 'l-ghinā
wa-lakinnamā 'l-maulā sharīkuka fī 'l-'udmi.

1) See about him: Ibn Ḥajar: *al-Iṣāba* No. 8777 (he cared for the widows of the Banū 'Adiyy).

2) al-Bālādhurī: *Ansāb*, ms. f. 869a.

3) Idem: *op. cit.*, ms. f. 144a; another version is given in the *Sīra* of Ibn Hishām I, 141.

Nuqāsimukum amwālanā wa-diyāranā
ka-qismati aysāri 'l-jazūri 'alā l-shaṭri[1])

"And we said to the people who immigrated to us: Welcome and secured are you from poverty
We shall share with you our property and abode
like the gamblers of *maysir*, who divide (in shares) the slaughtered camel".

Traditions about Ḥakīm b. Ḥizām record that he used to distribute the profits of his caravans among the poor and needy of his clan[2]).

The traditions quoted above seem to reflect clearly the tendency of care for poor and needy in the clan. Hāshim, establishing the *īlāf*, could successfully expand the trade; rich and poor participated in the caravan. A caravan became a joint enterprise. Even if a merchant sent on his own risk a caravan—other merchants tried to join him and invest in his caravan[3]). The following remark of al-Qummī about the social conceptions of the Meccans and their care for the poor is remarkable.

Wa-kānat Qurayshun yatafaḥḥaṣūna 'an ḥālati 'l-fuqarā'i wa-yasuddūna khallata 'l-maḥāwīji[4]).

Hāshim seems to have expanded the tendency of care for the needy into a social principle. Al-Diyārbakrī records a tradition about Hāshim on the authority of Ibn 'Abbās, reporting that the people of Mecca were in a state of neediness till they were rallied by Hāshim for sending of the caravans to Syria and al-Yaman. They used to divide their profits among the rich and poor, so that the poor became like the rich[5]). Ibn Ḥabīb, reporting about the men of the *īlāf* says that through them Allah raised the Quraysh and turned rich their poor". (*Aṣḥābu*

---

1) Ibn Ḥajar: *al-Iṣāba*, No. 8747; Ibn 'Abd al-Barr: *al-Istī'āb*, p. 298.
2) al-Zubayr b. Bakkār: *Nasab Quraysh* I, 367 (No. 644).
3) Idem: *op. cit.*, I, 371 (No. 645, 646).
4) al Qummī: *Gharā'ib al-Qur'ān* (on margin of Ṭabarī's *Tafsīr*, Būlāq 1229 AH) XXX, 169.
5) al-Diyārbakrī: *Ta'rīkh al-Khamīs* I, 156.

'l-īlāfi min Qurayshin 'lladhīna rafa'a 'llāhu bihim Qurayshan wa-na'asha fuqarā'ahā . .) [1]).

One is inclined to find some resemblance between the "mixing of the poor and the rich" (mukhālaṭa) and the *mu'ākhāt* [2]).

The conclusion of the *īlāf* agreements was accompanied by the improvement of the internal conditions in Mecca and the provision of amenities for the pilgrims. The first houses in Mecca were built by Quṣayy [3]). It may be assumed that these houses were very modest. The cutting of the trees in Mecca formed a serious problem, because of the sanctity of Mecca. But Quṣayy ordered to cut the trees and to build the houses [4]). The houses seem to have been circular in order to avoid the imitation of the shape of the Ka'ba [5]). Mu'arrij al-Sadūsī reports that Zubayr b. al-Ḥārith b. Asad was the first who covered a house (with a roof). Quraysh demolished the house out of reverence for the Ka'ba [6]). It was Ḥumayd b. Zubayr b. al-Ḥārith b. Asad b. 'Abd al-'Uzzā who built the first square house in Mecca [7]). When he built his house Quraysh feared the punishment (of Allah). The rajaz poets composed verses:

> *Al-yauma yubnā li-Ḥumaydin baytuh*
> *Immā ḥayātuhu wa-immā mautuh.*
> "Today for Ḥumayd his house is built
> (This means for him) either his life or his death" [8]).

When he was not afflicted by punishment Quraysh started to build square houses.

---

1) Muḥ. b. Ḥabīb: *al-Muḥabbar*, p. 162.

2) Comp. al-Sulamī: *Ādāb al-ṣuḥba* p. 50: . .*wa-kāna* (*al-nabiyyu ṣal'am*) *yanbasiṭu fī māli Abī Bakrin kamā yanbasiṭu fī mālihi wa-yaḥkumu fīhi kamā yaḥkumu fī mālihi*".

3) See Abū 'l-Baqā': *Manāqib*, ms. f. 85a.

4) See Ibn Sa'd: *Ṭabaqāt* I, 71 (ed. Beirut); al-Balādhurī: *Ansāb*, I, 58; Caetani: *Annali* I, 103 (78); al-Ya'qūbī: *Ta'rīkh* I, 197 (ed. Najaf); al-Ḥalabī: *Insān al-'uyūn* I, 14.

5) al-Tha'ālibī: *Thimār al-qulūb*, p. 13.

6) Mu'arrij al-Sadūsī: *al-Ḥadhf min nasab Quraysh*, p. 54.

7) al-Zubayr b. Bakkār: *Nasab Quraysh* I, 443.

8) These verses are attributed to Duwayd: see al-Zubayr b. Bakkār, *op. cit.*, ib. n. 2.

If this tradition be true—the time of the changes in building of houses was the second half of the 6th century. The sister of this Ḥumayd was the mother of Ḥakīm b. Ḥizām. The son of Ḥumayd, ʿAbdallah b. Ḥumayd fought at Uḥud [1]). The time of the significant changes in the building of houses may thus be fixed in the last decades of the 6th century.

The nobles of Mecca vied in providing amenities for the pilgrims. Hāshim is said to have taken care to supply the pilgrims with food [2]), ʿAbd al-Muṭṭalib to have been the first who provided them with sweet water [3]). He dug the well of Zamzam in the times of Kisrā b. Qubādh [4]). The water of Zamzam, although having medicinal qualities [5]) was not palatable and was mixed by ʿAbd al-Muṭṭalib with raisins. He also gave the pilgrims milk with honey [6]). ʿAbbās continued the tradition of ʿAbd al-Muṭṭalib and supplied drinking water for the pilgrims. The Prophet drank from his *siqāya* and the drinking from the *siqāya* of the family of ʿAbbās is considered as *sunna* [7]). There are traditions about digging of wells and rivalry between nobles of Mecca in providing drinks for pilgrims [8]). Suwayd b. Harmī is said to have been the first who gave the pilgrims milk (to drink) [9]). Abū Umayya b. al-Mughīra al-Makhzūmī (*Zād al-rakb*) and Abū Wadāʿa al-Sahmī gave the pilgrims honey [10])

The traditions about the *īlāf*, about the improvements in Mecca, about the provisions of food and drinks for the pilgrims—all this points to the efforts to increase the prestige of the city and to secure the

---

1) See Ibn Hishām: *Sīra* III, 135; al-Balādhurī: *Ansāb* I, 319: he made an oath to kill the Prophet at Uḥud.
2) al-Balādhurī: *Ansāb* I, 60-61; al-Azraqī: *Akhbār* p. 67 (Wüstenfeld).
3) al-Masʿūdī: *Murūj* II, 46;
4) *ib.*
5) Rathjens: *Die Pilgerfahrt*, pp. 42, 45.
6) Al-Azraqī; *Akhbār* p. 70 (ed. Wüstenfeld); comp. Abū Dharr: *Sharḥ*, p. 42 (ed. Brönnle).
7) See al-Suyūṭī: *al-Durr al-manthūr* III, 219.
8) Comp. al-Muṣʿab al-Zubayrī: *Nasab Quraysh*, pp. 32, 197-198.
9) *ib.* p. 342; al-Zubayr b. Bakkār: *Nasab Quraysh*, ms. f. 153a.
10) Muḥ. b. Ḥabīb: *al-Muḥabbar*, p. 177.

pilgrimage and trade. Special arrangements were made for individual merchants proceeding to Mecca for a pilgrimage [1]). Elaborate provisions were made for the caravans for which consent of the tribes was gained.

In this system Tamīm played a considerable role. This can be gauged from some passages of the report about the markets of the Jahīliyya, recorded by Muḥ. b. Ḥabīb [2]).

Reporting about the market of Dūmat al-Jandal Ibn Ḥabīb states that "every merchant who set out from al-Yaman and the Ḥijāz asked for the escort of Quraysh as long as he travelled in the abode of Muḍar; for the Muḍar did not harass Muḍarī merchants, nor were they (i.e. the merchants) troubled by an ally of Muḍar. That was the accepted custom between them. So did Kalb not trouble them, because of their alliance with Tamīm [3]). The Ṭayy also did not harass them because of their alliance with the Asad. Muḍar used to say: "Quraysh carried out for us the obligation of religious duties inherited to us by Ismāʿīl" [4]) (i.e. bequeathed to us).

This report is recorded in al-Marzūqī's *Amkina* with important

---

1) al-Marzūqī: *al-Amkina* II, 166; see the translation in Muh. Hamidullah: *Le prophète de l'Islam* II, 606.

2) Muḥ. b. Ḥabīb: *al-Muḥabbar*, pp. 264-265.

3) Hamidullah in *Muslim conduct of state* p. 54 (101); "as they were allied (i.e. the Kalb) to the Banū Jusham" (evidently a misprint).

4) Hamidullah translates: Les Mudarites avaient l'habitude de dire (avec fierté) "Les Quraichites ont payé la dette de honte que nous avions contractée au nom d'Ismaël (par les guerres fraticides et par le bellum omnium contra omnes)" — *Le Prophète de l'Islam*, II, 600—This translation seems however to be inaccurate. In order to translate "que nous avions contractée au nom d'Ismaël"—Hamidullah must have read *mā aurathnā Ismāʿīla* which is an error. The phrase has to be read: *mā aurathanā Ismāʿīlu.* The sentence is of the greatest importance for the understanding of the attitude of the tribes towards Quraysh. For the correct interpretation of the sentence a passage from al-Kalāʿī's *al-Iktifāʾ* (I, 150) may be quoted. Al-Kalāʿī, discussing the qualities of Quraysh, records the following passage: ..*wa-kānū ʿalā irthin min dīni Ibrāhīma wa-Ismāʿīla min qirā l-ḍayfi wa-rifdi ʾl-ḥajji wa-taʿẓīmi ʾl-ḥarami wa-manʿihi min al-baghyi fīhi wa-l-ilḥādi wa-qamʿi ʾl-ẓālimi wa-manʿi ʾl-maẓlūmi.* The passage commencing with *min qirā* is an explanation of *irthin min dīn Ibrahim wa-Ismāʿīl.*—The passage in Marzūqī's *Amkina* II, 162 does not leave any doubt about the meaning of the sentence: *mā aurathanā abūnā Ismāʿīlu*, "what our father (ancestor) Ismāʿīl inherited us" (bequeathed to us). And comp. al-Majlisī: *Biḥār al-anwār* VI, 42.

variants [1]). Quraysh used to set out (to Dūmat al-Jandal) from Mecca. If they took the way of al-Ḥazn [2]) they did not require the protection of any of the tribes till they came back, and that was because Muḍar . . . etc. [3]). And when they departed from al-Ḥazn or went to al-Ḥazn they reached the waters (i.e. the abode, the pasturing places) of Kalb. Kalb were allies of Tamīm and therefore they did not harass them. When they went on to the lowland they passed the Asad and arrived at the Ṭayy . . ."

The account of Marzūqī supplements the report of Ibn Ḥabīb. The vague expression of Ibn Ḥabīb *fī bilād Muḍar* is here more precise. The road leading from Mecca to al-Ḥazn [4]), which was under the control of the tribes of Muḍar. The Ḥazn itself was the territory of Tamīm [5]).

The two significant accounts, of Ibn Ḥabīb and al-Marzūqī give some idea how the system set up by Mecca worked in the area of Mecca-al-Ḥazn and its extension. Two tribal units of Muḍar, closely linked with Mecca by the Muḍar alliance, Tamīm and Asad—made it possible, due to the alliance of Tamīm with Kalb (Quḍāʿa) and the alliance of Asad with Ṭayy (Qaḥṭānī), to Quraysh to send in full security their caravans and to control the trade on these routes. It is these two tribes—Ṭayy and Kalb—who were especially dangerous for Mecca, as the majority of these two tribes did not respect the sanctity of Mecca and of the sacred months. It is significant that al-Marzūqī records about the Ṭayy: " . .and (arriving in the territory of Ṭayy) they (i.e. the merchants) gave them some pay and they (i.e. Ṭayy) guided them (in the direction) wherever they wanted" [6]).

---

1) al-Marzūqī: *al-Amkina*, II, 162.

2) Hamidullah translates *fa-in akhadhat ʿalā l-ḥazni* "et s'ils prenaient le chemin montagneux" (*Le Prophète*, II, 604). That seems, however, not to be accurate.

3) There is perhaps some misprint or error; perhaps one has to read "au ʿalau ʾl-Ḥazn".

4) See Thilo: *Die Ortsnamen* p. 56; and see Yāqūt: *Buldān* and al-Bakrī — *Muʿjam ma ʾstaʿjam*, s.v. "Ḥazn".

5) See von Oppenheim-Caskel: *Die Beduinen* III, 164.

6) al-Marzūqī: *al-Amkina* II, 162.

The attitude of the Ṭayy and Kalb towards Mecca will be touched upon later.

Merchants proceeding to the important trade-centre of al-Mushaqqar had also to require the escort of Quraysh, because the road led through the territory of Muḍar. This harbour-city frequented by merchants from Persia, an important base of Persian rule—had a market governed by men from Tamīm [1]).

In examination of the accounts about Dūmat al-Jandal [2]) one may assume that the Tamīm played a most important role in the control of the roads to these two markets and in securing of the caravans of Mecca.

Some Tamīmīs frequented Mecca for trade. An iniquity committed to a Tamīmī visiting Mecca caused a conflict between the leaders of Quraysh. The story is recorded by Ibn Abī ʾl-Ḥadīd on the authority of al-Wāqidī [3]). Abdallah b. Jaʿfar contested in glory Yazīd b. Muʿāwiya in the presence of Muʿāwiya [4]). He asked him: "By which of your ancestors do you rival in pride? By Ḥarb, whom we sheltered or by Umayya..?" We are here concerned with the story of Ḥarb sheltered by ʿAbd al-Muṭṭalib, which is given as follows:

Quraysh had the privilege of priority in passing the ʿAqaba, when travelling. Anybody had to wait till they passed. Ḥarb went out one night and when passing the ʿAqaba he met a man from the family of Ḥājib b. Zurāra, proceeding to Mecca for business. Ḥarb leaned forward and announced his name and so did the Tamīmī. He stated to be the "son" of Ḥājib b. Zurāra. The Tamīmī passed the ʿAqaba together with Ḥarb. Ḥarb was enraged and swore that he would never allow him to stay in Mecca as long as he lived. The Tamīmī spent some time outside Mecca. But—as his business was in Mecca (*wa-kāna matjaruhu bi-Makkata*)—he decided to enter and enquired

1) Ibn Ḥabīb: *al-Muḥabbar*, p. 265.
2) See the article *Dūmat al-Jandal* of L. Veccia Vaglieri in EI².
3) Ibn Abī l-Ḥadīd: *Sharḥ nahj al-balāgha* III, 465; Ibn ʿAsākir: *Taʾrīkh* VII, 329.
4) See the account of this event in Daḥlān's *Sīra* I, 22 (on the margin of "*Insān al-ʿuyūn*"): the talk was between Ibn ʿAbbās and Muʿāwiya; and see Ibn al-ʿArabī: *Muḥāḍarat al-abrār* I, 179.

about the man, who could give him protection against Ḥarb. The Tamīmī (the "son" of Zurārā) entered Mecca at night and went to the house of ʿAbd al-Muṭṭalib. He recited a poem in which the event was recorded and the protection of al Zubayr b. Abd al-Muṭṭalib [1]) was requested. He was granted the requested protection. In the morning al-Zubayr b. ʿAbd al-Muṭṭalib summoned his brother, al-Ghaydāq, and they went out girded with swords, escorting the Tamīmī. Ḥarb met them, assaulted the Tamīmī and slapped him on his face. A quarrel ensued between the sons of ʿAbd al-Muṭṭalib and Ḥarb. Ḥarb managed to escape and sought refuge in the house of Abd al-Muṭṭalib who granted him protection.

This narrative probably points to relations between the Banū Hāshim and the Dārim. Tradition mentions the names of some people of Dārim, who were in touch with the Banū Hāshim. One of them was the *ḥirmiyy* of the Prophet.

The prestige enjoyed by the Tamīm in Mecca was based mainly on their strength and their services for the external trade of Mecca. The Tamīm were strong and their leaders were highly respected. The prestige of the leaders of Tamīm (of the branch of the Dārim) is reflected in a remarkable anecdote attributed to the Prophet: A man (a Muslim) married a woman from a lower social class and was reproached by his brother. The Prophet was told about it, he was told as well about the virtues of the woman whom he married. He said in a talk with the husband: "You are not to be blamed for not marrying a woman (so aristocratic) as the daughter of Ḥājib b. Zurāra. Allah brought Islam and made all men equal. A Muslim is not to be rebuked" (for such a marriage) [2]).

Some groups of Tamīm were even included in the body politic of Mecca. They were given a share in the Meccan dominance and contributed to increase the influence of Mecca in the tribal society

---

1) Al-Zubayr b. ʿAbd al-Muṭṭalib was the leader of the Banū Hāshim at the "Day of al-Fijār"; see Muḥ. b. Ḥabīb: *al Muḥabbar*, p. 169; Ibn Durayd: *al-Ishtiqāq*, p. 47; al-Balādhurī: *Ansāb* I, 102.

2) Al-Fāsī: *Shifā al-gharām* (Wüstenfeld, II, 141).

and its prestige. The organization we refer to is the organization of the Ḥums.

Ibn Saʿd counts as Ḥums: Quraysh, Khuzāʿa and people of the Arabs "born by Quraysh". (According to another version of Ibn Saʿd: "and the allies of Quraysh") [1]).

Ibn Isḥāq records as Ḥums: Quraysh, Khuzāʿa and Kināna; Ibn Hishām adds (on the authority of Abū ʿUbayda al-Naḥwī) the ʿĀmir b. Ṣaʿṣaʿa [2]).

Ibn Qutayba mentions in his *Maʿārif* as Ḥums Quraysh and people from Kināna [3]). But in his *al-Maʿānī al-Kabīr* he counts as Ḥums: Quraysh their descendants and their allies [4]).

Al-Jāḥiẓ counts as Ḥums: Quraysh, ʿĀmir b. Ṣaʿṣaʿa and al-Ḥārith b. Kaʿb [5]).

Al-Anbārī [6]) and al-Marzūqī [7]) count: Quraysh, Kināna, Khuzāʿa and ʿĀmir b. Ṣaʿṣaʿa.

Abū Ḥayyān in his commentary of the Qurʾān has the following list: Quraysh, Kināna, Khuzāʿa, Thaqīf, Khathʿam, Āmir b. Ṣaʿṣaʿa and Naṣr b. Muʿāwiya [8]). An almost identical list is given by al-Qurṭubī; instead of Khathʿam—he has Jusham [9]).

The L. ʿA. records as Ḥums: Quraysh and "whom Quraysh had born" (i.e. descendants of men or women from Quraysh), Kināna, Fahm, ʿAdwān, ʿĀmir b. Ṣaʿṣaʿa and Khuzāʿa [10]).

The lists of the Ḥums quoted above are contradictory. The examination of these lists shows doubtless that Ḥums included the Quraysh, the inhabitants of Mecca, and people outside Mecca. According to

---

1) Ibn Saʿd: *Ṭabāqāt*, I, 72.
2) Ibn Hishām: *Sīra* I, 212; al-Kalāʿī: *al-Iktifāʾ* I, 272.
3) Ibn Qutayba: *al-Maʿārif*, p. 269.
4) Ibn Qutayba: *al-Maʿānī ʾl-Kabīr*, p. 989.
5) al-Jāḥiẓ: *Mukhtārāt fuṣūl*, ms. f. 208 b.
6) *al-Mufaḍḍaliyyāt* XXXIV, 14 (Lyall).
7) al-Marzūqī: *Sharḥ al-Ḥamāsa*, p. 31.
8) Abū Ḥayyān: *al-Baḥr al-muḥīṭ* II, 63.
9) al-Qurṭubī: *al-Jāmiʿ li-aḥkām al-Qurʾān* II, 345 (*Sura* II, 189); and see Blachére: *Coran* II, 782, n. 185.
10) L. ʿA., s.v. "Ḥms".

Arendonk: "The Ḥums is the name traditionally given to the inhabitants of Mecca at Muḥamad's appearance in so far as they were distinguished by special customs during the Iḥrām from the other tribes, who were together known as al-Ḥilla". [1])—This definition has to be altered.

A detailed list of the tribes of the Ḥums is given by Muḥ. b. Ḥabīb. "Ḥums were—reports Ibn Ḥabīb—all Quraysh, Khuzā'a (because they had dwelled in Mecca and were neighbours of Quraysh), people being descendents of Quraysh ("born by Quraysh"), clans dwelling in Mecca.

Descendants of Quraysh ("born by Quraysh") were: Kilāb, Ka'b, 'Āmir and Kalb i.e. the Banū Rabī'a b. 'Āmir b. Ṣa'ṣa'a. Their mother was Majd bint Taym b. Ghālib b. Fihr. To her referred Labīd saying:

Saqā qaumī banī Majdin wa-asqā
Numayran wa-l-qabā'ila min Hilāli [2]).

and al-Ḥārith b. 'Abd Manāt b. Kināna and Mudlij b. Murra b. 'Abd Manāt b. Kināna due to their dwelling near Mecca. And 'Āmir b. 'Abd Manāt b. Kināna and Mālik and Milkān b. Kināna and Thaqīf and 'Adwān. And Yarbū' b. Ḥanẓala and Māzin b. Mālik b. 'Amr b. Tamīm, whose mother (of both of them) was Jandala bint Fihr b. Mālik b. al-Naḍr [3]). Some maintain that all the 'Āmir (i.e. 'Āmir b. Ṣa'ṣa'a) are Ḥums, because their brethren, the Rabī'a b. 'Āmir became Ḥums. And 'Ilāf i.e. Rabbān b. Ḥulwān b. 'Imrān b. al-Ḥāf b. Quḍā'a. And Janāb b. Hubal b. Abdallah [4]), from Kalb. His mother was Āmina

1) EI, s.v. "Ḥums".

2) See Ibn 'Abd al-Barr: *al-Inbāh*, p. 87; Labīd: *Dīwān*, p. 93 (ed. I. 'Abbās); Ibn al-Kalbī: *Jamhara*, ms. f. 120 b. (In *Jamhara*: *Majd bint Taym b. Murra b. Ghālib b. Fihr*. The term used in *Jamhara* is of interest: *wa-hiya 'llatī ḥammasat Banī 'Āmirin, ja'alathum Ḥumsan*).

3) Jandala bint Fihr b. Mālik b. al-Naḍr b. Kināna was the wife of Ḥanẓala b. Mālik b. Zayd Manāt b. Tamīm. She gave birth to Qays, Yarbū', Rabī'a and 'Amr—the sons of Ḥanẓala b. Mālik b. Zayd Manāt. After the death of Ḥanẓala b. Mālik she married Mālik b. 'Amr b. Tamīm and gave birth to Māzin, Ghaylān, Aslam and Ghassān—the sons of Mālik b. 'Amr. See: Ibn al-Kalbī: *Jamhara*, ms. ff. 62a, 90a; al-Balādhurī: *Ansāb*, ms. f. 958b.

4) See Ibn Durayd: *al-Ishtiqāq*, p. 540.

bint Rabīʿa b. ʿĀmir b. Ṣaʿṣaʿa; her mother was Majd bint Taym al-Adram b. Ghālib b. Fihr" [1]).

The list of Ibn Ḥabīb shows a peculiar fact: the tribes allied in the organization of the Ḥums are of different origin and belong to various tribal divisions. The ʿĀmir b. Ṣaʿṣaʿa are Muḍarites. Kalb belonged to Quḍāʿa. The origin of Thaqīf is disputed. (According to some traditions they are considered as descendants of Qays ʿAylān). ʿAdwān belonged to Qays ʿAylān, Khuzāʿa were of South-Arabian origin [2]). The more important is the fact, that these tribes lived in different areas of the peninsula. The Thaqīf dwelt to the South-East of Mecca, the Kināna to the South, controlling the route Mecca-al-Yaman, the ʿĀmir b. Ṣaʿṣaʿa to the North East of Mecca, the Quḍāʿa (Kalb) in the North, controlling the trade-route to Syria; Yarbūʿ and Māzin controlled the route to al-Ḥīra and Persia.

Of special interest is the case of Zuhayr b. Janāb al-Kalbī. The Ghaṭafān decided—according to tradition—to establish a *ḥaram* like that of Mecca. Zuhayr b. Janāb raided them and destroyed their *ḥaram* [3]). This tradition explains why the group of Janāb of Kalb were included in the organization of the Ḥums

One may find some connection between the *īlāf* discussed above and the Ḥums. The expression of al-Thaʿālibī that Hāshim "took the *īlāf* from the enemies" [4]) means in fact, that the *īlāf* were a complementary system for the Ḥums. The *īlāf* were intended for tribes who did not respect the sacred months, or—although performing the pilgrimage—were in the sphere of influence of the client kingdoms. These clans and tribes—like Ṭayy, Khathʿam, clans of Quḍaʿa [5]), Ghifār from the Kināna [6]) were given some shares of profit and gave

1) Muḥ. b. Ḥabīb: *al-Muḥabbar*, p. 178-179.

2) See Ibn Durayd: *al-Ishtiqāq*, p. 468 seq.

3) *Aghānī* XII, 121; XXI, 63.

4) *Thimār al-Qulūb*, p. 89.

5) al-Balādhurī: *Ansāb*, ms. f. 900b; al-Jāḥiẓ: *al-Ḥayawān* VII, 216; see al-Balādhurī: *Ansāb*, ms. 366a: the talk between Muʿāwiya and ʿAdiyy b. Ḥātim in which Muʿāwiya accused Ṭayy of not respecting the sanctity of Mecca. Ṭayy and Khathʿam did not perform the pilgrimage to Mecca and were called *al-Afjarāni*.

6) See al-Dhahabī: *Siyar aʿlām al-nubalāʾ* II, 34 (*wa-kānū yuḥillūna al-shahra l-ḥarāma*); and see *Usd al-ghāba* I, 160.

security to the caravans. How much Mecca was dependent on these tribes and eager to carry out the terms of the *īlāf* can be gauged from some records preserved. Al-ʿAbbās was present when Abū Dharr was beaten violently in Mecca after he had embraced Islam. He reproached his people saying: "Woe to you, you are about to kill a man from Ghifār whilst your business and your passing by is through the territory of Ghifār". They let him go [1]). Thumāma b. Uthāl of the Ḥanīfa could threaten Quraysh with cutting of supplies from the Yamāma and even realized his threat [2]). Saʿd b. Muʿādh could threaten Abū Jahl, that if he prevents him to circumambulate the Kaʿba—he would cut his trade with Syria [3]). One is even tempted to think that there is some connection between the term *allafahum* "he concluded pacts of *īlāf* with them", and the term *al-mu'allafa qulūbuhum* "people whose hearts were gained (for Islam) by some gifts". But Ḥums denotes people strong in their conviction of the sanctity of Mecca, admitting the distinguished position of Quraysh, enjoying a special status in the rites of the *ḥajj* and ready to struggle for their ideas.

Some features of the Ḥums can be gauged from the chapters of al-Jāḥiẓ dealing with the virtues of Quraysh. Al-Jāḥiẓ records that never did a Qurashī allege his origin to another tribe, whilst till today "noble Arabs—like Banū Murra b. ʿAuf, some of the Banū Sulaym, Khuzāʿa and others—allege being of Qurashī origin. Quraysh did never bury their (female) babies alive. That was followed by the inhabitants of al-Ṭā'if, because they were neighbours and related with them by marriage and because they were Ḥums, and it was Quraysh who made them Ḥums . ." [4]).

When Islam appeared—continues al-Jāḥiẓ—there was no Qurashī woman who had been taken captive by the Arab tribes, nor was there

---

1) al-Dhahabī: *Siyar aʿlām al-nubalā'* II, 37 (*taqtulūna rajulan min Ghifārin wa-matjarukum wa-mamarrukum ʿalā Ghifār?*).

2) Ibn ʿAbd al-Barr: *al-Istīʿāb*, p. 79; al-Qasṭallānī: *Irshād* VI, 433; al-Qurṭubī: *al-Jāmiʿ li-aḥkām al-Qur'ān*, XII, 143; al-Ḥalabī: *Insān al-ʿuyūn* III, 198.

3) Ibn al-ʿArabī: *Muḥāḍarat al-abrār* II, 266; *Ṣifat al-ṣafwa* I, 37 (*la-aqṭaʿanna matjaraka ilā 'l-Shāmi*).

4) al-Jāḥiẓ: *Mukhtārāt fuṣūl*, ms. f. 202 seq.

any captive among them whose mother was a Qurashī woman. The Quraysh distinguished themselves from other tribes, that they did not give their daughters in marriage to the nobles of other tribes, unless they had got an assurance, that they would embrance the idea of the Ḥums. (They themselves—stresses al-Jāḥiẓ—married the daughters of other tribes without conditions to be imposed on them.) These tribes were: ʿĀmir b. Ṣaʿṣaʿa, Thaqīf, Khuzāʿa and al-Ḥārith b. Kaʿb. They were people of devotion (*wakānū dayyānīna*) and therefore they renounced raiding. That was in order to avoid pillage, injustice, robbery and rape".

In another passage al-Jāḥiẓ, discussing the qualities of Quraysh, remarks that Quraysh remained generous although their profits were not big since they refrained from raiding. Al-Jāḥiẓ emphasizes the hospitality of Quraysh, their care for the pilgrims and their care for kinsfolk. They allotted the men of the tribes to the different clans of Mecca—says al-Jāḥiẓ. Ghaṭafān were assigned to (the care of) al-Mughīra (i.e. al-Makhzūmī), Banū ʿĀmir went to someone else, the Tamīm to somebody else. They (i.e. the Quraysh) compelled them to perform the rites and cared for all their needs [1]). Al-Jāḥiẓ stresses that Quraysh

---

1) al-Jāḥiẓ: *Mukhtārāt fuṣūl*, ms. f. 204a (..*fa-yaqtasimūnahum, fa-takūnu Ghaṭafān li-l-Mughīrati wa-Banū ʿĀmirin li-kadhā, wa-Tamīmun li-kadhā*..). In al-Zubayr b. Bakkār's *Nasab Quraysh*, ms. f. 128 b. an interesting report is given about the allotment of the clans of Quraysh. They (i.e. the Quraysh) used to give them clothes in which they used to circumambulate the Kaʿba; they (i.e. the Bedouins) used to throw away the clothes which they wore when they came to Mecca. The host (i.e. the clan who lodged the Bedouins frequenting Mecca) used to get (scil. a share of) the meat of the slaughtered camels. The Banū Fazāra alighted in the house of al-Mughīra b. ʿAbdallah b. ʿAmr b. Makhzūm. The first who prevented him (i.e. al-Mughīra) to get (his share of) the slaughtered camel was Khushayn b. La'y al-Fazārī al-Shamkhī..; comp. Ibn Abī 'l-Ḥadīd: *Sharḥ nahj al-balāgha* IV, 296; and see Ibn Durayd: *al-Ishtiqāq* p. 282 (*Ẓuwaylim*). The word *ḥarīm* not recorded in the vocabularies as "payment for Quraysh from the alighting Bedouins" is recorded in the story of Ẓuwaylim reported by al-Balādhurī in his *Ansāb*, ms. f. 1101a. The quoted verse is of interest:

Wa-naḥnu manaʿnā min Qurayshin ḥarīmahā
bi-Makkata, ayyāma 'l-taḥāluqi wa-l-naḥri

Al-Balādhurī records also the story of ʿAmr b. Jābir b. Khushayn who used to get from every captive of the Ghaṭafān 2 camels. That was stopped by Ẓuwaylim b. ʿArīn (comp. the version of Ibn Durayd, *ib.*).

remained *Laqāḥ*, independent. They did not pay any tax and to them were entrusted the functions of *rifāda*, *siqāya*, etc.

In a third passage al-Jāḥiẓ repeats once more that all Quraysh were Ḥums, devoted to their *dīn*, a fact which prevented them from raiding, capture, intercourse with captive women and from burying alive their female babies. Once more al-Jāḥiẓ emphasizes that the Quraysh gave not their daughters in marriage unless on the condition that the children would become Ḥums. They were compelled—dwelling in a barren valley—to find means of livelihood and they got the *īlāf* and made journeys to kings . ." [1]).

In a fourth passage of al-Jāḥiẓ the report about the Ḥums is repeated. But there are some details which deserve attention. Mentioning the caravans—al-Jāḥiẓ reports that the merchants went to (the land of) Qayṣar in Byzantium, to al-Najāshī in Abyssinia, and to al-Muqauqis in Egypt. It is the only case in which Egypt is mentioned as destination of the merchants of Mecca. Al-Jāḥiẓ draws in this passage a line between the Ḥums of Quraysh and the converted Ḥums of the ʿĀmir b. Ṣaʿṣaʿa and al-Ḥārith b. Kaʿb. The Quraysh, being Ḥums, refrained from raiding, whereas the tribes who accepted the ideas of the Ḥums continued to raid, to have intercourse with captured women and to take spoils. But Quraysh remained courageous [2]).

Ibn al-Faqīh's account records that Khuzāʿa, ʿĀmir b. Ṣaʿṣaʿa, Thaqīf and "men of tribes" embraced the creed of the Ḥums. He records the tradition about the condition imposed on the nobles of the tribes marrying the daughters of Quraysh and gives details about the restrictions imposed on the pilgrims, not belonging to the Ḥums. They had to leave their travelling provision when entering Mecca, to take off their clothes which they wore outside the area of Mecca and to wear clothes of the Ḥaram (buying the clothes or borrowing them or as gifts). If they did not find clothes of the Ḥaram they per-

---

1) al-Jāḥiẓ: *Mukhtarāt fuṣūl*, ms. f. 16b. seq.

2) al-Jāḥiẓ: *Mukhtārāt fuṣūl*, ms. f. 208b. seq.; comp. al-Thaʿālibī: *Thimār al-qulūb*, p. 8 seq. (*Ahlu ʾllāh*); (significant is the expression *wa-ṣārū bi-ajmaʿihim tujjāran khulaṭāʾa*).

formed the circumambulation naked. They obliged the pilgrims to start the *ifāḍa* from al-Muzdalifa. They were *laqāḥ*, they did not pay any tax, nor did any king rule over them [1]).

Yāqūt mentions the Ḥums. According to him Quraysh gained for the idea of the Ḥums: Kināna, Jadīlat Qays, Fahm and ʿAdwān, Thaqīf and ʿĀmir b. Ṣaʿṣaʿa. He records the hardship which they imposed on themselves, the restrictions imposed on the pilgrims, and emphasizes that the people of Mecca were *laqāḥ*. Kings of Ḥimyar, Kinda, Ghassān and Lakhm used to perform the pilgrimage to Mecca and obeyed the Ḥums of Quraysh, considering as obliging to respect them . . [2]).

Mecca is mentioned as *Dār al-Ḥums* in the verses attributed to a Kāhin of the Lihb [3]) in the record of al-Ḥalabī. Al-Ḥalabī mentions the conditions of marriage of the Quraysh and their renouncing of raiding, which is connected with pillaging and rape [4]).

Sources give details about the rites of the Ḥums and of the imposed hardships [5]). They performed the *wuqūf* at al-Muzdalifa instead of at ʿArafāt [6]). They confined themselves during the *ḥajj* to the boundaries of the Ḥaram. During the *ḥajj* they did not eat meat, nor did they prepare curd, they did not stay in the shade of a house, they did not enter their houses through their doors [7]), etc. It is evident that by the hardship imposed on themselves they wanted to express their veneration for the Kaʿba and the Ḥaram. Al-Zamakhsharī connects the root *ḥms* with the root *ḥrm*. They acquired their distinct position

---

1) Ibn al-Faqīh: *Kitāb al-buldān*, p. 18.

2) Yāqūt: *Muʿjam al-buldān*, s.v. Makka.

3) The Lihb were known as men of special knowledge in augury (from the flight of birds) see: Wellhausen: *Reste*, p. 134; Ibn Durayd: *al-Ishtiqāq*, p. 491; al-Suhaylī: *al-Rauḍ al-unuf* I, 118.

4) al-Ḥalabī: *Insān al-ʿuyūn* I, 242.

5) See Muḥ. b. Ḥabīb: *al-Muḥabbar*, p. 180; Yāqūt: *Muʿjam al-buldān*, s.v. "Makka"; Ibn al-ʿArabī: *Muḥāḍarat al-abrār I*, 162, 150.

6) See Wellhausen: *Reste*, p. 77; Rathjens: *Die Pilgerfahrt*, pp. 72-73; but the Prophet did not follow the Ḥums in their *wuqūf*—see: al-Dhahabī: *Taʾrīkh al-Islām* I, 49.

7) But see the contradictory traditions in al-Ṭabarī's *Tafsīr* (*Sūra* II, 189) and al-Suyūṭī: *al-Durr al-manthūr I*, 204 seq.

of sanctity because they dwelt in the Ḥaram. They called themselves *Ahlu ʾllāh* [1]). That the idea of Ḥums was in fact connected with the cult of the Kaʿba is plainly attested by the fact, that the Kaʿba was called al-Ḥamsāʾ [2]).

It is evident that this link between Quraysh and the tribes attached to the Ḥums influenced their relations. Caskel remarks that the ʿĀmir b. Ṣaʿṣaʿa, being Ḥums, were on good terms with the inhabitants of Mecca [3]). An ʿĀmirī poet and chief, ʿAuf b. al-Aḥwaṣ b. Jaʿfar b. Kilāb, swears on the sacred month [4]) of the Banū Umayya, the sacred places of Quraysh, the sacrificed victims [5]). Khālid b. Jaʿfar, the uncle of ʿAuf, is said to have been the first who covered the Kaʿba with brocade (dībāj) which he got from a caravan looted by him [6]). The Kaʿb and Kilāb of the ʿĀmir were called *Kaʿb Quraysh* and *Kilāb Quraysh* [7]). Mālik b. Nuwayra of the Yarbūʿ (of Tamīm), who belonged to the Ḥums, mentions a group of horsemen who informed Quraysh (as *ʿUmmār*) about some battle [8]).

The Prophet himself belonged to the Ḥums [9]). He was the *ḥirmī* of ʿIyāḍ b. Ḥimār al-Mujāshiʿī ʾl-Tamīmī. The Prophet lent him his clothes and ʿIyāḍ used to perform the circumambulation of the Kaʿba in the clothes of the Prophet [10]).

---

1) al-Zamakhsharī: *al-Fāʾiq*, s.v. *ḥums*.
2) al-Fayrūzābādī: *al-Qāmūs*, s.v. *ḥms*. A curious explanation is given for the Ḥums in al-Maghribī's *Īnās*, ms. f. 26b: "They were called Ḥums, because they refrained from the service of labour.."
3) EI², s.v. ʿĀmir b. Ṣaʿṣaʿa.
4) i.e. Dhū ʾl-ḥijja.
5) al-Ḍabbī: *al-Mufaḍḍaliyyāt* XXXV, 4-5 (ed. Lyall):
wa-innī wa-ʾlladhī ḥajjat Qurayshun
maḥārimahū wa-mā jamaʿat Ḥirāʾu
Wa-shahri Banī Umayyata wa-l-hadāyā
idhā ḥubisat muḍarrijahā ʾl-dimāʾu
6) al-Suhaylī: *al-Rauḍ al-unuf* I, 77; al-Alūsī: *Bulūgh al-arab* I, 234.
7) al-Ḍabbī: *al-Mufaḍḍaliyyāt*, p. 259 (ed. Lyall).
8) *al-Aṣmaʿiyyāt* XXVI, 3 (ed. Ahlwardt); Ibn Abī ʾl-Ḥadīd: *Sharḥ nahj al-Balāgha* IV, 292.
9) See al-Azraqī: *Akhbār* (Wüstenfeld) I, 124; al-Suyūṭī: *al-Durr al-manthūr* I, 204 seq.
10) See: Muḥ. b. Ḥabīb: *al-Muḥabbar*, p. 181; Ibn Qutayba: *al-Maʿārif*, p. 147;

From the traditions quoted above one can gain a rough idea about the Ḥums. The fundamental principles of the Ḥums were the inviolability of the area of the Ḥaram, the independence[1]) and neutrality of Mecca.

The feeling of security in Mecca is described by one of the nobles of Mecca in the following verses:

Fakharnā wa-l-umūru lahā qarārun
bi-Makkatinā wa-bi-l-baladi 'l-ḥarāmi.
Wa-annā lā yurāmu lanā ḥarīmun
wa-annā lā nurawwaʿu fī 'l-manāmi.
Wa-annā lā tusāqu lanā kiʿābun
khilāla 'l-naqʿi bādiyatu l-khidāmi.
Maʿādha 'llāhi min hādhā wa-hādhā
fa-inna 'llāha laysa lahū musāmī[2]).

A Bedouin could not accustom himself to the quiet life of Mecca; Qays b. Zuhayr al-ʿAbsī said:

Tufākhirunī maʿāshiru min Qurayshin
bi-Kaʿbatihim wa-bi-l-bayti 'l-ḥarāmi
Fa-akrim bi-'lladhī fākharū wa-lākin
maghāẓī 'l-khayli dāmiyatu 'l-kilāmi.
Wa-ṭaʿnun fī 'l-ʿajājati kulla yaumin
nuḥūra 'l-khayli bi 'l-asali l-dawāmī.
Aḥabbu ilayya min ʿayshin rakhiyyin

Abū ʿUbayd: *Kit. al-amwāl*, p. 256; Ibn al-Kalbī: *Jamhara*, ms. f. 66a; al-Ṭabarānī: *al-Muʿjam al-ṣaghīr*, p. 3; Ibn al-Jārūd: *al-Muntaqā*, p. 500; al-Balādhurī: *Ansāb*, ms. f. 981a; Ibn Ḥazm: *Jawāmiʿ al-sīra*, p. 25 (reporting that he was a cousin of al-Aqraʿ b. Ḥābis); Ibn Ḥazm: *Jamharat ansāb al-ʿArab*, p. 219; Yāqūt: *Muʿjam al-buldān*, s.v. *ḥaram*; Ibn Ḥajar: *al-Iṣāba*, N. 6123; Abū Nuʿaym: *Ḥilya* II, 16 (mentioned as one of the *Ahl al-Ṣuffa*).

1) The fierce reaction of the Meccans when their independence was threatened can be gauged from the story of ʿUthmān b. Ḥuwayrith. See al-Zubayr b. Bakkār: *Nasab Quraysh*, ms. f. 76b; al Muṣʿab al-Zubayrī: *Nasab Quraysh*, p. 210; L.ʿA., s.v. *lqḥ*: Abū 'l-Baqā': *Manāqib*, ms. f. 10 b; al-Balādhurī: *Ansāb* IV B, 126 (and see "Annotations").

2) al-Balādhurī: *Ansāb*, ms. f. 1094a.

ma'a 'l-Qurashiyyi Ḥarbin au Hishāmi.
Wa-mā 'ayshu 'bni Jud'ānin bi-'ayshin
yajurru 'l-khazza fī 'l-baladi 'l-tihāmī [1])

The observation of some rites and customs was in fact an expression of their veneration of the sanctuary of Mecca. This organization, including different tribal units—among them units of Tamīm, who dwelled in different areas of the peninsula, had a militant character. They were ready to struggle for their ideas of the sanctity of Mecca. The *īlāf* seem to have been built up on the base of Ḥums. The Ḥums were the élite group distinct by their close relations with the Meccans, by their rites and customs. Both the organizations, the Ḥums and *īlāf* had economic significance. The religious "colouring" is not surprising [2]).

People not belonging to the Ḥums were "Ḥilla". The Ḥilla included—according to the report of Ibn Ḥabīb—all the Tamīm (except Yarbū', Māzin, Ḍabba, Ḥumays, Ẓā'ina, al-Ghauth b. Murr), all the Qays 'Aylān (except Thaqīf, 'Adwān and 'Āmir b. Ṣa'ṣa'a), all Rabī'a b. Nizār, all Quḍā'a (except 'Ilāf and Janāb), the Anṣār, Khath'am, Bajīla, Bakr b. 'Abd Manāt b. Kināna (other divisions of Kināna were Ḥums), Hudhayl, Asad, Ṭayy and Bāriq [3]). These Ḥilla—when performing the *ḥajj*—were quite different in their rites during the *iḥrām* and during the *ṭawāf*. A third group mentioned by Ibn Ḥabīb were the *Ṭuls*, including tribes from al-Yaman and Ḥaḍramaut, 'Akk, Ujayb and Iyād [4]).

The division into the three groups—Ḥums, Ḥilla, Ṭuls—is confronted

---

1) *Ib.*
2) Comp. Rathjens: *Die Pilgerfahrt*, p. 80 (.."Teilweise religiös getarnt..").
3) Muḥ. b. Ḥabīb: *al-Muḥabbar*, p. 179.
4) *ib.*; A special group, which deserves to be mentioned, were the *Basl*. The word *basl* denotes ideas similar to the ideas inherent in the word *ḥums*: courage, bravery, intrepid fighting on one hand, and the *ḥaram* the forbidden on the other hand. The *Basl* were the 'Āmir b. Lu'ayy (or 'Auf b. Lu'ayy, or Murra b. 'Auf b. Lu'ayy). They maintained, that the number of the sacred months is 8. The tribes granted them security during these months. See al-Kalā'ī: *al-Iktifā'*, I, 78; Ibn Kathīr: *al-Bidāya* II, 204; L.'A., s.v. *bsl*; Abū Dharr: *Sharḥ al-sīra* (ed. Brönnle) p. 233 (the *Basl* were Quraysh, because they were the people of Mecca and Mecca is *ḥaram*).

by another division. This scheme divides the tribes according to their recognition of the sanctity of Mecca: (1) the *muḥrimūn* and (2) the *muḥillun*. The *muḥrimūn* included the Ḥums and these tribes of the Ḥilla who in fact performed the pilgrimage. The *muḥillūn* did not recognize the sanctity of Mecca nor did they respect the sacred months. These *muḥillūn* constituted a real danger for Mecca.

Al-Jāḥiẓ counts as *muḥillūn* all the Ṭayy and Khathʿam (*mimman kāna lā yarā li-l-ḥarami wa-lā li-l-shahri ʾl-ḥarāmi ḥurmatan*). Muḥillūn—says al-Jāḥiẓ—were as well many clans of Quḍāʿa, Yashkur, and al-Ḥārith b. Kaʿb. They were enemies because of their (different) *dīn* and their (different) pedigree [1]).

Against these *muḥillūn* the intercalator uttered his famour declaration, making lawful the shedding of their blood. "I make lawful to shed the blood of the *muḥillūn*, Ṭayy and Khathʿam. Kill them, wherever you meet them if they harass you" [2]).

Al-Yaʿqūbī mentions as *muḥillūn*, people who considered as lawful to commit iniquities in these markets. They were groups from Asad, Ṭayy, Bakr b. ʿAbd Manāt b. Kināna and of ʿAmir b. Ṣaʿṣaʿa [3]).

It is evident, that it was necessary to take some steps to guard the free markets [4]) of Mecca from hostile tribes and unruly elements like brigands and robbers.

In fact al-Yaʿqūbī states: And among the tribes there were people, who condemned this and devoted themselves (*naṣabū anfusahum*) to the help of oppressed and to prevent bloodshed and committing of ini-

---

1) al-Jāḥiẓ: *al-Ḥayawān* VII, 216 seq.; comp. al-Najīramī: *Aymān al-ʿArab*, p. 12; Muḥ. b. Ḥabīb: *al-Muḥabbar*, p. 319 inf.

2) al-Balādhurī: *Ansāb*, ms. f. 900b (..*wa-innī qad aḥlaltu dimāʾa ʾl-muḥillīna min Ṭayyin wa-Khathʿam fa-ʾqtulūhum ḥaythu wajadtumūhum idhā ʿaraḍū lakum*); of interest is the following verse of al-Ḥuṭayʾa.

Alam akun muḥriman fa-yakūna baynī
wa-baynakumu ʾl-mawaddatu wa-l-ikhāʾu

(*Dīwān* (ed. Ṭāhā) 40, 1.7.). The commentary says:

al-muḥrimu al-musālimu ʾlladhī yaḥramu damuhu ʿalayka wa-damuka ʿalayhi.

3) al-Yaʿqūbī: *Taʾrīkh* I, 221 (ed. Najaf).

4) Comp. Muḥ. b. Ḥabīb: *al-Muḥabbar* p. 267 (*wa-lam takun fīhi* (i.e. *ʿUkāẓ*) *ʿushūrun wa-lā khufāratun*).

quities. They were called *al-Dhāda al-Muḥrimūna* (The *Muḥrimūn*, "the Defenders"). They were from the ʿAmr b. Tamīm, the Banū Ḥanẓala b. Zayd Manāt (b. Tamīm), Hudhayl, Shaybān and Kalb b. Wabara. They used to carry weapons (in the sacred months). The tribes were divided into people who took off their weapons during the sacred months and (lacuna; apparently: people who carried arms during these months—K).

This report of al-Yaʿqūbī is of importance; it sheds some light on the role of some groups of Tamīm who served in an inter-tribal militia, set up to defend Mecca and the markets of Mecca.

One may recall the remarkable passage of al-Jāḥiẓ quoted above [1]), in which *īlāf* was explained as a tax, imposed on the tribes in order to defend Mecca from the "wolves of the tribes", brigands and hostile tribes. It cannot be ruled out that the *īlāf* might have included some point about a pay for the militia to guard the markets and to guard Mecca.

Additional details about this militia are given by al-Marzūqī [2]): The tribes (al-ʿArab) were divided according to three different conceptions about the sacred months: (1) people who perpetrated unlawful deeds; these are the *muḥillūn*, who do not respect the sanctity of the *ḥaram*, steal in the *ḥaram* and kill. (2) people who refrain from it and respect the sacred months (*yuḥrimūna 'l-ashhura 'l-ḥuruma*). (3) people sharing the principle set up [3]) by Ṣulṣul b. Aus b. Mukhāshin b. Muʿā-

---

1) See p. 119 n. 2 above; the passage in al-Jāḥiẓ's *Rasa'il* runs as follows: *Wa-qad fassarahu qaumun bi-ghayri dhālika. Qālū: inna Hāshiman jaʿala ʿala ru'ūsi 'l-qabā'ili ḍarā'iba yu'addūnahā ilayhi li-yaḥmiya bihā ahla Makkata. Fa-inna dhu'-bāna l-ʿArabi wa-ṣaʿālīka 'l-aḥyā'i wa-aṣḥāba 'l-ṭawā'ili kānū lā yu'manūna ʿalā 'l-ḥarami; lā siyyāma wa-nāsun min al-ʿArabi kānū lā yarauna li-l-ḥarami ḥurmatan wa-lā li-l-shahri 'l-ḥarāmi qadran, mithlu Ṭayyin wa-Khathʿamin wa-Quḍāʿata wa-baʿḍi Balḥārithi bni Kaʿbin*".

2) al-Marzūqī: *al-Amkina* II, 166.

3) The translation of Hamidullah (*Le Prophète*, p. 605) is not accurate. He renders the text as follows:.. mais les gens se partageaient en trois groupes à ce propos: ceux qui pratiquaient l'abomination...ceux qui s'en abstenaient..et enfin les fantaisistes (*ahl al-ahwā'*), partisans du Tamīmite.." The text tells about three conceptions according to which people were divided. *Wa-kanāt al-ʿArabu fī ashhuri*

wiya b. Shurayf of the ʿAmr b. Tamīm; it is he who made lawful for them the fight of the *muḥillūn*.

This tradition transmitted by Ibn al-Kalbī (on the authority of his father) is refuted by Ibn al-Kalbī and Abū Khirāsh. They state: "That is the claim of the Banū Tamīm. Certain is in our opinion that it was the Qalammas and his ancestors. And it was he who intercalated the months". The refutation of Ibn al-Kalbī and Abū Khirāsh does not refer to the whole tradition about Ṣulṣul. It refers only to the phrase *fa-innahu aḥalla qitāla ʾl-muḥillīn* "and he made lawful to fight the *muḥillīn.*"Ibn al-Kalbī seems to refer to the declaration uttered by the intercalator. It was in fact the intercalator who uttered this declaration. But it was the group of Ṣulṣul, the *muḥrimūn—dhāda* who carried out the implication of this declaration.

A peculiar tradition recorded by al-Shahrastānī (*al-Milal*, p. 443—ed. Cureton) claims that the Qalammas (in text *al-Mutalammis*) *b. Umayya al-Kinānī* was of the *dīn* of Tamīm (*ʿalā dīni banī Tamīm*).

The tradition about the *muḥrimūn—dhāda* seems to be trustworthy. The Usayyid, the clan of Ṣulṣul, were in close connections with Mecca. Some of the Banū Usayyid came to Mecca, became allies of influential families, gained wealth, married daughters of aristocratic families, and became respected citizens of Mecca. Influential was the Usayyidī family of Nabbāsh. Their houses were in the vicinity of the Kaʿba [1]). Al-Aʿshā b. Zurāra b. al-Nabbāsh mourned Nubayh and Munabbih, the two sons of al-Ḥajjāj b. ʿĀmir, killed at Badr [2]). The mother of Baghīḍ b. ʿĀmir b. Hāshim b. ʿAbd Manāf b. ʿAbd al-Dār was the daughter of al-

---

ʾl-ḥajji ʿalā thalāthati ahwāʾin: minhum...wa-minhum..wa-minhum ahlu hawan sharaʿahu lahum Ṣulṣul... The group set up by Ṣulṣul were not "fantaisistes". The expression *ahlu hawan* is not pejorative; it is equal in its denotation to the expression used for the preceding groups.

1) al-Zubayr b. Bakkār: *Nasab Quraysh*, ms. f. 88b; al-Fāsī: *Shifāʾ al-gharām* (Wüstenfeld, II, 140 seq.).

2) Ibn Hishām: *Sīra* III, 16; al-Zubayr b. Bakkār: *Nasab Quraysh*, ms. f. 182 b; Abū ʾl-Faraj: *al-Aghānī* XVI, 60.

Nabbāsh b. Zurāra [1]). One of the mountains of Mecca belonged to the Banū Nabbāsh [2]). A spurious tradition—which may, however, contain some grain of truth—claims that Aktham b. Ṣayfī, the famous sage of the Usayyid, acquired his wisdom from Quṣayy, ʿAbd Manāf, Hāshim and Abū Ṭālib [3]). Another spurious tradition claims that Aktham learned *nasab* from ʿAbd al Muṭṭalib [4]). To the Usayyid belonged as well the first (or second) husband of Khadīja, Abū Hāla.

The family of Aus b. Mukhāshin was a noble one. The descendants of Aus b. Mukhāshin were the guardians of the sanctuary of Shums, the idol worshipped by the Ḍabba, Tamīm, ʿUkl, ʿAdiyy and Thaur [5]). This idol was pulled down by Hind, the son of Khadīja and by Ṣafwān b. Usayyid of the Mukhāshin [6]). This Ṣafwān married Durra, the daughter of Abū Lahab, and she gave birth to two of his sons Auf and al-Qaʿqāʿ [7]). Mukhāshin b. Muʿāwiya b. Jurwa b. Usayyid was called *Dhū ʾl-aʿwād* [8]). Ṣayfī b. Riyāḥ b. al-Ḥārith b. Mukhāshin b. Muʿāwiya b. Jurwa b. Usayyid, the father of Aktham was called *Dhū ʾl-ḥilm* or *Dhū ʾl-aubār* (because of the copious herds he possessed) [9]). Rabīʿa b. Mukhāshin and his father Mukhāshin were respected "judges of the tribes" [10]).

Ṣulṣul to whom the setting up of the *muḥrimūn-dhāda* is attributed was in very close relations with Mecca: he was in charge of the *mausim* and a judge at ʿUkāẓ [11]).

---

1) al-Zubayr b. Bakkār, *op. cit.*, ms. f. 89b; al-Muṣʿab al-Zubayrī: *Nasab Quraysh* p. 254; and see the discussion about the writer of the *ṣaḥīfa* in Suhaylī's *al-Rauḍ al-unuf* I, 232.

2) al-Azraqī: *Akhbār* (Wüstenfeld I, 490); Yāqūt: *Buldān*, s.v. *Shayba.*

3) al-Majlisī: *Biḥār al-anwār* VI, 39. 4) Abu l-Baqāʾ: *Manāqib*, ms. f. 96a.

5) Muḥ. b. Ḥabīb: *al-Muḥabbar*, p. 316.

6) *ib*; and see Ibn Ḥajar: *al-Iṣāba*, No. 4067, 4071.

7) Ibn Ḥazm: *Jamharat ansāb al-ʿArab*, p. 199, inf.

8) al-Hamdānī: *Iklīl* I/II, ms. f. 178a (Mukhāshin); Muḥ. b. Ḥabīb: *al-Muḥabbar*, p. 134 (Rabīʿa b. Mukhāshin). al-Anbārī: *Mufaḍḍaliyyāt* (Lyall) 447 (Rabīʿā); al-Yaʿqūbī: *Taʾrīkh* I, 214 (ed. Najaf: Mukhāshin); al-Farazdaq: *Dīwān*, p. 503, n. 2; Ibn Abī ʾl-Ḥadīd: *Sharḥ nahj al-Balāgha* III, 427.

9) al-Hamdānī: *ib.* Ibn al-Athīr; *al-Muraṣṣaʿ* (ed. Seybold) p. 82 (also attributed to Aktham).

10) Muḥ. b. Ḥabīb: *al-Muḥabbar*, p. 134; al-ʿAskarī: *Jamharat al-amthāl*, p. 104.

11) Muḥ. b. Ḥabīb: *al-Muḥabbar*, p. 182.

The duties entrusted to Tamīm in Mecca and in the markets of Mecca are a convincing evidence of the important role played by Tamīm in establishing of the economic power of Mecca. Tamīm were invested with the *ifāḍa* in Mecca itself and with the control of the market of ʿUkāẓ. ʿUkāẓ was one of the important markets because here the public opinion of the tribes could express itself in its literary, political and social aspects [1]). It was the co-operation with Tamīm in the market of ʿUkāẓ which helped Quraysh to avoid competition and secured for the Quraysh the influence in these markets [2]).

The share of Tamīm in the Meccan system is defined by Ibn Ḥabīb as follows: "The leaders (Aʾimma) of the tribes (after ʿĀmir b. al-Ẓarib) in the mawasim and their judges at ʿUkāz were the Banū Tamīm. The guardians of their *dīn* and the trustees of their *qibla* were the Quraysh. The authoritative interpreters of the *dīn* were the Banū Mālik b. Kināna [3])". Ibn Ḥabīb gives a list of chiefs of Tamīm who acted both as leaders of the mausim and as judges of ʿUkāẓ. (1) Saʿd b. Zayd Manāt b. Tamīm, (2) Ḥanẓala b. Zayd Manāt b. Tamīm, (3) Dhuʾayb b. Kaʿb b. ʿAmr b. Tamīm, (4) Māzin b. Mālik b. ʿAmr b. Tamīm, (5) Thaʿlaba b. Yarbūʿ b. Ḥanẓala b. Mālik b. Zayd Manāt, (6) Muʿāwiya b. Shurayf b. Jurwa b. Usayyid b. ʿAmr b. Tamīm, (7) al-Aḍbaṭ b. Qurayʿ b. ʿAuf b. Kaʿb b. Saʿd b. Zayd Manāt, (8) Ṣulṣul b. Aus b. Mukhāshin b. Muʿāwiya b. Shurayf b. Jurwa b. Usayyid, (9) Sufyān b. Mujāshiʿ; Sufyān was the last man who combined the two functions: of a judge and a leader of the mausim. After his death these duties were performed by two different persons. Muḥammad b. Sufyān performed the duties of a judge at ʿUkāẓ. At the appearance of Islam the judge was al-Aqraʿ b. Ḥābis b. ʿIqāl b. Muḥammad b. Sufyān b. Mujāshiʿ. After Ṣulṣul the "ijāza" of the mausim was entrusted to ʿAllāq b. Shihāb b. Laʾy of the ʿUwāfa (of the Banū

1) Comp. al-Marzūqī: *al-Amkina* II, 165, 170; al-Marzūqī: *Sharḥ al-Ḥamāsa*, p. 1514; Wellhausen: *Reste*, p. 84-87; Buhl: *Das Leben Muhammeds*, pp. 49-50, 105.

2) The opinion of Rathjens (*Die Pilgerfahrt*, p. 70), that there was competition between the market of Mecca and ʿUkāẓ seems to be without basis.

3) Muḥ. b. Ḥabīb: *al-Muḥabbar*, p. 181 inf.; the Mālik b. Kināna were the clan of the intercalators.

Sa'd)[1]. The last man who performed the duty of "ijāza" when Islam appeared was Karib b. Ṣafwān[2].

The list of the Tamīmī judges given by al-Balādhurī on the authority of Ibn Kunāsa is almost identical with the list of *al-Muḥabbar*[3]. Identical are as well the lists of the *Naqā'iḍ*[4] and al-Marzūqī's *Amkina*[5]. Ibn Ḥazm reports in a chapter omitted in the edition of Lévi Provençal[6], that the Tamīm got the duty of the judges at 'Ukāẓ and the *ifāḍa* after it had been performed by 'Adwān. The last of the 'Adwān were 'Āmir b. al-Ẓarib and Abū Sayyāra. The last man who performed the *ifāḍa* at the appearance of Islam was Karib b. Ṣafwān; the last judge was al-Aqra' b. Ḥābis. The Tamīm inherited the duties of the *ramy*, *nafr* and the *ijāẓa* from Ṣūfa—reports Ibn Ḥazm.

Tamīmī poets recall in their poems the duties performed by Tamīm. Al-Farazdaq boasts of the duty of the *ḥakam* performed by one of his ancestors:

Wa-'ammī 'lladhī 'khtārat Ma'addun ḥukūmatan
'alā 'l-nāsi idh wafau 'Ukāẓa bihā ma'ā
Huwa 'l-Aqra'u 'l-khayru 'lladhī kāna yabtanī
awākhiya majdin thābitin an yunaẓẓa'ā[7]

1) Zaynab bint 'Allāq b. Shihāb b. 'Amr of the Banū 'Uwāfa b. Sa'd b. Zayd Manāt was the grandmother of 'Umar b. 'Abd al-'Azīz (see Ibn Ḥabīb: *al-Muḥabbar*, p. 27; al-Balādhurī: *Ansāb*, ms. f. 1049 b). His son 'Attāb got the pay (*'aṭā'*) of 2,500 dirham by 'Umar (al-Balādhurī, *op. cit.* f. 1050a; Ibn al-Kalbī: *Jamhara*, ms. f. 83a). 'Allāq is said to have believed in God and in the Day of Resurrection (al-Shahrastānī, *al-Milal*, p. 439, ed. Cureton).

2) See Ibn al-Kalbī: *Jamhara*, ms. f. 81a; Ibn Ḥazm: *Jamharat ansāb al-'Arab*, p. 208; al-Balādhurī: *Ansāb*, ms. f. 1044a, 957a; Ḍamra b. Jābir b. Nahshal married his daughter Hind (al-Ḍabbī: *Amthāl al-'Arab*, p. 8).

3) al-Balādhurī: *Ansāb*, ms. f. 1044 b (but Māzin is followed by Mu'āwiya b. Shurayf; Ṣulṣul is followed by 'Allāq).

4) *Naqā'iḍ* 438 (Tha'laba b. Yarbū' is followed by Mu'āwiya b. Shurayf; but Mu'āwiya b. Shurayf is followed by Jurwa b. Usayyid. That is apparently an error; read for *thumma*: *bn*).

5) al-Marzūqī: *al-Amkina* II, 167.

6) Ḥamd al-Jāsir: *Naẓratun fī kitābi Jamharati ansābi l-'Arabi*, RAAD, 1950, p. 248 seq.

7) al-Farazdaq: *Dīwān*, p. 502 (ed. Ṣāwī).

The function of the judge boasts as well Jarīr:

Wa-naḥnu 'l-ḥākimūna 'alā Qulākhin
kafaynā dhā 'l-jarīrati wa-l-muṣāba [1])

(There is a variant: *Wa-ṇaḥnu 'l-ḥākimūna 'alā 'Ukāẓin*) [2]).

A significant verse of Ḥassān b. Thābit refers to the duties of Tamīm in the markets:

Wa-afḍalu mā niltum min al-majdi wa-l-'ulā
ridāfatunā 'inda 'ḥtiḍāri 'l-mawāsimi [3])
"And the best which you gained from glory and loftiness
Is (to be) our helpers at the attending of markets."

This verse is the 14th of a poem of Ḥassān, which was an answer to the poem of the delegation of Tamīm, which came to Mecca to meet the prophet anno 9 H. Arafat analysed the poem [4]) and came to the conclusion that though attributed to Ḥassān, it was actually composed by an Anṣārī in a later period. Unfortunately Arafat did not analyse this verse. The conclusion of Arafat is, however, not acceptable as far as this verse is concerned. Taking for granted that there was an Anṣārī poet interested to insult the Tamīm—he would not have recalled this relation of the Tamīm with Mecca. In later times when Quraysh were highly respected in the Islamic society—the *ridāfa* for Quraysh was not an insult.

Arafat remarks that the poem of Ḥassān "is clearly divided into two sections. The first eight lines are boasting in the first person plural in precisely the same manner which characterizes the poems of the later Anṣārīs some of which were attributed to Ḥassān. The remaining six lines are threats and insults addressed to the Banū Dārim" [5]). We are here not concerned with the eight verses of the poem containing

---

1) Jarīr: *Dīwān*, p. 67; *Naqā'iḍ*, p. 437.
2) See *Naqā'iḍ*, p. 438; Jarīr: *Dīwān*, ib.; Yāqūt: *Buldān*, s.v. Qulākh.
3) Ḥassān: *Dīwān* p. 385 (ed. Barqūqī).
4) W. Arafat: "An interpretation of the different accounts of the visit of the Tamīm delegation to the Prophet A.H. 9", BSOAS 1955, pp. 416-25.
5) *ib.* p. 422.

praises of the Anṣār and stressing the aid of the Anṣār for the Prophet. Arafat may be right assuming that these verses were composed by an Anṣārī of a later generation. But why did an Anṣārī of a later generation slander the Tamīm in such a vehement manner.

To start with, one may observe that the six verses of Ḥassān (9-14) are an answer for the poem of al-Zibriqān b. Badr [1]). In the four verses recorded al-Zibriqān praises his tribe and their deeds. The verses of Ḥassān form, in fact, an answer, a *naqīḍa* for the verses of al-Zibriqān. The verse of Ḥassān quoted above forms an answer for the first verse of al-Zibriqān:

> *Ataynāka kaymā yaʿlama ʾl-nāsu faḍlanā*
> *idhā ʾḥtafalū ʿinda ʾḥtiḍāri ʾl-mawāsimi*
> "We came to you in order that people may know our excellence
> When they rally attending the markets".

The verse seems to point to the duty of the Tamīm performed in the markets. The answer of Ḥassān—on behalf of the Prophet—is explicit: you were merely our chamberlains, *ardāf*, at these markets. That is the utmost of excellence which you could attain. It would be, in fact, probably better to put this verse after verse 10 of the poem. That would give 3 verses in which Ḥassān refutes the claim of the excellence of the Tamīm. The three other verses (11-13) would form the unity of threat and urge to embrace Islam.

The violent insults in the verses of Ḥassān are not surprising. Ḥassān was known as the poet who mentioned in his verses in the defense of the Prophet the faults of his opponents, their lost battles and some flaws in their pedigree [2]).

Arafat refuting the authenticity of the verses of Ḥassān remarks: "However, it is doubtful whether it would be in keeping with the

---

1) Ibn Hishām: *Sīra* IV, 211; two verses are quoted in al-Marzubānī's *Muʿjam al-shuʿarāʾ*, p. 299 and attributed to ʿUṭārid b. Ḥājib (attributed as well to al-Aqraʿ b. Ḥābis).

2) al-Dhahabī: *Siyar aʿlām al-nubalāʾ* II, 376; al-Zurqānī: *Sharḥ al-mawahib* III, 376.

character of the Prophet, always a great statesman, to allow such insults and threats to be used on such an occasion against the well known representatives of a great tribe" [1]). The argument of Arafat is a sound one. But there is a report which may give a reasonable answer to the question put forward by Arafat. According to an account given in the *Sīra Ḥalabiyya* [2]) there was a contest between al-Aqraʿ of the Tamīm [3]) and Ḥassān (*mufākhara*), which was attended by the Prophet. Al-Aqraʿ recited his poem and Ḥassān responded with his *naqīḍa*. The Prophet, hearing the verses of Ḥassān, said to al-Aqraʿ: "You did not need (*laqad kunta ghaniyyan*) to be reminded of things which you understand that people already forgot". This utterance of the Prophet—says al-Kalbī—was more grave for al-Aqraʿ than the verses of Ḥassān.

It is not surprising that this verse (14) of Ḥassān was omitted in later sources. The duty of Tamīm fell in oblivion and was mentioned only by early Islamic Tamīmī poets. The old markets had already ceased to exist. The verse could not serve as argument of boasting or of insult. The modern commentary of Barqūqī gives the following explanation: "It is better for you (says Ḥassān) because if you embrace Islam—you would gain the highest glory (*sharaf*), because you will attend with us all gatherings and that is the best thing you strive at" [4]). This explanation is hardly acceptable. *Wa-afḍalu mā niltum* does not denote future, but past. The verse was, in fact, an insult in the time of Ḥassān, anno 9 H.: you were merely helpers of ours (of Quraysh) in the markets.

Verses 11-12 of the poem (verse 3 of the second division) describe a real situation. "If you have come to save your lives and your property lest you be divided among the booty, then admit no rival to God, and become Muslims and wear not a similar attire to that of foreigners" [5]).

---

1) Arafat, *op. cit.*, p. 423.

2) al-Ḥalabī: *Insān al-ʿuyūn*, III, 228-29.

3) It is more plausible that the verses of the Tamīmī poet may be attributed to al-Aqraʿ or ʿUṭārid b. Ḥājib. It is hardly conceivable that the Saʿdī al-Zibriqān would have praised the Dārim: *wa-an laysa fī arḍi 'l-Ḥijāzi ka-Dārimi*. The verses of Ḥassān are as well addressed to the Dārim: *Banī Dārimin, lā tafkharū*.

4) Ḥassān: *Dīwān*, *ib.*

5) Arafat, *op. cit.*, p. 423.

The situation referred to in these verses is plainly mentioned in the verses of al-Farazdaq. The threat of Ḥassān that the Tamīmī prisoners might have been sold in the markets—cannot be considered as a void threat. Al-Farazdaq boasts of the Dārim:

Wa-ʿinda rasūli ʾllāhi idh shadda qabḍahu
wa-mulliʾa min asrā Tamīmin adāhimuh
Farajnā ʿani ʾl-asrā ʾl-adāhima baʿda mā
takhammaṭa wa-ʾshtaddat ʿalayhim shakāʾimuh [1])

In another poem al-Farazdaq stresses that the freeing of the captives was due to the intercession of al-Aqraʿ with the Prophet for them.

Wa-ʿinda rasūli ʾllāhi qāma ʾbnu Ḥābisin
bi-khuṭṭati sawwārin ilā ʾl-majdi, ḥāzimi.
Lahū aṭlaqa ʾl-asrā ʾllatī fī ḥibālihi
mughallaqatan aʿnāquhā fī ʾl-adāhimi.
Kafā ummahāti ʾl-khāʾifīna ʿalayhim
ʿalāʾa l-mufādī au sihāma l-musāhimi [2]).

A tradition recorded on the authority of al-Kalbī (forming a commentary of these verses) states that al-Aqraʿ interceded for the captives of the ʿAmr b. Jundab b. al-ʿAnbar b. ʿAmr b. Tamīm and promised to pay the bloodwit. The Prophet freed the captives and al-Aqraʿ paid the bloodwit on behalf of his people [3]). The verses of Ḥassān about Tamīm seem to be authentic.

One may agree with Arafat about the inferiority of these verses of Ḥassān—but that is not a sufficient proof that these verses were not composed by Ḥassān. Such verses are not surprising in political *hijāʾ*.

The problem of the delegation of Tamīm deserves to be treated separately.

The secular duties of Tamīm at the market, discussed above, were

---

1) al-Farazdaq: *Dīwān*, p. 767; *Naqāʾiḍ*, p. 748.
2) al-Farazdaq: *Dīwān*, p. 862; *Naqāʾid*, p. 747 (*mughallalatan aʿnāquhā*).
3) Naqāʾiḍ, p. 747; it is significant that versions "L", "O" of the *Naqāʾiḍ* have *au sihāma l-muqāsimi* resembling closely the expression of the verse of Ḥassān.

complemented by remarkable duties performed by the relatives of Tamīm during the festivities of the pilgrimage. The *Sīra* of Ibn Hishām supplies the following account about the Tamīmī leaders at the pilgrimage festivities:

"Al-Ghauth b. Murr b. Udd b. al-Ya's b. Muḍar used to give permission to men on pilgrimage to leave ʿArafa, and this function descended to his children after him. He and his sons used to be called Ṣūfa. Al-Ghauth used to exercise this function because his mother was a woman of Jurhum who had been barren and vowed to Allah that if she bore a son she would give him to the Kaʿba as a slave to serve it and to look after it. In course of time she gave birth to al-Ghauth and he used to look after the Kaʿba in early times with his Jurhum uncles and presided over the order of departure from ʿArafa because of the office which he held in the Kaʿba. His sons carried on the practice until they were cut off. Murr b. Udd, referring to the fulfilment of the mother's oath, said:

O Lord, I have made one of my sons
A devotee in Mecca the exalted.
So bless me for the vow fulfilled,
And make him the best of creatures to my credit.

Al-Ghauth, so they allege, used to say when he sent the people away:

O God I am following the example of others.
If that is wrong the fault is Quḍāʿa's.

Yaḥyā b. ʿAbbād b. ʿAbdullah b. al-Zubayr from his father ʿAbbād said: Ṣūfa used to send the people away from ʿArafa and give them permission to depart when they left Minā. When the day of departure arrived they used to come to throw pebbles, and a man of Ṣūfa used to throw for the men, none throwing until he had thrown. Those who had urgent business used to come and say to him: "Get up and throw so that we may throw with you", and he would say, "No, by God, not until the sun goes down"; and those who wanted to leave quickly used to throw stones at him to hurry him, saying, "Confound you, get up and throw". But he refused until the sun went down and then he would get up and throw while the men threw stones with him.

When they had finished the stoning and wanted to leave Minā, Ṣūfa held both sides of the hill and kept the men back. They said: "Give the order to depart, Ṣūfa". No one left until they had gone first. When Ṣūfa left and had passed on, men were left to go their own way and followed them. This was the practice until they were cut off. After them the next of kin inherited. They were of B. Sa'd in the family of Ṣāfwān b. al-Ḥārith b. Shijna. It was Ṣafwān who gave permission to the pilgrims to depart from 'Arafa, and this right was maintained by them up to Islam, the last being Karib b. Ṣafwān.

Aus b. Tamīm b. Maghrā' al-Sa'dī said:

> The pilgrims do not quit their halting-place at 'Arafa
> Until it is said, "Give permission O family of Ṣafwān [1])".

The verses of Abū Maghrā' are often quoted and the importance of the duty of Karib b. Ṣafwān is stressed [2]). It is a significant verse of Aus b. Maghrā':

> *Tarā thinānā, idhā mā jā'a, bad'ahumū*
> *wa-bad'uhum, in atānā, kāna thunyānā* [3])

The *ijāza* of Ṣūfa is mentioned in the verses of Murra b. Khulayf:

> *Idhā mā ajāzat Ṣūfatu 'l-naqba min Minan*
> *wa-lāḥa qutārun fauqahū safa'u 'l-dami*
> *Ra'aytu 'l-iyāba 'ājilan wa-taba''athat*
> *'alayna dawā'in li-l-Rabābi wa-Kalthami* [4])

The two poets of Tamīm, al-Farazdaq and Jarīr mention boasting

1) Ibn Hishām: *Sīra* I, 125 seq.; the translation of the whole quoted passage is taken from Guillaume: *The Life of Muhammad*, p. 49-50; comp. Ibn Kathīr: *al-Bidāya* II, 206.

2) al-Mubarrad: *Nasab*, p. 9; Muḥ. b. Ḥabīb: *al-Muḥabbar*, p. 183; al-Balādhurī: *Ansāb*, ms. f. 1044a; al-Qālī: *Amālī*, II, 176; al-Bakrī: *Simṭ*, p. 795-96; Ibn Qutayba: *al-Shi'r*, p. 264; Ibn 'Abd Rabbihi: *al-'Iqd al-farīd* II, 222; Ibn Abī 'l-Ḥadīd: *Sharḥ nahj al-balāgha* III, 426. Ibn Wallād: *al-Maqṣūr wa-l-mamdūd*, p. 24.

3) L. 'A., s.v. *th . n . y*.

4) al-Marzubānī: *Mu'jam al-shu'arā'*, p. 382.

the *ijāza* of their tribe [1]) in Mecca. A verse of al-Farazdaq about the *ijāza* of Tamīm was considered as unsurpassed (*afkhar*) in boasting:

Idhā habaṭa 'l-nāsu 'l-Muḥaṣṣaba min Minan
'ashiyyata yaumi 'l-naḥri min ḥaythu 'arrafū
Tarā 'l-nāsa mā sirnā yasīrūna khalfanā
wa-in naḥnu auma'nā ilā 'l-nāsi waqqafū [2])

Jarīr says:

Wa-jawwāzu 'l-ḥajīji lanā 'alaykum
wa-'ādiyyu 'l-makārimi wa-l-manāri [3])

---

1) The tradition stating that Ṣūfa were the descendants of al-Ghauth b. Murr (called al-Rabīṭ, or Ṣūfa) is recorded by Ibn al-Kalbī: *Jamhara*, ms. f. 60a (they perished; Muḥ. b. Ḥabīb: *Mukhtalif al-qabā'il*; al-Balādhurī: *Ansāb*, ms. f. 956b; Ibn Qutayba: *al-Ma'ārif*, p. 34 (al-Ghauth b. Murr moved to al-Yaman and were called Ṣūfa); al-Kalā'ī: *al-Iktifā'*, I, 132 seq.; and see Wellhausen: *Reste*, p. 77; Caetani: *Annali* I, p. 105 (79).

There are however contradictory traditions about Ṣūfa. Al-Azraqī: *Akhbār* (Wüstenfeld, I, 128) reports that the men, who were entrusted with the duty of the *ifāḍa* were descendants of Ṣūfa, whose name was Akhzam; he was from the Māzin b. Asad. Al-Ghauth b. Ṣūfa, the son of Ṣūfa and a woman from Jurhum, was entrusted with the *ijāza* by Ḥubshiyya of the Khuzā'a. His descendants performed the *ifāḍa* in the times of Jurhum and Khuzā'a till they perished. In the times of Quraysh the *ifāḍa* passed to the 'Adwān (of Qays 'Aylān), to Zayd b. 'Adwān. The last man, who performed this duty when Islam appeared was Abū Sayyāra.

Al-Maqdisī (*Kit. al-Bad'* IV, 127-ed. Huart) records that Ṣūfa were a group from Jurhum, given the privilege of the *ijāza*. They were defeated in the battle with Quṣayy.

Yāqūt reports that the *ijāza* was in the beginning entrusted to people from Khuzā'a, passed to 'Adwān and became the privilege of Abū Sayyāra; finally it became the privilege of al-Ghauth b. Murr b. Udd (*al-Buldān*, s.v. Thabīr).

In another passage Yāqūt reports that a group of Jurhum, called Ṣūfa, used to perform the *ijāza*. The poet said about them:

Wa-lā yarīmūna fī 'l-ta'rīfi mauqi'ahum
ḥattā yuqāla: "*ajīzū āla Ṣūfānā*"

(Yāqūt: *al-Buldān*, s.v. Makka). The privilege passed to Khuzā'a, was later transferred to 'Adwān (Abū Sayyāra). Quṣayy removed Abū Sayyāra and his people.

According to al-Sijistānī (*al-Mu'ammarūn*, p. 51 ed. Goldziher) Ṣūfa performed the duty of the *ijāza* one day; on another day the duty was performed by 'Adwān. (see n. 34 of Goldziher.)

2) Ibn Rashīq: *al-'Umda* II, 137; al-'Askari: *Dīwān al-Ma'ānī*, I, 78; al-Farazdaq: *Dīwān*, p. 5667 (ed. al-Ṣāwī; there is a misprint: *auma'nā ilā 'l-nāri*, instead of *ilā 'l-nāsi*); but see al-Qālī: *al-Amālī* (Dhayl 119 inf.) and Ibn Rashīq: *al-'Umda II*, 269.

3) Jarīr: *Dīwān*, p. 298.

Al ʿAjjāj says describing the multitude of the pilgrims:

Ḥattā idhā mā ḥāna fiṭru ʾl-ṣuwwami
ajāza minnā jāʾizun lam yūqami [1])

These verses of the Tamīmī poets clearly point to the above co-operation between Quraysh and Tamīm. The fact that Quraysh invested Tamīm with the two most important duties in their religions and economic life: the *ḥukūma* and the *ijāza* [2]) shows that the Tamīm were in fact strong and influential and rendered considerable services to Mecca.

The suggestion of Wellhausen, that the granting of the *ijāza* to Ṣūfa (and later to Tamīm—K) shows, that Mecca was not the center of the *ḥajj* [3]) seems not to be adequate. Quraysh ceded their authority or invested a clan with some duties in their territory or in the territory in which the exertion of influence was vital for Quraysh (the markets), because they could in this way more efficiently control the activities of the tribes and gain the security of their territory. There were precedents of this kind and this principle was already applied by the rulers of the border kingdoms [4]). About the investment of some duties in the market, we can gauge from a significant passage in al-Marzūqī's *Amkina* [5]):

Wa-kāna ashrāfu ʾl-ʿArabi yatawāfauna bi-tilka ʾl-aswāqi maʿa ʾl-tujjāri min ajli anna ʾl-mulūka kānat tarḍakhu li-l-ashrāfi, li-kulli sharīfin bi-sahmin

---

1) al-ʿAjjāj: *Dīwān*, p. 60 (ed. Ahlwardt).

2) For the *ijāza* see: von Grunebaum: *Muhammadan Festivals*, p. 32-33: Wellhausen: *Reste*, pp. 57, 75-80; about *ashriq Thabīr* see Abū Misḥal: *Nawādir*, p. 452; and see L. ʿA., s.v. *th b r* and *Sh r q*.

3) Wellhausen: *Reste*, p. 77: "Das Recht, das Zeichen zum Beginne des Laufes zu geben, die sogenannte *Iğāza* stand in alter Zeit den Çufa d. i. den Āl Çafwān zu, nicht den Quraisch (B. Hischām 77_{12}, 80_5, 82_5, vrgl, Agh. III, 4_{17}, seq.). Das ist bemerkenswert. Hätte Mekka im Mittelpunkt gestanden, so hätten es auch die Quraisch getan; statt dessen wird berichtet, dass sie in der heidnischen Zeit sich gar nicht an der Festversammlung zu ʿArafa beteiligten, sondern erst an einem späteren Punkte zu der Prozession stiessen".

4) Comp. Ibn Ḥabīb: *Asmāʾ al-mughtālīn* (*Nawādir al-makṭūṭāt*, ed. A. S. Hārūn 6, 221). But perhaps to read *mulayk* not *malīk* (*ay laysa bi-l-maliki l-tāmmi*).

5) al-Marzūqī: *al-Amkina*, II, 166.

min al-arbāḥi. Fa-kāna sharīfu kulli baladin yaḥḍuru sūqa baladihi, illā ʿUkāẓa, fa-innahum kānū yatawāfauna bihā min kulli aubin.

"And the nobles (leaders of the tribes) used to frequent these markets with the merchants, because the kings used to allot to every leader (*sharīf*, noble), a share of the profits. The leader of every area used to attend the market of this district, except ʿUkāẓ, as they flocked to ʿUkāẓ from every side".

This passage gives some idea about the relations between the rulers and the Bedouin chiefs. They were granted some share in the profits. Such apparently was the situation in Dūmat al-Jandal, at Hajar, at Ṣuḥār-at Dabā and in other markets, controlled by rulers of client kingdoms in which there were taxes levied. In the same way Quraysh invested the Tamīm with the privilege of the leadership of the market of ʿUkāẓ. But this was not based on some paltry reward. ʿUkāẓ was a free market where no taxes were paid. There is no indication what this reward was. The expression *aʾimmat al-ʿArab* points to some principle of mutual co-operation. As an ideological base served the principle of the respect for the sanctuary of Mecca and the sacred months. It is clear that the consent of the tribes was necessary for the performing of this duty.

The control of the markets and the *ijāza* were of importance not only for the tribes. It was of the concern of some rulers as well. This can be gauged from a significant tradition reported by Suhaylī: *wa-qāla baʿḍu naqalati ʾl-akhbāri inna wilāyata ʾl-Ghauthi kānat min qibali mulūki Kindata.* "Some transmitters of historical records say that the appointment of al-Ghauth (b. Murr) was done by the kings of Kinda"[1]). These Ghauth b. Murr are said to have left for al-Yaman [2]). The traditions that al-Ghauth b. Murr emigrated to al-Yaman point clearly to their connections with South Arabia. According to tradition, after Ṣūfa were extinguished, the duty was inherited by the Ṣafwān b. al-Ḥārith b. Shijna of the Saʿd, who were next in kin (*fa warithahum dhālika min baʿdihim bi-l-quʿdudi*). One may remember that this family had close connections

1) al-Suhaylī: *al-Rauḍ al-unuf I*, 84 inf.

2) See above, p. 154, n. 1.

with the Kinda family. It was Uwayr b. Shijna who sheltered some members of the defeated family of Kinda and was praised by Imru 'l-Qays. It was Karib b. Ṣafwān who refused to join the other clans of Tamīm in their attack against the ʿĀmir b. Ṣaʿṣaʿa, who belonged to the Ḥums, at the battle of Jabala. One may venture to suggest that there is a grain of truth in this tradition. The Kinda co-operated with Quraysh in the escort of caravans [1]) and it is plausible that they influenced at least the appointment of the man and the clan who performed the *ijāza*.

A Saʿdī leader and poet, al-Zibriqān b. Badr, reproached a man who dared to slander Abū Jahl. He said:

Atadrī man hajauta Abā Ḥabībin
salīla khaḍārimin sakanū 'l-biṭāḥa
A "Zāda 'l-Rakbi" tadhkuru am Hishāman
wa-bayta 'llāhi wa-l-balada
l-laqāḥa [2])

The verses express loyalty and respect to the aristocratic Qurashite (Abū Jahl) and devotion for Mecca.

The branch of Tamīm to whom the function of the judge at Ukāẓ was entrusted were the Mujāshiʿ of the Dārim, a clan influential at the court of al-Ḥīra [3]).

The tradition discussed in this paper give us a rough idea how the clans of Tamīm became linked with Mecca: some of them by the organization of the Ḥums, some of them by the pacts of *īlāf*, some of them by getting the authority at the markets and in performing of the rites of the *ḥajj*, some of them by participating in the intertribal militia to guard Mecca.

It is plausible that we find in Mecca men from Tamīm as *ḥulafāʾ* and daughters of Tamīmī chiefs married by leaders of Meccan clans. This fact may deserve to be stressed. According to some traditions, Quraysh

1) Comp. Muḥ. b. Ḥabīb: *al-Muḥabbar*, p. 267 (about the market of al-Rābiya in Ḥaḍramaut): "..the Quraysh used to request the escort of Kinda..and the Banū Ākil al-Murār gained power, owing to Quraysh, over other people"..

2) Yāqūt: *Buldān*, s.v. Makka.

3) See Oppenheim — Caskel: *Die Beduinen*, III, 166.

refrained from marrying daughters of some tribes. Tumāḍir bint al-Asbagh of Kalb, the wife of ʿAbd al-Raḥmān b. ʿAuf was the first Kalbī woman married by a Qurashite. Quraysh did not enter into marriages with Kalb [1]). About a family of Tamīm tradition emphasizes that Quraysh entered into marriages with this family [2]).

The wife of the noble Makhzūmite, Hishām b. al-Mughīra, the mother of the famous Abū Jahl, was Asmāʾ bint Mukharriba b. Jandal b. Ubayr b. Nahshal b. Dārim. She was as well the mother of ʿAbdallah b. Abī Rabīʿa and ʿAyyāsh b. Abī Rabīʾa [3]). ʿAyyāsh b. Abī Rabīʿa [4]) married Asmāʾ bint Salāma b. Mukharriba b. Jandal [5]). ʿAbdallah b. ʿAyyāsh b. Abī Rabīʿa married Hind bint Muṭarrif b. Salāma b. Mukharriba [6]). ʿAbdallah b. Abī Rabīʿa married the daughter of the Tamīmī leader ʿUṭārid b. Ḥājib b. Zurāra - Laylā [7]). Abū Jahl married the daughter of ʿUmayr b. Maʿbad b. Zurāra [8]). ʿUbaydullah b. ʿUmar b. al-Khaṭṭāb married Asmāʾ bint ʿUṭārid b. Ḥājib b. Zurāra [9]). Khaula bint al-Qaʿqāʿ b. Maʿbad b. Zurāra b. ʿUdas married Talḥa b. ʿUbaydallah; her second marriage was with Abū Jahm b. Ḥudhayfa [10]). Laylā bint

1) al-Muṣʿab al-Zubayrī: *Nasab Quraysh*, p. 267; al-Zubayr b. Bakkār: *Nasab Quraysh*, ms. f. 95 b.

2) al-Balādhurī: *Ansāb*, ms. f. 989 b: ..*kāna sharīfan wa-qad nakaḥat ilayhi Qurayshun*..

3) Ibn al-Kalbī: *Jamhara*, ms. f. 36a, 67b; al-Jumaḥī: *Ṭabaqāt fuḥūl al-shuʿarāʾ*, p. 123; al-Zubayr b. Bakkār: *Nasab Quraysh*, ms. f. 135a, 140 b; al-Muṣʿab al-Zubayrī: *Nasab Quraysh*, pp. 317, 301; al-Wāqidī: *Maghāzī*, pp. 83-84; Abū ʾl-Faraj: *al-Aghānī* I, 29 seq.; *Naqāʾiḍ*, p. 607; al-Balādhurī: *Ansāb*, ms. f. 986 b, 804a; Ibn ʿAbd al-Barr: *al-Istīʿāb*, p. 495; al-Balādhurī; *Ansāb* I, 298, 209, 235; Ibn Ḥajar: *al-Iṣāba* VIII, 10 (No. 55 women).

4) See about him: Ibn Ḥajar: *al-Iṣaba*, No. 6118.

5) Ibn Hishām: *Sīra* I, 273; Ibn ʿAbd al-Barr: *al-Istīʿāb*, p. 705; al-Muṣʿab al-Zubayri: *Nasab Quraysh*, pp. 267, 319; al-Zubayr b. Bakkār: *Nasab Quraysh*, ms. f. 96a.

6) al-Muṣʿab al-Zubayrī: *Nasab Quraysh*, p. 319; Ibn Saʿd: *Ṭabaqāt* V, 28.

7) al-Muṣʿab al-Zubayrī: *Nasab Quraysh*, p. 318; al-Zubayr b. Bakkār: *Nasab Quraysh*, ms. f. 141a; Ibn Ḥajar: *al-Iṣāba* VIII, 182; al-Balādhurī: *Ansāb*, ms. f. 804 b.

8) al-Muṣʿab al-Zubayrī: *op. cit.*, p. 312; al-Zubayr b. Bakkār, *op. cit.* f. 135 b.

9) al-Jumaḥī: *Ṭabaqāt fuḥūl al-shuʿarāʾ*, p. 488 n. 3.

10) al-Zubayr b. Bakkār, *op. cit.*, ms. f. 118a, 171a; al-Balādhurī: *Ansāb*, ms. f. 871a; al-Muṣʿab al-Zubayrī, *op. cit.*, pp. 372, 281; Ibn Ḥajar: *al-Iṣāba* VIII, 71 (No. 371); Ibn Saʿd: *Ṭabaqāt* III I, 152; V, 120; VI, 147 (ed. Leiden).

Mas'ūd b. Khālid b. Mālik b. Rib'ī b. Sulmī b. Jandal b. Nahshal married 'Alī b. Abī Ṭālib; her second marriage was with 'Abdallah b. Ja'far b. Abī Ṭālib [1]). 'Aqīl b. Abī Ṭālib married the daughter of Sinān b. al-Ḥautakiyya of the Sa'd b. Zayd Manāt [2]). The daughters of al-Zibriqān b. Badr married Sa'd b. Abī Waqqaṣ, al-Musawwir b. Makhrama al-Zuhrī, 'Amr b. Umayya al-Ḍamrī, al-Ḥārith b. al-Ḥakam b. Abī 'l-'Āṣ b. Umayya b. 'Abd Shams, 'Uthmān b. Abī 'l-'Āṣ, al-Ḥakam b. Abī 'l-'Āṣ, Umayya b. Abī 'l-'Āṣ [3]).

Umayya al-Aṣghar, 'Abd Umayya, Naufal and Ama were the children of 'Abd Shams b. 'Abd Manāf, born by his wife, 'Abla bint 'Ubayd b. Jādhil b. Qays b. Ḥanẓala b. Mālik b. Zayd Manāt; their descendants were called *al-'Abalāt* [4]). Naufal b. 'Abd Manāf b. Quṣayy married Fukayha bint Jandal b. Ubayr b. Nahshal b. Dārim [5]). One of the wives of al-Muṭṭalib b. 'Abd Manāf b. Quṣayy was Umm al-Ḥārith bint al-Ḥārith b. Salīṭ b. Yarbū' b. Ḥanẓala b. Mālik b. Zayd Manāt [6]). Umayya b. Khalaf married a Tamīmī woman, Salmā bint 'Auf; she gave birth to 'Alī b. Umayya killed at Badr [7]). Wahb b. 'Uthmān b. Abī Ṭalḥa of the 'Abd al-Dār b. Quṣayy married Su'da bint Zayd b. Laqīṭ of the Māzin b. 'Amr b. Tamīm [8]). Ḥarb b. Umayya married a Tamīmī woman [9]).

Nāfi' b. Ṭarīf b. 'Amr b. Naufal b. 'Abd Manāf married Ghaniyya bint Abī Ihāb b. 'Azīz b. Qays b. Suwayd b. Rabī'a b. Zayd b. 'Abd b. Dārim [10]). Abū Ihāb was a descendant of Suwayd b. Rabī'a who

1) Ibn al-Kalbī, *Jamhara*, ms. f. 9a: al-Balādhurī's *Ansāb*, ms. f. 153a: al Muṣ'ab al-Zubayrī, *op. cit.*, pp. 44, 83; Ibn Ḥajar: *al-Iṣāba* No. 8404; Ibn Sa'd: *Ṭabaqat* III, 19.

2) al-Balādhurī: *Ansāb*, ms. f. 154a, 1050a.

3) al-Balādhurī: *Ansāb*, ms. f. 1044a; al-Muṣ'ab al-Zubayrī, *op. cit.*, p. 169.

4) Ibn al-Kalbī *Jamhara*, ms. f. 116; al-Muṣ'ab al-Zubayrī, *op. cit.*, p. 98; Mu'arrij al-Sadūsī: *Ḥadhf*, p. 30; al-Balādhurī: *Ansāb*, ms. f. 345, 806; Abū 'l-Faraj: *Aghānī* I, 82.

5) al-Muṣ'ab al-Zubayrī: *op. cit.*, p. 198; al-Balādhurī: *Ansāb*, ms. f. 808a (Kuhayfa bint Jandal—not Fukayha); Ibn al-Kalbī: *Jamhara*, ms. f. 21a.

6) Ibn al-Kalbī: *Jamhara*, ms. f. 20; al Muṣ'ab al-Zubayrī, *op. cit.*, pp. 44, 83; Ibn Ḥajar: *al-Iṣāba* No. 8404; Ibn Sa'd: *Ṭabaqat* III, 19.

7) al-Zubayr b. Bakkār, *op. cit.*, f. 176 b; al Muṣ'ab al-Zubayrī, *op. cit.*, p. 387 inc.

8) al-Zubayr b. Bakkār, *op. cit.*, f. 88a.

9) al-Muṣ'ab al-Zubayrī, *op. cit.*, p. 123.

10) al-Muṣ'ab al-Zubayri, *op. cit.*, p. 204.

killed a son of the ruler of al-Ḥīra and escaped to Mecca. He became an ally of the Naufal b. ʿAbd Manāf. The grandfather of Ghaniyya, ʿAzīz b. Qays married Fākhita bint ʿĀmir b. Naufal b. ʿAbd Manāf [1]). Abū Ihāb b. ʿAzīz, the father of Ghaniyya married Durra bint Abī Lahab, the uncle of the prophet [2]). The daughter of Abū Ihāb married ʿAbd al-Raḥmān b. ʿAttāb b. Asīd b. Abī ʾl-ʿĪṣ b. Umayya b. ʿAbd Shams [3]).

The granddaughter of Abū Lahab, Durra bint ʿUtba b. Abī Lahab married a Tamīmī: Hind b. Hind b. Abī Hāla the grandson of Khadīja from her first (or second) husband, the Tamīmī Abū Hāla [4]). The daughter of Naufal b. al-Ḥārith b. ʿAbd al-Muṭṭalib [5]) married the Tamīmī Ḥanẓala b. al-Rabīʿa, the secretary of the Prophet [6]), the nephew of Aktham b. Ṣayfī [7]).

The list of the Tamīmī women who married the men of the aristocratic families of Quraysh is not comprehensive at all. There seems to have been a considerable number of Tamīmī women who married the sons of distinguished families of Mecca. It points to the close relations between Quraysh and Tamīm. These marriages may have been intended to strengthen the ties with the chiefs of Tamīm, who contributed considerably to strengthen the position of Mecca in the tribal society.

---

1) al-Muṣʿab al-Zubayrī, *op. cit.*, pp. 204, 420; al-Zubayr. b. Bakkār, *op. cit.*, f. 186a; Abū'l-Baqā', *op. cit.*, f. 150b.
2) Ibn al-Kalbī: *Jamhara*, ms. f. 116 b.
3) al-Muṣʿab al-Zubayrī, *op. cit.*, p. 193.
4) Ibn al-Kalbī: *Jamhara*, ms. f. 118b.
5) See about him: Ibn Ḥajar: *al-Iṣāba*, No. 8827.
6) Ibn al-Kalbī: *Jamhara*, ms. f. 118a.
7) See about him: Ibn Ḥajar: *al-Iṣāba*, No. 1855.

BIBLIOGRAPHY

al-ʿAbbāsī: *Maʿāhid al-tanṣīṣ*, Cairo 1316 A.H.
Abū ʾl-Baqāʾ Hibatu ʾllāh: *al-Manāqib al-mazyadiyya fī akhbār al-mulūk al-asadiyya*, ms. Br. Mus., add. 23, 296.
Abū Dharr: *Sharḥ* al-Sīra ed. Brönnle, Cairo 1911.
Abū Ḥātim al-Sijistānī: *Kitāb al-Muʿammarīn*, ed. I. Goldziher, Leiden 1899.
Abū Ḥayyān: *Tafsīr al-baḥr al-muḥīṭ*, I-VIII, Cairo 1328 A.H.

Abū Mishal, Abd al-Wahhāb b. Ḥarīsh; *al-Nawādir*, ed. ʿIzzat Ḥasan, Damascus 1961.
Abū Nuʿaym al-Iṣbahānī: *Ḥilyat al-awliyā*, I-X, Cairo 1932-1938.
Abū ʿUbayd: *Kitāb al-amwāl*, Cairo 1353 A.H.
al-ʿAjjāj: *Dīwān*, ed. W. Ahlwardt, Berlin 1903.
al-Alūsī: *Bulūgh al-Arab*, Cairo 1940.
W. Arafat: "An Interpretation of the Different Accounts of the Visit of the Tamīm Delegation to the Prophet in A.H. 9", *BSOAS* (1955), pp. 416-425.
al-Aʿshā: *Dīwān*, ed. R. Geyer, Wien 1928 (Gibb Memorial Series, VI).
al-ʿAskarī: *Dīwān al-maʿānī*, I-II, Cairo 1352 A.H.
al-Aṣmaʿiyyāt, ed. W. Ahlwardt,
al-Azraqī: *Akhbār Makka*, ed. F. Wüstenfeld *Die Chroniken der Stadt Mekka*), Leipzig 1858.
al-Bakrī, Abū ʿUbayd ʿAbdallah b. ʿAbd al-ʿAzīz: *Muʿjam maʾstaʿjam*, ed. M. al-Saqqā, Cairo 1945-1951.
——: *Simṭ al-laʾālī*, ed. ʿAbd al-ʿAzīz al-Maymanī, Cairo 1936.
al-Balādhurī, Aḥmad b. Yaḥyā: *Ansāb al-ashrāf*, ms. Ashir Efendi, 597/8, Istanbul; vol. I, ed. Muḥ. Ḥamīdullāh, Cairo 1959; vol. IV/B, ed. M. Schloessinger, Jerusalem 1938; vol. V, ed. S. D. Goitein, Jerusalem 1936.
H. Birkeland: *The Lord Guideth*, Oslo 1956.
F. Buhl: *Das Leben Muhammeds*, trans. H. H. Schaeder, Heidelberg 1955.
L. Caetani: *Annali dell'Islam*, I-II, Milano 1905-1907.
al-Ḍabbī: *Amthāl al-ʿArab*, Constantinople, 1300 A.H.
Daḥlān: *al-Sīra al-nabawiyya*, on margin of al-Ḥalabī's *Insān al-ʿUyūn*, I-III, Cairo 1932-1935.
al-Dhahabī: *Siyar aʿlām al-nubalāʾ*, I-II, ed. Ṣalāḥ al-Dīn al-Munajjid - I. al-Abyārī, Cairo 1956-1957.
——: *Taʾrīkh al-Islām*, I-V, Cairo 1367-1369 A.H.
al-Diyārbakrī, Ḥusayn b. Muḥ.: *Taʾrīkh al-Khamīs*, I-II, Cairo 1283 A.H.
al-Farazdaq: *Dīwān*, ed. al-Ṣāwī, Cairo 1936.
al-Fāsī, Abū 'l-Ṭayyib, Muḥ b. Abdallah b. Alī: Shifāʾu 'l-gharām, ed. F. Wüstenfeld (*Die Chroniken der Stadt Mekka*), Leipzig 1859.
G. von Grunebaum: *Muhammadan Festivals*, New York 1951.
A. Guillaume: *The Life of Muhammad*, Oxford University Press, 1955.
al-Ḥalabī, ʿAlī b. Burhān al-Dīn: *Insān al-ʿuyūn*, I-III, Cairo 1932-1935.
al-Hamdānī: *al-Iklīl*, I-II, ms. facsimile, Berlin 1943.
M. Hamidullah: "al-Īlāf ou les rapports économico-diplomatiques de la Mecque pré-Islamique", *Mélanges Louis Massignon*, II, p. 293 sep.
——: *Muslim Conduct of State*, Lahore 1961.
——: *Le Prophète de l'Islam*, Paris 1959.
Ḥassān b. Thābit: *Dīwān*, ed. A.R. al-Barqūqī, Cairo 1929.
al-Ḥutayʾa: *Dīwān* ed. A.R. al-Barqūqī, Cairo 1929.
al-Ḥuṭayʾa: *Dīwān*, ed. N. A. Ṭāhā, Cairo 1958.
Ibn ʿAbd al-Barr: *al-Inbāh ʿalā qabāʾil al-ruwāh*, Cairo 1350 A.H.
——: *al-Istīʿāb fī maʿrifat al-aṣḥāb*, Hyderabad 1336 A.H.
Ibn ʿAbd Rabbihi: *al-ʿIqd al-Farīd*, I-IV, Cairo 1935.
Ibn al-Jauzī: *Ṣifat al-Ṣafwa*, Hyderabad 1355-57 A.H.
Ibn Abī 'l-Ḥadīd: *Sharḥ nahj al-balāgha*, I-IV, Cairo 1329 A.H.
Ibn al-ʿArabi: *Muḥāḍarat al-Abrār*, I-II, Cairo 1906.

Ibn al-Athīr: *al-Muraṣṣaʿ*, ed. C. F. Seybold, Weimar 1896.
Ibn Durayd: *al-Ishtiqāq*, ed. A. S. Harun, Cairo 1958.
Ibn al-Faqīh: *Kitāb al-buldān*, ed. de Goeje, Leiden 1885.
Ibn Ḥabīb, Muḥammad: *Asmāʾ al-mughtālīn min al-ashrāf*, ed. A. S. Hārūn (*Nawādir al-makhṭuṭāt* VI).
——: *al-Muḥabbar*, ed. Ilse Lichtenstädter, Hyderabad 1942.
——: *Muktalif al-qabāʾil*, ed. F. Wüstenfeld, Göttingen 1850.
ibn Ḥajar: *al-Iṣāba fī tamyīẓ al-ṣahāba*, I-VIII, Cairo 1323-1327 A.H.
Ibn Ḥazm: *Jamharat ansāb al-ʿArab*, ed. E. Lévi-Provençal, Cairo 1948.
——: *Jawāmiʿ al-sīra*, ed. I. ʿAbbās — Nāṣir al-Dīn al-Asad, A.M. Shākir.
Ibn Hishām: *al-Sīra al-nabawiyya*, I-IV, ed. Muṣtafā al-Saqqā — Ibrāhīm al-Abyārī — ʿAbd al-Ḥāfiẓ Shalabī.
Ibn al-Jārūd: *al-Muntaqā*, Hyderabad 1309 A.H.
Ibn al-Kalbī, Hishām b. Muḥ.: *Jamharat al-nasab*, ms. Br. Mus. add. 23297.
Ibn Kathīr: *al-Bidāya wa-l-nihāya*, I-XIV, Cairo 1351-1358 A.H.
Ibn Qutayba: al-Maʿānī 'l-Kabīr, I-III, Hyderabad 1949.
——: *al-Maʿārif*, Cairo 1935.
——: *al-Shiʿr wal-lʾshuʿarāʾ*, ed. M. al-Saqqā, Cairo 1932.
Ibn Rashīq: *al-ʿUmda*, I-II, ed. M. Muḥyi 'l-Dīn ʿAbd al-Ḥamīd, Cairo 1934.
Ibn Saʿd: *al- Ṭabaqāt al-Kubrā*, I-VIII, ed. Beirut 1960.
Ibn al-Shajarī: *al-Ḥamāsa*, Hyderabad 1345 A.H.
Ibn Sharaf: *Rasāʾil al-intiqād* (in *Rasāʾil al-bulaghāʾ*, ed. Muḥammad Kurd ʿAlī, Cairo 1946).
al-Jāḥiẓ: *al-Ḥayawān*, I-VII, ed. A. S. Hārūn, Cairo 1938-1945.
——: *Mukhtārāt fuṣūl al-Jāḥiẓ*, ms. Br. Mus., Or. 3183 (Catalogue Rieu, suppl. p. 709).
——: *Rasāʾil*, ed. H. al-Sandūbī, Cairo 1933.
Jarīr: *Dīwān*, ed. al-Ṣāwī, Cairo 1353 A.H.
al-Jumaḥī: *Ṭabaqāt fuḥūl al-shuʿarāʾ*, ed. M. M. Shākir, Cairo 1952.
al-Kalāʿī, Abū 'l-Rabīʿ Sulayman b. Sālim: *Kitāb al-Iktifāʾ*, I, ed. H. Masse, Alger 1931.
al-Khālidiyyāni: *al-Ashbāh wa-l-naẓāʾir*, ed. Muḥ. Yūsuf, Cairo 1958.
Labīd: *Dīwān*, ed. I. ʿAbbās, Kuwayt 1962.
G. Levi della Vida: "Pre-Islamic Arabia" in N. A. Faris (ed.), *The Arab Heritage*, Princeton 1944.
al-Maghribī, al-Wazīr, al-Ḥusayn b. ʿAlī: *al-Īnās bi-ʿilmi 'l-ansāb*, ms. Br. Mus., Or. 3620.
al-Majlisī: *Biḥār al-anwār*, vol. VI, 1302 A.H.
al-Maqdisī, Muṭahhar b. Ṭāhir: *al-Badʿ wa-l-taʾrīkh*, ed. U. Huart, Paris 1899-1919.
al-Marzubānī: *Muʿjam al-shuʿarāʾ*, ed. F. Krenkow, Cairo 1354 A.H.
al-Marzūqī: *al-Azmina wa-l-amkina*, I-II, Hyderabad 1332 A.H.
——: *Sharḥ dīwan al-ḥamāsa*, ed. A. Amīn — A. S. Hārūn, Cairo 1953.
al-Masʿūdī: *Muruj al-Dhahab*, ed.Muḥ. Muḥyi al-Dīn ʿAbd al-Ḥamīd, Cairo 1357 A.H.
Muʾarrij al-Sadūsī: *al-Ḥadhf min nasab Quraysh*, ed. Ṣalāḥ al-Dīn al-Munajjid, Cairo 1960.
al-Mubarrad: *Nasab ʿAdnān wa-Qaḥṭān*, ed. ʿAbd al-ʿAzīz al-Maymanī, Cairo 1936.
al-Mufaḍḍal al-Ḍabbī: *al-Mufaḍḍaliyyāt*, ed. C. Lyall, Oxford 1918-1921; ed. A. M. Shākir — A. S. Hārūn, Cairo 1952.

Muṣ'ab b. 'Abdallah al-Zubayrī: *Nasab Quraysh*, ed. E. Lévi-Provençal, Cairo 1953.
al-Najīramī: *Aymān al-'Arab*, ed. Muḥibb al-Dīn al-Khaṭīb, Cairo 1928.
Naqā'iḍ Jarīr wa-l-Farazdaq, ed. A. A. Bevan, Leiden 1905-1912.
T. Nöldeke: *Geschichte der Perser und Araber zur Zeit der Sassaniden*, Leiden 1879.
M. von Oppenheim — W. Caskel — E. Bräunlich: *Die Beduinen*, I-III, Wiesbaden 1939-1952.
al-Qālī: *Dhayl al-amālī*, and "*Nawādir*", ed. 'Abd al-'Azīz al-Maymanī, Cairo 1926.
al-Qummī- *Gharā'ib al-qur'ān*, on margin of Ṭabarī's Tafsīr, Būlāq 1323-1329 A.H.
al-Qurṭubī: *al-Jāmi' li-aḥkām al-qur'ān*, ed. Cairo, 1935-46.
C. Rathjens: *Die Pilgerfahrt nach Mecca*, Hamburg 1948.
G. Rothstein: *Die Dynastie der Laḥmiden in al-Ḥīra*, Berlin 1899.
al-Shahrastānī: *al-Milal wa-l-niḥal*, ed. W. Cureton, London 1846.
al-Suhaylī: *al-Rauḍ al-unuf*, I-II, Cairo 1914.
al-Suyūṭī: *al-Durr al-manthūr fi 'l-tafsīr bi-l-ma'thūr*, I-VI, Teheran 1377 A.H.
al-Ṭabarānī: *al-Mu'jam al-ṣaghīr*, Delhi 1311 A.H.
al-Ṭabarī, Muḥ. b. Jarīr: *Ta'rīkh al-umam wa-l-mulūk*, I-VIII, Cairo 1939.
al-Ṭabarsī: *Majma' al-bayān*, I-XXX, Beirut 1957.
al-Tha'ālibī: *Laṭā'if al-ma'ānī*, ed. de Jong, Leiden 1867.
——: *Thimār al-qulūb fī 'l-muḍāf wa-l-mansūb*, Cairo 1908.
U. Thilo: *Die Ortsnamen in der altarabischen Poesie*, Wiesbaden 1958.
al-Wāqidī: *al-Maghāzī*, ed. A. von Kremer, Calcutta 1856.
J. Wellhausen: *Reste arabischen Heidentums*, Berlin 1887.
E. R. Wolf: "The Social Organization of Mecca and the Origins of Islam", *Southwestern Journal of Anthropology* (1951), 330-337.
al-Ya'qūbī: *Ta'rīkh*, I-III, al-Najaf 1358 A.H.
Yāqūt: *Mu'jam al-buldān*, I-VIII, Cairo 1906.
Ẓāfir al-Qāsimī: *al-Īlaf wa-l-ma'ūnāt ghayru 'l-mashrūṭa*, *RAAD*, XXXIV.
al-Zubayr b. Bakkār: *Jamharat nasab Quraysh wa-akhbārihā*, ms. Bodley. Marsh. 384; vol. I, ed. Maḥmūd Muḥ. Shākir, Cairo 1381 A.H.
al-Zurqānī: *Sharḥ al-mawahib al-ladunniyya*, Cairo 1325-1328 A.H.

ADDITIONAL NOTES

ad p.118, note 2: Comp. Ibn Ẓafar al-Ṣaqalī, *Anbāʾ nujabāʾ al-abnāʾ*, ed. Muṣṭafā al-Qabānī, Cairo n.d., pp. 66-68; al-ʿIṣāmī, *Simṭ al-nujūm al-ʿawālī*, Cairo 1380 AH, I, 214-215; *Siyar al-mulūk*, Ms. Br. Mus., Add. 23298, fol. 174a.

p.119, 1.10: A significant report, quoted from *al-Kamāʾim* (not extant) is given by Ibn Saʿīd in his *Nashwat al-ṭarab*, Ms. Tübingen, fol. 97 r-v.: *qāla ṣāḥibu l-kamāʾimi: kānat qurayshun qad inqaṭaʿat ʿinda l-bayti wa-kānat al-ʿarabu llatī ḥaulahā tamnaʿuhum min al-khurūji fī ṭalabi l-maʿāshi, wa-lam yakun lahum ʿayshun illā mā yaʾtī l-mausimu ayyāma l-ḥajji; fa-lammā nashaʾa banū ʿabdi manāfin l-madhkūrūna akhadhū l-ʿaraba bi-l-siyāsati wa-l-muhādāt ilā an inqādū lahum wa-fataḥū l-ṭarīqa li-suffārihim ḥaythu shāʾū fa-khtaraʿū l-īlāfa lladhī dhakarahu llāhu ʿazza wa-jalla.*

p.121, note 1: And see on *Īlāf*: al-Mauṣilī, *Ghāyat al-wasāʾil ilā maʿrifati l-awāʾil*, Ms. Cambridge Qq·33, fol. 16b-17a; Anonymous, *al-Taʾrīkh al-muḥkam fīman intasaba ilā l-nabiyyi ṣallā llāhu ʿalayhi wa-sallam*, Ms. Br. Mus., Or. 8653, fol. 60b-61a; Ibn Nāṣir al-Dīn al-Dimashqī, *Jāmiʿ al-āthār fī maulidi l-nabiyyi l-mukhtār*, Ms. Cambridge Or. 913, fols. 111a-b; cf. al-Subkī, *Ṭabaqāt al-shāfiʿiyya*, ed. al-Ḥulw and al-Ṭanāḥī, Cairo 1385/1966, IV, 400-401.

ad p.121, note 3: See Ibn Kathīr, *al-Bidāya*, II, 316-317; *Siyar al-mulūk*, Ms. fol. 173b: Abū Ḥayyān al-Tauḥīdī, *al-Baṣāʾir wa-l-dhakhāʾir*, ed. Ibrāhīm al-Kaylānī, Damascus 1964, II, 222-223; Ibn ʿAsākir, *Taʾrīkh Dimashq (Tahdhīb)* VI, 118; Ibn Nāṣir al-Dīn, *op.cit.*, fol. 112a.

p.122, note 1: cf. Mughulṭāy, *al-Zahr al-bāsim fī sīrat abī l-qāsim*, Ms. Leiden, Or. 370, fol. 64b.

ad. p.123, note 1: *Siyar al-mulūk*, Ms. fol. 173a.

ad. p.126, note 5: See al-Mauṣilī, *Ghāyat al-wasāʾil ilā maʿrifati l-awāʾil*, Ms. Cambridge, Qq 33, fol. 58: ... *wa-qīla: awwalu man banā bihā baytan saʿdu bnu sahmin* (but see al-Fāsī, *Shifāʾu l-gharām*, Cairo 1956, I, 19: *saʿīd b. ʿamr b. ḥuṣayṣ al-sahmī;* comp. however Muṣʿab b. ʿAbdallah, *Nasab Quraysh*, p.400, 1.10) *fa-qāla ʿabdu llāhi bnu wādiʿata* (read: *bnu wadāʿata*; see Muṣʿab, *op.cit.*, p.406; and comp. al-Fāsī, *op. cit.*, I, 19: *wa-dhakara l-zubayru bnu bakkārin ʿan abī sufyāna bni abī wadāʿata* - which is the correct reading) *yaftakhiru:*

wa-saʿdu l-suʿūdi jāmiʿu l-shamli innahū: badā l-ḥilfa wa-l-aḥyāʾu ghayru ḥilāfi

fa-ausaqa ʿahda l-ḥilfi wa-l-wuddi baynahum: bi-amrin ḥaṣīfin fīhimū wa-naṣāfi

wa-dhālika mā arsā thabīru makānahū: wa-mā balla baḥrun ṣufatan bi-niṭāfi

wa-awwalu man bawwā bi-makkata baytahū: wa sawwara fīhi ***sākinan bi-athāfi*

**Ms. *saknan*; but see al-Fāsī, *op.cit.*, ib./. Al-Mauṣilī records (ib.) that the first who built a square house in Mecca was Budayl b. Warqā al-Khuzāʿī (the Companion of the Prophet - K).

Al-Wāqidī reports on the authority of al-Zuhrī (al-Fākihī, *Taʾrīkh Makkata*, Ms. Leiden, Or. 463, fol. 444b) that the first square house was built in Mecca during the *fitna* of ʿUthmān *(qāla l-wāqidī wa-ḥaddathanī muḥammadu bnu ʿabdi llāhi ʿan al-zuhrī qāla: mā buniya bi-makkata baytun murabbaʿun ḥattā kānat fitnatu ʿuthmāna raḍiya llāhu ʿanhu)*.

ad p.126, note 7: and see al-Fākihī, *op.cit.*, fol. 440b about the shape of the houses: ... *wa-innamā kānat ʿāmmata buyūtihim ʿurūshun min khaṣāṣifa wa-saʿafin wa-jarīdin, wa-kānū yusammūnahā l-ʿurūsha.*

p.130, note 4: and see al-Muʿāfā b. Zakariyyā, *al-Jalīs al-ṣāliḥ al-kāfī wa-l-anīs al-nāṣiḥ al-shāfī*, Ms. Topkapi Saray, Ahmet III, 2321, fol. 170a; Ali-Khān al-Madanī al-Shīrāzī, *al-Darajāt al-rafīʿa fī ṭabaqāt al-shīʿa*, ed. Muḥammad Ṣādiq Baḥr al-ʿulūm, Najaf 1381/1962, pp. 173-174.

ad p.132, note 1: and see Ibn Ẓafar al-Ṣaqalī, *op,cit.*, pp. 69-70.

ad p.132, note 7: and see al-Marzubānī, *Nūr al-qabas*, ed. F. Sellheim, Wiesbaden 1964, 258 (on the authority of al-Kalbī); Ibn Ḥabīb, *al-Munammaq*, ed. Khurshīd Aḥmad Fāriq, Hyderabad 1964, pp. 143-146; Muqātil, *Tafsīr al-khamsi miʾati āya*, Ms. Br. Mus., or. 6333, fol. 28b; idem, *Tafsīr*, Ḥamīdiyya 58, fols. 29b, 31b, 87b; about the peculiar customs of *ṭawāf* of the Thaqīf, Āmir b. Ṣaʿṣaʿa, Khuzā a Banū Mudlij and al-Ḥārith b. ʿAbd Manāt see ib., fol. 123a.

ad p.137, note 2: For the expression *"ahlu llāh"* see al-Fākihī, *op. cit.*, fol. 415b-416a; al-Azraqī, *op.cit.*, 380-381; Muḥ. Ḥusayn al-

Qazwīnī, *Sharḥ shawāhid majmaʿ al-bayān* Tehran 1338 H Sh., II, 62, no. 336; *Siyar al-mulūk*, Ms. fol. 177a.

p.138, note 5: and see about the Hums: Ibn Nāṣir al-Dīn, *op,cit.*, fol. 119a; al-Fāsī, *al-ʿIqd al-thamīn fī taʾrīkh al-balad al-amīn*, ed. Fuʾād Sayyid, Cairo 1378/1958, I, 140-141; al-Suyūṭī, *al-Durr al-manthūr*, I, 226-227; al-Taḥāwī, *Mushkil al-āthār*, Hyderabad 1333, II, 75-76; Muqātil, *Tafsīr*, Ms. Ahmet III, 74, I, 29b, 91a; Ibn al-ʿArabī, *Aḥkām al-Qurʾān*, ed. ʿAlī al-Bijāwī, Cairo 1387/1967, pp. 767-768; al-Muḥibb al-Ṭabarī, *al-Qirā li-qāṣidi ummi l-qurā*, ed. Muṣṭafā l-Saqā, Cairo 1390/1970, pp. 381-382; Ibn Junghul, *Taʾrīkh* Ms. Br. Mus., Or. 5912, I, 158b; al-Wāḥidī, *Asbāb al-nuzūl*, Cairo 1388/1968, p.152; Ibn Qutayba, *al-Maʿānī l-kabīr*, Hyderabad 1368/1949, pp. 989, 998; al-Ḥāzimī, *al-Iʿtibār fī bayāni l-nāsikh wa-l-munsūkh min al-āthār*, Hyderabad 1359, p. 150; Amīn Maḥmūd al-Khaṭṭāb, *Fatḥu l-maliki l-maʿbūd, takmilatu l-manhali l-ʿadhbi l-maurūd, sharḥ sunan abī dāwūd*, Cairo 1394/1974, pp. 40-41; and see art. II, 63, note 5.

ad p.139, note 2: and see al-ʿIṣāmī, *op.cit.*, I, 218: *wa-innamā summū l-ḥumsa bi-l-kaʿbati li-annahā ḥamsaʾu, ḥajaruhā abyaḍu yaḍribu ilā l-sawādi;* and see a significant definition of the Ḥums, ib, p. 219: *lam takun al-ḥums bi-ḥilfin wa-lakinnahu dīnun sharaʿathu Qurayshun wa-ajmaʿū ʿalayhi.*

ad p.139, note 10: al-Majlisī, *Biḥār al-anwār*, Tehran, new ed., XXII, 294 (reporting that Iyāḍ was a *qāḍī* at Ukāẓ).

ad p.140, note 1: and see al-Zamakhsharī, *Rabīʿ al-abrār*, Ms. Br. Mus. Or. 6511, fol. 83b: ... *lam tazal makkatu ḥarasahā llāhu amnan wa-laqāḥan; qāla ḥarbu bnu umayyata:*

abā maṭarin halumma ila ṣalāḥin:

fa-nakfiyaka l-nadāmā min qurayshi

fa-ta mana wasṭahum wa-taʿīsha fīhim: abā maṭarin mudidta bi-khayri ʿayshi

wa-tanzila baldatan ʿamirat laqāḥan; wa-taʾmana an yazūraka rabbu jayshi.

The word "*ṣalāḥ*" is explained as a name of Mecca.

and see *ib.*, fol. 113a: the king of Abyssinia demanded from ʿAbd al-Muṭṭalib to obey him (*an yadīna lahu*), but Mecca was *laqāḥ*; and see *ib.*, fol. 83b: the people of Mecca were demanded by some king to pay *itāwa*, but ʿAbd al- Muṭṭalib refused, (and comp. "Arabica", XV, (1968) p. 144, note 5); and see al-ʿIṣāmī, *op.cit.*, I, 213-214; Ibn Saʿīd, *op.cit.*, fol. 103 v.

ad p.141, note 3: and comp. al-ʿIṣāmī, *op.cit.*, I, 219.

ad p.144, 1.16 add: Al-ʿIṣāmī (*op.cit.*, I, 333) records the tradition of Ibn al-Kalbī, quoting it from Fākihī's *Taʾrīkh Makkata*. This tradition has an additional passage, which seems to be of some importance: The group of Ṣulṣul - says the tradition - used to alight at a well in the neibourhood of Minā called Biʾr Ṣulṣul; from this place they used to disperse in order to join the different groups of people. (About this well see al-Azraqī, *op.cit.*, p. 442).

II

SOME REPORTS CONCERNING MECCA

FROM JĀHILIYYA TO ISLAM [1]

Information about the conditions in Mecca in the period preceding Islam is scarce, and there are few accounts about the relations of Mecca with tribes and vassal kingdoms. Some data from hitherto unpublished Mss., or those published only recently may elucidate certain aspects of the inner situation in Mecca, and shed some light on the relations of Mecca with the tribes and the vassal kingdoms.

I

A passage in the anonymous *Nihāyat al-irab fī akhbār al-furs wa-l-ʿarab* [2]) gives some details about the activity of Hāshim b. ʿAbd Manāf and about the Expedition of the Elephant. It is noticeable that this report stresses especially the relations of Mecca with Abyssinia, not emphasized in other sources.

Hāshim, says the tradition, took from the kings of Abyssinia, al-Yaman, Persia and Syria charters permitting the merchants of Mecca to frequent these territories with their merchandise [3]). It is emphasized that the first king who granted him the charter was al-Najāshī and that "Abyssinia was the best land in which the Meccan merchants traded [4])." After receiving of the charter from the Najāshī Hāshim went to Yemen. The report furnishes us with some information about the kings who ruled in that period: in Yemen ruled Abraha b. al-Ashram who bore the *kunya* Abū Yaksūm [5]); he granted Hāshim the requested charter.

1) The reader's attention is called to the Addenda at the end of this article. Places in the text and the notes referred to in the Addenda are marked by asterisks.

2) See about this Ms.: E. G. Browne, *Some Account of the Arabic Work entitled Nihāyatu l-irab fī akhbāri l Fursi wa-l-ʿArab*, JRAS, 1900, pp. 195-204.

3) *Nihāyat al-irab*, Ms. Br. Mus., Add. 23298, fol. 174a: ... *wa-inna hāshiman sāra ilā l-mulūki fa-akhadha minhum al-ʿuhūda wa-l-ʿuqūda: lā yumnaʿu qaumuhu min al-tijārāti fī buldānihim wa-arḍihim.*

4) *Ibid.*: ... *wa-kānat arḍu l-ḥabashati min afḍali l-amākini llatī yatjaru fīhā qurayshun.*

5) It may be noticed that the social conditions in the army of the Abyssinians and

From the Yemen Hāshim journeyed to Jabala b. Ayham, the king of Syria; from Syria he proceeded to ʿIrāq, to Qubādh; from both of them he got the required charters. The final sentences of the report tell us about the results of the efforts of Hāshim and give a description of the changes which occurred in the relations of Mecca with the tribes and the neighbouring kingdoms as a result of the granted charters. "... Thus Quraysh traded in these territories and got profits and became rich; their wealth increased, their trade expanded; thus the Arabs overcame the *ʿAjam* by the abundance of wealth, generosity and excellence; they (i.e. Quraysh) were men of mind, reason, dignity, generosity, excellence, staid behaviour and nobility; they are the chosen people of God's servants, the best of His creature and the noblest of His peoples [1])."

---

the causes which brought about the fight between Aryāṭ and Abraha are given in the *Nihāyat al-irab* in more detail than in other sources. Aryāṭ, a nephew of the Najāshī, divided gifts and products after the conquest of the Yemen among the chiefs and nobles of the Abyssinians, treating scornfully the weak (i.e. the poor) and depriving them of his gifts (fol. 151a: ... *wa-farraqa l-ṣilāti wa-l-ḥawāʾija ʿalā ʿuẓamāʾi l-ḥabashati wa-ashrāfihim wa-ḥarama ḍuʿafāʾahum wa-ẓdarāhum fa-ghaḍibū min dhālika ghaḍaban shadīdan* ...). They appealed to Abraha, one of the officers of the army sent with Aryāṭ, and swore their allegiance to him. The weak part of the army stood behind Abraha, the strong and the noble behind Aryāṭ. In the well-known fight between them Abraha killed Aryāṭ. The declaration issued by Abraha after the duel stresses again the social aspect of the rebellion: "O Abyssinian people, God is our Lord, Jesus is our Prophet, the Gospel is our Book, the Najāshī is our king. I rebelled against Aryāṭ only because he abandoned equality amongst you. Therefore stand fast for equality amongst you, as God will not be pleased by preference in division (i.e. of spoils and grants—K) and by depriving the weak of their share of booty." (fol. 151b: *yā maʿshara l-ḥabashati llāhu rabbunā wa-ʿīsā nabiyyunā wa-l-injīlu kitābunā wa-l-najāshiyyu malikunā, wa-innī innamā kharajtu ʿalā aryāṭa li-tarkihi l-sawiyyata baynakum, fa-thbutū li-l-stiwāʾi baynakum, fa-inna llāha lā yarḍā bi-l-atharati fī l-qasmi wa-lā an yuḥrama l-ḍuʿafāʾu l-maghnama* ...) Abraha, stressing in his letter to the Najāshī his allegiance and loyalty, repeats his argument that Aryāṭ treated the weak unjustly (fol. 152a: ... *wa-innamā qataltu aryāṭa illā li-īthārihi l-aqwiyāʾa ʿalā l-ḍuʿafāʾi min jundika, fa-lam yakun dhālika min sīratika wa-lā raʾyika* ...). The lowly origin of Abraha is indicated in the remark of the Najāshī: ... *wa-innamā huwa qirdun min al-qurūdi, laysa lahu sharafun fī l-ḥabashati wa-lā aṣlun*. Cf. the account of Procopius in Sidney Smith's *Events in Arabia in the 6th Century AD*, BSOAS XVI (1954), pp. 431-432; and see Mughulṭāy, *al-Zahr al-bāsim*, Ms. Leiden, Or. 370, fol. 32a (quoted from Wāqidī): ... *fa-aʿṭā* (i.e. Aryāṭ) *l-mulūka wa-stadhalla l-fuqarāʾa.*

1) *Nihāyat al-irab*, fol. 174a, inf.: *fa-atjarat qurayshun fī hādhihi l-amākini kullihā fa-rabiḥū wa-athrau wa-kathurat amwāluhum wa-aẓumat tijāratuhum wa-sāda l-ʿarabu*

After the death of Hāshim his son ʿAbd al-Muṭṭalib took over his duties and mission; he died during the reign of Anūshirwān b. Qubādh [1]) In his time the well-known expedition of Abraha against Mecca took place.

According to Arab tradition Abraha built a temple (*haykal*, *qullays*) and tried to divert the pilgrimage to Mecca to his temple. The immediate cause for the expedition of Abraha was the desecration of this temple. We have conflicting traditions about the location of the temple (Ṣanʿāʾ, Najrān, a place on the sea shore) and the persons who burnt it, robbed it or relieved their bowels in it. According to the traditions the desecration was committed by Nufayl b. Ḥabīb al-Khathʿamī, [2]) by a man (or men) from Kināna [3]), or more accurately by a man from the *Nasaʾa* [4]) or by a group of Arabs.

The reports about the desecration (or the unintentional burning) of the temple point to Quraysh as the initiators of this action. The tradition that the deed was carried out by men from Kināna, or a group of *nasaʾa* or *ḥums* [5]) deserves special attention; these groups were closely related to Quraysh. A tribal leader of al-Ḥārith b. ʿAbd

---

ʿalā l-ʿajami bi-kathrati l-amwāli wa-l-sakhāʾi wa-l-faḍli; wa-kānū dhawī aḥlāmin wa-ʿuqūlin wa-bahāʾin wa-sakhāʾin wa-faḍlin wa-waqārin wa-nublin; fa-hum ṣafwatu llāhi min ʿibādihi wa-khīratuhu min jamīʿi khalqihi wa-afḍalu bariyyatihi.

1) *Ibid.*, fol. 174b, sup.

2) Al-Ṭabarī, *Taʾrīkh*, Cairo 1939, I, 556; Mughulṭāy, *op. cit.*, fol. 32a; al-Zurqānī, *Sharḥ al-mawāhib*, Cairo 1325, I, 83; *Nihāyat al-irab*, fol. 174a.

3) Muḥammad b. Ḥabīb, *al-Munammaq*, ed. Khurshīd Aḥmad Fāriq, Hyderabad 1384/1964, p. 68; al-Ṭabarī, *Taʾrīkh*, I, 551; al-Zurqānī, *op. cit.*, I, 83; al-Damīrī, *Ḥayāt al-ḥayawān*, Cairo 1383-1963, II, 230; and see al-Bayhaqī, *Dalāʾil al-nubuwwa*, Ms. Br. Mus., Or. 3013, fol. 13a: ... *anna rajulan min banī milkān b. kināna, wa-huwa min al-ḥums* ...

4) Al-Ṭabarī, *Taʾrīkh*, I, 550 inf.; al-Qurṭubī, *al-Jāmiʿ li-aḥkāmi l-qurʾān*, Cairo 1387/1967, XX, 188, 1.1; al-Kalāʿī, *al-Iktifāʾ*, ed. H. Massé, Paris 1931, I, 188 ult.; Ibn Hishām, *al-Sīra al-nabawiyya*, ed. al-Saqā, al-Abyārī, Shalabī, Cairo 1355/1936, I, 44 ult.; Ibn Kathīr, *al-Sīra al-nabawīyya*, ed. Muṣṭafā ʿAbd al-Wāḥid, Cairo 1384/1964, I, 30.

5) See about *al-ḥums* al-Shāṭibī, *al-Jumān fī akhbāri l-zamān*, Ms. Br. Mus., Or. 3008, fols. 43b, 55a; al-Ḥākim, *al-Mustadrak*, Hyderabad 1342, I, 483; al-Suyūṭī, *Lubāb al-nuqūl*, Cairo 1373/1954, pp. 25-26; al-Bakrī, *Muʿjam mā staʿjam*, ed. Muṣṭafā al-Saqā, Cairo 1364/1945, I, 245, s.v. *Birk*; Muqātil, *Tafsīr*, Ms. Ḥāmidiyya 58, fols. 87a, 103a; Ibn Ḥabīb, *al-Munammaq*, pp. 143-146; al-ʿIṣāmī, *Simṭ al-nujūm al-ʿawālī*, Cairo 1380, I, 218-219.

Manāt b. Kināna came to Mecca in order to conclude an alliance with a clan of Quraysh [1]. Kināna were the allies of Quraysh in the wars of *al-Fijār* [2]. The close co-operation of Kināna with Quraysh is reflected in a short passage recorded by al-Fākihī on the authority of al-Zuhrī where the crucial event of the boycott of the Banū Hāshim is recounted. When Quraysh decided to impose a boycott on the Banū Hāshim in connection with missionary activities of the Prophet, they allied with the Banū Kināna. The terms of the agreement between the two parties entailed that they should cease trading with the Banū Hāshim and desist from giving them shelter [3]. This passage may help us to evaluate the story of the boycott [4] and the reports about the co-operation of Quraysh with the neighbouring tribes and clans. It is not surprising to find traditions according to which a leader of Kināna participated in the delegation to Abraha, when he came with his army to destroy the Kaʿba. Consequently the version that men from Kināna committed the desecration seems to be preferable.

The reports usually describe the wrath of Abraha when he received the information about the desecration of his temple. The *Nihāyat al-irab* has a short but important passage about his reaction. Two men of Khathʿam, says the report, desecrated the temple of Abraha. Upon hearing about it he said: "This was committed by agents of Quraysh as they are angry for the sake of their House to which the Arabs resort for their pilgrimage." He swore to destroy the Kaʿba so that pilgrimage should be to the temple of Ṣanʿāʾ exclusively. "In Ṣanʿāʾ there were (at that time—K) Qurashī merchants", states the report. "Among them was Hishām b. al-Mughīra [5]." Abraha summoned

---

1) Ibn Ḥabīb, *al-Munammaq*, p. 288.

2) See e.g. *al-Munammaq*, p. 201 seq., al-Bakrī, *op. cit.*, s.v. ʿUkāẓ.

3) Al-Fākihī, *Taʾrīkh Makka*, Ms. Leiden, Or. 463, fol. 444b: ... *qāla l-zuhriyyu: wa-l-khayfu l-wādī ḥaythu taqāsamat qurayshun ʿalā l-kufri, wa-dhālika anna banī kinānata ḥālafat qurayshan ʿalā banī hāshimin an lā yubāyiʿūhum wa-lā yuʾwūhum*; and see this report: al-Bakrī, *op. cit.*, s.v. Khayf.; Aḥmad b. Ḥanbal, *Musnad*, ed. Shākir, XII 230, no. 7239.

4) Cf. W. Montgomery Watt, *Muhammad at Mecca*, Oxford 1953, pp. 119-122.

5) See on him Muṣʿab al-Zubayrī, *Nasab quraysh*, ed. E. Lévi Provençal, Cairo 1953, p. 301; al-Zubayr b. Bakkār, *Jamharat nasab quraysh*, Ms. Bodley, Marsh. 384, fols. 129a-130a.

the Qurashī merchants and asked them: "Have I not allowed you to trade freely in my country and ordered to protect you and to treat you honourably"? They said: "Yes, o king, so it was." Abraha asked: "So why did you secretly send men to the church built for the king, al-Najāshī, to defecate and to smear the walls with excrements?"' They answered: "We do not know about it." Abraha said: "I thought that you did it indeed out of anger for the sake of your House to which the Arabs go on pilgrimage, when I ordered to direct the pilgrims to this church." Hishām b. al-Mughīra then said: "Our House is (a place of) shelter and security; there gather there prey-beasts with wild animals, prey birds with innocous ones and they do not attack each other. Pilgrimage to your temple should be performed by those who follow your faith, but adherents of the faith of the Arabs [1]) will not choose or adopt anything (else) in preference to the House (i.e. the Kaʿba—K) [2])." Abraha swore to demolish the Kaʿba. Hishām b. al-Mughīra said that more then one king had intended to pull down the Kaʿba, but had failed to get there, as the House has a Lord who protects it. "Do what you like" (*sha'naka wa-mā aradta*) he finally said.

This seems to be an early tradition, reflecting as it does the conditions at the period preceding the expedition of Abraha and

---

1) For *dīnu l-ʿarab* see G. E. von Grunebaum, *The Nature of Arab Unity before Islam*, Arabica X (1963) p. 15.

2) *Nihāyat al-irab*, fols. 174b-175a: ...*fa-ukhbira bi-dhālika abrahatu fa-qāla: hādhā dasīsu qurayshin, li-ghaḍabihim li-baytihim lladhī* (text: llatī) *taḥujju ilayhi l-ʿarabu, wa-l-masīḥi la-ahdimanna dhālika l-bayta ḥajaran ḥajaran ḥattā yakhluṣa l-ḥajju ilā mā hā-hunā; wa-kāna bi-ṣanʿāʾa tujjārun min qurayshin, fīhim hishāmu bnu l-mughīrati, fa-arsala ilayhim* (text: *ilayhi*) *abrahatu, fa-aqbalū ḥattā dakhalū ʿalayhi, fa-qāla lahum: a-lam uṭliq lakum al-matjara fī arḍī wa-amartu bi-ḥifẓikum wa-ikrāmikum? qālū: balā, qad kāna dhālika; qāla: fa-mā ḥamalakum ʿalā an dasastum ilā hādhihi l-bīʿati llatī banaytuhā li-l-maliki l-najāshiyyi man* (text: *ḥattā*) *aḥdatha fīhā l-ʿadhirata wa-laṭakha bihā ḥīṭānahā? qālū: mā lanā bi-dhālika ʿilmun; qāla: qad ẓanantu annakum innamā faʿaltum dhālika ghaḍaban li-baytikum lladhī* (text: *llatī*) *taḥujju ilayhi l-ʿarabu ʿindamā amartu min taṣyīri l-ḥujjāji ilayhā; qāla hishāmu bnu l-mughīrati: inna baytanā ḥirzun wa-amnun yajtamiʿu fīhi l-sibāʿu maʿa l-waḥshi wa-jawāriḥu l-ṭayri maʿa l-bughāthi, wa-lā yaʿriḍu shayʾun minhā li-ṣāḥibihi; wa-innamā yanbaghī an yaḥujja ilā bīʿatika man kāna ʿalā dīnika; ammā man kāna ʿalā dīni l-ʿarabi fa-laysa bi-mukhtārin wa-lā muʾthirin ʿalā dhālika l-bayti shayʾan.*

corroborating the reports about commercial relations between Mecca and the Yemen in that period. There is little ground for suspicion that the story was fabricated: it contains no favourable features, heroic or Islamic, which would explain why it should have been invented; Makhzūm could have hardly any interest in forging it as one of the many "praises" of Hishām [1]). It remained in fact peripheral, not included in any of the reports of the expedition of Abraha.

The answer of Hishām in his talk with Abraha contains an interesting definition of the position of Mecca and its role as conceived by a Meccan leader. Mecca, in this concept, was a neutral city, not involved in intertribal wars, a place of security and a sanctuary to which every Arab had the right to make pilgrimage. Only adherents of a state religion should be ordered to perform their pilgrimage to a temple established by the ruler. It is hardly necessary to observe that this neutral position enabled Mecca to expand its commercial relations with the tribes.

A similar opinion about Mecca was expressed by Qurra b. Hubayra, a tribal leader, in a decisive moment of the history of Mecca: in the first phase of the *ridda*. His view mirrors the attitude of the tribal groups, according to their established relations with Mecca. When ʿAmr b. al-ʿĀṣ was on his way from ʿUmān to Medina, when the revolt of the *ridda* started, he came to Qurra b. Hubayra al-Qushayrī [2]). Qurra received him hospitably and gave him escort to Medina. When ʿAmr b. al-ʿĀṣ was about to leave, Qurra gave him his advice: "You people of Quraysh lived in your *ḥaram* with security both for yourselves and for (other) people (i.e. the tribes—K) with regard to you. Then there appeared a man from amongst you and announced what you heard. When this (information) reached us we did not dislike it; we said: "A man from Muḍar is (going) to lead the people" (i.e. the tribes—K). This man has (now) died. People (i.e. the tribes—K) are hurrying to you not offering you anything. Therefore go back to your *ḥaram* and live there in security. If you do not act (according to

1) See Ibn Abī l-Ḥadīd: *Sharḥ nahj al-balāgha*, ed. Muḥammad Abū l-Faḍl Ibrāhīm, Cairo 1963, XVIII, 285-300.

2) See on him "*Arabica*" XV (1968) p. 155, note 2; Ibn ʿAbd al-Barr, *al-Istīʿāb*, ed. ʿAlī Muḥammad al-Bijāwī, Cairo n.d., III, 1281, no. 2114.

my advice—K) I am ready to meet you (in fight—K) wherever you will fix the place [1])." The intent of Qurra was that Mecca should return to its former position as a place of security. Quraysh had to refrain from getting involved in a new political plan "to lead the people"; this plan had come to its end, in his opinion, with the death of the Prophet. Quraysh should revert to its previous relations with the tribes upon conditions of equality, with co-operation and confidence. Because of this saying Khālid b. al-Walīd demanded to execute Qurra when he was taken prisoner [2]).

There are conflicting traditions about the troops which took part in the expedition of Abraha. Ibn Isḥāq mentions only the Abyssinians as the force of Abraha, reporting that the Arabs went out against him. The two leaders who fought Abraha, aided by their tribes and the Arabs who considered it their duty to fight him, were Dhū Nafar al-Ḥimyarī and Nufayl b. Ḥabīb al-Khathʿamī: they were defeated and captured. Abraha marched towards Mecca and passed by al-Ṭā'if where he was received with hospitality by Muʿattib b. Mālik al-Thaqafī and directed towards Mecca. This story is followed by the report of the seizing of the herd of ʿAbd al-Muṭṭalib, the talk of ʿAbd al-Muṭṭalib with Abraha and the miracle of the birds who destroyed the army of Abraha. Ibn Isḥāq mentions also another tradition according to which ʿAbd al-Muṭṭalib went to Abraha in the company of the leaders of Kināna and Hudhayl (Yaʿmar b. Nufātha al-Kinānī and Khuwaylid al-Hudhalī) and offered him a third part of the goods of the Tihāma [3]).

Muqātil (d. 150 H) reports (as quoted from his *Tafsīr*) about the following two expeditions of Abraha al-Ashram al-Yamanī against

---

1) Ibn Ḥubaysh, *al-Maghāzī*, Ms. Leiden, Or. 343, p. 24: . . . *wa-innakum, yā maʿshara qurayshin, kuntum fī ḥaramikum ta'manūna fīhi wa-ya'manukum l-nāsu; thumma kharaja minkum rajulun yaqūlu mā samiʿta; fa-lammā balaghanā dhālika lam nakrahhu, wa-qulnā: rajulun min muḍara yasūqu l-nāsa; wa-qad tuwuffiya wa-l-nāsu ilaykum sirāʿun, wa-innahum ghayru muʿṭīkum shay'an, fa-lḥaqū bi-ḥaramikum fa-'manū fīhi; wa-in kunta ghayra fāʿilin fa-ʿidnī ḥaythu shi'ta ātika* . . . *

2) *Ibid.*, p. 24, ll. 4-5; p. 26, ll. 1-2.

3) Ibn Hishām, *op. cit.*, I, 47, 63; al-Ṭabarī, *Ta'rīkh*, I, 551-556 (from Ibn Isḥāq); Ibn Kathīr, *al-Sīra*, I, 30-41 (from Ibn Isḥāq); al-Azraqī, *Akhbār Makka*, ed. F. Wüstenfeld, Leipzig 1858, pp. 87-92.

Mecca: the first one was headed by Abū Yaksūm b. (!) Abraha in order to destroy the Kaʿba and establish the elephant as object of worship; this expedition failed. The second one occurred after some Qurashites came to a Christian church called *al-Haykal* (called by the Najāshī *Māsirḥasān*), sat down to roast meat, forgot to extinguish the fire and as a result the church went up in flames. This happened a year or two after the first expedition and was the cause for the second expedition. When the Najāshī was informed about the burning of the church he became enraged and decided to go out against Mecca. Ḥujr b. Shurāḥīl al-Kindī, Abū Yaksūm al-Kindi (!) and Abraha b. al-Ṣabbāḥ promised him their help. It was the Najāshī who headed the expedition and who talked with ʿAbd al-Muṭṭalib and returned him the seized herd. When ʿAbd al-Muṭṭalib came back to Mecca, he was advised by Abū Masʿūd al-Thaqafī to leave the city and to stay in the surrounding mountains. "This House has a Lord Who protects it"—said Abū Masʿūd [1]). Then the miracle of the birds appeared, Abraha's army was destroyed and ʿAbd al-Mutṭṭalib and Abū Masʿūd both collected the discarded jewels and gold [2]).

Ibn Isḥāq gives a different version in his *Mubtada*ʾ: the grandson of Abraha, the king of the Ḥabash (the son of his daughter), Aksūm b. al-Ṣabbāḥ came as pilgrim to Mecca. On his way back he stopped in a church in Najrān. There he was attacked by men from Mecca who robbed his luggage and looted the church. When the grandfather heard about it from his grandson, he sent against Mecca an army of twenty thousand men headed by Shamir b. Maqṣūd.

The short report contains the story of the seizing of the herd of ʿAbd al-Muṭṭalib and the miracle of the birds [3]). Two poems of ʿAbd al-Muṭṭalib (14 verses ending in *mū* and 10 verses ending in *mā*) are also quoted from the *Mubtada*ʾ [4]).

---

1) Comp. above, p. 65: the answer of Hishām b. al-Mughīra to Abraha.

2) Mughulṭāy, *op. cit.*, fol. 25a-26b sup. (See a short passage of the version of Muqātil in Majlisī's *Biḥār*, XV, 137; other fragments :al-ʿIṣāmī, *op. cit.*, I, 232-233; al-Thaʿlabī, *Qiṣaṣ al-anbiyā*ʾ, Cairo n.d., pp. 602-603).*

3) Mughulṭāy, *op. cit.*, fol. 26b.

4) *Ibid.*, fol. 27a-b.

But Mughulṭāy seems to have recorded only a part of the report of the *Mubtada'*. The whole report is recorded by Abū Nuʿaym al-Iṣfahānī in his *Dalā'il al-nubuwwa* [1]). The isnād of Abū Nuʿaym does not include the name of Ibn Isḥāq; but the fragment of the *Mubtada'* recorded by Mughulṭāy is identical with the first part of Abū Nuʿaym's report [2]). According to this report the army of Shamir consisted of Khaulān and a group of Ashʿariyyīn. The army was joined by al-Taqāl al-Khathʿamī. The talk of ʿAbd al-Muṭṭalib with Abraha and the story of the miracle of the birds are given at length.

The combined report of al-Ṭabarī [3]) is based on the account of al-Wāqidī. It is recorded by Ibn Saʿd [4]), Abū Nuʿaym [5]), Mughulṭāy [6]), and al-Thaʿlabī [7]). According to this tradition ʿAbd al-Muṭṭalib stayed at the mountain of Ḥirā' with ʿAmr b. ʿĀ'idh al-Makhzūmī, Muṭʿim b. ʿAdiyy and Abū Masʿūd al-Thaqafī.

An anonymous report claims that the father of ʿUthmān b. ʿAffān, was close to ʿAbd al-Muṭṭalib on the mountain; the first who descended in order to collect the spoils of the army of Abraha were ʿAbd al-Muṭṭalib, ʿAffān and Abū Masʿūd al-Thaqafī. The father of ʿUthmān then became a rich man [8]). According to the report of the *Nihāyat al-irab* ʿAbd al-Muṭṭatlib descendend with Ḥakīm b. Ḥizām [9]).

A significant report is recorded by al-Ṭabarsī [10]) and Majlisī [11]). The majority of the followers of Abraha in his army were people from ʿAkk, Ashʿar and Khathʿam. When the troops of Abraha reached

---

1) Hyderabad 1369/1950, pp. 101-105; see al-Suyūṭī, *al-Durr al-manthūr*, Cairo 1314, VI, 394 (quoted from the *Dalā'il*).

2) Mughulṭāy perused the text of Abū Nuʿaym and remarks (fol. 25b, l.7) that Abū Nuʿaym recorded the name of the commander Shamir b. Maṣfūd (see Abū Nuʿaym, *Dalā'il*, p. 101, note 1).

3) *Ta'rīkh*, I, 556-557.

4) *Ṭabaqāt*, Beirut 1956, I, 90-92.

5) *Dalā'il*, pp. 106-107.

6) *Al-Zahr*, fol. 32a.

7) *Qiṣaṣ al-anbiyā'*, pp. 603-604.

8) Al-Ḥalabī, *Insān al-ʿuyūn* (= *al-Sīra al-ḥalabiyya*), Cairo 1351/1932, I, 73.

9) Fol. 176b.

10) Al-Ṭabarsī, *Majmaʿ al-bayān*, Beirut 1380/1961, XXX, 234-237.

11) *Biḥār al-anwār*, Teheran 1379, XV, 134-137.

Mecca, the people left the city and sought shelter in the mountains. There were left in Mecca only ʿAbd al-Muṭṭalib carrying out the duty of the *siqāya* and Shayba b. ʿUthmān b. ʿAbd al-Dār carrying out the duty of the *ḥijāba*. The story of the seizure of the herd of ʿAbd al-Muṭṭalib is followed by the story of the meeting of ʿAbd al-Muṭṭalib with Abū Yaksūm. The details about the events following the meeting are of special interest. The Ashʿariyyūn and the Khathʿam broke their swords and spears and declared themselves innocent before God of any intention to destroy the House. When the miracle of the birds occurred, the troops who marched against Mecca being killed by the stones thrown by the birds, the Kathʿam and Ashʿar were saved from being harmed by the stones.

This report, recorded by the Shīʿī Ṭabarsi and Majlisī, is recorded by the Sunnī al-Bayhaqī in his *Dalāʾil al-nubuwwa* [1]). It is evident that the tradition has a South-Arabian tendency. The South-Arabian tradition also adopts the version that Dhū Nafar and Naufal b. Ḥabīb were taken prisoners by Abraha and forced to follow him. Naufal (or Nufayl) was the man who desecrated the temple of Abraha in order to keep the pilgrimage to Mecca and Dhū Nafar was a friend of ʿAbd al-Muṭṭalib, who advised him when he came to meet Abraha [2]). These are apparent attempts to clear the South-Arabian tribes from any accusation of aiding Abraha in his activities against the *ḥaram* of Mecca.

The version recorded by Muḥammad b. Ḥabīb [3]) differs from those mentioned above. Abraha built the church in Ṣanʿāʾ according to the plan of the Kaʿba. It was desecrated by a group of Kināna. Abraha decided to march against Mecca, to destroy the Kaʿba and afterwards to raid Najd. He gathered people of low extraction and brigands and listed them in his army. He was followed by the leader of Khathʿam, Nufayl, on the head of huge groups of his tribe and by the Munabbih b. Kaʿb of the Balḥārith, who did not recognize the sanctity of the

---

1) Fols. 13a-14a.
2) Cf. al-Hamdānī, *al-Iklīl*, ed. Muḥibb al-Dīn al-Khaṭīb, X, 25. (Cairo 1368).
3) *Al-Munammaq*, pp. 68-80.

Ka'ba and the *ḥaram*. Ṭarafa, who stayed at that time in Najrān, warned Qatāda b. Salama al-Ḥanafī [1]) of the planned attack of Abraha against Najd. Verses of Kulthūm b. 'Umays al-Kinānī, who was captured by the army of Abraha and put in chains, give a vivid description of the army of Abraha.

O, may God let hear a call:
and send between the mountains of Mecca (*al-Akhshabāni*) a herald.
There came upon you the troops of al-Ashram, among them an elephant:
and black men riding (beasts like) ogers.
And infantry troops, stout ones, whose number cannot be counted:
by al-Lāt, they swing their javelines thirsty (of blood).
They came upon you, they came upon you! The earth is too narrow to bear them:
like a gush of water flowing overpowers the valley.

On their way the troops of Abraha were attacked by the Azd who defeated them. Abraha and his army were however received hospitably in al-Ṭā'if by Mas'ūd b. Mu'attib, who explained to Abraha that the sanctuary of al-Ṭa'if is small and that his goal is the Ka'ba of Mecca, which should be destroyed in revenge for the desecration of his temple. When the army of Abraha approached Mecca, the people of city left, seeking refuge in the mountains; only 'Abd al-Muṭṭalib and 'Amr b. 'Ā'idh al-Makhzūmī remained in the city [2]): they fed the people (scil. remaining in Mecca). Further the report gives the story of the meeting of Abraha with 'Abd al-Muṭṭalib and the miracle of the birds. The appended verses give the description of the disastrous end of Abraha's army.

The quoted traditions are, in fact, contradictory and the picture they give is blurred. Miraculous and legendary elements [3]) are evident and form a part of every report. There are however some details which deserve to be considered. Muqātil's version, as recorded by Mughulṭāy, is the only one in which two expeditions are mentioned: a first one which failed to reach the precincts of Mecca, and a second one, which

1) See *Dīwān de Ṭarafa*, ed. M. Seligsohn, Paris 1901, p. 146 (VII, appendix). And see *ibid.*, p. 90; and see *al-Munammaq*, p. 69, note 3.

2) Cf. al-Balādhurī, *Ansāb al-ashrāf*, ed. Muḥammad Ḥamīdullah, Cairo 1959, I, 68; al-Maqdisī, *al-Bad' wa-l-ta'rīkh*, ed. Cl. Huart, Paris 1899, III, 186.

3) See the legendary report of Abū l-Ḥasan al-Bakrī in Majlisī's *Biḥār* XV, 65-74.

occurred a year or two later. In this expedition the army was led by the Najāshī, some troops entered Mecca, but the expedition ended with the disastrous fate of the army. This tradition suits the assumption of W. Caskel, who considered the inscription Ry 506 referring to an expedition preceding the Expedition of the Elephant [1]).

The troops in the army of Abraha seem to have been from both South and North Arabia. Khath'am, Balḥārith, 'Akk, Ash'ar, Khaulān are the names of South-Arabian troops, mentioned in the reports. The presence of Muḍarī troops is implied in the story of the meal of testicles prepared for Khath'am, which the Muḍarī (Northern) troops refused to eat [2]). When the Muḍarīs refused to eat the testicles and to prostrate before the cross, Abraha ordered to summon them; they explained that they do not eat testicles, nor do they prostrate to the cross; they follow the tenets of their people (*wa-naḥnu, abayta l-la'na, fī dīni qauminā*). Abraha freed them, stating: *kullu qaumin wa-dīnahum* [3]). There was also a troop of Abyssinians. The verses of Qays b. Khuzā'ī (al-Sulamī) in praise of Abraha describe a selected unit of Abyssinians surrounding Abraha:

v. 3 The sons of Abyssinia around him:
wrapped in Abyssinian silk clothes
4. 4 With white faces and black faces:
their hair (curly) like long peppers [4]).

The information that Abraha intended to raid Najd after he would destroy the Ka'ba is noteworthy. The attack on Najd, as attested by the verses of Ṭarafa, seems to have been planned on the background of the struggle between Persia and Byzantium and the raids of the tribes being under the sway of al-Ḥīra on the territories of tribes in the region of Najrān being under the sway of Abraha [5]). It is notice-

---

1) W. Caskel, *Entdeckungen in Arabien*, Köln und Opladen 1954, p. 30 inf.

2) *Al-Munammaq*, p. 70: *ayyuhā l-maliku, inna man ma'aka min muḍara abau an ya'kulū min hādhihi l-khuṣā shay'an ... wa-arsala, fa-ukhidha lahu nāsun min muḍara ...*

3) *Ibid.*, p. 71. The saying of Abraha reminds the idea advocated by Hishām b. al-Mughīra in his talk with Abraha.

4) *Al-Munammaq*, p. 70.

5) See Caskel, *op. cit.*, p. 30.

able that Abraha chose Najrān as halting place in his march, where, as Ṭarafa says, "the kings took their decisions." (*bi-najrāna mā qaḍḍā l-mulūku qaḍā'ahum*) 1). The people of Najrān were devoted Christians and certainly sympathised with Abraha; 2) groups of Balḥārith in this region aided him.

The information about the leaders of Mecca who remained with ʿAbd al-Muṭṭalib deserves to be examined. ʿAmr b. ʿĀʾidh al-Makhzūmī was apparently in close contact with ʿAbd al-Muṭṭalib; ʿAbd al-Muṭṭalib married his daughter Fāṭima and she gave birth to his son ʿAbdallah, the father of the Prophet 3). The Makhzūm, as mentioned in the *Nihāyat al-irab* had trade relations with the Yemen. It is not surprising to find that Abyssinians dwelt in the *Dār al ʿUlūj*, in the quarter of the Banū Makhzūm 4). The Makhzūm seem to have had financial relations with Najrān as well: when al-Walīd b. al-Mughīra died he mentioned to his sons that he owed the bishop of Najrān a hundred dīnārs 5). It is thus plausible that Makhzūm had to be consulted

1) Cf. al-Hamdānī, *op. cit.*, II, 157 (ed. Muḥammad al-Akwaʿ al-Ḥiwālī, Cairo 1386/1966): . . . *ʿalā Ḥububāna idh tuqaḍḍā maḥāṣiluh*; and see *ibid.*, p. 157: . .. *ḍarabū li-abrahata l-umūra.*

2) See Ibn ʿAbd al-Ḥakam, *Futūḥ Miṣr*, ed. C. Torrey, New Haven 1922, p. 301, 1.5, the saying of the Prophet about his tiring discussions with the delegation of Najrān: . . . *la-wadidtu anna baynī wa-bayna ahli najrāna ḥijāban* (min shiddati mā kānū yujādilūnahu).*

3) See Ibn Ḥabīb, *al-Muḥabbar*, ed. Ilse Lichtenstaedter, Hyderabad 1361/1942, p. 51; Ibn al-Kalbī, *Jamharat al-nasab*, Ms. Br. Mus., Add. 23297, fols. 8a, 1.3; 8b, 1.3 bot.; Ibn Ḥabīb, *Ummahāt al-nabī*, ed. Ḥusayn ʿAlī Maḥfūẓ, Baghdād 1372/1952, p. 10 (fol. 1b).

4) Al-Fākihī, *op. cit.*, fol. 458a; the Prophet was informed that these Abyssinians wanted to come to him in order to embrace Islam; they feared however that the Prophet might repel them. The Prophet said: "There is nothing good in Abyssinians: when they are hungry they steal, when they are sated they drink; they have two good qualities: they feed people and are courageous." ʿAṭā b. Abī Rabāḥ is said to have been born in this house. When ʿUmar came to Mecca he distributed money amongst Quraysh, Arabs, Mawālī, Persians and Abyssinians (al-Fākihī, *op. cit.*, fol. 397a, inf.). When ʿAbdallah b. al-Zubayr pulled down the Kaʿba he used Abyssinian slaves for this task. He hoped that amongst them there would be the Abyssinian about whom the Prophet foretold that he would destroy the Kaʿba (al-Azraqī, *op. cit.*, p. 141 inf.; al-ʿIṣāmī, *op. cit.*, I, 169 inf.) About the Abyssinian who will destroy the Kaʿba see al-Azraqī, *op. cit.*, p. 193; al-Fāsī, *Shifāʾ al-gharām*, Cairo 1956, I, 127-128.*

5) Al-Zubayr b. Bakkār, *op. cit.*, Ms. fol. 145b, 1.8.*

at the arrival of the army of Abraha and shared in the decisions. The Kināna as mentioned above, had close relations with Mecca. It is thus probable that Muḥammad b. Khuzāʿī (al-Sulamī) was sent by Abraha to the Banū Kināna, that a Kinānī was captured and compiled the verses to warn Quraysh of the danger of the approaching army of Abraha and that a Kinānī, from the clan of Diʾl was said to have been a member of the delegation who negotiated with Abraha. The verse recited by a Diʾlī woman to Muʿāwiya seems to refer to the role played by the Kināna in the Expedition of the Elephant:

hum manaʿū jaysha l-aḥābīshi ʿanwatan:
wa-hum nahnahū ʿannā ghuwāta banī bakri
They (i.e. the Diʾl) resisted the army of the Abyssinians forcibly:
and they repelled from us those who allure, the Banū Bakr [1])

It is plausible to find also a chief of the Hudhayl in the delegation. Hudhayl had good relations with Mecca and played a considerable role in stopping the expedition of Abraha against Mecca [2]).

It is also quite likely that ʿAbd al-Muṭṭalib consulted the leader of the Thaqīf in his decisions. Thaqīf had very close financial relations with Makhzūm and common financial enterprises [3]). It is noteworthy too that ʿAbd al-Muṭṭalib himself had property in al-Ṭāʾif [4]). He had

---

1) Al-Balādhurī, *Ansāb al-ashrāf*, ed. M. Schloessinger, Jerusalem 1971, IV A, p. 18; Bakr apparently refers to Bakr b. ʿAbd Manāt (see Watt, Muḥammad at Medina, p. 83); and see the story of the alliance concluded between Quraysh and the Aḥābīsh by ʿAbd Muṭṭalib to face the Banū Bakr—al-Balādhurī, *Ansāb*, fol. 902a; but see the second hemistich in the poem of Ḥudhāfa b. Ghānim al-Jumaḥī, al-Azraqī, *op. cit.*, p. 69:
humū malakū l-baṭhāʾa majdan wa-suʾdadan:
wa-hum ṭaradū ʿanhā ghuwāta banī bakri
(*malakū*, perhaps preferable *malaʾū*).

2) See EI², s.v. *Hudhayl* (G. Rentz) and W. Caskel, *op. cit.*, p. 31, ll.10-16.

3) See al-Wāḥidī, *Asbāb al-nuzūl*, Cairo 1388/1968, pp. 58-59; al-Suyūṭī, *Lubāb al-nuqūl*, p. 42; al-Ṭabarī, *Tafsīr*, ed. Maḥmūd and Aḥmad Shākir, Cairo n.d., VI, 22-23; (nos. 6258-6259); and see Muqātil, *Tafsīr*, Ms. Ḥāmidiyya 58, fol. 46 a: *...fa-lammā aẓhara llāhu ʿazza wa-jalla l-nabiyya (ṣ) ʿalā l-tāʾifi shtaraṭat thaqīfun anna kulla riban lahum ʿalā l-nāsi fa-huwa lahum wa-kulla ribā l-nāsi ʿalayhim fa-huwa mauḍūʿun ʿanhum ...*; and see Mughulṭāy, *op. cit.*, fols., 171b-172a; and see al-Suyūṭī, *al-Durr al-manthūr*, I, 366-367.

4) Ibn Ḥabīb, *al-Munammaq*, op. cit., p. 98 ult.

also relations with the Yemen; this can be deduced from a tradition about a document of a debt owed to him by a man from Ṣanʿāʾ [1]).

ʿAbd al-Muṭṭalib acted of course as a representative of the *ḥaram*, as the dignitary of the Kaʿba, in charge of the *siqāya*. This is especially emphasized in the tradition that he remained in Mecca with another dignitary Shayba b. ʿUthmān, who held the office of the *ḥijāba*. They both fed the people; this reflects the concept of responsibility of the dignitaries of the Kaʿba.*

It would be vain to try to establish who in fact led Mecca in the decisive moment of the raid of Abraha. What can be deduced from the traditions is only what were the tribal elements which influenced the policy of Mecca and who were the representatives of the clans of Mecca deciding at that time.

Details about the expedition are indeed meagre [2]). But information about the results of the expedition is instructive. According to the report of the *Nihāyat al-irab* "Quraysh gained prestige in the eyes of the Arabs (i.e. the tribes) and they called them *Ālu llāhi*; they said: "God repelled from them the evil (of the enemy) who plotted against them [3])." ʿAbd al-Muṭṭalib became wealthy, bought every year many camels and slaughtered them for the people of Mecca [4]). He bought the wells called *al-Ajbāb* from the Banū Naṣr b. Muʿāwiya [5]), obviously in order to secure the water supply of Mecca in addition to the well of Zamzam which he dug.

Arabic tradition stresses that the institution of the *ḥums* was established after the Expedition of the Elephant [6]). Some sources are doubtful about the date of the establishment of the *ḥums* [7]). But it is

---

1) Al-Majlisī, *op. cit.*, XV, 160, no. 90; cf. Yāqūt, *Muʿjam al-buldān*, s.v. *Zaul.*

2) See Caskel, *op. cit.*, p. 31 sup.: "*Es geht daraus hervor, wie dürftig die einheimischen Quellen*"...

3) *Nihāyat al-irab*, fol. 177a; and see al-Azraqī, *op. cit.*, p. 98.*

4) *Nihāyat al-irab*, fol. 177a.

5) *Ibid.*, fol. 191b, inf.

6) Ibn al-Athīr, *al-Kāmil fī l-taʾrīkh*, ed. ʿAbd al-Wahhāb al-Najjār, Cairo 1348, I, 266.

7) Ibn Hishām, *op. cit.*, I, 211: *qāla ibnu isḥāqa: wa-qad kānat qurayshun—lā adrī a-qabla l-fīli am baʿdahu—btadaʿat raʾya l-ḥumsi* ...

evident that the failure of the expedition helped to expand the trade of Mecca, to set up close relations with the tribes, to establish its influence and to strengthen the institutions already built up by Quraysh. The market of ʿUkāẓ was established fifteen years after the Expedition of the Elephant [1]). ʿAbd al-Muṭṭalib was one of the members of the delegation who came to Sayf b. dhī Yazan to congratulate him on his victory [2]). According to a tradition recorded by al-Majlisī on the authority of al-Wāqidī, Sayf b. dhī Yazan sent his son to Mecca as a *governor* on his behalf [3]). The report of Wāqidī is probably exaggerated; he may have been sent merely as a *representative*, not as governor. But both the reports indicate that the relations of Mecca with the Yemen were re-established and the commercial ties renewed.

II

Mecca owed its existence to trade. Pilgrimage rite and trade were indivisible in this city. It is thus plausible that in the young Muslim community one of the most vital questions which could be asked was the question whether trade could be conducted during the *ḥajj*. This question was positively answered in Sūra II, 198: "It is no fault in you, that you should seek bounty from your Lord . . ." [4]) Trade in Mecca

---

1) Mughulṭāy, *op. cit.*, fol. 170a, ult.; al-Bakrī, *op. cit.*, III, 959; al-Tauḥīdī considers these markets of the Arabs as marks of nobility in both societies of the Arabs, amongst the bedouins and the sedentary: . . . *wa-mimmā yadullu ʿalā tahadduribim fī bādiyatihim wa-tabaddīhim fī taḥaḍḍurihim wa-taḥallīhim bi-ashrafi aḥwāli l-amrayni aswāquhum llatī lahum fī l-jāhiliyyati* . . . (*al-Imtāʿ wa-l-muʾānasa*, ed. Aḥmad Amīn, Aḥmad al-Zayn, Beirut (reprint—n.d.), I, 83).

2) See e.g. Ibn Kathīr, *al-Bidāya wa-l-nihāya*, Beirut—al-Riyāḍ 1966, II, 178; Ibn al-Jauzī, *al-Wafā bi-aḥwāl al-muṣṭafā*, ed. Muṣṭafā ʿAbd al-Wāḥid, Cairo 1386/1966, I, 122-128.

3) *Biḥār al-anwār*, XV, 146, no. 80: *qāla l-wāqidiyyū: kāna fī zamāni ʿabdi l-muṭṭalibi rajulun yuqālu lahu sayfu bnu dhī yazana wa-kāna min mulūki l-yamani wa-qad anfadha bnahu ilā makkata wāliyan min qibalihi, wa-taqaddama ilayhi bi-stiʿmāli l-ʿadli wa-l-inṣāfi* . . .

4) See al-Ṭabari, *Tafsīr*, IV, 163-169 (nos. 3761-3791); al-Bakrī, *op. cit.*, III, 960; al-Ḥākim, *op. cit.*, I, 449, 482; Muqātil, *op. cit.*, fol. 31b; al-Suyūṭī, *Lubāb*, p. 30; al-Shaybānī, *al-Iktisāb fī l-rizq al-mustaṭāb*, ed. Muḥammad ʿArnūs, Cairo 1357/1938, p. 21; Ibn Kathīr, *Tafsīr*, Beirut 1385/1966, I, 424-426; and see Ch. C. Torrey, *The Commercial-Theological Terms in the Koran*, Leyden 1892, p. 5; but see al-Fasawī, *al-Maʿrifa wa-l-taʾrīkh*, Ms. Esad Ef. 2391, fol. 67b, 1. 14 (on Ayyūb al-Sakhtiyānī): . . . *wa-kāna lā yashtarī wa-lā yabīʿu fī l-ḥajji.**

remained thus inseparably connected with religious rites, as it was in the times of the Jāhiliyya. Caravans with wares used to pour into Mecca, [1]) protected by the established institutions of the Sacred Months, *Ḥums* and *Dhāda* and enjoying free access to the markets.* Caravans departed from Mecca loaded with wares for Syria, Persia or Yemen.

The following information about the import of wares from Egypt is of particular interest. In the lower part of Mecca there was the "Court of Egypt" (*Dār Miṣr*) [2]) which belonged to Ṣafwān b. Umayya al-Jumaḥī [3]). He used to deposit the wares which arrived from Egypt in this court. People would come to the lower part of Mecca and buy these wares. "His trade", says the report, "was confined to Egypt;" therefore the court was named "*Dār Miṣr*", referring to the wares which were sold in it [4]).

In the quarter of the Banū Makhzūm was the court of al-Sā'ib b. Abī l-Sā'ib; in one of its departments the wares of the Prophet and of al-Sā'ib were stored [5]). Al-Sā'ib was the Prophet's partner before he received the revelation [6]). According to al-Shaybānī they traded with skins [7]). According to a tradition recorded by al-Balādhurī, the Prophet

---

1) See E. R. Wolf: *The Social Organization of Mecca and the Origins of Islam*, Southwestern Journal of Anthropology 1951, pp. 330-337; and comp. about the trade of Qurayẓa and Naḍīr the report about the seven caravans which arrived on the same day from Buṣrā and Adhruʿāt, carrying clothes, perfumes, jewels and "sea-goods" (*amtiʿat al-baḥr*)—al-Wāḥidī, *op. cit.*, p. 187; al-Qurṭubī, *op. cit.*, X, 56.*

2) See al-Azraqī, *op. cit.*, p. 474 penult.

3) See on him Ibn ʿAbd al-Barr, *op. cit.*, II, 718, no. 1214; Ibn Ḥajar, *al-Iṣāba*, Cairo 1325/1907, III, 246, no. 4068; Ibn Saʿd, *op. cit.*, V, 449.

4) Al-Fākihī, *op. cit.*, fol. 461b: ... *wa-lahum dārun bi-asfali makkata yuqālu lahā dāru miṣra, fīhā l-dabbāghūna, kānat li-ṣafwāna bni umayyata; wa-innamā summiyat dāra miṣra anna ṣafwāna bna umayyata kāna yaʾtīhi min miṣra tijārātun wa-amtiʿatun, fa-kāna idhā atathu unīkhat fī dārihi tilka, fa-yaʾtīhi l-nāsu ilā asfali makkata fa-yashtarūna minhu l-matāʿa; wa-lā tajūzu tijāratuhu ilā ghayri miṣra, fa-nusibat al-dāru ilā mā kāna yubāʿu fīhā min matāʿi miṣra.*

5) Al-Fākihī, *op. cit.*, fol. 458b; al-Azraqī, *op. cit.*, pp. 470-471.

6) Al-Fākihī, *op. cit.*, fol. 458b; Ibn ʿAbd al-Barr, *op. cit.*, p. 572, no. 892 (and see *ib.*, p. 1288); Ibn al-Kalbī, *op. cit.*, fol. 102a; Ibn Ḥajar, *al-Iṣāba*, III, 60, no. 3060; al-Zubayr b. Bakkār, *op. cit.*, fol. 186b (al-Sāʾib b. Wadāʿa); *ibid.*, fol. 149b, 1.23; Ibn al-Jauzī, *al-Wafā*, I, 142 inf.; al-Ṭabarī, *Dhayl al-mudhayyal*, Cairo 1939, p. 60.

7) *Al-Iktisāb*, p. 17 ult.—p. 18 sup.

invested in some wares carried by Abū Sufyān from Syria and got profit [1]).

The intricate trade-transactions gave rise to various partnerships. Al-ʿAbbās was a partner of Khālid b. al-Walīd; they both used to lend money for interest; when Islam appeared they had big sums lent for interest [2]). According to another tradition al-ʿAbbās was a partner of Abū Sufyān [3]). Al-Dhahabī records a tradition stating that Naufal b. al-Ḥārith b. ʿAbd al-Muṭṭalib was a partner of ʿAbbās [4]). Al-Balādhurī reports about a partnership between two Sulamī leaders and Ḥarb b. Umayya; Ḥarb invested the money necessary for the cultivation of the land owned by them [5]).

It is evident that the trade of Mecca necessitated free traffic, free access to the markets of Mecca and free markets, without taxes. In fact, when the Prophet came to Medina he decided to turn Medina into a *ḥaram* and to establish in Medina a free market, without taxes [6]). The fundamental change occurred when Sūra IX, 28 was revealed: "O believers, the idolaters are indeed unclean; so let them not come near the Holy Mosque after this year of theirs. If you fear poverty, God shall surely enrich you of His bounty, if He will . . ." The verse

---

1) Al-Balādhurī, *Ansāb al-ashrāf*, IVa, 9; and see another version (Muḥammad refuses to accept a reduction in the commision of Abū Sufyān) ʿAbd al-Jabbār, *Tathbīt dalāʾil al-nubuwwa*, ed. ʿAbd al-Karīm ʿUthmān, Beirut 1386/1966, II, 591.

2) Al-Wāḥidī, *op. cit.*, p. 59; Mughulṭāy, *op. cit.*, fol. 170b, penult.

3) Mughulṭāy, *op. cit.*, fol. 313a; cf. Ibn Ḥabīb, *al-Munammaq*, p. 27 (al-Abbās was the *nadīm* of Abū Sufyān; according to a report of al-Zubayr b. Bakkār, *op. cit.*, fol. 94b, penult. ʿAuf b. ʿAbd ʿAuf (see on him al-Kalbī, *op. cit.*, 28a) was a *nadīm* of al-Fākih b. al-Mughīra al-Makhzūmī. About the companionship of Ḥarb b. Umayya, ʿAbdallah b. Judʿān and Hishām b. al-Mughīra see al-Zubayr b. Bakkār, *op. cit.*, fol. 126b inf.); Ḥarb b. Umayya was a *nadīm* of ʿAbd al-Muṭṭalib (al-Balādhurī, IVa, p. 3).

4) *Siyar aʿlām al-nubalāʾ*, I, 144.

5) Al-Baladhurī, *Ansāb* IVA, p. 3.

6) Al-Balādhurī, *Futuḥ al-buldān*, ed. ʿAbdallah and ʿUmar al-Ṭabbāʿ, Beirut 1377/1957, p. 24: . . . *wa-lammā arāda rasūlu llāhi an yattakhidha l-sūqa bi-l-madīnati, qāla: hādhā sūqukum, lā kharāja ʿalaykum fīhi*. Consequently there were no taxes imposed on markets. The first who levied taxes from markets was Ziyād b. Abīhi (see al-Shiblī: *Maḥāsin al-wasāʾil*, Ms. Br. Mus., or. 1530, fol. 121b: *awwalu man akhadha min al-sūqi ajran ziyādun*).

was revealed in year 9 of the *hijra* [1]). The Muslims were afraid that the prohibition to approach the Kaʿba by the unbelievers may endanger their trade, as the unbelievers used to bring their merchandise to Mecca during their *ḥajj*. Allah promised the faithful to enrich them [2]).

It is evident that this crucial verse was revealed after Mecca had been conquered, when the roads of trade were secured and controlled by chiefs and leaders who had sworn loyalty to the Prophet. They changed in fact their former loyalty to Quraysh into a new loyalty: to the Prophet and the Muslim community. Unbelievers who returned from this *ḥajj* could sadly remark: "What can you do, as Quraysh had already embraced Islām [3])." Muqātil reports that the people of Judda, Ḥunayn and Ṣanʿāʾ embraced Islām and brought food to Mecca: they had thus no need to trade with the unbelievers [4]).

The *ḥaram* became a Muslim sanctuary; its functionaries were appointed by the Prophet. It is the Muslim community and its representatives who decide who will bring merchandise to Mecca and its markets. The former institutions of *īlāf*, *ḥums*, *dhāda* were fundamentally transformed [5]). Their functions and authority were transferred to the loyal tribes, who had to ensure the safety of the roads and of the trade traffic. They had to pay taxes and yield to the authority of the chiefs appointed by the Prophet. Profits could be kept, as before, for the tribes (or their chiefs respectively) and the established authorities of the two *ḥarams*, Mecca and Medina.

It is significant that when the crisis of the establishment of Medina occurred after the death of the Prophet, when the chiefs of tribes

---

1) See F. Buhl, *Das Leben Muhammeds* (transl. H. H. Schaeder), Heidelberg 1955, pp. 338-339, notes 58-60.

2) Al-Ṭabarī, *Tafsīr*, XIV, 192-195 (nos. 16597-16608); al-Qurṭubī, *op. cit.*, VIII, 106; Ibn Kathīr, *Tafsīr*, III, 382; Ibn Hishām, *op. cit.*, IV, 192; al-Rāzī, *Tafsīr*, Cairo, 1357/1938, XVI, 24-26.

3) Al-Ṭabarī, *Taʾrīkh*, II, 383: *fa-rajaʿa l-mushrikūna fa-lāma baʿḍuhum baʿḍan wa-qālū*: "*mā taṣnaʿūna, wa-qad aslamat qurayshun*", *fa-aslamū.*

4) Al-Rāzī, *op. cit.*, XVI, 26 inf.*

5) Comp. al-Tauḥīdī, *al-Imtāʿ*, I, 85 about ʿUkāẓ: ... *wa-man lahu ḥukūmatun irtafaʿa ilā lladhī yaqūmu bi-amri l-ḥukūmati min banī tamīmin, wa-kāna ākhirahum al-aqraʿu bnu ḥābisin.* Al-Aqraʿ was in the new system appointed by the Prophet as *muṣaddiq.*

attempted to free themselves from their dependence on Medina, they tried to return to relations of a different kind than the *īlāf-ḥums* with Mecca. According to a tradition recorded by Ibn Ḥubaysh al-Aqraʿ b. Ḥābis and ʿUyayna b. Ḥiṣn came at the outbreak of the *ridda* to Medina accompanied by chiefs of tribes, met some *Muhājirūn* and informed them about the *ridda* in their tribes; the tribes, they said, refuse to pay to the authority of Medina the payments which they paid to the Prophet. They suggested that they would assure that their tribes would not attack Medina if they were given a certain payment. The *Muhājirūn* came to Abū Bakr and advised him to accept the offer; Abū Bakr however refused [1]).

Another tradition recorded by Ibn Ḥubaysh corroborates this report. When ʿAmr b. al-ʿAṣ was on his way to Medina he met people renouncing Islam (*murtaddīn*). When he arrived at Dhū l-Qaṣṣa [2]) he met ʿUyayna b. Ḥiṣn, who returned from his visit to Medina. ʿUyayna met Abū Bakr and told him: "If you pay us a (defined) sum, we shall keep you from (every attack occurring from) our territory." ʿAmr. b. al-ʿĀṣ asked him about the events (which happened in his absence), and ʿUyayna informed him that Abū Bakr headed the Muslim community. "Now we are equal, you and we, "added ʿUyayna. ʿAmr said: "You are lying, O son of the mischievous of Muḍar [3])."

ʿUyayna b. Ḥiṣn, the chief of Fazāra, was aware of the weakness

---

1) *Al-Maghāzī*, p. 9: . . . *wa-qadima ʿalā abī bakrin ʿuyaynatu bnu ḥiṣnin wa-l-aqraʿu bnu ḥābisin fī rijālin min ashrāfi l-ʿarabi, fa-dakhalū ʿalā rijālin min al-muhājirīna fa-qālū innahu qad irtadda ʿāmmatu man warāʾanā ʿan al-islāmi wa-laysa fī anfusihim an yuʾaddū ilaykum min amwālihim mā kānū yuʾaddūna ilā rasūli llāhi* (*ṣ*); *fa-in tajʿalū lanā juʿlan narjiʿ fa-nakfīkum man warāʾanā*; *fa-dakhala l-muhājirūna wa-l-anṣāru ʿalā abī bakrin fa-ʿaraḍū ʿalayhi lladhī ʿaraḍū ʿalayhim wa-qālū*: *narā an tuṭʿima l-aqraʿa wa-ʿuyaynata ṭuʿmatan yarḍayāni bihā wa-yakfiyānika man warāʾahumā ḥattā yarjiʿa ilayka usāmatu wa-jayshuhu wa-yashtadda amruka, fa-innā l-yauma qalīlun fī kathīrin, wa-lā ṭaqata lanā bi-qitāli l-ʿarabi* . . .

2) See Yāqūt, *Muʿjam al-buldān*, s.v. Qaṣṣa.

3) *Al-Maghāzī*, p. 25, l. 10: . . . *aqbala ʿamru bnu l-ʿāṣi yalqā l-nāsa murtaddīna ḥattā atā ʿalā dhī l-qaṣṣati, fa-laqiya ʿuyaynata bna ḥiṣnin khārijan min al-madīnati, wa-dhālika ḥīna qadima ʿalā abī bakrin al-ṣiddīqi yaqūlu*: "*in jaʿalta lanā shayʾan kafaynāka ma warāʾanā*"; *fa-qāla lahu ʿamru bnu l-ʿāṣi*: "*mā warāʾaka*"; *fa-qāla ʿuyaynatu*: "*ibnu abī quḥāfata wālī l-nāsi, yā ʿamru, wa-stawaynā naḥnu wa-antum*"; *fa-qāla ʿamrun*: "*kadhabta yā bna l-akhābithi min muḍar*". . .

of Medina. He suggested to Abū Bakr that Fazāra should protect Medina from attacks from their territory against an agreed payment. Abū Bakr could not accept the offer: acceptance of this offer might have meant giving up the idea of continuity of the work of the Prophet and yielding to the force of bedouin tribes, thus conceding to the disintegration of the Madinian commonwealth, which took up, in fact, the legacy of Mecca. Abū Bakr had to refuse the offer, which meant *ridda*. For the sake of Medina, he had to decide to crush the *ridda*.

III

The development of Mecca was accompanied by a continuous struggle between the factions of Quraysh, which brought about the formation of alliances of clans and sometimes led to clashes and bloodshed. The best known alliance is the one of the *Muṭayyabūn* and their adversaries, the *Aḥlāf* [1]). The reports about the role of the Banū l-Ḥārith b. Fihr in this alliance may be of some interest.

The Ḥārith b. Fihr belonged to *Quraysh al-ẓawāhir*. The *Quraysh al-ẓawāhir*, although closely co-operating with the *Quraysh al-biṭāḥ*, attended fights and raids in their own tribal units [2]). Sometimes their actions seem to have collided with the policy of Mecca [3]). They concluded alliances with tribes and carried out joint raids against tribes [4]). Members of defeated groups of *Quraysh al-ẓawāhir* sought refuge in Mecca and dispersed amongst families of the *Abṭahiyyīn*. It is of interest that persons of these Ḥārith b. Fihr who already merged into clans of the *Abṭaḥīs* were "repatriated" by ʿUmar into their former tribal units [5]). Ibn Ḥabīb mentions a group of the Ḥārith b. Fihr (the clan

---

1) See Ibn Hishām, *op. cit.*, I, 138-140; W. M. Watt, *Muhammad at Mecca*, pp. 5-8.

2) Cf. al-Balādhurī, *Ansāb*, Ms. fol. 882a: . . . *wa-kāna ḍirāru bnu l-khaṭṭābi raʾīsa muḥāribi bni fihrin wa-qāʾidahā fī l-fijāri.*

3) Cf. al-ʿIṣāmī, *op. cit.*, I, 163: . . *kānat qurayshu l-ẓawāhir yughīrūna ʿalā banī kinānata, yughīruhum ʿamru bnu waddin al-ʿāmiriyyu.*

4) Cf. al-Balādhurī, *Ansāb*, Ms. fol. 882a: . . . *wa-ghazat banū fihrin wa-banū ʿabsin, wa-kāna baynahum yaumaʾidhin baʿdu l-ḥilfi, ʿalā l-yamani; fa-qāla ḍirāru bnu l-khaṭṭābi . . .*

5) Al-Zubayr b. Bakkār, *op. cit.*, fol. 128b, inf.: . . . *ʿan ibni shihābin, sababu maqtali fahmin banī l-ḥārithi bni fihrin bi-farthah* (?), *fa-lam yabqa min banī l-ḥārithi illā l-shurādāt fa-taqassamthum qurayshun; fa-kāna fī banī ʿimrāna bni makhzūmin iyāsun wa-huwa*

of Abū ʿUbayda) who came down to Mecca and joined the *Muṭayyabūn* [1]); he counts them, in fact, in the list of the *Muṭayyabūn* [2]) and records that they were put as adversaries of the ʿAdiyy b. Kaʿb during the mobilization of the rival forces [3]). The ʿAdiyy b. Kaʿb were a weak tribal unit; they were the only group of Quraysh, who "had no *sayyid* who could cope with their problems and avenge their shed blood [4])." According to another tradition the Ḥārith b. Fihr were attached to ʿAbd Manāf and had jointly to face Sahm and Jumaḥ [5]). It is evident that these Banū l-Ḥārith b. Fihr were not a strong group; they were accepted by the *Muṭayyabūn* into their alliance in order to strengthen the alliance. The attachment of the Ḥārith b. Fihr to the *Abṭaḥīs* was reinforced by mutual marriages: ʿAbd al-ʿUzzā b. ʿĀmir married Qilāba bint ʿAbd Manāf; the mother of Ḥarb b. Umayya was Umayma bint Abī Hamhama of al-Ḥārith b. Fihr [6]). Abū Hamhama went out with Umayya when the latter contested Hāshim b. ʿAbd Manāf [7]). Due to these marriages the Banū l-Ḥārith b. Fihr became a part of the *Abṭaḥīs* and consequently of the *Muṭayyabūn* [8]). The case of the Banū l-Ḥārith is instructive and points to the policy followed by Quraysh of adopting clans and attaching families and individuals into their community [9]).

---

lladhī qāla lahu abū ṭālibin:

khālī l-walīdu qad raʾaytum makānahu:

wa-khālu abī lʿāṣi iyāsu bnu maʿbadi

wa-kāna maʿbadu bnu wahbin tabannāhu, fa-kāna yuqālu iyāsu bnu maʿbadin; fa-lammā kānat khilāfatu ʿumara bni l-khaṭṭābi (r) wajadahum fī buṭūni qurayshin, fa-jamaʿahum fa-ḥamalahum ilā gaumihim wa-ʿalā ʿarāfatihim.

1) *Al-Munammaq*, pp. 18, 84, 237.

2) *Ibid.*, pp. 20 ult., 223; and see al-ʿIṣāmī, *op. cit.*, I, 163.

3) *Al-Munammaq*, pp. 20, 44.

4) *Ibid.*, p. 146.

5) *Ibid.*, p. 334 ult.

6) Al-Balādhurī, *Ansāb*, fol. 833a, inf.; Ibn Ḥabīb, *al-Munammaq*, pp. 324-326; Muṣʿab b. ʿAbdallah, *op. cit.*, pp. 443 ult.-444, 1.7; al-Zubayr b. Bakkār, *op. cit.*, fol. 200b.

7) Al-Maqrīzī, *al-Nizāʿ wa-l-takhāṣum*, ed. Maḥmūd ʿArnūs, Cairo 1917, p. 20.

8) Al-Zubayr b. Bakkār, *op. cit.*, fol. 200b: *wa-qadima* (i.e. *ʿabd al-ʿuzzā b. ʿāmir*) *makkata fa-zawwajahu ʿabdu manāfin wa-aqāma maʿahu wa-ʿāqadahu fa-ṣāra banū l-ḥārithi bni fihrin maʿa banī ʿabdi manāfi bni quṣayyin ilā l-yaumi, wa-bi-dhālika l-sababi ṣārū min ahli l-biṭāhi, dūna banī muḥāribi bni fihrin wa-bi-dhālika l-sababi ayḍan dakhalū fī l-muṭayyabīn.*

9) See e.g. Ibn Ḥabīb, *al-Munammaq*, pp. 275-332.

The high position which a *ḥalīf* could achieve in Mecca can be deduced for instance from the fact that a man from Sulaym was appointed by Quraysh as "*muḥtasib*" in Mecca [1]).

The two groups of the *Muṭayyabūn* and the *Aḥlāf* could be mobilized with no difficulty. This can be gauged from the report about the murder of Abū Uzayhir; both groups stood ready to fight and the Prophet ordered Ḥassān to spur them to fight each other. Only due to the wise intervention of Abū Sufyān was bloodshed prevented. The date of the event is given with precision: after the battle of Badr [2]).

The cohesive force of this alliance can be gauged from the report of al-Fākihī, that there were two separate cemeteries in Mecca: one of the *Muṭayyabūn*, and another of the *Aḥlāf* [3]). At the "Day of Uḥud" Quraysh fought under the banners of the *Muṭayyabūn* and *Aḥlāf* [4]).

A story told on the authority of Ibn Abī Mulayka [5]) records a talk between ʿAbdallah b. Safwān b. Umayya and Ibn ʿAbbās. The story exposes problems discussed in connection with the role of Mecca and its development and attests the persistence of the idea of division between the *Muṭayyabūn* and *Aḥlāf*. Ibn ʿAbbās attended the *siqāya* [6]); ʿAbdallah b. Ṣafwān passed by and said: "How pleasant is the rule (*imāra*) of the *Aḥlāf* with regard to you" ("What he in fact said was: How did you assess the imāra of the *Aḥlāf* with regard to you"). Ibn ʿAbbās answered: "The *imāra* of the *Muṭayyabūn* before that was better than that"; he referred to the caliphate of Abū Bakr and ʿUmar. Ibn Ṣafwān said: "ʿUmar ordered to close the well of Zamzam in the interval between the periods of the *ḥajj*" (i.e. to open the well only in the period of the *ḥajj*—K). Ibn ʿAbbās said: "Do you strive for the

1) Al-Fākihī, *op. cit.*, fol. 449b; Ibn Ḥabīb, *al-Munammaq*, p. 286; al-Azraqī, *op. cit.* p. 454; al-Zubayr b. Bakkār, *op. cit.*, fol. 129a; L.ʿA, s.v. *sh r d*; Ibn Abī l-Ḥadīd, *op. cit.*, XVIII, 299.*

2) Al-Zubayr b. Bakkār, *op. cit.*, fol. 145b; Ibn Ḥabīb, *al-Munammaq*, pp. 237-241.

3) *Op. cit.*, fol. 480a: ... *wa-kānat maqbaratu l-muṭayyabīna bi-aʿlā makkata wa-maqbaratu l-aḥlāfi bi-asfali makkata*; see details about the *Muṭayyabūn* and *Aḥlāf*, al-Zubayr b. Bakkār, *op. cit.*, fols. 174b, 184a.

4) Al-Zubayr b. Bakkār, *op. cit.*, fol. 86b.

5) See on him Ibn Ḥajar, *Tahdhīb al-tahdhīb*, V, 306, no. 523.

6) About the privilege of the *siqāya* granted by the Prophet to ʿAbbās see Muqātil, *op. cit.*, fol. 74a; al-Azraqī, *op, cit.*, pp. 337-338; al-ʿIṣāmī, *op. cit.*, I, 207.

sunna of ʿUmar? ʿUmar ordered to turn the upper and lower parts of the valley (i.e. the valley of Mecca) into a resting place for the pilgrims and to turn Ajyadayn and Quʿayqiʿān into a place for walking and resting for them. Then you and your "patron" (*ṣāḥibuka*) started to build up the place with houses ("he perhaps said: 'you built it up with houses and palaces'"); within this is your house and property; after that (i.e. after all your actions contrary to the prescriptions and interdictions of ʿUmar—K) you come and ask (for the application of—K) the *sunna* of ʿUmar? How far is it! You left the *sunna* of ʿUmar far behind [1])."

The quoted passage shows clearly how firm the consciousness of the division between the *Muṭayyabūn* and *Aḥlāf* was in the minds of the Qurashites in the times of ʿUthmān. The rule of Abū Bakr (*muṭayyabūn*) and ʿUmar (*aḥlāf*) was assessed according to which faction they belonged to.

The questions discussed in this talk were connected with the conflicting views about the role of Mecca and whether it was legitimate to develop it. It was a fundamental question whether Mecca had to be kept as a center of pilgrimage, in which building new residential quarters was to be forbidden and the original character of the city preserved as it was in the times of the Prophet. As we can see from the quoted passage changes did take place early.

A considerable wave of building activity is attested in the times of Muʿāwiya. The number of houses and courts bought by Muʿāwiya at Mecca is surprising. He bought from the Banū Mulayl of Khuzāʿa the court called *Dār Ibrāhīm* or *Dār Aus*, located in the lane of the shoemakers, in the quarter of the allies of the Banū Hāshim [2]). In the quarter of the Banū ʿAbd Shams he acquired by exchange the *Dār al-Ḥammām* [3]). In the same quarter he got hold of an unoccupied piece of land in the neighbourhood of the court of al-Ḥakam b.

---

1) Al-Fākihī, *op. cit.*, fol. 443b; al-Azraqī, *op. cit.*, p. 392.

2) Al-Fākihī, *op. cit.*, fol. 448b, ll. 11-12; in this court the shoe-makers and butchers had their shops (*ib.*, fol. 451a, l. 16).

3) *Ibid.*, fol. 449a, l. 4.

Abī l-ʿĀṣ and built there the court of Ziyād b. Abīhi [1]). To Muʿāwiya belonged the *Dār al-Raqṭāʾ* (built with read bricks and gypsum-mortar), the White Court (*al-Dār al-Bayḍāʾ*—the plastered court), the *Dār al-Marājil* (bought by Muʿāwiya from the family of al-Muʾammal of the ʿAdiyy b. Kaʿb), [2]) the *Dār Babba* (=ʿAbdallah b. al-Ḥārith b. Naufal b. al-Ḥarith b. ʿAbd al-Muṭṭalib), the *Dār Salm* (a court located opposite the *Dār al-Ḥammām*), *Dār al-Shiʿb*, a court in the lane of the blacksmiths called *Dār Māli Llāhi* (in which the diseased were housed), the *Dār Saʿd* (built of carved stones, with figures carved in the stones).[3]) In the quarter of the ʿAbd al-Dār Muʿāwiya bought the *Dār al-Nadwa* from Ibn al-Rahīn [4]) and paid for it 100,000 dirham [5]). In this quarter he bought also the court of Saʿīd b. Abī Ṭalḥa [6]). In the quarter of the Banū Zuhra he bought some courts from the ʿAbd ʿAuf [7]). Muʿāwiya bought also the house of Khadīja, in which the Prophet lived until the *hijra*, and turned it into a mosque [8]). According to tradition, Muʿāwiya was the first who built in Mecca houses with baked bricks and gypsum mortar [9]). The sums spent on buildings can be gauged from the report about the building of the court of al-Ḥajjāj. He bought the court of ʿAbd al-Muṭṭalib and deposited thirty thousand dīnārs, as expenses of the building, with the pious ʿAṭāʾ b. Abī Rabāḥ [10]). For the court of Ḥuwayṭib b. ʿAbd al-ʿUzzā Muʿāwiya paid fourty five thousand dīnār [11]). In some of the courts

1) *Ibid.*, fol. 449a, ll. 18-19; the spot between the court of Abū Sufyān and Ḥanẓala b. Abī Sufyān, facing the court of Saʿīd b. al-ʿĀṣ and the court of al-Ḥakam was called *Bayna l-Dārayni*; it was a place where the caravans with wheat and corn used to make halt.

2) In this court there were pots of brass in which meals for the pilgrims and meals of Ramaḍān were prepared in the time of Muʿāwiya.

3) Al-Fākihī, *op. cit.*, fols. 450b, inf.-451b, 460b, l.5.

4) See on him *ibid.*, fol. 424a.

5) *Ibid.*, fol. 455b; and see other versions about this transactions: al-Zubayr b. Bakkār, *op. cit.*, fol. 88b; Mughulṭāy, *op. cit.*, fol. 28b, ult.; Ibn al-Kalbī, *op. cit.*, fol. 24a; *al-Sīra al-ḥalabiyya*, I, 17 inf.; al-Balādhurī, *Futūḥ*, p. 70.

6) Al-Fākihī, *op. cit.*, fols. 456a, l. 6; 496a.

7) *Ibid.*, fol. 456b, l. 5.

8) *Ibid.*, fol. 470b; cf. al-Azraqī, *op. cit.*, p. 457 inf.

9) Al-Fākihī, *op. cit.*, fol. 441a.

10) *Ibid.*, fol. 447a.

11) Al-Balādhurī, *Ansāb* IVA, 47, l. 17 (and see the references of the editor).

acquired by Muʿāwiya there seem to have been workshops of craftsmen, stores and magazines [1]), which secured income and profit.

The vigorous building activities of Muʿāwiya were met with opposition by the orthodox circles, who looked with disapproval at the changes in the city. They wanted it to be a city for pilgrims, with wide, unbuilt spaces, preserved for pilgrims and their riding beasts. A comprehensive chapter in al-Fākihī's *Taʾrīkh*, dealing with these problems, is entitled: "*dhikru karāhiyati kirāʾi buyūti makkata wa-ijāratihā wa-bayʿi ribāʿihā wa-mā jāʾa fī dhālika wa-tafsīruhu*" [2]). The arguments of the scholars are based on the utterances of the Prophet. He is said to have stated, that Mecca had to be put freely at the disposal of the pilgrims: houses should not be rented nor sold (*makkatu mubāḥun au munākhun* [3]), *lā tubāʿu ribāʿuhā wa-lā tuʾājaru buyūtuhā*).[4]) ʿĀʾisha is said to have asked the Prophet to set up for him a building in Mecca in order to find shade from the sun; but the Prophet answered: "Mecca is an alighting place for these who come first" (*innamā hiya munākhu man sabaqa*).[5]) "He who eats (the income) of the rent of houses in Mecca, eats fire" (i.e. he will enter Hell-K).[6])

According to tradition, the houses of Mecca were during the time of the Prophet Abū Bakr and ʿUmar called "*al-sawāʾib*", free possessions, accessible to everyone: they were not sold nor bought; he who needed dwelt in them; he who did not, lodged others in them [7]). People coming

---

1) For the dimensions of a court (*dār*) see e.g. the report of al-Yaʿqūbī, *Mushākalat al-nās bi-zamānihim*, ed. W. Millward, Beirut 1962, p. 13: *fa-banā l-zubayru bnu l-ʿawwāmi dārahu l-mashhūrata bi-l-baṣrati wa-fīhā l-aswāqu wa-l-tijārātu* . . .

2) Fols. 443b-444b.

3) The difference of version مباح, مناخ may be regarded as variants in the written text, the two words looking alike in the Arabic script.

4) Al-Fākihī, *op. cit.*, fol. 443b, l. 2; al-Qurṭubī, *op. cit.*, XI, 33 ult.; and al-Balādhurī, *Futūḥ*, p. 58: *makkatu ḥaramun lā yaḥillu bayʿu ribāʿihā wa-lā ujūru buyūtihā*; al-Fākihī, *op. cit.*, 444a, l. 1; and see al-Ṭaḥāwī, *Sharḥ maʿānī l-āthār*, ed. Muḥammad Zuhrī l-Najjār, Cairo 1388/1968; al-ʿAzīzī, *al-Sirāj al-munīr*, Cairo 1377/1957, III, 305; cf. Aḥmad b. Ḥanbal, *Kitāb al-waraʿ*, Cairo 1340, pp. 80-81.

5) Al-Balādhurī, *Futūḥ*, p. 58; al-Qurṭubī, *op. cit.*, XI, 34; Abū ʿUbayd, *al-Amwāl*, ed. Muḥammad Ḥāmid al-Fiqqī, Cairo 1353, p. 65, no. 160.

6) Al-Qurṭubī, *op. cit.*, XI, 33; Abū ʿUbayd, *op. cit.*, p. 66, no. 163.

7) Al-Qurṭubī, *op. cit.*, XI, 33; al-Ṭaḥāwī, *op. cit.*, IV, 29; Ibn al-ʿArabī, *Aḥkām al-qurʾān*, III, 1264 sup.

to Mecca used to pitch their tents everywhere, even in the open spaces of the courts [1]).

The discussion of this problem centered around the interpretation of Sūra XXII, 25: "... and the Holy Mosque that We have appointed equal unto men, alike him who cleaves to it and the tent dweller" ... "*Sawā'un al-ʿākifu fīhi wa-l-bādi*" was interpreted by some of the scholars as equal rights of the residents of Mecca and the visitors in relation to the courts and houses. The residents have no more rights in relation to these places than the new-comers. "The visitor may alight at any place he finds; the householder has to shelter him, whether he wants to or not [2])." One of the interpretations has a cautious remark: ... "they are equal and they are entitled to alight wherever they want, *without driving out anyone from the house* [3])."

Another problem, a legal one, closely connected with the discussed question, was whether Mecca was conquered by force (*ʿanwatan*) or by a peace-agreement. According to the former opinion (represented by Mālik, Abū Ḥanīfa, Auzāʿī) the houses should be considered as spoil; the Prophet did not distribute the houses and let the owners stay in their lodgings gratuitously, leaving these rights for their progeny too. Therefore, the courts of Mecca are at the disposal of residents and visitors alike. The contradictory opinion, represented by al-Shāfiʿī, stated that Mecca was conquered by a treaty; the courts are thus in the ownership of householders [4]).

The practical application of these views is mirrored in early traditions about ʿUmar. He is said to have forbidden to build doors for the courts of Mecca [5]). The courts of Mecca had no doors; the first who installed a door in his court was Ayman b. Ḥāṭib b. Abī Baltaʿa (according to another tradition: Muʿāwiya).[6]) ʿUmar b. ʿAbd al-ʿAzīz in a letter

1) Al-Fākihī, *op. cit.*, 444a, inf.; Ibn al-ʿArabī, *op. cit.*, III, 1264.
2) See al-Qurṭubī, *op. cit.*, XI, 32; Ibn al-ʿArabī, *op. cit.*, III, 1263; and see al-Balādhurī, *Futūḥ*, p. 59.
3) Al-Balādhurī, *op. cit.*, p. 59, ll. 4-5.
4) Al-Qurṭubī, *op. cit.*, XI, 33; Ibn al-ʿArabī, *op. cit.*, III, 1263 inf.-1264 (see esp. ll. 4-7).
5) Al-Balādhurī, *Futūḥ*, p. 59; al-Fākihī, *op. cit.*, fol. 444b, sup.
6) Al-Fākihī, *op. cit.*, fol. 444a.

to the *amīr* of Mecca prohibited the renting of houses in the city [1]).

There are compromise utterances, in which the interdiction is restricted. Al-Ṭaḥāwī records the tradition about the proposal of ʿĀʾisha to set up a building for the Prophet in *Minā*; the refusal of the Prophet and the interdiction of building is thus limited to Minā [2]). Further, according to al-Ṭaḥāwī, the idea of equal rights to residents and pilgrims is confined to public places; but places owned by people are not included in this category;[3]) this is the concept of al—Layth b. Saʿd: rents of houses are permitted, pilgrims may freely alight in open spaces of houses, ways, waste spaces and plains [4]).

According to another compromise opinion, the renting of houses is unlawful during the *ḥajj*; but it is permissible if the rent is taken from a man who is resident of Mecca (*mujāwir*) and not in the period of the *ḥajj* [5]). A special chapter in al-Fākihī's *Taʾrīkh* deals with the permissibility of buying and renting houses (*dhikru man rakhkhaṣa fī kirāʾi buyūti makkata wa-bayʿi ribāʿihā*).[6]) Houses were in fact bought and sold and the transactions were accurately registered [7]).

The changes in Mecca and the reaction of the orthodox circles are mirrored in a talk between ʿĀʾisha and Muʿāwiya. ʿĀʾisha reproved Muʿāwiya that he built the city into townships and palaces, while the Prophet had made it free for all the Muslims. No one has more right in it (i.e. in the land and buildings—K) than the other. Muʿāwiya answered: "O Mother of the Faithful, so indeed is Mecca and they do not find anything which would shelter them from sun and rain. I ask you to bear witness that it is a *ṣadaqa* for them" (i.e. that my possession in Mecca be considered as a charitable endownment for the Muslim

---

1) Al-Balādhurī, *Futūḥ*, p. 58 ult.-59sup.; al-Fākihī, *op. cit.*, fol. 444b, l. 2.

2) Al-Taḥāwī, *op. cit.*, IV, 50-51; and see the discussion on this subject al-Fāsī, *Shifāʾ al-gharām*, I, 320-321.

3) *Ibid.*, IV, 50.

4) Al-Balādhurī, *Futūḥ*, p. 60.

5) *Ibid.*, p. 60.

6) Fols. 444b-445b.

7) *Ibid.*, fol. 447a: ...*fa-khāṣamahu al-ḥajjāju bnu ʿabdi l-maliki bni l-ḥajjāji bni yūsufa, fa-naẓarū fī l-dawāwīn fa-wajadū l-nafaqata wa-l-thamana min ʿindi l-ḥajjāji.*

community—K).[1]) This solemn promise was never fulfilled, of course.

The growth of Mecca in the early period of Islam was impressive. Houses climbed up the mountains. They were built above the highly placed well of Jubayr b. Muṭʿim, an area where houses were never built before [2]), and on the hill of Abū Qubays [3]). The attitude of the pious men of Mecca is reflected in the saying of Ibn ʿUmar when he saw the houses built on Abū Qubays: "O Mujāhid, when you see houses appearing on its mountains and water flowing in its thoroughfares, then beware"! [4]) The intent of the warning is made clear in another saying of ʿAbdallah b. ʿAmr: "When you see rivers bursting in Mecca and buildings on the tops of the mountains, then know that you are already in the shade of the Day of Judgment".[5])

In fact Muʿāwiya's activity of buying and building houses was accompanied by his energetic activity of digging wells, canals and planting gardens and orchards and cultivating the land in Mecca. Al-Azraqī mentions the wells dug by Muʿāwiya and the orchards in

1) Al-Fākihī, *op. cit.*, fol. 451b: ... *ʿan dhakwāna maulā ʿāʾishata qāla: inna muʿāwiyata (r) dakhala ʿalā ʿāʾishata (r) manzilahā, fa-qālat: anta lladhī ʿamadta ilā makkata fa-banaytahā madāʾina wa-quṣūran, wa-qad abāḥahā llāhu ʿazza wa-jalla li-l-muslimīna, wa-laysa aḥadun aḥaqqu bihā min aḥadin; qāla: yā umma l-muʾminīna, inna makkata kadhā wa-lā yajidūna mā yukinnuhum min al-shamsi wa-l-maṭari; wa-anā ushhiduki annahā ṣadaqatun ʿalayhim.*

2) Al-Fākihī, *op. cit.*, fol. 472b, penult.: ... *wa-samiʿtu baʿḍa ahli makkata min al-fuqahāʾi yaqūlu: kāna l-nāsu lā yujāwizūna fī l-sakani fī qadīmi l-dahri hādhihi l-biʾra; innamā kāna l-nāsu fīmā dūnahā ilā l-masjidi, wa-mā fauqa dhālika khālin min al-nāsi* ...

3) *Ibid.*, fol. 472a, l. 2: *wa-lam yakun yaumaʾidhin ʿalā abī qubaysin buyūtun, innamā ḥadathat baʿdu.*

4) Nuʿaym b. Ḥammād, *Kitāb al-fitan*, Ms. Atif Ef. 602, fol. 4a: "*yā mujāhidu, idhā raʾayta buyūta makkata qad ẓaharat ʿalā akhshābihā wa-jarā l-māʾu fī ṭuruqihā fa-khudh ḥidhraka*. Cf. al-Fākihī, *op. cit.*, fol. 414a: *qāla ʿabdu llāhi bnu ʿamrin (r): yā mujāhidu idhā raʾayta l-māʾa bi-ṭarīqi makkata wa-raʾayta l-bināʾa yaʿlū akhāshibahā, fa-khudh ḥidhraka.*

5) Al-Fākihī, *op. cit.*, fol. 414a, inf.: *idhā raʾayta makkata qad buʿijat kiẓāman, wa-raʾayta l-bināʾa qad ʿalā ʿalā ruʾūsi l-jibāli fa-ʿlam anna l-amra qad aẓallaka*; Abū ʿUbayd, *Gharīb al-ḥadīth*, Hyderabad 1384/1964, I, 269; cf. similar traditions about Medina in Samhūdī's *Wafāʾu l-Wafā*, ed. Muḥammad Muḥyī l-Dīn ʿAbd al-Ḥamīd, Cairo 1374/1955, I, 119: ... *yūshiku l-bunyānu an yaʾtiya hādhā l-makāna* (Ihāb); and see *ibid.*, the recommendation of the Prophet to Abū Dharr: *idhā balagha l-bināʾu salʿan fa-rtaḥil ilā l-shāmi*; cf. Ibn Kathīr, *Nihāyat al-bidāya wa-l-nihāya fī l-fitan wa-l-malāḥim*, ed. Muḥammad Fahīm Abū ʿUbayd, Riyāḍ 1968, I, 80: *tablughu l-masākinu ihāba.*

which palm-trees and plants were grown [1]). Activities of this kind were never before carried out in the city. Sources stress that he was the first who dug wells in Mecca and planted orchards [2]).

The aim and purpose of these investments can be deduced from a talk between ʿAbdallah b. ʿAbbās and Muʿāwiya. Ibn ʿAbbās said in his talk when he visited Muʿāwiya: "I know a valley flowing with gold." Muʿāwiya remained silent and did not ask him (scil. about the valley). Afterwards he granted him the place which is called al-ʿAbbāsiyya; Ibn ʿAbbās turned it into an orchard and dug a well in it. Afterwards Muʿāwiya set up the orchards (in Mecca).[3]) The expression "a valley flowing with gold" points clearly to the aims of setting up the orchards; they were obviously profitable.

Muʿāwiya's activity of digging up wells and canals met with opposition like the building of houses and palaces. ʿAbdallah b. Ṣafwān rebuked Muʿāwiya for his growing orchards in the "valley where there is no sown land" (i.e. Mecca),[4]) contrary to the words of Allah [5]). Scholars of law discussed the problem whether the fruit of trees and vegetables grown in Mecca are permissible to be picked and eaten and whether it is permissible to cut in Mecca trees planted by men [6]). It is evident that cutting trees not planted by men is forbidden in the *ḥaram* area [7]).

The governors and the officials of the Umayyads cared also for the supply of water for the city and for the pilgrims on their way. ʿAbdallah b. ʿĀmir b. Kurayz built cisterns for the pilgrims in ʿArafa [8]). He dug

1) Al-Azraqī, *op. cit.*, p.p 442-444; al-Fākihī, *op. cit.*, fols. 490a-491b.
2) Al-Fākihī, *op. cit.*, fol. 441a-b.
3) Al-Fākihī, *op. cit.*, fol. 441b: *wa-yuqālu*: *bal awwalu ḥāʾiṭin ujriya bi-aʿrāḍi makkata al-ʿabbāsiyyatu*; *yuqālu inna bna ʿabbāsin* (*r*) *qāla yauman, wa-huwa ʿinda muʿāwiyata* (*r*): *innī la-aʿlamu wādiyan yajrī bi-l-dhahabi jaryan*; *qāla, fa-sakata muʿāwiyatu* (*r*) *wa-lam yasʾalhu*; *fa-lammā kāna baʿdu aqṭaʿahu mauḍiʿa al-ʿabbāsiyyati, fa-ajrāhā ʿaynan*; *fa-lammā ʿamilahā akhadha muʿāwiyatu* (*r*) *fī ʿamali l-ḥawāʾiṭi.*
4) *Qurʾān*, Sūra XIV, (Ibrāhīm) 37.
5) Al-Fākihī, *op. cit.*, fol. 490b; al-Balādhurī, *Ansāb*, IV A, 16.
6) Al-Balādhurī, *Futūḥ*, pp. 60-61.
7) See al-Azraqī, *op. cit.*, pp. 372-374.
8) Al-Balādhurī, *Ansāb*, Ms. fol. 799b: ... *wa-ttakhadha bi-ʿarafata ḥiyāḍan wa-siqāyātin*; Ibn ʿAbd al-Barr, *al-Istīʿāb*, p. 932 inf., no. 1587.

wells for pilgrims on their way from al-ʿIrāq to Mecca and said some day: "Had I been left (i.e. to do as I think fit—K) a woman would journey alighting every day at a well (literally a water—K) and a market until reaching Mecca".[1]) Later Khālid b. ʿAbdallah al-Qasrī dug a well (between the passes of Dhū Ṭuwā and Ḥajūn) on the order of al-Walīd b. ʿAbd al-Malik and drew the water from the well to the *ḥaram*. The water was sweet and Khālid urged the people to drink it. He spoke scornfully about Zamzam calling it "Mother of the black-beetles" (*umm al-jiʿlān*) [2]) and stressed its preference over Zamzam [3]). He was so proud of the deed of al-Walīd that he tried to deduce from it the superiority of the Caliph of God (i.e. al-Walīd) over the Messenger of God. "Abraham asked God rain water and He gave salty water (i.e. Zamzam); the Commander of the Faithful asked Him rain water and He gave him sweet water" (i.e. the well dug on the order of the Caliph).[4]) It was in fact a shameless saying. This covered pool located in the *ḥaram*, having its waters supplied from the well dug by Khālid al-Qasrī, was destroyed by Dāwūd b. ʿAlī b. ʿAbdallah b. ʿAbbās to the joy of the people; they preferred the water of Zamzam [5]).

After the period of the first Umayyads the building activities came to what amounts to a standstill. Such activities were only resumed with the advent of the Abbasids [6]).

1) *Ibid.*, fol. 799b.

2) There was however a well called "*umm jiʿlān*" belonging to the ʿAbd Shams (see al-Azraqī, *op. cit.*, p. 438; al-Fākihī, *op. cit.*, fol. 487b, l.4).

3) Al-ʿIṣāmī, *op. cit.*, I, 228.

4) Al-Fākihī, *op. cit.*, fol. 415a.

5) Al-Mauṣilī, *Ghāyat al-wasāʾil*, Ms. Cambridge Qq 33, fol. 14a: *awwalu mā aḥdatha dāwūd b. ʿalī b. ʿabdillāh . . . an hadama l-birkata llatī ʿamilahā khālid b. ʿabdillāh al-qushayrī* (read: *al-qasrī*) . . . *wa-kāna amarahu bi-ʿamali hādhihi l-birkati sulaymānu b. ʿabdi l-maliki wa-an yujriya minhā māʾan ʿadhban fa-kharaja bayna zamzam wa-l-rukn al-aswad yuḍāhī bihā niʿama zamzam . . . wa-kānū fī shurbi māʾi zamzam arghaba minhum fīhā ilā an qadima dāwūd b. ʿalī fa-hadamahā wa-surra l-nāsu bi-dhālika surūran ʿaẓīman.*

6) Cf. al-Fāsī, *op. cit.*, I, 346: . . . *wa-qad kānat ʿuyūnu muʿāwiyata tilka nqaṭaʿat wa-dhahabat fa-amara amīru l-muʾminīna l-rashīdu bi-tajdīdihā.*

ADDENDA

P. 67 note 1

Comp. Ibn Aʿtham, *al-Futūḥ*, Hyderabad 1388/1968, I, 17-18.

P. 68 note 2

See al-Khāzin, *Lubāb al-ta'wīl*, Cairo 1381, VII, 244-245; al-Baghawī, *Maʿālim al-tanzīl* (on margin of *Lubāb al-ta'wīl*), *ib.*

P. 73 note 2

The forces which could be levied in the region of Najrān seem to have been considerable. This can be gauged from the report of Sālim b. abī l-Ja'd (d. 98H at the age of 115; on him see *Tahdhīb al-tahdhīb*, III, 432, no. 799) as transmitted by al-Aʿmash (on him see al-Dhahabī, *Tadhkirat al-ḥuffāẓ*, I, 154, no. 149). When the (Christian) population of Najrān, says the report, increased in number so that the number of the men able to fight became forty thousand—the Muslims were afraid that they would turn against them. ʿUmar then decided to exile them. He deported a group of them to Syria, another one to ʿIrāq and another one to another region. (See Muqātil, *Tafsīr*, Ms. Ḥamidiyya 58, fol. 66b: ... *kathurū ḥattā ṣārū arbaʿīna alfa muqātilin, fa-khāfa l-muslimūna an yamīlū ʿalayhim .... fa-akhraja* (i.e. ʿUmar) *firqatan ilā l-shāmi, wa-firqatan ilā l-ʿirāqi wa-firqatan ilā arḍin ukhrā*). The number of the fighting men given in this account may be exaggerated; it points nevertheless to the strenght of the forces which could be levied in Najrān. (Al-Balādhurī's account of the event [*Futūḥ*, p. 89, ll.1-2] is very laconic: "... they [i.e. the people of Najrān] lent money at interest and increased in number; therefore ʿUmar feared them and expelled them").

P. 73 note 4

About Persian craftsmen engaged in the building of the Kaʿba during its restoration by ʿAbdallah b. al-Zubayr (or in the building of the houses for Muʿāwiya) see al-Mauṣilī, *Ghāyat al-wasā'il*, Ms. Cambridge Qq 33, fol. 231b, inf. (*wa-kāna marra bi-l-fursi wa-hum yabnūna l-masjida l-ḥarāma fī fitnati bni l-zubayri, wa-qīla yabnūna dūra muʿāwiyata....*).

P. 73 note 5

The extent of the trade of the family of Hishām b. al-Mughīra can be gauged from the following verses of al-Ḥuṭay'a (*Dīwān*, ed. Nuʿmān Amīn Ṭāhā, Cairo 1378/1958, p. 320):

fa-hallā amarti bnay hishāmin fa-yamkuthā:
ʿalā mā aṣābā min mi'īna wa-min alfi
min al-rūmi wa-l-uḥbūshi ḥattā tanāwalā:
bi-bayʿihimā māla l-marāzibati l-ghulfi
wa-mā kāna mimmā aṣbaḥā yajmaʿānihi:
min al-māli illā bi-l-taḥarrufi wa-l-ṣarfi

(See the commentary *ib.*, p. 322).

P. 75 l. 8

The principle that the dignitaries of the *ḥaram* have to stay in Mecca, carrying out their duties in the Kaʿba, was followed by the Prophet. Al-ʿAbbās and Shayba were freed from the obligation of the *hijra* and remained in Mecca. (See Ibn ʿAsākir, *Taʾrīkh*, VI, 349: *kāna l-ʿabbāsu wa-shaybatu umanāʾa* [perhaps *min al-umanāʾi*] *wa-lam yuhājirā; fa-aqāma l-ʿabbāsu ʿalā siqāyatihi wa-shaybatu ʿalā l-ḥijābati*...). And see Ibn Ḥajar, *al-Iṣāba*, III, 218, ll. 18-19, no. 3490.

P. 75 note 3

See al-Mauṣilī, *op. cit.*, fol. 156a: *awwalu mā ʿaẓuma amru qurayshin fa-summiyat āla llāhi wa-qarābatahu ḥīna hazama llāhu jaysha l-fīli.*

P. 76 note 4

See al-Khāzin, *op. cit.*, I, 154: *wa-qāla baʿḍu l-ʿulamāʾi inna l-tijarata in waqqʿat naqṣan fī aʿmāli l-ḥajji lam takun mubāḥatan wa-in lam tuwaqqiʿ naqṣan fīhi kānat min al-mubāḥāti llatī al-aulā tarkuhā li-tajrīdi l-ʿibādati min ghayrihā li-anna l-ḥajja bi-dūni l-tijārati afḍalu wa-akmalu.*

P. 77 l. 4

About the encampment of the *Dhāda* at the well called Biʾr Ṣulṣul (in the neighbourhood of Minā) see al-ʿIṣāmī, *op. cit.*, I, 333. (About this well see al-Azraqī, *op. cit.*, p. 442).

P. 77 note 1

The Companions of the Prophet used to trade with Syria by sea; among them were Ṭalḥa and Saʿīd b. Zayd. (See Aḥmad b. Ḥanbal, *al-ʿIlal*, ed. T. Koçyiğit—İ. Cerrahoğlu, Ankara 1963, I, 224, no. 1410: *kāna aṣḥābu rasūli llāhi* [ṣ] *yatjarūna fī l-baḥri ilā l-rūmi, minhum ṭalḥatu bnu ʿubaydi llāhi wa-saʿīdu bnu zaydin*...); and see al-Ṭabarānī, *al-Muʿjam al-ṣaghīr*, ed. ʿAbd al-Raḥmān Muḥ. ʿUthmān, al-Madīna 1388/1968, I, 113,

P. 79 note 4

See al-Jāwī, *Marāḥ labīd*, Cairo n.d., I, 336: .... *wa-aslama ahlu juddata wa-ḥunaynin wa-ṣanʿāʾa wa-tabālata wa-jurasha fa-ḥamalū l-ṭaʿāma ilā makkata*...; and see al-Khāzin, *op. cit.*, III, 64.

P. 83, note 1

See Ibn Ḥazm, *Jamharat ansāb al-ʿArab*, ed. Levi Provençal, Cairo 1948, p. 251, l.20: *kāna bi-makkata fī l-jāhiliyyati muḥtasiban yaʾmuru bi-l-maʿrūfi wa-yanhā ʿan al-munkari*...

ADDITIONAL NOTES

ad p.64, note 3: See Muḥibb al-Dīn al-Ṭabarī, *al-Qirā li-qāṣidi ummi l-qurā*, p.547-548; ʿAlī-al-Ḥalabī, *al-Sira l-ḥalabiyya*, Cairo 1382/1962, III, 98 inf.; Ibn Ḥazm, *Ḥajjāt al-wadāʾ*, ed. Mamdūḥ Ḥaqqī, Beirut 1966, p.148;

p.78, note 1: And see Ibn Nāṣir al-Dīn, *op.cit.*, fol.72a.

p.78, note 3: Al-ʿAbbās was a friend of al-Walīd b. ʿUtba b. Rabīʿa; see al-Suyūṭī, *al-Durr al-manthūr*, III, 164, inf.

p.78, note 4: And see Ibn ʿAbd al-Barr, *al-Istīʿāb*, p.1512, no. 2642.

p.79, note 2: And see al-Samarqandī , *Tafsīr*, Ms. Chester Beatty 3668/I, fol.268b:... *fa-aslama ahlu juddata wa-ṣinfun min ahli l-yamani fa-ḥamalū l-ṭaʿāma ilā makkata mina l-barri wa-l-baḥri wa-aghnāhumu llāhu bi-dhālika, yaʿnī aghnāhum ʿan tujjāri l-kuffāri bi-l-muʾminīn.*

ad p.83, note 1: See Ibn al-Kalbī, *Jamhara*, Ms. Br. Mus. Add. 23297, fol.162a, inf.-162b, 1.1:... *minhum ḥakīmu bnu umayyata... bnu hilālin, ḥalīfu banī umayyata; kāna ḥakīmun muḥtasiban fi l-jāhiliyyati yanhā ʿani l- munkari, wa-fīhi yaqūlu rajulun min qurayshin, yuqālu innahu ʿuthmānu bnu ʿaffāna:*

uṭawwifu bi-l-maṭābikhi kulla yaumin:
makhāfata an yusharridanī ḥakīmu.

ad p.86, note 4: See Ibn Zanjawayh, *al-Amwāl*, Ms. Burdur 183, fol.24a-b; al-Fāsī, *Shifāʾ*, I, 26-46: *dhikru ḥukmi bayʿi dūri makkata wa-ijāratihā;* Ibn Kathir, *Tafsīr*, Beirut 1385/1966, IV, 628-629; al-Jaṣṣāṣ, *Aḥkām al-Qurʾān*, Quṣṭanṭiniyya 1338, III, 228-232; al-Majlisī, *Biḥār al-anwār*, new ed. XCIX, 81, no.28.

ad p.86, note 5: al-Munāwī, *Fayḍ al-qadīr*, VI, 3, no.8202 (see the comment of al-Munāwī: ... *wa-lā tuʾājaru buyūtuhā: li-annahā ghayru mukhtaṣṣatin bi-aḥadin bal hiya mauḍiʿun li-adāʾi l-manāsiki; qāla abū ḥanīfata: fa-arḍu l-ḥarami mauqūfatun, fa-lā yajūzu tamallukuhā li-aḥadin...;* al-Wāqidī, *Maghāzī*, ed. M. Jones, p.1101 (...*fa-abā rasūlu llāhi* [*ṣ*] *wa-qāla: minan manzilu man sabaqa...);* al-Fākihī, *op.cit.*, fol.516b: (...*innamā minan munākhu man sabaqa ilayhi;* and see *ib.*, ...*kānat ʿāʾishatu* [*r*] *takrahu l-bunyāna bi-minan;* and see *ib.* about the place of the merchants frequenting *minā*: ʿUmar asks Zayd b. Ṣūḥān about his place [scil. at-Minā-K]; when answered that he was used to alight in the left half of the spot ʿUmar stated that it was the place where the *dājj* used to alight; *dājj* is explained by Saʿīd b. Jubayr as denoting merchants).

ad p.86, note 5: al-Fāsī, *Shifāʾ*, I, 320-322, 1.2: *dhikru ḥukmi l-bināʾi bi-minan;* Ibn Zanjawayh, *op.cit.*, fol.24a.

p.86, note 6: al-Suyūṭī, *al-Durr al-manthūr*, IV, 351; Ibn Zanjawayh, *op.cit.*, fol.24a.

p.86, note 7: Ibn Zanjawayh, *op.cit.*, fol.24a.

ad p.87, note 6: Ibn Kathīr, *al-Bidāya*, VIII, 139, sup.; idem, *al-Tafsīr*, IV, 629; al-Shiblī, *Maḥāsin al-wasāʾil*, Ms. Br. Mus., Or.1530, fol.30a; al-Majlisī, *Biḥār al-anwār*, XCIX, 81, nos.29, 31.

ad p.90, note 6: And see al-Fākihī, *op.cit.*, fols.465a-466a; al-Shiblī, *Maḥāsin al-wasā'il*, fol.27b.

ad p.91, note 3: And see al-Fākihī, *op.cit.*, fol.429b.

ad p.91, note 4: See al-Fāsī, *al-ʿIqd al-thamīn*, IV, 280 (from Ṭabarī).

ad p.91, note 5: And see al-Fākihī, *op.cit.*, fol.429b; al-Fāsī, *al-ʿIqd*, IV, 274 (from al-Azraqī).

III

AL-ḤĪRA

Some notes on its relations with Arabia

THE RIVALRY between the Persian and Byzantine Empires over the control of the regions of the Arab Peninsula at the end of the sixth and the beginning of the seventh century is reflected in a number of traditions attributed to the Prophet and recorded in some commentaries of the *Qur'ān*. Qatāda (died 117 AH) [1] gives a description of the sad situation of the Arab population of the Peninsula before they embraced Islam, commenting on *Qur'ān*, VIII, 26: "And remember when you were few and abased in the land and were fearful that the people (*al-nās*) would snatch you away" [2]. He describes their sorrowful economic situation, their going astray and their weakness, and states that they were "confined on a top of a rock between Fāris and Rūm" (*maʿkūfīna ʿalā ra'si ḥağarin bayna Fārisa wa-l-Rūmi*) [3]. "The people" (*al-nās*) mentioned in the verse of the *Qur'ān* are said to refer to Persians and Byzantines [4]. A ḥadīṯ reported on the authority of Ibn ʿAbbās (died 68 AH) states that the Prophet interpreted *al-nās* as

1. See about him IBN ḤAĞAR : *Tahḏīb al-tahḏīb*, VIII, 355 (Hyderabad 1327 AH); AL-ḎAHABĪ: *Mīzān al-iʿtidāl*, III, 385, No. 6864 (ed. AL-BIĞĀWĪ, Cairo 1963).

2. Translation of A. J. ARBERRY : *The Koran Interpreted*, p. 172 (London 1964).

3. AL-SUYŪṬĪ, *al-Durr al-manṯūr*, III, 177 (Cairo 1314 AH); ṬABARĪ's *Tafsīr*, XIII, 478 (ed. Maḥmūd Muḥ. ŠĀKIR and Aḥmad Muḥ. ŠĀKIR, Cairo 1958) contains the comment of Qatāda, but the mentioned phrase is inserted by the Editors with variants: "*between the two lions* (*asadayni*) *Fāris and Rūm*" and "*makʿūmīna*" instead of "*maʿkūfīna*"; AL-ŠAWKĀNĪ, *Fatḥ al-Qadīr*, II, 287 (Cairo 1932—but the phrase is omitted); IBN KAṮĪR, *Tafsīr*, III, 303 (Beirut 1966—the phrase is omitted); AL-SAMARQANDĪ, *Tafsīr*, Ms. Chester Beatty, I, f. 252b (*kānū bayna asadayni bayna Qayṣara wa-Kisrā*).

4. AL-SUYŪṬĪ, *op. cit.*, ib.; AL-ṬABARĪ, *op. cit.*, ib.—but al-Ṭabarī prefers another interpretation, according to which "*al-nās*" refers to Qurayš, ib. p. 379; AL-FAYRŪZABĀDĪ, *Tanwīr al-miqbās*, p. 138 (Cairo 1290 AH) records that *al-nās* refers to Qurayš; AL-SAMARQANDĪ, *op. cit.*, ib.: *al-nās* refers to Persians, Byzantines and "*ʿArab*" who dwelt around Mecca; AL-BAYḌĀWĪ, *Tafsīr*, I, 183 (Cairo 1355 AH) . . . *wa-qīla li-l-ʿArabi kāffatan fa-innahum kānū aḏillā'a fī aydī Fārisa wa-l-Rūmi*.

referring to Persians [1]. Whatever the interpretation of the phrase in the verse discussed above, these early commentaries seem to mirror the apprehensions felt by the people of the Peninsula concerning the power of the two rival Empires and to bring out the impact of this rivalry on the life of the communities in the Peninsula.

The struggle between the two Empires, in which the two vassal-kingdoms of al-Ḥīra and Ġassān took active part, was closely watched by the unbelievers and Muslims in the different stages of their context. According to the commentaries on *Qur'ān*, XXX, 1-2, the sympathies of the unbelievers of Mecca were with Persia whereas the Muslim community inclined towards the Byzantines [2]. The victories of the Byzantines, it is stressed, coincided with the victories of the Prophet [3].

The efforts of Persia to gain control over the region of al-Ḥiǧāz were noticed by R. Růžička, who assumed that the waning of the influence of Tamīm and the rise of the influence of Ġaṭafān were caused by the action of Persian policy performed through the medium of the Laḫmid kingdom in order to get a foothold in this region [4].

A tradition recorded by Ibn Sa'īd in his *Našwat al-ṭarab* [5] reports

1. AL-SUYŪṬĪ, *op. cit.*, ib; but in ṬABARĪ's *Ṭafsīr*, p. 478 the comment is attributed to Wahb b. Munabbih.

2. AL-ṬABARĪ, *op. cit.*, XXI, 16 (Cairo 1954, printed by Muṣṭafā al-Bābī AL-ḤALABĪ); AL-QURṬUBĪ, *al-Ǧāmi' li-aḥkām al-Qur'ān*, XIV, 1 seq. (Cairo 1945); IBN KAṮĪR, *op. cit.*, V, 342-43; ABŪ NU'AYM: *Dalā'il al-nubuwwa*, p. 296 (Hyderabad 1950); ABŪ ḤAYYĀN: *Tafsīr al-Baḥr al-Muḥīṭ*, VII, 161 (Cairo 1328 AH); ABŪ L-MAḤĀSIN YŪSUF B. MŪSĀ AL-ḤANAFĪ, *al-Mu'taṣar min al-muḫtaṣar*, II, 189-190 (Hyderabad 1362 AH); and see M. HARTMANN, *Der Islamische Orient*, II (Die arabische Frage), pp. 50-51, 511-514 (Leipzig 1909); R. BLACHÈRE, *Le Coran*, I, 418-20 (Paris 1920); MUḤ. HAMIDULLAH, *Le Prophète de l'Islam*, I, 18 (Paris 1959).

3. AL-QURṬUBĪ, *op. cit.*, XIV, 1-5; AL-ṬABARĪ, *op. cit.*, XXI, 16 seq.; IBN KAṮĪR, *op. cit.*, V, 348; of interest is a record reported by al-Qurṭubī: when the tidings of the victory of the Byzantines arrived many people embraced Islam, *op. cit.*, XIV, 2; and see F. ALTHEIM and R. STIEHL: *Finanzgeschichte der Spätantike*, pp. 158-60 (Frankfurt am Main 1957).

4. R. RŮŽIČKA: *Duraid b. aṣ-Ṣimma*, I, 55 (Praha 1930): *"Zda se, že v zaniknuti nadvlady Tamimovcu a v převladnuti vlivu Ġaṭafanovcu třeba spatřovati učinky politiky perské, jež se snažila postřednictvim političky vladnouti"* . . . ["Il semble qu'il faille voir dans la disparition de la prépondérance de Tamīm et la montée de celle de Ġaṭafān les effets de la politique perse, qui s'efforçait d'assurer sa domination en mettant en œuvre de petits moyens" (N.D.L.R.)].

5. Ms. Tübingen, f. 96 v. (See F. TRUMMETER, *Ibn Sa'īd's Geschichte der vorislamischen Araber*, Stuttgart 1928; and see G. POTIRON: *Un polygraphe andalou du XIIIe Siècle*, in *Arabica* 1966, p. 164).

an interesting attempt of Persia to cast its power over Mecca. When Qubāḏ embraced the faith of Mazdak [1] and deposed the Banū Naṣr who refused to accept it, al-Ḥāriṯ al-Kindī followed suit. Qubāḏ, the story relates, ordered al-Ḥāriṯ to impose this faith on the Arabs of Naǧd and Tihāma [2]. When these tidings reached Mecca some people embraced the faith of Mazdak (*fa-minhum man tazandaqa*) and when Islam appeared there was a group (scil. in Mecca-K.) of people who were indicated as former Mazdakites [3]. There were however people who refrained from embracing this faith. Among them was ʿAbd Manāf, who gathered his people and stated that he would not abandon the religion of Ismāʿīl and Abraham and follow a religion imposed by the sword. When al-Ḥāriṯ came to know about it he reported it to Qubāḏ. Qubāḏ ordered him to rush upon Mecca, to destroy the Kaʿba, to kill ʿAbd Manāf and to abolish the leadership of the Banū Quṣayy [4]. Al-Ḥāriṯ was not willing to comply with the order; because of his partisanship of the Arabs he prevented Qubāḏ from it and Qubāḏ was busy with other people than Qurayš [5]. The tendency of this tradition is obvious: it tries to lay a heavy stress on the behaviour of ʿAbd Manāf who remained faithful to the religion of Qurayš, the *dīn Ismāʿīl*. The tradition may be spurious, but it points to the contacts which seem to have existed between al-Ḥīra and Mecca.

Ibn Ḫurdāḏbeh in his *Kitāb al-masālik wa-l-mamālik* [6] records a tradition according to which the *marzubān al-bādiya* appointed an *ʿāmil* on al-Madīna, who collected the taxes. The Qurayẓa and the Naḍīr—says the tradition—were kings who were appointed by them on al-Madīna, upon the Aws and the Ḫazraǧ. A verse to this effect by an Anṣārī poet is quoted. It says:

---

1. *fī zamani Qubāḏa sulṭāni l-Fursi llaḏī tazandaqa wa-ttabaʿa maḏhaba Mazdaqa.*
2. *wa-amara l-Ḥāriṯa an yaʾḫuḏa ahla Naǧdin wa-Tihāmata bi-ḏālika.*
3. See Ǧawād ʿAlī, *Taʾrīḫ al-ʿArab qabla l-Islām*, VI, 287-88 (Baghdād 1957); he assumes that these "*zanādiqa*" of Qurayš embraced the *maǧūsiyya*; this passage of *Našwat al-ṭarab* seems to give a new interpretation of the well known tradition about the "*zandaqa*" of some Qurayš. And see the list of these "*zanādiqa*" of Qurayš in Ibn Ḥabīb's *al-Muḥabbar*, p. 161 (ed. Ilse Lichtenstädter, Hyderabad 1942).
4. "*fa-amarahu an yanhaḍa ilā Makkata wa-yahdima l-bayta wa-yanḥara ʿAbda Manāfin wa-yuzīla riʾāsata bani Quṣayyin*".
5. "*fa-kariha ḏālika al-Ḥāriṯu wa-dāḫalathu ḥamiyyatun li-l-ʿArabi fa-dāraʾa ʿanhum wa-šuġila Qubāḏu bi-ġayrihim*".
6. p. 128 (ed. de Goeje, Leiden 1889).

"You pay the tax after the tax of Kisrā: and the tax of Qurayẓa and Naḍīr" [1]. Yāqūt quotes the tradition that the Qurayẓa and Naḍīr were kings driven out by the Aws and Ḫazraǧ; the Aws and Ḫazraǧ used formerly to pay tax to the Jews [2].

W. Caskel doubts whether Ibn Ḫurdāḏbeh had had another source than this verse of one of the Anṣār [3]. Caskel's assumption can however hardly be accepted. The record given by Ibn Ḫurdāḏbeh and Yāqūt seems to be based on a separate tradition to which the verse was attached. This verse attributed here to an Anṣārī poet occurs in the well-known poem of Ibn Buqayla; in the poem this verse has quite a different connotation [4].

This tradition was discussed by H. Z. Hirschberg in his *Yisrael be-ʿArav* [5]. Hirschberg does not accept the tradition as valid, arguing that this report is not confirmed by another independent source. He maintains that the people of al-Madīna were free (*bnei ḥorin*) with regard to Persia and Byzantium. It is not plausible—argues Hirschberg—that the *ʿāmil* of the *marzubān* of Haǧar, whose power was so weak in Baḥrayn, could have levied taxes in the North of Ḥiǧāz.

Altheim and Stiehl consider the tradition sound. The *ʿāmil* of al-Madīna represented the king of al-Ḥīra, on his side stood the "kings" of Qurayẓa and Naḍīr. This state of affairs—according to Altheim-Stiehl—could endure as long as the Jewish tribes dominated the immigrant Aws and Ḫazraǧ, i.e. till the middle of the sixth century. How things went on later with the Sassanid *ʿāmil* is unknown—state the authors [6].

---

1. "*Tuʾaddī l-ḫarǧa baʿda ḫarāǧi Kisrā*: *wa-ḫarǧin min Qurayẓata wa-l-Naḍīri*".

"*Min Qurayẓata*" would mean "for *Qurayẓa*". The variant given in Yāqūt's *Muʿǧam al-buldān*, IV, 460 is "*wa-ḫarǧi banī Qurayẓata wa-l-Naḍīri*".

2. Yāqūt, *op. cit.*, ib.; and see Altheim-Stiehl, *op. cit.*, p. 150, l. 4-5.

3. F. Altheim-R. Stiehl, *op. cit.*, p. 149, n. 63.

4. See the poem al-Ṭabarī, *Taʾrīḫ*, I, 2042; al-Masʿūdī, *Murūǧ*, I, 221-222 (ed. Barbier de Meynard, Paris 1861). A significant variant is given in Abū l-Baqāʾ's *al-Manāqib al-Mazyadiyya*, f. 34b (Ms. Br. Mus.): "*ka-ḫarǧi banī-Qurayẓata*". Abū l-Baqāʾ states that ʿAbd al-Masīḥ composed this poem eulogising al-Nuʿmān, his son and his grandfather and wailing them after Ḫālid b. al-Walīd "imposed (scil. upon his people—K.) the *ǧizya*" (*lammā ẓahara l-Islāmu wa-ḍaraba Ḫālidu bnu l-Walīdi l-ǧizyata*).

5. p. 122, n. 99, Tel-Aviv 1946; in this note an additional reference is given: al-Samhūdī, *Wafāʾ al-wafā*, II, 269 (quoted from Ibn Ḫurdāḏbeh, but without the verse).

6. *Op. cit.*, pp. 149-150.

Altheim-Stiehl are probably right in their assumption. A significant record of Ibn Sa'īd in his *Našwat al-ṭarab* gives important details about the continuity of the Sassanid control of al-Madīna after the Jewish domination had come to an end.

Ibn Sa'īd reports that battles often took place between the two fighting groups (i.e. the Jews, Aws and Ḫazraǧ) [1] and no rule was imposed on them until 'Amr b. al-Iṭnāba al-Ḫazraǧī entered the court of al-Nu'mān b. al-Mundir, the king of al-Ḥīra and was appointed by him (as king) on al-Madīna [2].

In another passage Ibn Sa'īd furnishes us with further details about this event. The author records that 'Amr b. al-Iṭnāba was appointed by al-Nu'mān b. al-Mundir as king of al-Madīna. The father of Ḥassān b. Ṯābit composed satirical verses about 'Amr and said:

"Aliknī ilā l-Nu'māni qawlan maḥaḍtuhu:
wa-fī l-nuṣḥi li-l-albābi yawman dalā'ilu
Ba'aṯṯa ilaynā ba'ḍanā wa-hwa aḥmaqun:
fa-yā laytahū min ġayrinā wa-hwa 'āqilu"

"Convey from me to al-Nu'mān a word which
[I said truthfully
for in good advise minds will have some day
[indications
You sent to us one from us—but he is a fool;
Lo! Would that he were from an alien people
[and be a wise man" [3].

Our knowledge of the life of 'Amr b. al-Iṭnāba is meagre. 'Amr b. 'Āmir b. Zayd Manāt b. Mālik b. Ṯa'laba b. Ka'b b. al-Ḫazraǧ is a well known poet often quoted in literary anthologies [4]. He is

---

1. See the interpretation of Hirschberg about the continuous penetration of the Bedouins and their raids against the Jewish population, *op. cit.*, 127 ult., 128 sup.

2. *Našwat al-ṭarab*, f. 55 v., inf.: *"illā annahu kānati l-ḥarbu kaṯīran mā taqa'u bayna l-farīqayni wa-lam yastaqim lahum an yastabidda bihim malikun ilā an daḫala ilā l-Nu'māni bni l-Mundiri maliki l-Ḥīrati 'Amru bnu l-Iṭnābati al-Ḫazraǧiyyu fa-mallakahu 'alā l-Madīnati"*.

3. ib., f. 57 v.: *wa-min ši'rihi fī 'Amri bni l-Iṭnābati l-Ḫazraǧiyyi lammā mallakahu l-Nu'mānu bnu l-Mundiri 'alā l-Madīnati: aliknī—etc.*

4. Ibn Ḥazm, *Ǧamharat ansāb al-'Arab*, p. 345, l. 17 (ed. Lévi-Provençal, Cairo 1948); Ṣadr al-Dīn, *al-Ḥamāsa al-Baṣriyya*, I, 3 (see the references supplied by the editor, Muḫtār al-Dīn Aḥmad, Hyderabad 1964); al-'Askarī, *al-Maṣūn*, p. 136 (see the references given by the editor 'Abd al-

described as "the most honoured of the Ḫazraǧ" [1], as the "best horseman of his people" [2], as a "king of al-Ḥiǧāz" [3]. The opinion of W. Caskel that the story of the meeting of ʿAmr b. al-Iṭnāba with al-Ḥāriṯ b. Ẓālim is of legendary character [4] seems to be sound. It is however noteworthy that Abū ʿUbayda stresses in his record that ʿAmr b. al-Iṭnāba was a friend of Ḫālid b. Ǧaʿfar, the leader of the Kilāb, who was in close contact with the ruler of al-Ḥīra and who was murdered by al-Ḥāriṯ b. Ẓālim [5] at the court of al-Nuʿmān. The names of the persons mentioned in the stories about ʿAmr b. al-Iṭnāba [6] like al-Ḥāriṯ b. Ẓālim, Zayd al-Ḫayl [7], Ḫālid b. Ǧaʿfar, al-Nuʿmān b. al-Munḏir, help us to fix the time of his life as the second half of the sixth century.

The tradition about the appointment of ʿAmr as a "king", which meant in fact as a representative of al-Ḥīra and a collector of the taxes on al-Madīna, by al-Nuʿmān seems authentic. Invention can hardly be suspected as there were no prominent men among the descendents of ʿAmr who would have been interested to boast of this appointment. The two verses of Ṯābit, the father of Ḥassān, confirm the authenticity of the story, which is thus complementary

---

Salām Hārūn, Kuweit 1960); Ibn al-Šaǧarī, *al-Ḥamāsa*, p. 112 (Hyderabad 1345 AH); Ibn Ḥabīb, *Man nusiba ilā ummihi min al-šuʿarāʾ* (*Nawādir al-maḫṭūṭāt*, I, 95, 201—ed. ʿAbd al-Salām Hārūn, Cairo 1951); al-Mubarrad, *al-Kāmil*, I, 89, IV, 68 (ed. Muḥ. Abū l-Faḍl Ibrāhīm, Cairo 1956); *L.ʿA.*, s.v. *ṭnb*; S. M. Ḥusain, *Early Arabic Odes*, p. 42-44 (Ar. text; and see the references of the Editor; and see pp. 41-42 of the English text—Dacca 1938). One of the descendants of ʿAmr b. al-Iṭnāba was Qaraẓa b. Kaʿb b. ʿAmr, a Companion of the Prophet. See Ibn Ḥazm, *op. cit.*, ib.; and see about Qaraẓa Ibn Ḥaǧar: *al-Iṣāba*, V, 236, No. 7092; Ibn Saʿd, *Ṭabaqat*, VI, 17 (Beirut 1957); al-Minqarī, *Waqʿat Ṣiffīn*, p. 17 (ed. ʿAbd al-Salām Hārūn, Cairo 1387 AH).

1. al-Marzubānī, *Muʿǧam al-Šuʿarāʾ*, p. 203 (ed. F. Krenkow, Cairo 1354 AH).
2. Ibn Durayd, *al-Ištiqāq*, p. 453 (ed. ʿAbd al-Salām Hārūn, Cairo 1958).
3. *al-Aġānī*, X, 28.
4. W. Caskel, *Ǧamharat an-Nasab, das genealogische Werk des Hišām b. Muḥ. al-Kalbī*, II, 170 (Leiden 1966).
5. *Aġānī*, X, 28; about the murder of Ḫālid b. Ǧaʿfar see *Aġānī*, X, 16; Ibn Ḥabīb, *al-Muḥabbar*, p. 193; idem, *Asmāʾ al-muġtālīna min al-ašrāf* (*Nawādir al-maḫṭūṭāt*, II, 134-135, ed. ʿAbd al-Salām Hārūn, Cairo 1954); Ibn al-Aṯīr, *al-Kāmil*, I, 338-39 (ed. ʿAbd al-Wahhāb al-Naǧǧār, Cairo 1348 AH).
6. In the record of the battle of Fāriʿ (Ibn al-Aṯīr: *al-Kāmil*, I, 409-410) the leader of the Ḫazraǧ is "ʿĀmir b. al-Iṭnāba", which seems to be an erroneous reading for "ʿAmr b. al-Iṭnāba. (The verses are by ʿAmr b. al-Iṭnāba).
7. *Aġānī*, XVI, 53.

to the tradition recorded by Ibn Ḫurdāḏbeh and attests the continuity of the Persian control over al-Madīna during the second part of the sixth century.

In order to secure the domination of al-Ḥīra the loyalty of the tribes was essential. Some formations of the tribes fought on the side of the military units of al-Ḥīra, tribal chiefs had to guarantee the security of the caravans sent by the rulers of al-Ḥīra which passed in their territory, rebellious chiefs had to be tamed and trade had to be made safe.

In order to secure the loyalty and co-operation of the chief of the tribe some prerogatives of the ruler were ceded to him. In this way the *ridāfa* was created. The *Ridf* sat—according to tradition—in the court of the king, on his right hand, rode with the king, got a fourth of the spoils and booty of the raids gained by the king and received some payment from the king's subjects [1]. The *ridf*s are said to have had at the court the position of the *wazīr*s in the Islamic period [2]. At the court of al-Ḥīra the clan of Yarbūʿ of Tamīm had the privilege of the *ridāfa*. Chamberlains, *ardāf*, of the kings, are mentioned as well in the tribe of Ḍabba [3], in the clan of Taym [4], in the clan of Sadūs (of Šaybān) [5] and in the tribe of Taġlib [6]. The institution of the *ridf* is often mentioned in ancient poetry. The Banū Yarbūʿ of Tamīm boasted that they were the *ardāf* of the kings of al-Ḥīra.

---

1. *al-Naqāʾiḍ*, pp. 66, 299, 809 (ed. BEVAN, Leiden 1905); AL-BALĀḎURĪ, *Ansāb al-ašrāf*, ms., f. 992 b; AL-KUTUBĪ, *Fawāt al-wafayāt*, II, 626 (ed. Muḥ. Muḥyī al-Dīn AL-ḪAṬĪB, Cairo 1951).

2. *L. ʿA.*, s.v. "*qṣr*"; KUṮAYYIR ʿAZZA, *Dīwān*, II, 49 (ed. Henri PÉRÈS, Alger-Paris 1930); and see ROTHSTEIN, *Die Dynastie der Laḫmīden*, p. 133.

3. IBN AL-KALBĪ, *Ǧamhara*, ms. f. 114 b; AL-BALĀḎURĪ, *Ansāb*, ms. f. 952 (Ḥulayla—or Ǧulayla—b. Ṯābit b. ʿAbd al-ʿUzzā).

4. AL-BALĀḎURĪ, *op. cit.*, f. 933 b (The Banū Šihāb).

5. IBN DURAYD, *al-Ištiqāq*, p. 352. IBN QUTAYBA, *al-Maʿārif*, p. 45 (Cairo 1935); they were the *ardāf* of Kinda; and see ROTHSTEIN, *op. cit.*, ib., n. 2; and see the verse of LABĪD "*wa-ardāfu l-mulūki šuhūdu*" in his *Dīwān*, p. 35 (ed. I. ʿABBĀS, Kuwait 1962); *L. ʿA.*, s.v. "*rdf*"; AL-ṮAʿĀLIBĪ, *Ṯimār al-qulūb*, p. 144 (Cairo 1908); YĀQŪT, *al-Buldān*, s.v. *Ufāqa*; *Naqāʾiḍ*, p. 299; ABŪ ʿUBAYDA, *Maǧāz al-Qurʾān*, I, 315 (ed. Fuʾād SEZGIN, Cairo 1955); for the *ridāfa* of Mālik b. Nuwayra, see NÖLDEKE, *Beiträge zur Kenntniss der Poesie der alten Araber*, pp. 126-27 (Hanover 1864); and compare the saying of Wāʾil b. Ḥuǧr al-Ḥaḍramī to Muʿāwiya: "*Mā aḏunnu ʿalayka bi-hāḏihi l-nāqati, wa-lākin lasta min ardāfi l-mulūki wa-akrahu an uʿayyara bika*"—AL-ṬABARĀNĪ, *al-Muʿǧam al-ṣaġīr*, p. 242 (Delhi 1311 AH); IBN KAṮĪR, *al-Sīra al-nabawiyya*, IV, 154-55 (ed. Muṣṭafā ʿABD AL-WĀḤID, Cairo 1966).

6. MUḤ. B. ḤABĪB, *al-Muḥabbar*, p. 204.

These socio-political conditions of the second part of the sixth century gave rise to another institution, that of the *Ḏawū l-ākāl*. Ibn Ḥabīb defines the *Ḏawū l-ākāl* as follows: "The *Ḏawū l-ākāl* are from Wā'il; they are the noble among them. The king used to grant them fiefs" [1]. A description of these *Ḏawū l-ākāl*, stressing their social position, is given by al-Aʿšā:

"Around me are the men of the fiefs of Wā'il
like the night (i.e. numerous), nomads and sedentary.
(Men) feeding on meat (i.e. the needy and the
[hungry—K.) in winter
and obliging the gambler of *maysir* to care for food
[(of the poor)" [2].

Further the *Ḏawū l-ākāl* are mentioned in another verse of al-Aʿšā in which the people of the *ākāl* are depicted as noble men serving the army of the king of al-Ḥīra.

"Your army is the inherited one, the excellent of
[the chiefs
The people of the leathern tents and the fiefs" [3].

Ibn Ḥabīb shows a clear line between the tribes whose chiefs co-operated with Persia or with the rulers of al-Ḥīra and were granted fiefs as a reward and the tribes who pursued a policy of independence towards al-Ḥīra. As to Muḍar—states Ibn Ḥabīb—they were *laqāḥ*. They did not submit to the obedience of the kings (*lā yadīnūna li-l-mulūki*) except some clans of Tamīm, namely those whose abode was Yamāma and the adjacent regions" [4].

The case of fiefs granted by the rulers of al-Ḥīra to the loyal chiefs is well illustrated by the story of Qays b. Masʿūd al-Šaybānī.

---

1. *Op. cit.*, p. 253; and see AL-MARZŪQĪ, *al-Azmina wa-l-amkina*, II, 191 (Hyderabad 1332 AH).

2. AL-AʿŠĀ, *Dīwān*, XVIII, 48-49 (p. 107)—ed. R. GEYER, London 1928:
"*Ḥawlī ḏawū l-ākāli min Wā'ilin*:
ka-l-layli min bādin wa-min ḥāḍiri
Al-muṭʿimū l-laḥma iḏā mā šataw
wa-l-ǧāʿilū l-qūta ʿalā l-yāsiri".

3. AL-AʿŠĀ, *op. cit.*, I, 56 (p. 11) "*Ǧunduka l-tālidu l-ʿatīqu min al-sādāti ahla l-qibābi wa-l-ākāli*"; and see commentary: "*al-ṭārifu l-talīdu*". AL-BAKRĪ, *Simṭ al-la'ālī*, p. 269 (ed. MAYMANĪ, Cairo 1936); but see AL-ZAWZANĪ, *Nayl al-arab*, p. 185 (Cairo 1328 AH): *ǧunduka l-tālidu l-ṭarīfu min al-ġārāti ahlu l-hibāti wa-l-ukāli*. The expression "people of leathern tents" denotes their high position in the tribe.

4. *Al-Muḥabbar*, p. 253.

Qays b. Mas'ūd was granted the lands of Ṭaff Ubulla by Khusrau II Parwez (after the death of al-Nu'mān III) against a guarantee that Bakr b. Wā'il would refrain from raiding the territory of the Sawād [1]. Contrary to Šaybān the Muḍar were independent. And it is noteworthy that one of the strongest tribes of the federation of Muḍar was Tamīm [2].

Traditions of some importance about the relations between al-Ḥīra and the tribes are recorded by Abū l-Baqā'. Discussing the position of the kings of al-Ḥīra Abū l-Baqā' remarks that the Bedouins (*al-'Arab*), being used to blowing up things and to exaggerate, used to call the rulers of al-Ḥīra "kings". The Chosroes of Persia—states Abū l-Baqā'—granted the rulers of al-Ḥīra some territories as fiefs and as assistance for them in their governorship (scil. on behalf of the kings of Persia—K.). They collected the taxes of these territories and used them for their expenses. They bestowed from it presents on some of their own people and on people (of the Bedouins—K.) whom they blandished and tried to win over. Sometimes they granted them localities from the fiefs presented to them [3].

Abū l-Baqā' points out that these fiefs granted by the Persian rulers were restricted to the border-lands in the vicinity of al-Ḥīra. The rulers of al-Ḥīra could not trespass these lands, because the territories (of Persia) belonged to the Dihqāns, who vied among themselves for their possession. Abū l-Baqā' remarks that the fiefs granted by the kings of al-Ḥīra were very meagre in comparison with the flourishing state of the country.

Of some interest is the passage in which Abū l-Baqā' records

---

1. *Al-Aġānī*, XX, 132: "*fa-wafada Qaysu bnu Mas'ūdin ilā Kisrā fa-sa'alahu an yaǧ'ala lahu uklan wa-ṭu'matan 'alā an yaḍmana lahu 'alā Bakri bni Wā'ilin an lā yadḫulū l-Sawāda wa-lā yufsidū fīhi; fa-aqṭa'ahu l-Ubullata wa-mā wālāhā*"; and see Rothstein, *op. cit.*, p. 122; E. Bräunlich, *Bisṭām b. Qais*, pp. 12, 30-33 (Leipzig 1923); W. Caskel, *al-A'šā*, in *EI*²; W. Caskel, *Ǧamharat an-Nasab*, II, 461.

2. Comp. Abū Zayd, *al-Nawādir*, p. 61 (ed. Sa'īd al-Šartūnī, Beirut 1894):

"*Fa-inna bayta Tamīmim ḏū sami'ta bihi:*
fīhi tanammat wa-arsat 'izzahā Muḍaru

3. Abū l-Baqā', *al-Manāqib*, ms. f. 145 a: "*... wa-innamā kānat al-Akāsiratu tuqṭi'uhum mawāḍi'a minhu mu'ayyanatan, musammātan, taǧ'aluhā aṭ'imatan lahum wa-ma'ūnatan 'alā 'amalihim. Wa-kānū yaǧtabūna ḫarāǧahā fa-ya'kulūnahu wa-yuṭ'imūna minhu man šā'ū min ahlihim wa-man kānū yuṣāni'ūnahu wa-yastamīlūnahu min al-'Arabi. Wa-rubbamā aqṭa'ūhum ayḍan quran min ǧumlati iqṭā'ihim ...*".

details about the amount of taxes collected by al-Nuʿmān from the fiefs granted to him by the Persian king [1]: "the sum of (the taxes collected from) the fiefs given by Kisrā to al-Nuʿmān was 100,000 dirham. In some of the books of al-Ḥīra it was mentioned, that the lands given by Kisrā as fief were the *rustāq* of Saylaḥīn, Qaṭāʾiʿ banī Ṭalḥa and Sanām Ṭibāq. This I have seen (i.e. read it) in a book".

The author identifies the names of the localities mentioned with names current in his time. They were located in the region of al-Naǧaf. The sum of the tax collected was a mere 100,000 dirhams, notwithstanding—as Abū l-Baqāʾ points out—the fertility of the lands, which yielded a yearly average of 30,000 *karr* in addition to fruits and other produce [2].

Al-Nuʿmān granted some of these lands to some important persons. Sawād b. ʿAdiyy (from Tamīm) was granted a place which was named after him "al-Sawādiyya" [3]. ʿAbd Hind b. Nuǧam al-Iyādī got al-Ḫuṣūṣ [4].

When Khusrau II Parvez appointed Iyās b. Qabīṣa as ruler over al-Ḥīra he granted him ʿAyn Tamr and eighty villages located on the border of the Sawād. Iyās b. Qabīṣa granted Aqsās as a fief to Mālik b. Qays and the place was later known as Aqsās Mālik [5].

The interrelation between the rulers of al-Ḥīra and the friendly chiefs of the tribes is defined by Abū l-Baqāʾ as follows: "They

---

1. Abū l-Baqāʾ, *op. cit.*, ib.: "*wa-kāna qadru iqṭāʿi l-Nuʿmāni min Kisrā miʾata alfi dirhamin. Ḏukira fī baʿḍi kutubi l-Ḥīrati anna llaḏī kāna Kisrā aqṭaʿa l-Nuʿmāna min al-bilādi rustāqu al-Saylaḥīn wa-Qaṭāʾiʿu banī Ṭalḥata wa-Sanāmu Ṭibāqin. Kaḏā raʾaytu fī nusḫatin*". For the Qaṭāʾiʿ Banī Ṭalḥa see Yāqūt, *al-Buldān*, s.v. *Našāstaǧ*. And see *op. cit.*, s.v. *Sanām*; and see al-Bakrī, *Muʿǧam*, s.v. *Safawān* and *Sanām*.

2. Abū l-Baqāʾ, *op. cit.*, f. 145 b: "*fa-kāna ḫarāǧu ḏālika yuǧbā li-l-Nuʿmāni fī kulli sanatin miʾata alfi dirhamin; hāḏā mā ḏukira ʿalā ʿiẓami irtifāʿihi li-ahlihi wa-kaṯrati mustaġallihi li-mullākihi; wa-ḏukira annahu lā yuʿrafu fī l-arḍi barriyyatun akṯaru rayʿan wa-lā aḫaffu ḫarāǧan wa-lā aqallu maʾūnatan minhā wa-annahā kānat tuġillu li-ahlihā fī kulli sanatin ṯalāṯīna alfa karrin ḥinṭatan bi-l-muʿaddal siwā ġayrihā min al-ġallāti wa-l-ṯamarāti wa-sāʾiri l-ašyāʾi.*

3. See Yāqūt, *op. cit.*, s.v. *al-Sawādiyya* and *al-Sawāriyya*.

4. See Yāqūt, *op. cit.*, s.v. *al-Ḫuṣūṣ*; this ʿAbd Hind is said to have been a friend of ʿAdiyy b. Zayd. (Abū l-Baqāʾ, *op. cit.*, f. 146 a; and see the *Dīwān* of ʿAdiyy b. Zayd, p. 68 (ed. Muḥ. Ǧabbār al-Muʿaybid, Baġdād 1965). From his descendants is said to have been the judge Abū Duʾād al-Iyādī. (Abū l-Baqāʾ, *op. cit.*, f. 146 a).

5. Abū l-Baqāʾ, *op cit.*., 145 b.; see Yāqūt, *op. cit.*, s.v. *Aqsās*, where the pedigree of Mālik is given as follows: Mālik b. ʿAbd Hind b. Nuǧam b. Manaʿa (but the story of the grant is not mentioned).

had governors on the borders of the country from al-ʿIrāq till al-Baḥrayn. Each of these governors ruled the Bedouins under his protection in the same way" [1].

But the kings of al-Ḥīra themselves were in fact merely governors on behalf of the Akāsira [2]. The Bedouins did not submit to their obedience. Only clans and tribes dwelling in territories under the control of the rulers of al-Ḥīra were compelled to submit and to pay some taxes (*itāwa*) as they dwelt in their territory. These tribes virtually feared to be crushed by their military forces. When the tribe departed and left the territory, thus being beyond the reach of the rulers of al-Ḥīra, it became unapproachable (*imtanaʿū*). "Obedience—maintains Abū l-Baqā'—did not mean for the tribes more than to refrain from raiding the Sawād and the border territories" [3].

Tribes could thus be divided—according to the classification of Abū l-Baqā'—into three groups: a) The independent tribes, *laqāḥ* [4], who raided the territory of the rulers of al-Ḥīra and were raided by them, b) tribes who concluded pacts with the rulers of al-Ḥīra on certain terms, and c) tribes who pastured in the vicinity of al-Ḥīra and were obedient to the rulers of al-Ḥīra. But even these tribes were blandished by the rulers of al-Ḥīra, who tried to win their hearts. The nearest neighbours of al-Ḥīra were Rabīʿa and Tamīm [5]. For the expression *laqāḥ* Abū l-Baqā' quotes the verses

---

1. Abū l-Baqā', *op. cit.*, f. 100 a: "*wa-kāna lahum ʿummālun ʿalā aṭrāfi l-bilādi min al-ʿIrāqi ilā l-Baḥrayni ḥakama kullu wāḥidin minhum maʿa* (sic!) *man bi-izā'ihi min al-ʿArabi fī ḥimāyatihi miṯla hāḏā l-ḥukmi*".

2. Comp. *Naqā'iḍ*, p. 299: "*wa-kānū ʿummāla l-akāsirati*"; al-Yaʿqūbī, *Ta'rīḫ*, I, 184 (al-Naǧaf 1964).

3. Abū l-Baqā', *op. cit.*, f. 99 b.

4. See *L. ʿA.* s.v. *lqḥ*; and see al-Ǧāḥiẓ, *Maǧmūʿat al-rasā'il*, p. 59 (*Faḫr al-Sūdān ʿalā l-bīḍān*, Cairo 1324 AH): "*fa-l-laqāḥu l-baladu llaḏī lā yu'addī ilā l-mulūki l-urbāna, wa-l-urbānu huwa l-ḫarāǧu wa-huwa l-itāwatu*"; in the new edition of ʿAbd al-Salām Hārūn, I, 187 (*Rasā'il al-Ǧāḥiẓ*, Cairo 1964) the word is read "*aryān*"; and see Nöldeke, *Delectus*, p. 42, l. 14.

5. Abū l-Baqā', *op. cit.*, f. 121 b: "*wa-ammā ḥaddu ʿizzihim fī l-ʿArabi llaḏīna kānū fī l-taqdīri riʿāyā lahum wa-lahum ismu l-mulki ʿalayhim fa-qad taqaddama ḏikru kawnihim maʿahum ʿalā ṭabaqātin ṯalāṯin: al-laqāḥi llaḏīna kānū yuġāzūnahum wa-ahli l-hudnati llaḏīna kānū yuʿāhidūnahum wa-yuwāṯiqūnahum, wa-hāḏihi mumāṯalatum wa-musāwātum min ahli hātayni l-manzilatayni li-l-mulūki, hum wa-iyyāhum ʿalā ḥaddi sawā'in. Wa-ammā l-ṭabaqatu l-ṯāliṯatu fa-humu llaḏīna kānū yadīnūna lahum fa-kānū fī akṯari zamānihim ayḍan yuṣāniʿūna ahla hāḏihi l-manzilati istimālatan lahum wa-taqawwiyan bihim ʿalā man siwāhum ḥattā anna l-malika kāna yakūnu maʿahum ka-l-muwallā ʿalayhi; wa-kāna aqraba l-ʿArabi minhum dāran*

of ʿAmr b. Ḥawṭ al-Riyāḥī [1] and the saying of Abū Zamʿa al-Aswad b. al-Muṭṭalib b. Asad when he opposed the crowning of ʿUṯmān b. al-Ḥuwayriṯ as "king" of Mecca on behalf of the Byzantine ruler [2].

As *Laqāḥ* the author mentions Asad b. Ḫuzayma and Ġaṭafān. They were independent in their relations with the kings of al-Ḥīra. Only few of them visited the court of al-Ḥira as merchants, relatives or visitors [3].

To the second group of tribes belonged Sulaym and Hawāzin. "Sulaym and Hawāzin—reports Abū l-Baqā'—used to conclude pacts with the kings of al-Ḥīra. They (nevertheless) were not submissive to them. They used to take their merchandise for them and to sell it at ʿUkāẓ and in other markets. Thus they got (in these relations) profits with them. Sometimes an individual or a group of them came to the king (of al-Ḥīra), took parts in his raids and shared with him (i.e. with the king) some spoils. Then they (i.e. the people of the tribe) departed. The caravans of the kings with their goods could only enter Naǧd and go beyond Naǧd with the escort of men of the tribes [4].

This passage may shed some light on the battles of al-Fiǧār caused by the murder of ʿUrwa al-Raḥḥāl (from ʿĀmir) by al-Barrāḍ (from Kināna) [5].

The changing relations between the kings of al-Ḥīra and the chiefs of the tribes are reflected in the story of Hubayra b. ʿĀmir b. Salama al-Qušayrī of the ʿĀmir b. Ṣaʿṣaʿa and his son Qurra b.

Rabīʿatu wa-Tamīmun. By Tamīm—of course—only some clans are meant, pasturing in the vicinity of al-Ḥīra.

1. See *Naqā'iḍ*, p. 69: "*Abaw dīna l-mulūki fa-hum laqāḥun*"; (about ʿAmr b. Ḥawṭ see W. Caskel, *Ǧamharat an-nasab* II, 176, l. 1 and al-Balāḏurī, *Ansāb al-ašrāf*, ms. f. 992 b).

2. Abū l-Baqā', *op. cit.*, f. 100 b; al-Muṣʿab al-Zubayrī, *Nasab Qurayš*, p. 210 (ed. E. Lévi-Provençal, Cairo 1953); al-Zubayr b. Bakkār, *Ǧamharat nasab Qurayš*, ms. Bodley, f. 74 b; al-Balāḏurī, *Ansāb al-ašrāf*, IV B, 126 (ed. M. Schloessinger, Jerusalem 1938); Ibn Ḥabīb, *al-Munammaq*, pp. 178-185 (ed. Ḫuršīd Aḥmad Fāriq, Hyderabad 1964).

3. Abū l-Baqā', *op. cit.*, f. 100 b.

4. ib., f. 102 a: "*wa-kānat Sulaymun wa-Hawāzinu tuwāṯiquhum wa-lā tadīnu lahum; wa-ya'ḫuḏūna lahumu l-taǧā'ira fa-yabīʿūna lahum bi-ʿUkāẓa wa-ġayrihā fa-yuṣībūna maʿahumu l-arbāḥa; wa-rubbamā atā 'l-malika minhumu l-raǧulu wa-l-nafaru fa-yašhadūna maʿahu maġāziyahu wa-yuṣībūna maʿahu min al-ġanā'imi wa-yanṣarifūna; wa-lam yakun laṭā'imu l-mulūki wa-tiǧārātuhum tadḫulu Naǧdan fa-mā warā'ahu illā bi-ḫafarin min al-qabā'ili*.

5. See W. M. Watt, *Muhammad at Mecca*, p. 11 (Oxford 1953).

Hubayra. Hubayra is said to have attacked the camp of al-Nuʿmān b. al-Munḏir, captured his wife al-Mutağarrida and taken booty and spoils [1]. His son Qurra [2] was entrusted by al-Nuʿmān to guard a caravan to ʿUkāẓ against Bedouins who were not obedient to the king of al-Ḥīra (*yaḫfiruhā ʿalā man laysa fī dīnihi min al-ʿArabi*). The events took place when al-Nuʿmān was compelled to flee before the Persian king. Qurra seized the caravan for himself. Then the Banū ʿUqayl came to the Banū Qušayr asking for a share in the seized caravan, arguing that they were afraid of the possible consequences of the action of Qurra. When the Qušayr refused to grant them a share, a quarrel flared up. Hostilities between the two clans were avoided when Qušayr and ʿUqayl agreed to take as arbiter the famous leader of ʿĀmir b. Ṣaʿṣaʿa, Muʿāwiya b. Mālik nicknamed "Muʿawwiḏ al-Ḥukamāʾ" [3].

This passage is instructive: while the father of Qurra is recorded to have attacked the camp of al-Nuʿmān, al-Nuʿmān was compelled to entrust the escort of his caravan to his son. It is an evidence of the weakness of the last ruler of al-Ḥīra and of fickle policy of al-Ḥīra toward the chiefs of the independent tribes of ʿĀmir b. Ṣaʿṣaʿa. It may be stressed that the ʿĀmir b. Ṣaʿṣaʿa were in close relations with Mecca and the interests of Mecca might have some bearings upon the attitudes and the actions of ʿĀmir b. Ṣaʿṣaʿa towards al-Ḥīra.

The clever use of intertribal feuds and hostilities by the rulers of al-Ḥīra to their own advantage is another aspect of the relations of al-Ḥīra with the tribes, analysed with deep insight by Abū l-Baqāʾ. There was always some fight between tribes—says Abū l-Baqāʾ. The kings of al-Ḥīra exploited it for their own ends; when they intended to raid a tribe they used to win the hearts of its enemies, to solicite the help of a group against another and "beat one by the

---

1. *Naqāʾiḍ*, p. 404; Abū l-Baqāʾ, *op. cit.*, f. 129 a; al-Nābiġa al-Ğaʿdī, *Dīwān* (ed. Maria Nallino, Roma 1953), pp. 117, 119; Ibn Ḥazm, *Ğamharat ansāb al-ʿArab*, p. 272; W. Caskel, *Ğamharat an-nasab*, II, 285.

2. See about him: *Naqāʾiḍ*, p. 405; Ibn Ḥağar, *al-Iṣāba*, No. 7010, vol. V, 238 (Cairo 1907); Ibn Ḥabīb, *Asmāʾ al-muġtālīna* (*Nawādir al-maḫṭūṭāt*, ed. ʿAbd al-Salām Hārūn, VII, 244); Ibn ʿAbd al-Barr, *al-Istīʿāb*, p. 532 (Hyderabad 1336 AH); W. Caskel, *op. cit.*, II, 472; Ṭabarī, *Taʾrīḫ*, II, 490 (Cairo 1939).

3. Abū l-Baqāʾ, *op. cit.*, f. 38 a; see about "*Muʿawwiḏ al-ḥukamāʾ*", Ibn Ḥabīb, *al-Muḥabbar*, p. 458; W. Caskel, *op. cit.*, II, 413.

other" [1]. Considerable forces of a tribe used in fact to rally and join the troops of al-Ḥīra in order to fight together against a hostile tribe or in the hope of getting spoils and booty. After the raid the forces of the tribe departed to their abode and the kings of al-Ḥīra were left with their own forces only.

The co-operation between the kings of al-Ḥīra and the tribes in their military actions is well illustrated by the story of the raid of al-Qurnatayn. According to the report of al-Balāḏurī [2] al-Nuʿmān equipped his brother (from his mother's side), Wabara b. Rūmānis with strong forces of the Maʿadd and others. He sent for Ḍirār b. ʿAmr al-Ḍabbī who came with 9 sons, each of whom already experienced in warfare and leadership [3]. Another leader of the Ḍabba, Ḥubayš b. Dulaf [4], came as well. Al-Nuʿmān sent with them to Mecca a caravan and instructed them to attack the Banū ʿĀmir b. Ṣaʿṣaʿa after they had finished their trading transactions. The cause of this raid is given in the version of Ibn al-Aṯīr [5]: the forces of al-Ḥīra and their allies were sent against the ʿĀmir b. Ṣaʿṣaʿa in retaliation for an attack of the Banū ʿĀmir on a caravan of al-Nuʿmān sent by him to ʿUkāẓ.

When Qurayš returned from ʿUkāẓ to Mecca, these forces of the king under the command of his brother attacked the Banū ʿĀmir. The Banū ʿĀmir, however, having been warned by ʿAbd Allāh b. Gudʿān, fought with great bravery and defeated the forces of the king of al-Ḥīra. Ḍirār b. ʿAmr, the leader of the Ḍabba, was rescued by his sons when he was attacked by Abū Barāʾa ʿĀmir b. Mālik (the brother of Muʿāwiya b. Mālik, the uncle of the poet ʿĀmir b. Ṭufayl), one of the leaders of the ʿĀmir b. Ṣaʿṣaʿa [6]. Ḥubayš b. Dulaf was captured by a sign of Ḍirār b. ʿAmr [7]. Wabara b.

---

1. Abū l-Baqāʾ, *op. cit.*, f. 100 a: "*wa-kānati l-ʿArabu ayḍan lā taḫlū fī ḏāti baynihā min al-dimāʾi wa-l-ḥurūbi wa-l-muġāwarāti fīmā baynahum ... wa-kāna l-maliku iḏā arāda ġazwata ḥayyin min al-ʿArabi istamāla aʿdāʾahum ʿalayhim ... wa-istanǧada bi-qawmin ʿalā qawmin wa-ḍaraba baʿḍahum bi-baʿḍin*".

2. al-Balāḏurī, *Ansāb*, ms. f. 948 b.

3. Ibn al-Kalbī, *Ǧamhara*, ms. f. 112 b; and see W. Caskel, *op. cit.*, II, 242.

4. See about him W. Caskel, *op. cit.*, II, 327.

5. Ibn al-Aṯīr, *al-Kāmil*, I, 391 ("*yawm al-Sullān*"); and comp. Ibn ʿAbd Rabbihi, *al-ʿIqd al-farīd*, III, 335 (Cairo 1935—"*yawm al-Sarayān*").

6. See Ibn Ḥaǧar, *al-Iṣāba*, No. 4417; W. Caskel, *op. cit.*, II, 161.

7. According to the version of Ibn al-Kalbī, as recorded by al-Balāḏurī, *Ansāb*, ms. ff. 949 a and 956 b he was killed at the "Day of al-Qurnatayn". (*wa-qāla bnu l-Kalbī: qutila Ḥubayšun fī yawmi l-Qurnatayn*).

Rūmānis was captured by the warrior and poet Yazīd b. al-Ṣaʿiq [1]. He freed him after he had paid a ransom of 1000 camels, 2 singing girls and an allotment of his possessions. The defeated forces were led back to al-Nuʿmān by Ḍirār b. ʿAmr. The victory of the ʿĀmir was mentioned in the verses of Yazīd b. al-Ṣaʿiq:

"Tarakna aḫā l-Nuʿmāni yarsufu ʿāniyan:
wa-ǧaddaʿna aǧnāda l-mulūki l-ṣanāʾiʿā"
"They left the brother of al-Nuʿmān walking in
[shackles as captive
and mutilated the troops of the kings, the *ṣanāʾiʿ*" [2].

An interesting aspect of the battle is brought out in the version of Abū l-Baqāʾ: Yazīd b. al-Ṣaʿiq came to al-Nuʿmān with his brother, the captive, asking the promised ransom. Al-Nuʿmān asked him how it happened that a corpulent man like his brother was captured by a Yazīd b. al-Ṣaʿiq (a man of short stature). Yazīd answered: "His people were absent, my people attended (the battle)". It is of course a hint, that his tribe, the attacked one (ʿĀmir) were superior in battle to the mercenary troops of the *Ṣanāʾiʿ* [3]. The Kalb, the tribe of Wabara, did not take part in the battle; Wabara was a leader appointed by the ruler of al-Ḥīra.

For understanding of the policy of al-Ḥīra it may be mentioned that this very Ḍirār b. ʿAmr—according to a tradition recorded by Abū l-Baqāʾ in his *Manāqib* [4]—attacked the camp of al-Mundir, the father of al-Nuʿmān. It happened when al-Mundir returned to al-Ḥīra from his visit to al-Ḥārit b. Ḥiṣn b. Ḍamḍam al-Kalbī [5],

1. See about him W. Caskel, *op. cit.*, II, 593; according to the version of al-Mufaḍḍal al-Ḍabbī recorded by al-Balāḏurī, *op. cit.*, f. 956 b, he captured Ḥassān b. Wabara, the brother of al-Nuʿmān (from his mother's side) who led the Ḍabba in this raid and who was appointed by his brother, al-Nuʿmān, on the Ribāb.

2. So in the account of Abū l-Baqāʾ, *op. cit.*, ms. f. 126 a, 21 b; in the account of al-Balāḏurī, *op. cit.*, 948 b.
"wa-ǧaddaʿna Murran wa-l-mulūka l-ṣanāʾiʿā".

3. Abū l-Baqā mentions as well another version recorded from the descendants of Ibn al-Ṣaʿiq (*"wa-fī riwāyatin uḫrā ʿan wuldi Yazīda bni l-Ṣaʿiq"*), according to which the king of al-Ḥīra was al-Mundir, not al-Nuʿmān. (About Muʿāḏ b. Yazīd b. al-Ṣaʿiq who opposed the *ridda* see: Ibn Ḥaǧar, *al-Iṣāba*, No. 8425; about Yazīd b. Qays b. Yazīd b. al-Ṣaʿiq see al-Balāḏurī, *Ansāb*, ms. f. 942 b); about Umāma bint Yazīd b. ʿAmr b. al-Ṣaʿiq see Ibn Ḥabīb, *al-Munammaq*, p. 8).

4. f. 128 b; another version: al-Ḍabbī, *Amṯāl al-ʿArab*, p. 6.

5. See Rothstein, *op. cit.*, p. 108, n. 3.

with the gift given to him by al-Ḥāriṯ: the bondwoman Salmā, his later wife, the mother of his son al-Nuʿmān. Only by the intercession of al-Ḥāriṯ b. Ḥiṣn—did Ḍirār agree to return the seized property of al-Mundir, inter alia the bondwoman Salmā.

Some time after the battle of al-Qurnatayn [1] Ḍirār attended the market of ʿUkāẓ [2]. Ḍirār attended the battle as an aged man. He is said to have visited the court of al-Mundir b. Māʾ al-Samāʾ, had quarrelled with Abū Marḥab, Rabīʿa b. Ḥaṣaba b. Aznam of the Yarbūʿ [3] and had cut his forearm. He asked for the protection of the king failed to grant him protection. He was granted the protection of Ǧušayš (or Ḥušayš) b. Nimrān al-Riyāḥī [4].

Of interest are the relations of Ḍirār with Tamīm; he gave his daughter Muʿāda as wife to Maʿbad b. Zurāra [5]. The version of Ibn al-Aṯīr states that al-Nuʿmān summoned with the Banū Ḍabba the Banū Ribāb and Tamīm; they responded and took part in the battle.

Some verses of Aws b. Ḥaǧar [6], Labīd [7] and Yazīd b. al-Ṣaʿiq [8] give the impression that the battle was a grave one.

It is noteworthy that Ibn al-Aṯīr stresses in his report (on the authority of Abū ʿUbayda), that the ʿĀmir b. Ṣaʿṣaʿa were *Ḥums*, kindred with the Qurayš and that they were *Laqāḥ*. (*kāna Banū ʿĀmiri bni Ṣaʿṣaʿata ḥumsan, wa-l-ḥumsu Qurayšun wa-man lahu fīhim wilādatun*). This points to the connections between Qurayš and the ʿĀmir and explains why ʿAbd Allāh b. Ǧudʿān [9] sent to

---

1. See about the battle: Yāqūt, *Buldān*, s.v. *Sullān*; Ibn Ḥazm, *Ǧamharat ansāb al-ʿArab*, p. 194; about the location of the place: U. Thilo, *Die Ortsnamen in der altarabischen Poesie*, s.v. *Lubān, ʿUyūn* (Wiesbaden 1958).

2. Ibn Abī l-Ḥadīd, *Šarḥ Nahǧ al-Balāġa*, IV, 308, 362 (Cairo 1329 AH).

3. About Abū Marḥab see: Ibn Ḥabīb, *Asmāʾ al-muġtālīna* (*Nawādir al-maḫṭūṭāt*, VII, 139); about the quarrel between Ḍirār and Abū Marḥab see al-Ḍabbī, *Amṯāl al-ʿArab*, p. 15; about Ḍirār at the court of al-Ḥīra see al-Maydānī, *Maǧmaʿ al-amṯāl*, I, 44 (Cairo 1352 AH).

4. Abū l-Baqāʾ, *op. cit.*, f. 137 b.

5. al-Balāḏurī, *Ansab*, ms. f. 948 b, 954 a; Ibn Abī l-Ḥadīd, *op. cit.*, IV, 308; al-Ǧāḥiẓ, *al-Bayān*, I, 168 (ed. al-Sandūbī, Cairo 1932).

6. *Dīwān*, p. 6 (ed. Muḥ. Yūsuf Naǧm, Beirut 1960).

7. *Šarḥ Dīwān Labīd*, p. 133 (ed. Iḥsān ʿAbbās, Kuwait 1962); see note 2 of the editor, who did not identify the battle.

8. Abū l-Baqāʾ, *op. cit.*, f. 126 b, inf.: *"wa-naḥnu ġadāta l-Qurnatayni tawāhaqat: ḫanāḏīḏu yamʿaǧna l-ġubāra ḍawāʾiʿā. Bi-kulli sinānin fī l-qanāti taḫāluhu: šihāban fī ẓulmati l-layli sāṭiʿā. [Ṯara]knā Ḥubayšan ḥīna arǧafa naǧduhu: yuʿāliǧu maʾsūran ʿalayhi l-ǧawāmiʿā"*.

9. See about him: Ibn Hišām, *al-Sīra*, I, 141 (ed. al-Saqqā, al-Abyārī, Šalabī, Cairo 1936); al-Balāḏurī, *Ansāb*, I, 74, 101 (ed. Muḥ. Hamidullah,

warn Banū ʿĀmir of the approaching forces of al-Ḥīra, enabling them to prepare themselves for battle. One may assume that there was some co-operation between Qurayš and ʿĀmir, that Mecca had some influence on the actions of ʿĀmir and that this had some bearing on the attitude of ʿĀmir towards al-Ḥīra.

It is plausible, that the booty of the raided caravan of the king of al-Ḥīra was sold at ʿUkāẓ; a case of this kind is recorded in Ibn Habīb's *al-Munammaq* [1].

For understanding of the relations between al-Ḥīra and the tribes the reports about the taxes collected by the kings of al-Ḥīra and the position of the tax-collectors are of some importance. Analyzing the sources of income of the rulers of al-Ḥīra and the position of al-Ḥīra Abū l-Baqāʾ mentions the income from the fiefs of al-ʿIrāq and states: "That was the amount of their income from al-ʿIrāq. But the bulk of their revenues for their livelihood and their profits was gained from trade, from booty of their raids against the Bedouins, against the border lands of Syria, against every territory they could raid and from collection of taxes from the obedient tribes; they collected in this way great quantities of cattle" [2].

The rulers of al-Ḥīra appointed the leaders of friendly tribes as collectors of taxes, as military leaders of divisions of their forces and as officials in territories in which they exercised some control. ʿAmr b. Šarīk, the father of al-Ḥawfazān, was in charge of the police troops of al-Mundir and al-Nuʿmān (*waliya šurața l-Mundiri wa-l-Nuʿmāni min baʿdihi*),[3] Sinān b. Mālik of the Aws Manāt (of the Namir b. Qāsiț) was appointed by al-Nuʿmān b. al-Mundir as governor of Ubulla [4].

In the service of ʿAmr b. Hind there was the Tamīmī al-Ġallāq b.

Cairo 1959); Ibn Kaṯīr, *al-Sīra al-nabawiyya*, I, 116-117 (ed. Muṣṭafā ʿAbd al-Wāḥid, Cairo 1964); al-Muṣʿab al-Zubayrī, *Nasab Qurayš*, p. 291.

1. Ibn Ḥabīb, *al-Munammaq*, p. 428-29.

2. Abū l-Baqāʾ, *op. cit.*, f. 145 a: "*fa-hāḏā kāna qadra naṣībi l-qawmi min al-ʿIrāqi. Wa-innamā kāna ğulla maʿāšihim wa-akṯara amwālihim mā kānū yuṣībūnahu min al-arbāḥi fī l-tiğārāti wa-yaġnimūnahu min al-maġāzī wa-l-iġārāti ʿalā l-ʿArabi wa-aṭrāfi l-Šāmi wa-kulli arḍin yumkinuhum ġazwuhā wa-yağtabūna l-itāwata mimman dāna lahum wa-ẓafirū bihi min al-ʿArabi; fa-yağtamiʿu lahum min ḏālika l-kaṯīru min al-anʿāmi*".

3. Ibn al-Kalbī, *op. cit.*, f. 205 a.

4. Ibn al-Kalbī, *op. cit.*, f. 232 a; W. Caskel, *op. cit.*, II, 513; these Aws Manāt were exterminated by Ḫālid b. al-Walīd in the wars of the *ridda*. (see Ibn Ḥazm, *Ğamharat ansāb al-ʿArab*, p. 284).

Qays b. ʿAbd Allāh b. ʿAmr b. Hammām [1]. He is mentioned in a verse of Diğāğa [2] b. ʿAbd Qays quoted in the *Iḫtiyārayn* [3] as a leader of an attacking troop together with al-Ḥāriṯ b. Bayba [4] and Ḥāğib [5]. Ġallāq was sent by ʿAmr b. Hind to submit the Taġlib; he raided them and killed many of them [6]. This event is mentioned by al-Ḥāriṯ b. Ḥilliza in his *Muʿallaqa* [7]. According to *Aġānī* [8] and the commentary of al-Tibrīzī [9] al-Ġallāq was in charge of the white camels (*hağā'in*) of al-Nuʿmān [10]. According to *Simṭ al-La'ālī* [11] he was appointed by al-Nuʿmān who put him in charge of the white camels of the tribes adjacent to his country (*istaʿmalahu l-Nuʿmānu bnu l-Munḏiri ʿalā hağā'ini man yalī arḍahu min al-ʿArab*). The report of al-Bakrī indicates that al-Ġallāq was entrusted with collecting taxes. ʿUqfān b. ʿĀṣim al-Yarbūʿī hid from al-Ġallāq—

---

1. So Ibn al-Kalbī, *op. cit.*, and al-Balāḏurī, *Ansāb*, "*Ġallāq*"; in some other sources "*ʿAllāq*"; see W. Caskel, *op. cit.*, II, 271.
2. Ibn al-Kalbī, *op. cit.*, f. 98; W. Caskel, *op. cit.*, II, 232; al-Wazīr al-Maġribī, *al-Īnās bi-ʿilmi l-ansāb*, Ms. Br. Mus., f. 37 b; he was from the Taym b. ʿAbd Manāt b. Udd. See al-Balāḏurī, *op. cit.*, f. 929 b.
3. S. M. Ḥusayn, *Early Arabic Odes*, p. 199, transl. p. 161, commentary p. 320. The pedigree in the commentary: ʿAllāq b. ʿAbdallah b. Hammām al-Riyāḥi (his brother Qays b. ʿAbd Allāh mentioned as well). Ḏū l-Kīr is said to have been al-Ḥāriṯ b. Munabbih b. Qurṭ b. Sufyān b. Muğāšiʿ. But Munabbih is a mistake; read: "al-Ḥārit b. Bayba" (Comp. v. 13 of the poem).
4. This verse:

   "*Tağarrada ʿAllāqun ilaynā wa-Ḥāğibun:*
   wa-Ḏū l-Kīri yadʿū yā-la Ḥanẓalata rkabū"

   is rendered by S. M. Ḥusayn:

   "There come helter-skelter to us ʿAllaq and Ḥāğib:
   and Ḏū l-Kīr crying: Ho Ḥanẓala: ride forth".

   About al-Ḥāriṯ b. Bayba see W. Caskel, *op. cit.*, II, 305, 221.
5. Ḥāğib—obviously Ḥāğib b. Zurāra.
6. Ibn Qutayba, *al-Maʿānī al-kabīr*, p. 1012 (ed. F. Krenkow, Hyderabad 1949).
7. And see Ibn al-Kalbī, *op. cit.*, f. 72 a and al-Balāḏurī, *op. cit.*, f. 993 b.
8. *Aġānī*, IX, 173.
9. *Šarḥ al-qaṣa'id al-ʿašr*, p. 275 ("*al-Munīriyya*" Print, 1352 AH).
10. See T. Nöldeke, *Fünf Moʿallaqāt*, I, 76. And see about his son al-ʿAffāq b. al-Ġallāq, who was killed by the ʿAbs: *Naqā'iḍ*, p. 336; al-Ḥuṭay'a, *Dīwān*, p. 323 (ed. Nuʿmān Amīn Ṭāhā, Cairo 1958); al-Balāḏurī, *op. cit.*, f. 929 b.
11. al-Bakrī, *Simṭ al-la'ālī*, p. 746 (ed. al-Maymanī, Cairo 1936); and see *L. ʿA.*, s.v. *zlf*; according to al-Balāḏurī, *op. cit.*, f. 798 b ʿUqfān b. Qays b. ʿĀṣim came to Arwā bint Kurayz (another version: the visitor was Mutammim b. Nuwayra). A verse of ʿUqfān see Ibn Qutayba, *al-Maʿānī al-kabīr* p. 105; and see al-Balāḏurī, *Ansāb*, V, 1 (ed. S. D. Goitein, Jerusalem 1936); he is said to have been a companion of the Prophet (see Ibn Ḥağar, *al-Iṣāba*, No. 5619).

according to this report—his white camels. When pursued by al-Ġallāq he went to al-Nuʿmān with the herd and asked for his protection. He was in fact granted protection and al-Nuʿmān "did not take anything from his herd" (*wa-lam yaʾḫuḏ minhā*—i.e. *al-ibil—šayʾan*).

The story of al-Ġallāq illustrates the relations which existed between al-Ḥīra and a chief of a tribal group. Al-Ġallāq was entrusted by the king of al-Ḥīra to subdue the Taġlib, he commanded a military unit and it is plausible that he had at his disposal some force for carrying out his task as tax collector. This may explain how the kings of al-Ḥīra could impose their rule on tribal groups in cooperation with friendly chiefs and loyal tribal forces.

A clash between the tax-collector of al-Ḥīra and a clan grew into a clash between tribal units. According to the tradition recorded in *al-ʿIqd* [1] on the authority of Abū ʿUbayda—the Banū Usayyid (a clan of the ʿAmr b. Tamīm) captured Wāʾil b. Ṣuraym al-Yaškurī (from Bakr b. Wāʾil) and killed him. When they killed him they chanted: "*Yā ayyuhā l-māʾiḥu dalwī dūnaka*" [2]. His brother Bāʿiṯ, raided the Usayyid, killed a nobleman of this clan and upon his body he killed 100 men of the same clan. This version is also given by al-Bakrī in *Muʿǧam mā staʿǧam* [3].

According to another version given by al-Bakrī [4] Wāʾil b. Ṣuraym was sent by ʿAmr b. Hind as tax-collector (*baʿaṯahu sāʿiyan*) of the Banū Tamīm. They threw him into a well and stoned him. He was killed by the clan of Usayyid.

A more detailed version is given by al-Riyāšī in his commentary of the *Ḥamāsa* [5]. All the clans of Tamīm paid the demanded tax (*al-itāwa*) to Wāʾil b. Ṣuraym. When he came to the Usayyid they collected the cattle and sheep (scil. of the tax) and ordered them to be counted. When he was sitting on the side of a well there came an elder of the Usayyid and catching him unaware pushed

---

1. IBN ʿABD RABBIHI, *al-ʿIqd al-farīd*, III, 354.
2. See this verse: AL-MARZŪQĪ, *al-Azmina wa-l-amkina*, II, 159; AL-FARRĀʾ, *Maʿānī al-Qurʾān*, I, 323, (ed. NAĞĀTĪ—AL-NAĞĞĀR, Cairo 1955); *L. ʿA.*, s.v. *myḥ*; AL-ANṢĀRĪ, *Šuḏūr al-ḏahab*, p. 436 (ed. Muḥ. Muḥyī al-Dīn ʿABD AL-ḤAMĪD, Cairo 1942).
3. *Muʿǧām mā staʿǧam*, s.v. *Ḥāğir*.
4. ib., s.v. *Ṭuwayliʿ*.
5. AL-TIBRĪZĪ, *Šarḥ Dīwān al-Ḥamāsa*, II, 112-13 (ed. Muḥ. Muḥyi al-Dīn ʿABD AL-ḤAMĪD, Cairo 1938); and see AL-BAKRĪ, *Simṭ*, pp. 286, 476 (see the references given by AL-MAYMANĪ in note 5).

him into the well. The clan assembled and stoned him to death. His brother Bā'iṯ decided to avenge him, and together with his clan the Ġubar of Yaškur, attacked the Banū Usayyid. His vow to fill the well with the blood of Usayyid was fulfilled; when some of them lowered the bucket into the well it came up full of blood.

Poets of Yaškur mentioned the event in their verses. The event is recorded in al-Wazīr al-Maġribī's *Īnās* [1] and Abū l-Baqā's *Manāqib* [2]. The clash lived long in the memory of the two clans, as is evident from the curses in these clans: *"Ta'isat Ġubar, ta'isat Usayyid"* [3].

W. Caskel denies the historical value of the story [4]. This may be true. But the story faithfully reflects the attitude of the tribes towards the tax-collectors, their hatred towards them and the acts of violence committed against them.

Refusal to pay taxes to the king of al-Ḥīra was the cause of a raid made by the troops of al-Nu'mān against Tamīm. The story recorded by al-Mubarrad [5] on the authority of Abū 'Ubayda says that Tamīm refused to pay the tax to al-Nu'mān. He sent against them his brother al-Rayyān b. al-Munḏir at the head of troops which belonged mainly to Bakr b. Wā'il. They raided the Tamīm, captured children and took their cattle as spoils. Abū l-Mušamraǧ al-Yaškurī ('Amr b. al-Mušamraǧ) composed a poem in which he described the defeat of Tamīm:

"Lammā ra'aw ra'yata l-Nu'māni muqbilatan:
qālū alā layta adnā dārinā 'Adanu
Yā layta umma Tamīmin lam takun 'arafat:
Murran wa-kānat ka-man awdā bihi l-zamanu
In taqtulūnā [6] *fa-a'yārun muǧadda'atun:*
aw tun'imū fa-qadīman minkumu l-minanu
Minhum Zuhayrun wa-'Attābun wa-Muḥtaḍarun:
wa-bnā Laqīṭin wa-awdā fī l-waġā Qaṭanu"

---

1. ff. 28 b-29 a.
2. f. 123.
3. AL-BALĀḎURĪ, *op. cit.*, p. 1075 b; AL-TIBRĪZĪ, *Šarḥ Dīwān al-Ḥamāsa*, II, 113; the grandson of Bā'iṯ, 'Amr b. Ǧabala b. Bā'iṯ, fought at Ḏū Qār (see AL-MARZUBĀNĪ, *Mu'ǧam al-šu'arā'*, p. 225).
4. W. CASKEL, *op. cit.*, II, 221, 585. (Bā'iṯ b. Ṣuraym and Wā'il b. Ṣuraym).
5. AL-MUBARRAD, *al-Kāmil*, II, 82-83 (ed. Muḥ. Abū l-Faḍl IBRĀHĪM—AL-SAYYID ŠAḤĀTA, Cairo 1956).
6. So AL-MUBARRAD, *op. cit.*, ib., and AL-MAYDĀNĪ, *Maǧma' al-amṯāl*, I, 439; AL-MARZUBĀNĪ, *Mu'ǧam al-šu'arā'*, p. 211: "*in taqtulūhum*", which seems to be the correct reading.

"When they saw the banner of al-Nuʿmān advancing
they said: "would that our nearest abode be ʿAdan
May the mother of Tamīm not have known Murr
and been like one destroyed by the (changes of) time".
If you kill them—they are (merely) asses with cut
[noses,
and if you show grace—since ancient time you have
[shown grace.
From among them are Zuhayr, ʿAttāb and Muḥtaḍar
and two sons of Laqīṭ; Qaṭan perished in the battle".

The leaders of Tamīm came to al-Nuʿmān asking him to release the captives. Al-Nuʿmān agreed that every woman who wished to return to her relatives should be returned. All the women questioned expressed the wish to be returned to their tribe except the daughter of Qays b. ʿĀṣim who preferred to remain with the man who captured her, ʿAmr b. al-Mušamraǧ. Qays then vowed to bury every female child, that would be born to him.

The version of *al-Aġānī* [1] does not mention that the cause of the raid was the refusal to pay taxes, does not contain the verses and records the story as a raid of al-Mušamraǧ. But in this version the raid is restricted to the Banū Saʿd and the name of the captured woman is given: Rumayma bint Aḥmar [2] b. Ǧandal; her mother was the sister of Qays b. ʿĀṣim.

Al-Mušamraǧ is mentioned in a short account of al-Balāḏurī [3]: some clans of Bakr b. Wāʾil raided the ʿUkl. They were however defeated by the ʿUkl under the command of al-Namir b. Tawlab [4]. In one of the verses quoted by al-Balāḏurī and attributed to al-Namir b. Tawlab, al-Mušamraǧ is mentioned as a captive of the ʿUkl [5].

For the assessment of the story of the raid the verse recited by

---

1. *Aġānī*, XII, 144.
2. In the text "*Aḥmad*", which is a mistake. Aḥmar b. Ǧandal was the brother of Salāma b. Ǧandal (See SALĀMA B. ǦANDAL, *Dīwān*, p. 21—ed. CHEIKHO; and see AL-ǦĀḤIẒ, *al-Bayān*, III, 318; AL-BAĠDĀDĪ: *Ḫizānat al-adab*, II, 86; ʿAMR B. KULṮŪM, *Dīwān*, p. 3—ed. KRENKOW; AL-BALĀḎURĪ, *op. cit.*, f. 1040 a; W. CASKEL, *op. cit.*, II, 146).
3. AL-BALĀḎURĪ, *op. cit.*, f. 928 a.
4. About him see W. CASKEL, *op. cit.*, II, 444.
5. "*Rāḥa l-Mušamraǧu li-l-rikābi ǧanībatan*:
fī l-qiddi maʾsūran ʿalā adbārihā"
(in text: *Mušamraḥ*, *ǧanbiyatan*).

al-Nu'mān—quoted by al-Mubarrad—is of some importance: when al-Nu'mān forgave the Tamīm he said:

"Mā kāna ḍarra Tamīman law taġammadahā:
min faḍlinā mā 'alayhi Qaysu 'Aylāni"
"What would harm the Banū Tamīm if they
[would be filled
with our favour like the Qays 'Aylān" [1].

Al-Nu'mān reminds the Banū Tamīm that by paying the *itāwa*, and by their loyalty they would enjoy the favour of the king. The expression seems to point to the benefits bestowed by the king on the chiefs of the tribe Qays 'Aylān, appointment of their chiefs as tax collectors, granting them pastures, etc. It is noteworthy that al-Mubarrad renders *itāwa* by *adyān*, pointing to obedience and submission [2]. The verse attributed to al-Nu'mān reflects the efforts of al-Ḥīra to gain the allegiance of some divisions of Tamīm (evidently the Sa'd), who tried to free themselves from the dependence of al-Ḥīra. That was manifested by the refusal to pay taxes.

Some light on the relations between al-Ḥīra and Asad and Ġaṭafān is shed by a story recorded by Muḥammad b. Ḥabīb [3]. These tribes—says Ibn Ḥabīb—were allies, not submitting to the obedience of the kings [4]. 'Amr b. Mas'ūd and Ḫālid b. Naḍla [5] of Asad used to visit every year the ruler of al-Ḥīra, stay with him and drink with him. During one of these visits al-Mundir al-Akbar suggested that they should accept his obedience. He said: "What prevents you from yielding to my obedience and to defend me like the Tamīm and Rabī'a?" They refused his offer, remarking: "These territories are not suitable for our herds. Besides (in the present situation) we are near to you; we are here in these sandy lands and if you summon us we will respond". Al-Mundir understood that they were not willing to accept his offer and ordered to poison them. Whether Ḫālid b. Naḍla was really poisoned is rather doubtful [6]; the story itself may be spurious. But the tendency of

1. AL-MUBARRAD, *op. cit.*, II, 84.
2. ib., p. 83, l. 2; and see above note 4, p. [11]. (*adyān* is identical with *urbān* and *aryān*).
3. IBN ḤABĪB, *Asmā' al-muġtālīna* (*Nawādir al-maḫṭūṭāt*, VI, 133).
4. Comp. p. 12, l. 3 of this paper (note 3).
5. SEE W. CASKEL, *op. cit.*, II, 179, 342.
6. See AL-BALĀḎURĪ, *Ansāb*, f. 903 a (with other versions about his death); AL-ḌABBĪ, *Mufaḍḍaliyyāt*, VII, 1 (LYALL notes p. 14); AL-QĀLĪ, *al-Nawādir*, p. 195; AL-A'ŠĀ, *Dīwān*, p. 306 (ed. GEYER—AL-ASWAD B. YA'FUR, XLIX,

the rulers of al-Ḥīra to widen their influence by gaining the obedience of independent tribes is evident from this story. The answer of the two leaders seems to indicate that the ruler of al-Ḥīra proposed that they should enter territories under his control, but that they refused to do so [1].

The rulers of al-Ḥīra could impose their sway on the tribes either by granting the chiefs benefits—as mentioned in the stories quoted above—or by force. The rulers based their power on their troops. The troops were, however, not levied from a certain tribe: there was no tribe ruling in al-Ḥīra; it was a family. The rulers of al-Ḥīra had therefore to rely on foreign troops or on mercenary troops. Only occasionally could they use a tribal force against another tribal unit, hostile to the first—as already mentioned.

The problem of the formations of *Dawsar*, *al-Šahbā'*, *al-Waḍā'iʿ*, *al-Ṣanā'iʿ* and *al-Rahā'in* was discussed by Rothstein [2]. Rothstein, quoting the sources [3] and arguing with Caussin de Perceval arrives at the conclusion that the *Ṣanā'iʿ* seem to have been a *Prätorianerschaar* [4]. This is confirmed by the commentary of the *Naqā'iḍ* [5]: Aḥmad b. ʿUbayd states that the *Ṣanā'iʿ* are people upon whom the king bestows his favours (*yaṣtaniʿuhumu l-maliku*) and they remain in his service. Another version is also given there: the *Ṣanā'iʿ* of the kings are the helpers of the king, who raid with him, by whom the king is aided. An additional information is given by al-Mubarrad [6]: most of them are from Bakr b. Wā'il.

The *Waḍā'iʿ* are defined by Rothstein as *Besatzungstruppen*. Rothstein argues that *Waḍā'iʿ* cannot refer to certain troops (... "dass damit unmöglich eine bestimmte Truppe gemeint sein kann"). He assumes that the *Waḍā'iʿ* may probably denote the troops of the garrisons and especially the border garrisons. *Dawsar* and *Šahbā'* refer probably—according to Rothstein—to the garrison-troops of al-Ḥīra.

v. 6-7); and see ǦAWĀD ʿALĪ, *Ta'rīḫ al-ʿArab qabla l-Islām*, IV, 73; ABŪ MISḤAL: *Nawādir*, I, 122-3 (ed. ʿIZZAT ḤASAN, Damascus 1961—see the notes of the editor).

1. "... *hāḏihi l-bilādu lā tulā'imu mawāšiyanā*" ... and see the variant of the question of the king (AL-BAĠDĀDĪ, *Ḫizāna*, IV, 151): "... *wa-an tadnū minnī kamā danat Tamīmun wa-Rabīʿatu*".

2. *Die Dynastie der Laḫmiden*, pp. 134-138.

3. *Al-Ḥamāsa, al-Aġānī, al-ʿIqd al-farīd*, AL-ǦAWHARĪ, *Ṣaḥāḥ*.

4. ROTHSTEIN, *op. cit.*, p. 137.

5. p. 884.

6. *Al-Kāmil*, II, 83.

The definition of the *Waḍā'i'* given by Aḥmad b. 'Ubayd is different. *Waḍā'i'*—says Ibn 'Ubayd—are the troops levied by the king, 100 from every tribal group (*qawm*), more or less according to their number. Another definition quoted in the same source [1] claims that the *Waḍā'i'* are the forces of the subjects of the kingdom. According to this definition Bevan renders *Waḍā'i'* in his glossary "levies, troops, raised by the Lakhmite king". Ibn al-Aṯīr, however, defines them as "semi-chiefs" [2].

The opinion about the *Rahā'in*, the hostages of the tribes is unanimous.

A detailed account about the troops of al-Ḥīra is given by Abū l-Baqā' [3]. Imru' l-Qays al-Badan [4]—records Abū l-Baqā'—was the man who, imitating the division of the troops of Kisrā, divided his troops and gave them names, which remained till the end of the kingdom of al-Ḥīra. People next in kinship to the king were called *Ahlu l-rifāda*. There were leaders of the troops marching in front of the troops in battles and raids [5]. The commanders of the divisions of the troops were the *Ardāf* [6].

A special division of the army of al-Ḥīra was levied from among the Laḫm. This troop was called *al-Ǧamarāt* or *al-Ǧimār*. As soldiers of this troop are mentioned the Urayš b. Irāš b. Ǧazīla [7] of Laḫm. Another version claims that this troop was formed from people levied from Laḫm and other groups. Mentioned are Banū Silsila from Ǧu'fī, Banū Māwiya from Kalb [8] and groups from Banū Salamān b. Ṯu'al [9] of Ṭayy.

The *Ṣana'i'* were a troop of outlaws from different tribes—records Abū l-Baqā'. Driven out from their tribes as murderers or culprits—they were protected by the king of al-Ḥīra and gained

---

1. *Naqā'iḍ*, p. 884.
2. See Ǧawād 'Alī, *Ta'rīḫ al-'Arab qabla l-Islām*, IV, 92 ("*al-waḍā'i' wa-humu llaḏīna kānū šibha l-mašāyiḫ*").
3. Abū l-Baqā', *op. cit.*, f. 21 a, seq.
4. See Ǧawād 'Alī, *op. cit.*, IV, 31; and see S. Smith, *Events in Arabia*, in *BSOAS*, 1954, p. 430, Table A.
5. The word denoting the title of these leaders cannot be deciphered. It is written والعرامى.
6. Abū l-Baqā', *op. cit.*, f. 21 a: "*wa-l-ardāf wa-hum 'urafā'u l-ǧundi wa-zu'amā'uhum wa-quwwāduhum wa-azimmatuhum*".
7. See Ibn Ḥazm, *op. cit.*, p. 396.
8. See W. Caskel, *op. cit.*, II, 405.
9. See Ibn Durayd, *al-Ištiqāq*, p. 386.

safety. They attended his battles and raids [1]. The other version about the *Ṣana'i'* is given as well, they were men from Bakr b. Wā'il, from the Lahāzim, from Qays and 'Abd al-Lāt and from Ṯa'laba b. 'Ukāba. Abū l-Baqā' prefers the first version.

The *Waḍā'i'*—says Abū l-Baqā'—were a Persian unit, sent by Kisrā to the kings of al-Ḥīra as reinforcements. They counted 1000 mounted soldiers (*asāwira*) and stayed a year at al-Ḥīra. After a year's service they used to return to Persia and were replaced by another troop sent from Persia. They formed in fact the strength of the ruler of al-Ḥīra and through their force the ruler of al-Ḥīra could compel the people of al-Ḥīra as well as the Bedouin tribes to yield obedience to him. Without these forces the rulers were weakened, so that they had to fear the people of al-Ḥīra [2].

The people of al-Ḥīra consisted of three divisions *Dawsar* (or *Dawsara*), an elite troop of valiant and courageous warriors; *al-Šahbā'*, (but according to a contradictory tradition this was the troop of the *Waḍā'i'*); *al-Malḥā'*, so called because of the colour of the iron (i.e. their coat-of-mail) [3].

The *Rahā'in* were youths from Arab tribes taken by the kings of al-Ḥīra as hostages guaranteeing that their tribes would not raid the territories of al-Ḥīra and that they would fulfil the terms of their pacts and obligations between them and the kings of al-Ḥīra. They counted—according to a tradition quoted by Abū l-Baqā'—500 youths and stayed 6 months at the court of al-Ḥīra. After this period they were replaced by others [4].

These forces—of the people of al-Ḥīra and the Persian troops—formed the strength, upon which the rulers of al-Ḥīra relied. They fought with the rulers of al-Ḥīra in obedience to Kisrā, in order to defend their abode, their families and possessions; they could not forsake them [5].

---

1. Two verses are quoted as evidence: the verse of Yazīd b. al-Ṣa'iq (see above, n. 2, p. [15]) and the verse of Ǧarīr:
   "Ḥamaynā yawma Ḏī Naǧabin ḥimānā:
   wa-aḥraznā l-ṣanā'i'a wa-l-nihābā"
   see his *Dīwān* (ed. al-Ṣāwī), p. 68, l. 1.
2. Abū l-Baqā', *op. cit.*, f. 99 b, seq.
3. ib., f. 22 b; Abū l-Baqā' records the opinion of Ṭabarī, that these two troops (*Šahbā'* and *Dawsar*) were Persian troops sent to al-Ḥīra.
4. ib., f. 21 b; Ǧawād 'Alī, *op. cit.*, IV, 93.
5. Abū l-Baqā', *op. cit.*, f. 99 b: *"wa-kāna ǧundahum llaḏīna bihimi mtinā'uhum wa-'izzuhum ahlu l-Ḥīrati l-musammawna bi-tilka l-asmā'i l-muqaddami ḏikruhā; fa-kānū yuḥāribūna ma'ahum ṭā'atan li-Kisrā wa-*

When the king of al-Ḥīra left with his troops for a military action, the people of al-Ḥīra afraid of an attack of the raiding Bedouins, used to stay in their fortified fortresses till the king returned with his troops. Sometimes the king concluded agreements with the neighbouring tribes—mainly from Bakr b. Wā'il and Tamīm—that they would not raid al-Ḥīra in his absence [1].

A peculiar aspect of the relations of the tribes with the rulers of al-Ḥīra is brought out by Abū l-Baqā': tribes pasturing in regions adjacent to the kingdom of al-Ḥīra were compelled to get their provisions (*al-mīra wa-l-kayl*) from the kingdom of al-Ḥīra and therefore had to submit to the obedience of its rulers [2].

The rulers of al-Ḥīra were well acquainted with the situation in the tribe itself and used to intervene in the internal affairs of the tribes. A case of this kind is illustrated by the story of Laqīṭ b. Zurāra, who was convinced by al-Mundir b. Mā' al-Samā' to return the children of Ḍamra b. Ǧābir al-Nahšalī [3]. His children were given as hostages to Laqīṭ for the children of Kubayš and Rušayya [4] and the Banū Nahšal requested the king to intervene [5]. Ḍamra himself was respected and liked by the king [6]. His son, Ḍamra b. Ḍamra, was favoured by al-Mundir and al-Nu'mān. He was one of his boon-companions and the king entrusted him with the care of his white camels [7].

Instructive is the case of Ḥāǧib b. Zurāra with the Banū 'Adiyy

---

ḥifẓan li-bayḍatihim wa-ahlihim wa-manāzilihim wa-ḥimāyatan li-anfusihim wa-amwālihim wa-lā yumkinuhum ḫidlānuhum wa-lā l-taḫallufu 'anhum.

1. ib. f. 102 a.

2. ib., f. 100 a; for the necessity of getting provisions comp. the story of "Yawm al-Mušaqqar".

3. He was the father of the famous Ḍamra b. Ḍamra. The name of Ḍamra b. Ḍamra was in fact Šiqqa b. Ḍamra; his mother was Hind bint Karib b. Ṣafwān, one of the leaders of Sa'd. About Ḍamra b. Ǧābir see W. Caskel, *op. cit.*, II, 241; about Šiqqa b. Ḍamra, ib., II, 530.

4. Al-Kalb b. Kunays (or Kubayš) b. Ǧābir, the son of Kunays and Rušayya married the mother of al-Ḥuṭay'a (see Abū l-Farağ, *al-Aġānī*, II, 43; *ZDMG*, XLIII, p. 3, n. 2).

5. al-Ḍabbī, *Amṯāl al-'Arab*, pp. 7-9; al-Mufaḍḍal b. Salama, *al-Fāḫir*, p. 53 (ed. C. A. Storey, Leiden 1915); al-Maydānī, *Maǧma' al-amṯāl*, I, 136.

6. See the sources given in the preceding note and see al-Balāḏurī, *op. cit.*, f. 986 b.

7. al-Balāḏurī, *op. cit.*, 987 a: "*wa-ǧa'alahu min ḥuddāṯihi wa-summārihi wa-dafa'a ilayhi ibilan kānat lahu fa-kānat fī yadihi wa-hiya haǧā'inuhu wa-haǧā'inu l-Nu'māni bnihi ba'dahu, wariṯahā 'an abīhi; wa-kānat min akrami l-ibili* . . .".

b. ʿAbd Manāt [1]. These ʿAdiyy were in the service of Ḥāǧib and Ḥāǧib intended to turn them into his slaves by a writ of al-Munḏir [2].

Chiefs of tribal divisions co-operating with the rulers of al-Ḥīra took part in their expeditions against Syria, visited their court and were favoured and respected. There was, however, no general line of continuous loyalty and allegiance to the rulers of al-Ḥīra. Contending leaders of clans revolted against the agreements concluded by their chiefs with al-Ḥira from which they could not get the desired share of profit. There was continuous contention between chiefs on the favour of the ruler, which strenghened the feeling of lack of confidence. Sudden changes in the policy of Persia towards the rulers of al-Ḥīra further enhanced the feeling of instability. The application of the method of "divide and impera" [3] as a means to control the tribes and the lack of sufficient and steady support for the loyal tribes—all this created a feeling of disappointment and bitterness.

The successful raids of small units of clans against al-Ḥīra undermined the prestige of its rulers. ʿUṣayma b. Ḥālid b. Minqar [4] could oppose the orders of the king al-Nuʿmān, when he demanded to extradite the man from ʿĀmir b. Ṣaʿṣaʿa to whom ʿUṣayma gave shelter. When raided by the troops of al-Nuʿmān ʿUṣayma summoned his people by the war-cry "*Kawṯar*" and defied the king. Directing the spear to the mane of his horse he said: "Go back, you wind-breaking king! Would I like to put the spear in another place—I would put it [5]. The Banū ʿAmr b. Tamīm when attacked by the forces of the king al-Nuʿmān succeeded in defeating his army and in plundering his camp [6]. The cases of the victory of Bedouin tribes over the royal troops of al-Ḥīra were sufficient proof of the weakness of the vassal kingdom of al-Ḥīra, presaging its fall.

It was concurrent with the rise of Mecca to authority and power.

---

1. Probably the ʿAdiyy b. ʿAbd Manāt b. Udd; see W. Caskel, *op. cit.*, II, 137.

2. Ibn Rašīq, *al-ʿUmda*, II, 174 (Cairo 1934).

3. W. Caskel, *Die Bedeutung der Beduinen in der Geschichte der Araber*, p. 15 (Köln 1953).

4. Apparently ʿIṣma b. Sinān b. Ḫālid b. Minqar as in Ibn al-Kalbī's *Ǧamhara*, f. 78 b and in al-Balāḏurī's *Ansāb*, f. 1030 a; see Ṭufayl al-Ġanawī, *Dīwān*, p. 59 (No. 19), éd. F. Krenkow; see W. Caskel, *Ǧamharat al-Nasab*, II, 359 (ʿIṣma b. Sinān).

5. Muḥ. Ibn Ḥabīb, *al-Muḥabbar*, p. 354.

6. Abū l-Baqāʾ, *op. cit.*, f. 126 a.

IV

THE CAMPAIGN OF ḤULUBĀN
A NEW LIGHT ON THE EXPEDITION OF ABRAHA

The record of the expedition of Abraha against the Maʿadd and especially against the ʿĀmir b. Ṣaʿṣaʿa deserves special mention. The record of this expedition found on an inscription on a rock in the vicinity of the well of al-Murayghān refers to a tribal division of Tamīm. It is the only case — as yet — in which a tribal division of Tamīm has been mentioned in an inscription.

This inscription « Ry 506 », found by the expedition of Professor G. Ryckmans, was published by him with a French translation and comments [1]. It was published with a German translation and valuable comments by W. Caskel [2], rendered into English with notes and remarks by Sidney Smith [3] and by F. Beeston [4], who gave a penetrating analysis of the text. Of importance are the remarks and studies of J. Ryckmans [5]. A comprehensive study of the inscription was given in Russian by A.G. Lundin [6]. The inscription was partly translated into Arabic and furnished with notes by Jawād ʿAlī [7]. The text given by Sidney Smith was translated into Arabic by Iḥsān ʿAbbās [8].

The rendering of F. Beeston of the inscription is here given in full :

« By the power of the Merciful One and His Messiah, the king Abraha (etc.) wrote this inscription when he had raided Maʿadd in the spring razzia in the month ḏtbtn (and) when all the Banū ʿĀmir had revolted. Now the king sent ʾBĞBR with the Kindites and ʿAlites and BŠR son of ḤṢN with the Saʿdites and these two commanders of the army did battle and fought, (namely) the Kindite column against the Banī ʿĀmir and the Murādite and Saʿdite column against ... in the valley on the TRBN route and they slew and made captive (the enemy) and took

[1] *Le Muséon*, 66 (1953), pp. 275-284.

[2] W. Caskel, *Entdeckungen in Arabien*, pp. 27-31.

[3] Sidney Smith, *Events in Arabia in the 6th century A.D.*, BSOAS, 1954, pp. 435-37.

[4] A.F.L. Beeston, *Notes on the Muraighān inscription*, BSOAS, 1954, pp. 389-92.

[5] *Le Muséon*, 66 (1953), pp. 339-42; B.O. XIV, p. 94.

[6] A.G. Lundin, *Yujnaya Arabia w VI weke* (*Palestynski Sbornik*, 1961, pp. 73-84).

[7] Jawād ʿAli, *Taʾrīkh al-ʿArab qabla ʾl-Islām*, IV, 396-98.

[8] Iḥsān ʿAbbās, *Sharḥ Dīwān Labīd b. Rabīʿa*, Introduction, p. 8 (al-Kuwayt, 1962).

satisfactory booty. The king, on the other hand, did battle at Ḥalibān and the (troops?) of Maʿadd were defeated and forced to give hostages. After all this ʿAmr son of al-Mundhir negotiated with Abraha [9] and agreed to give hostages to Abraha from al-Mundhir, for al-Mundhir had invested him (ʿAmr) with the governorship over Maʿadd. So Abraha returned from Ḥalibān by the power of the Merciful One (etc.). »

Beeston's comment [10] shows clearly that the description deals with two campaigns : the campaign of the king, Abraha, at Ḥalibān [11] and the campaign of Kinda and Saʿd - Murād at TRBN [12]. It is evident that we are concerned here with an enormous encounter in which many tribal forces participated.

Caskel remarks that the expedition might be considered a sa « Vorübung » for the expedition of Abraha towards the North of the Ar. peninsula, which stopped near Mecca [13]. J. Ryckmans states : « Cette expédition aurait partiellement servi de base à la tradition d'une campagne de Abraha contre la Mecque » [14]. Altheim and Stiehl state that the expedition of Abraha recorded in the inscription « Ry 506 »

[9] The phrase : « wbʿdnhw/wsʿhmw/ʿmrm/bn/mḏrm/wrhnmw/bnhw/wsḫtlfw/ʿaly/mʿdm» is obscure. « wsʿ » may probably denote — as pointed out by Caskel, *op. cit.*, p. 29, ad « Z » 7 — « aus einer drückenden Lage befreien ». A verse of Zabbān b. Sayyār may be consulted : « Wasiʿnā, wasiʿnā fī umūrin tamahhalat : ʿalā 'l-ṭālibi 'l-mautūri ayya tamahhuli » (al Zubayr b. Bakkār, *Nasab Quraysh*, ed. Shākir, p. 15). Perhaps the translation may be : Afterwards ʿAmr b. al-Mundhir gave them sufficient succour; his son (ʿAmr — see Caskel, *op. cit.*, p. 29, ad « L » 7) gave hostages for them and he (i.e. Abraha) made him governor over Maʿadd.

[10] BSOAS, 1954, p. 391.

[11] So vowelled in al-Bakrī, *Muʿjam mā 'staʿjam*, s.v. Ḥlbān. Yāqūt vowels : Ḥalabān (*Buldān*, s.v. Ḥlbān). Al-Bakrī states that it is « a city in al-Yaman, in the lowland of al Ḥaḍūr ». Yāqūt states that it was « a place in al-Yaman in the vicinity of Najrān ». He also quotes another opinion, that it was a water-place of the Banū Qushayr. Thilo locates the place according to Yāqūt and states that it is a wādī starting in the mountain-chain of ʿArwā and flowing into the Rikā' Sirra. It is located in the vicinity of Yadhbul - see Thilo, *Ortsnamen*, s.v. Ḥalabān.

[12] See Beeston, *op. cit.*, p. 391; Lundin, *op. cit.*, pp. 76-77 (n. 66-67). See esp. al-Bakrī, *Muʿjam mā 'staʿjam*, s.v. Turaba : « It is a place in the territory of the Banū ʿĀmir »; see ʿArrām b. al-Asbagh, *Asmā' jibāl Tihāma* (*Nawādir al-makhṭuṭāt*, ed. Hārūn, VIII, 146).

[13] Caskel, *op. cit.*, p. 30.

[14] J. Ryckmans, *Inscriptions historiques Sabéennes, Le Muséon*, 1953, p. 342; Lundin, *op. cit.*, p. 82.

is in fact the « Expedition of the Elephant » mentioned in the Qur'ān [15]. Lundin devotes a comprehensive discussion to the proposition of Altheim - Stiehl and refutes their assumption stating that the « Expedition of the Elephant » is not connected with the events of 547 A.D., recorded in the inscription « Ry 506 » [16]. He assumes that the « Expedition of the Elephant » took place about 563 A.D. [17].

Some remarks concerning this controversy may be made here. The tradition of Ibn al-Kalbī stating that the Prophet was born 23 years after the « Expedition of the Elephant » is not « an isolated one » (« Danniye Muh. b. al-Kalbī stoyat osobnyakom ») - as Lundin claims. There are many traditions stating that the Prophet was not born on the « Day of the Elephant » or in the year of « the Elephant »; these can, however, not be discussed here. One of these traditions, an important one, may be quoted here.

Ḥaddathanā al-Zubayru qāla : wa-ḥaddathanī ʿUmaru bnu Abī Bakrin al-Mu'ammilī ʿan Zakariyā 'bni Abī ʿĪsā ʿan 'bni Shihābin anna Qurayshan kānat taʿuddu qabla ʿadadi rasūli 'llahi (ṣ) min zamani 'l-fīli. Kānū yaʿuddūna bayna 'l-fīli wa-bayna 'l-fijāri arbaʿīna sanatan. Wa-kānū yaʿuddūna bayna 'l-fijāri wa-bayna wafāti Hishāmi 'bni l-Mughīrati sitta sinīna. Wa-kānū yaʿuddūna bayna wafāti Hishāmin wa-bayna bunyāni l-kaʿbati tisʿa sinīna. Wa-kānū yaʿuddūna bayna bunyāni l-kaʿbati wa-bayna an kharaja rasūlu 'llāhi ilā l-madīnati khamsa ʿashrata sanatan. Minhā khamsu sinīna qabla an yunzala ʿalayhi. Thumma kāna l-ʿadadu yuʿaddu.

... « Ībn Shihâb (i.e. al-Zuhrī - K) : Quraysh counted, before the chronology of the Prophet, from the time of the 'Elephant'. Between the Elephant and the (battle of the) Fijār they counted 40 years. Between the Fijār and the death of Hishām b. al-Mughīra they counted 6 years. Between the death of Hishām and the building of the Kaʿba they counted 9 years. Between the building of the Kaʿba and the departure of the Prophet for al-Madīna (i.e. the Hijra - K) they counted 15 years; he stayed 5 years (of these 15) not receiving the revelation. Then the counting (of the usual chronology) was as follows. »

This tradition of al-Zuhrī is recorded by al-Zubayr b. Bakkār in

[15] F. Altheim - R. Stiehl, *Araber und Sassaniden* (*Edwin Redslob zum 70 Geburtstag*, Berlin 1954, pp. 200-207 : Mohammeds Geburtsjahr); F. Altheim - R. Stiehl, *Finanzgeschichte der Spätantike*, pp. 145-148 and 353-355.

[16] Lundin, *op. cit.*, pp. 82-83.

[17] Lundin, *op. cit.*, pp. 83-84.

his « Nasab Quraysh »[18] and is quoted in Ibn 'Asākir's « Ta'rīkh Dimashq »[19]. This tradition is not connected directly with the date of the birth of the Prophet and seems to be trustworthy. It fixes the date of the « Expedition of the Elephant» at 552 A.D. It is exactly the date fixed for the inscription « Ry 506 » by Beeston[20]. The proposition of Altheim-Stiehl seems to be correct : the inscription « Ry 506 » is apparently a record of the « Expedition of the Elephant ». The problem of the date of the birth of the Prophet deserves to be dealt with in a separate study.

Some additional details about the « Expedition of the Elephant », hitherto unknown, may here be quoted as well. Al-Balādhurī records a tradition on the authority of Ibn Da'b : Jābir b. Sufyān, the father of Ta'abbaṭa Sharran (Ibn al-Kalbī says : Jābir b. Sufyān b. 'Adiyy. Others say : Sufyān b. 'Amaythil b. 'Adiyy) said about the « Day of the Elephant » :

Atānā rākibun fa-na'ā Unāsan
wa-'Abbāsan wa-nāsan ākharīnā
Aqamnā bi-l-Mughammasi niṣfa shahrin
wa ...[21] hum bihā mutajāwirīnā[22]

A horseman came to us and announced the death of Unās[23]
and the death of 'Abbās and other people
We stayed at al-Mughammas half a month
and ... them in it, staying close together.

There is no intimation as to who the persons, mentioned in the verses, were. They were evidently from the tribe of Jābir b. Sufyān, from the Fahm. From the verses we gather that the father of Ta'abbaṭa Sharran witnessed the battle. They clearly point to the fact that Fahm took part in the battle against Abraha.

It may be of some interest to mention, that the family of Ta'abbaṭa Sharran had some relations with Mecca. Umayya[24], the daughter

[18] Ms. Bodley, f. 129b.

[19] I, 28 (ed. al-Munajjid); comp. a tradition recounted by Mūsā b. 'Uqba on the authority of Zuhrī : Al-Dhahabī, *Ta'rīkh al-Islām*, I, 22; and see Ibn Kathīr, *al-Bidāya*, II, 260-62.

[20] BSOAS, 1954, p. 391, n. 2.

[21] I could not decipher the word. It is written ويحروهم.

[22] al-Balādhurī, *Ansāb*, ms. f. 1125a.

[23] Perhaps Iyās (instead of Unās).

[24] In the « Iṣāba » : Āmina; al-Istī'āb : Āmina bint Naufal b. Jābir.

of Jābir b. Sufyān, the sister of Ta'abbaṭa Sharran, married Naufal b. Asad [25]. Her son 'Adiyy b. Naufal b. Asad, the brother of Waraqa b. Naufal, was appointed by 'Umar or 'Uthmān as governor of Ḥaḍramaut.

Lundin discussing whether the inscription of « Ry 506 » can be connected with the « Expedition of the Elephant » argues, that the inscription does not contain the names of the men mentioned in the North-Arabian tradition : Nufayl b. Ḥabīb, the guide of Abraha, Muḥammad b. Khuzā'ī, claimed to have been appointed over Ma'add [26], the Khath'am etc. One may remark, that the tradition of Ṭabarī explicitly says that Muḥ. b. Khuzā'ī was killed by the Kināna. Abraha advancing against Kināna intended to avenge the murder of Muḥ. b. Khuzā'ī [27]. A contradictory tradition, recorded by Muḥ. b. Ḥabīb, states that Muḥ. b. Khuzā'ī was with the army of Abraha with the Elephant [28]. In both cases (whether Muḥ. b. Khuzā'ī was alive or dead) there was no reason to mention his name on an inscription recording the events of a battle between the forces of Abraha and of revolting tribes. That seems to have been the reason that the name of the guide of Abraha was not mentioned either.

It is a fact that in a relatively short time the decisive events fell into oblivion, poems composed on the occasion of the battles were lost. Only dim memories of the campaigns were preserved in a few verses.

A peculiar passage in al Balādhurī's « Ansāb » [29] may shed new light on the relations between Abraha and Mecca, emphasizing the economic aspect :

... Minhumu 'l-Ḥārithu bnu 'Alqamata 'bni Kaladata 'bni 'Abdi Manāfi 'bni 'Abdi l-Dāri, rahīnatu Qurayshin 'inda Abī Yaksūma l-Ḥabashiyyi,

[25] See al-Muṣ'ab, *Nasab Quraysh*, p. 209; al-Zubayr b. Bakkār, *Jamharat Nasab Quraysh*, I, 421, 423 (ed. Shākir); Ibn Ḥajar, *al-Iṣāba*, nº 5484; Ibn'Abd al-Barr, *al-Istī'āb*, p. 502.

[26] In the tradition of al-Ṭabarī (I, 551; ed. Cairo 1939) he was appointed over Muḍar, not over Ma'add.

[27] al-Ṭabarī, *Ta'rīkh*, *ib.*; al-Ṭabarsī in his *Majma' al-Bayān* XXX, 191 seq. tells that Abraha — when on his way against Mecca with his army — sent a man from Sulaym as a missionary to summon the people to make the pilgrimage to his church, which he had built. A man from the Kināna, from the Ḥums, met him and fought him. That increased the wrath of Abraha.

[28] al-Muḥabbar, p. 130.

[29] Ms. f. 811a.

ḥīna dakhala Makkata qaumun min tujjārihim fī ḥaṭmatin kānat, fa-wathaba aḥdāthun ʿalā baʿḍi mā kāna maʿahum fa-'ntahabūhu fa-waqaʿat baynahum munāfaratun, thumma 'ṣṭalaḥū baʿda an maḍat ʿiddatun min wujūhi Qurayshin ilā Abī Yaksūma wa-sa'alūhu allā yaqṭaʿa tujjāra ahli mamlakatihi ʿanhum. Fa-dufiʿa l-Ḥārithu wa-ghayruhu rahīnatan. Fa-kāna yukrimuhum wa-yaṣiluhum wa-kānū yubḍiʿūna l-baḍā'iʿa ilā Makkata li-anfusihim.

... « From them (i.e. the Banū ʿAbd al-Dār - K) was al-Ḥārith b. ʿAlqama b. Kalada b. ʿAbd Manāf b. ʿAbd al Dār, the hostage of Quraysh handed over to Abū Yaksūm, the Abyssinian. (It happened) when a group of their merchants entered Mecca in a barren year. Some young men attacked and robbed them of their merchandise. Then discord broke out among them. They were later reconciled, after a group of nobles of Quraysh went to Abū Yaksūm and requested him not to cut off the merchants of his kingdom from (coming to) them. Al-Ḥārith and others were handed over as hostages to him (i.e. to Abraha -K). He honoured them and showed them friendship and they sent merchandise for themselves to Mecca. »

Al-Ḥārith b. ʿAlqama is also mentioned as hostage of Quraysh with Abū Yaksūm the Abyssinian in al-Zubayr b. Bakkār's « Nasab Quraysh » [30].

This passage of the « Ansāb » is quoted by M. Ḥamīdullah in his *Les rapports économico - diplomatiques de la Mecque* (*Mélanges L. Massignon*, II, 302) and in his *Le Prophète de l'Islam*, p. 195. Unfortunately Ḥamīdullah misinterpreted an expression of the report of al Balādhurī. Ḥamīdullah renders the text as follows : « ... ils s'excusèrent donc auprès du Négus ... Le Négus Abū Yaksūm (c.à.d. le roi de la dynastie d'Axoum) traita ces otages avec bonté ...» (*Les rapports*, *ib.*). And in his *Le Prophète de l'Islam* : « Le ʿAbdarite al-Ḥārith b. ʿAlqamah fut l'otage quraichite entre les mains du roi d'Abyssinie Abū Yaksūm (= aksoumite) ... furent allés auprès de l'Aksoumite... »

But in the text quoted above there is no mention of the Negus at all. The expression « Abū Yaksūm al-Ḥabashī » refers to *A b r a h a*, whose « Kunya » was *A b ū Y a k s ū m*, because he had a son called Yaksūm, who ruled after his death. The merchants who were attacked at Mecca were not necessarily Abyssinians; they were evidently Yamanī merchants.

It is of interest to note that Thaqīf also surrendered hostages to

[30] Ms. Bodley, f. 69a; and see Ibn Ḥajar, *al-Iṣāba*, nº 8705 and nº 8714.

Abraha. Al-Balādhurī records that ʻUtbān b. Mālik b. Kaʻb b. ʻAmr was « the hostage of Abū Yaksūm the Abyssinian » [31]. This tradition confirms the North-Ar. story about some contacts between Abraha and Ṭā'if.

The tradition here quoted point to the direction of the activity of Abraha : Ṭhaqīf (Ṭā'if), Fahm, Kināna and Hudhayl — all these tribes staying in the vicinity of Mecca. One is inclined to trust to some degree the North-Arabian tradition stating that the expedition was directed against Mecca and her allies.

It may be remarked here that there is a rather diverging tradition about the cause of the expedition of Abraha against Mecca : The grandson of Abraha (the son of his daughter), Aksūm b. al-Ṣabbāḥ al-Ḥimyarī went to Mecca to perform his pilgrimage. On his way back from Mecca he stayed in a church in Najrān. He was attacked by men from Mecca, who robbed him of his luggage and looted the church. Aksūm went to his grandfather, and complained about the behaviour of the men from Mecca. Abraha vowed to destroy the sanctuary of Mecca [32].

The inscription mentions tribal troops of the army of Abraha despatched by the king : Kinda sent against the ʻĀmīr, and Saʻd-Murād sent towards TRBN.

The troop of Saʻd, which we are interested in, was identified by Smith as a « sept of Quraysh » [33]. Caskel identified the Saʻd as Saʻd al-ʻAshīra [34]. Caskel's assumption was accepted by Lundin [35]. It was Jawād ʻAlī, who for the first time quoted two verses of al-Mukhabbal al-Saʻdī from the « Muʻjam mā 'staʻjam », in which the help of the Saʻd for Abraha was mentioned [36]. It is rather important to stress that *these Saʻd are in fact Saʻd of Tamīm.*

The passage of al-Bakrī [37] states that al-Mukhabbal al-Saʻdī boasted

[31] al-Balādhurī, *Ansāb*, ms. f. 1139a.

[32] al-Iṣbahānī, *Dalāʼil al-nubuwwa*, p. 100-101 (ed. 1950); al-Suyūṭī, *al-Durr al-manthūr*, VI, 394 (quoted from the Dalā'il).

[33] Smith, *op. cit.*, p. 436, n. 2.

[34] W. Caskel, *op. cit.*, p. 29, n. 124.

[35] A.G. Lundin, *op. cit.*, p. 76, n. 63.

[36] Jawād ʻAli, *op. cit.*, IV, 397.

[37] al-Bakrī, *Muʻjam mā 'staʻjam*, s.v. Ḥulubān; the first verse is quoted in L. ʻA. s.v. « ḥlb » and in Tāj al-ʻArūs (s.v. ḥlb); for the expression « ṣaramū l-umūra » see al-Balādhurī's *Ansāb*, IV, 158 (ed. Schloessinger) : « wa-naḥnu ṣaramnā amra Bakri 'bni

of their (i.e. of the Sa'd - K) help extended to Abraha b. al-Ṣabbāḥ, the king of al-Yaman; it was in fact Khindif who were his followers. He said :

Ḍarabū li-Abrahata 'l-umūra maḥalluhā
Ḥulubānu, fa-'nṭalaqū ma'a l-aqwāli
Wa-Muḥarriqun wa-l-Ḥārithāni kilāhumā
shurakā'unā fī l-ṣihri wa-l-amwāli

They decided for Abraha the actions (of war); the place
of it was Ḥulubān, and they rushed with the « qayls »
Muḥarriq and the two al Ḥārith both of them were
our partners in kinship and possessions.

Al-Hamdānī quotes these very verses in his « Iklīl » remarking : ... « about Abraha the Qayl » says al-Mukhabbal mentioning their (i.e. of the Sa'd) loyalty (« mayl ») for him». Further al-Hamdānī says : « About him (i.e. about Abraha) he said boasting of their deeds in war with him (i.e. fighting on his side — K) :

Wa-yauma Abī Yaksūma wa-l-nāsu ḥuḍḍarun
'alā Ḥulubānin idh tuqaḍḍā maḥamiluh [38]
Fataḥnā lahū bāba 'l-Ḥuḍayri wa-rabbuhu
'azīzun yumashshī bi-l-suyūfi arājiluh [39].

These two verses are found in a qaṣīda of al-Mukhabbal in the « Ikhtiyārayn » (al-Mufaḍḍal - al-Aṣma'ī) edited by S.H. Husain [40]. The verses in the « Ikhtiyārayn » contain, however, some variants which deserve to be mentioned :

Verse 1. taqaḍḍā maḥāsiluh (instead maḥāmiluh)
Verse 2. Ṭawaynā lahum bāba l-ḥuṣayni wa-dūnahu
'azīzum yumashshi bi-l-ḥirābi maqāwiluh.

The two verses, for which the editor could nowhere find parallels, are rendered by him as follows :

And on the day of Abū Yaksūm when the people were present
at Ḥalibān after its products were consumed

Wā'ilin »; and see the explanation of the expression in al-'Askarī's *Jamharat al-amthāl*, p. 62.

[38] Perhaps to be read « mahāfiluh ».

[39] al-Hamdānī, *al-Iklīl*, ms. Berlin, I/II f. 109b.

[40] P. 204 (*The University of Dacca, Bulletin*, XIX).

We closed against them the gate of the fortress in front of which was a prince whose chiefs went forth with the javelins [41].

The commentary of the « Ikhtiyārayn » has « maḥāsiluhu » and explains « mā tajamma'a minhu », « what comes together, combines ». « Abū Yaksūm » is explained : « a king »; « al ḥuṣayn » is explained « a fortress, a palace »; « bi-l-ḥirāb » is explained : « he meant to say : his horsemen and his infantry ».

Al-Hamdānī's comments are of some importance : « Ḥulubān — says Hamdānī — is located in Ḥaḍūr. Those who transmitted « Khaḍīr » refer to some king (wa-man rawāhu al-Khaḍīr arāda malikan min al-mulūki); he who transmits it « al-Ḥuḍayr » refers to al-Ḥaḍr. The commentaries do not help us to understand this crucial verse of al-Mukhabbal. The commentary of « al-Ikhtiyārayn » does not explain the situation and does not say anything about the fortress (al-ḥuṣayn) mentioned in the verse. The commentary of al-Hamdānī does not elucidate the situation.

What can be deduced is that the Banū Sa'd of Tamīm were the decisive factor at Ḥulubān, where the king Abraha decided about the movements of the troops (maḥāfil). They opened (or « folded up ») for the king a gate of a fortress, belonging to a mighty king and defended by well armed guards. This fortress must have hindered the advance of the troops of Abraha.

Of importance is the remark of al-Bakrī, that Khindif [42] were the followers of Abraha. Tradition is silent about the Northern tribes that aided Abraha : only the Southern Khaulān and Ash'ar are mentioned as his followers. It is only the Northern Ḥumays b. Udd who are mentioned as having fought on the side of Abraha in his expedition against Mecca [43].

Other verses quoted by al-Hamdānī are 2 well-known verses of

[41] *Op. cit.*, p. 168 (English text).

[42] See CASKEL, *Die Bedeutung der Beduinen*, p. 15; and comp. Naqā'iḍ, index (Khindif); al-Balādhurī, *Ansāb*, I, 32-34; al-Muṣ'ab al-Zubayrī, *Nasab Quraysh*, p. 7-8; al 'Ajjāj, Dīwān, p. 60 (Ar. text; ed. AHLWARDT).

[43] See Ibn al-Kalbī, *Jamhara*, ms. f. 115b; « Ḥarb b. Ḥumays b. Udd, they were with Abraha b. al-Ashram and perished on the « Day of the Elephant »; 60 of them were saved », etc.

Labīd [44] and the often quoted verse of Qays b. al-Khaṭīm [45]. They do not help us to know more about the expedition of Abraha.

***

Lundin remarks that none of the scholars who published the inscription tried to identify the persons of Abū Jabr and Bishr b. Ḥiṣn (or Bashīr, or Basshār; b. Ḥuṣayn or b. Ḥaṣṣān) [46]. Lundin stresses that in the case of Abū Jabr only his « Kunya » is known; his name is missing. He therefore attempted only to identify the person of Bishr b. Ḥiṣn.

The following lines can assist in identifying the person of Abū Jabr al Kindī :

In the « Maqṣūra » of Ibn Durayd [47] a remarkable verse refers to Abū l-Jabr :

Wa-khāmarat nafsa Abī l-Jabri l-jawā :
ḥattā ḥawāhu l-ḥatfu fī man qad ḥawā

And passion pervaded the soul of Abū 'l-Jabr :
till death took possession of him among those
whom he (i.e. death) took possession of.

The commentary supplies important details about Abū l-Jabr. He was a Kindī, from the kings of Kinda (i.e. from the royal family of Kinda - K). His « kunya » Abū 'l-Jabr was his name. He went to Kisrā, asking for aid against his people. Kisrā gave him a force of his mounted troops (al Asāwira). When Abū 'l-Jabr with his troop reached Kāẓima — the troop saw the wilderness of the Arab land and decided to return. They put poison into the food of Abū 'l-Jabr. When he was overwhelmed with pain they asked him to write a letter to Kisrā, stating that he gave them permission to return. He gave them the required letter. When they left he felt relief and journeyed

44 *Dīwān*, p. 108 (ed. Iḥsān ʿAbbās); see Beeston, E.I. ², art. « Abraha », bibliography. The verse of Labīd : « Wa-ghalabna Abrahata 'lladhī alfaynahu » (*Dīwān*, p. 275) is however explained by al-Hamdānī as referring to Abraha b. al-Ṣabbāḥ b. Shuraḥbīl b. Lahīʿa. « Some people say — remarks al-Hamdānī — that he referred to Abī Abraha Dhū 'l-Manār ».

45 *Dīwān*, p. 61 (ed. Samarrā'ī - Matloub); see Beeston, E.I. ², *op. cit.*, bibliography.

46 Lundin, *op. cit.*, p. 76.

47 Ibn Durayd, *al-Maqṣūra*, p. 82 (ed. al-Jawā'ib, 1300 A.H.).

to al-Ṭā'if, to the Arab physician al-Ḥārith b. Kalada al-Thaqafī[48]. He recovered from his illness due to the treatment of al-Ḥārith b. Kalada. He left for al-Yaman. But on his way back the illness returned and he died. He was mourned by his aunt (on his father's side), Kabsha, who composed the following dirge on his death.

Layta shiʿrī wa-qad shaʿartu abā l-Jabri bi-mā qad laqīta fī 'l-tarḥāli
A-tamaṭṭat bika l-rikābu, abayta l-
laʿna, ḥattā ḥalalta fī l-aqtāli
A-shujāʿu fa-anta ashjaʿu min lay-
thin hamūsi 'l-surā, abī ashbāli
A-jawādu fa-anta ajwadu min say-
lin tadāʿā min musbilin haṭṭāli[49]
A-karīmu fa-anta akramu man ḍam-
mat ḥaṣānun wa-man mashā fi 'l-niʿāli
Anta khayrun min ʿĀmirin wa-'bni Waqqā-
ṣin wa-man jammaʿū li-yaumi 'l-miḥāli
Anta khayrun min alfi alfin min al-qau-
mi idhā kunta fī wujūhi l-rījali

Ibn Durayd in his «Ishtiqa»[50] and Ibn 'Abd Rabbihi in his «'Iqd»[51] mention that Kisrā gave Abū l-Jabr as gift Sumayya, a girl from Zardaward[52]. Abū 'l-Jabr cured by al-Ḥārith b. Kalada gratefully gave him Sumayya as a gift[53].

The story of Abū 'l-Jabr as given in the commentary of the « Maqṣūra » is recorded by Ibn Khallikān[54]. Ibn Khallikān quotes the verse of Ibn Durayd and the narrative about Sumayya. The record of Ibn Khallikān contains, however, a detail of great importance : two versions of the name of Abū 'l-Jabr. According to version (1) his name was Yazīd b. Shuraḥīl al-Kindī; according to version (2) his name was Abū 'l-Jabr b. 'Amr.

48 See about him Ibn Ḥazm, *Jamharat ansāb al-ʿArab*, p. 256; Ibn Ḥajar, *al-Isāba*, nº 1472; al-Balādhurī, *Ansāb*, ms. f. 116a; Ibn 'Abd al-Barr, *al-Istīʿāb*, pp. 109, 304.

49 Added from the ed. Cairo, 1324 AH, p. 82.

50 Ibn Durayd, *al-Ishtiqāq*, pp. 305-306.

51 Ibn 'Abd Rabbihi, *al-ʿIqd al-farīd*, V, 4.

52 Comp. Yāqūt, *al-Buldān*, s.v. Zandaward : it was al-Nushjānī who was cured by al-Ḥārith b. Kalada and gave him as gift Sumayya, the mother of Ziyād b. Sufyān (or b. Abīhi, or b. 'Ubayd, or b. Abī Sufyān).

53 But see contradictory traditions : al-Balādhurī's *Ansāb*, I, 489 and Ibn Ḥajar, *al-Iṣāba*, VIII, 119 (nº 611 - women).

54 Ibn Khallikān, *Wafayāt*, II, 388 (ed. Būlāq, 1299 A.H.).

Examining these narratives in the light of the two versions about Kabsha as recorded in the MS. of al-Balādhuri [55], one may assume that Abū Jabr of the inscription is identical with Abū 'l-Jabr (or Abū-Jabr) [56] of the traditions quoted above and that he was from the branch of Āl al-Jaun.

Nothing could be found about the commander of the troop of Sa'd, Bishr (or Bashīr, or Bashshār) b. Ḥiṣn (or Ḥuṣayn). The suggestion of Lundin that he might have been a prince of Kinda [57] can hardly be accepted. There is evidence that the reading « Ḥisn » in the text of Ibn Khaldūn is merely a clerical error (al-Balādhurī Ansāb, MS. f. 996b.) It may be supposed that as a commander of a Khindif troop — and Khindif were the supporters of Abraha at Ḥulubān — a chief from among them would have been nominated. Were the Sa'd of the inscription a southern tribe — as assumed by Lundin — the appointment of a Kinda chief would have been plausible. It may be pointed out that Bishr and Ḥuṣayn are names frequently occurring in North-Arabian genealogies. The silence about the leader of the Sa'd in the battle of Ḥulubān can be explained by the fact that nobody of the Sa'd was interested to recall the deeds of the ancestors, who had served the cause of Abraha and participated in the attack led against the 'Āmir b. Ṣa'ṣa'a and apparently intended against Mecca.

Jerusalem

[55] See al-Balādhurī, *Ansāb,* Ms. f. 985b, 996b.

[56] So mentioned once in the report of Ibn Khallikān and in the « risāla » of Abū Yaḥyā b. Mas'ada (*Nawādir al-makhṭūṭāt,* III, 267 - ed. A.S. Hārūn). The *Mukhtaṣar Jamharāt al-Ansāb* (Ms. Rāghib Pasha, nº 999, f. 233a, line 2) mentions Abū 'l-Jabr, poisoned by the forces of Misrā.

[57] Lundin, *op. cit.,* p. 76, n. 64-65.

V

AL-TAḤANNUTH
AN INQUIRY INTO THE MEANING OF A TERM

The expression *taḥannuth* mentioned in some traditions in connexion with the first revelation of the Prophet was variously interpreted by Muslim philologists and commentators of *ḥadīth*. Several meanings have been attached to it by modern scholars. A re-examination of the material seems to give us a clue for elucidation of the meaning of *taḥannuth* and the ideas connected with it. This may also be helpful towards understanding the circumstances of the 'Call to Prophecy' of Muḥammad.

I

The word *al-taḥannuth* occurs in the famous tradition recorded in the *Sīra* of Ibn Isḥāq concerning the 'Beginning of the Prophethood'.[1] The tradition is quoted on the authority of 'Ubayd b. 'Umayr b. Qatāda al-Laythī[2] and reported by Wahb b. Kaysān.[3] 'Ubayd b. 'Umayr related the tradition in the presence of 'Abdullāh b. al-Zubayr and other people; among them was Wahb b. Kaysān. 'The Prophet—says the tradition—used to sojourn (*yujāwiru*) on Mt. Ḥirā'[4] for a month every year. That was the *taḥannuth* which Quraysh used to practise in the period of the Jāhiliyya (*wa-kāna dhālika mimmā taḥannatha bihi Qurayshun fi 'l-Jāhiliyyati*). The Prophet used to sojourn during that month every year, feeding[5] the poor who called on him. After the conclusion of that month of sojourn, before entering his house, he would go to the Ka'ba and circumambulate it seven times or as many times as it pleased God. Then he would go back to his home. When the month came in which God wished to grant him His grace (*karāma*), in the year when God sent him and it was the month of Ramaḍān[6] the Prophet went out to Ḥirā' as was his custom for his sojourn (*li-jiwārihi*). With him was his family.'

[1] Ibn Hishām, *al-Sīra al-nabawiyya*, ed. al-Saqqā, al-Abyārī, Shalabī, Cairo, 1936, I, 251; see A. Guillaume (tr.), *The life of Muhammad*, London, 1955, 105.

[2] See Ibn Ḥajar, *Tahdhīb al-tahdhīb*, VII, 71 (died A.H. 67; he was the Qāṣṣ of the people of Mecca); al-Dhahabī, *Tadhkirat al-ḥuffāẓ*, I, 50 (records that he died A.H. 74); *idem*, *Ta'rīkh al-Islām*, Cairo, 1368/1948–9, III, 190. The date of his death given by F. Buhl, *Das Leben Muhammeds*, second ed., transl. H. H. Schaeder, Heidelberg, 1955, p. 134, n. 24, as A.H. 98 seems to be an error; see A. Sprenger, *Das Leben und die Lehre des Moḥammad, zweite Auflage*, Berlin, 1869, I, 339.

[3] See Ibn Ḥajar, *Tahdhīb al-tahdhīb*, XI, 166 (died A.H. 126 or 129); al-Suyūṭī, *Is'āf al-mubaṭṭa*, Cairo, n.d., 41 (gives the date of his death as A.H. 127).

[4] For the location of the place see Muḥammad Ḥamīdullāh, *Le Prophète de l'Islam*, Paris, 1959, I, 64: 'situé à un kilomètre a peine de l'emplacement de la maison de Muhammad le Mount Nur présente . . .'; and see 'Arrām b. al-Aṣbagh, *Asmā' jibāl Tihāma*, ed. 'Abd al-Salām Hārūn, Cairo, 1956, (*Nawādir al-makhṭūṭāt*, VIII, 419); al-Fāsī, *Shifā' al-gharām*, Cairo, 1956, I, 280–1.

[5] In the translation of Guillaume: '. . . the apostle would *pray* in seclusion *and* give food to the poor . . .'.

[6] See al-Ḥalabī, *Insān al-'uyūn*, I, 272 (the discussion as to whether it happened in Ramaḍān, or in the month of Rabī' al-awwal or in the month of Rajab). And see Ibn al-Jauzī, *Ṣifat al-ṣafwa*,

The tradition giving an account of the same events in al-Bukhārī's *Ṣaḥīḥ* [7] is told on the authority of 'Ā'isha. The chain of the *isnād* includes Yaḥyā b. Bukayr [8]—al-Layth [9]—'Uqayl [10]—Ibn Shihāb (i.e. al-Zuhrī)—'Urwa b. al-Zubayr—'Ā'isha. The tradition [11] contains the expression *taḥannatha*, but differs in many respects from the tradition of Ibn Isḥāq. The passage we are concerned with runs in the *Ṣaḥīḥ* as follows:

'... Then he was made to cherish solitude and he sojourned alone in the cave of Ḥirā' and practised *taḥannuth* a number of nights before he returned to his family; and he used to take provisions for it (i.e. the sojourn). Then he would go back to Khadīja and take provisions for a similar (period of sojourn). So things went on till the Truth came upon him (*jā'ahu 'l-ḥaqqu*) [12] when he was in the cave of Ḥirā' '.[13]

Hyderabad, 1355/1936–7, I, 27, and al-Majlisī, *Biḥār*, XVIII, 189 inf. (stating that it happened in Rajab); J. Fück, 'Sechs Ergänzungen zu Sachaus Ausgabe von al-Bīrūnīs "Chronologie orientalischer Völker"', in J. Fück (ed.), *Documenta Islamica inedita*, Berlin, 1952, 97 (Rabī' al-awwal or Rajab).

[7] Al-Bukhārī, *Ṣaḥīḥ*, Cairo, n.d., I, 5—*Bāb kayfa kāna bad'u 'l-waḥyi ilā rasūli 'llāhi.*

[8] In fact Yaḥyā b. 'Abdullāh b. Bukayr: see Ibn Ḥajar, *Tahdhīb*, XI, 237; al-Dhahabī, *Tadhkirat al-ḥuffāẓ*, II, 420; al-'Aynī, *'Umdat al-qārī'*, Cairo, 1308/1890–1, I, 56.

[9] See al-Khaṭīb al-Baghdādī, *Ta'rīkh Baghdād*, XIII, 3–14; al-Dhahabī, *Mīzān al-i'tidāl*, ed. 'Alī Muḥ. al-Bajāwī, Cairo, 1963, III, 423, no. 6998; Ibn Ḥajar, *Tahdhīb*, VIII, 459; al-'Aynī, op. cit., I, 56.

[10] See al-Sam'ānī, *al-Ansāb*, ed. 'Abd al-Raḥmān al-Mu'allamī, Hyderabad, 1962, I, 410; Ibn Ḥajar, *Tahdhīb*, VII, 255.

[11] See the rendering of the tradition in Richard Bell, 'Mohammed's Call', *Moslem World*, XXIV, 1, 1934, 13.

[12] In the tradition of Ibn Sa'd, *Ṭabaqāt*, Beirut, 1960, I, 194, l. 16, *ḥattā faji'ahu 'l-ḥaqqu* 'till Truth came upon him suddenly'. Likewise, Ibn Sayyid al-Nās, *'Uyūn al-athar*, Cairo, 1356/1937–8, I, 84, l. 4 from bottom; al-Balādhurī, *Ansāb al-ashrāf*, ed. Muḥammad Ḥamīdullāh, Cairo, 1959, I, 105, l. 6; al-'Aynī, op. cit., I, 63, l. 4 from bottom; al-Majlisī, *Biḥār al-anwār*, Tehran, 1380/1960–1, XVIII, p. 227, n. 6; al-Zurqānī, *Sharḥ*, I, 211, l. 4; Ibn al-Athīr, *al-Kāmil*, Cairo, 1357/1938–9, II, 31; etc. The importance of this expression may be stressed as it is opposed by the expression *fa-ẓanantuhā faj'ata 'l-jinni*. See Abū Nu'aym, *Dalā'il al-nubuwwa*, Hyderabad, 1950, 171, l. 5; al-Suyūṭī, *al-Khaṣā'iṣ al-kubrā*, Hyderabad, 1319/1901–2, I, 96, l. 6 from bottom; *idem*, *al-Durr al-manthūr*, Cairo, 1314/1896–7, VI, 369, l. 6.

[13] According to the tradition of al-Bukhārī the Prophet returned to his wife Khadīja, his heart fluttering, asked her to wrap him up, told her about the revelation, and found comfort in her words. She took him to Waraqa b. Naufal, her cousin, and he assured the Prophet that the revelation had been a true one and that it had been the *Nāmūs* sent down upon Moses. According to a tradition reported on the authority of Mūsā b. 'Uqba and Sulaymān al-Taymī (al-Suyūṭī, *al-Khaṣā'iṣ al-kubrā*, I, 93; al-Zurqānī, *Sharḥ al-mawāhib al-ladunniya*, I, 213; and cf. al-Majlisī, *Biḥār al-anwār*, XVIII, 228) Khadīja went with the Prophet to 'Addās, a servant (*ghulām*) of 'Utba b. Rabī'a. He was a Christian from the people of Niniveh and she asked him about Jibrīl. He shouted *Quddūs, quddūs, quddūs*. He asked her: 'O, Lady of the women of Quraysh, how is Jibrīl mentioned in this country of the worshippers of idols?' She urged him to tell her about Jibrīl and he stated that Jibrīl was the trustee (*amīn*) of Allāh over the Prophets. He is the angel-guardian (*ṣāḥib*) of Mūsā and 'Īsā. And cf. al-Balādhurī, *Ansāb*, I, 111.

According to a version recorded by al-Balādhurī, *Ansāb*, I, 105–6, Khadīja asked Abū Bakr to go with the Prophet to Waraqa. (The tradition is reported on the authority of Ibn Isḥāq—Abū Maysara ['Amr b. Shuraḥbīl al-Hamdānī al-Kūfī—see Ibn Ḥajar, *Tahdhīb*, VIII, 47].) This tradition is reported also by: al-Suhaylī, *al-Rauḍ al-unuf*, Cairo, 1914, I, 157 (on the authority of Yūnus b. Bukayr—Ibn Isḥāq); al-Diyārbakrī, *Ta'rīkh al-Khamīs*, I, 282; al-Ḥalabī, *Insān al-'uyūn*, Cairo, 1354/1935–6, I, 275; Ibn Sayyid al-Nās, *'Uyūn al-athar*, I, 83.

It is evident that this tradition is of importance: it states that the first believer was Abū Bakr.

The differences between the two traditions are crucial: according to the tradition of Ibn Isḥāq the sojourn of Muḥammad on Mt. Ḥirā' was in accordance with the custom of Quraysh to practise *taḥannuth* for a month every year; according to the tradition of al-Bukhārī the Prophet was made to like solitude.[14] Whereas the tradition of Ibn Isḥāq states that he went out with his family,[15] i.e. Khadīja—the tradition of al-Bukhārī maintains that the Prophet went out alone and used to come back at certain intervals[16] in order to get provisions.[17]

(There is even a tradition stating that the Prophet reported his apprehensions in connexion with the summons he heard to Abū Bakr, who was his companion—al-Suyūṭī, *al-Khaṣā'iṣ al-kubrā*, I, 95.)

This tradition stands in opposition to the Shī'ī version that the first believer was 'Alī b. Abī Ṭālib. ' The first who prayed with the Prophet was 'Alī b. Abī Ṭālib ' (al-Majlisī, op. cit., XXXVIII, 202, 203—the chapter '... *annahu sabaqa 'l-nāsa fi 'l-islāmi wa 'l-īmāni*', pp. 201–88; Ibn Shahrāshūb, *Manāqib āl Abī Ṭālib*, Najaf, 1956, I, 288–303; al-Ya'qūbī, *Ta'rīkh*, Najaf, 1964, II, 18–19; al-Karājakī, *Kanz al-fawā'id*, lithograph, 1322/1904–5, 117–28; al-Shaykh al-Ṭūsī, *al-Amālī*, Najaf, 1964, I, 265, 267; and see al-Suyūṭī, *al-La'ālī al-maṣnū'a*, Cairo, al-Maktaba al-Tijāriyya, n.d., I, 322–4). '*I am al-Ṣiddīq al-akbar*,' states 'Alī, ' whoever says it after me is merely a liar or forger; I prayed with the Prophet seven years ' (al-Majlisī, op. cit., XXXVIII, 204). ' When the revelation was sent down on the Prophet he came to the *masjid* and stood up praying; 'Alī passed by the Prophet—and he was nine years old—and the Prophet summoned him: " O, 'Alī, come to me (*aqbil*) " ... ' (ibid., 207). ' I was the first of people who embraced Islam: the Prophet received his call on Monday and I prayed with him on Tuesday; I remained with him praying for seven years till a group embraced Islam ', says 'Alī (ibid., 209—cf. Ibn Sayyid al-Nās, op. cit., I, 92; see al-Nasā'ī, *Khaṣā'iṣ Amīr al-Mu'minīna*, Cairo, 1308/1890–1, 2–3; see the discussion about the first to embrace Islam in al-Tirmidhī's *Ṣaḥīḥ*, Cairo, 1934, XIII, 177; and see Ibn al-Athīr, *Jāmi' al-uṣūl min aḥādīth al-rasūl*, Cairo, 1952, IX, 440, no. 6412; Ibn Abi 'l-Ḥadīd, *Sharḥ nahj al-balāgha*, ed. Muḥammad Abu 'l-Faḍl Ibrāhīm, Cairo, 1959, IV, 116 et seq.); 'Alī states plainly on the minbar of al-Baṣra that he is *al-Ṣiddīq al-akbar*, that he believed before Abū Bakr and embraced Islam before Abū Bakr did (al-Mufīd, *Irshād*, Najaf, 1962, 21).

The tradition in favour of Abū Bakr maintains that he was the first one to embrace Islam (al-Suyūṭī, *Ta'rīkh al-khulafā'*, ed. Muḥammad Muḥyi al-Dīn 'Abd al-Ḥamīd, Cairo, 1952, 33). He even believed in the mission of the Prophet in the time of Baḥīrā, the monk (ibid.). There is, in fact, a tendency towards harmonization: the first *man* who embraced Islam was Abū Bakr; the first *boy* was 'Alī (ibid., 34). The tradition of al-Jāḥiẓ that Abū Bakr was the first to embrace Islam (al-Jāḥiẓ, *al-'Uthmāniyya*, ed. 'Abd al-Salām Hārūn, Cairo, 1955, 3; and see there other versions about the first who embraced Islam: Zayd b. Ḥāritha, Khabbāb b. Aratt; 'Alī is not mentioned) is fiercely denied by al-Iskāfī (ibid., 286 et seq.). Of interest is the tradition recorded by al-Khaṭīb al-Baghdādī, *Mūḍiḥ auhām al-jam' wa 'l-tafrīq*, Hyderabad, 1960, II, 321, on the authority of Maymūn b. Mihrān: ' Abū Bakr believed in the Prophet in the time of Baḥīrā, the monk; Abū Bakr was the match-maker who arranged the Prophet's marriage with Khadīja, and all that before 'Alī was born '. And see the chapter ' *Awwalu 'l-nāsi īmānan bi-'llāhi wa-rasūlihi* ' in Ibn Sayyid al-Nās, '*Uyūn al-athar*, I, 91 et seq.; and 'Abd al-Razzāq, *al-Muṣannaf*, MS Murād Molla, 604, f. 67b inf.; the traditions that 'Alī was the first who embraced Islam are opposed by the tradition of al-Zuhrī that the first was Zayd b. Ḥāritha.

[14] The expression *ḥubbiba ilayhi al-khalā'* etc. is explained by Ibn Ḥazm, *Jawāmi' al-Sīra*, ed. Iḥsān 'Abbās, Nāṣir al-Dīn al-Asad, A. M. Shākir, Cairo, n.d., 44, that nobody did order him to do it, nor did he see anybody do it whom he could imitate; it was merely Allāh who wanted him to do it and he remained there (i.e. in the cave) for days and nights.

[15] See the combined tradition in al-Maqrīzī, *Imtā' al-asmā'*, ed. Maḥmūd Muḥammad Shākir, Cairo, 1941, I, 12, l. 10: *wa-ḥubbiba ilayhi 'l-khalā'u fa-kāna yakhlū bi-ghāri Ḥirā'a kamā kāna yaf'alu dhālika muta'abbidū dhālika 'l-zamāni fa-yuqīmu fīhi 'l-layāliya dhawāti 'l-'adad thumma yarji'u ilā ahlihi fa-yatazawwadu li-mithlihā yataḥannathu bi-Ḥirā'a wa-ma'ahu Khadījatu*. But see the discussion of the contradictory traditions in al-Ḥalabī's *Insān al-'uyūn*, I, 274.

[16] On these periods see e.g. al-Zurqānī, *Sharḥ al-mawāhib*, I, 211.

[17] On the kinds of provisions see al-Ḥalabī, op. cit., I, 271; and see Muṭahhar b. Ṭāhir

Furthermore, the cave where he retired for solitude, according to the tradition of al-Bukhārī, is not mentioned in the tradition recorded by Ibn Isḥāq. The information about the feeding of the poor is missing in the tradition of al-Bukhārī. Consequently other differences occur stemming from the fundamental divergences between the two traditions: according to the tradition of Ibn Isḥāq, Khadīja sent messengers to look for the Prophet: they went out and reached the upper part of Mecca in their search for the Prophet. They were, of course, sent by Khadīja from the mountain of Ḥirā' where they both sojourned. After the talk of Khadīja with the Prophet she descended from the mountain, went to Waraqa, and told him the story of the Call to Prophecy. According to the tradition recorded by al-Bukhārī, the Prophet sojourned in solitude in the cave and went to Khadīja at Mecca after receiving the Call, and she went with him to Waraqa.

II

The explanation of the word *taḥannuth* is differently given in the two traditions. In the tradition of Ibn Isḥāq it is glossed by *tabarrur*; in the tradition of al-Bukhārī it is glossed by *ta'abbud*.[18] Ibn Hishām replaces it by *taḥannuf*, i.e. professing the Ḥanīfiyya, performing the actions of a Ḥanīf.[19] There are other traditions in which the expression *tanassaka* is mentioned instead of *taḥannatha*.[20] Al-Balādhurī in his report about the revelation, recorded on the authority of 'Ā'isha,[21] glosses *taḥannuth* as *al-ta'abbud wa 'l-tabarrur*. It is evident that al-Balādhurī referred to the glosses of the two different traditions.[22]

al-Maqdisī, *al-Bad' wa'l-ta'rīkh*, ed. Huart, IV, 141: he sojourned at Ḥirā' with provisions of dates and milk feeding people.

[18] According to Ibn Ḥajar, *Fatḥ al-bārī*, Cairo, 1348/1929–30, I, 18, the word *taḥannuth* was glossed *ta'abbud* by al-Zuhrī.

[19] Abū Dharr considers this explanation as unnecessary. See his commentary, Brönnle, Cairo, 1911, 75.

[20] Al-Dhahabī, *Ta'rīkh al-Islām*, I, 74: *wa-kāna yakhruju ilā Ḥirā'a fī kulli 'āmin shahran min al-sanati yansuku fīhi*; Ibn Kathīr, *al-Sīra al-nabawiyya*, ed. Muṣṭafā 'Abd al-Wāḥid, Cairo, 1964, I, 390: *wa-kāna yakhruju ilā Ḥirā'a fī kulli 'āmin shahran min al-sanati yatanassaku fīhi, wa-kāna min nusuk Qurayshin fi 'l-jāhiliyyati, yuṭ'imu man jā'ahu min al-masākīn*. This expression is used as well in the MS of the *Sīra* in the Qarawīyūn library at Fez, no. 727, as mentioned by A. Guillaume, *New light on the life of Muhammad* (*Journal of Semitic Studies*. Monograph No. 1), [1960], p. 29, ll. 5–7: 'The word used of Muḥammad's devotions, is *nasak*, and it is said that members of Quraysh who practised such devotions in the pagan era used to feed any of the poor who came to them'. And see al-Suyūṭī, *al-Khaṣā'iṣ al-kubrā*, I, 94, *kāna rasūlu 'llāhi ṣallā 'llāhu 'alayhi wa-sallama yakhruju ilā Ḥirā'a fī kulli 'āmin shahran min al-sanati yatanassaku fīhi* . . . (but feeding the poor is not mentioned here).

[21] *Ansāb al-ashrāf*, ed. Muḥammad Ḥamīdullāh, Cairo, 1959, I, 105, no. 191: . . . *fa-yataḥannathu fīhi wa-yamkuthu al-layāliya qabla an* . . .; in the *Ṣaḥīḥ* of Muslim, Cairo, 1334/1915–16, I, 97, . . . *al-layāliya ulāt al-'adad*; the *Tafsīr* of al-Ṭabarī, Būlāq, 1329/1911, XXX, 161, and the *Muṣannaf* of 'Abd al-Razzāq, MS Murād Molla, 604, f. 67a, inf., have (like al-Bukhārī) *dhawāt al-'adad*. A version recorded by 'Abd al-Razzāq deserves mention: the Prophet started to practise *taḥannuth* and he was made to like solitude after some of his daughters were born (*wa-ṭafiqa rasūlu 'llāhi ṣallā 'llahu 'alayhi wa-sallama ba'da mā wulidat lahu ba'ḍu banātihi yataḥannathu wa-ḥubbiba ilayhi 'l-khalā'u*—op. cit., f. 67a, l. 6 from bottom).

[22] Ibn Sa'd, *Ṭabaqāt*, Beirut, 1960, I, 194, records a tradition on the authority of 'Ā'isha, but does not, however, gloss the term *taḥannuth*.

The obscure expression *taḥannuth* caused some difficulties to the philologists, lexicographers, and commentators of *ḥadīth*. The famous scholars Ibn al-A'rābī and Ibn 'Amr al-Shaybānī stated that they did not know the expression *taḥannuth*.[23] The explanation commonly given was that *taḥannuth* means 'to remove sin (*ḥinth*) from oneself'; some other examples of similar verbs having the form *tafa''ala* with a cognate are quoted (*ta'aththama, taḥarraja, taḥawwaba*).[24]

In the tradition of al-Bukhārī *taḥannuth* is glossed by *ta'abbud*. *Ta'abbud* has a wide range of meanings and commentators are at pains to define the *ta'abbud* of the Prophet. Al-Qasṭallānī states that the Prophet performed three devotional practices (*'ibādāt*): seclusion (*khalwa*), *taḥannuth*, and the watching of the Ka'ba (*al-naẓar ila 'l-Ka'ba*). Comparing the expression in the tradition of Ibn Isḥāq, *ya'takifu shahra Ramaḍāna*, in which there is no clear definition of the kind of *ta'abbud*, with the expression of the tradition of 'Ā'isha, al-Qasṭallānī remarks that 'Ā'isha assigned the idea of *ta'abbud* exclusively (*bi-mujarradihā*) to seclusion because withdrawal from people, and especially people living in falsehood (*man kāna 'alā bāṭilin*), is a kind of *'ibāda*. Finally al-Qasṭallānī quotes an anonymous opinion that the *ta'abbud* of the Prophet was meditation (*tafakkur*).[25]

The discussion of the term in al-Qasṭallānī's *Irshād* does not add much to our understanding of the meaning of the expression. *Taḥannuth* is identified with *ta'abbud*; *ta'abbud* is identified with *khalwa*, which was, however, the cause or means of *ta'abbud*. Further, *taḥannuth* is stated to be one of the three *'ibādāt*, and lastly *ta'abbud* is stated to be contemplation.

The mention of the word *i'takafa* in connexion with *taḥannuth* does not, by itself, lend more definition to the obscure expression *taḥannuth*. It is noteworthy that the expression *i'takafa* is used for *taḥannatha* in the traditions recorded by Abū Nu'aym [26] and al-Suyūṭī,[27] stating that the Prophet vowed to sojourn with Khadīja for a month at Ḥirā'.

The identification of *ta'abbud* with *taḥannuth* raised consequently the question of the religious basis of this devotion, the *ta'abbud* of the Prophet.

[23] Al-Kirmānī, *Sharḥ Ṣaḥīḥ al-Bukhārī*, Cairo, 1932, I, 32; Abū 'Amr read the word *yataḥannafu* (ibid.); al-'Aynī, '*Umdat al-qārī*', I, 58.

[24] Rāghib al-Iṣfahānī, *al-Mufradāt*, Cairo, 1324/1906–7, 132, s.v. *ḥnth*; Ibn Ḥajar, *Fatḥ al-bārī*, I, 18; al-Kirmānī, op. cit., I, 32; al-Zarkashī, *Sharḥ Ṣaḥīḥ al-Bukhārī*, I, 6; al-Zamakhsharī, *al-Fā'iq*, ed. al-Bajāwī and Abu 'l-Faḍl Ibrāhīm, Cairo, 1945, I, 250; Ibn al-Athīr, *al-Nihāya*, s.v. *ḥnth*; *L'A* and *T'A*, s.v. *ḥnth*. It is noteworthy that beside the definition 'removing sin from oneself, keeping away from sin' there is also a definition 'acting so (*yaf'alu fi'lan*) as to cause sin to be removed' (*al-Nihāya*, *T'A*, *L'A*, etc.). And see al-'Aynī, '*Umdat al-qārī*', I, 58. (*Taḥannatha* means as well 'to commit a sin' and belongs to the *aḍdād*. See Ibn al-Dahhān al-Naḥwī, '*al-Aḍdād*', in *Nafā'is al-makhṭūṭāt*, ed. Muḥammad Ḥasan Āl Yāsīn, Baghdād, 1964, 96; and see al-Zurqānī, *Sharḥ al-mawāhib*, I, 210, l. 20.)

[25] Al-Qasṭallānī, *Irshād al-sārī*, Cairo, 1326/1908–9, I, 172; and see Ibn Ẓahīra, *al-Jāmi' al-laṭīf fī faḍli Makkata wa-ahlihā wa-binā'i 'l-bayti 'l-sharīf*, Cairo, 1921, 342.

[26] Abū Nu'aym, *Dalā'il al-nubuwwa*, 171, l. 3, *anna rasūla 'llāhi nadhara an ya'takifa shahran huwa wa-Khadījatu bi-Ḥirā'a*.

[27] Al-Suyūṭī, *al-Durr al-manthūr*, VI, 369, l. 5.

Opinions varied about whether the *taʿabbud* was according to the *sharīʿa* of Ibrāhīm or Mūsā or ʿĪsā or Nūḥ or Ādam or according to the *sharīʿa* of some of his predecessors, or whether he did or did not follow before his Call any other *sharīʿa*.[28]

On the form of his *taʿabbud* at Ḥirāʾ, Sirāj al-Bulqaynī could plainly state that the manner of the *taʿabbud* was not specified in the traditions which he had perused.[29]

III

Modern scholars have been divided in their opinions as to the origin of the term *taḥannuth* and its meaning, and have reached a number of divergent conclusions.

Sprenger collected a good deal of material about the beginning of the revelation [30] and took great pains to analyse the various traditions. He considered *taḥannuth* as a ' Kraftausdruck ' repeated by the men of *ḥadīth* in almost all versions of this tradition. ' Ein unverdaulicher Ausdruck ' sums up Sprenger's view of the word.[31] He based his opinion about the character of the sojourn of the Prophet on Mt. Ḥirāʾ on a passage of Balʿamī's translation of al-Ṭabarī. Sprenger refutes the possibility of devotional practices of the Meccans at Ḥirāʾ as incompatible with the spirit of the Jāhiliyya and supposes that Ḥirāʾ served as a summer resort for these Meccans who could not afford to spend the summer in al-Ṭāʾif or Wādi ʾl-Qurā. Muḥammad dwelt in the hot month of Ramaḍān in a cave at Ḥirāʾ. One may imagine—continues Sprenger—that he might have pitched a tent in front of the cave ; of course, he could not find there a place for his wife and children : the cave was too small.[32]

Nöldeke rendered *taḥannuth* by ' living a solitary life '.[33] Pautz—quoting the tradition of Ibn Isḥāq with the gloss *tabarrur*—renders it by ' Andachtsübungen '.[34]

Grimme renders the gloss of Ibn Isḥāq, *al-tabarrur*, by ' fromm sein '. He also records the gloss of Ibn Hishām, *taḥannuf*, explaining it by ' sich für sündig halten ' and follows it by a question mark. Quoting the gloss *taʿabbud*

[28] See al-Zurqānī, *Sharḥ al-mawāhib*, I, 210 ; al-Jāḥiẓ, *al-ʿUthmāniyya*, 305, ult. (al-Iskāfī) ; al-Māwardī, *Aʿlām al-nubuwwa*, Cairo, 1935, 173–4 ; al-ʿAynī, ʿ*Umdat al-qāri*ʾ, I, 72.

[29] Al-Ḥalabī, *Insān al-ʿuyūn*, I, 271 ; on al-Sirāj al-Bulqaynī see al-Samʿānī, *Ansāb*, II, p. 317, n. 7.

[30] A. Sprenger, *Das Leben und die Lehre des Moḥammad, zweite Auflage*, I, 330–49.

[31] ibid., 330 : ' In Traditionen kommen nicht selten Kraftausdrücke und obsolete Worte vor, und diese werden gewöhnlich in allen, dem Sinne nach auch so verschiedenen Versionen einer und derselben Erzählung festgehalten : die Kraftausdrücke, weil sie den Ueberlieferern gefielen, die obsoleten, unverständlichen Worte, weil sie sie nicht verdauen konnten und darunter etwas mysteriöses suchten, und auch weil sie sich darauf etwas einbildeten, mit solchen gelehrten Brocken um sich werfen zu können. Ein solcher unverdaulicher Ausdruck ist in dieser Tradition taḥannoth '.

[32] ibid., 295–6.

[33] Th. Nöldeke, *Geschichte des Qorans, bearbeitet von F. Schwally*, Leipzig, 1909, I, 84 : ' . . . als er noch in den Bergen ein einsames Leben führte (*taḥannatha*) '.

[34] O. Pautz, *Muhammeds Lehre von der Offenbarung*, Leipzig, 1898, 16 ; and see ibid., 17, ' *yataḥannathu*, " andächtig war " '.

of the tradition of al-Bukhārī he asks whether it did not mean a kind of service at the temple ('eine Art Tempeldienst') like the later *Mujāwir*.[35]

Tor Andrae renders *taḥannuth* (like Pautz), by 'einsame Andachtsübungen' and finds similarity between these practices and the practices of Syrian Christianity.[36]

Buhl does not differ from Andrae in his rendering of the expression.[37] He defines it, however, more precisely: 'eine asketische Observanz, die die Mekkaner im Monat Ramaḍān auf dem Berge Ḥirā' vollzogen haben und die im Fasten und sexueller Enthaltsamkeit bestand'.[38]

Hirschfeld suggests that *taḥannuth* is nothing but the Hebrew *teḥinnoth* 'prayers', a word very common among the Jews to express voluntary devotions apart from official liturgy. 'There is little doubt', says Hirschfeld, 'that Muḥammad heard this word often in Medina before he framed his report of the affair and employed it readily on account of its strange and sacred character.'[39]

Lyall accepts Hirschfeld's suggestion about the Hebrew origin of the word *taḥannuth*, rejects the connexion between *taḥannuf* and *taḥannuth*, and thinks that 'the proposal to take *taḥannuth* as a private formation, doing that by which a sin is expelled, appears to be unnecessary'.[40]

Caetani is inclined to accept Hirschfeld's suggestion; he remarks, however, that it may be a more modern expression used in the legendary story about the Call to Prophecy in the second part of the first century of the Hijra, although it cannot be excluded that the word was known in the time of Muḥammad in Mecca and might denote retirement into solitude and prayer.[41]

W. M. Watt gives a compound version of the views quoted. He suggests that Muḥammad's going to Ḥirā' 'might be a method of escaping from the heat of Mecca in an unpleasant season for those who could not afford to go to al-Ṭā'if'[42]: 'Judaeo-Christian influence, such as the example of monks, or a little personal experience', continues Watt, 'would show the need and desirability of solitude'.[43] 'The precise meaning and derivation of *taḥannuth*', says Watt, 'is uncertain, though it is evidently some sort of devotional practice. The best suggestion is perhaps that of H. Hirschfeld, that it comes from the Hebrew *teḥinnot* or *teḥinnoth*, meaning prayers for God's favour. The meaning may have been influenced by the Arabic root, however. *Ḥinth* is properly the

[35] H. Grimme, *Mohammed*, Münster, 1892, I, p. 10, n. 1.

[36] Tor Andrae, *Mohammed, sein Leben und Glaube*, Göttingen, 1932, 34–5.

[37] F. Buhl, *Das Leben Muhammeds*, 134: 'um sich Andachtsübungen hinzugeben ...'; see ibid., p. 68, n. 167.

[38] ibid., p. 88, n. 244.

[39] H. Hirschfeld, *New researches into the composition and exegesis of the Qoran*, London, 1902, 19.

[40] Ch. J. Lyall, 'The words Ḥanīf and Muslim', *JRAS*, 1903, 780.

[41] L. Caetani, *Annali dell Islam*, Milano, 1905, I, 222, 'Introduzione', § 208, n. 2.

[42] W. M. Watt, *Muhammad at Mecca*, London, 1953, 44: this opinion of Watt's is reminiscent of the proposition of Sprenger mentioned above, which is not, however, referred to by Watt.

[43] op. cit., 44. There seems to be some connexion between the proposition of Tor Andrae and the opinion of Watt; Tor Andrae is not mentioned.

violation of or failure to perform an oath, and so more generally sin; and *taḥannuth* is accordingly said to mean "doing some work so as to escape from sin or crime". The use of the word *taḥannuth* here is probably a mark that the material is old and in this respect genuine.'[44]

In his article '*Ḥanīf*' Watt repeats the assertion that *taḥannuth* is almost certainly from Hebrew and means devotional exercises.[45]

Bell remarks that *taḥannuth* is explained as meaning 'worship'. The real meaning of the word, says Bell, is uncertain, but is probably something like 'bewailing of sin'.[46] Bell, doubting the truth of the story, argues as follows: 'That *taḥannuth* was a Quraish practice may well be doubted, because of the character of the Meccans as depicted in the Koran, the absence of any record of such a practice in pre-Islamic Arabia, and the fact that the Koran makes no reference to any such practice. In fact, the ascetic note in such a practice was entirely alien to Mohammed's nature, and the accompanying fasts, so often imaginatively decked out even by Western scholars, as predisposing the future prophet to seeing visions at this stage, have no support whatever in the early parts of the Koran. Fasting was not introduced until the Medinan period, and then as an imitation of Jewish practice. . . . The whole story is the invention of a later age. It is founded probably on Christian ascetic practice'.[47]

Chelhod, stressing the ambivalence of the root *ḥnf*, compares it with *ḥnth*, remarking that it is probable that *ḥnth* is derived from *ḥnf*. The meaning of *ḥinth* is perjury; *taḥannuth* means refusal ('rejet') of paganism.[48]

None of the opinions about the meaning of *taḥannuth* quoted above seems entirely satisfactory. Sprenger's proposition about Ḥirā' as 'summer resort' for the Prophet was rejected by Caetani, who considered the whole story of little historical value.[49]

The opinion of Nöldeke about Muḥammad's life of solitude in the mountains fits the tradition of al-Bukhārī and corresponds to the idea of *khalā'*, seclusion; *khalā'* cannot, however, be rendered by *taḥannuth*. Neither does it agree with the tradition of Ibn Isḥāq, where it is explicitly stated that the Prophet went out to Ḥirā' with his family.

Fasting—as assumed by Buhl—cannot be accepted; sources do not mention fasting by the Prophet at Ḥirā' at all.[50] Further: the tradition of al-Bukhārī on which Buhl relied states explicitly that the Prophet used to come back in order to take provisions for his sojourn. According to the tradition of Ibn Isḥāq the Prophet went out to Ḥirā' with Khadīja and thus the idea of sexual abstention seems to be excluded.

[44] op. cit., 44; Watt quotes in a note the contrasting opinion of Caetani.

[45] *EI*, second ed., s.v. *ḥanīf*.

[46] R. Bell, 'Mohammed's Call', *Moslem World*, XXIV, 1, 1934, p. 13, n. 1.

[47] ibid., 16; and see *idem, Introduction to the Qur'an*, Edinburgh, 1953, 104–5: 'it was apparently some sort of pious exercise expressing repentance or doing penance for sin'.

[48] J. Chelhod, *Introduction à la sociologie de l'Islam*, Paris, 1958, 137.

[49] Caetani, op. cit., 'Introduzione', § 208, n. 1.

[50] See Bell, art. cit., 16 (quoted in n. 46 above).

Hirschfeld's assumption about the derivation of the word *taḥannuth* from the Hebrew *teḥinnoth* was convincingly refuted by Goitein: this Hebrew word, states Goitein, was used in that technical sense only in far later times.[51]

Grimme's rendering for *taḥannuth*, 'sich sündig halten', is not based on lexicographical grounds. *Ta'abbud* here cannot be connected with the later *mujāwir*, denoting 'service at the Temple'.

Whether the Prophet was influenced by Christian monks as suggested by Andrae or whether his 'crise mystique' was influenced by the *ḥunafā'* as assumed by Blachère [52] cannot be discussed here.[53]

It is doubtful whether *yujāwiru* can be translated 'to pray in seclusion', as was rendered by Guillaume,[54] or whether *tabarrur* may be rendered by 'religious devotion'.[55]

Bell's assertion about the 'absence of any record of such a practice in pre-Islamic Arabia' is not accurate: there are some records of such *taḥannuth*. His opinion about the character of Quraysh cannot be discussed within the limits of the present article. The question of whether ascetic practices were alien to the Prophet or not may be preceded by a discussion of the question of whether *taḥannuth* is an ascetic practice.

IV

The expression *taḥannuth* occurs not only in the tradition about the Call of the Prophet. Stories in which this expression appears may be quoted here.

There is a significant tradition reported by Muḥammad b. Ḥabīb about an alliance made between a leader of al-Ḥārith b. 'Abd Manāt b. Kināna, a tribal group which entered the federation of the Aḥābīsh [56] and a clan of Quraysh. The leader, Khālid b. al-Ḥārith b. 'Ubayd b. Taym b. 'Amr b. al-Ḥārith b. Mabdhūl b. al-Ḥārith b. 'Abd Manāt b. Kināna, came to Mecca. Every clan of Quraysh was eager to get him as its ally. Every clan invited him to be its guest or offered to give him one of its daughters in marriage. Khālid did not want to give preference to any one of those clans. He asked for a delay of three days and 'he went out to Ḥirā' and practised *ta'abbud* three nights on the top of the mountain and went down'. He decided to be an ally of the (clan of the) first man whom he would meet. The first man was 'Abd 'Auf b. 'Abd al-Ḥārith b. Zuhra b. Kilāb. He tied his garment with the garments of 'Abd 'Auf, took his hand, and they continued until they entered the *masjid*

[51] S. D. Goitein, *Studies in Islamic history and institutions*, Leiden, 1966, p. 93, n. 2.

[52] R. Blachère, *Le problème de Mahomet*, Paris, 1952, 37.

[53] See H. A. R. Gibb, 'Pre-Islamic monotheism in Arabia', *Harvard Theological Review*, LV, 4, 1962, 269–80.

[54] A. Guillaume (tr.), *The life of Muhammed*, 105.

[55] ibid.

[56] See Muḥammad b. Ḥabīb, *al-Muḥabbar*, ed. Ilse Lichtenstaedter, Hyderabad, 1942, 178 (al-Ḥārith b. 'Abd Manāt b. Kināna were included in the organization of the Ḥums), 267; al-Balādhurī, *Ansāb al-ashrāf*, MS, f. 959a; Ibn al-Kalbī, *Jamharat al-nasab*, MS, f. 48b et seq.; W. Caskel, *Ǧamharat an-nasab*, Leiden, 1966, II, 145; Watt, *Muhammed at Mecca*, 154 et seq.; al-'Iṣāmī, *Simṭ al-nujūm al-'awālī*, Cairo, 1380/1960–1, I, 192 inf.

al-ḥarām (i.e. the Ka'ba—K); they stood at the House and the alliance was accomplished.[57]

The expression occurring in this tradition is *ta'abbada*. It is exactly the expression used for glossing the word *taḥannuth* in some of the traditions of the Call to Prophecy. The setting in which *ta'abbud* takes place in this tradition deserves to be stressed. *Ta'abbud* is practised before making an important decision and is followed by a solemn ceremony at the Ka'ba. It seems to be quite clear that the expression *ta'abbada* in this tradition corresponds to the expression *taḥannatha* in the tradition of the Call to Prophecy and in the traditions about the practices of Quraysh mentioned below. In these traditions the *taḥannuth* is followed by a circumambulation of the Ka'ba several times before the *mutaḥannith* returns to his home.

Several traditions about the Ḥanīf Zayd b. 'Amr b. Nufayl are connected with Ḥirā'; in some of them *taḥannuth* or a similar expression occurs. Ibn Isḥāq reports that Zayd was expelled from Mecca and sojourned at Ḥirā'.[58] Al-Balādhurī records that Zayd 'pitched a tent at Ḥirā' practising in it *taḥannuth*. He withdrew from Quraysh and they named him *al-Rāhib*. He died and was buried inside Mt. Ḥirā''.[59] Ibn Ḥabīb reports about him that he practised *taḥannuf* at Ḥirā'.[60] This tradition seems to have been recorded with a significant variant: *kāna yakhruju li 'l-taḥawwub* (or *li 'l-taḥayyub*). *Taḥawwub* is glossed by *al-ta'abbud wa 'l-tajannub li 'l-ma'tham* (*ta'abbud* and refraining from sin).[61]

The first man who practised *taḥannuth* at Ḥirā' is said to have been 'Abd al-Muṭṭalib. A tradition with the *isnād* al-Wāqidī—'Abdullāh b. Ja'far—Makhrama b. Naufal—al-Zuhrī relates that 'he was the first who practised *taḥannuth* at Ḥirā'. (*Taḥannuth*, says the gloss, is *ta'alluh* and *tabarrur*.) When the moon of Ramaḍān appeared he used to enter Ḥirā' and did not leave till the end of the month and fed the poor. He was distressed by the iniquity of the people of Mecca and would perform circumambulation of the Ka'ba many times'.[62]

A tradition recorded by al-Balādhurī gives some information about

[57] Muḥammad b. Ḥabīb, *al-Munammaq*, ed. Khursheed Aḥmad Fāriq, Hyderabad, 1964, 288: *fa-kharaja ilā Ḥirā'a fa-ta'abbada tilka 'l-thalātha fī ra'sihi thumma nazala.*

[58] Ibn Hishām, *al-Sīra*, I, 246; al-Kalā'ī, *al-Iktifā'*, ed. H. Massé, Alger-Paris, 1931, I, 320; Ibn 'Asākir, *Tahdhīb ta'rīkh*, VI, 29, l. 9; Ibn Kathīr, *al-Sīra al-nabawiyya*, I, 154–5 (but the words *fa-nazala Ḥirā'a* are omitted); and see Ibn 'Asākir, op. cit., VI, 34; Ibn Kathīr, op. cit., I, 162; al-Suyūṭī, *al-Khaṣā'iṣ al-kubrā*, I, 24, l. 3 from bottom; al-Dhahabī, *Siyar a'lām al-nubalā'*, ed. Ṣalāḥ al-Dīn al-Munajjid, Cairo, 1956, I, 86, 90.

[59] Al-Balādhurī, *Ansāb al-ashrāf*, MS, f. 867b; and see Ibn Sa'd, *Ṭabaqāt*, Beirut, 1957, III, 381: he was buried inside Ḥirā'.

[60] *Al-Munammaq*, 532, l. 3.

[61] Abū 'Ubayd, *Gharīb al-ḥadīth*, ed. M. 'Abd al-Mu'īd Khān, Hyderabad, 1965, II, 21; and see the explanation of *taḥawwub* on the authority of Abū 'Ubayd in *L'A*, s.v. *ḥwb*, where the story of Zayd b. 'Amr is not, however, recorded.

[62] Al-Balādhurī, *Ansāb*, I, 84; see Daḥlān, *Sīra*, I, 20 sup. (on margin of the *Sīra Ḥalabiyya*); al-Zurqānī, *Sharḥ al-mawāhib*, I, 71: ... *idhā dakhala shahru ramaḍāna ṣa'idahu wa-aṭ'ama 'l-masākīna* ....

Qurashites who practised *taḥannuth* at Ḥirā' (the *isnād* is: Muḥammad b. Sa'd—al-Wāqidī—Talḥa b. 'Amr—Ibn 'Abbās): 'When the month of Ramaḍān began people of Quraysh—these intending *taḥannuth*—used to leave for Ḥirā' and stayed there a month and fed the poor who called on them. When they saw the moon of Shawwāl they (descended and) did not enter their homes until they had performed the circumambulation of the Ka'ba for a week. The Prophet used to perform it (i.e. this custom)'.[63]

It is noteworthy that in both these traditions about *taḥannuth* at Ḥirā', the one about 'Abd al-Muṭṭalib and the one about the people of Quraysh, two elements are emphasized: the feeding of the poor and the ritual practices of the circumambulation of the Ka'ba, a token of the veneration of the House. These are exactly the elements of *taḥannuth* as related in the tradition of Ibn Isḥāq about the Call of Prophecy.

A group of traditions about *taḥannuth* is connected with the person of Ḥakīm b. Ḥizām and refers to his deeds in the period before he embraced Islam. A tradition (with the *isnād* al-Zuhrī—'Urwa b. al-Zubayr—Ḥakīm b. Ḥizām) runs as follows: 'Ḥakīm b. Ḥizām asked the Prophet: What is your opinion about things which I used to do, practising thus *taḥannuth* (*a-ra'ayta umūran kuntu ataḥannathu bihā*) in the period of the Jāhiliyya, viz. doing good to my people, freeing slaves and giving alms; shall I be rewarded for it? The Prophet answered: You embraced Islam having the credit of the good (deeds of your) past'.[64]

In another tradition recorded on the authority of Ḥakīm b. Ḥizām, Ḥakīm says about himself: 'I was a man of good luck in trade. I never bought a thing without gaining profit (scil. in selling). Quraysh used to send their merchandise and I used to send my merchandise (scil. separately). It happened sometimes that a man from among them (i.e. the Quraysh) asked me to allow him to share with me in his expenditures (scil. concerning the merchandise), aiming by it (scil. to benefit from) the good luck in (the profit of) my merchandise (I refused—K) and that (was) because of this, viz. whatever I got of profit I used to spend (*taḥannathtu bihi*) it (partly?) or wholly, intending by that (deed) the increase of wealth and (increase of) friendship (*al-maḥabba*) in the clan'.[65]

[63] Al-Balādhurī, *Ansāb*, I, 105.

[64] Al-Bukhārī, *al-Adab al-mufrad*, ed. Muḥibb al-Dīn al-Khaṭīb, Cairo, 1379/1959–60, p. 38, no. 70, under the heading *Bāb man waṣala raḥimahu fī 'l-jāhiliyyati thumma aslama* (and see the references given by the editor); al-Zubayr b. Bakkār, *Jamharat nasab Quraysh*, ed. Maḥmūd Muḥ. Shākir, Cairo, 1381/1961–2, I, 362, no. 637 (see the parallels recorded by the editor); *L'A*, *T'A*, and Ibn al-Athīr, *Nihāya*, s.v. *ḥnth*, with a comment *ay ataqarrabu ila 'llāhi ta'ālā bi-af'ālin fī 'l-jāhiliyyati*; al-Nabulusī, *Dhakhā'ir al-mawārīth*, Cairo, 1934, I, 198, no. 1790; and see Abū 'Awāna, *Musnad*, Hyderabad, 1362/1943, I, 72–3 (*taḥannuth* is glossed by *ta'abbud*, p. 72); in a variant of this tradition Ḥakīm, assured by the Prophet that he would receive the reward for his *taḥannuth* in the period of the Jāhiliyya, promises to do as a Muslim these deeds which he did as a pagan. These deeds in the Jāhiliyya are explained as freeing 100 slaves and driving 100 victims for sacrifice at Mecca (scil. to feed the people; another version, ibid.: and providing 100 men with camels).

[65] Al-Zubayr b. Bakkār, op. cit., I, 371, no. 645.

In a very similar passage Ḥakīm states: 'I used to make many profits and I used to distribute them among the poor of my people—and we did not worship anything (*wa-naḥnu lā na'budu shay'an*)—intending the (increase of) wealth and friendship in the clan'.[66] In this tradition the word *taḥannatha* is missing. But the phrase *fa-a'ūdu 'alā fuqarā'i qaumī* explains the action of *taḥannuth* and the motive of the deed is given in an explanatory phrase: *kuntu u'āliju 'l-birra fī 'l-jāhiliyyati* 'I used to perform good deeds towards kinsmen in the Jāhiliyya'.

It is evident that the expression *taḥannatha* in the traditions of Ḥakīm b. Ḥizām denotes good deeds towards poor kinsmen, freeing of slaves, giving alms to the needy and poor. That is plainly indicated in the tradition of al-Bukhārī on the authority of Ḥakīm b. Ḥizām: the word *ataḥannathu* is followed by an explicative phrase: *min ṣilatin wa-'atāqatin wa-ṣadaqatin*. *Taḥannuth* here is identical with the term *birr*. This is indeed confirmed by another version of this tradition; *L'A* s.v. *brr* records the tradition as follows: *a-ra'ayta umūran kuntu abrartuhā*. This expression is glossed: *ay aṭlubu biha 'l-birra wa 'l-iḥsāna ila 'l-nāsi wa 'l-taqarruba ila 'llāhi ta'ālā*. The first part of this gloss is accurate; but the second part, *wa 'l-taqarruba ila 'llāhi ta'ālā*, is a Muslim interpretation of a Jāhiliyya tradition.

The sentence inserted in the tradition of Ḥakīm quoted above, *wa-naḥnu lā na'budu shay'an*, is significant. It indicates that his *birr*, or his *taḥannuth*, was not connected with ritual practices. A line is thus drawn between the *taḥannuth* of Ḥakīm b. Ḥizām, consisting of good deeds, and the *taḥannuth* of the leader of al-Ḥārith b. 'Abd Manāt of Kināna, Zayd b. 'Amr, and the *taḥannuth* of the Prophet according to the tradition of the Call as recorded by al-Bukhārī in which only the *ta'abbud* is mentioned. The *taḥannuth* of 'Abd al-Muṭṭalib, the *taḥannuth* of some groups of Quraysh, and the *taḥannuth* of the Prophet according to the tradition of Ibn Isḥāq included two elements: *ta'abbud* and *tabarrur*. It consisted in feeding the poor and in the practice of veneration at the Ka'ba.

The traditions about Ḥakīm b. Ḥizām are apparently very early ones and the expression *taḥannuth* in these traditions is, no doubt, original. The argument of Sprenger[67] that the tradition is forged ('gewiss unecht') and fairly late ('ziemlich neu') is unfounded. If there were any doubt about the usage of the term *taḥannuth* in the tradition of the talk of Ḥakīm with the Prophet, the expression *taḥannuth* is evidently genuine in the story of his deeds towards his kinsmen. Here there was no need to put in the word *taḥannatha*.

There is also no reason to entertain doubts about the genuineness of the expression *taḥannuth* in the traditions about the practices of Quraysh at Ḥirā'. The feeding of the poor at Ḥirā' in the month of Ramaḍān belonged to the category of *birr*. The identity of *taḥannuth* with *birr* is plainly seen in a state-

[66] Al-Zubayr b. Bakkār, op. cit., I, 367, no. 644; and see Ibn 'Asākir, *Tahdhīb ta'rīkh*, IV, 414; al-Dhahabī, *Siyar a'lām al-nubalā'*, ed. As'ad Ṭalas, Cairo, 1962, III, 32, l. 1–2.

[67] Sprenger, op. cit., I, 331, ll. 16–20.

ment of Muṭahhar b. Ṭāhir where it is also seen that this was the Prophet's only purpose in practising *taḥannuth*: *wa-kāna Qurayshun yataḥannathūna bi-Ḥirā' fī Ramaḍāna wa-kāna rasūlu 'llāhi yaf'alu dhālika li-annahu min al-birri* 'Quraysh used to practise *taḥannuth* during the month of Ramaḍān and the Prophet did it because it was a kind of good deed towards his fellow men (*birr*)'.[68] The meaning attached to *taḥannatha* here fully corresponds to the meaning of the traditions of Ḥakīm, as pointed out above, and to the meaning of the tradition of the Call to Prophecy in the *Sīra* of Ibn Isḥāq. Muḥammad's reinterpretation and revaluation of this simple meaning of the Jāhilī term of *birr* were fully explained by H. A. R. Gibb: 'In its secular use the root (i.e. *birr*) indicates the paternal and filial relation, with its attitudes of affection, obedience and loyalty. To Muḥammad, as to all other prophetic teachers, the test of true belief lay in character and works. If the repeated insistence of the Koran upon good works were not enough, it would be conclusively proved by the comprehensive definition of *birr* in the noble verse Sūra 2, 172: not only belief in God, the Last Day, the angels, the Scripture and the prophets, but charity to all for the love of God, steadfastness in prayers, loyalty to the plighted word, and patience under all afflictions—these are the qualities that mark out the truly believing and the truly God-fearing. *Birr* is thus the crown of true belief, when the believer at last realizes and responds to the ever-presence of God in all his thoughts and conduct'.[69] In the light of this passage we can understand the essential changes in the Muslim interpretation of *birr* and consequently in the meaning of *taḥannuth* which is identical with *birr*. In the tradition of Ibn Isḥāq about the Call it denotes thus merely good deeds, charity and giving alms to the poor.

A crucial question which remains to be answered is that of the sojourn on Mt. Ḥirā'. Why did these groups of Quraysh who practised *taḥannuth* perform it there? The answer can be gauged from the traditions quoted above including variants of *taḥannuth*. Ḥirā' was a *mansik*, a place of ritual practices of some groups of Quraysh; these practices were apparently connected with the veneration of the Ka'ba. This assumption is confirmed by such terms as *tanassaka, jāwara, i'takafa, ta'abbada*, and the significant sentence in all the traditions (except these of Ḥakīm) about the numerous circumambulations of the Ka'ba. The word *ta'abbada* in the tradition of Khālid b. al-Ḥārith of the 'Abd Manāt of Kināna indicates various practices (probably austerities, hardships, and perhaps some good deeds) connected with the cult of the Ka'ba. This assumption is further confirmed by an interesting interpretation recorded by al-Ḥalabī: 'The Prophet used to sojourn (scil. on Mt. Ḥirā') feeding the

[68] *Al-Bad' wa 'l-ta'rīkh*, ed. Huart, IV, 141.

[69] H. A. R. Gibb: *Studies on the civilization of Islam*, ed. S. J. Shaw and W. R. Polk, Boston, 1962, 191–2; and see the significant traditions about a peculiar kind of *birr* of the Jāhiliyya versus *tuqā* of Islam: Ibn Qutayba, *Tafsīr gharīb al-Qur'ān*, ed. Aḥmad Saqr, Cairo, 1958, 76; al-Suyūṭī, *al-Durr al-manthūr*, I, 204; and see T. Izutsu, *The structure of the ethical terms in the Koran*, Tokyo, 1959, 210–12.

poor who called on him i.e. because it was a ritual practice (*nusuk*) [70] of Quraysh in the period of the Jāhiliyya, i.e. in this place the man used to feed the poor who came to him. It has been said that this was the *ta'abbud* of the Prophet in the cave of Ḥirā' '.[71] The tradition of *ta'abbud* of the Prophet on Mt. Ḥirā' has thus to be understood according to the quoted traditions: he followed an old custom of his predecessors and sojourned at Ḥirā' performing some ritual practices and deeds of charity towards the needy and the poor. That was the *taḥannuth* of the Jāhiliyya and the Prophet practised it before he received his Call to Prophecy.[72] The discussion about what was the *sharī'a* adopted by the Prophet for his *ta'abbud* before he received his revelation is, of course, an expression of a later Muslim attitude with regard to an ancient Jāhilī term.

It was while Muḥammad was practising *taḥannuth*, which consisted, as we have seen, of the veneration of the Ka'ba and of doing charitable deeds towards one's fellow men on Mt. Ḥirā', that he received—according to Muslim tradition—his first revelation. In so doing he was following the ancient custom of Quraysh.

[70] In text, *min nsl*; this is an error—read *min nusuk*.

[71] Al-Ḥalabī, *Insān al-'uyūn*, I, 271 inf., 272 sup.

[72] See H. Birkeland, *The Lord guideth*, Oslo, 1956, 40–1: ' About 100 H. no Muslim doubted that Muhammad was a pagan before he was called by Allah at the age of 40 '.

VI

'A BAG OF MEAT': A STUDY OF AN EARLY *ḤADĪTH*

The manuscript Qarawīyūn 727 in Fez contains on folios 37b–38a a tradition reported by Yūnus b. Bukayr on the authority of Ibn Isḥāq. The tradition tells of a meeting between the Prophet and Zayd b. 'Amr b. Nufayl, one of the *ḥunafā'* in Mecca. During the meeting Zayd b. 'Amr was offered meat which he, however, refused to eat, arguing that he never ate meat sacrificed before idols.

This tradition was published and translated by A. Guillaume in his *New light on the life of Muhammad.*[1] It runs in his translation as follows:

'I was told that the apostle of God while speaking of Zayd ibn 'Amr ibn Nufayl said, "He was the first to blame me for worshipping idols and forbade me to do so. I had come from al-Ṭā'if with Zayd ibn Ḥāritha when I passed by Zayd ibn 'Amr on the high ground above Mecca, for Quraysh had made a public example of him (*shaharathu*) for abandoning their religion, so that he went forth from among them and (stayed) in the high ground of Mecca. I went and sat with him. I had with me a bag of meat from our sacrifices to our idols which Zayd ibn Ḥāritha was carrying, and I offered it to him. I was a young lad at the time. I said 'Eat some of this food, O my uncle'. He replied 'Nephew, it is a part of those sacrifices of yours which you offer to your idols, isn't it?' When I answered that it was he said 'If you were to ask the daughters of 'Abdu'l-Muṭṭalib they would tell you that I never eat of these sacrifices and I want nothing to do with them'. Then he blamed me and those who worship idols and sacrifice to them saying 'They are futile: they can do neither good nor harm', or words to that effect." The apostle added "After that with that knowledge I never stroked an idol of theirs nor did I sacrifice to them until God honoured me with His apostleship"'.

Guillaume considers this report as 'a tradition of outstanding importance'. 'It is the only extant evidence', he says, 'of the influence of a monotheist on Muhammad by way of admonition.'[2]

Guillaume remarks that 'this tradition has been expunged from Ibn Hishām's recension altogether, but there are traces of it in S. [al-Suhaylī's *al-Rauḍ al-unuf*] (p. 146) and Bukhārī (K. p. 63, bāb 24) where there is an imposing *isnād* going back to 'Abdullāh ibn 'Umar to the effect that the Prophet met Zayd in the lower part of Baldaḥ before his apostleship. "A bag was brought to the prophet *or the prophet brought it to him* and he refused to eat of it saying 'I never eat what you sacrifice before your idols. I eat only that over which the name of God has been mentioned'. *He blamed Quraysh* for their sacrifices"'.

[1] (*Journal of Semitic Studies.* Monograph No. 1), Manchester University Press, [1960], 27–8; Ar. text, 59.

[2] ibid., 27; see L. Caetani, *Annali dell'Islam,* Milano, 1905, I, 190, § 186: 'Se la tradizione è vera dovremmo ritenere che egli conoscesse Maometto prima dell'inizio della missione, e la condotta di questo originale e i discorsi del medesimo possono forse aver influitto sull' animo di Maometto'; T. Nöldeke, *Geschichte des Qorāns, bearbeitet von F. Schwally,* Leipzig, 1909, I, 18.

Guillaume surveys the discussion of the tradition in Suhaylī's *Rauḍ* and remarks that Ibn Kathīr ' (p. 239) also retains part of the original tradition which our MS contains. He says : " Zayd ibn 'Amr came to the apostle who was with Zayd ibn Ḥāritha as they were eating from a bag they had with them. When *they* invited him to eat with them he said, ' O nephew, I never eat from what has been offered to idols ' " '.[3]

The different versions of the tradition concerning the meeting of the Prophet with Zayd b. 'Amr deserve to be surveyed. The tradition of al-Bukhārī [4] (with the *isnād* Mūsā (b. 'Uqba) > Sālim b. 'Abdallāh > 'Abdallāh b. 'Umar) is recorded by Ibn 'Abd al-Barr,[5] Ibn Sa'd,[6] al-Bakrī,[7] Ibn Kathīr,[8] Aḥmad b. Ḥanbal,[9] Ibn 'Asākir,[10] al-Dhahabī,[11] and al-Ḥalabī.[12] A tradition recorded by Ibn Durayd [13] has a quite different setting : the Prophet was made to cherish solitude before he received the revelation and he sojourned in the folds of the mountains of Mecca. He said (i.e. the Prophet) : ' I saw Zayd b. 'Amr in one of the folds when he too secluded himself from the world. I sat down in his company and I offered him a meal containing meat. He then said " O nephew, I do not eat from these sacrifices (*innī lā ākulu min hādhihi 'l-dhabā'iḥi*) " '. In this tradition the Prophet was alone ; Zayd b. Ḥāritha is not mentioned. One may only deduce from the expression *hādhihi 'l-dhabā'iḥ* that meat of sacrifices slaughtered before idols is intended.

A similar tradition is recorded by al-Khargūshī.[14] The Prophet said ' Zayd b. 'Amr came to me when I was pasturing ; with me was cooked meat. I invited him to (eat) it and adjured him to do it (i.e. to eat). He answered " O nephew, if you were to ask your aunts they would tell you that I do not eat meat offered to any god other than God, who is Exalted " '. The difference between the tradition recorded by Ibn Durayd and the tradition of al-Khargūshī is noteworthy : the tradition of Ibn Durayd refers to the story of the solitude of the Prophet before he received the apostleship ; the tradition of al-Khargūshī refers to the story that the Prophet pastured the cattle of some people of Mecca.

[3] op. cit., 28.

[4] With the version *fa-quddimat ilā 'l-nabiyyi sufratun*, v, 50, Cairo, n. d. (Muḥ. 'Alī Ṣubayḥ and Sons printers).

[5] *Al-Istī'āb*, ed. 'Alī Muḥ. al-Bijāwī, Cairo, 1960, 617, with the version : *fa-qaddama ilayhi rasūlu 'llāhi ṣallā 'llāhu 'alayhi wa-sallama sufratan fīhā laḥmun.*

[6] *Ṭabaqāt*, Beirut, 1957, III, 380.

[7] *Mu'jam mā sta'jam*, ed. al-Saqā, Cairo, 1945, I, 273.

[8] *Al-Bidāya wa 'l-nihāya*, Beirut and al-Riyāḍ, 1966, II, 240 (quoted from al-Bukhārī).

[9] *Al-Musnad*, ed. Aḥmad Muḥammad Shākir, Cairo, 1949, VII, 225–6, no. 5369.

[10] *Tahdhīb ta'rīkh Dimashq*, VI, 32.

[11] *Ta'rīkh al-Islām*, Cairo, 1367/1947–8, I, 52 ; *Siyar a'lām al-nubalā'*, ed. Ṣalāḥ al-Dīn al-Munajjid, Cairo, 1956, I, 90 ; and see A. Sprenger, *Das Leben und die Lehre des Moḥammad, zweite Auflage*, Berlin, 1869, I, 119.

[12] 'Alī b. Burhān al-Dīn al-Ḥalabī, *Insān al-'uyūn fī sīrat al-amīn al-ma'mūn = al-Sīra al-ḥalabiyya*, Cairo, 1932, I, 147.

[13] *Al-Ishtiqāq*, ed. 'Abd al-Salām Hārūn, Cairo, 1958, 134.

[14] *Sharaf al-Muṣṭafā*, BM MS Or. 3014, fol. 28a.

Significant is the phrase 'if you were to ask your aunts . . .' which is almost identical with that in the tradition of Yūnus b. Bukayr.

A certain divergence is seen in a tradition recorded on the authority of 'Ā'isha (with an *isnād*: Hishām b. 'Urwa > 'Urwa > 'Ā'isha) who heard the Prophet say 'I heard Zayd b. 'Amr b. Nufayl condemning the eating of meat of sacrifices offered to someone other than God. So I did not taste anything (slaughtered) on the *nuṣub*[15] until God honoured me by the Call'.[16] In this tradition there is no mention of a bag of meat, nor that the Prophet invited Zayd b. 'Amr to eat meat. The Prophet merely heard Zayd b. 'Amr condemn the eating of such meat.

The person of Zayd b. Ḥāritha is mentioned in a tradition recorded by Aḥmad b. Ḥanbal[17] with the following *isnād*: Yazīd > al-Mas'ūdī > Nufayl b. Hishām b. Sa'īd b. Zayd b. 'Amr b. Nufayl > Hishām b. Sa'īd > Sa'īd b. Zayd.[18] 'When the Prophet and Zayd b. Ḥāritha', says the tradition, 'stayed in Mecca, Zayd b. 'Amr passed by. They invited him to (share) a bag of theirs. Zayd b. 'Amr answered "O nephew, I do not eat what has been sacrificed on the *nuṣub*".' The transmitter (i.e. Sa'īd b. Zayd b. 'Amr) said: 'the Prophet was after this never seen eating something sacrificed on the *nuṣub*'.

This tradition with the same *isnād* is recorded by al-Ṭayālisī.[19] It contains, however, a slight variant. Zayd b. 'Amr passed by the Prophet who was in the company of Zayd b. Ḥāritha; they both (i.e. the Prophet and Zayd b. Ḥāritha) ate from a bag of theirs. They invited him, etc. . . . This is, of course, the source of the tradition of Ibn Kathīr (II, 239) mentioned above.

An almost identical tradition is recorded by Ibn 'Abd al-Barr.[20] It is in fact a combined tradition containing details about the search for a true religion by Zayd b. 'Amr and Waraqa b. Naufal; the report concerning the invitation to Zayd b. 'Amr to eat meat from a bag is only a part of the tradition. The important difference is that the Prophet was in the company of Abū Sufyān b. al-Ḥārith[21] (not Zayd b. Ḥāritha).

The tradition recorded in MS Fez, Qarawīyūn 727, and translated by Guillaume, is not an isolated one. The tradition is recorded in the *Musnad* of al-Rabī' b. Ḥabīb[22] on the authority of Abū 'Ubayda. The variants are few:

[15] For the explanation of the word see al-Ṭabarī, *Tafsīr*, ed. Maḥmūd and Aḥmad Muḥammad Shākir, Cairo, 1957, IX, 508–9.

[16] Al-Khargūshī, op. cit., fol. 27b; al-Suyūṭī, *al-Khaṣā'iṣ al-kubrā*, Hyderabad, 1319/1901–2, I, 89; 'Alī b. Burhān al-Dīn al-Ḥalabī, op. cit., I, 146; al-Muttaqī al-Hindī, *Kanz al-'ummāl*, Hyderabad, 1965, XIII, 68, no. 387.

[17] *Al-Musnad*, III, 116–17, no. 1648; Ibn Kathīr, *al-Bidāya*, II, 239; Ibn Ḥajar, *Fatḥ al-bārī*, Cairo, 1325/1907–8, VII, 98; al-Dhahabī, *Siyar a'lām al-nubalā'*, I, 87 (on the authority of Yūnus b. Bukayr).

[18] See the editor's remarks on the men of the *isnād*, *al-Musnad*, loc. cit., III, 116–17, no. 1648.

[19] Abu Dā'ūd al-Ṭayālisī, *Musnad*, Hyderabad, 1311/1893–4, p. 32, no. 234.

[20] *Al-Istī'āb*, 616; al-Muḥibb al-Ṭabarī, *al-Riyāḍ al-naḍira fī manāqib al-'ashara*, Cairo, 1953, II, 405.

[21] See on him Ibn Ḥajar, *al-Iṣāba*, Cairo, 1907, VII, 86, no. 535; Ibn 'Abd al-Barr, op. cit., p. 1673, no. 3002.

[22] *Al-Jāmi' al-ṣaḥīḥ, Musnad al-Rabī' b. Ḥabīb b. 'Umar al-Azdī al-Baṣrī, 'alā tartīb al-shaykh Abī Ya'qūb Yūsuf b. Ibrāhīm al-Wārjilānī*, Cairo, 1349/1930–1, I, 18.

the phrase ' if you were to ask the daughters of 'Abd al-Muṭṭalib they would tell you that I never eat of these sacrifices . . . ' is missing. The question of Zayd b. 'Amr here was quite frank: ' O nephew, do you indeed sacrifice before these idols of yours ? (*yā bna akhī antum tadhbaḥūna 'alā aṣnāmikum hādhihi ?*) '. The Prophet answered ' Yes '. Then Zayd b. 'Amr said ' I shall not eat it (i.e. the meat from the bag) '. He condemned the idols (*thumma 'āba 'l-aṣnāma wa 'l-authāna*) and those who fed and approached them with reverence. The Prophet said ' By God, I did not draw near the idols at all until God granted me prophethood '.

A significant tradition, lengthy and detailed, is recorded by al-Khargūshī.[23] It is reported by Usāma b. Zayd on the authority of his father Zayd b. Ḥāritha. ' The Prophet ', says the report, ' slaughtered a ewe for a *nuṣub* of the *anṣāb* (*dhabaḥa rasūlu 'llāhi ṣallā 'llāhu 'alayhi wa-sallama shātan li-nuṣubin min al-anṣābi*); then he roasted it and carried it with him (*qāla: thumma shawāhā fa-ḥtamalahā ma'ahu*). Then Zayd b. 'Amr b. Nufayl met us in the upper part of the valley; (it was) on one of the hot days of Mecca. When we met, we greeted each other with the greeting of the Jāhiliyya, *in'am ṣabāḥan*. The Prophet said " Why do I see you, O son of 'Amr, hated by your people ? " [24] He said " This (happened) without me being the cause of their hatred (*qāla: dhāka li-ghayri thā'iratin kānat minnī fīhim*) [25]; but I found them associating divinities with God and I was reluctant to do the same. I wanted (to worship God according to) the religion of Ibrāhīm. I came to the learned men (*aḥbār*) of Yathrib and I found them worshipping God, but associating other divinities with Him. Then I said (in my soul): this is not the religion that I seek and I travelled till I came to the learned men of the Jews in Syria. Then a man from among them said ' You are asking about a religion which no one we know of follows, except an old man in the Jazīra '. I came to him and he asked me ' Which people do you belong to ? ' I said ' I am from the people of thorns and acacia trees (*al-shauk wa 'l-qaraẓ*),[26] from the people of the *Ḥaram* of God '. He told me ' Return, as God who is blessed and exalted caused to rise the star of a prophet who has already appeared, or is about to appear; follow him, because he will worship God according to the religion about which you are inquiring '." He (i.e. Zayd b. 'Amr) said " So I came, but—by God— I do not notice [27] anything ". The Prophet said " Would you like some food ? " He (i.e. Zayd b. 'Amr) said " Yes ". Then he (i.e. the Prophet) put before him the (meat of the) ewe. He said (i.e. Zayd b. 'Amr) " What did you sacrifice it to, O Muḥammad (*li-ayyi*

[23] *Sharaf al-Muṣṭafā*, fols. 27b–28a.

[24] In MS, *shaqaqaka*; in other parallels *shanifū laka*; and see *Lisān*, s.v., *sh n f*: *wa-fī ḥadīthi Zaydi bni 'Amri bni Nufaylin: qāla li-rasūli 'llāhi ṣallā 'llāhu 'alayhi wa-sallama: mā lī arā qaumaka qad shanifūka*. In our MS, correctly: *qāla lahu 'l-nabiyyu ṣallā 'llāhu 'alayhi wa-ṣallama: mā lī arāka yā bna 'Amrin* . . . etc.

[25] In MS, *thā'iratin*; other parallels: *nā'ilatin* and *nā'iratin*.

[26] In MS, *min ahli bayti 'l-shirki wa 'l-qaraẓi*; in *Siyar a'lām al-nubalā'*, I, 161, *min ahli bayti 'llāhi*; in *Majma' al-zawā'id*, IX, 418, *ahl al-shauk wa 'l-qaraẓ*.

[27] In MS, *uḥsinu*; in *Siyar a'lām*, correctly *uḥissu*; *al-Mustadrak*, like our MS, *uḥsinu*.

shay'in dhabaḥta yā Muḥammadu) ? " He (i.e. the Prophet) said " To one of the *anṣāb* (*qāla : li-nuṣubin min al-anṣābi*) ". He (i.e. Zayd b. 'Amr) said " I am not the one to eat anything slaughtered for a divinity other than God ". The Prophet went on his way and after a short time he was given the prophethood. He (i.e. Zayd b. Ḥāritha) said " Zayd b. 'Amr was mentioned to the Prophet and he (i.e. the Prophet) said ' He (i.e. Zayd b. 'Amr) will rise in the Resurrection as a people by himself ' ".' [28]

This tradition with slight variants is recorded in al-Ḥākim's *Mustadrak*,[29] in al-Haythamī's *Zawā'id*,[30] and in al-Dhahabī's *Siyar* [31] and his *Ta'rīkh al-Islām*.[32] In the *Mustadrak, Siyar*, and *Ta'rīkh* the tradition is traced back to Usāma b. Zayd, told on the authority of his father, Zayd b. Ḥāritha and is followed by an appended tradition that the Prophet went afterwards to the Ka'ba and performed the circumambulation accompanied by Zayd b. Ḥāritha. He forbade Zayd b. Ḥāritha to stroke the idols of Isāf and Nā'ila.[33] The slight variants may be of some importance. In some of the sources, instead of the learned men of Yathrib (*aḥbār*) the scholars of Fadak are mentioned. In some sources, the scholars of Khaybar are mentioned; others mention the scholars of Ayla. All the sources, except al-Khargūshī, tell the tradition in the first person plural: ' *and we slaughtered a ewe . . . and he* (i.e. Zayd b. 'Amr) *asked " What is it ? " We said " It is a ewe which we slaughtered for this nuṣub ". . .* '.[34]

By examining these traditions, one can discern the diverging details. Some of the traditions report that the Prophet heard from Zayd and refrained from eating meat offered to the *nuṣub*, other traditions state that the Prophet met Zayd and offered him the meat; some traditions state that the Prophet was alone; other traditions report that he was in the company of Zayd b. Ḥāritha or in the company of Abū Sufyān b. al-Ḥārith. Some of the traditions state that Zayd b. Ḥāritha slaughtered the animal, others claim that both he and the Prophet slaughtered it. The only tradition stating frankly that the Prophet himself offered the ewe to a *nuṣub* is the tradition of al-Khargūshī.

The slight variants of the traditions were closely examined by Muslim scholars. Guillaume quotes al-Suhaylī discussing the question as to ' how it could be thought that God allowed Zayd to give up meat offered to idols when the apostle had the better right to such a privilege. He says that the *ḥadīth* does not say that the apostle actually ate of it; merely that Zayd refused to do so.

[28] For the expression *ummatan wāḥidatan* and *ummatan waḥdahu* see Aḥmad b. Ḥanbal, op. cit., III, 117, no. 1648, note; *Lisān*, s.v. *umm*; Ibn Kathīr, op. cit., II, 241; al-Dhahabī, *Siyar a'lām*, I, 88; and see al-Muttaqī al-Hindī, op. cit., XIII, 67–8, nos. 384–6.

[29] Hyderabad, 1334/1915–16—1342/1923–4, III, 216–17.

[30] *Majma' al-zawā'id wa-manba' al-fawā'id*, Cairo, 1353/1934–5, IX, 417–18.

[31] I, 90–1, 160–1.

[32] I, 53.

[33] This tradition is recorded as an independent report in al-Suyūṭī's *al-Khaṣā'iṣ al-kubrā*, I, 89.

[34] In al-Dhahabī's *Ta'rīkh*: *shātun dhubiḥat li 'l-nuṣubi* against *thumma qaddamna ilayhi 'l-sufrata* in *al-Mustadrak*; al-Dhahabī's *Siyar a'lām*, I, 161, has *fa-qarraba ilayhi 'l-sufrata* (i.e. Muḥammad).

Secondly Zayd was simply following his own opinion, and not obeying an earlier law, for the law of Abraham forbade the eating of the flesh of animals that had died, not the flesh of animals that had been sacrificed to idols. Before Islam came to forbid the practice there was nothing against it, so that if the apostle did eat of such meat he did what was permissible, and if he did not, there is no difficulty. The truth is that it was neither expressly permitted nor forbidden '.[35]

The arguments of Suhaylī were not unanimously accepted by the scholars. The opinion that ' the law of Abraham (*shar'u Ibrāhīm*) forbade the eating of the flesh of animals that had died, not the flesh of animals that had been sacrificed to idols ' was refuted by some scholars, who argued that the law of Abraham forbade the eating of the flesh of animals sacrificed to a divinity other than God (i.e. to the idols) as he was an enemy of the idols.[36]

Three hundred years before al-Suhaylī (d. 581/1285) the tradition was discussed by Ibrāhīm al-Ḥarbī (d. 285/898) [37] as reported by al-Dhahabī.[38] The expression discussed is ' and we slaughtered for him ' (*fa-dhabaḥnā lahu*) in the first person plural. Al-Ḥarbī argues: ' in the slaughter (of the ewe) on the *nuṣub* there are two possibilities: (1) either Zayd (b. Ḥāritha) performed it (i.e. the slaughter) without being ordered by the Prophet, but as he was in his company the deed (of slaughter) was attributed to him (which is indicated by the usage of the plural first person—*dhabaḥnā*); Zayd (b. Ḥāritha) had not the immunity from sin (*'iṣma*) and God's guidance (*taufīq*), granted to the Prophet by God. How would it be possible (to think that the Prophet ordered him to do so) as the Prophet forbade Zayd to touch an idol and (indeed) he (i.e. the Prophet) did not touch it before he received prophethood ? So how could he acquiesce in the thought that he may slaughter for an idol ? That is impossible. (2) (It may be that) he slaughtered for God and it happened that it was done in front of an idol before which they (i.e. Quraysh) used to slaughter '.

Ibn Manẓūr records the opinion of Ibrāhīm al-Ḥarbī [39] as quoted by Ibn al-Athīr; in this record the second possibility is more plainly discussed: he (i.e. Zayd b. Ḥāritha) slaughtered the ewe in front of an idol (at a spot) at which they (i.e. Quraysh) used to slaughter; but he did not slaughter for the idol. This is the explanation of the phrase, if *nuṣub* denotes an idol. If, however, *nuṣub* denotes a stone, there was a semantic misunderstanding: when the Prophet was asked by Zayd b. 'Amr about the bag of meat he answered that the ewe was slaughtered on a *nuṣub*, on a stone, but Zayd b. 'Amr understood that it had been slaughtered for a *nuṣub*, an idol, and refused to eat it, remarking that he did not eat the meat of animals slaughtered for idols.

It is evident that we face here attempts of the commentators to interpret

[35] Guillaume, op. cit., 27–8; 'Alī b. Burhān al-Dīn, op. cit., I, 147 (quoting al-Suhaylī).

[36] Al-Qasṭallānī, *Irshād al-sārī*, Cairo, 1326/1908, VII, 427.

[37] On whom, see al-Dhahabī, *Tadhkirat al-ḥuffāẓ*, Hyderabad, 1956, II, 584, no. 609; al-Khatīb al-Baghdādī, *Ta'rīkh Baghdād*, Cairo, 1931, VI, 27; al-Subkī, *Ṭabaqāt al-shāfi'iyya*, ed. al-Ḥilw and al-Ṭanāḥī, Cairo, 1964, II, 256 (see the additional references supplied by the editors, ibid.).

[38] *Siyar a'lām*, I, 91.

[39] *Lisān*, s.v. *n ṣ b*; and see ibid., s.v. *s f r*.

these *ḥadīths* in a way showing that the Prophet did not slaughter for idols, nor did he eat meat slaughtered for idols.

This path is followed by al-Dhahabī who endeavours to interpret the opening phrases of this tradition.[40] 'Zayd b. Ḥāritha said "I went out with the Prophet, mounted behind him (on the riding beast) to one of the *anṣāb* and we slaughtered for him a ewe"' (*kharajtu ma'a rasūli 'llāhi ṣallā 'llāhu 'alayhi wa-sallama, wa-huwa murdifī, ilā nuṣubin min al-anṣābi fa-dhabaḥnā lahu shātan*). The crucial problem is, of course, the slaughter. The key for the interpretation of the sentence is the suffixed pronoun *hu* in *lahu*. If *lahu* is referred to *nuṣub* it would mean that the Prophet and Zayd b. Ḥāritha offered the ewe to the idol. This is evaded by the attribution of the suffixed pronoun to the Prophet. 'The suffixed pronoun in *lahu* refers to the Prophet', says al-Dhahabī (*ḍamīru lahu rāji'un ilā rasūli 'llāhi ṣallā 'llāhu 'alayhi wa-sallama*). Zayd used the first person plural, 'we slaughtered for him (i.e. for the Prophet) a ewe', but it was Zayd who slaughtered it. Consequently when Zayd b. 'Amr asks during the conversation about the contents of the bag, 'What is it?', the phrase *qulnā shātun dhabaḥnāhā li 'l-nuṣubi kadhā* 'we said "A ewe which we slaughtered for a certain *nuṣub*"' may form the answer of Zayd b. Ḥāritha or the answer of the Prophet on behalf of Zayd b. Ḥāritha who actually slaughtered the ewe, not being guided by God to refrain from sacrificing before the *nuṣub*.

The reading *quddimat lahu sufratun* (another version: *fa-quddimat ilā 'l-nabiyyi ṣallā 'llāhu 'alayhi wa-sallama sufratun*) in the tradition of al-Bukhārī gave the opportunity for a peculiar interpretation recorded by Ibn Ḥajar al-'Asqalānī.[41] Ibn Baṭṭāl (d. 449/1057) said that the bag was offered (*quddimat*) to the Prophet by Quraysh but he refused to eat it and offered it to Zayd b. 'Amr, who refused to eat it too. Ibn Ḥajar remarks: 'That is possible, but I do not know whence he could determine it, because I did not find it (i.e. this form of the tradition) in the transmission of anyone'.

Ibn Ḥajar prefers [42] the explanation given by al-Khaṭṭābī (d. 388/998): 'the Prophet did not eat meat of sacrifices slaughtered on the *nuṣub* for the idols, but he ate everything else, even if the name of God was not mentioned (during the slaughter), because the law had not been revealed then. The law prohibiting consumption of the meat of animals (over which during the slaughter the name of God was not mentioned) was not revealed until a long time after the Call'.

Ibn Ḥajar interprets *nuṣub* as 'stone' and concludes that Zayd b. Ḥāritha slaughtered the ewe on a stone, not intending to sacrifice for an idol. He accepts further the opinion of Suhaylī that Zayd b. 'Amr was 'following his own opinion' and refutes the assumption that he adopted the opinion of the *Ahl al-Kitāb*.

Of some interest is the interpretation of the expression about the bag in the

[40] *Siyar a'lām*, I, 90.

[41] *Fatḥ al-bārī*, VII, 98; al-Qasṭallānī, op. cit., VII, 427; al-'Aynī, '*Umdat al-qāri*', VIII, 36.

[42] *Fatḥ al-bārī*, VII, 98; al-'Aynī, op. cit., VIII, 36.

tradition of al-Bukhārī given by al-Kirmānī (d. 786/1384). The fact that the meat was in the bag does not indicate that the Prophet did eat of it, argues al-Kirmānī. In many cases food from a traveller's bag is not consumed by the traveller but by his companions. The Prophet did not forbid the persons in his company to consume it because he had not received the revelation at that time and had not been told to make known anything of order or prohibition.[43]

Shī'ī scholars strongly rejected the tradition of the bag of meat. Ibn Ṭāwūs in his *Ṭarā'if 'Abd al-Maḥmūd* [44] says: ' O you, may God have mercy upon you, look at this story the validity of which they attested, (alleging) that their Prophet was among those who slaughtered on the *anṣāb* and ate (the meat) and at the same time recording in their books that God undertook to educate and instruct him and Jibrīl undertook to see to his formation [45] (and stating further) that he did not follow (the customs of) the Jāhiliyya and did not accept anything of their manners. How did they bespeak themselves in this matter and in (the records of) the praise of God and their praise for His First and His Last, His Inward and His Outward, and with all this they attest that Zayd b. 'Amr knew God more than he and was more strict in keeping the observances of God (*kāna a'rafa bi-'llāhi minhu wa-atamma ḥifẓan li-jānibi 'llāhi*). How can I and others among the wise imitate people who record things like this and consider them sound? I asked scholars of the family of the Prophet (*'ulamā'a ahli 'l-'itrati*) about it, from their Shī'a, and they totally refused to accept the soundness of the tradition '.

The same arguments are put forth against this tradition by al-Ḥasan b. Yūsuf al-Ḥillī in his *Nahj al-ḥaqq wa-kashf al-ṣidq*.[46] Al-Faḍl b. Rūzbahān in a polemic against al-Ḥillī in his *Nahj al-ta'ṭīl* claims that al-Ḥillī deleted the final part of the saying of the Prophet (as recorded by al-Bukhārī). ' When Zayd (b. 'Amr) said " I do not eat from the meat of the sacrifices offered to the idols ", the Prophet said " I also do not eat from their sacrifices nor from that upon which God's name was not mentioned ". So they both ate (sc. the meat).' Muḥammad Ḥasan al-Muẓaffar denies the claim of al-Faḍl b. Rūzbahān and states that this addition (recorded by al-Faḍl) could not be found in the *Ṣaḥīḥ* of al-Bukhārī.[47]

In conclusion, it may be said that the discussion in connexion with the tradition concerning the conversation of the Prophet with Zayd b. 'Amr and the offer of the bag of meat was concerned with the essential problem of the *'iṣma* of the Prophet before he was granted prophethood. The main effort of the Muslim scholars was to prove that the Prophet did not eat meat slaughtered for

[43] Al-'Aynī, op. cit., VIII, 36.

[44] Ibn Ṭāwūs, *Ṭarā'if 'Abd al-Maḥmūd*, Tehran, n. d., 110.

[45] *Tahdhībahu* glossed in the text by *khidmatahu*.

[46] Muḥammad al-Ḥasan al-Muẓaffar, *Dalā'il al-ṣidq*, no place of publication given, 1389/1969(?), I, 409.

[47] ibid.

idols, nor did he slaughter it, as he was granted immunity from sin before he received prophethood.

The tradition of Ibn Isḥāq in the recension of Yūnus b. Bukayr discussed by Guillaume ' is given us ', as stated by Guillaume, ' in what must have been its original form '.[48] It is not a unique tradition, but it is undoubtedly an early one.

The lengthy tradition recorded by al-Khargūshī belongs to the same category: it plainly states that the Prophet offered the ewe to the idol and he admitted it in his talk with Zayd b. ʿAmr. The phrases mentioning that the Prophet and Zayd greeted each other with the greeting of the Jāhiliyya [49] are significant. The tradition explicitly points to the fact that the Prophet followed, before his prophethood, the practices of his people and corroborates the tradition of Ibn al-Kalbī that the Prophet ' offered a white ewe to al-ʿUzzā following the religious practices of his people ' (*laqad ahdaytu li 'l-ʿuzzā shātan ʿafrāʾa wa-anā ʿalā dīni qaumī*).[50]

The tradition of al-Khargūshī based on the idea that the Prophet had no *ʿiṣma* [51] before his Call belongs to the earliest layer of *ḥadīth*—traditions which fell later into oblivion or were re-shaped or expunged.

[48] *New light on the life of Muhammad*, 7.

[49] See I. Goldziher, *Muslim studies*, ed. S. M. Stern, London, 1967, 239.

[50] Ibn al-Kalbī, *Kitāb al-aṣnām*, ed. Aḥmad Zakī Pasha, Cairo, 1914, 19; J. Wellhausen, *Reste arabischen Heidentums*, Berlin, 1887, 30.

[51] See Ibn Taymiyya, *Minhāj al-sunna al-nabawiyya*, ed. Muḥammad Rashād Sālim, Cairo, 1964, II, 308, 311; H. Birkeland, *The Lord guideth*, Oslo, 1956, 40–1.

VII

"GOD WILL NEVER DISGRACE THEE"

(The Interpretation of an Early Ḥadīth)

The well known tradition in al-Bukhārī, told on the authority of al-Zuhrī—'Urwa—'Ā'isha, about the conversation between the Prophet and Khadīja after he received his first revelation[1] contains at the end a phrase variously interpreted by Muslim scholars and translated in modern times in various manners.

The contents of the ḥadīth are as follows: After the Prophet had heard the call to prophecy, he came to Khadīja with a trembling heart, asking her to cover him. He informed her about his experience and told her of his anxiety for himself. Khadīja encouraged him and assured him, that God would not disgrace him because of his good qualities. "Nay, by God" she said, "God will never disgrace you; you do good unto the kindred, bear the burden of the infirm, bestow alms on the poor, entertain the guest." The last phrase of this ḥadīth is: *wa-tu'īnu 'alā nawā'ibi 'l-ḥaqqi.* An attempt is here made to elucidate the meaning of this obscure phrase, and the problem of the originality of the ḥadīth is briefly discussed.

I

To start with, there are two interesting variants of this phrase. Al-Maqrīzī's version is: *wa-tu'īnu 'alā nawā'ibi 'l-dahri,*[2] you help against the misfortunes of time, whereas Ibn Kathīr quotes a version *nawā'ibu 'l-khairi*[3] and interprets it: "If a misfortune befalls somebody in a righteous case (*idhā waqa'at nā'ibatun li-aḥadin fī khairin*), you extend your help and aid him till he finds means of living or sustenance."

Al-Qasṭallānī[4] does not quote the version *tu'īnu 'alā nawā'ibi 'l-khairi* but interprets the saying in a corresponding manner by giving to the word *ḥaqq* a meaning similar to that of *khair*: "*Nawā'ib* means vicissitudes (*ḥawādith*); she (i.e. Khadīja) said *nawā'ibu 'l-ḥaqqi* because vicissitudes affect the righteous and unrighteous (*li-annahā takūnu fī 'l-ḥaqqi wa-l-bāṭili*). Labīd said: *Nawā'ibu min khairin wa-sharrin kilāhumā: fa-lā 'l-khairu mamdūdun wa-lā 'l-sharru lāzibu.*"

Al-Qasṭallānī thus contrasts *ḥaqq* with *bāṭil*; the phrase according to him would mean: you help in vicissitudes of a righteous case (as opposed to bāṭil, an unrighteous one). The verse of Labīd, quoted as *shāhid*, does not, however, confirm this interpretation. Labīd wanted to say: Vicissitudes of good and evil both (exist), the good is not prolonged, nor the evil lasting—and not "vicissitudes in a good or an evil cause". Labīd's verse can be compared with the one by al-Nābigha al-Dhubyānī.[5]

Wa-lā yaḥsabūna 'l-khaira lā sharra ba'dahu:
Wa-lā yaḥsabūna 'l-sharra ḍarbata lāzibi

[1] Al-Bukhārī: *Ṣaḥīḥ*, Bāb kaifa kāna bad'u l-waḥyi, I, 3 (ed. Cairo, A.H. 1286); Muslim: *Ṣaḥīḥ*, I, 97 (ed. Cairo, A.H. 1334); comp.: Ibn Sa'd: *Ṭabaqāt*, I, 195 (ed. Beirut, 1960); al-Balādhurī: *Ansāb al-ashrāf*, I, 106 (ed. M. Ḥamidullah); Abū Nu'aim: *Dalā'il al-nubuwwa*, p. 68 (ed. Hyderabad A.H. 1320); *al-Sīra al-ḥalabiyya*, I, 277 (ed. Cairo, A.H. 1351).

[2] *Imtā' al-asmā'*, I, 13, inf. (ed. Cairo, 1941).

[3] *Al-bidāya wa-l-nihāya*, III, 7 (ed. Cairo, 1932); and see W. Sakakīnī: *Ummahāt al-mu'minīn*, p. 16 (Cairo, n.d.).

[4] *Irshād al-sārī*, I, 65 (ed. Būlāq, A.H. 1323).

[5] *Dīwān*, p. 12 (ed. Muḥ. Jamāl, Beirut, 1929).

which conveys the same idea of changes in the conditions of the tribe. The idea of *ḥaqq* and *bāṭil* cannot be traced in the verses of either Labīd or al-Nābigha.

Al-Qasṭallānī's interpretation was copied by al-Zurqānī[1]; al-Sīra al-Ḥalabiyya only comments on the word *nawā'ib* rendering it *ḥawādith*.[2] A quite different interpretation of the phrase is given by al-Kashmīrī in his "Faiḍ al-bārī"[3]: *Tu'īnu 'alā nawā'ibi 'l-ḥaqqi* is a comprehensive expression for (qualities) mentioned (in this ḥadīth) and not mentioned. The Banū Hāshim gained fame by these features of character. (awṣāf)." ...

II

Let us turn to the translators: Houdas-Marçais translate[4]: ... "et tu secours les victimes des vicissitues du droit": the words "victims of the vicissitudes of right" are not, however, found in the text: *nawā'ibu 'l-ḥaqqi*. Sprenger translates[5]: "und unterstützest Leute in unverdientem Unglück," which again can hardly be deduced from the text. Mirza Bashīr al-Dīn Maḥmūd Aḥmad's translation reads[6]: "and you help those who are in distress," which corresponds to the version of al-Maqrīzī mentioned above.[7] An unusual rendering is given by W. M. Watt[8]: "you succour the agents of the truth." This translation (although followed by a question mark) is erroneous and was probably caused by confusing *nuwwāb* with *nawā'ib*. R. V. C. Bodley's translation[9]: "Hast thou not been loving to thy kinsfolk ... faithful to thy word and ever a defender of the truth" ... merely glosses over the difficulty.

III

For the elucidation of the phrase under discussion early poetry and prose have to be consulted.

A remarkable verse of 'Urwa b. al-Ward runs as follows[10]:

Atahza'u minnī an saminta wa-qad tarā
Bi-jismiya massa[11] *'l-ḥaqqi wa-l-ḥaqqu jāhidu*

The verse is rendered by Nöldëke[12]: "Spottest Du über mich dass Du fett geworden. Während Du an meinen Leibe den Eindruck der Pflicht (welche Andern zuerst Nahrung giebt und mir nichts lässt) siehst? Denn die Pflicht greift an." Nöldëke's rendering is based on the commentary on the words: "Duty is exhausting"; "this means that duties (obligations) come upon him (*yaṭruquhu*) and he prefers the fulfilment of duties to his own interest (*yu'thiruhu 'alā nafsihi*) and to the interest of his family; he is enduring hunger and drinks cold water. The *ḥaqq* mentioned means doing good to kindred, bestowing upon the beggar and the kinsman; everybody who practices it is exhausted by it."

This meaning of *ḥaqq* as a social obligation of the noble member of a tribe towards

1 *Sharḥ al-mawāhib*, I, 212–13 (ed. Cairo, A.H. 1325).
2 Op. cit., ib.
3 I, 28–29 (ed. Cairo, 1938).
4 El-Bokhārī: *Les traditions islamiques*, I, 3 (Paris, 1903).
5 *Die Lehre des Mohammad*, I, 333 (Berlin, 1869).
6 *Introduction to the Study of the Holy Quran*, p. 144 (London, 1949).
7 Vide above, n. 2, p. 27.
8 *Muḥammad at Mecca*, p. 40 (Oxford, 1953).
9 *The Messenger*, p. 52 (Lahore, 1954).
10 Th. Nöldëke: *Die Gedichte des 'Urwa b. al-Ward*, p. 41 (Göttingen, 1863).
11 In Ḥamāsa: *shuḥūba 'l-ḥaqqi* (Freytag, p. 723).
12 Op. cit., p. 78.

the poor, the needy and the kinsfolk in the *Jāhiliyya* is further elucidated by the response of Qays b. Zuhayr, quoted by al-Bakrī[1]:

Lā tashtumannī yā 'bna Wardin fa-innanī
Ta'ūdu 'alā mālī 'l-ḥuqūqu 'l-'awā'idu
Fa-man yu'thiri 'l-ḥaqqa 'l-na'ūba[2] *takun bihi*
Khuṣāṣatu jismin wa-hwa ṭayyānu mājidu

"Do not revile me, O son of Ward for obligations which come up again and again are turning upon my property;

and whoever prefers to fulfil the recurring obligation, his body will turn hollow shaped; he is hungry but noble."

We have here the expression *al-ḥaqqu al-na'ūbu*, "the recurring obligation" which explains the phrase of the ḥadīth. The same expression is found in a verse of Mu'āwiya b. Mālīk, the "Mu'awwidu l-Ḥukamā' "; he gained his sobriquet by this verse[3]:

U'awwidu mithlahā 'l-ḥukamā'a ba'dī:
Idhā mā 'l-ḥaqqu fī 'l-ashyā'i nābā

"I accustom the wise men after me to do the like
Whenever obligations come upon the tribal groups"

Al-Anbārī gives a pertinent explanation of the word *ḥaqq* as understood by the Beduins, in which obligations like paying the bloodwit for men, who have no means to pay it, and entertaining guests are included. The translation of *ḥaqq* by Lyall as "just claims" seems not to be justified. A similar explanation of *ḥaqq* by al-Anbārī is found in this commentary on the verse *Mufaḍḍaliyyāt* IV, 9, where a herd is described which has been diminished by changes of time and fulfilment of social obligations. Mu'āwiya b. Mālik mentions the idea of recurring obligations in another verse[4]:

Qālat Zunaybatu qad ghawaita li-an rā'at
Ḥaqqan yunāwibu mālana wa-wufūdu

"Zunayba said: you err, as she saw that obligations keep recurring upon our property, and deputations (asking our help)"

An anonymous verse[5] conveys the same idea of the obligations of a noble man:

Wa-lā arba'u 'l-māla min ḥubbihi, wa-lā li-l-fikhāri
wa-lā li-l-bakhal
Wa-lākin li-ḥaqqin idhā nābanī, wa-ikrāmi ḍayfin
idhā mā nazal

"I do not care for property for the love of it or for the sake of boasting, or because of avarice; but only for fulfilling obligations when they come upon me, and to honour a guest should he alight."

[1] *Simṭ al-La'ālī*, p. 822 (ed. al-Maimanī).
[2] Al-Qālī: *Amālī*, II, 204: *al-nadūba* (ed. al-Maimanī).
[3] *Mufaḍḍaliyyāt*, CV, 15 (ed. Lyall); al-Bakrī: *Simṭ* 190 (*idhā mu'ḍilu l-ḥadathāni nāba*); Ibn Ḥabīb: *Alqābu 'l-shu'arā*, *Nawādir al-makhṭūṭāt*, VII, 313 (ed. 'Abd al-Salām Hārūn).
[4] Abū Zaid: *Nawādir*, p. 148 (ed. al-Shartūnī, Beirut, 1894).
[5] I, 68—T. 'A.

An Umayyad poet, Shabīb b. al-Barṣā' uses the expression in a reverse order[1]:

Wa-aḥbisu fī 'l-ḥaqqi 'l-karīmata, innamā
Yaqūmu biḥaqqi 'l-nā'ibāti ṣabūruhā

"And I reserve for obligations the valuable (property); for it is only he who endures that can fulfil the duty of recurring obligations"

The same poet mentions this idea in another verse[2]:

Wa-li-l-ḥaqqi min māli idhā huwa ḍāfanī
Naṣībun wa-li-l-nafsi 'l-sha'ā'i naṣību
Wa-lā khayra fīman lā yuwaṭṭinu nafsahu
'Alā nāi'bāti 'l-dahri ḥīna tanūbu

"A share of my property is for an obligation should it come to me; and a share for the unsettled soul. And no good is in a man who cannot train himself to bear the misfortunes of time when they come (upon him)"

The word *ḥaqq* is joined by another verb (*alamma*) in a verse the *mukhadram* poet 'Amr b. al-Ahtam[3]:

Wa-l-badhlu min mu'dimīha in alamma bihā
Ḥaqqun wa-lā yashtakīhā man yunādīhā

"And its poor (of the tribe) give freely when an obligation draws near, and he who calls on them (for help) does not complain of them."

In another poem by 'Amr[4] obligations are mentioned together with misfortunes[5]:

Wa-innī karīmun dhū 'iyālin tuhimmunī
Nawā'ibu yaghshā ruz'uhā wa-ḥuqūqu

"I am a noble man, with a household to look after; I take care of misfortunes (entailing) losses, and of obligations."

The translation by Lyall of *huqūq* as: "calls for brotherly help" seems to be inaccurate.

Poets sometimes boast that the noble men of their tribe fulfil their social obligations towards the poor and the needy, holding lightly their property in their generosity. Rabī'a b. Maqrūm, one of the warriors and poets of Ḍabba, says[6]:

Yuhīnūna fī-l-ḥaqqi amwālahum
Idhā 'l-lazibātu iltaḥayna 'l-musīma

"They hold lightly their property in fulfilment of their obligations; when barren years wear away the (herds) of the owner of the cattle." Lyall translates: "claims on them."

The commentary of al-Anbārī repeats the explanation of "*ḥaqq*" quoted above as including

[1] *Aghānī* (3rd ed.), 12, 275.
[2] Al-Āmidī: *al-Mu'talif*, p. 68 (ed. Krenkow).
[3] Ibn al-Shajarī, *Ḥamāsa*, p. 50 (ed. Krenkow).
[4] *Mufaḍḍaliyyāt*, XXIII, 6.
[5] Comp. op. cit., IV, 9, mentioned above.
[6] *Mufaḍḍaliyyāt*, XXXVIII, 26; T. 'A., I, 470; comp. the verse of Miskīn al-Dārimī: *wa-in ḥaqqun 'arānī ahantuhā* al-'Askarī: *Dīwān al-Ma'ānī*, I, 29 (ed. A.H. 1352).

the expenditure in order to help in cases of bloodwit, bestowing camels, and entertaining guests. The Umayyad Ibn Rumma says[1]:

Wa-innā lakhushnun fī 'l-liqā'i a'izzatun
Wa-fī 'l-ḥaqqi waḍḍāḥūna, bīḍun, qalāmisu

"We are harsh and mighty in battle, and in fulfilling obligations bright, shining and generous."

In all these cases *ḥaqq* means obligation, duty. The verbs attached such as *'arā, alamma, ṭaraqa, 'āda, ḍāfa, nazala,*[2] denote the appearing of the obligation, and are synonymous with *nāba*, mentioned in the *ḥadīth* of 'Ā'isha. It is clear, then, that the phrase *Nawā'ibu 'l-ḥaqq* like *'awāi'du 'l-ḥaqq* means cases of obligations coming upon the tribe, or the community. The expression "*tu'īnu 'alā nawā'ibi 'l-ḥaqqi*" is a *Jāhiliyya* term used in praise of tribe and its leaders and was adopted in Islam. It can now be seen that the commentators and translators did not grasp its correct meaning.

IV

It may be remarked, that the qualities enumerated by Khadīja in the tradition discussed here are not attributed to the Prophet alone; we find a similar tradition also about Abū Bakr. When the leader of the Aḥābīsh, Ibn al-Dughunna met Abū Bakr, who was intending to leave Mecca, he laid stress on his behaviour in his clan and mentioned his qualities. He said[3]: "You are the splendour of your people, you help them (to overcome) the misfortunes (tu'īnu 'alā 'l-nawā'ibi), you act righteously, you bestow upon the poor. Return . . . etc."

There is however another version of this story; and it is striking to find that the text is almost identical to the ḥadīth of 'Ā'isha discussed here. This version is recorded by al-Bukhārī[4] on the authority of al-Zuhrī—'Urwa—'Ā'isha: Ibn al-Dughunna says addressing Abū Bakr: "A man like you should not be driven out. You bestow on the poor, you do good to your kindred, you bear the burden (of the poor, forlorn or needy), you entertain the guest, you help in the fulfilment of obligations (tu'īnu 'alā nawā'ibi l-ḥaqqi). I am your protector. Return etc. . . ."

The similarity of the ḥadīth about the conversation between Khadīja and the Prophet, and the story of the conversation between Ibn al-Dughunna and Abū Bakr in the version of al-Bukhārī, suggests that this kind of address was a coined formula of praise, current at that period. We find for instance a description of Hāshim[5] written in a similar style. Many other descriptions of noble men of the *Jāhiliyya* emphasize exactly these qualities.

In later times, even a *mawlā* could be addressed in the same way. When Jarīr came with a group of Yarbū'ites asking the help of Fayrūz Ḥuṣayn (a *mawlā* of Tamīm) because the people were driven away by drought, he said: "you are the splendour of the people, you help (to overcome) the misfortune (*tu'īnu 'alā 'l-nā'ibati*), you bear the burden (of the

[1] Ibn al-Shajarī: *Ḥamāsa*, p. 54.
[2] Comp. Al-Balādhurī: *Ansāb*, MS. 1025a: *wa-lā yadfa'u l-ḥaqqa idhā nazala bihi.*
[3] Ibn Hishām: *Sīra*, II, 12; and see Suhailī: *al-Rauḍ al-Unuf*, I, 231 (ed. Cairo, 1917).
[4] *Ṣaḥīḥ*, II, 268; and see: Al-Dhahabī: *Ta'rīkh*, I, 190; Ibn Kathīr: *al-Bidāya*, III, 173. It is obvious, that the mention of these qualities is more relevant in the case of Abū Bakr; here his social activity is rightly stressed.
[5] *Wa-kāna yaḥmilu 'bna 'l-sabīli wa-yu'addī 'l-ḥaqā'iqa* . . . al-Zurqānī: *Sharḥ al-Mawāhib*, I, 73.

needy and the poor)."[1] Fayrūz handed over 1,000 dirhems to Jarīr. Here the praise used in honour of the Prophet and Abū Bakr is applied to a *mawlā*!

In conclusion it may be said, that the phrase *tu'īnu 'alā nawā'ibi 'l-ḥaqqi* is closely connected with the *Jāhiliyya* social ideal about the fulfilment of duties towards the poor and the needy and it tallies well in the ḥadīth about the Prophet with the other qualities mentioned in it. The phrase has to be translated: "and thou helpest in cases of recurring obligations."

The ḥadīth on the conversation between the Prophet and Khadīja shows a striking similarity to the tradition about the conversation between Abū Bakr and Ibn al-Dughunna; this seems to suggest that we have here a current panegyrical formula.

[1] Al-Balādhurī: *Ansāb*, MS. 1012b.

VIII

'A BOOTH LIKE THE BOOTH OF MOSES...' A STUDY OF AN EARLY *ḤADĪTH* [1]

The chapter about innovations in mosques in al-Ṭurṭūshī's *Kitāb al-ḥawādith wa-'l-bidaʿ* [2] contains a remarkable tradition about the building of the mosque of the Prophet in Medina which deserves special attention. This tradition, not included in the orthodox collections of *ḥadīth*, is of considerable importance: it seems to belong to a large body of early traditions omitted by later collectors of *ḥadīth*, and it may throw some light on an attitude of the Prophet which was later ignored by Muslim scholars. This tradition may help us to understand the views and opinions of the early Muslim scholars.

The *ḥadīth* referred to is told anonymously and runs as follows: 'Abu'l-Dardā' and Ubayy b. Kaʿb measured the mosque; they came afterwards to the Prophet with the rod of the cubit. The Prophet then said: " Nay, a booth like the booth of Moses: *thumām* and wood, because the affair (will happen) sooner than that (*bal ʿarīsh^{un} ka-ʿarīsh^{i} Mūsā thumām^{un} wa-khashab^{un} fa-'l-amr^{u} aʿjal^{u} min dhālika* [3]) " '. The *ḥadīth* is obscure and abstruse and the editor, Muḥammad al-Ṭālibī, remarks that he could not find this story in the collections of traditions about the building of the mosque in Medina, or about the building of the three mosques, nor in the *Nihāya* of Ibn al-Athīr; he could not find anything which may elucidate the text in the collections of the biographies of the Companions of the Prophet, nor in the stories about the life of Moses.[4]

This tradition is, however, given in al-Suyūṭī's *al-Jāmiʿ al-ṣaghīr* [5] in two versions: (*a*) a version which contains only a part of the tradition, and (*b*) a version in which the tradition is reported in full; both versions contain some slight deviations from the text of al-Ṭurṭūshī. The two versions of al-Suyūṭī were copied by al-Nabhānī in his book *al-Fatḥ al-kabīr*.[6]

The second part of the tradition is found in quite a different context, without being connected with the building of the mosque in Medina or with that of any mosque at all. It is reported by al-Tirmidhī [7] in the *Bāb qiṣar al-amal* and by

1 Professor R. B. Serjeant kindly agreed to read this article in typescript and has added a few valuable notes, the contents of which are given below. The author wishes to express sincere thanks for the interest Professor Serjeant has shown and for his comments.

2 Abū Bakr Muḥammad b. al-Walīd al-Ṭurṭūshī, *Kitāb al-ḥawādith wa-'l-bidaʿ*, ed. Muḥammad al-Ṭālibī, Tunis, 1959, pp. 93–9.

3 Professor Serjeant remarks that he has often seen roofs built in such a way in South Arabia. He writes (in a letter): '*Khashab* would be beams, perhaps palm-trunks. These would be covered with smaller branches, and then with *thumām*. On top of this would be added some wet *ṭīn* and *tibn*, clay mixed with chopped straw, and this would form the roof. *Khushaybāt* is better than *khashab* because it would mean presumably little branches'.

4 P. 94, n. 6.

5 II, 58, *ʿarsh ka-ʿarsh Mūsā*; 59, *ʿarīsh ka-ʿarīsh Mūsā thumām wa-khushaybāt wa-'l-amr aʿjal min dhālika.*

6 II, 226, 228.

7 IX, 204, ed. Cairo, A.H. 1353.

Ibn Māja in the *Bāb al-binā' wa-'l-kharāb*[1]; Abū Dā'ūd quotes the tradition in the *Kitāb al-adab*, in *Bāb mā jā'a fi'l-binā'*.[2] The tradition, told on the authority of al-A'mash, runs, in the report of al-Tirmidhī, as follows: ' 'Abdullah b. 'Amr said: The Messenger of God passed by us when we were busy (repairing) a hut of ours and asked us: " What is this ? " We answered: " It threatened to fall, therefore we repair it ". The Prophet said: " I think the affair will outstrip that " '. In the collections of Ibn Māja and of Abū Dā'ūd the tradition is also reported on the authority of al-A'mash, but there are some differences in the formulation of the statement of the Prophet: *Mā arā al-amr illā a'jal min dhālika*, and *al-amr asra' min dhālika*. This saying of the Prophet is thus the same as that reported in the second part of our tradition. There is, however, a difference of meaning between the saying as quoted by al-Ṭurṭūshī and the same saying as reported by Ibn Māja, Abū Dā'ūd, and al-Tirmidhī. The key-word for the understanding of the two traditions is the word *amr* 'affair'. This word must be interpreted in the tradition of al-Tirmidhī, Ibn Māja, and Abū Dā'ūd as meaning 'death'.[3] This is actually the interpretation given by Muḥammad b. 'Abd al-Hādī al-Ḥanafī al-Sindī in his commentary on Ibn Māja. In the same way we can also explain the saying of al-Ḥasan who, when asked why he did not wash his shirt, said: *al-amr asra' min dhālika*.[4] The meaning of the tradition would be: there is no need to repair (or to plaster a wall with clay, as in one of the versions of Abū Dā'ūd) even huts; death will outstrip your efforts. This saying is in harmony with other statements of the Prophet and his utterances in the *Bāb qiṣar al-amal* (e.g. ' . . . Be in this world like a wayfarer . . . Ibn 'Umar said: getting up do not hope for the evening . . .') and in the *Bāb al-binā' wa-'l-kharāb* (' . . . Every expense of the believer will be rewarded except the expense of building . . .').[5]

The meaning 'death' can, however, hardly apply to the word *amr* in the tradition of al-Ṭurṭūshī. The Prophet can hardly be assumed to have told Abu'l-Dardā' and Ubayy not to build mosques because death (i.e. his or theirs) would outstrip the completion of the building; the Prophet's death or that of the builders can hardly be a reason for an injunction to build the mosque in a provisional way, like the booth of Moses, for the mosque could well serve the believers even after their death. The meaning of al-Ṭurṭūshī's tradition seems thus to be quite different: *amr* denotes here an affair which will put an end to life in general; it will put an end to worship as well. It means in this

[1] II, 540, ed. Cairo, A.H. 1349.

[2] II, 347, ed. Cairo, A.H. 1348.

[3] ' In a modern text from al-Shiḥr: *idhā jarā amr Allāh 'alā [fulān]* " if so and so dies ". I am translating this phrase as " God's command ". The context is that if a fisherman dies, i.e. God's command comes to him, yet his family will continue to receive his share in the fishing crew's earnings till the end of the fishing season ' (R. B. Serjeant).

[4] Ibn al-'Arabī, *Muḥāḍarāt al-abrār*, I, 193.

[5] This tradition was emended; the clause added states, ' except the expenses of building mosques '. These expenses will, of course, be rewarded. See *al-Iktisāb*, 79. Cf. *Musnad al-Ṭayālisī*, p. 341: ' Ibn 'Abbās: the Prophet said: He who builds a mosque for Allah even like a hollow (dug by) a sand grouse (for laying eggs), Allah will build for him a house in Paradise '.

context destruction, disaster, calamity in which everything will perish. In this tradition of al-Ṭurṭūshī *amr* is identical in meaning with *al-sāʿa*, the time of total calamity which will be followed by the resurrection. The Prophet said to Abu'l-Dardā': 'The *amr*, the Day of Judgment, may be sooner than that', for he believed that the *sāʿa* was at hand; there was no need, therefore, to erect sumptuous buildings, not even for mosques. A remarkable tradition quoted by al-Bayhaqī on the authority of Ibn 'Abbās may be mentioned to strengthen this point. 'The Prophet said: I have not been ordered to build the mosque sumptuously (*mā umirtu bi-tashyīd al-masjid*)'.[1] This meaning of *amr* as identical with *al-sāʿa* can already be detected in the Qur'ān, XVI, 1; this is also the explanation given there by the commentators.[2]

The fact that the Prophet was overpowered by the feeling of the approaching Day of Judgment, which was duly stressed by Buhl [3] and T. Andrae,[4] may be illustrated by a tradition comprehensively explained by al-Sharīf al-Raḍī.[5] 'The Prophet said: I was sent at the breath of the Day of Judgment; the Day almost outstripped me' (*buʿithtu fī nasam al-sāʿa, in kādat la-tasbiqunī* [the *in* here is *mukhaffafa min al-thaqīla*]). Another version of this tradition is also mentioned by the author; it has *nafas* instead of *nasam*. The first version is explained as denoting beginning, and should therefore be literally translated: 'I was sent at the first blowing of the wind of the *sāʿa*'; the meaning is derived from the idea of a breath of wind at the beginning of the day. The second version, *nafas*, is said to be derived from the idea of delay, pause. Thus the tradition can be interpreted in two different ways: (*a*) the Prophet was sent at a time when the Day of Judgment was just about to begin; (*b*) the Prophet was sent at a time when the Day of Judgment was almost at hand; Allah postponed it for a while, and during this pause the Prophet was sent. A similar tradition is quoted by al-Tirmidhī [6] and by Ibn Ḥibbān.[7]

It is obvious why this tradition about the building of the mosque of the Prophet as quoted in the book of al-Ṭurṭūshī was omitted by Muslim scholars. The Day of Judgment did not come in the days of the Prophet and there was no reason to quote a tradition which stated clearly that the Prophet believed that the *sāʿa* would happen in his own lifetime.

II

We can, fortunately, trace the first part of the tradition in other sources. It served as an argument for scholars who claimed that mosques should be built in an austere and modest style, like the mosque of the Prophet. Thus we have

[1] *Kitāb al-sunan al-kubrā*, II, 439.
[2] Ibn Qutayba, *al-Qurṭayn*, I, 242, ed. Cairo, A.H. 1355; cf. P. Casanova, *Mohammed et la fin du monde*, 15.
[3] *Das Leben Muhammeds*, 145, 157.
[4] *Mohammed*, 43.
[5] *al-Majāzāt al-nabawiyya*, p. 36; cf. Casanova, op. cit., 18 (1), 20, 57.
[6] *Bāb al-fitan*, IX, 60.
[7] I, 9.

the following tradition, told on the authority of Sālim b. ʿAṭiyya: 'The Prophet said: A booth like the booth of Moses'. The explanation given says: 'He did not like arches [1] about the mosques' (*yaʿnī annahu kāna yakrahu al-ṭāq fī ḥawālī al-masājid*).[2] A slightly different interpretation is given to this tradition in *Kitāb al-waraʿ* of Aḥmad b. Ḥanbal.[3] The circumstances in which this saying was uttered according to Ibn Ḥanbal are also different. People asked the Prophet to adorn the walls of the mosque (*an yukaḥḥil[a] al-masjid*), and the Prophet said: 'No, a booth like the booth of Moses'. The compiler, Aḥmad b. Ḥanbal, explains: 'It is a varnish like antimony (*kuḥl*); the Prophet did not allow it'.

Quite a different version of this tradition is given in an early treatise compiled by Muḥammad b. Ḥasan al-Shaybānī (died A.H. 189), summarized by his pupil Muḥammad b. Samāʿa (died A.H. 233), in his book *al-Iktisāb fī al-rizq al-mustaṭāb*: 'People offered the Prophet to pull down his mosque and to build it anew. The Prophet answered: No, a booth like the booth of Moses'.[4]

The tradition is also quoted in the book of Naṣr b. Muzāḥim, *Waqʿat Ṣiffīn*.[5] It is quoted there on the authority of al-Ḥasan: 'When the Prophet intended to build his mosque he said: Build for me a booth like the booth of Moses'.

In the sources quoted above the expression about the dry branches and *thumām* is missing; the second part of the tradition, about the *amr* which will outstrip the effort of the builders, has been cut off.

III

The whole tradition of al-Ṭurṭūshī is found in the *Ṭabaqāt* of Ibn Saʿd (I, 2, p. 2; in the edition of Cairo, A.H. 1358, vol. II, p. 5). The Prophet, says the tradition of Ibn Saʿd, covered the mosque with palm branches. He was asked: Why not cover with a ceiling? The Prophet answered: 'A booth

[1] The word 'arch' is used here to translate Arabic *ṭāq*. According to Professor Serjeant (letter dated 20 August 1960), '*ṭāq* or *ṭāqa* is in South Arabian usage a window, an aperture (especially in a technical sense, to a tomb), a niche in a wall for holding a lamp or something of the kind. Such a niche in my experience is usually made in a clay wall and may be topped by a round arch or pointed arch (in clay), or it could simply have a wooden top on the post and lintel principle'. These features of building, mentioned by Professor Serjeant, did not exist in the mosque of the Prophet, and orthodox circles were opposed to them. It was ʿUmar b. ʿAbd al-ʿAzīz who was the first to build the *miḥrāb* in the form of a niche when he rebuilt the mosque in Medina by order of al-Walīd (details about this innovation, Creswell, *A short account of early Muslim architecture*, 44). The *ṭāq al-imām* in the traditions quoted by al-Ṭurṭūshī seems thus to be identical with the *miḥrāb* (cf., eg., p. 94, *fa-min dhālika al-maḥārīb . . . fa-taqaddama al-Ḥasan wa-ʿtazala al-ṭāq an yuṣalliya fīhi . . . wa-kariha al-ṣalāt fī ṭāq al-imām al-Nakhaʿī . . .*). The fundamental sense of *miḥrāb*, as elucidated by Professor Serjeant, was in fact columns and a space between them. *Miḥrāb* in the form of an arched niche was an innovation; it was introduced at the end of the seventh century and was fiercely opposed by the orthodox. *Ṭāq* as *miḥrāb* was considered as *bidʿa*.

[2] Al-Bayhaqī, *al-Sunan*, II, 439.

[3] Ed. Cairo, A.H. 1340, p. 107; compiled by Abū Bakr Aḥmad b. Muḥammad al-Marwazī.

[4] P. 78

[5] Ed. Beirut, p. 238. Also *ʿUmdat al-akhbār*, p. 81. Cf. Ibn Qayyim al-Jauziyya, *Zād al-maʿād*, II, 146.

like the booth of Moses, wood pieces and *thumām*; the affair (will happen) sooner than that'.[1]

The same tradition, told on the authority of Shahr b. Ḥaushab [2] and quoted in the *Sīra Ḥalabiyya*,[3] contains a few interesting additions: 'When the Prophet wanted to build the mosque he said: "Build for me a booth like the booth of Moses, *thumāmāt* and dry branches and a covering like the covering of Moses, and the affair (will happen) sooner than that". He was asked: "What is a covering of Moses?" and he answered: "When he stood up his head touched the ceiling"'. This very tradition is quoted by Aḥmad b. 'Abd al-Ḥamīd al-'Abbāsī in his *'Umdat al-akhbār fī madīnat al-mukhtār* [4]; the source given is the collection of Razīn.[5]

Another version of this tradition, in a slightly different form, is given by the *'Umdat al-akhbār* and the *Sīra Ḥalabiyya*: 'When the Prophet wanted to build the mosque he was told [the *Sīra Ḥalabiyya* comments: Gabriel told him]: "A booth like the booth of Moses, thy brother". Anas said: Thus the Prophet built it the first time from palm-branches; four years after the *hijra* he built the mosque from bricks'.[6]

A tradition quoted in both books mentions a different situation upon which the saying was uttered. Rain used to drip into the mosque. Since the covering contained little clay, the mosque was filled with muddy water. The believers then came to the Prophet and asked him to give an order that the ceiling be plastered with clay, in order to prevent the rain from dripping into the mosque. The Prophet answered: 'No, a booth like the booth of Moses'. The mosque was left in this state until the death of the Prophet.[7]

In conclusion we may assume that the tradition quoted by al-Ṭurṭūshī was already widely spread in the circles of Muslim scholars at the beginning of the third century of the *hijra*, or even at the end of the second century.

[1] Quoted from Ibn Sa'd in Nuwayrī, *Nihāyat al-arab*, XVI, 345.

[2] See his biography, *Tahdhīb al-tahdhīb*, IV, 369.

[3] Ed. Cairo, A.H. 1320, II, 71; *Sīrat Dahlān* (on margin of *Ḥalabiyya*), I, 357.

[4] Ed. As'ad Ṭarābzūnī, p. 80. According to a tradition mentioned in the *Sīrat al-Dimyāṭī*, quoted in the *Ḥalabiyya* (loc. cit.), the explanation of the booth of Moses is given by al-Ḥasan, who reported the tradition.

[5] Razīn b. Mu'āwiya b. 'Ammār al-'Abdārī (d. 535/1140), cf. Brockelmann, *GAL, Suppl.*, I, 630.

[6] The saying of Anas is not mentioned in the *Ḥalabiyya*. *Libn*, here translated 'bricks', means, as Professor Serjeant points out, fundamentally clay bricks, but one may assume fairly safely that in a hastily constructed building they would be of unbaked clay, cf. Landberg, *Gloss. daṯ.*, III, Leiden, 1942, 2611 [reference supplied by Professor Serjeant, who also refers to the terms *ājur* and *libn* in *RSO*, XXVIII, 1953, 8, and *madra* and *lubna* in *Le Muséon*, LXII 1–2, 1949, 160]. In the sources relating to our tradition there is, however, a controversy over the question of these bricks and their form. Some support for taking *libn* to mean unbaked clay bricks in this tradition may be adduced from the following tradition about the mosque built in Baṣra by Abū Mūsā al-Ash'arī: *wa-banā Abū Mūsā al-Ash'arī al-masjid wa-dār al-imāra bi-libn wa-ṭīn wa-saqqafahā bi-'l-'ushb* (al-Balādhurī, *Futūḥ*, ed. Cairo, A.H. 1319, p. 355)—he built it from clay bricks and clay and covered it with brushwood [using this word for '*ushb* at Professor Serjeant's suggestion].

[7] *'Umdat al-akhbār*, 81; *al-Ḥalabiyya*, loc. cit.

That is evident from the quotation in the *Ṭabaqāt* of Ibn Sa'd. The mosque of the Prophet was in fact built in a very simple, even primitive, way,[1] and resembled a booth.[2] The saying of the Prophet about the Day of Judgment seems to reflect truly his feeling in the first period of his stay in Medina. The comparison with the booth of Moses in this period is not surprising: his relations with the Jews in Medina were not yet hostile. This tradition seems thus to belong to an early layer of *ḥadīth* of considerable importance.

[1] See Ibn Sa'd, loc. cit.; Yāqūt, *Buldān*, s.v. *Yathrib*; *EI*, s.v. 'Masdjid' (Pedersen); Creswell, *Early Muslim architecture*, 2–11, 25.

[2] cf. Tha'lab's explanation of the verse of al-A'shā (*Dīwān*, ed. Geiger, XXIX, 4). It was a construction of trunks covered with dry branches, where people used to seek shelter from the heat. Cf. Abū Dharr's commentary, ed. Brönnle, p. 424, and cf. the verse of Mutawakkil al-Laythī, *Aghānī*, XI, 38.

IX

THE MARKET OF THE PROPHET

The reasons given by the Arabic sources for the assassination of Kaʿb b. al-Ashraf are that he stirred up the Meccans to fight the Prophet and to avenge their defeat at Badr, that he composed anti-Muslim verses defaming Muslim women or that he plotted with a group of Jews to kill the Prophet [1]). These reasons are also accepted or quoted in the works of scholars, analysing the attitude of the Prophet towards Kaʿb b. al-Ashraf [2]).

---

1) Ibn Hishām: *al-Sīra* III, 54-61, 206-210 (ed. al-Saqā'-Abyārī-Shalabī, Cairo 1936); al-Shaybānī: *Kitāb al-Siyar al-Kabīr* I, 270-77 (ed. Ṣalāḥ al-Dīn al-Munajjid, Cairo 1957); al-Wāqidī: *al-Maghāzī*, 184-90 (ed. von Kremer, Calcutta 1856); Ibn Saʿd: *Ṭabaqāt* II, 31-34 (ed. Beirut 1957); Muḥ. b. Ḥabīb: *Asmā' al-mughtālīn* (*Nawādir al-makhṭūṭāt* VI, 144-46, ed. ʿAbd al-Salām Hārūn); al-Balādhurī: *Ansāb al-Ashrāf* I, 284, 374 (ed. Muḥ. Ḥamīdullāh, Cairo 1959); al-Bukhārī: *Ṣaḥīḥ* V, 115-16 (ed. Cairo, Muḥ ʿAlī Ṣubayḥ, n.d.); Muslim: *Ṣaḥīḥ* V, 184-85 (ed. Cairo 1334 AH); al-Ṭabarī: *Ta'rīkh* II, 177-80 (ed. Cairo 1939); Aghānī XIX, 106-107; al-Khaṭṭābī: *Maʿālim al-Sunan* II, 336-38 (Sharḥ Sunan Abī Da'ūd, Cairo 1933); al-Bayhaqī: *al-Sunan al-Kubrā* IX, 81 (ed. Hyderabad 1356 AH); al-Maqdisī: *al-Bad' wa-l-Ta'rīkh* IV, 197 (ed. Huart, Paris 1907); Ibn Kathīr: *al-Bidāya* IV, 5-9 (ed. Cairo 1932); Abū Ḥayyān: *Tafsīr al-baḥr al-muḥīṭ* III, 135 (ed. Cairo 1328 AH.); al-Maqrīzī: *Imtāʿ al-Asmāʿ* I, 108-110 (ed. Maḥmūd Muḥ. Shākir, Cairo 1941); Al-Suhaylī: *al-Rauḍ al-Unuf* II, 123- 25 (ed. Cairo 1914); al-Suyūṭī: *al-Durr al-Manthūr* II, 107 (reprint Teheran 1377 AH); Ibn Qayyim al-Jauziyya: *Badā'iʿ al-Fawā'id*, III, 210 (Cairo, Munīriyya Print, n.d.); Ibn Sayyid al-Nās: *ʿUyūn al-Athar* I, 298-301 (ed. Cairo 1356 AH); Ibn Ḥajar al-Haythamī: *Majmaʿ al-zawā'id* VI, 195-96 (ed. Cairo 1353 AH); ʿAlī b. Burhān al-Dīn al-Ḥalabī: *Insān al-ʿuyūn* III, 181 (ed. Cairo 1354 AH); Daḥlān: *al-Sīra* (on margin of *Insān al-ʿuyūn* II, 13-20); al-Ṭabarsī: *Iʿlām al-warā*, 56 (ed. 1312 AH); al-Majlisī: *Biḥār al-Anwār* IX, 74; XX, 10-11 (ed. Teheran 1376-85 AH); al-Samhūdī: *Wafā' al-Wafā* I, 199 (ed. Cairo 1326 AH); al-Diyārbakrī: *Ta'rīkh al-Khamīs* I, 464-66 (ed. 1302 AH); al-Zurqānī: *Sharḥ al-Mawāhib* II, 8-14 (ed. Cairo 1325 AH).

2) L. Caetani: *Annali* I, 534-37 (ed. Milano 1905); H. Grimme: *Mohammed* I, 94 (ed. Münster i. W. 1892); A. J. Wensinck: *Mohammed en de Joden te Medina*, 152-55 (ed. Leiden 1908); R. Leszynsky: *Die Juden in Arabien zur Zeit Mohammeds*, 66-69 (ed. Berlin 1910); F. Buhl: *EI*[1], s.v. Kaʿb b. al-Ashraf; F. Buhl: *Das Leben Muhammeds*, 250-51 (transl. H. H. Schaeder, Heidelberg 1955, second ed.); H. Z. Hirschberg: *Yisra'el ba-ʿArav*, 143 (ed. Tel-Aviv 1943); S. D. Goitein: *Ha-Islām shel Muḥammad*, 215 (ed. Jerusalem 1955); M. Gaudefroy-Demombynes: *Mahomet*, 135 (ed. Paris

A passage in Samhūdī's *Wafā' al-Wafā* [1]) reveals another aspect of the enmity between Kaʿb b. al-Ashraf and the Prophet and sheds some light on the economic activities of the Prophet and the Muslim community in Medina. The event recorded in this passage on the authority of Ibn Shabba [2]) runs as follows:

Ibn Shabba-Ṣāliḥ b. Kaysān [3]): "The Prophet pitched a tent in the *Baqīʿ al-Zubayr* and said: This is your market. Then Kaʿb b. al-Ashraf came up, entered inside and cut its ropes. The Prophet then said: Indeed, I shall move it into a place which will be more grievous for him than this place. And he moved into the place of the "Market of Medina" (scil. the place which was later the Market of Medina -K). Then he said: This is your market. Do not set up sections in it and do not impose taxes for it".

The problem that faces us is why did Kaʿb b. al-Ashraf cut the ropes of the tent of the Prophet. Some conclusion can be drawn from another fragment of this tradition [4]) of ʿUmar b. Shabba, stating that al-Zubayr asked the Prophet to grant him *al-Baqīʿ* after the assassination of Kaʿb [5]).

1957); M. Hamidullah: *Le Prophete de l'Islam*, index (ed. Paris 1959); W. Montgomery Watt: *Muhammed at Medina*, index (ed. Oxford 1956); M. Rodinson: *Mahomet*, 173 (ed. Paris 1961).

1) I 540.

2) See about him: Yāqūt: *Muʿjam al-Udabā'* XVI, 60-62 (ed. Cairo 1938); al-Khaṭīb al-Baghdādī: *Ta'rīkh Baghdād* XI, 208-210 (ed. Cairo 1931); Ibn Ḥajar: *Tahdhīb al-Tahdhīb* VII, 460 (ed. Hyderabad 1326 AH); Saleh Ahmed al-Ali: *Studies in the Topography of Medina, I.C.* 1961, pp. 66-67; Ṣāliḥ Aḥmad al-ʿAlī: *al-Mu'allafāt al-ʿarabiyya ʿan al-Madīna wa-l-Ḥijāz, Majallat al-Majmaʿ al-ʿIlmī al-ʿIrāqī*, 1964, pp. 131-134.

3) See about him: al-Dhahabī: *Mīzān al-iʿtidāl* II, 299, No. 3823 (ed. al-Bijāwī, Cairo 1963); idem: *Tadhkirat al-ḥuffāẓ* I, 148, No. 142 (ed. Hyderabad 1958); Ibn Ḥajar: *Tahdhīb al-Tahdhīb* IV, 399-400; Aḥmad b. Ḥanbal: *Kitāb al-ʿIlal* I, 359 (ed. Koçyiğit-Cerrahoğlu, Ankara 1963); and see E. L. Petersen: *ʿAlī and Muʿāwiya in Early Arabic Tradition*, index (ed. Copenhagen 1964).

4) Samhūdī, *op. cit.*, II, 265.

5) About the topography of Baqīʿ al-Zubayr see S. A. al-Ali: *Studies*, p. 79; about grants of the Prophet to al-Zubayr see: Abū ʿUbayd: *al-Amwāl* p. 272 — No. 675; p. 279 — No. 691 (ed. Cairo 1353 AH); Abū Yūsuf: *Kit. al-Kharāj*, p. 61 (ed. Cairo 1382 AH); al-Hindī: *Kanz al-ʿummāl* III, 524 — No. 4022 (ed. Hyderabad 1951); Ibn Zanjawayh: *Kitāb al-Amwāl*, MS. f. 99b-100a; al-Shaybānī: *Kit. al-Siyar al-Kabīr* II, 611.

This *Baqīʿ* became—of course later—known as *Baqīʿ al-Zubayr*. It is obvious that Kaʿb tried to prevent the Prophet from establishing the market on his land. This was the cause of the clash between the Prophet and Kaʿb.

Other traditions supply more details about the event of the establishment of the market, although the clash between the Prophet and Kaʿb is not mentioned. Ibn Zubāla [1]) reports on the authority of Yazīd b. ʿUbayd Allāh b. Qusayṭ [2]) that the market (scil. of Medina) was in (the quarter of) the Banū Qaynuqāʿ until it was moved afterwards (into another place) [3]). A corroborative tradition reported by ʿUmar b. Shabba on the authority of ʿAṭāʾ b. Yasār [4]) states that the Prophet decided to establish a market for Medina. He came to the market of the Banū Qaynuqāʿ, then he went to (the place later known as -K) the market of Medina. He stamped its ground with his foot and said: This is your market; let it not be narrowed (*fa-lā yuḍayyaq*) and let no tax (*kharāj*) be taken on it [5]). A tradition quoted on the authority of Ibn Asīd reports that the place of the market of Medina was proposed to the Prophet by a man (scil. one of the adherents of the Prophet); the Prophet visited the place, stamped the ground with his foot and uttered his saying that it might not be diminished nor might a tax be imposed on it [6]).

A slightly different tradition is recorded by Ibn Mājah [7]) on the authority of Abū Usayd [8]). The Prophet went to the market of the

1) See about him Ibn Ḥajar: *Tahdhīb* IX, 115-17; al-Suyūṭī: *al-Laʾālī al-maṣnūʿa* I, 24 penult. (ed. Cairo, al-Maktaba al-Tijāriyya, n.d.); al-Dhahabī: *Mīzān al-iʿtidāl* III, 514. No. 7380; S.A.: al.Ali *Studies* p. 66-67; idem: *Muʾallafāt*, pp. 127-29.

2) See about him Ibn Ḥajar: *Tahdhīb* XI, 342 (his name is Yazīd b. ʿAbd Allāh (not ʿUbayd Allāh) b. Qusayṭ); al-Dhahabī: *Mīzān* IV, 430; al-Suyūṭī: *Isʿāf al-mubaṭṭaʾ bi-rijāl al-Muwaṭṭaʾ*, p. 42 (printed with *Tanwīr al-ḥawālik sharḥ ʿalā Muwaṭṭaʾ Mālik*, Cairo n.d.).

3) al-Samhūdī, *op. cit.*, I, 539 inf.

4) See about him: al-Dhahabī: *Tadkhkira* I, 90 (No. 80); idem: *Mīzān* III, 77 (No. 5654); Ibn Ḥajar: *Tahdhīb* VII, 217-18 (No. 399).

5) al-Samhūdī, *op. cit.*, I, 539.

6) al-Samhūdī, *op. cit.*, I, 540.

7) *Sunan al-Muṣṭafā* II, 28 (ed. Cairo 1349 AH).

8) His name was Mālik b. Rabīʿa al-Sāʿidī; see about him: al-Nābulusī: *Dhakhāʾir al-mawārīth* III, 91 — No. 6160 (ed. Cairo 1934); Ibn Ḥajar: *Iṣāba* IV, 23 — No. 7622; Ibn Saʿd: *Ṭabaqāt* III, 557-58 (ed. Beirut 1957).

Nabīṭ looked at it and said: This is not a market for you. Then he went to a market (i.e. to another market), looked at it and said: This is not a market for you. Then he returned to this market, circumambulated it and said: This is your market; let it not be diminished, and let no tax be levied on it [1]).

The place chosen by the Prophet was in the quarter of the Banū Sā'ida and served as a cemetery. The Banū Sā'ida objected at first but gave their consent later [2]). It was an open space and a rider could put his saddle in the market, go round the market in every direction and see his saddle [3]). Attempts to erect some buildings or to pitch tents in the market were prevented by the Prophet and later by 'Umar b. al-Khaṭṭāb [4]). It was Mu'āwiya who for the first time built two houses in the market: The *Dār al-Qaṭirān* and *Dār al-Nuqṣān* [5]) and levied taxes. Hishām built a big building which included the whole market; on the ground floor were shops, on the upper floor were rooms for letting. This building was demolished by the people of Medina when the news of the death of Hishām reached them [6]). The reason for this mutinous action seems to be that the people considered the building of the house in the market and the levying of taxes by the governor of the Caliph as unlawful innovations.

In fact the pious 'Umar b. 'Abd al-'Azīz is reported to have forbidden to levy any fee (*kirā'*) in the market on the grounds that "the market is a charitable endowment" (*al-sūq ṣadaqa*) [7]). The meaning of this utterance of 'Umar b. 'Abd al-'Azīz is elucidated by a report of Ibn Zubāla and Ibn Shabba, told on the authority of Muḥammad b. 'Abd

1) The text has *fa-lā yuntaqaṣanna*; the commentator reads and explains *fa-lā yuntaqaḍanna*, which seems to be an error.

2) al-Samhūdi, *op. cit.*, I, 540.

3) *ib.*, I 541.

4) *ib.* I, 540 inf. — 541 sup.; al-Hindī: *Kanz al-'ummāl* V, 488 .

5) al-Samhūdī: *op. cit.*, I. 541; *Dār al-Qaṭirān* and *Dār al-Nuqṣān* appear to be pejorative nicknames coined by the people who objected to the principle of building the houses and levying taxes.

6) Saleh Ahmed al-Ali: *Studies*, p. 86-87.

7) Reported by Ibn Zubāla on the authority of Khālid b. Ilyās al-'Adawī as recorded by al-Samhūdī, *op. cit.*, I, 540; about Khālid b. Ilyās see Ibn Ḥajar: *Tahdhīb* III, 80 and Dhahabī: *Mīzān* I, 627 (No. 2408).

Allāh b. Ḥasan [1]) stating that the Prophet granted the Muslims their markets as charitable endowment (*taṣaddaqa ʿalā ʾl-muslimīna bi-aswāqihim*) [2]). The letter of ʿUmar b. ʿAbd al-ʿAzīz abolished apparently the levying of taxes imposed on the market by Muʿāwiya.

The scanty reports about the market established by the Prophet in Medina seem to be trustworthy. They are recorded by ʿUmar b. Shabba and Ibn Zubāla, both competent authorities on the history of Medina. These reports were omitted in other sources because the event of the market was not enough important in shaping the image of the Prophet and the early community by later authors as the market itself did not survive and did not serve as place of devotion.

The establishment of the market by the Prophet a short time after his arrival in Medina [3]) seems to be of some importance. There is no indication of the intention of the Prophet; but the principle to establish a new market without taxes may imply that the Prophet intended to adopt the practice of the market at Ukāẓ where taxes were not levied. The later interpretation of this event was the idea of *al-sūq ṣādaqa*.

The clash with Kaʿb b. al-Ashraf [4]) seems to indicate that Kaʿb considered the establishment of the new market as competition to the existing one of the Banū Qaynuqāʿ. The story of the market supplies us with an additional aspect of the contention between the Prophet and the Jews in Medina.

---

1) See about him: Abū ʾl-Faraj al-Iṣfahānī: *Maqātil al-Ṭālibiyyīn*, index (ed. A. Ṣaqr, Cairo 1949); Ibn Ḥajar: *Tahdhīb* IX, 252; al-Dhahabī: *Mīzān* III, 591 (No. 7736).

2) al-Samhūdī, *op. cit.*, I, 540; comp. the utterance of ʿAlī: *Sūqu ʾl-muslimīna kamuṣallā ʾl-muṣallīna, man sabaqa ilā shayʾin fa-huwa lahu yaumahu ḥattā yadaʿahu* — al-Hindī: *Kanz al-ʿummāl* V, 488, No. 2688; and see al-Kulīnī: *al-Kāfī* II, 662 (ed. Teheran 1381 AH).

3) The date can be fixed by the date of the assassination of Kaʿb b. al-Ashraf. See Jones: *The Chronology of the Maghāzī*, BSOAS, 1957 p. 248, 262.

4) Kaʿb was elected as chief of the Jews, replacing Mālik b. al-Ṣayf; see ʿAli b. Burhān al-Dīn al-Ḥalabī: *Insān al-ʿuyūn* II, 116.

ADDITIONAL NOTES

ad p.274, note 3: Cf. al-Hindī, *Kanz al-ʿummāl* IV, 79, no.714: *ʿan ʿuthmāna qāla: kuntu abtāʿu l-tamra min baṭnin min al-yahūdi yuqālu lahum banū qaynuqāʿ wa-abī-ʿuhu bi-ribḥin...;* no.715: *ʿan ʿuthmāna: kuntu abīʿu l-tamra fī sūqi banī qaynuqāʿ...*

ad p.274, note 6: And see Nūr al-Dīn al-Haythamī, *Majmaʿ al-zawāʾid,* IV, 76.

ad p.276, note 2: Cf. Wakīʿ, *Akhbār al-quḍāt*, ed. ʿAbd al-ʿAzīz al-Marāghī, Cairo 1366/1947, I, 339: ... *anna iyāsa bna muʿāwiyata kāna yaqḍī fī sūqi l-baṣrati: hiya mithlu masjidi l-jāmiʿ, man sabaqa ilā makānin fahuwa aḥaqqu bihi mā jalasa ʿalayhi; fa-idhā qāma ākharu fa-jalasa ʿalayhi fa-huwa aḥaqqu bihi.....* The unjust deed of ʿUthmān who disregarded the order of the Prophet about the market of Medina to keep it as a charitable endowment for the Muslim community and gave it as grant to one of his relatives, al-Ḥārith b. al-Ḥakam, caused discontent among the Muslims. (See Ibn Qutayba, *al-Maʿārif*, ed. Tharwat ʿUkāsha, Cairo 1969, p.195: *qālū: wa-taṣaddaqa rasūlu llāhi (ṣ) bi-mahzūrin, mauḍiʿi sūqi l-madīnati ʿalā l-muslimīna, fa-aqṭaʿahā ʿuthmānu l-ḥāritha bna l-ḥakami akhā marwāna bni l-ḥakami).* And see Abū Nuʿaym, *Ḥilyat al-auliyāʾ*, IX, 48:... *saʾaltu l-ḥasana ʿan bayʿi dakākīni l-sūqi, fa-kariha bayʿahā wa-shirāʾahā wa-ijāratahā.* And cf. al-Bukhārī, *al-Taʾrīkh al-kabīr*, Hyderabad 1378, VI (=III/II) 218, no.2215: ... *anna ḥaddādan btanā kīran bi-l-sūqi fa-qāla: intaqiḍhu min al-sūqi, [fa-] qāma bihi fa-hudima.*

X

THE EXPEDITION OF BI'R MA'ŪNA

The character of the expedition sent by the Prophet in the month of Safar 4 H., [1] which ended in the killing of the participants at Bi'r Ma'ūna, is rather obscure. Traditions about this expedition are contradictory: [2] the aim of the expedition can hardly be determined; the number of the participants is variously stated in the divergent traditions; the tribal composition of the participants is disputed; the details about the attackers are few; the reason for their attack on the Muslim party is not clear. It may therefore be useful to present a survey of some of the traditions concerning this encounter, in course of which a version apparently hitherto unknown is presented.

I

The traditional account of the story as reported by Ibn Isḥāq (d. 151 H.) [3] forms a composite narrative, based on the authority of a number of Muslim traditionists. According to this account, one of the chiefs of ʿĀmir b. Ṣaʿṣaʿa, Abū Barāʾ ʿĀmir b. Mālik, [4] nicknamed "Mulāʿib al-Asinna" ("The Player with the Spears"), [5] came to the Prophet and was invited by him to accept Islam. Although he did not embrace Islam, he was not far removed from it. He asked the Prophet to send some of his Companions to Najd to summon its people to embrace Islam, and expressed the hope that they would respond. He assured the Prophet of his protection of the Companions. The Prophet sent forty of his Companions with al-Mundhir b. ʿAmr

---

[1] Cf. J. M. B. Jones, "The Chronology of the Maghāzī—a textual survey," in *BSOAS* (*Bulletin of the School of Oriental and African Studies* **XXI**,1957), 249, 267: the anonymous tradition fixing the date of the expedition in Muharram (p. 249 n. 10) is quoted as well in Samhūdī's *Wafāʾ al-wafāʾ*, I, 211.

[2] See Max v. Oppenheim, *Die Beduinen*, rev. and ed. W. Caskel, III, 9.

[3] In Ibn Hishām's *Sīra*.

[4] See his biography in Ibn Ḥajar, *Iṣāba* nº 4417.

[5] For this nickname, see Ibn al-Kalbī, *Ansāb al-Khail*, ed. Aḥmad Zakī Pasha (Cairo, 1946), 77; Aus b. Ḥajar, *Dīwān*, ed. Geyer, XVII, 7, 8; XXI, 3; Ibn ʿAbd Rabbihi, *ʿIqd*, III (Cairo, 1935), 335; Yāqūt, *Buldān*, s.v. "Sullān"; al-Zurqanī; *Sharḥ ʿalā ʾl-mawāhib*, II (1325 H.), 75; al-Suhailī: *al-Rauḍ al-unuf*, II (Cairo, 1914), 174.

al-Sāʿidī.[1] When the party reached Biʾr Maʿūna,[2] they sent Ḥarām b. Milḥān with the Prophet's letter to ʿĀmir b. al-Ṭufail.[3] He, however, killed the envoy, without even looking at the letter. ʿĀmir b. al-Ṭufail summoned his people (that is, the ʿĀmir b. Ṣaʿṣaʿa) to attack the party of the Muslims. But they respected the protection of Abū Barāʾ, and refused to join him. He then summoned the clans of Sulaim: ʿUṣaiya, Riʿl and Dhakwān. They responded and attacked the Muslim party. The Muslims fought, but were killed to the last man.[4]

Two men of the expedition, ʿAmr b. Umaiya al-Ḍamrī and a man from the Anṣār, who were engaged in pasturing the camels of the party, noticed some vultures hovering about the camp. When they drew near, they saw the dead bodies of their companions. The Anṣārī decided to fight, and was slain by the polytheists. ʿAmr b. Umaiya was captured, but was released by ʿĀmir b. al-Ṭufail, when he stated that he was from Muḍar.[5] On his way, he killed two men of ʿĀmir b. Ṣaʿṣaʿa, whom he accidentally met, not being aware that they had been granted protection by the Prophet. The Prophet paid their bloodwit.

Abū Barāʾ was grieved by the violation of his protection by ʿĀmir b. al-Ṭufail, and the death of the Prophet's companions. Ḥassān b. Thābit composed verses inciting the son of Abū Barāʾ, Rabīʿa, against ʿĀmir b. al-Ṭufail.[6]

---

[1] See, about him, Ibn Saʿd, *Ṭabaqāt*, III (Beirut), 555, 618; Ibn Duraid, *Ishtiqāq*, ed. A.S. Hārūn, 456; Ibn ʿAbd al-Barr, *Istīʿāb*, 275; Ibn Ḥajar, *Iṣāba*, nº 8220.

[2] For the location of the place, see ʿArrām b. al-Aṣbagh al-Sulamī, *Asmāʾ Jibāl Tihāma*, ed. A. S. Hārūn, (*Nawādir al-Makhṭūṭāt*) VIII, 429; Yāqūt, *Buldān*, s.v. "Biʾr Maʿūna", "Ublā"; Samhūdī, *Wafāʾ al-wafāʾ*, II, 256-57; Thilo, *Die Ortsnamen in altarabischen Poesie*, s.v. "Ublā".

[3] See *EI*², s.v. "ʿĀmir b. al-Ṭufail" (W. Caskel).

[4] Only one man, wounded seriously, was left. He survived till the Battle of the Trench.

[5] Ibn al-Kalbī, *Jamhara*, MS British Museum, fº 45b; al-Balādhurī, *Ansab*, MS, fº 896a.

[6] The rendering of these verses by Nabia Abbott (*Studies in Arabic Papyri*, [Chicago, 1957], 69) is rather inaccurate. "Alā abligh Rabīʿata dhā 'l-masāʿī: fa-mā aḥdathta fī 'l-ḥadathāni baʿdī" is not "*Verily I shall inform Rabīʿah, he of the highest distinctions, of the event you caused to happen* (*right*) *behind me.*" "Alam yaruʿkum" cannot be rendered: "surely you will make amends": the correct translation is: "were you not shocked (or stirred)." "Wa-mā khaṭaʾun ka-ʿamdi" cannot be translated: "and he (the latter) did not do wrong (to the man of Biʾr Maʿūna) intentionally." It should be rendered: "a mistake is not the same as an intentional act" (that is, an intentionally committed crime). Cf. the translations of Guillaume, *The Life of Muhammad*, 435; Lyall, *The Dīwāns of ʿAbīd b. al-Abraṣ*

Rabīʿa b. ʿĀmir, the son of Abū Barāʾ attacked ʿĀmir b. al-Ṭufail, trying to kill him, but he failed.

Anas b. ʿAbbās al-Sulamī, a maternal uncle of Ṭuʿaima b. ʿAdī b. Naufal, boasted of his killing Nāfiʿ b. Budail al-Khuzāʿī, one of the members of the Muslim party. The martyrs were mourned in verses by ʿAbd Allāh b. Rawāḥa and Ḥassān b. Thābit. Kaʿb b. Mālik composed verses blaming the Jaʿfar b. Kilāb (of ʿĀmir b. Ṣaʿṣaʿa) for not carrying out the obligation of protection granted to the Muslim party. [1]

This account of Ibn Isḥāq [2] differs in very essential points from the account of Mūsā b. ʿUqba (d. 141 H.). [3] His account is traced to al-Zuhrī (d. 124 H.). [4] Abū Barāʾ refused to accept Islam. He offered the Prophet a gift, but the Prophet refused to accept the gift of a polytheist. [5] The number of the Companions sent by the Prophet is rendered by the word *rahṭ*, denoting rather a small group.

As in the account of Ibn Isḥāq, ʿĀmir b. al-Ṭufail summons his people to attack the Muslim party. When they refused, he appealed to the clans of Sulaim. They joined him, attacked the Muslim party and killed all the men, except ʿAmr b. Umaiya al-Ḍamrī, who was released by ʿĀmir b. al-Ṭufail. [6]

The same account is partly quoted by Ibn Ḥajar, [7] with an explicit statement that it is taken from the book of the *Maghāzī* by Mūsā b. ʿUqba.

The most important detail in the account of Mūsā b. ʿUqba is the

---

and ʿĀmir b. al-Ṭufail, 87; W. Arafat, "The Development of a Dramatic Theme in the Story of Khubaib," *BSOAS* XXI (1958), 19, line 12.

[1] The verses of Kaʿb b. Mālik were added by Ibn Hishām; see Guillaume, *op. cit.*, 762 (678).

[2] Ibn Hishām, *Sīra*, ed. Saqqā, Abyārī, Shalabī, III, 193-99; Guillaume, *op. cit.*, 433-36.

[3] Sachau, "*Das Berliner Fragment des Mūsā b. ʿUqba*," *Sitzungsberichte der phil. Classe, Preussische Akademie der Wissenschaften* (1904), 468.

[4] See A. A. Duri, "A Study on the Beginnings of History Writing in Islam," *BSOAS* XX (1957).

[5] The same saying of refusal uttered by the Prophet when ʿIyāḍ b. Ḥimār al-Mujāshiʿī offered him the gift of a horse; see Ibn Qutaiba, *al-Maʿārif*, (Cairo, 1935), 147; al-Ṭabarānī, *al-Muʿjam al-ṣaghīr* (Delhi), 3; Abū ʿUbaid, *Amwāl*, 256; Ibn al-Kalbī, *Jamhara*, f° 66a; Ibn Ḥajar, *Iṣāba*, n° 6123. The same expression occurs again, when the Prophet refused to accept the gift of Ḥakīm b. Ḥizām; see Zubair b. Bakkār, *Nasab Quraish*, MS Bodl., f° 65b; *Lisān al-ʿArab*, s.v. "ZBD"; and see the discussion in Abū ʿUbaid's *Amwāl*, 257, whether the gift was presented by ʿĀmir b. Tufail or by ʿĀmir b. Mālik.

[6] See the translation of this document in Guillaume, *op. cit.*, p. xliv (Introduction).

[7] *Iṣāba*, n° 8220.

phrase that al-Mundhir b. ʿAmr al-Sāʿidī was sent by the Prophet with the group as "his spy in Najd" (ʿainan lahu fī ahli Najd). It points to the fact, that the expedition was not a peaceful missionary enterprise.

The papyrus about the campaigns of Muḥammad, edited by Nabia Abbott, [1] contains the story of the expedition of Bi'r Maʿūna. The date of the papyrus is fixed by Professor Abbott at the end of the second century of the Hijra and it is attributed by her to Maʿmar b. Rāshid (d. 154 H.). The story of the expedition shows close affinity to the account of Ibn Isḥāq. It may be remarked that a list of the Anṣār, killed at Bi'r Maʿūna, is given. According to the version of the papyrus, three men were pasturing the cattle of the party. One of them preferred to fight the polytheists, and was killed. The other two went back to Medina, and, on their way back, they killed the two men of Kilāb who had been granted a safeconduct by the Prophet.

The composite account of al-Wāqidī (d. 207 H.) [2] contains quite divergent details. According to this account, the Prophet sent seventy young men of the Anṣār, distinguished by their piety and called *al-qurrāʾ*. The version giving the number as seventy is told on the authority of Abū Saʿīd al-Khudrī (d. 63 or 74 H.) and is repeated by a saying about four battles, in each of which seventy Anṣār were killed, [3] but al-Wāqidī prefers the version of forty men. Further, al-Wāqidī mentions that a guide of Sulaim, called al-Muṭālib (read: al-Muṭṭalib), [4] was sent with the party. Al-Wāqidī gives the name of the man of the Anṣār, who was sent with ʿAmr b. Umaiya to pasture the camels of the party, as al-Ḥārith b. al-Ṣimma. [5] A passage is devoted to the description of the heroic death of the leader of the party, al-Mundhir b. ʿAmr; he refused to be pardoned by the attackers, fought and was killed. Also al-Ḥārith b. al-Ṣimma preferred to die fighting. A special passage, told on the authority of ʿUrwa, reports the death of ʿUrwa (b. Asmāʾ) b. al-Ṣalt, who was on friendly terms with ʿĀmir b. al-Ṭufail, and whom his people, the Sulaim, tried to spare and par-

[1] N. Abbott, *Studies in Arabic Papyri*, Document 5 (Chicago, 1957), 65-79.

[2] *al-Maghāzī*, ed. v. Kremer, 337-44.

[3] al-Wāqidī, *al-Maghāzī*, 338, 341; Ibn ʿAsākir, *Taʾrīkh*, VII (Damascus, 1932), 198; Zurqānī, *Sharḥ ʿalā ʾl-mawāhib*, II, 77.

[4] See Ibn Ḥajar, *Iṣāba*, nº 8024.

[5] See Ibn ʿAbd al-Barr, *Istīʿāb*, 112; Ibn Ḥajar, *Iṣāba*, nº 1423. According to Ibn Hishām, *Sīra*, III, 195 the name of the Anṣārī who pastured with ʿAmr b. Umaiya was al-Mundhir b. Muḥammad b. ʿUqba b. Uḥaiḥa b. al-Julāḥ (see, about him, Ibn Duraid, *Ishtiqāq*, ed. A.S. Hārūn, 441; Ibn ʿAbd al-Barr, *Istīʿāb*, 276; Ibn Ḥajar, *Iṣāba*, nº 8225).

doned. He, however, preferred to fight and was killed. [1] The story about the gift offered to the Prophet by Abū Barāʾ is recorded, but another version of this story is added as well. Abū Barāʾ sent Labīd and his son Rabīʿa with a gift to the Prophet. The Prophet refused to accept the gift. He sent him, however, a remedy for the tumor of which Abū Barāʾ suffered, as he did request it. According to the account of al-Wāqidī, Rabīʿa, the son of Abū Barāʾ, attempted to kill ʿĀmir b. al-Ṭufail after a talk with the Prophet.

Al-Wāqidī devotes special passages to the story about the Prophet's curse on Muḍar and the clans of Sulaim, [2] mentions the verse of the Koran revealed to the Prophet on the occasion of the slaughter of the Companions (later abrogated) and gives a list of the killed members of the expedition.

Of special importance is a version given by al-Wāqidī, stating that Saʿd b. Abī Waqqāṣ returned to the Prophet with ʿAmr b. Umaiya. Al-Wāqidī refutes this version, on the ground that only Anṣār participated in this expedition. [3] Also of importance is the remark of al-Wāqidī about Anas b. ʿAbbās al-Riʿlī al-Sulamī, who killed Nāfiʿ b. Budail al-Khuzāʿī: "He went out on the Day of Bi'r Maʿūna, inciting his people to fight the Muslim party, in order to avenge the blood of the son of his sister, [4] Ṭu'aima b. ʿAdī."

Ibn Saʿd (d. 230 H.) has two versions: [5] (1) a version similar to that of al-Wāqidī, including the description of the expedition as a group of pious young Readers, the action of ʿĀmir b. al-Ṭufail and his killing of Ḥarām b. Milḥān, the curse of the Prophet, the *āya* revealed to the Prophet and the return of ʿAmr b. Umaiya; (2) a tradition transmitted by Ibn Abī ʿArūba-Qatāda-Anas b. Mālik, giving quite a different explanation of the affair of Bi'r Maʿūna. Riʿl, Dhakwān, ʿUṣaiya and Liḥyān [6] came to the Prophet and sought his

---

[1] See, about him, Ibn Saʿd, *Ṭabaqāt*, IV (Beirut), 377; al-Balādhurī, *Ansāb*, MS f° 1131b; Ibn ʿAbd al-Barr, *Istīʿāb*, 491; Ibn Ḥazm, *Jamharat ansāb al-ʿArab*, ed. Levi-Provençal, 250; Ibn Ḥajar, *Iṣāba*, n° 5509.

[2] See Ṭabarī, *Tafsīr*, ed. A. M. Shākir, n° 7821 (Kor. 3, 128); al-Naḥās, *al-Nāsikh* (Cairo, 1938), 91; Marzūqī, *Azmina*, II (Hyderabad, 1332 H.), 33; J. Kowalski, *O pewnych potrawach spozywanych w Arabii podczas głodu* (R.O. 1914), 223 ; al-Baghdādī, *Khizāna*, III, 142.

[3] Al-Wāqidī, however, contradicts himself by giving the list of the martyrs: ʿĀmir b. Fuhaira was a maulā of Abū Bakr; Nāfiʿ b. Budail was from Khuzāʿa; ʿUrwa b. Asmāʾ b. al-Ṣalt was from Sulaim; al-Ḥakam b. Kaisān was a maulā of Makhzūm; ʿAmr b. Umaiya (the survivor of the expedition) was from Kināna.

[4] In the text: *ibni akhīhi*, read *ibni ukhtihi*; al-*Maghāzī*, 344.

[5] *Ṭabaqāt*, II (Beirut), 51-54.

[6] The Liḥyān were in fact cursed by the Prophet with Dhakwān, ʿUṣaiya

aid against their people (probably the unbelievers among their people). The Prophet sent with them seventy pious men of the Anṣār, called *al-qurrā'*. When they reached Bi'r Ma'ūna, these clans betrayed them and killed them. The Prophet cursed these clans daily for a month in his morning prayer. A revelation had been sent down to the Prophet: "Inform your people, that we met our Lord and He was pleased with us and contented us."

Two other versions recorded by Ibn Sa'd in the biography of Ḥarām b. Milḥān deserve attention. Both versions are told on the authority of Anas b. Mālik. The first version states that some people came to the Prophet and asked him to send men to teach them Koran and Sunna. The Prophet sent seventy pious men called *al-qurrā'*. This Muslim party was attacked by these people and slaughtered before they reached their destination. Ḥarām b. Milḥān was pierced with a spear by a man who came from behind and killed him. This version, rather a vague one, is followed by a version more clear and detailed: The Prophet sent seventy men with Ḥarām b. Milḥān to the Banū 'Āmir b. Ṣa'ṣa'a. Ḥarām volunteered to precede the party. He came to the unbelievers and got a promise of safety. When he talked with them about the Prophet they signaled to one of them, who attacked him and pierced him with a spear. [1]

It may be remarked that the three versions recorded by Ibn Sa'd contradict the version that 'Āmir b. al-Ṭufail killed Ḥarām. In these three versions 'Āmir b. al-Ṭufail is not mentioned at all.

Muḥammad b. Ḥabīb (d. 245 H.) gives a very short account about the expedition. The Prophet sent al-Mundhir b. 'Amr al-Sā'idī with thirty men to Bi'r Ma'ūna; twenty-six of them were Anṣār, four were Muhājirūn. All of them were killed, except 'Amr b. Umaiya al-Kinānī. [2]

The number of the members of the expedition, given by Ibn Ḥabīb as thirty, is the smallest one mentioned in the sources. Nothing in this account is said about the course of the encounter about the aim of the expedition.

An important tradition in connection with the expedition of Bi'r

---

and Ri'l. The Liḥyān were responsible for the slaughter of the Companions at the Day of al-Rajī'. The information about the two disasters reached the Prophet on the same day and he cursed the clans of Sulaim together with Liḥyān; see Lyall, *The Dīwāns of 'Abīd b. al-Abraṣ and 'Āmir b. al-Ṭufail*, 86 n. 4; 'Ali b. Burhān al-Dīn, *Insān al-'Uyūn*, III, 195.

1 *Ṭabaqāt*, III, 514-15.

2 *al-Muḥabbar*, 118.

Ma'ūna is given by Ibn Ḥabīb in a chapter devoted to "Stories of men who drank undiluted wine till death, because of anger or disdain." [1]

According to this tradition, it was 'Āmir b. al-Ṭufail who went out against the Companions sent by the Prophet on the request of Abū Barā' to teach his people Islam, and killed them all, except one. Abū Barā' became angry, because 'Āmir b. al-Ṭufail violated his promised protection of the Companions. When the people of Abū Barā' were informed that 'Āmir b. al-Ṭufail had died on his way home from a visit to the Prophet, they decided to leave their abode and seek new pastures. When Abū Barā' asked about the unwonted movement in the camp he was informed: "They are departing because of the event which happened." He was surprised to learn that they were about to depart without his order. One of his relatives told him that they suspected that he had had a fit of mental aberration when he was sent to "that man." Abū Barā' became enraged and decided to drink himself to death. "There is no good in life when the Banū 'Āmir disobeyed me." [2]

The tribal tradition of the Banū 'Āmir b. Ṣa'ṣa'a is reflected in a peculiar sentence quoted by Ibn Ḥabīb: "The Banū 'Āmir say that he did not kill himself. He died as Muslim."

The tradition recorded by Ibn Ḥabīb is a significant and a rare one, stating that Abū Barā' lost influence in his tribe and that he outlived 'Āmir b. al-Ṭufail.

Al-Balādhurī (d. 279 H.) has a short record of the expedition. The number of the men was forty or seventy. They went out at the request of Abū Barā' as missionaries, and were killed in an attack launched against them by 'Āmir b. al-Ṭufail, aided by the clans of Sulaim. [3]

Al-Bukhārī (d. 256 H.) quotes the tradition of Qatāda on the authority of Anas, already mentioned above (see Ibn Sa'd), according to which the Companions were treacherously killed by the clans of Sulaim and Liḥyān who invited them. The tradition in which the role of Ḥarām b. Milḥān is stressed, already mentioned above as well, is also recorded. (See, above, Ibn Sa'd, the biography of Ḥarām.) A

---

[1] *Op. cit.*, 472; this version is given by Bakrī in his *Mu'jam mā 'sta'jam*, s.v. "Ma'ūna". The version is divergent on a detail: 'Amr b. Umaiya and Ḥarām b. Milḥān pastured the camels of the Muslims. Ḥarām decided to fight the polytheists and was killed. 'Amr b. Umaiya returned to the Prophet.

[2] About his drinking of wine till his death, see, Jarīr wa 'l-Farazdaq, *Naqā'iḍ*, ed. Bevan, 199; Ibn Qutaiba, *al-Shi'r wa 'l-shu'arā'*, ed. de Goeje, 224

[3] *Ansāb al-ashrāf*, ed. Hamidullah, I, 375.

peculiar tradition told as well on the authority of Anas deserves to be mentioned: the Prophet sent seventy men called *al-qurrā'* for some purpose. They were met by two clans of Sulaim, Riʿl and Dhakwān, at the well of Bi'r Maʿūna. The men of the Muslim party said to them: "By God, we do not intend you, we are merely passing by to carry out some purpose of the Prophet." They (that is, the clans of Sulaim) killed the men of the Muslim party, and the Prophet cursed them daily for a month in his morning prayer. [1]

Al-Ṭabarī (d. 310 H.) records the account of Ibn Isḥāq but mentions the other versions as well. Both versions about the death of Ḥarām are given: (1) that he was killed by ʿĀmir b. al-Ṭufail, and (2) that he was killed by a man from the people of Bi'r Maʿūna. Four verses of Ḥassān (already mentioned) and nine verses of Kaʿb b. Mālik, blaming the relatives of Abū Barā' for not helping the attacked Muslim party, and reproaching the violators of the promise of protection given to the Prophet, are quoted as well. [2].

Al-Masʿūdī (d. 345 H.) blames ʿĀmir b. al-Ṭufail of the killing of seventy Anṣār sent to Najd by the Prophet, to teach the people the Koran. [3]

A tradition closely resembling the tradition recorded by al-Bukhārī, in which it was stressed that the missionaries did not intend the clans of Sulaim, is given by al-Ṭabarānī (d. 360 H.). [4] Some details in this account may be stressed: the expedition was sent by the Prophet after the death of Khubaib. It was Ḥarām b. Milḥān who informed the men of Sulaim, that the party had no intentions concerning them (*annā lasnā īyāhum nurīdu*) in order to gain their consent to their passage. There is a description of how the men of Sulaim killed Ḥarām and the Muslim party. [5]

An important version, differing from other accounts, is given by al-Samarqandī (d. 393 H.) in his *Tafsīr*. [6] The Prophet sent a troop commanded by al-Mundhir b. ʿAmr. The Banū ʿĀmir b. Ṣaʿṣaʿa went out against them, ambushed them and killed them. Three men of the participants of the expedition came back. In the neighborhood of Medina they met two men of Sulaim, who stated that they were of

---

1 *Ṣaḥīḥ*, III (Cairo, 1286 H.), 23-25.
2 Ṭabarī, *Ta'rīkh*, II (Cairo 1939), 219-223.
3 *al-Tanbīh wa 'l-ishrāf* (Cairo, 1938), 212.
4 *al-Muʿjam al-ṣaghīr*, 110.
5 This tradition is quoted in Abū Nuʿaim's *Ḥilyat al-auliyā'*, I, 123.
6 MS Chester Beatty, II, fº 228a.

'Āmir b. Ṣa'ṣa'a, and killed them. About these three men, *āya* one of sura forty-nine was revealed.

Abū Nu'aim al-Iṣbahānī (d. 430 H.) records, in his *Ḥilya*, the version of Qatāda about the treacherous slaughter of the seventy Anṣār by the clans of Sulaim who invited them. He also records a tradition related on the authority of Ka'b b. Mā'ik, according to which 'Āmir b. al-Ṭufail attacked and killed a small group (*nafar*) of Companions sent to the Banū Sulaim. [1] In his *Dalā'il al-nubūwa*, Abū Nu'aim records the version about the sending of a small group (*rahṭ*) of pious Companions at the request of Abū Barā', and their slaughter by 'Āmir b. al-Ṭufail. From al-Wāqidī are quoted the passages about the heroic death of 'Āmir b. Fuhaira, and about the gift sent to the Prophet by Abū Barā', with Labīd. [2]

A unique tradition is recorded by Abū' l-Baqā' Hibat Allāh.[3] According to this version ten survivors of the Muslim party returned to Medina.

Later sources do not contribute much to the elucidation of the event. The account of Ibn 'Asākir (d. 686 H.) is mainly based on that of al-Wāqidī. [4] On Wāqidī's account is also based the version of al-Maqrīzī (d. 845 H.).[5] Al-Suyūṭī (d. 911 H.) records the version[6] given by al-Ṭabarī, [7] on the authority of Isḥāq b. Abī Ṭalḥa—Anas: the forty or seventy Companions were sent to Bi'r Ma'ūna. There stayed 'Āmir b. al-Ṭufail. The Muslims entered a cave and sent Ḥarām b. Milḥān to the people of Bi'r Ma'ūna to convey the message of the Prophet. He was killed by a man of the people of Bi'r Ma'ūna. 'Āmir b. al-Ṭufail, with the people of Bi'r Ma'ūna, attacked the Muslims in the cave and killed them. The *āya* revealed to the Prophet in connection with this event was replaced by *āya* 169 of sura 3. [8]

The account of 'Alī b. Burhān al-Dīn (d. 1044 H.) [9] is mainly based on the accounts of Ibn Isḥāq and al-Wāqidī. The contradictory accounts are quoted, and attempts of scholars to smooth out the con-

---

[1] *Ḥilyat al-auliyā'*, I, 123.

[2] Pp. 185-86 (Hyderabad, 1320 H.).

[3] *al-Manāqib al-Mazyadīya*, MS British Museum f° 8a.

[4] *Ta'rīkh*, VII, 195-199.

[5] *Imtā' al-asmā'*, ed. A. M. Shākir, I (Cairo, 1941), 170-73.

[6] *al-Durr al-manthūr*, II, 95.

[7] *Ta'rīkh*, II, 222; and cf. Ṭabarī, *Tafsīr*, ed. A. M. Shākir, n° 8224 (Kor. 3, 169).

[8] See also Ibn Kathīr, *Tafsīr*, Kor. 3, 169.

[9] *Insān al-'uyūn*, III (1353 H.), 194-97.

tradictions are recorded. (The number of the members of the party, the curse of Liḥyān with the clans of Sulaim, etc.)

Al-Samhūdī (d. 1056 H.) quotes the traditions of Ibn Isḥāq and al-Bukhārī. Contradictory traditions are discussed (the tribal composition of the expedition, whether Abū Barā' drank wine till death, or accepted Islam and died a Muslim in battle). [1]

The path of reconciliation between contradictory traditions is followed by al-Zurqānī (d. 1122 H.). [2] A case of plausible reconciliation may be quoted here. Quoting the tradition that Ḥarām was killed by ʿĀmir b. al-Ṭufail and the tradition that he was killed by a man of Sulaim, al-Zurqānī states that ʿĀmir b. al-Ṭufail was the leader of the people, so the deed was attributed to him. [3]

In summary, it may be said that the traditions about this expedition are contradictory as to whether the expedition was a peaceful one sent to teach Islam and the Koran, or a military enterprise; whether it was sent to the Banū ʿĀmir or to Sulaim; whether the members of the expedition were slain by clans of Sulaim, by clans of ʿĀmir b. Ṣaʿṣaʿa, by clans of Sulaim led by ʿĀmir b. al-Ṭufail; whether the envoy, Ḥarām, was killed by ʿĀmir b. al-Ṭufail; or by a man of Sulaim; whether the ʿĀmir b. Ṣaʿṣaʿa opposed the relations between Abū Barā' and the Prophet or supported it; whether ten or three or two or one of the members of the party survived and returned to Medina; whether Saʿd b. Abī Waqqās was among the members of the party or not; whether three or two men who returned to Medina killed the two men of Sulaim (or ʿĀmir b. Ṣaʿṣaʿa), or whether it was ʿAmr b. Umaiya alone who killed them; whether the members of the party were Anṣār only, or Anṣār and Muhājirūn.

II

Scholars have tried to find an answer to the riddle of the expedition. Muir [4] assumes that "perhaps there were divided opinions in the tribe [that is, ʿĀmir b. Ṣaʿṣaʿa]." Muir points out that the Prophet, almost immediately after the massacre, entered into communication with ʿĀmir b. al-Ṭufail, on the subject of the latter's claim for blood-money for the two ʿĀmirites killed by the returning ʿAmr b. Umaiya, without making any counterclaim for the blood of the martyrs, and

---

1 *Wafā' al-wafā'*, I (1326 H.), 211.

2 *Sharḥ ʿalā 'l-mawāhib*, II (Cairo, 1325 H.), 74-79.

3 *fa-kāna nisbatu dhālika ilaihi ʿalā sabīli 'l-taǰauwuzi.*

4 *The life of Moḥammad*, ed. Weir (Edinburgh, 1912), 280 n. 2.

remarks that (all this) "looks as if the attack was not so gratuitous as might appear."

Caetani mentions the same argument (of paying ʿĀmir b. al-Ṭufail the bloodwite for the two men from Kilāb who had been killed). Caetani supposes that the disaster of Biʾr Maʿūna was the consequence of a military expedition, not of a peaceful missionary enterprise. He suggests that there might have been some violation of a pact by the Muslims, and that therefore the massacre was an act of legitimate defense or revenge. [1]

Lyall makes a comprehensive study of the question of the aim of the expedition. [2] He reaches the conclusion that it was a warlike expedition "sent by the Prophet to help one section of the Banū Sulaim against another." "The Prophet had reason to think, from his relations with Abū Barāʾ, that the ʿĀmir b. Ṣaʿṣaʿa were friendly to him and might have been expected to help. In this he was disappointed. The Sulamīs proved to be treacherous, and ʿĀmir b. al-Ṭufail perhaps joined them in the attack on the Prophet's party." The payment of the bloodwit by the Prophet for the two ʿĀmirites serves as evidence, for Lyall, that ʿĀmir b. al-Ṭufail did not in fact violate an express pledge of protection given by Abū Barāʾ.

Buhl gives the traditional account of the expedition as a peaceful missionary enterprise. [3]

Watt, trying to solve the problem of the blood money paid by the Prophet to ʿĀmir b. al-Ṭufail, without any counterclaim for the martyrs of Biʾr Maʿūna, declares that it is improbable, as has been suggested, "that the Muslims had done something which caused them to forfeit the right to blood money." [4] Watt suggests that ʿĀmir b. al-Ṭufail encouraged the Sulamī clans to massacre the Muslims. "He was morally responsible, he was not their leader in any sense and so not technically responsible." [5] "It was probably also they who killed the letter carrier." Watt suggests that the appeal of Abū Barāʾ to Muhammad "was at bottom an appeal for help against rivals within his tribe. Muḥammad, anxious to bring Banū ʿĀmir to his own side, decided to interfere in the internal politics of the tribe,

---

1 Caetani, *Annali dellʾIslam*, I (Milano 1905), 578-80.

2 *The Dīwāns of ʿAbīd b. al-Abraṣ and ʿĀmir b. al-Ṭufail* (Leiden, 1913), 84-89.

3 *Das Leben Muhammeds* (Heidelberg, 1955), 261-62.

4 Cf. Caetani, *op. cit.*, *loc. cit.*

5 Cf. the opinion of Lyall, *op. cit.*, 89: "The Sulamīs proved to be treacherous and ʿĀmir b. al-Ṭufail perhaps joined them."

though he realized the riskiness of doing so." [1] 'Āmir b. al-Ṭufail was not strong enough to bring the tribe to disown Abū Barā''s protection, and "persuaded his neighbours of B. Sulaim to attack the Muslims, and doubtless gave them help by way of information." [2]

C. E. Bosworth suggests [3] that "Muḥammad had apparently been invited to intervene in an internal dispute of Sulaim, but the incident is also mixed up with the quarrel within 'Āmir between Abū Barā' and 'Āmir b. al-Ṭufail."

W. Caskel states that "there was an engagement of protection entered into by the uncle of 'Āmir b. al-Ṭufail, only that 'Āmir could not fulfil it among Sulaim, who had killed the 'holy band', in reality a pillaging expedition." [4] Caskel states that after the death of Abū Barā', 'Āmir b. al-Ṭufail became formally the head of the Ja'far.

Nabia Abbott assumes that "this was not a military expedition but a proselytizing mission to a large confederation of tribes in the prosperous and coveted Najd." [5]

Muhammad Hamidullah mentions the massacre of the seventy missionaries, treacherously slain by 'Āmir b. al-Ṭufail in the territory of Sulaim. The Sulaim were evidently discontented, assumes Hamidullah, because of the Muslim expeditions in their territory, in the preceding months. [6]

III

As mentioned above, al-Wāqidī quotes a version stating that Sa'd b. Abī Waqqāṣ returned with 'Amr b. Umaiya al-Ḍamrī to the Prophet, after the massacre of Bi'r Ma'ūna. Al-Wāqidī seems to refute this information, stressing that only men of the Anṣār participated in this expedition. [7]

The information about the participation of Sa'd b. Abī Waqqāṣ in the expedition of Bi'r Ma'ūna is included in a significant account recorded by Abu 'l-Laith al-Samarqandī (d. 393 H.): [8]

> 'Āmir b. Mālik, one of the horsemen of the Arabs (his nickname was Mulā'ib al-Asinna) wrote to the Prophet: 'Send me men to teach us the Koran and instruct us in religion. They will be under my pro-

---

1 Cf. Muir, above, about "The divided opinions in the tribe."

2 W. M. Watt, *Muhammad at Medina* (Oxford, 1956), 31-33, 97-98.

3 *EI*², s.v. "Bi'r Ma'ūna."

4 *EI*², s.v. "'Āmir b. al-Ṭufail."

5 *Studies in Arabic Papyri*, 76-79.

6 *Le Prophète de l'Islam*, I (1959), 312.

7 Wāqidī, *op. cit.*, 342 *infra*—343 *supra.*

8 *Bustān al-'ārifīn* (on margin of *Tanbīh al-ghāfilīn*), 207.

> tection.' The Prophet sent him Mundhir b. 'Amr al-Sā'idī with fourteen men, Muhājirūn and Anṣār. After a night's march, they heard that 'Āmir b. Mālik had died. They wrote to the Prophet and he sent four men to help them. They travelled together till they reached Bi'r Ma'ūna. Then they were attacked by 'Āmir b. al-Ṭufail with some clans of the Bedouins, Ri'l, Dhakwān, Liḥyān and 'Uṣaiya, who killed them all at Bi'r Ma'ūna, except for 'Amr b. Umaiya al-Ḍamrī, Sa'd b. Abī Waqqāṣ and another person. That was because they had dropped behind the party. When they [that is, the three men] learned that the party had been wiped out, they returned to Medina. The Prophet cursed these clans in his prayers for forty days.

This account, quite different from the stories of the heroic death of al-Mundhir b. 'Amr, 'Āmir b. Fuhaira, Ḥarām b. Milḥān and others, was not admitted into the current collections of traditions about the *maghāzī*.

It seems, however, to be an abridged version. Some additional details are given in a narrative recorded by al-Samarqandī in his *Tafsīr*. [1]

> 'Āmir b. Mālik wrote to the Prophet: 'Send me men to teach us the Koran and instruct us in religion. They will be under my protection.' The Prophet sent al-Mundhir b. 'Amr al-Sā'idī with fourteen men, Muhājirūn and Anṣār and they set out in the direction of Bi'r Ma'ūna. When they were a night's march from Medina, they heard that 'Āmir b. Mālik had died. Al-Mundhir b. 'Amr wrote to the Prophet, asking him to send aid, and the Prophet sent four men: 'Amr b. Umaiya al-Ḍamrī, al-Ḥārith b. al-Ṣimma, Sa'd b. Abī Waqqāṣ and another man. They travelled till they reached Bi'r Ma'ūna. Then they wrote to Rabī'a b. Mālik [that is, to Rabī'a b. 'Āmir b. Mālik]: 'We are under your protection and the protection of your father. Shall we proceed to you or not?' He said: 'You are under my protection, so come.'
>
> Then 'Āmir b. al-Ṭufail set out against them and asked assistance of Ri'l, Dhakwān and 'Uṣaiya. They went out against the Muslims who fought them until they killed all of them, except 'Amr b. Umaiya, al-Ḥārith b. al-Ṣimma and Sa'd b. Abī Waqqāṣ.
>
> (These three) had lagged behind (the Muslim party) and alighted under a tree. A bird perched on the tree let drop a clot of blood upon them. They understood that the bird had drunk blood, and said: 'Our friends have been killed.' They climbed a mountain and saw the dead bodies of their friends, the birds hovering over them.

Further on, a passage is devoted to the description of the heroic death of al-Ḥārith b. al-Ṣimma. He refused to save his own life and fought the polytheists till he was killed.

'Amr b. Umaiya al-Ḍamrī and, with him, two other men returned to the Prophet. The account contains the story of the murder of the

---

[1] MS Chester Beatty, II, 263 f.

two men of Kilāb by ʿAmr b. Umaiya, and the curse of the Prophet on Muḍar and the clans of Sulaim.

It may be remarked that whereas in the version of *Bustān al-ʿĀrifīn*, al-Samarqandī states explicitly that the persons who returned to Medina were ʿAmr b. Umaiya al-Ḍamrī, Saʿd b. Abī Waqqāṣ and a third person—he mentions, in the account of his *Tafsīr*, ʿAmr b. Umaiya, not giving the name of Saʿd b. Abī Waqqāṣ.

This account is unique in giving the number of the participants of the expedition as fourteen plus four. From among the eighteen participants fifteen were killed. It is evident that this is the account referred to and refuted by al-Wāqidī. The account states explicitly that Saʿd b. Abī Waqqāṣ took part in the expedition, and that both the Muhājirūn and the Anṣār participated in it.

One may venture to say that we have here a very early account. It may be accepted with certainty that this version of the tradition was known and even disputed at the end of the second century.

IV

The assumptions put forward by the scholars, surveyed briefly above, are divergent. Some of them are contradictory. They give rise to a number of questions. One is tempted to ask, why did the Prophet decide to interfere in the internal politics of a polytheist tribe, "though he realized the riskiness of doing so," as assumed by Watt? It is not plausible that the Prophet would have risked the lives of his Companions, if not for the cause of Islam and in the interest of the Muslim community. Further, how could ʿĀmir b. al-Ṭufail succeed in persuading the clans of Sulaim to attack the Muslims and kill them, as proposed by Watt, when he failed to convince his own people that they should do so? What was the relationship between ʿĀmir b. al-Ṭufail and the clans of Sulaim?

There is some hope of finding some of the answers and to arrive at some solutions which may elucidate the story of Biʾr Maʿūna. Some details may give a clue to this.

Going through the different accounts of the story of Biʾr Maʿūna one notes that, of the party of the polytheists who massacred the Muslims, only two names are mentioned in the sources: Jabbār b. Salmā b. Mālik b. Jaʿfar [1] killed ʿĀmir b. Fuhaira. [2] Anas b. ʿAbbās al-

---

[1] Ibn al-Kalbī, *Jamhara*, MS f° 123a; Ibn ʿAbd al-Barr, *Istīʿāb*, 88; Ibn Ḥajar, *Iṣāba*, n° 1051; Ibn Hishām, *Sīra*, III, 196.

[2] Cf. Ibn Saʿd, *Ṭabaqāt*, III, 231; Ibn Duraid, *Ishtiqāq*, 25; Ibn Ḥajar, *Iṣāba*,

Ri'lī killed Nāfi' b. Budail b. Warqā' al-Khuzā'ī.[1] We are here especially concerned with the case of Anas b. 'Abbās.

Anas boasted of the killing of Nāfi' b. Budail. In one of the two verses of Anas there is mention of Abū Raiyān whose blood Anas avenged. This Abū Raiyān is said to have been Ṭu'aima b. Adī b. Naufal b. 'Abd Manāf. Anas was his maternal uncle.[2] Al-Wāqidī says a little more about Anas and about the role he played at Bi'r Ma'ūna. Quoting the two verses of Anas, al-Wāqidī remarks: "Anas went out on the Day of Bi'r Ma'ūna inciting his people (to attack the Muslims), in order to avenge the blood of his sister's son."[3]

Some details about Ṭu'aima may help to elucidate the course of events.

Ṭu'aima b. 'Adī b. Naufal b. 'Abd Manāf b. Quṣaiy belonged to the nobility of Quraish in Mecca.[4] His boon companion was one of the noble quraishites of Mecca, Munabbih b. al-Ḥajjāj al-Sahmī.[5] Like Munabbih, Ṭu'aima was a fierce opponent of the Prophet.[6] According to one of the traditions, the document about the boycott of the Banū Hāshim was entrusted to Ṭu'aima.[7] He attended the meeting at the Dār al-Nadwa at which the problem of the expulsion of the Prophet was discussed, representing the Banū Naufal.[8] He incited the Quraish to fight on the eve of the battle of Badr,[9] and was one of the *muṭ'imūn* during the march.[10] He is said to have killed, at Badr, Sa'd b. Khaithama[11] and Sahl b. al-Baiḍā'.[12] According to a tradition of al-Wāqidī, he killed Ṣafwān b. al-Baiḍā'.[13] Traditions are not unanimous about his death: whether he was captured at Badr and the Prophet ordered Ḥamza to kill him in cold blood,[14] or whe-

---

nº 4408; Sakhāwī, *al-Tuḥfa al-laṭīfa*, ed. As'ad Darabzūnī (Cairo, 1957-8), nº 1908.

1 See Ibn Ḥajar, Iṣāba, nº 8644.

2 Ibn Hishām, *Sīra*, III, 197-98.

3 Wāqidī, *op. cit.*, 344.

4 Mu'arrij, *al-Ḥadhf min nasab Quraish*, 42.

5 Muḥammad b. Ḥabīb, *Muḥabbar*, ed. Lichtenstadter, 177.

6 al-Balādhurī, *Ansāb*, MS, fº 808b; *idem*, *Ansāb al-ashrāf*, ed. Hamidullah, I, 153-54.

7 *Ibid.*, I, 235.

8 Ibn Hishām, *Sīra*, II, 125.

9 al-Balādhūrī, *Ansāb al-ashrāf*, I, 292.

10 Ibn Hishām, *Sīra*, II, 320.

11 al-Balādhurī, *op. cit.*, I, 296.

12 *Ibid.*, I, 225; but see Ibn Sa'd, *Ṭabaqāt*, IV, 213.

13 *al-Maghāzī*, 141; but see Ibn Sa'd, *Ṭabaqāt*, III, 416.

14 Ibn Qutaiba, *Ma'ārif*, 68: "Three were killed in cold blood at Badr: 'Uqba, Ṭu'aima and al-Naḍr"; al-Balādhurī, *Ansāb*, MS, fº 808b; *idem*, *Ansāb al-ashrāf*, ed. Hamidullah, I, 148; Ibn Ḥazm *Jawāmi' al-sīra*, 148.

ther he was killed in an encounter with ʿAlī and Ḥamza. Some sources record a vivid description of this encounter. Al-Wāqidī gives this description, [1] but omits the name of Ṭuʿaima. The story is quoted by Muṣʿab al-Zubairī,[2] by Abū 'l-Baqā' Hibat Allāh [3] and by al-Majlisī. [4] Some sources mention only that he was killed at Badr. [5]

The clan of Naufal b. ʿAbd Manāf were opposed to the Hāshim b. ʿAbd Manāf and Muṭṭalib b. ʿAbd Manāf, and were allies of the ʿAbd Shams b. ʿAbd Manāf. [6] ʿAdī b. Naufal competed with ʿAbd al-Muṭṭalib in supplying beverages for the pilgrims: al-Muṭṭalib supplied the beverages at Zamzam, ʿAdī b. Naufal, at a spot between al-Ṣafā and al-Marwa; the latter offered them honey and milk. [7] The mother of ʿAdī was Hind, Umm al-Khiyār bint Wuhaib, of Māzin the kindred of Sulaim.

The mother of his sons, Muṭʿim and Ṭuʿaima, was Fākhita bint ʿAbbās b. ʿĀmir b. Ḥuyaiy b. Riʿl, of Sulaim. [8] Of special importance is the information stating that the Sulaim were allies of the Banū Naufal. [9]

It is thus conceivable why the clans of Sulaim responded, according to some accounts, when ʿĀmir b. al-Ṭufail summoned them to attack the Muslim party. The reasons are clearly expounded in a significant passage of the *Nasab Quraish*: [10]

> The Banū Riʿl and Dhakwān, and they are allies of the Banū Naufal (and they are of Sulaim), gave aid to ʿĀmir b. al-Ṭufail against the Companions of the Prophet, who were killed at Bi'r Maʿūna, because of Ṭuʿaima.[11] He who aided ʿĀmir b. al-Ṭufail was Anas b. ʿAbbās al-Riʿlī, called al-Aṣamm. With him went out (to the attack) the Riʿl, Dhakwān and ʿUṣaiya. The ʿĀmir b. Ṣaʿṣaʿa refused to aid

---

1 *Maghāzī*, 87.

2 *Nasab Quraish*, 199-200.

3 *al-Manāqib al-Mazyadīya*, MS, fº 8a.

4 *Biḥār al-anwār*, VI "*Bāb ghazwat Badr al-kubrā*" (quoted from al-Wāqidī).

5 Mu'arrij, *al-Ḥadhf min nasab Quraish*, 42; Ibn Hishām, *Sīra*, II, 366; Muḥammad b. Ḥabīb, *Muḥabbar*, 177.

6 Mu'arrij, *al-Ḥadhf min nasab Quraish*, p. 41; al-Balādhurī, *Ansāb*, MS, fº 808a: "Zaʿamū anna Banī Naufal b. ʿAbd Manāf kānū yadan maʿa ʿAbd Shams ʿalā sā'iri Banī ʿAbd Manāf."

7 Muṣʿab, *Nasab Quraish*, 32, 197 (cf. the expression "Ibn al-Siqāyatain").

8 *Ibid.*, 198; al-Samʿānī, *Ansāb*, fº 255a.

9 Muṣʿab, *op. cit.*, 97, 198.

10 *Ibid.*, 198-199.

11 Jubair b. Muṭʿim b. ʿAdī promised to free his slave Waḥshī, if he would kill Ḥamza (Ḥamza, as mentioned, killed Ṭuʿaima). Wahshī succeeded, in fact, in killing Ḥamza at Uḥud and was freed by Jubair. (See Ibn Hishām, *Sīra*, III, 65, 76.)

ʿĀmir b. al-Ṭufail, because Abū Barā' was the protector of the Companions who were killled by ʿĀmir b. al-Ṭufail at Bi'r Maʿūna.

We shall now follow the thread of Anas b. ʿAbbās who seems to have been the driving spirit behind the attack on the Muslim party.

W. Arafat, in his penetrating study of the story of Khubaib, analyses a verse of Ḥassān in which the name Anas is mentioned, and says: "Anas, according to Ibn Hishām and the note to the poem in the Dīwān, was from the tribe of Sulaim and nothing else seems to be known about him." [1] Every bit of information about Anas may be helpful to elucidate the case of Bi'r Maʿūna.

The name Anas is glossed by Ibn Hishām as follows: "Anas al-Aṣamm al-Sulamī, the maternal uncle of Muṭʿim b. ʿAdī b. Naufal b. ʿAbd Manāf." [2] He can thus easily be identified with the chief of the clan of Riʿl, Anas b. ʿAbbās b. ʿĀmir b. Ḥuyaiy b. Riʿl b. Mālik b. ʿAuf b. Imra'al-Qais b. Buhtha b. Sulaim, as mentioned in Muṣʿab's *Nasab.* [3] His sister was Fākhita bint ʿAbbās, the wife of ʿAdī, the mother of Ṭuʿaima b. ʿAdī, whose blood Anas avenged at Bi'r Maʿūna. His father, ʿAbbās, known as ʿAbbās b. Raiṭa, was a highly respected chief of his people, and the Sulaim intended to "put a crown on his head." ʿAbbās had as antagonist one of his relatives, who offended him, and he left his tribe. He joined the Fazāra.[4] According to al-Jāḥiẓ, he was compelled to leave his tribe because of the small number of his kin in the tribe. [5] ʿAbbās was a poet, [6] but his verses were sometimes attributed to his son Anas, [7] who was also a poet. [8]

Anas b. ʿAbbās, according to Ibn al-Kalbī, [9] al-Balādhurī [10] and Ibn Ḥazm, [11] was a chief of his people, and was killed by the

---

1 W. C. Arafat, "A Dramatic Theme in the Story of Khubaib b. ʿAdiy," *BSOAS* **XXI (1958), 26.**

2 Ibn Hishām, *Sīra*, III, 188.

3 Page 198; the same genealogy is recorded in al-Zubair b. Bakkār's *Nasab Quraish*, MS Bodl., f° 191a (in the genealogy of "Zainab bint ʿAdī b. Naufal").

4 *Aghānī*, XVI, 55 (his name is given as "al-ʿAbbās b. Anas," but see al-Jāḥiẓ, *Ḥayawān*, quoted below); Nallino, *Raccolta*, III, 66.

5 *al-Ḥayawān*, I, 359; V, 30, 31.

6 al-Bakrī, *Simṭ*, 513; Jarīr wa 'l-Farazdaq, *Naqāʾiḍ*, ed. Bevan, 392.

7 al-Marzubānī, *Muʿjam*, ed. Krenkow, 263; Yāqūt, *Buldān*, s.v. "Dafīna."

8 Sībawaihi, *Kitāb*, I (Būlāq, 1316 H.), 349; Abū Tammām, *al-Waḥshīyāt* (ed. Maimanī), 231.

9 *Jamhara*, MS, f° 160a.

10 *al-Ansāb*, MS, f° 1132a.

11 *Jamharat ansāb al-ʿArab*, 250 (erroneously "Ibn Jubair b. Riʿl" instead of "Ibn Ḥuyaiy").

Khath'am.[1] A story told on the authority of Abū 'Ubaida states that Anas raided, together with Ṣakhr b. 'Amr al-Sulamī, the Banū Asad.[2] Ibn Sa'd mentions that Anas was a member of the delegation of Sulaim who visited the Prophet. He is said to have embraced Islam.[3]

Of special importance for the elucidation of the relations between Ri'l and 'Āmir b. Ṣa'ṣa'a, and especially between Anas and the 'Āmir b. Ṣa'ṣa'a, is the story of *Yaum al-Raghām* reported by Abū 'Ubaida. When the Tha'laba b. Yarbū' attacked the 'Āmir b. Ṣa'ṣa'a, Anas b. 'Abbās stayed with the 'Āmir b. Ṣa'ṣa'a. He acted in the in-interest of the 'Āmir b. Ṣa'ṣa'a, trying by a stratagem to make possible a counterattack of the Kilāb against the Tha'laba b. Yarbū'. He was captured and released after paying a ransom of 200 camels.[4] The place of the encounter between the Yarbū' and the Kilāb seems to have been al-Ẓilāl. Yāqūt mentions that as the place, stating that it belonged to the Ja'far b. Kilāb. "They (that is, the Ja'far b. Kilāb) were attacked at this spot by 'Utaiba b. al-Ḥārith b. Shihāb. He seized their cattle and the cattle of the men of Sulaim."[5] The *Naqā'iḍ* have an additional phrase, which is of some importance:[6] "...of the men of Sulaim, being under their protection. One of them was Anas b. 'Abbās al-Ri'lī." This phrase supplies a clue for the understanding of the relations between the clan of Ri'l and the Ja'far of 'Āmir b. Ṣa'ṣa'a, and throws light on the action of 'Āmir b. al-Ṭufail.

V

It is not easy to establish the true facts about the expedition. In the light of the version recorded by al-Samarqandī, which was omitted

---

1 The information of Ibn al-Kalbī is quoted in Ibn Ḥajar's *Iṣāba*, nº 269.

2 *Aghānī*, XIII, 130.

3 *Ṭabaqāt*, I, 307 (erroneously "Anas b. 'Iyāḍ al-Ri'lī"); this information is also recorded in Ibn 'Asākir's *Ta'rīkh*, III, 137, and in Ibn Ḥajar's *Iṣāba*, nº 269. About the son of Anas, Razīn, see Ibn Ḥajar, *Iṣāba*, nº 2645. About his father, 'Abbās, see Ibn Ḥajar, *Iṣāba*, nº 4496 (al-'Abbās b. Anas b. 'Āmir al-Ri'lī) and al-Balādhurī, *Ansāb*, MS, fº 1138b ('Abbās b. Anas al-Aṣamm).

4 Jarīr wa 'l-Farardaq, *Naqā'iḍ*, ed. Bevan, 410; *Aghānī*, XIV, 84; al-Balādhurī, *Ansāb*, MS, fº 997b f. Other versions about the capture of Anas by 'Utaiba b. al-Ḥārith: (1) Anas came to 'Utaiba as a guest and was treacherously put in fetters, and released after he paid a ransom; (2) he was under the protection of 'Utaiba and was treacherously tied, put in fetters, and released after paying ransom; see al-Balādhurī, *Ansāb*, MS, fº 997b and fº 1138b ("Anas b. 'Iyāḍ" and "Anas b. Mirdās," in the MS, are errors).

5 So Yāqūt, *Buldān*, s.v. "*Ẓilāl*"; *amwāla 'l-muslimīna*, in the *Naqā'iḍ*, 302, is an error; read: "*amwāla 'l-sulamīyīna*". 6 *Naqā'iḍ*, 302.

in the traditional accounts, and after a closer study of the data quoted above, some suggestions about this expedition may be propounded.

Abū Barā', one of the leaders of the 'Āmir b. Ṣa'ṣa'a came into touch with the Prophet. He was an aged man and was summoned by the Prophet to accept Islam. Neither he nor his son Rabī'a [1] embraced Islam, although the tribal tradition of the 'Āmir b. Ṣa'ṣa'a tried to show that Abū Barā' later embraced Islam, fought and fell in battle. According to the traditions, he agreed to give the Muslim group safe conduct and consented to the propagation of Islam in his tribe. That is quite plausible, and Abū Barā' might have hoped that he would strengthen his influence in the tribe by accepting the Muslim group. A significant phrase in Ibn Qutaiba's *al-Shi'r wa' l-shu'arā'* seems to point to this fact. [2] The Prophet obviously hoped to win over parts of the 'Āmir b. Ṣa'ṣa'a to the cause of Islam. The action brings to mind the despatch of missionaries to Medina before the Hijra. After the defeat at Uḥud, it was the only way of propagating Islam.

The Prophet sent a group of fourteen Companions, relying upon the promise of Abū Barā'. The Companions might have realized on their way that they were only a few, and sent to ask for aid. They received the aid of four men. Two of the four were famous for their valor: Sa'd b. Abī Waqqāṣ was an excellent fighter; 'Amr b. Umaiya was a reckless warrior, although the Prophet's opinion on his moral qualities was rather unfavorable. [3] It is also plausible to assume that the Muslim troop sent word to Rabī'a, the son of the aged Abū Barā', asking him to reaffirm the promise of safe conduct and protection. They wanted to be sure that he would stand by his father's pledge. Whether Abū Barā' died exactly on the night when the Companions set out is rather doubtful. The tradition that he lived a short time after the massacre of Bi'r Ma'ūna seems to be more trustworthy.

The Muslim troop alighted at Bi'r Ma'ūna. Here evidently the clans of Sulaim led by Anas b. 'Abbās al-Ri'lī camped under the protection of the Kilāb. Groups of Kilāb stayed there also. This is indicated by the fact that 'Āmir b. Fuhaira was killed by Jabbār b. Salmā of the Banū Ja'far of 'Āmir b. Ṣa'ṣa'a. The expedition took place in a

---

[1] See, about him, Ibn Ḥajar, *Iṣāba*, n° 2627.

[2] Ibn Qutaiba, *al-Shi'r wa 'l-shu'arā'*, ed. de Goeje, 224, var. "q": *li-yuqārrūhu 'alā riyāsatihi*. In the edition of Muṣṭafā al-Saqqā (Cairo, 1932) it is rendered: *li-yuqātilūhu 'alā riyāsatihi*. In the edition of Shākir(Cairo, 1364 H.) the phrase has been omitted.

[3] See Abū Dā'ūd, *Sunan*, II, 296, "Bāb fī 'l-ḥidhr."

very hot month (Safar/July-August, 4 H.), and the clans evidently gathered with their herds around the well. The envoy of the Muslim troop came to the people staying at the well and informed them that they were not the object of their expedition. The envoy, Ḥarām b. Milḥān, was killed by one of the people.

The attack was a sudden one, as attested by a verse of the sister of al-Mundhir b. ʿAmr. [1]

The attack was led by Anas b. ʿAbbās al-Riʿlī. He fulfilled his obligation as a relative of Ṭuʿaima b. ʿAdī to avenge his death at Badr. The clans who followed him fulfilled their obligation as allies of the Banū Naufal. [2] Some units or individuals of Jaʿfar b. Kilāb might have taken part in the attack. This is indicated by a verse of the sister of al-Mundhir b. ʾAmr, in which she mentions "the wolves of the Ḥijāz, the Banū Buhtha [that is, the Banū Sulaim] and Banū Jaʿfar" [that is, Jaʿfar b. Kilāb of the ʿĀmir b. Ṣaʿṣaʿa].[3] ʿĀmir b. al-Ṭufail might have approved the action of Anas or even taken part in the attack. But the responsibility was on the Riʿl and the other clans of Sulaim. It was the Riʿl and clans of Sulaim who were cursed by the Prophet. The action is connected with Mecca and the Naufal b. ʿAbd Manaf were the cause for the launching of the attack on their enemies. The attack was apparently inspired by Mecca.

In fact, the ʿĀmir b. Ṣaʿṣaʿa are merely reproached for not standing by the pledge of protection. Kaʿb b. Mālik reproaches the ʿĀmir that they did not come to the aid of those attacked when they asked for help. They refrained from coming to their aid, because they knew that the battle would be a seroius one. [4] ʿĀmir b. al-Ṭufail is reproached by Ḥassān for violation of the pledge of Abū Barāʾ, obviously because he did not prevent the clans of Sulaim, his clients, to attack the Muslim troop. [5]

It is conceivable that Abū Barāʾ was grieved by the violation of

[1] "Had the group been wary of these troops," Ḥassān, *Dīwān*, ed. Hirschfeld, 57.

[2] The case of al-Rajīʿ is also connected with the clan of Naufal b. ʿAbd Manāf: Khubaib was killed in revenge for al-Ḥārith b. ʿĀmir b. Naufal. Khubaib was bought by Ḥujair b. Abī Ihāb, an ally of the Banū Naufal. He was executed by the son of al-Ḥārith with the assistance of Abū Maisara of the ʿAbd al-Dār. See Ibn Hishām, *Sīra*, III, 182.

[3] Ḥassān, *Dīwān*, ed. Hirschfeld, 57-58.

[4] Ṭabarī, *Taʾrīkh*, II, 221-22.

[5] Cf. Ibn Hishām, *Sīra*, III, 198: "You left your 'jār' (that is, the Muslim group) to the Banū Sulaim, fearing their hostile action, in (your) abjection and weakness."

his protection. According to the record of Ibn Qutaiba, [1] he commanded his people to kill 'Āmir b. al-Ṭufail, but they disobeyed. The affair had evidently, in their opinion nothing to do with them. It was the Banū Sulaim who had settled their accounts with the Muslims. They, the 'Āmir b. Ṣa'ṣa'a, considered the sending of Abū Barā' to "that man" as a fit of mental aberration. [2] It was only the son of Abū Barā' who tried to kill 'Āmir b. al-Ṭufail, but failed. Abū Barā', feeling that he had lost authority in his tribe, started to imbibe undiluted wine and drank himself to death. It may be remarked that the verses of Ḥassān are addressed to Abū Barā''s son, Rabī'a; not one verse is addressed to Abū Barā'. He lost influence in his tribe, and must have died shorthly after the massacre of Bi'r Ma'ūna, probably from his tumor.

The tradition about the attendance of Sa'd b. Abī Waqqāṣ was not admitted into the traditional accounts, because of the case of the murder of the two men of Kilāb (or Sulaim) granted safe conduct by the Prophet. The report of Qatāda, as quoted by al-Samarqandī, [3] states explicitly that the two men were killed by the three Companions, returning from Bi'r Ma'ūna. The report of the papyrus states that the two returning Companions killed the two men of Kilāb. [4] Later collections of the *maghāzī* preferred not to mention the version claimiing that Sa'd b. Abī Waqqāṣ, the first who shed blood for the cause of Islam, the hero of al-Qādisīya, did not take part in the battle of Bi'r Ma'ūna but saved his own life, while the other Companions died the death of martyrs, or was involved in the murder of the two men of Kilāb. The blame of the murder of the two men of Kilāb was put solely on 'Amr b. Umaiya al-Ḍamrī.

The Prophet could not demand the bloodwite for the martyrs from the Banū Sulaim, nor from the 'Āmir b. Ṣa'ṣa'a. He promised to pay the bloodwite for the two men of Kilāb, killed by his Companion (or Companions) and started to collect the money of the indemnity. He summoned the Banū Naḍīr to contribute a portion of it. That led to the encounter with the Naḍīr and to their expulsion.

---

1 *al-Shi'r wa 'l-shu'arā'*, ed. de Goeje, 224.
2 Muḥammad b. Ḥabīb, *Muḥabbar*, 472.
3 MS Chester Beatty, I, 228a.
4 Nabia Abbott, *Studies in Arabic Papyri*, Document 5 (verso), 69, lines 11-12.

Hebrew University, Jerusalem

XI

SOME REPORTS CONCERNING AL-ṬĀ'IF

In memory of Yuval Taglicht

The battle of Ḥunayn (8H/630), in which the Muslim troops defeated the joint forces of the Hawāzin and Thaqīf, heralded the submission of al-Ṭā'if. The expedition of the Prophet against al-Ṭā'if is reflected in a peculiar utterance attributed to him: "God's last tread was at Wajj (. . . *wa-inna ākhira waṭ'atin waṭi'ahā llāhu bi-wajj;* in another version: *inna ākhira waṭ'atin li-llāhi yaumu wajj*)[1] and interpreted as referring to the last campaign of the Prophet (aided by God's power, indicated by the word *"waṭ'a"* – K) against the unbelievers. The conversion of al-Ṭā'if to Islam marked in fact the last victorious stage of the Prophet's struggle for control over the three important cities in the Arabian peninsula: Mecca, Medina and al-Ṭā'if.

The reports about the negotiations between the Prophet and the deputation of Thaqīf (in 9 H), and the concessions and privileges granted by him to Thaqīf, are divergent and even contradictory. By surveying these traditions it is possible to elucidate some points of the negotiated conditions, which shed light on certain essential details of the concessions granted.

A report on the administrative and military steps taken by Mu'āwiya with regard to al-Ṭā'if may expose the changes in the structure of the population of al-Ṭā'if in that period.

I

According to the most widely quoted traditions,[2] the Prophet rejected all the requests submitted to him by the delegation of Thaqīf, including the permission to profit from financial transactions based on usury, permission to have inter-

---

1 Al-Bakrī, *Mu'jam mā sta'jam*, ed. Muṣṭafā l-Saqā, Cairo, 1368/1949, p. 1369; Yāqūt, *Mu'jam al-buldān*, Beirut, 1376/1957, V, 361; Ibn al-Athīr, *al-Nihāya fī gharībi l-ḥadīthi wa-l-athar*, ed. al-Ṭanāḥī, Cairo, 1385/1965, V, 200; al-Zamakhsharī, *al-Fā'iq*, ed. Muḥammad Abū l-Faḍl Ibrāhīm, 'Alī Muḥammad al-Bijāwī, Cairo, 1971, I, 185; Nūr al-Dīn al-Haythamī, *Majma' al-zawā'id*, Beirut, 1967, X, 54; *L'A*, s.v. w ṭ 'a, w j j; P.H. Lammens, *La Cité Arabe de Ṭā'if à la Veille de l'Hegire*, Beyrouth, 1922, p. 28.

2 See Ibn Hishām, *al-Sīra al-nabawiyya*, ed. al-Saqā, al Abyārī, Shalabī, Cairo, 1355/1936, IV, 182-7; al-Wāqidī, *al-Maghāzī*, ed. Marsden Jones, Oxford, 1966, III, 960–73; Ibn Sa'd, *Ṭabaqāt*, Beirut, 1380/1960, I, 312–13; al-Ṭabarī, *Ta'rīkh al-umam wa-l-mulūk*, Cairo, 1357/

course with prostitutes (during their journeys), permission to drink wine and, finally, the concession to worship al-Lāt (*al-Rabba*) for a period; all these demands were refused by the Prophet, save the concession that the idol of al-Lāt be destroyed not by themselves but by others.

Watt, in scrutinizing the negotiations of the delegation with the Prophet, notices that there is no mention of anyone being commissioned to collect any contribution or tax from Thaqīf; he remarks that "this might be a reason for the disappearance of the text of the treaty with al-Ṭā'if."[3] Some fifty years earlier Buhl, pointing out that the Prophet granted to Thaqīf as a privilege recognition of their valley, Wajj, as *ḥaram,*[4] had suggested that he might have granted them additional concessions, not mentioned in the traditions.[5] This line was followed by Sperber in his study of the letters of the Prophet.[6]

As a matter of fact there are reports which attribute to the Prophet far-reaching concessions granted to Thaqīf. According to one of them Thaqīf embraced Islam on condition that their people would be free from paying the *ṣadaqa* and

---

1939, II, 364-6; al-Kalā'ī, *al-Iktifā' fī maghāzī rasūli llāhi wa-l-thalāthati l-khulafā*, ed. Mustafā 'Abd al-Wāḥid, Cairo, 1389/1970, II, 398–408; Ibn Kathīr, *al-Bidāya wa-l-nihāya*, Beirut al-Riyād, 1966, V, 29–34; Ibn Sayyid al-Nās, *'Uyūn al-athar fī funūn al-maghāzī wa-l-shamā'il wa-l-siyar*, Cairo, 1356, II, 228-31; al-Maqrīzī, *Imtā' al-asmā' bi-mā li-l-rasūli min al-anbā'i wa-l-amwāli wa-l-ḥafadati wa-l-matā'*, ed. Maḥmūd Muḥammad Shākir, Cairo, 1941, I, 491-4; al-Zurqānī, *Sharḥ al-mawāhib al-laduniyya*, Cairo 1327, IV, 6–10; Ibn al-Athīr, *al-Kāmil fī l-ta'rīkh*, ed. 'Abd al-Wahhāb al-Najjār, Cairo, 1349, II, 193-4; 'Alī b. Burhān al-Dīn al-Ḥalabī, *Insān al-'uyūn fī sīrati l-amīni l-ma'mūn* (*=al-Sīra al-ḥalabiyya*), Cairo, n.d., III, 243-6; Ibn 'Abd al-Barr, *al-Durar fī khtiṣāri l-maghāzī wa-l-siyar*, ed. Shauqī Ḍayf, Cairo, 1386/1966, pp. 262-5; Daḥlān, *al-Sīra al-nabawiyya*, Cairo, 1310, II, 145 inf.-147; al-Diyārbakrī, *Ta'rīkh al-khamīs fī aḥwāl anfas nafīs*, Cairo, 1238, II, 134 inf.-138 1.1; Ibn Ḥazm, *Jawāmi' al-sīra*, ed. Iḥsān 'Abbās, Nāṣir al-Dīn al-Asad, Cairo, n.d., pp. 255-8; Ibn Qayyim al-Jauziyya, *Zād al-ma'ād*, Beirut, n.d., II, 197-9, III, 26-9; Ibn Abī Shayba, *al-Muṣannaf*, ed. 'Abd al-Khāliq al-Afghānī, Hyderabad, 1388/1968, III, 197; al-Balādhurī, *Futūḥ al-buldān, ed.* 'Abdallah and 'Umar al-Ṭabbā', Beirut, 1377/1958, p. 75.

[3] W. Montgomery Watt, *Muhammad at Medina*, Oxford, 1956, p. 104.

[4] See on *taḥrīm wajj:* al-Fākihī, *Ta'rīkh Makka*, Ms. Leiden Or. 463, fol. 539b; Ibn Sa'd, *op. cit.*, I, 284-5; Muḥibb al-Dīn al-Ṭabarī, *al-Qirā li-qāṣidi ummi l-qurā*, ed. Muṣṭafā l-Saqā, Cairo, 1390/1970, p. 666 (see the remarks of the author about the nature of *taḥrīm*: whether it was merely given the status of a *ḥimā*, or whether the privilege was later annulled); al-Samhūdī, *Wafā'u l-wafā bi-akhbāri dāri l-muṣṭafā*, ed. Muḥammad Muḥyī l-Dīn 'Abd al-Ḥamīd, Cairo, 1374/1955, p. 1036; Abū 'Ubayd, *al-Amwāl*, ed. Muḥammad Ḥāmid al-Fiqī, Cairo, 1353, p. 193, no. 507, *L'A*, s. v. w j j; al-Zurqānī, *op. cit.*, IV, 10 (discussing contradictory opinions of scholars about the status of Wajj); al-Shaukānī, *Nayl al-auṭār*, Cairo, 1372/1953, V, 39–40 (see the discussion about the validity of the tradition and the position of Wajj); Ibn Zanjawayh, *Kitāb al-amwāl*, Ms. Burdur 183, fol. 68a; al-Diyārbakrī, *op. cit.*, II, 110, 11.2-6; al-Maqrīzī, *op. cit.*, I, 493; Amīn Maḥmūd Khaṭṭāb, *Fatḥ al-malik al-ma'būd, Takmilat al-manhal al-'adhb al-maurūd*, Cairo, 1394/1974, II, 231-3; Muḥammad Ḥamīdullāh, *Majmū'at al-wathā'iq al-siyāsiyya*, Cairo, 1376/1956, no. 182; Shakīb Arslān, *al-Irtisāmāt al-liṭāf fī khāṭiri l-ḥājji ilā aqdasi maṭāf*, ed. Muḥammad Rashīd Riḍā, Cairo, 1350, p. 135 (see the quotation from Ibn Fahd's *Tuḥfat al-laṭā'if fī faḍā'ili l-ḥabri bni l-'abbāsi wa-wajjin wa-l-ṭā'if*).

[5] F. Buhl, *Das Leben Muhammeds*, transl. H.H. Schaeder, Heidelberg, 1955 (repr.), p. 332.

[6] J. Sperber, "Die Schreiben Mohammeds an die Stämme Arabiens", *MSOS* 19 (1916), 71-2.

exempted from obligatory participation in the expeditions of *jihād*. The Prophet then noted that in the future they would pay the poor tax, the *ṣadaqa*, and participate in the holy war (*jihād*).[7] It is evident that, according to this version of the tradition, the Prophet freed Thaqīf from the poor tax and from participation in war expeditions. The version which contains the final restrictive clause (*idhā aslamū*) is, however, interpreted in a different way: the convert is granted a respite from the obligation till a prescribed time or within specific circumstances. In this case Thaqīf would be obliged to pay the *ṣadaqa*, the poor tax, when the fixed time came and to participate in *jihād* whenever announced.[8] It can thus be deduced, according to this interpretation, that the Prophet merely postponed for Thaqīf the fulfillment of some obligations.

The exemption of Thaqīf from paying the poor tax (*ṣadaqa*) and *jihād* is plainly reported in a *ḥadīth* in which the Prophet conceded payment of the tithe (*'ushr*) as well as conscription (*lakum an lā tuḥsharū wa-lā tu'sharū*); their third demand, not to perform prostration in prayer (*an lā yujabbū*) was refused by the Prophet, on the grounds that faith without prostration was devoid of good.[9] The two concessions of *'ushr* and *ḥashr* are in fact included in the official epistle issued by the Prophet for Thaqīf as recorded by Abū 'Ubayd.[10]

The request of the deputation to exempt Thaqīf from prayer deserves particular attention. When the Prophet refused this demand he is said to have remarked: "A faith without prayer is devoid of good" (*lā khayra fī dīnin lā ṣalāta fīhi*);[11] the deputation, in accepting the Prophet's decision, said: "We grant you that even

---

[7] Ibn Rajab, *Jāmi' al-'ulūm wa-l-ḥikam*, ed. Muḥammad al-Aḥmadī Abū l-Nūr, Cairo, 1389/1969, I, 180 inf.: . . . *wa-anna rasūla llāhi ṣallā llāhu 'alayhi wa-sallama qāla: sa-yaṣṣaddaqūna wa-yujāhidūna* (quoted from Aḥmad b. Ḥanbal's *Musnad*); Abū Dāwūd, *Sunan*, Cairo, 1348, II, 42; Ibn Kathīr, *al-Bidāya*, V, 30 (In both sources the utterance of the Prophet ends with an additional clause: *idhā aslamū*. They will pay the *ṣadaqa* and take part in the expeditions of the holy war "when they will embrace Islam"); al-Suyūṭī, *al-Khaṣā'iṣ al-kubrā*, ed. Muḥammad Khalīl Harās, Cairo, 1386/1967, II, 145; Ibn al-Athīr, *al-Nihāya* I, 238, records a different version of the tradition. It was Jābir who explained the reason for the Prophet's dispensation: "he knew that they would fight and pay the *ṣadaqa* when they convert."

[8] See Ibn al-Athīr, *al-Nihāya* I, 238, ll. 5-6: "*. . .wa-lam yurakhkhiṣ lahum fī tarki l-ṣalāti li-anna waqtahā ḥāḍirun mutakarrirun bi-khilāfi waqti l-zakāti wa-l-jihādi.*"

[9] Abū Dāwūd, *op. cit.*, II, 42: . . . *wa-lā khayra fī dīnin laysa fīhi rukū'un;* Ibn Kathīr, *al-Bidāya*, V, 30; Aḥmad b. Ḥanbal, *Musnad*, Būlāq, 1313, IV, 218 (with an additional request of the delegation: that the governor of al-Ṭā'if would be appointed from among themselves; this was granted by the Prophet).

[10] Abū 'Ubayd, *al-Amwāl*, pp. 190-3, no. 506. (The crucial expression *lā yuḥsharūna* is glossed by Abū 'Ubayd: *tu'khadhu minhum ṣadaqatu l-mawāshī bi-afniyatihim, ya'tīhimu l-muṣaddiqu hunāka, wa-lā ya'muruhum an yajlibūhā ilayhi.* But *L'A* s. v. ḥ sh r, referring to the conditions of the deputation of Thaqīf, explains *lā yuḥsharūna: ay lā yundabūna ilā l-maghāzī wa-lā tuḍrabu 'alayhimu l-bu'ūthu. L'A* also mentions the interpretation as recorded by Abū 'Ubayd. Both these explanations are recorded by Ibn al-Athīr in his *Nihāya*, s. v. ḥ sh r; and see Ibn Zanjawayh, *op. cit.*, fol. 67a; Muḥammad Ḥamīdullah, *op. cit.*, no. 181; cf. Abū 'Ubayd, *Gharību l-ḥadīth*, Hyderabad, 1385/1966, III, 197 ult.- 198.

[11] See e.g. al-Wāqidī, *op. cit.*, p. 968.

though it be humiliation" (*fa-qālū sa-nu'tīkahā wa-in kānat danā'atan*).[12] The expression *danā'a*, baseness, or humiliation, seems at first blush somewhat odd in this context. However, its connotation may become apparent from additional reports. The requests of the deputation are recorded in several commentaries to the Qur'ān (Sūra XVII, 75): "Indeed they were near to seducing thee from that We revealed to thee..." Al-Khāzin[13] and al-Baghawī[14] record a tradition according to which the deputation asked the Prophet to grant them the following concessions: not to bend (or prostrate) in prayer; not to destroy their idols by themselves; and to be allowed to keep al-Lāt for a period of a year, on condition that the goddess would not be worshipped (by them). The Prophet conceded that other people should pull down their idol, but refused to allow its demolition to be delayed; concerning prostration in prayer he remarked: "A faith in which there is no prostration is devoid of good" (*lā khayra fī dīnin lā rukū'a fīhi*).[15] It is thus clear that the deputation did not seek exemption from prayer, but from prostration. According to Arab concepts of honor prostration was deemed demeaning. This is well reflected in the reply of Abū Ṭālib, when invited by the Prophet to join him in prayer: "I know that you are on the right path, but I do not like to prostrate so that my hindquarter is higher than (the rest of) me" (... *wa-lākinnī akrahu an asjuda fa-ta'luwanī stī*).[16] It is indeed instructive to find that Musaylima, when praying in front of Arabs, ordered them to perform the prayer upright, in the manner of noblemen.[17] The opinion of the other false prophet, Ṭulayḥa, about prostrations was also unfavourable and he forbade his followers to prostrate in prayer.[18] The idea regarding prostration as humiliating, in the Arab society of the Jāhiliyya, is clearly reflected in Ibn 'Arabī's commentary to the Qur'ān.[19]

*

The economic factor behind the request to preserve their idol, though com-

---

[12] See e.g. Ibn Kathīr, *al-Bidāya*, V, 30.

[13] Al-Khāzin, *Tafsīr* (= *Lubāb al-ta'wīl fī ma'ānī l-tanzīl*), Cairo, 1381, IV, 140 (the text here: *lā naḥnī fī l-ṣalāt*, with the gloss: *ay: lā nanḥanī*).

[14] Al-Baghawī, *Tafsīr* (= *Ma'ālim al-tanzīl*) on margin of al-Khāzin's *Tafsīr*, IV, 140 (with the reading *lā nanḥanī fī l-ṣalāt*); and see Ibn al-Athīr, *al-Nihāya*, I, 237 ult.- 238; *L'A* s.v. j b ā (quoted from Ibn al-Athīr).

[15] See this version as variant: 'Alī b. Burhān al-Dīn, *op. cit.*, III, 245, l. 3; Daḥlān, *op. cit.*, II, 147; Ibn Kathīr, *al-Bidāya*, V, 30.

[16] Al-Khaṭīb al-Baghdādī, *Ta'rīkh Baghdād*, Cairo, 1349/1931, II, 274.

[17] Nashwān, *Mulūk ḥimyar wa-aqyāl al-yaman*, ed. 'Alī al-Mu'ayyad, Ismā'īl al-Jarāfī, Cairo, 1378, p. 176: ... *wa-kāna musaylimatu idhā ṣallā bi-l-'arabi qāla: mā yurīdu llāhu bi-tauliyati adbārikum wa-sujūdikum 'alā jibāhikum, ṣallū li-llāhi qiyāman, kirāman.*

[18] Ibn al-Athīr, *al Kāmil fī l-ta'rīkh*, II, 232;... *wa-kāna ya'muruhum bi-tarki l-sujūdi fī l-ṣalāti, yaqūlu: inna llāha lā yaṣna'u bi-ta'affuri wujūhikum wa-taqabbuḥi (?) adbārikum shay'an.*

[19] See e.g. Ibn 'Arabī, *Aḥkām al-Qur'ān*, ed. 'Alī Muḥammad al-Bijāwī, Cairo, 1387/1967, I, 21:... *wa-qad kāna l-rukū'u athqala shay'in 'alā l-qaumi fī l-jāhiliyyati, ḥattā qāla ba'du man aslama li-l-nabiyyi (ṣ): 'alā allā akhirra illā qā'iman, fa-min ta'awwulihi: 'alā allā arka'a.*

mitting themselves to eschew its worship, is given in a commentary to the Qur'ān: Thaqīf would indeed refrain during the year from worshipping their idol, but other people would come to worship it and bring offerings which will form part of the revenue of Thaqīf.[20]

*

Some of the traditions relate a remarkable story about the intervention of 'Umar during the negotiations of the Prophet with the delegation of Thaqīf. At a certain point in the negotiations, when the delegation enumerated its insolent and excessive demands, 'Umar noticed vexation on the face of the Prophet; he stood up and stopped the negotiations by forceful interference. Then God revealed the verse: "Indeed they were near to seducing thee. . . "

According to a tradition recorded by al-Zamakhshari, the deputation came forward with a considerable list of conditions, demanding exemption from the tithe, from participation in military expeditions and from prostration. Whatever was coming to them in usury was to remain due, but everything they owed in usury to others was to be cancelled; al-Lāt was to remain intact for a year, at the end of which the idol was to be destroyed by others, not by themselves; entrance to Wajj was to be forbidden to those seeking to cut trees in the area. Further, the deputation tried to persuade the Prophet, that if asked by the Arab tribes, he should claim that God had ordered him to grant these exceptional privileges and concessions to Thaqīf. The deputation came prepared with a letter in order to record the conditions agreed upon. They had written in the letter: "In the name of the Merciful, the Compassionate. This is the letter from Muḥammad, the Messenger of God, to Thaqīf. They will not pay the *'ushr* (i.e. the tithe) and they will not be recruited for military expeditions." Then they added: "They will not prostrate in prayer." The Prophet kept silent. They said to the scribe: "Write: 'and they will not prostrate in prayer'." The scribe looked at the Prophet (waiting for his assent – K). At that moment 'Umar stood up, drew his sword and said: "You burnt the heart of our Prophet, O men of Thaqīf, may God burn your hearts" (literally: your livers)." The Thaqafites replied that they had not come to talk with him, but with the Prophet. It was then that the verse mentioned above was revealed.[21] There is no indication in this report whether the negotiations, broken off by 'Umar's interference, were resumed after the verse was revealed; whether the demands of Thaqīf which were accepted by the Prophet, were later confirmed, and whether the docu-

---

[20] Al-Qurṭubī, *Tafsīr* (= *al-Jāmi' li-akḥāmi l-qur'ān*), Cairo, 1387/1967, X, 299; al-Ṭabarsī, *Majma' l-bayān fī tafsīri l-qur'ān*, Beirut, 1380/1961, XV, 81.

[21] Al-Zamakhsharī, *al-Kashshāf*, Cairo, 1354, II, 370; Ibn Ḥajar, *al-Kāfī al-shāf fī takhrīji aḥādīthi l-kashshāf*, Cairo, 1354, p. 100, no 296, states that he could not find this *ḥadīth*, but remarks that al-Tha'labī recorded it (evidently in his *Tafsīr* – K) on the authority of Ibn 'Abbās, though without *isnād*; al-Naysābūrī, *Gharā'ib al-qur'ān wa-raghā'ib al-furqān*, Cairo, 1384/1965, XV, 64 (the text has: . . . *wa-lā nujabbiya fī ṣalātinā* with a gloss: *ay lā nasjuda*; 'Umar's remark is different in style from that recorded in the *Kashshāf*); al-Rāzī, *al-Tafsīr al-kabīr* (*Mafātīḥ al-ghayb*), Cairo, 1357/1938, XXI, 20.

ment was signed by the Prophet. It is however explicit in the report that the reason why the negotiations broke off was the demand for exemption from prostration in prayer.

The report recorded by the early Qur'ān commentator Muqātil b. Sulaymān (d. 150 H) is more detailed and divergent in certain essential points. The deputation of Thaqīf stressed in its speech the strong position of Thaqīf and their influence on other tribes. If they accepted Islam, they said, the whole of Najd would follow suit; if they fought, all their allies would join them against the Prophet and his community. On this basis they appealed to the Prophet to accept their demands. Their conditions for converting to Islam included exemption from conscription, from tithes and from prostration in prayer, cancellation of their debts of usury while affirming suit debts owed to them by others; bestowing on the Wajj valley the status of the sacred *ḥaram* of Mecca, to prevent outsiders from trespassing in order to cut trees there; having the Prophet appoint governors from Thaqīf over the Banū Mālik and the Aḥlāf; the preservation of al-Lāt and al-'Uzzā (sic!) for a year, though they were not to be worshipped by Thaqīf, after which time the idols would be demolished by others. They urged the Prophet to accept their demands in order to demonstrate to the Arab tribes the Prophet's regard for them and their superiority over the other tribes. The Prophet acceded, in so far as he exempted them from the tithe, released them from conscription, promised to let their idols be destroyed by others, and granted them the privileges of usury; but he would not dispense them from prostrating in prayer. The crisis occurred when the deputation insisted on preserving al-Lāt for a year. The Prophet remained silent, unwilling to refuse them and say "no"; the deputation remained equally adamant in their demand but for which they would not convert. They tried to persuade the Prophet that, if the Arab tribes blamed him for destroying their own idols while allowing that of Thaqīf to remain, he could claim that God ordered him to do so It was at that instant that 'Umar intervened, holding that the deputation had vexed the Prophet. He emphasized that God could not allow heathen belief in a territory where He was worshipped, and demanded that they choose between conversion to Islam and return to their abode.[22]

---

[22] Muqātil, *Tafsīr*, Ms. Ahmet III, 74/I, fols. 217b–218a: . . .*wa-dhālika anna thaqīfan atau l-nabiyya (ṣ) fa-qālū: naḥnu ikhwānuka wa-aṣhāruka wa-jīrānuka wa-naḥnu khayru ahli najdin laka silman wa-aḍarruhu 'alayka ḥarban, fa-in nuslim tuslim najdun kulluhā, wa-in nuḥāribka yuḥāribka man warā'anā, fa-a'ṭinā lladhī nurīdu; fa-qāla l-nabiyyu (ṣ): wa-mā turīdūna? qālū: nuslimu 'alā an lā nuḥshara wa-lā nu'shara wa-lā naḥniya, – yaqūlūna: 'alā an lā nuṣalliya wa-lā naksira aṣnāmanā bi-aydīnā; wa-kullu riban lanā 'alā l-nāsi fa-huwa lanā, wa-kullu riban li-l-nāsi fa-huwa 'annā mauḍū'un; wa-man wajadnāhu fī wādī wajjin yaqṭa'u shajarahā ntaza'nā 'anhu thiyābahu wa-ḍarabnā ẓahrahu wa-baṭnahu, wa-ḥurmatuhu ka-ḥurmati makkata wa-ṣayduhu wa-ṭayruhu wa-shajaruhu (?); wa-tasta'mila 'alā banī mālikin rajulan wa-'alā l-aḥlāfi rajulan; wa-an tumatti'nā bi-l-lāti wa-l-'uzzā sanatan wa-lā naksirahā (!) bi-aydīnā, min ghayri an na'budahā, li-ya'rifa l-nāsu karāmatanā 'alayka wa-faḍlanā 'alayhim; fa-qāla lahum rasūlu llāhi (ṣ): ammā qaulukum lā nuḥsharu wa-lā nu'sharu wa-l-ribā, fa-lakum; wa-ammā qaulukum lā naḥnī, fa-innahu lā khayra fī dīnin laysa fīhi rukū'un wa-lā sujūdun; qālū: naf'alu dhālika wa-in kāna 'alaynā fīhi danā'atun; wa-ammā qaulukum lā naksiru aṣnāmanā bi-aydīnā, fa-innā sa-na'muru man yaksiruhā ghayrakum; thumma sakata l-nabiyyu*

The crisis in the negotiations, according to the report of Muqātil, occurred when the deputation insisted on their demand to keep the idol for a year; this was the cause why the negotiations failed, rather than their demand to be excused from prostration. There is nothing in this report on the reaction of the deputation, whether it yielded to having their idol destroyed without delay and whether the Prophet ratified the document on the basis of the concessions which he granted. It is noteworthy that this report explicitly states that the Prophet conceded to them profits from usury. Some questions which remain unanswered in this report can probably be answered by comparing it with the documents recorded by Abū 'Ubayd, and by comparing other accounts of the concession of usury, the privilege of the *ḥaram* of Wajj, the exemption from tithes and from the military levy.

A concise version recorded by Abū 'Ubayd indeed mentions that the deputation returned home after the Prophet rejected their requests for concessions concerning usury, prostration and wine. Subsequently, they willingly returned to convert to Islam, and then the Prophet issued the document to them, as recorded by Abū 'Ubayd.[23] Although the setting of this tradition is different, the passage referring to the return of the deputation may be linked with the report recorded by Muqātil. The conditions agreed upon between the deputation and the Prophet, as given by Muqātil, seem to have served as basis for the letter of the Prophet.

Abū 'Ubayd emphasizes that the Prophet granted Thaqīf special privileges not given to other peoples. He concludes that the Prophet did this so as to reconcile their hearts to Islam, and he mentions precedents in which the enemy's strength was feared and could be diverted by concessions, or in which conversion to Islam was made conditional to certain privileges. In such cases the Prophet was wont to accede to the demands made.[24]

Abū 'Ubayd stresses that the Prophet did not grant Thaqīf permission for transactions based on usury.[25] This statement is true, for in the negotiations the Prophet indeed upheld his interdiction of usury; but he granted Thaqīf the privilege of collecting the debts owed to them up to the day of their conversion, including the interest, whilst in paying their own debts to other peoples they would only pay the capital without interest.

(ṣ), fa-qālū: tumatti'unā bi-l-lāti sanatan; fa-a'raḍa 'anhum wa-ja'ala yakrahu an yaqūla lā, fa-ya'bauna l-islāma; fa-qālat thaqīfun li-l-nabiyyi (ṣ): in kāna bika malāmatu l-'arabi fī kasri aṣnāmihim wa-tarki aṣnāminā, fa-qul lahum: inna rabbī amaranī an uqirra l-lāta bi-arḍihim sanatan; fa-qāla 'umaru bnu l-khaṭṭābi (r) 'inda dhālika: aḥraqtum qalba l-nabiyyi (ṣ) bi-dhikri l-lāti, aḥraqa llāhu akbādakum, lā, wa-lā ni'mata 'aynin, inna llāha 'azza wa-jalla lā yada'u l-shirka fī arḍin yu'badu llāhu ta'ālā fīhā, fa-immā tuslimū kamā yuslimu l-nāsu, fa-immā talḥaqū bi-arḍikum; fa-anzala llāhu 'azza wa-jalla: "wa-in kādū la-yaftinūnaka – ay yaṣuddūnaka 'ani lladhī auḥaynā ilayka".

[23] Abū 'Ubayd, *al-Amwāl*, p. 194.

[24] Abū 'Ubayd, *al-Amwāl*, pp. 193 penult. - 194.

[25] Abū 'Ubayd, *al-Amwāl*, p. 194: . . . *wa-yubayyinu dhālika anna rasūla llāhi (ṣ) lam yaj'al lahum, fīmā a'ṭāhum taḥlīla l-ribā.*

The fact that the Prophet did grant them this concession can be deduced from the traditions concerning a law suit brought before 'Attāb b. Asīd, governor of Mecca in the period following the conversion of al-Ṭā'if. The Banū Mughīra (a branch of Makhzūm), the traditions say, had close financial relations with the Banū 'Amr from al-Ṭā'if based on the lending of money. In their suit the Banū 'Amr demanded payment of the debt owed them by the Banū Mughīra, arguing that the Prophet had permitted them to collect such debts with all due interest. The Banū Mughīra argued, in their defence, that they were in difficult straits, for usury was forbidden by Islam and consequently they had lost considerable sums of money owed to them. 'Attāb b. Asīd wrote to the Prophet in Medina asking him for a decision in the matter. Then verse 278 of *Sūrat al-Baqara* was revealed: "O believers, fear God and give up the usury that is outstanding. . . " The Prophet conveyed the verse to 'Attāb, who summoned the Banū 'Amr from al-Tā'if and read before them the revealed verse. They promised to obey and act accordingly,[26] and dropped their suit.

The report about the suit of the Banū 'Amr against the Banū Mughīra[27] supplements the tradition of Muqātil and supports its validity. The Prophet apparently granted Thaqīf the concession to collect the debts owed to them with all due interest up to the date of their conversion. The privilege granted seems, however, to have remained in force for a very short period and was abrogated by the verse of the Qur'ān mentioned above. The date of the revelation of this verse can be fixed in the period after the visit of the deputation in 9 H and before the death of the Prophet in 11 H.

The terms granted to Thaqīf by the Prophet were considered by Muslim scholars as exceptionally favourable.[28] The privileged status granted to Thaqīf was

---

[26] Muqātil, *op. cit.*, I, fol. 47a; and see al-Suyūṭī, *al-Durr al-manthūr*, Cairo, 1314, I, 366, ll. 12-18, 25-34; cf. al-Suyūṭī, *Lubāb al-nuqūl fī asbābi l-nuzūl*, Cairo, 1373/1954, p. 42inf.-43; al-Wāḥidī, *Asbāb al-nuzūl*, Cairo, 1388/1968, pp. 58-9; al-Naysābūrī, *op. cit.*, III, 79; al-Qurṭubī, *Tafsīr*, III, 363; Ibn Ḥajar, *al-Iṣāba*, ed. 'Alī Muḥammad al-Bijāwī, Cairo, 1392/1972, VI, 551-2.

[27] See al-Samarqandī, *Tafsīr*, Ms. Chester Beatty 3668, I, 70b: *. . .nazalat hādhihi l-āyatu fī nafarin min banī thaqīfin wa-fī banī l-mughīrati min qurayshin, wa-kānat thaqīfun yurbūna li-banī l-mughīrati fī l-jāhiliyyati, wa-kānū arba'ata ikhwatin minhum mas'ūdun wa-'abdu yālīla wa-akhawāhumā yurbiyānī li-banī l-mughīrati; fa-lammā ẓahara l-nabiyyu 'alā ahli makkata waḍa'a l-ribā, wa-kāna ahlu l-ṭā'ifi qad ṣālaḥū 'alā anna lahum ribāhum 'alā l-nāsi ya'khudhūnahu, wa-mā kāna 'alayhim min ribā l-nāsi fa-huwa mauḍū'un 'anhum, lā yu'khadhu minhum; wa-qad kāna rasūlu llāhi (ṣ) kataba lahum kitāban wa-kataba fī asfali kitābihim: inna lakum mā li-l-muslimīna wa-'alaykum mā 'alayhim; fa-lammā ḥalla l-ajalu ṭalaba thaqīfun ribāhum, fa-khāṣamū ilā amīri makkata wa-huwa 'attābu bnu asīdin. . .*; and see this tradition (with slight variants) in al-Suyūṭī's *al-Durr al-manthūr*, I, 364, 11. 3-8; cf. the concise comment on the verse of the Qur'ān given by al-Jaṣṣāṣ, *Aḥkām al-qur'ān*, Istanbul, 1338, I, 470: *. . . .fa-abṭala minhu mā baqiya mimmā lam yuqbaḍ wa-lam yubṭil al-maqbūḍ* (the abrogation referred to sums to be paid, but not to sums already paid).

[28] See A. Ben-Shemesh, *Taxation in Islam* III (Qudāma b. Ja'far, *Kit. al-kharāj*), Leiden, 1965, II, 30 (Ar. text, fol. 83a: *. . . annahu wa-in kāna bayna man aslama ṭā'i'an wa-man ukriha 'alā l-islāmi farqun qad abānahu rasūlu llāhi (ṣ) bi-l-fi'li, wa-dhālika annahu ja'ala li-ahli*

clearly expressed in the stipulation that Wajj was their exclusive domain (*wa-thaqīfun aḥaqqu l-nāsi bi-wajjin*), that no one could enter the city of al-Ṭā'if without their permission, that they could plan the building of their city according to will, and that the governors would be appointed only from amongst themselves. The document of the Prophet formed, in fact, a definite solution to the long-standing competition between al-Ṭā'if and Mecca in the Jāhiliyya. Tradition says that Quraysh increased in number in the period of the Jāhiliyya and coveted the valley of Wajj; they proposed to Thaqīf that they share the *ḥaram* (of Mecca – K) and Wajj on equal terms. Thaqīf refused, arguing that Wajj had been built up by their ancestors (they having therefore exclusive right of control over the land and the city – K), whilst the *ḥaram* of Mecca was established by Abraham (and was thus a place open to all – K). Quraysh then threatened to deny Thaqīf access to Mecca; Thaqīf, fearing war with Quraysh and their allies from Khuzā'a and Bakr b. 'Abd Manāt, were compelled to concede and entered into alliance with Quraysh.[29] This alliance tightened their mutual relations; Thaqīf were granted entrance into the Qurashī controlled Ḥums organization and intermarried with Quraysh.[30] The agreement, however, also facilitated the purchase of land in Wajj by Qurashites, and reports of Qurashī possessions in Wajj and in al-Ṭā'if substantiate it.[31]

---

l-ṭā'ifi lladhīna kāna islāmuhum ṭau'an mā lam yaj'alhu li-ghayrihim mithla taḥrīmi wādīhim wa-allā yu'bara ṭā'ifuhum...; the translation: "declared their water-sources protected areas" is slightly inaccurate; it should, of course, be rendered: "and he declared their valley as *ḥaram*".

[29] Muḥammad b. Ḥabīb, *al-Munammaq*, ed. Khursheed Aḥmad Fāriq, Hyderabad, 1384/1964, pp. 280-1.

[30] Al-Jāḥiẓ, Kitāb al-amṣār wa-'aja'ib al-buldān, ed. Charles Pellat, *Al-Mashriq* 60 (1966), pp. 175-76 (The passage referred to: *wa-mimmā bānat* [*bihi*] *qurayshun annahā lam talid fī l-jāhiliyyati waladan* [*majnūnan*] *qaṭṭu wa-la-qad akhadha dhālika minhum sukkānu l-ṭā'ifi li-qurbi l-jiwāri wa-ba'ḍi l-muṣāharati wa-li- annahum kānū ḥumsan wa-qurayshun ḥammasa thum*, seems to contain a misreading, the amendment of which may here be suggested. The reading *waladat* is erroneous and consequently the addition [*majnūnan*] is unwarranted. The reading that Quraysh "never gave birth to a mad child in the period of the Jāhiliyya" is incompatible with the following sentence, stating that the people of al-Ṭā'if "took it over (learnt it – K) from them". The correct reading is apparently "*lam ta'id*": Quraysh never buried a [living female] child in the period of the Jāhiliyya; Thaqīf took over this custom (i.e. learnt it, adopted it – K) from Quraysh. In the following passage: *"wa-laysa fī aydī jamī'i l-'arabi nisbatun min jamī'i nisā'i quraysh"*, read correctly: *sabiyyatun*; when Islam came there was no captive Qurashī woman among all the tribes of the Arabs. [See the verse of al-'Āṣ b. Wā'il in al-Balādhurī's *Ansāb al-ashrāf*, Ms. fol. 1154a, about the women of Mecca: *wa-innā lā tusāqu lanā ki'ābun: khilāla l-naq'i bādiyata l-khidāmi*]. The word *al-qasm* [p. 176, l. 3] should be read *al-ghashm*).

[31] Al-Balādhurī, *Futūḥ*, p. 75; al-Ṭabarī, *Ta'rīkh*, II, 68: *...wa-qadima nāsun min al-ṭā'ifi min qurayshin lahum amwālun...*; and see Abū l-Baqā' Muḥammad b. al-Ḍiyā' al-Makkī l-'Adawī, *Aḥwāl Makka wa-l-Madīna*, Ms. Br. Mus., Or. 11865, fol. 38b: *...wa-kāna li-l-'abbāsi karmun bi-l-ṭā'ifi, wa-kāna yaḥmilu zabībahu ilayhā wa-kāna yudāyinu ahla l-ṭā'ifi wa-yaqtaḍī minhum al-zabība...*; *ibid.*, fol. 39b sup.: *...fa-kānat fī yadi 'aliyyi bni 'abdi llāhi bni 'abbāsin..... ya'tīhi l-zabību min mālihi bi-l-ṭā'if...*; Muqātil, *op. cit.*, II, 215a: ... *wa-ja'altu lahu mālan mamdūdan* (Sūra LXXIV, 13) *ya'nī bi-l-māli bustānahu lladhī lahu bi-l-ṭā'ifi, wa-l-mamdūdu lladhī lā yanqaṭi'u khayruhu shitā'an wa-lā ṣayfan*. The person referred to,

It may be of some importance to elucidate a peculiar passage in the letter of the Prophet concerning the real estate of Quraysh in the region of al-Ṭā'if. "Half of the (crops of – K) vineyards of Quraysh watered by Thaqīf will be (the lot – K) of them," says the stipulation in the document of the Prophet.[32] It is evident that this decision aimed at regulating the partnership relations between the Qurashī owners of the land and their Thaqafī partners, who saw to the tilling and watering of the vineyards. The Thaqafites, perceiving the weakness of the Qurashites who had been involved in the bloody struggle with the Prophet, tried apparently to change the terms of the partnership in their own favour, or even to take over the property of their Qurashī partners. This can be gauged from a tradition recorded by al-Balādhurī: when Mecca was conquered by the Prophet and Quraysh embraced Islam, the Thaqafites coveted the land property of the Qurashites (scil. in the region of al-Ṭā'if – K); when al-Ṭā'if was conquered (for Islam) the rights to ownership of the property were confirmed.[33] The stipulation in the document of the Prophet seems to have settled the problem of the ownership of the land property of the Meccans and the conditions of their partnership with the Thaqafites.

The privileges granted to Thaqīf by the Prophet included exemption from *'ushr* and *ḥashr*. The meanings attached to these two words are divergent, and Muslim scholars differed concerning their definition already in the second century H. Abū 'Ubayd states that the exemption from *'ushr* means that they would not pay the tenth of their property, and that the tax paid by them would be confined to payment of *ṣadaqa*, i.e. five dirhams of every two hundred and fifty dirhams. The exemption from *ḥashr* is interpreted as meaning that they would not be ordered to gather their flocks and bring them to the tax-collector, who would come to them to their court-yards to levy their taxes.[34] Other scholars, quoting the interpretation of Jābir,[35] state that the Prophet in fact exempted them from payment of the poor tax, the *ṣadaqa*, but only for a very short period; as the time came to pay the tax of *ṣadaqa*, he postponed their payment until the end of the year. Comparing the decision of the Prophet to exempt Thaqīf from *ṣadaqa* and *jihād* with his refusal to exempt Bashīr b. al-Khaṣāṣiyya from these two prescriptions, Ibn al-Athīr explains that Bashīr was an individual, whereas Thaqīf were a community group (*jamā'a*), and that Thaqīf would not have converted in contrast to Bashīr, of whom the Prophet knew that he desired to embrace Islam. Therefore the Prophet sought to reconcile them and to bring them into Islam by stages.[36]

according to the commentary is al-Walīd b. al-Mughīra; cf. al-Qurṭubī, *Tafsīr*, XIX, 71; al-Naysābūrī, *Gharā'ib*, XXIX, 91.

[32] Abū 'Ubayd, *al-Amwāl*, p. 191, ll. 18–19.

[33] Al-Balādhurī, *Futūḥ*, p. 75 (. . .*wa-kānat li-'āmmati qurayshin amwālun bi-l-ṭā'ifi ya'tūnahā min makkata fa-yuṣliḥūnahā; fa-lammā futiḥat makkatu wa-aslama ahluhā ṭami'at thaqīfun fīhā, ḥattā idhā futiḥat al-ṭā'ifu uqirrat fī aydī al-makkiyyīn*. . .).

[34] Abū 'Ubayd, *al-Amwāl*, p. 192.

[35] See note 7 above.

[36] Ibn al-Athīr, *al-Nihāya*, III, 239 inf.- 240; *L'A*, s.v 'a sh r; (see on Bashīr b. al-Khaṣāṣiyya: Ibn al-Athīr, *Usd al-ghāba*, Būlāq, 1280, I, 193-4).

Some scholars explain *ḥashr* (*lā yuḥsharūna*), contrary to the interpretation of Abū 'Ubayd, as denoting that Thaqīf would not be summoned for fighting in military expeditions.[37] Abū 'Ubayd's interpretation of *'ushr* and *ḥashr* reflects in fact the Muslim opinion on the tax " *'ushr* ", the tithe collected only from Jewish and Christian merchants, but from which Muslims were exempt[38] and on "*ḥashr*" the forbidden practice of driving the flocks to a specific location for the purpose of taxation (taxes were to be collected "on the spot", *'alā miyāhihim wa-bi-afniya-tihim*).[39] The intricate and crucial problem of the meaning of these two terms was authoritatively solved by the late D.C. Baneth: "Der mehrfach vorkommende Ausdruck *lā yuḥsharūna wa-lā yu'sharūna* ist überall zu deuten: sie sollen weder zu Kriegsdiensten noch zum Zehnt herangezogen werden."[40] The Prophet apparently exempted Thaqīf from the prescribed poor tax, *ṣadaqa* (=*zakāt*) and *jihād*, in his endeavour to gain their cooperation and thus secure control over a city of considerable economic importance.

The destruction of the heathen sanctuary of al-Lāt according to the stipulations of the letter of the Prophet[41] marked the conversion of Thaqīf to Islam. The mosque of al-Ṭā'if was erected on the spot on which al-Lāt had been worshipped,[42] a visible mark of the victory of Islam over paganism. The Prophet, of course, knew that Thaqīf, after their conversion to Islam, would become loyal members of the Islamic community and perform fully the prescriptions of the new faith.

*

The privileges bestowed upon Thaqīf by the Prophet were generous and amounted almost to a measure of autonomy. The granted concessions, however, very soon lost their importance, when al-Ṭā'if was incorporated into the body politic of the nascent Muslim commonwealth. The Prophet sent 'Uthmān b. abī l-'Āṣ to al-Ṭā'if as governor[43] and Sālif b. 'Uthmān b. Mu'attib as tax collector.[44]

[37] Ibn al-Athīr, *al-Nihāya*, I, 389; *L'A*, s.v. ḥ sh r; cf. al-Zamakhsharī, *al-Fā'iq*, II, 433 sup., I, 180, ll. 13–14.

[38] See Abū 'Ubayd, *al-Amwāl*, pp. 528–30, nos. 1631-43 (and see esp. no. 1638); and see al-Ṭaḥāwī, *Sharḥ ma'ānī l-āthār*, ed. Muḥammad Zuhrī l-Najjār, Cairo, 1388/1968, II, 30-3.

[39] See e.g. Abū 'Ubayd, *al-Amwāl*, p. 404, no. 1092; and see above, notes 7, 10.

[40] D.H. Baneth, *Beiträge Zur Kritik und zum sprachlichen Verständnis der Schreiben Mohammeds* (Résumé of thesis, 1920).

[41] See e.g. al-Wāqidī, *op. cit.*, pp. 971-2.

[42] See Yāqūt, *Mu'jam al-buldān*, s.v. al-Lāt; Ibn al-Kalbī, *Kit. al-aṣnām*, ed. Aḥmad Zakī Pāshā, Cairo, 1343/1934, p. 16. (Comp. the story of the destruction of Dhū l-Khalasa: Ibn al-Kalbī, *op. cit.*, pp. 35inf.- 36; the mosque of 'Ablā', was erected on the spot of the sanctuary of Dhū Khalaṣa [see al-Balādhurī, *Ansāb al-ashrāf*, Ms. fol. 1175a inf.: . . .*thumma innahu ḥajja ilā dhī l-khalaṣata wa-huwa baytun bi-l-'ablā' kānat khath'amun wa-man yalīhim min qaysin wa-ghayrihim yaḥujjūnahu, wa-huwa l-yauma mauḍi'u masjidi l-'ablā'i. . .*]).

[43] Al-Balādhurī, *Futūḥ*, p. 79; Ibn Qutayba, *al-Ma'ārif*, ed. Tharwat 'Ukāsha, Cairo, 1969, pp. 268-9; al-Fāsī, *al-'Iqd al-thamīn fī ta'rīkh al-balad al-amīn*, ed. Fu'ād Sayyid, Cairo, 1386/1966, VI, 24-5; al-Zurqānī, *Sharḥ al-mawāhib*, IV, 10; Khalīfa b. Khayyāṭ, *Ta'rīkh*, ed. Akram Ḍiyā' al-'Umarī, al-Najaf, 1386/1967, pp. 61, 91; al-Dhahabī, *Siyar a'lām al-nubalā'*, ed. Ibrāhīm al-Abyārī, Cairo, 1957, II, 269.

[44] Al-Balādhurī, *Ansāb al-ashrāf*, ed. Muḥammad Ḥamīdullāh, Cairo, 1959, I, 531; Ibn

Sa'd b. abī Waqqāṣ was appointed by the Prophet over the *ḥimā* of Wajj.[45] This marked, of course, the full absorption of Thaqīf into the activities of the Muslim community. Later al-Ṭā'if became a district of Mecca.[46] Abū Bakr appointed 'Attāb b. Asīd as governor of Mecca and al-Ṭā'if, but later 'Uthmān b. abī l-'Āṣ was reappointed governor of al-Ṭā'if, leaving 'Attāb solely as governor of Mecca.[47] 'Umar appointed Nāfi' b. 'Abd al-Ḥārith from Khuzā'a as governor of Mecca and al-Ṭā'if, but later dismissed him[48] and appointed Sufyān b. 'Abdallāh al-Thaqafī as governor of Ṭā'if;[49] other sources record that 'Umar sent him to al-Ṭā'if as tax-collector.[50] In his questions addressed to 'Umar concerning taxes imposed on cattle, fruits and honey, and in 'Umar's instructions there is no trace of a privileged position for al-Ṭā'if,[51] nor is there any such position in the taxation on land. Al-Ṭā'if had become equal to all other regions of the Arabian peninsula.[52] The stipulation concerning the *taḥrīm* of the entire area of al-Ṭā'if seems to have lost its validity and the privately owned *ḥimās* fell under the control of the governor and received formal acknowledgement and protection upon due payment of taxes.[53]

Shortly after the Prophet's death Thaqīf were summoned to participate in the enormous effort of the Muslim conquests: on the eve of the expedition against Syria, Abū Bakr called upon the people of al-Ṭā'if to join the forces being despatched towards the borders of the Byzantine empire.[54] It is noteworthy that as early as 13 H, 'Umar appointed Abū 'Ubayd al-Thaqafī, the martyr of the Battle of the Bridge, as the commander of the Muslim forces fighting on the Persian frontier.[55]

Ḥajar, *al-Iṣāba*, III, 8, no. 3041; . . . *fa-lammā aslamū sta'mala min al-aḥlāfi sālifa bna 'uthmāna 'alā ṣadaqati thaqīfin*. . . ; Ibn al-Athīr, *Usd*, III, 245; and see Ibn al-Kalbī, *Jamhara*, Ms. Br. Mus., Add. 23297, fol. 155a, ll.3-5.

[45] Al-Wāqidī, *op. cit.*, p. 973, ll. 7-8.

[46] Al-Balādhurī, *Futūḥ*, p. 75 (. . .*wa-ṣārat arḍu l-ṭā'ifi mikhlāfan min makhālīfi makkata*).

[47] Al-Balādhurī, *Ansāb*, I, 529.

[48] Al-Fāsī, *al-'Iqd al-thamīn*, VII, 320-2, no. 2574; Ibn al-Athīr, *Usd*, V, 7-8; cf. Ibn Ḥajar, *al-Iṣāba*, VI, 408.

[49] Al-Balādhurī, *Futūḥ*, pp. 77, 79; see on him Ibn Ḥajar, *al-Iṣāba*, III, 124, no. 3317; Ibn al-Athīr, *Usd*, II, 319–20; al-Fāsī, *al-'Iqd*, IV, 590, no. 1308; Khalīfa b. Khayyāṭ, *op. cit.*, p. 129.

[50] 'Abd al-Razzāq, *al-Muṣannaf*, ed. Ḥabīburraḥmān al-A'ẓamī, Beirut, 1391/1972, IV, 10, no. 6806 (. . . *anna 'umara bna l-khaṭṭābi ba'atha sufyāna bna 'abdi llāhi l-thaqafiyya sā'iyan* . . .), II, no. 6808 (. . .*anna sufyāna bna 'abdi llāhi wa-huwa yuṣaddiqu fī makhālīfi l-ṭā'ifi*. . .)

[51] See 'Abd al-Razzāq, *op. cit.*, IV, 14, no. 6816; al-Balādhurī, *Futūḥ*, pp. 76-8; cf. Yaḥyā b. Ādam, *Kit. al-kharāj*, ed. Aḥmad Muḥammad Shākir, Cairo, 1347, p. 155, no. 548.

[52] See Abū Yūsuf, *Kit. al-kharāj*, Cairo, 1382, pp. 58inf., 63; Abū 'Ubayd, *al-Amwāl*, p. 512, no. 1560.

[53] See 'Abd al-Razzāq, *op. cit.*, IV, 62, no. 6969; Abū Yūsuf, *op. cit*, pp. 55 inf., 70 inf.- 71 sup.; Abū 'Ubayd, *al-Amwāl*, p. 497, no. 1488; Ibn Abī Shayba, *al-Muṣannaf*, III, 141; and see F. Lokkegaard, *Islamic Taxation*, Copenhagen, 1950, p. 31 (and see *ib.*, pp. 22–35 on *ḥaram* and *ḥimā*).

[54] Al-Balādhurī, *Futūḥ*, p. 149.

[55] See e.g. al-Balādhurī, *Futūḥ*, pp. 350-2; al-Ṭabarī, *Ta'rīkh*, II, 630-2; Ibn A'tham, *al-Futūḥ*, Hyderabad, 1388/1968, I, 164.

As equal but not privileged members of the emerging society of the Arab Empire, the Thaqafites migrated to the various regions of the conquered lands and produced quite a few well known leaders and administrators, as well as rebels.

II

The wars of the *ridda* and the subsequent wars of conquest and expansion brought about fundamental changes in the population structure of the Arabian peninsula. As a result of the fact that tribal units emigrated by waves to the newly-conquered territories, bonds between clans and tribes were loosened, weakening the units and groups which remained in the peninsula; this led to the necessity to form new bonds amongst these tribal groups. Furthermore, small and weak tribal units, which had split away from their main tribe and had come to dwell among other tribal divisions, detached themselves during this stormy period of migrations, and tried to find the way back to their original tribes.

The changes which the re-distribution of land by the rulers in the Arabian peninsula introduced were considerable: vast areas of pasture land were expropriated and turned into *ḥimā* territory; lands of the expelled Jews and Christians in Najrān were divided and leased out on terms now fixed by the Caliph[56] and exacted by his governors.

Large estates were established by members of the Meccan aristocracy, and wells were dug (especially on the routes of the *ḥajj*), providing them with water. Captives from the conquered territories were brought to the Arabian peninsula and employed by land owners in building up their estates.

The rapid development of Mecca, as a center of pilgrimage for the rising Empire, called for large supplies of vegetables and fruits. This was the impetus for the growth of well-cultivated farms and estates in the vicinity of Mecca and Medina, providing for the needs of the population and the pilgrims to these two cities.

Mu'āwiya's grasp of the economic importance of real estate led him to acquire lands in the area of Mecca and Medina, where he also purchased buildings and courts. He did the same in al-Ṭā'if, buying land from Jews who had settled there as merchants after being expelled from al-Yaman and Medina.[57] It is obvious

---

[56] See Ibn Abī Shayba, *Ta'rīkh*, Ms. Berlin 9409 (Sprenger 104), fol. 100b: *ḥaddathanā abū khālidin al-aḥmaru 'an yaḥyā bni sa'īdin anna 'umara ajlā ahla najrāna l-yahūda wa-l-naṣārā wa-shtarā* (text: *wa-starā*) *bayāḍa arḍihim wa-kurūmihim, fa-'āmala 'umaru l-nāsa: in hum jā'ū bi-l-baqari wa-l-hadīdi min 'indihim fa-lahumu l-thulthāni wa-li-'umara l-thulthu; wa-in jā'a 'umaru bi-l-badhri min 'indihi fa-lahu l-shaṭru; wa-'āmalahum al-nakhl* (sic!) *'alā anna lahumu l-khumsa wa-li-'umara arba'atu akhmāsin; wa-'āmalahum al-karm* (sic!) *'alā anna lahumu l-thultha wa-li-'umara l-thulthāni*. 'Umar denotes in this report (. . . *wa-li-'umara, . . . wa-in jā'a 'umaru. . .*) the Muslim government of Medina. It is obvious that the government established a new order of the agrarian organization of Najrān and supplied, in certain cases, the peasants with means of cultivation of the land.

[57] See al-Balādhurī, *Futūḥ*, p. 75.

that Mu'āwiya needed labourers to cultivate his lands, as well as reliable personnel for maintaining his houses and managing his enterprises.[58] The thread which may lead us to a better understanding of Mu'āwiya's policy against the background of the contemporary social and economic situation is provided in a concise account which states that Mu'āwiya affiliated the 'Ā'idhat Quraysh (i.e. the Khuzayma b. Lu'ayy) to Quraysh in order to strengthen his power by them (*yatakaththaru bihim*).[59] The expression *"yatakaththaru bihim"*, in the context of the reports on the power struggle between the various parties, denotes the affiliation or adoption of a group of people by one of the parties in order to overcome a contending party.[60] The application of this principle in relation to the Banū Sāma is recorded in a significant report, transmitted by al-Zubayr b. Bakkār and Muḥammad b. Ḥabīb, on the authority of al-Zuhrī. Abū Jahm b. Ḥudhayfa[61] came to Mu'āwiya who enquired about his fight and dissension with Thaqīf, for the latter had submitted a complaint against him to Mu'āwiya. Abū Jahm's succinct reply was: he would not be reconciled with them until they said: "Quraysh and Thaqīf, Liyya

---

[58] See M. Rosen-Ayalon (ed.), *Studies in Memory of Gaston Wiet*, Jerusalem 1977, p. 44, notes 52-5.

[59] See *Oriens* 25-26 (1976) 56, note 42; and see on 'Ā'idhat Quraysh: al-Zubayr b. Bakkār, *Jamharat nasab quraysh wa-akhbārihā*, Ms. Bodley, Marsh 384, fol. 199a-b; Muṣ'ab al-Zubayrī, *Nasab quraysh*, ed. Levi Provençal, Cairo, 1953, p. 442 sup.; al-'Iṣāmī, *Simṭ al-nujūm al-'awālī*, Cairo, 1380, I, 164. (And see about the different petty tribal divisions alleging a Qurashī pedigree: *Oriens* 25-26 (1976) 55–56, notes 33-41; and see about the Murra b. 'Auf alleging Qurashī origin: al-Balādhurī, *Ansāb*, Ms., fol. 1143b; and see about the expulsion of Āl Junayda b. Qays from amongst Quraysh by 'Umar: al-Zubayr b. Bakkār, *op. cit.*, fol. 201b; and see about alliances of certain small tribal factions: al-Zubayr b. Bakkār, *op. cit.*, fol. 199b: *wa-kāna banū ma'īṣi bni 'āmiri bni lu'ayyin wa-banū l-adrami wa-banū muḥāribi bni fihrin ḥulafā'a*. . . ; cf. al-'Iṣāmī, *op. cit.*, I, 164: *wa-fī qurayshin rahṭun yuqālu lahu l-ajrabāni wa-hum banū baghīḍi* (read correctly: *ma'īṣi*) *bni 'āmiri bni lu'ayyin wa-banū muhāribi bni fihrin, wa-kāna hādhāni l-rahṭāni mutaḥālifayni wa-kānā yud'ayāni l-ajrabayni*. . .).

[60] The accusation of 'Abd al-Raḥmān b. al-Ḥakam raised against Mu'āwiya: *lau lam tajid illā l-zanja la-takaththarta bihim 'alaynā*. . . was mistranslated and misinterpreted by Lammens, *Études sur la Règne du Calife Omaiyade Mo'āwia Ier*, Beyrouth, 1906, p. 11: . . . *Par Dieu si les nègres pouvaient te rendre service tu n'hésiterais pas à les employer pour affermir ton pouvoir*. . given as proof for the preceding assumption of Lammens: . . . *Ainsi, dans le gouvernement de l'islam, agissaient Mo'āwia et, à son exemple, les Omaiyades; chez le premier surtout, la raison d'état a généralement primé les autres considérations*. . . This utterance was as well mistranslated and misinterpreted by W. Hoenerbach, "Araber und Mittelmeer, Anfänge und Probleme Arabischer Seegeschichte" in: *Zeki Velidi Togan'a Armağan*, Istanbul, 1950-5, p. 385: *"Wenn du Profit haben könntest durch die Zanǧ so würdest du Profit durch sie haben*. . . *tatsächlich kennzeichnet sie seine stete Bereitschaft zur Übernahme alter Einrichtungen*. . . The correct translation should be: ". . . If you found none but negroes, you would strive to out-number us by [adopting or attaching] them [scil. to your clan – K]", as I gave it in *Studies in Memory of Gaston Wiet*, p. 44, note 57.

[61] See on him Ibn Ḥajar, *al-Iṣāba*, VII, 71, no. 9691; Ibn 'Abd al-Barr, *al-Istī'āb*, ed. 'Alī Muḥammad al-Bijāwī, Cairo, 1380/1960, pp. 1623-4, no. 2899; Ibn al-Athīr, *Usd*, V, 163-4; Muṣ'ab, *Nasab*, pp. 369, 371; al-Fāsī, *al-'Iqd*, VIII, 34, no 2846; Anonymous, *al-Ta'rīkh al-muḥkam fī man intasaba ilā l-nabiyyi ṣallā llāhu 'alayhi wa-sallam*, Ms. Br. Mus., Or. 8653, fol. 178a.

and Wajj."[62] "By God," said Abū Jahm, "only a fool from among them will like us and only a fool from among us will like them; by this we discern our fools."[63] Another report, also related on the authority of al-Zuhrī, tells of the conversation between Mu'āwiya and Abū Jahm on the latter's second visit[64] to Mu'āwiya, complementing and elucidating the policy which Quraysh were pressing with regard to the Bakr b. 'Abd Manāt, a Kinānī division which had long sojourned at Mecca, and towards Thaqīf in al-Ṭā'if. Abū Jahm gives details of the situation and explains his plan of action; Mu'āwiya relates the steps taken. "The Banū Bakr (i.e. Banū Bakr b. 'Abd Manāt b. Kināna) are increasing in numbers, surpassing us" (thus forming a danger to our authority in the city – K),"[65] said Abū Jahm, advising Mu'āwiya to send to the Banū Sāma and to settle them beyond the Ditch (*khandaq*) opposite the best of the Banū Bakr;[66] he further proposed to grant to the Banū

---

[62] The reading in *al-Munammaq*, p. 397, l. 7: *wa-lītā wajj* is erroneous; read: *wa-liyatu wa-wajj.*

[63] The passage in *al-Munammaq*, p. 397, l. 7: *wa-lā yuḥibbūna minnā illā aḥmaqa, wa-lā yuḥibbuhum minnā illā aḥmaqu wa-bi-dhālika na'tabiruka min ḥamqānā*, is erroneous; read: *wa-lā yuḥibbunā minhum illā aḥmaqu, wa-lā yuḥibbuhum minnā illā aḥmaqu, wa-bi-dhālika na'tabiru ḥamqānā*; and see al-Bakrī, *Mu'jam mā sta'jam*, p. 1168.

[64] The text in *al-Munammaq*, p. 397, l. 8: *fī qal'atin ukhrā* is erroneous; read as in al-Zubayr's *Jamhara: fī wafdatin ukhrā wafadahā ilayhi.*

[65] For the expression *yatakaththarūna 'alaynā* see e.g. al-Zubayr b. Bakkār, *op. cit.*, fol. 184a: . . . *fa-inna banī kilābi bni murrata takaththarū 'alā buṭūni banī ka'bi bni lu'ayyin fa-taḥālafat 'alayhim tilka l-aḥlāf. . .*

[66] In al-Munammaq: *fa-j'alhum janāba banī bakr*; in al-Zubayr's *Jamhara: fa-j'alhum 'alā suyyābi banī bakr.*

The pedigree of the Banū Sāma is obscure, their relation with Quraysh is disputed and the reports of the scholars of *nasab* about their ancestor Sāma b. Lu'ayy are divergent and contradictory. According to tradition Sāma was compelled to leave his tribe. He escaped to 'Umān where he married the Quḍā'ī Nājiya bint Jarm b. Rabbān. The report that Sāma died childless is corroborated by an utterance of the Prophet that he left no progeny. But a contradictory *ḥadīth* attributed to the Prophet says that the Prophet asked a man about his pedigree. He said he was a descendant of Sāma and the Prophet asked: "The poet?", referring to a widely circulated verse of Sāma. This may obviously point to the fact that the Prophet confirmed the existence of descendants of Sāma. Somewhat clearer information can be obtained from an account according to which the Prophet received a delegation of the Banū Sāma and remarked that they were the relatives of Quraysh.

Some genealogical accounts say that Sāma's son from his first marriage (with Hind bint Taym al-Adram b. Ghālib), al-Ḥārith, married after the death of Sāma his stepmother Nājiya bint Jarm in accordance with the custom of *nikāḥ al-maqt*. The Banū Sama are thus the descendants of al-Ḥārith b. Sāma and Nājiya and are known as the Banū Nājiya. Another report says that Sāma and Nājiya had only a daughter, 'Āja, and the Banū Sāma (or Banū Nājiya) are the progeny of this daughter. A divergent account reports that Sāma died childless; Nājiya married after his death a man from Baḥrayn and gave birth to a child named al-Ḥārith. When her second husband died she went with her child, al-Ḥārith, to Mecca claiming falsely that al-Ḥārith was the child of Sāma b. Lu'ayy. She was welcomed by Ka'b b. Lu'ayy and accommodated by him with her child in Mecca. But when after some time a group of people from al-Baḥrayn divulged her lie, Ka'b b. Lu'ayy banned Nājiya with her son from Mecca; they returned to al-Baḥrayn. Another report states that Sāma did not beget children; he adopted a child of Nājiya and the Banū Sāma are in fact descendants of this adopted son.

Sāma as a source of sustenance the (income of the – K) settlements of Fadak, Khaybar and Wādī l-Qurā. Further, Abū Jahm described the situation in al-Ṭā'if, saying that Thaqīf would surpass Quraysh in numbers in Wajj and proposed that Mu'āwiya send many Byzantines and Persians[67] to settle densely in the Wajj valley, so that "we may devour them (i.e. Thaqīf) by them (i.e. the Byzantines and Persians).[68] Mu'āwiya expressed his full assent and told Abu Jahm that he fully settled[69] the (quarters of the – K) Banū Bakr with warriors and troops, so that if a Qurashite were to become enraged[70] he would send for one of the Banū Bakr; the Bakrī would be brought before him[71] and would do what he (i.e. the Qurashī) would wish him to do. Mu'āwiya emphasized what he did with Thaqīf, driving them from their abode and resettling them in the high mountains of al-Sarāt. They asked to be given their pay in 'Irāq, but Mu'āwiya insisted upon paying them in Syria, the country of plagues[72] in order to be rid of them. All their property

---

After the rise of Islam a delegation of the Banū Sāma asked to be affiliated to Quraysh, tracing their pedigree back to Sāma b. Lu'ayy, the ancestor of Quraysh. Both 'Umar and 'Alī denied any connection of Quraysh with them, refusing to include them in the pay-roll of Quraysh. A statement of 'Alī that the Banū Sāma were descendants of a bondsmaid of Sāma raped by one of his black slaves, is said to have led to a rebellion of the troop of the Banū Nājiya numbering 300 warriors. They openly revolted under their leader, al-Khirrīt b. Rāshid (from the Sāmī clan of 'Abd al-Bayt). They left 'Alī's camp and were joined by Muslim political malcontents, as well as by local inhabitants who refused to pay the land-tax (*kharāj*) and by Kurds and Bedouins. 'Alī was compelled to levy a strong force under the command of Ma'qil b. Qays al-Riyāḥī who succeeded to defeat al-Khirrīt's force in the region of al-Ahwāz. Al-Khirrīt retreated to the coastal territory of the Persian Gulf where he managed to rally the Banū Sāma, some of the 'Abd Qays, as well as Christians and converts to Islam from Christianity, who wanted to revert to their former faith. A strong force dispatched by 'Alī defeated the rebelling troop and al-Khirrīt was killed in the battle. The captives were sold to Maṣqala b. Hubayra al-Shaybānī, who freed them; he failed, however, to pay the promised sum, absconded and joined Mu'āwiya. The Banu Sāma were later known by their hostile attitude towards 'Alī. (See: al-Ḥusayn b. 'Alī al-Maghribī, *al-Īnās bi-'ilmi l-ansāb*, Ms. Br. Mus., Or. 3620, fols. 51a–55a; *al-Aghānī*, index; al-Ṭabarī, *Ta'rīkh*. index; Ibn A'tham, *al-Futūḥ*, Hyderabad 1391/1971, IV, 75–88; Ibn Abī l-Ḥadīd, *Sharḥ nahj al-balāgha*, ed. Muḥammad Abū l-Faḍl Ibrāhīm, Cairo, 1385/1965, III, 119–122, 126–151; Ibn Ḥazm, *Jamharat ansāb al-'arab*, ed. 'Abd al-Salām Hārūn, Cairo, 1962, p. 173; Ibn al-Athīr, *Usd*, II, 110; Ibn 'Abd al-Barr, *al-Istī'āb*, pp. 458-9; al-Balādhurī, *Ansāb al-ashrāf*, Ms., fol 1054a; and see W. Caskel, *Ǧamharat an-nasab, das genealogische Werk des Hišām ibn Muḥammad al-Kalbī*, II, 123, s.v. 'Abdalbait b. al-Ḥāriṯ; *Oriens* 25–26, 56 (1976), note 38).

[67] In al-Zubayr's *Jamhara: fa-akthir min* [*al-aḥrāri min*] *al-rūmi wa-l-fursi* [*wa-mla' wajjan minhum*]; the words in brackets are missing in *al-Munammaq*.

[68] The reading *ḥattā ta'kulahum* is erroneous; read: *ḥatta na'kulahum*. For the expression *na'kulu bi* see al-Ṭabarī, *Ta'rīkh*, II, 84: *wa-llāhi lau annī akhadhtu hādhā l-fatā min qurayshin la-akaltu bihi l-'araba.*

[69] The reading *mala'ahum* in *al-Munammaq* is erroneous; read: *fa-qad mala'tuhum.*

[70] The correct reading is: *ḥattā anna aḥadakum la-yaghḍabu l-ghadbata* as in al-Zubayr's *Jamhara.*

[71] Read as in the *Jamhara: fa-yuqādu ilayhi* (not: *fa-yanqādu*); the correct reading is given in *al-Munammaq*, p. 398, note 9.

[72] The reading *arḍu l-miṭwā'īn*, the "land of the obedient", is erroneous; the correct reading is *arḍu l-ṭawā'īn*, the land of plagues and pestilences. This latter reading is corroborated by

(lands – K) were taken over by Quraysh and Mu'āwiya settled the territory with Byzantines and Persians.[73]

The quoted traditions indeed explain the report stating that Mu'āwiya affiliated the Banū Sāma to Quraysh, with the aim of gaining strength for his clan through this extension. They were settled in Mecca and served as his loyal supporters, increasing his authority and reducing the power of the Bakr b. 'Abd Manāt, a tribal division which had played a considerable role in the relations between Quraysh and the Prophet.

Mu'āwiya's policy in relation to al-Ṭā'if is fully expounded in this report. He strived, like his father, to acquire lands in al-Ṭā'if and its surrounding territories and to widen Qurashī influence there. The Qurashī aim is expressed in the saying of Abū Jahm: "There will be no reconciliation with Thaqīf until they say Liyya and Wajj, Quraysh and Thaqīf." The intention seems to be that Thaqīf should acknowledge the demands of Quraysh to share in Liyya and Wajj as equal partners. The Qurashī pressure was reinforced by the dispersion of Thaqīf in the mountains of al-Sarāt and by necessitating them to go to Syria, considered a country exposed to plagues, in order to collect their pay. The Persians and Byzantines mentioned in the report were, in all probability, captives employed as labourers on the large estates.

*

Al-Ṭā'if after that played no political role in the history of the Muslim Empire. Praised for its good climate it remained a summer resort for the wealthy of Mecca and Medina. The descendants of Thaqīf clung fondly to the document of the Prophet about Wajj;[74] the fertile lands in the vicinity of al-Ṭā'if seem to have been considered a good investment and it is quite plausible that Hishām b. 'Abd al-Malik purchased real estate there.[75] As a place of pilgrimage al-Ṭā'if became coupled with Mecca[76] or given a twofold sanctity comprising that of Mecca and of the Holy Land: al-Ṭā'if was a piece of Palestine transferred by God to the Arabian peninsula and placed in the spot of al-Ṭā'if after having performed the *ṭawāf* around the Ka'ba.[77] The traditions attributed to the Prophet, in which he

---

the phrase: "so that you and I may be rid of them", i.e. they would perish, afflicted by plagues in Syria. See on the "*ṭawā'īn al-shām*" al-Tha'ālibī, *Thimār al-qulūb*, ed. Muḥammad Abū l-Faḍl Ibrāhīm, Cairo, 1384/1965, p. 547, no. 896. And see about the deportation of people suspected of rebellious actions to Syria, the country of plagues: al-Balādhurī, Ansāb IVA, 232, ll. 5-6: *wa-wadidtu annī kuntu ḥabastuhu wa-aṣḥābahu au farraqtuhum fī kūri l-shāmi fa-kafatnīhimu l-ṭawā'īnu.*

[73] Al-Zubayr b. Bakkār, *op. cit.*, fol. 170b; Muḥammad b. Ḥabīb, *al-Munammaq*, pp. 397-9.

[74] Shakīb Arslān, *op. cit.*, p. 119: *...wa-kānat thaqīfun tatawārathu hādhā l-kitāba wa-tatabarraku bihi* (quoted from Ibn Fahd's *Tuḥfat al-laṭā'if*).

[75] Al-Balādhurī, *Ansāb*, Ms. fol. 1225b: *...ittakhadha hishāmun mālan bi-l-ṭā'if...*

[76] Shakīb Arslān, *op. cit.*, p. 136: *inna l-ṭā'ifa min makkata wa-makkatu min al-ṭā'ifi* (quoted from al-'Ujaymī's *Iḥdā'u l-laṭā'if*).

[77] See *Le Muséon* 82 (1969), 206, note 92; and see al-Ṭabarī, *Tafsīr*, ed. Shākir, III 52; al-'Ayyāshī, *Tafsīr*, ed. Hāshim al-Rasūlī l-Maḥallātī, Qumm, 1380, I, 60; al-Mas'ūdī,

asserted that Thaqīf were among the worst of the Arab tribes,[78] were replaced by traditions of praise. "The first for whom I shall intercede on the Day of Resurrection will be the people of Mecca, Medina and al-Ṭā'if,"[79] said a tradition attributed to the Prophet. "Thaqīf are God's deputation," says another tradition alleged to have been uttered by the Prophet.[80] Current stories predicted that during the period of disasters at the end of time the best people would dwell in the neighbourhood of al-Ṭā'if.[81] "Wajj is a sacred valley," says a *ḥadīth* recorded in the early compilation of Maʿmar b. Rāshid.[82] In the vein of this trend the tradition of God's last tread seems to have been altered: "Wajj is a sacred valley; from Wajj God, may He be blessed and exalted, ascended to Heaven after He had accomplished the creation of heaven and earth."[83] Wajj seems thus to have turned into the last spot on earth on which God trod and from which He ascended to Heaven, against the claims made on behalf of the Rock of the Dome in Jerusalem.

Ithbāt al-waṣiyya, Najaf, 1374/1955, p. 39; Ibn Bābūyah, *'Ilal al-sharā'i'*, Najaf, 1385/1966, pp. 442-3; al-Suyūṭī, *al-Durr al-manthūr*, I, 124; al-Majlisī, *Biḥār al-anwār*, Tehran, 1378, XII, 109; Hāshim al-Baḥrānī al-Taubalī al-Katkānī, *al-Burhān fī tafsīri l-qur'ān*, ed. Maḥmūd al-Mūsawī al-Zarandī, Tehran, 1375, I, 155, no. 8 and II, 319, nos. 4-5; Shakīb Arslān, *op. cit.*, p. 133.

[78] See Ibn Kathīr, *al-Bidāya*, VI, 236: . . .*sharru qabā'ili l-'arabi banū umayyata wa-banū ḥanīfata wa-thaqīfun*; al-Daylamī, *al-Firdaus*, Ms. Chester Beatty 3037, fol. 94a.

[79] Al-Nabīl, *al-Awā'il*, Ms. Ẓāhiriyya, ḥadīth 297/I, fol. 22a; Ibn 'Abd al-Barr, *al-Istī'āb*, p. 1007; al-Muḥibb al-Ṭabarī, *al-Qirā li-qāṣidi umm al-qurā*, ed. Muṣṭafā l-Saqā, Cairo, 1390/1970, p. 666.

[80] Ibn Hibbān al-Bustī, *Kit. al-majrūḥīn*, ed. 'Azīz al-Qādirī, Hyderabad, 1390/1970, I, 148: . . . *thaqīfun wafdu llāhi 'azza wa-jalla*; and see Ahmad b. Ḥanbal, *Musnad*, III, 342inf.: *qāla rasūlu llāhi (ṣ): allāhumma hdi thaqīfan.*

[81] Shakīb Arslān, *op. cit.*, p. 136 (quoted from al-Māyurqī's *Bahjat al-muhaj fī ba'ḍi faḍā'il al-ṭa'if wa-wajj*).

[82] 'Abd al Razzāq, *al-Muṣannaf*, XI, 134, no. 20125; al-Muhibb al-Ṭabarī, *op. cit.*, p. 666.

[83] Al-Bakrī, *Mu'jam*, p. 1370.

XII

"RAJAB IS THE MONTH OF GOD . . ."

A Study in the Persistence of an Early Tradition

in memory of my student DAVID S. ELLER

The holy month of Rajab was observed during the period of the Jāhiliyya in spring.[1] It was the month of the *'umra* and of offering of the sacrifices of the *'atā'ir* to the pagan deities.[2] The people of the Jāhiliyya kept the sanctity of the month by refraining from raids and warfare.[3] It is said to have been a month of devotional practices and of fasting.[4] According to some traditions swearing

[1] See EI, *s.v.* "*Radjab*" (M. Plessner); S. D. Goitein, *Studies in Islamic History and Institutions* (Leiden 1966), pp. 92–93; J. Wellhausen, *Reste arabischen Heidentums* (Skizzen und Vorarbeiten) (Berlin 1887), pp. 74, 93; G. E. von Grunebaum, *Muhammadan Festivals* (New York 1951), p. 36; W. Gottschalk, *Das Gelübde nach älterer arabischer Auffassung* (Berlin 1919), pp. 106–107; K. Wagtendonk, *Fasting in the Koran* (Leiden 1968), p. 106; M. Gaudefroy-Demombynes, *Le Pèlerinage à la Mekke* (Paris 1923), pp. IV, 192–198; C. Rathjens, *Die Pilgerfahrt nach Mekka* (Hamburg 1948), p. 66. [The above books are quoted by the names of their authors.]

[2] See EI[2] *s.v.* "*'Atīra*" (Ch. Pellat); F. Buhl, *Das Leben Muhammeds* (Heidelberg 1955), p. 88 (and see note 246, *ibid.*); al-Anbārī, *Sharḥ al-qaṣā'id al-sab' al-ṭiwāl*, ed. 'Abd al-Salām Hārūn (Cairo 1963), pp. 294, 484; Ibn Qutayba, *al-Ma'ānī al-kabīr* (Hyderabad 1949), I, 67; al-Nuwayrī, *Nihāyat al-arab* (repr. Cairo 1964), III, 120; Ibn Durayd, *al-Ishtiqāq*, ed. 'Abd al-Salām Hārūn (Cairo 1958), p. 280 (with a divergent version: *inna 'alā kulli muslimin fī kulli 'āmin 'atīratan, wa-hiya shātun kānat tudhbaḥu fī l-muḥarrami fa-nasakha dhālika l-aḍḥā.* The month of sacrifice here is Muḥarram, not Rajab); J. Wellhausen, pp. 94, 115–116; W. Gottschalk, p. 119; W. Robertson Smith, *Lectures on the Religion of the Semites* (London 1914), pp. 227–228; K. Wagtendonk, p. 36; al-Jāḥiẓ, *Kit. al-ḥayawān*, ed. 'Abd al-Salām Hārūn (Cairo 1965), I, 18.

[3] See J. Wellhausen, p. 94; al-Farrā', *al-Ayyām wa-l-layālī wa-l-shuhūr*, ed. Ibrāhīm al-Ibyārī (Cairo 1956), pp. 12–13; al-Marzūqī, *al-Azmina wa-l-amkina* (Hyderabad 1332 AH), I, 282, 90, 278; al-Jumaḥī, *Ṭabaqāt fuḥūl al-shu'arā'*, ed. Maḥmūd Muḥ. Shākir (Cairo 1952), p. 61; L'A, *s.v.* "*ṣmm, nṣl, rjb*"; al-Ṭurṭūshī, *Kit. al-ḥawādith wa-l-bida'*, ed. Muḥ. al-Ṭālibī (Tunis 1959), pp. 123, 125; 'Alī al-Qāri', *al-Adab fī rajab*, Paris, Bibliothèque Nationale, Ms. Arabe 6084, Majmū'a, fol. 65a (*wa-yuqālu rajabun al-aṣammu li-annahu lā yunādā fīhi "yā qaumāh" wa-"yā ṣabāḥāh" wa-li-annahu lā yusma'u fīhi ḥissu l-silāḥi lā fī l-ṣabāḥi wa-lā fī l-rawāḥi*); Ibn Qutayba, *Tafsīr gharīb al-Qur'ān*, ed. Aḥmad Ṣaqr (Cairo 1958), p. 185.

[4] See S. D. Goitein, pp. 92–93; K. Wagtendonk, pp. 117, 120–122.

against the iniquitous and wrong-doers in this month was especially efficacious.[5]

The veneration of this month seems to have continued in the period of Islam and to have survived until recent times. Contradictory traditions attributed to the Prophet, recommending some practices of Rajab or interdicting it, bear evidence of divergent opinion on this subject in the Muslim community during the early centuries of Islam. Heated discussions among Muslim scholars concerning different aspects of these practices make it possible to understand them better. These Rajab traditions are to be surveyed in the following pages of this paper.

I

The widely circulated utterance of the Prophet *lā faraʿa wa-lā ʿatīrata*, "no sacrifice of the firstlings (of the flock) nor of the animals slaughtered in Rajab",[6] indicates explicitly the interdiction to perform the sacrifices of Rajab. This *ḥadīth* is however contradicted by a tradition reported by ʿAmr b. Shuʿayb.[7] The Prophet, when asked about the *ʿaqīqa*, the *faraʿa* and the *ʿatīra*, stated concerning the *ʿatīra*: *al-ʿatīratu ḥaqqun*, "the *ʿatīra* is obligatory" (verbatim: the *ʿatīra* is an obligation). The word *ʿatīra* is explained in the tradition as a sacrifice of a ewe, which the people of the Jāhiliyya used in Rajab to slaughter, cook, and whose meat they used to consume and feed from (scil. the needy and poor).[8]

More explicit about the obligatory character of the *ʿatīra*, the sacrifice of Rajab, is the tradition reported on the authority of Mikhnaf b. Sulaym.[9] "Upon the people of every house, stated the Prophet, there is an obligation every

[5] See al-Kalāʿī, *al-Iktifāʾ fī maghāzī l-muṣṭafā wa-l-thalāthati l-khulafāʾ*, ed. H. Massé (Alger 1931), I, 123–124; al-Jīlānī, *al-Ghunya li-ṭālibi ṭarīqi l-ḥaqqi ʿazza wa-jalla* (Cairo 1322 AH), I, 196.

[6] Aḥmad b. Ḥanbal, *Musnad*, ed. Aḥmad Muḥ. Shākir (Cairo 1949–1956), XII, 104, No. 7135 and XIV, 171, No. 7737; al-Suyūṭī, *al-Jāmiʿ al-ṣaghīr* (Cairo 1320 AH), II, 202; L ʿA, *s.v.* "*frʿ*"; comp. W. Robertson Smith, pp. 227, note 3, and pp. 462–465; al-Shaukānī, *Nayl al-auṭār* (Cairo 1347 AH), V, 119; Abū l-Maḥāsin al-Ḥanāfī, *al-Muʿtaṣar min al-mukhtaṣar* (Hyderabad 1362 AH), I, 274; Abū Dāʾūd, *Ṣaḥīḥ sunan al-muṣṭafā* (Cairo 1348 AH), II, 8; al-Ḥākim, *al-Mustadrak* (Hyderabad 1342 AH), IV, 236; al-Muttaqī al-Hindī, *Kanz al-ʿummāl* (Hyderabad 1954), V, 48, No. 428; al-Tirmidhī, *Ṣaḥīḥ* (Cairo 1931), VI, 311–312; Muslim, *Ṣaḥīḥ* (Cairo 1285 AH), II, 159; al-ʿAzīzī, *al-Sirāj al-munīr* (Cairo 1957), III, 473, ult.; al-Tibrīzī, *Mishkāt al-maṣābīḥ* (Karachi), p. 129.

[7] See on him al-Dhahabī, *Mīzān al-iʿtidāl*, ed. ʿAlī Muḥ. al-Bijāwī (Cairo 1963), III, 263–268, No. 6383; Ibn Ḥajar, *Tahdhīb al-tahdhīb* (Hyderabad 1326 AH), VIII, 48–55, No. 80.

[8] Aḥmad b. Ḥanbal, XI, 4–7, No. 6713; al-Shaukānī, *Nayl*, V, 119; al-Suyūṭī, *al-Jāmiʿ al-ṣaghīr*, II, 67; al-Muttaqī al-Hindī, V, 48, No. 427; al-ʿAzīzī, II, 467, inf.

[9] See on him Ibn ʿAbd al-Barr, *al-Istīʿāb*, ed. ʿAlī Muḥ. al-Bijāwī (Cairo, n.d.), p. 1467, No. 2534; Ibn Ḥajar, *Tahdhīb*, X, 78; idem, *al-Iṣāba*, VI, 72, No. 7842.

year (to slaughter) a victim (scil. of the Sacrificial Feast) and a *ʿatīra*". The *ʿatīra* is glossed in the tradition as "*al-rajabiyya*". (*ʿAlā kulli ahli baytin fī kulli ʿāmin uḍḥiyyatun*[10] *wa-ʿatīratun: hal tadrūna mā l-ʿatīratu? hiya l-rajabiyyatu*).[11]

It is evident that these traditions are contradictory and reflect two diverse attitudes towards the continuation of the practices of the sacrifices of Rajab in Islam: the one approving of the *rajabiyya* and incorporating it into the body of Islamic sacrifices, authorized by the utterance of the Prophet; the other one aiming at the abolition of the Rajab sacrifice, it too basing its arguments on the utterances of the Prophet.

The two contradictory traditions (*lā faraʿa wa-lā ʿatīrata* and *inna ʿalā kulli ahli baytin*) are discussed by Abū ʿUbayd (d. 224 AH). Stressing the Jāhilī character of the *ʿatīra*, he remarks that this sacrifice was abolished by Islam. In his opinion, the *ḥadīth* of "*lā faraʿa*" abrogates the *ḥadīth* of "*ʿalā kulli ahli baytin...*" (*wa-l-ḥadīthu l-awwalu nāsikhun li-hādhā*).[12]

Al-Khaṭṭābī (d. 388 AH) records the opinion of Abū Dā'ūd (d. 275 AH) about the tradition of Mikhnaf b. Sulaym, which is identical with the opinion of Abū ʿUbayd. "The *ʿatīra*, says Abū Dā'ūd, is (an) abrogated (practice)", *al-ʿatīratu mansūkhatun.*[13] Al-Khaṭṭābī emphasizes the difference between the meaning of *ʿatīra* in the times of the Jāhiliyya and that of Islam. In the period of the Jāhiliyya *ʿatīra* denoted a ewe sacrificed for the idol; its blood was poured on the head of the idol — argues al-Khaṭṭābī. But in this *ḥadīth* (i.e. in the *ḥadīth* of Mikhnaf b. Sulaym) it denotes the sacrifices of an animal in Rajab. This, says al-Khaṭṭābī, fits the intent of the *ḥadīth* and is compatible with the prescription of the religion.[14] Al Khaṭṭābī does not consider the

10 In some traditions "*aḍḥātun*".

11 Ibn Ḥajar, *al-Iṣāba*, VI, 72; Abū Nuʿaym, *Akhbār Iṣfahān*, ed. S. Dedering (Leiden 1931). I, 73; al-Shaukānī, *Nayl*, V, 117; L'A, *s.v.* "*ʿatr*"; Abū l-Maḥāsin al-Ḥanafī, I, 274; ʿAbd al-Ghanī al-Nābulsī, *Dhakhā'ir al-mawārīth* (Cairo 1934), III, 95; al-Suyūṭī, *al-Jāmiʿ al-ṣaghīr*, II, 60 (with a slightly different version: *ʿalā ahli kulli baytin an yadhbaḥū shātan fī kulli rajabin wa-fī kulli aḍḥā shātan*); al-Muttaqī al-Hindī, V, 48, No. 429 and V, 57, No. 500–502; al-Bayhaqī, *al-Sunan al-kubrā* (Hyderabad 1356 AH), IX, 260; Muslim, II, 159; Abū Dā'ūd, II, 2; Ibn al-Athīr, *al-Nihāya*, ed. al-Ṭanāḥī (Cairo 1963), III, 178 (*ʿalā kulli muslimin aḍḥātun wa-ʿatīratun*); Ibn al-Athīr, *Jāmiʿ al-uṣūl min aḥādīth al-rasūl*, ed. Muḥ. Ḥāmid al-Fiqqī (Cairo 1950), IV, 121, No. 1624.

12 Abū ʿUbayd, *Gharīb al-ḥadīth*, ed. Muḥ. ʿAẓim al-Dīn (Hyderabad 1964), I, 194–195; L'A, *s.v.* "*ʿatr*" (where the opinion of Abū ʿUbayd is recorded differently: *wa-l-ḥadīthu l-awwalu aṣaḥḥu*); and see the note of the editor in Ibn al-Athīr's *Jāmiʿ al-uṣūl* IV, 122 (Abū ʿUbayda stated that the *ḥadīth*: "*lā faraʿa...*" abrogated the ḥadīth: "*ʿalā ahli kulli baytin...*").

13 Ḥamd b. Muḥ. al-Khaṭṭābī, *Maʿālim al-sunan* (Ḥalab 1933), II, 226.

14 *Ib.*, (...*al-ʿatīratu tafsīruhā fī l-ḥadīthi annahā shātun tudhbaḥu fī rajabin wa-hādhā huwa lladhī yushbihu maʿnā l-ḥadīthi wa-yalīqu bi-ḥukmi l-dīni* [in text: *l-tadayyuni*]); L'A, *s.v.* "*ʿatr*" (correctly: *l-dīni*); Ibn al-Athīr, *al-Nihāya*, III, 178 (correctly: *l-dīni*).

'atīra as abrogated; he seems to consider it lawful, although he has some reservations in connection with one of the transmitters of the *ḥadīth*.[15]

The opinion that the *'atīra* was abrogated by the Sacrificial Feast is plainly reflected in the *ḥadīth* reported on the authority of 'Alī. The Prophet said: "The Sacrificial Feast abrogated every sacrifice, the fasting of Ramaḍān abrogated every fasting... etc. (*nasakha l-aḍhā kulla dhabḥin wa-ṣaumu ramaḍāna kulla ṣaumin*...).[16]

Between the two poles of interdiction of the *'atīra* and its recommendation, there are some traditions which reflect an attitude of toleration. This can be gauged in the tradition recorded on the authority of Abū Razīn.[17] Abū Razīn said, asking the Prophet about the sacrifice of Rajab: "We used to slaughter in Rajab, to eat (scil. from the meat of the slaughtered animal) and to feed people who came to us." The Prophet then said: "There is no objection to it" (*lā ba'sa bihi*).[18] Wakī' b. 'Udus[19] the transmitter of Abū Razīn stated that he would never, following this tradition, abandon the sacrifice in Rajab.[20] Ibn 'Aun and Ibn Sīrīn used to sacrifice in Rajab.[21]

Slightly different is the tradition reported on the authority of al-Ḥārith b. 'Amr.[22] The Prophet, when asked about the *farā'i'* and *'atā'ir*, said: "He who wants to sacrifice the firstlings (of the flock) may do so; he who does not — may desist. He who wants to sacrifice the *'atīra* may do so, he who does not —may desist; there is a sacrifice on sheep" (*man shā'a farra'a wa-man shā'a lam yufarri'; wa-man shā'a 'atara wa-man shā'a lam ya'tir; wa-fī l-ghanami uḍḥiyatuhā*).[23] It may be pointed out that this utterance of the Prophet, as reported by al-Ḥārith b. 'Amr, was given by the Prophet

15 Comp. Ibn al-Athīr, *Jāmi' al-uṣūl* IV, 122, note 1: *wa-qāla l-Khaṭṭābī: hādhā l-ḥadīthu ḍa'īfu l-mukharraji, wa-Abū Ramlata majhūlun.*

16 al-Bayhaqī, IX, 262 sup.; al-Tirmidhī, VI, 312 (quoted in the commentary of Ibn al-'Arabī).

17 See on him Ibn 'Abd al-Barr, p. 1657, No. 2952; Ibn Ḥajar, *al-Iṣāba*, VI, 8, No. 7549.

18 Al-Khaṭīb al-Baghdādī, *Mūḍiḥ auhām al-jam' wa-l-tafrīq* (Hyderabad 1960), II, 333, No. 177 (*kunnā nadhbaḥu fī rajab*); Abū l-Maḥāsin al-Ḥanafī, I, 274; al-Bayhaqī, IX, 312; al-Shaukānī, *Nayl*, V, 118; Muslim, II, 159 (in the commentary of al-Nawawī).

19 See on him Ibn Ḥajar, *Tahdhīb*, XI, 131, No. 212.

20 Al-Bayhaqī, IX, 312.

21 Abū l-Maḥāsin al-Ḥanafī, I, 274; and see Ibn al-Athīr, *Jāmi' al-uṣūl*, IV, 122, note 1: *wa-kāna Ibn Sīrīn min bayni ahli l-'ilmi yadhbaḥu l-'atīrata fī shahri rajabin wa-kāna yarwī fīhā shay'an wa-lam yarahu mansūkhan.*

22 See on him Ibn 'Abd al-Barr, p. 294, No. 417; Ibn Ḥajar, *al-Iṣāba*, I, 298, No. 1454; idem, *Tahdhīb*, II, 151, No. 257.

23 Al-Ḥākim, IV, 232; Ibn Sa'd, *Ṭabaqāt* (Beirut 1958), VII, 64; al-Muttaqī al-Hindī, V, 48, No. 430; Abū l-Maḥāsin al-Ḥanafī, I, 257; al-Shaukānī, *Nayl*, V, 118; Muslim, II, 159 (in the commentary of al-Nawawī).

at the *ḥajjat al-wadāʿ*, forming thus his last and definitive utterance in this matter. This cannot be changed of course by an abrogating tradition.

Close to the preceding tradition is the *ḥadīth* reported on the authority of Nubaysha.[24] When asked about the sacrifices of Rajab, the Prophet said: "Slaughter for God in any month (you like), bestow upon people (graces) for the sake of God and feed (poor people)" (*idhbaḥū li-llāhi fī ayyi shahrin kāna wa-birrū li-llāhi ʿazza wa-jalla wa-aṭʿimū*).[25]

The difference between the tradition of Abū Razīn and the two preceding traditions is substantial: while in the tradition of Abū Razīn the *ʿatīra* is considered as lawful (*lā ba'sa bihā*) and meritorious, in the two preceding traditions no merit is attached to the sacrifice in Rajab at all; animals may be slaughtered in any month of the year; reward is given according to the good deed: the animals have to be slaughtered for God and their meat has to be given to the poor and needy.

The tendency of Muslim scholars, as might be foreseen, is to try and reconcile the conflicting opinions. Abū l-Maḥāsin al-Ḥanafī concludes that it may be supposed that the obligatory character of the *ʿatīra* (in Rajab) was abolished, but that it was left as a permitted and lawful sacrifice (*yuḥtamalu naskhu mā kāna wājiban wa-baqiya jā'izan*).[26] This definition mirrors the opinion of al-Shāfiʿī; *lā faraʿa wa-lā ʿatīra* does not indicate interdiction, it merely negates the obligation, but leaves the *ʿatīra* as permissible and lawful sacrifice.[27] Some Muslim scholars even considered it favoured (*mustaḥabb*).[28] Some scholars considered the *ʿatīra* obligatory in Islam.[29]

The contradictory traditions surveyed above concerning the sacrifice of Rajab, the *ʿatīra*, reflect already the struggle between the different groups of Muslim scholars over the subject of sanctity of Rajab in Islam. The pivot of the polemic is in fact the problem whether the sanctity of Rajab continues

24 See on him Ibn ʿAbd al-Barr, p. 1523, No. 2652; Ibn Ḥajar, *al-Iṣāba*, VI, 231, No. 8674; idem, *Tahdhīb*, X, 417, No. 751.

25 Al-Ḥākim, IV, 235; Abū Dā'ūd, II, 8; Muslim, II, 159 (in the commentary of al-Nawawī); Abū l-Maḥāsin al-Ḥanafī, I, 274; al-Muttaqī al-Hindī, V, 56, No. 490 (and comp. *ibid.*, 57, No. 499); al-Shaukānī, *Nayl* V, 118; al-ʿAzīzī, I, 189.

26 Abū l-Maḥāsin al-Ḥanafī, I, 274 inf.–275 sup.; and see al-ʿAzīzī, I, 189.

27 See al-Bayhaqī, IX, 313; al-Shaukānī, *Nayl*, V, 119; and see Ibn al-Athīr, *Jāmiʿ al-uṣūl*, IV, 122, note 1: *wa-qīla "lā faraʿa wājiban wa-lā ʿatīrata wājibatan" li-yakūna jamʿan bayna l-aḥādīthi.*

28 Al-ʿAzīzī, I, 189, line 9, from bottom; Muslim, II, 159 (in Nawawī's commentary); al-Bayhaqī quoted in Ibn al-Athīr's *Jāmiʿ al-uṣūl*, IV, 122 commenting on the tradition of Mikhnaf b. Sulaym: *Hādhā l-ḥadīthu, in ṣaḥḥa, fa-l-murādu ʿalā ṭarīqi l-istiḥbābi, idh qad jamaʿa baynahā wa-bayna l-ʿatīrati; wa-l-ʿatīratu ghayru wājibatin bi-l-ijmāʿ.*

29 See Ibn al-Athīr, *Jāmiʿ al-uṣūl*, IV, 122, note 1: *wa-qāla l-Yaḥṣubī: wa-qāla baʿḍu l-salafi bi-baqā'i ḥukmihā.*

in Islam and thus its merits were approved of by the Prophet, or whether its sanctity was annulled by the Prophet and thus its practices are reprehensible or at least of no value whatsoever. The opinion of Lammens that the Prophet forbade or prohibited the *ʿatīra* (*ḥarramahā au manaʿahā*)[30] and the opinion of Jawād ʿAlī that Islam abolished it (*wa-qad abṭala l-islāmu l-rajabiyyata, wa-hiya l-ʿatīratu, kamā abṭala l-faraʿa*)[31] can hardly be accepted.

The *ʿatīra* forms in fact one aspect of this struggle. The controversy between the different groups of Muslim scholars extends to other observances of Rajab, like fasting, prayer and other acts of piety.

II

The partisans of the sanctity of Rajab emphasized the qualities of this month, basing their arguments — as usual — on the alleged utterances of the Prophet. In a tradition reported on the authority of ʿĀ'isha the Prophet is said to have stated that Rajab was the month of God;[32] it is called "the Deaf", *al-aṣamm*, because the people of the Jāhiliyya used to put down their weapons and refrained from fighting; people lived in security during this month.[33] An almost identical tradition is recorded in Shīʿī sources.[34]

Ibn Ḥajar (d. 852 AH) comments on this tradition that although the content of this tradition might be true, it cannot be attributed to the Prophet (*lā yaṣiḥḥu ʿan rasūli llāhi*). Two transmitters of this tradition, Ubayn b. Sufyān[35] and Ghālib b. ʿUbaydullah,[36] argues Ibn Ḥajar, were known as forgers of *ḥadīth*.[37]

The idea of the continuity of the sanctity of Rajab in Islam is plainly expressed in a significant saying of Abū l-Dardā' about the fasting of Rajab: it was a month honoured in the times of the Jāhiliyya; Islam only enhanced its merit

30 H. Lammens, *al-Ḥijāra al-mu'allaha* (al-Mashriq 1939), p. 97.

31 Jawād ʿAlī, *Ta'rīkh al-ʿarab qabla l-islām* (Baghdad), V, 238.

32 But see al-Bayhaqī, III, 4 and IV, 291 where al-Muḥarram is designated as "the month of God" (*wa-inna afḍala l-ṣiyāmi baʿda shahri ramaḍāna shahru llāhi lladhī tadʿūnahu l-muḥarrama*); Abū Ṭālib al-Makkī, *Qūt al-qulūb* (Cairo 1932), I, 111, line 7; Ibn Mājah, *Sunan al-muṣṭafā* (Cairo 1349 AH), I, 530, ult. (and see *ibid.*, the commentary of Muḥ. b. ʿAbd al-Hādī al-Hanafī).

33 Ibn Ḥajar, *Tabyīn al-ʿajab bi-mā warada fī faḍli rajab* (Cairo 1351 AH), p. 14; L'A, *s.v.* "*ṣmm*" (but there are two versions recorded: according to one version it was the Prophet who called Rajab "the month of God"; according to the other one the people of the Jāhilliyya named Rajab "the month of God").

34 See Ibn Bābūyah, *Thawāb al-aʿmāl wa-ʿiqāb al-aʿmāl* (Teheran 1385 AH), p. 52.

35 See on him al-Dhahabī, *Mīzān al-iʿtidāl*, I, 78, No. 272.

36 See on him al-Dhahabī, III, 331, No. 6645.

37 *Tabyīn al-ʿajab*, p. 14.

(*kānat al-jāhiliyyatu tuʿaẓẓimuhu fī jāhiliyyatihā wa-mā zādahu l-islāmu illā faḍlan*).[38] This view is fairly exposed in Shīʿī tradition as well.[39]

The elements of "holiness" required for localities and cities, as analysed by G. E. von Grunebaum,[40] are inherent in the traditions of Rajab. The Prophet, claim some traditions, was born in Rajab.[41] Al-Qasṭallānī (d. 923 AH) rejects this tradition. The Prophet, argues al-Qasṭallānī, was not born in Ramaḍān, Muḥarram or Rajab, nor in any other of the honoured months, as the Prophet is not honoured by time; on the contrary: time is honoured by him. If he had been born in one of these (honoured) months, one might have imagined that he was honoured by them. Therefore God fixed the date of his birth in another month in order to show His concern for him and the grace bestowed upon him.[42]

According to another tradition, he "was put into the womb of his mother" in the first eve of Rajab; it was the eve of Friday, and God ordered Riḍwān to announce the tidings in Heaven.[43] Muslim scholars remark that this date (i.e. the first of Rajab as the date of beginning of pregnancy) fits the date established by tradition as the date of birth of the Prophet: Rabīʿ al-awwal.[44]

Some traditions maintain that he received his revelation in Rajab.[45] This date is given as well by some Shīʿī sources.[46] Some traditions assert that the event of *laylat al-miʿrāj* occurred in Rajab.[47]

The Prophet gathered the people in Rajab, according to a tradition reported

[38] *Ibid.*, p. 29.

[39] See Muḥ. b. Fattāl, *Rauḍat al-wāʿiẓīn* (Najaf 1966), p. 396; Ibn Bābūyah, p. 52.

[40] G. E. von Grunebaum, "The Sacred Character of Islamic Cities", *Mélanges Taha Husain*, ed. Abdurrahman Badawi (Cairo 1962), pp. 26–27.

[41] Al-Zurqānī, *Sharḥ ʿalā l-mawāhib al-ladunniyya* (Cairo 1325 AH), I, 131, line 4; Ibn Ḥajar al-Haythamī, *al-Niʿma al-kubrā ʿalā l-ʿālam bi-maulidi sayyidi banī Ādam*, Ms (in my possession), fol. 19a, line 1.

[42] Al-Zurqānī, I, 132, line 19 (quoted from ʿAbdarī's *Mudkhal*); and see Ibn Ḥajar al-Haythamī, *al-Niʿma al-kubrā*, fol. 19a, lines 3–6; al-Majlisī, *Biḥār al-anwār*, XX, 113, line 25 (lithogr. ed.); and comp. al-Suyūṭī, *al-Ḥāwī*, I, 305 sup.

[43] Ibn Ḥajar al-Haythamī, *al-Niʿma al-kubrā*, fol. 12b; al-Shāṭibī, *al-Jumān fī akhbar al-zamān*, Ms. Br. Mus., Or. 3008, fol. 48a.

[44] Al-Ḥalabī, *Insān al-ʿuyūn* (Cairo 1932), I, 68; al-Zurqānī, I, 105, line 10.

[45] Al-Suyūṭī, *al-Durr al-manthūr* (Cairo 1314 AH), II, 235 ult.; Ibn Qayyim al-Jauziyya, *Zād al-maʿād* (on margin of Zurqānī's *Sharḥ* I, 58); Ibn al-Jauzī, *Ṣifat al-ṣafwa* (Hyderabad 1355 AH), I, 27; al-Ghazālī, *Iḥyāʾ ʿulūm al-dīn*, (Cairo 1933), I, 328.

[46] Ibn Bābūyah, p. 57; al-Ṭūsī, *Amālī* (Najaf 1964), I, 44; al-Baḥrānī, *al-Ḥadāʾiq an-nāḍira fī aḥkām al-ʿitra al-ṭāhira* (Najaf 1384 AH), XIII, 362–363; al-Majlisī (Teheran 1386 AH), XVIII, 189.

[47] Al-Zurqānī, I, 306, 308; al-ʿAbdarī, *al-Mudkhal* (Cairo 1929), I, 294, line 10; see al-Dīrīnī, *Ṭahārat al-qulūb* (Kafr al-Zaghārā 1354 AH), p. 93, line 11; EI, *s.v.* "*Miʿrādj*"; Abū Ṭālib al-Makkī, I, 93; al-Ghazzālī, I, 328; ʿAlī al-Qāriʾ, *al-Adab*, fol. 66a.

on the authority of Ibn ʿAbbās, and informed them about the virtues of his pedigree.[48] All the rivers of the world visit in Rajab the well of Zamzam — according to a tradition reported by Wahb b. Munabbih.[49]

The sanctity of Rajab was assessed in comparison with that of the other months in a peculiar utterance attributed to the Prophet. The Prophet said: "Rajab is the month of God, Shaʿbān is my month, Ramaḍān is the month of my people."[50]

Close to this tradition is a *ḥadīth* counting the rewards for the believers observing Rajab, Shaʿbān and Ramaḍān and reported on the authority of Anas b. Mālik. It is recorded in al-Bayhaqī's (d. 458 AH) *Faḍā'il al-auqāt* and quoted by Ibn Ḥajar. "The month chosen by God is Rajab" — says the Prophet. "He who honours the month of Rajab — honours the order of God and he who honours the order of God — God will introduce him into the Gardens of Paradise and grant him His favour", etc.[51] Al-Bayhaqī marks the *ḥadīth* as *munkar*, but Ibn Ḥajar differs, classifying it as "forged with obvious features of forgery" (*bal huwa mauḍūʿun ẓāhiru l-waḍʿi*) and attributes the forgery to one of the transmitters, Nūḥ al-Jāmiʿ, "Nuḥ the Collector", about whom people used to say that "he collected everything except truth."[52] Nevertheless al-Suyūṭī (d. 911 AH) recorded this tradition in his commentary of the Qur'ān.[53]

A peculiar Shīʿī tradition sheds some light on the similarity of growth of pro-Rajab tenets in Sunnī and Shīʿī societies as well as on the manner of casting of the Shīʿī traditions in this matter. ʿAlī, says the tradition, used to fast the whole month of Rajab, and he used to say: "Rajab is my month, Shaʿbān is the month of the Messenger of God, Ramaḍān is the month of God."[54] It is evident that this is a Shīʿī re-moulding of the ḥadīth "Rajab is the month

48 al-Qandūzī, *Yanābiʿ al-mawadda* (Najaf 1965), p. 16.

49 Al-Dīrīnī, p. 93.

50 Al-Sahmī, *Ta'rīkh Jurjān* (Hyderabad 1950), p. 184; al-Sakhāwī, *al-Maqāṣid al-ḥasana fī bayān kathīr min al-aḥādīth al-mushtahira*, ed. ʿAbdallah Muḥ. al-Ṣadīq (Cairo 1956), p. 224, No. 510; al-Jarrāḥī, *Kashf al-khafā' wa-muzīl al-ilbās* (Cairo 1351 AH), I, 423, No. 1358; al-Suyūṭī, *al-Jāmiʿ al-ṣaghīr*, II, 21 inf.; Ibn Ḥajar, *Tabyīn al-ʿajab*, p. 10 sup.; al-Jīlānī, I, 200; al-Shaukānī, *al-Fawā'id al-majmūʿa fī l-aḥādīth al-mauḍūʿa*, ed. ʿAbd al-Raḥmān al-Muʿallamī al-Yamanī (Cairo 1960), p. 439, ult.; idem, *Nayl*, IV, 210; Ibn Bābūyah, p. 52; al-Pattanī, *Tadhkirat al-mauḍūʿāt* (Cairo 1343 AH), p. 116 inf.; and see a divergent tradition: *shaʿbān shahrī wa-ramaḍān shahru llāhi...*, in al-Jarrāḥī's *Kashf* II, 9, No. 1551 and in Ibn Bābūyah's *Amālī*, p. 13; and see ʿAlī al-Qāri', *al-Adab*, fol. 65a inf.; idem, *Risālat al-aḥādīth al-mauḍūʿa*, *Majmūʿa*, fol. 61a.

51 Ibn Ḥajar, *Tabyīn al-ʿajab*, p. 13.

52 See on Nūḥ al-Jāmiʿ: al-Dhahabī, *Mīzān al-iʿtidāl*, IV, 279, No. 9143.

53 *Al-Durr al-manthūr*, III, 236 sup.; (and see Qāsim al-Qaysī, *Ta'rīkh al-tafsīr* (Baghdād 1966), p. 132, about weak and forged traditions in the commentaries of al-Suyūṭī).

54 Al-Baḥrānī, XIII, 381 inf.; cp. Jaʿfar Manṣūr al-Yaman, *Ta'wīl al-zakāt*, Ms. Leiden

of God, Sha'bān is my month (i.e. of the Prophet), Ramaḍān is the month of my people".

Another assessment of Rajab in relation to other months is reported in a *ḥadīth* recorded on the authority of Anas b. Mālik. The Prophet said:

> "The superiority of Rajab over other months is like the superiority of the Qur'ān over other speech; the superiority of Sha'bān over other months is like my superiority over other prophets; the superiority of Ramaḍān over other months is like the superiority of God over (His) believers."[55]

The scale of qualities is, in this *ḥadīth*, rather different. The highest rank is, like in the Shī'ī tradition mentioned above, given to Ramaḍān.

III

One of the most controversial practices of Rajab was the practice of fasting. Just as in the case of the sacrifices of Rajab, the partisans of fasting in Rajab took recourse to alleged utterances of the Prophet[56] pointing to the merits of fasting and the efficacy of fasting during some particular days in this month. The antagonists rejected the sanctity of the month altogether, basing their arguments again on alleged utterances of the Prophet and marking the traditions in favour of fasting in Rajab as weak, untrustworthy or even forged. The lines of discussion on fasting resemble those of the discussion about the sacrifices.

> "In Paradise there is a river called Rajab" — says a tradition attributed to the Prophet. "This river is whiter than milk and sweeter than honey.

Or. 1971, fol. 38a: *wa-qāla rajabun shahru llāhi wa-sha'bānu shahrī wa-ramaḍānu shahru 'aliyyin.*

55 Al-Samarqandī, *Tanbīh al-ghāfilīn* (Cairo 1347 AH), p. 116; Ibn Ḥajar, *Tabyīn al-'ajab*, p. 14; al-Pattanī, p. 116 inf.; al-Sakhāwī, p. 299, No. 740; Ibn al-Dayba', *Tamyīz al-ṭayyib min al-khabīth fīma yadūru 'alā alsinati l-nāsi min al-ḥadīth* (Cairo 1324 AH), p. 137; al-Shaukānī, *al-Fawā'id*, p. 440 sup.; and see an interesting Shī'ī tradition in al-Majlisī's *Biḥār* XXXVII, 53 (new ed.): Muḥammad among his believers is like Ramaḍān in relation to other months, the family of Muḥammad among the believers is like Sha'bān in relation to other months, 'Alī among the family of Muḥammad is like the best of the days of Sha'bān, i.e. the fifteenth day of this month. The believers of the family of Muḥammad are like Rajab in relation to Sha'bān.

56 Comp. J. Goldziher, "Neue Materialien zur Litteratur des Überlieferungwesens bei den Muhammedanern", *ZDMG* L (1896), p. 482: "allerdings haben die Theologen mit seltener Kühnheit in jedem auftauchenden Falle, den sie zu entscheiden hatten, ihre eigene Ansicht oder die der Lehrpartei der sie angeherten als Spruch des Propheten ausgegeben, zuweilen Sprüche die lange Zeit als Urtheile angesehener Leute aus der Gemeinde des Islam bekannt waren, an den Propheten selbst angelehnt um dadurch grössere Authorität für dieselben zu erlangen."

He who fasts one day of the month of Rajab — God will give him to drink from that river."[57]

"In Paradise" — asserts another tradition — "there is a palace (prepared) for the people fasting in Rajab."[58]

The obligation of fasting in Rajab is motivated by miracles of God, His aid and deliverance of the righteous after plight and distress and His favour and grace granted to His believers in this month. Fasting is in fact an act of gratitude. God bade Nūḥ to set out on his ark in Rajab. He fasted this month, thanking God for His grace and ordered the people of the ark to fast this month according to some traditions.[59] In Rajab God split the sea for Moses; Ibrāhīm and ʿĪsā were born during Rajab. God forgave the people of Yūnus their sins in Rajab; in this month too God forgave Ādam.[60] Rajab is nicknamed "the Deaf" (*al-aṣamm*), because the wrath of God was never heard of during this month; God punished peoples in other months, but never in Rajab.[61] Rajab was also nicknamed *al-aṣabb*, "the Pouring", because the mercy of God poured forth during this month and flooded His servants; God bestows on them in this month graces and rewards which never an eye has seen, nor an ear heard, nor had it occurred to the mind of a man.[62]

Special rewards were promised, according to some traditions, for fasting on some particular days in Rajab. One of these especially venerated days is the twenty-seventh day of Rajab. On this day Muhammad was granted his prophethood. "He who fasts on the twenty-seventh day of Rajab will be granted by God the reward (otherwise) due for fasting sixty months", says a tradition reported on the authority of Abū Hurayra and attributed to the Prophet.[63] In another version of this *ḥadīth*, he who fasts the twenty-seventh day of Rajab, and spends the preceding night awake (praying) will be rewarded just

[57] Al-Jīlānī, I, 200; al-Suyūṭī, *al-Jāmiʿ al-ṣaghīr*, I, 91 inf.; al-ʿAzīzī, I, 513; al-Dhahabī, *Mīzān al-iʿtidāl*, IV, 189, No. 8797; al-Baḥrānī, XIII, 381; Ibn Bābūyah, p. 52; Ibn Ḥajar, *Tabyīn al-ʿajab*, pp. 5–8; Muḥ. b. Fattāl, p. 401; al-Muttaqī al-Hindī, VIII, 360, No. 2646; al-Zurqānī, VIII, 128; al-Ṭurṭūshī, p. 125; ʿAlī al-Qāri', *al-Adab*, fol. 65a; al-Suyūṭī, *al-Ḥāwī li-l-fatāwī*, ed. Muḥ. Muhyī l-Dīn ʿAbd al-Ḥamīd (Cairo 1959), I, 145; and comp. al-Asyūṭī, *al-Kanz al-madfūn* (Cairo 1288 AH), p. 74.

[58] Ibn ʿAsākir, *Ta'rīkh* (*Tahdhīb*), ed. Aḥmad ʿUbayd (Damascus 1351 AH), VII, 137; al-ʿAzīzī, I, 513; al-Suyūṭī, *al-Durr al-manthūr* ,III, 235; al-Muttaqī al-Hindī, VIII, 409, No. 2967–2968; al-Dīrīnī, p. 93, line 3; al-Zurqānī, VIII, 128; Abū Shāma, *al-Bāʿith ʿalā inkāri l-bidaʿi wa-l-ḥawādith*, ed. Maḥmūd Fu'ād Minqāra al-Ṭarābulsi (Cairo 1955), p. 55.

[59] Al-Jīlānī, I, 197; Ibn Ḥajar, *Tabyin al-ʿajab*, p. 17; al-Suyūṭī, *al-Durr al-manthūr*, III, 235; and see al-Shaukānī, *al-Fawā'id*, p. 440, line 12; ʿAlī al-Qāri', *al-Adab*, fol. 65a.

[60] Ibn Ḥajar, *Tabyīn al-ʿajab*, p. 17.

[61] Al-Jīlānī, I, 196 inf.

[62] *Ibid.*, I, 197.

[63] Ibn Ḥajar, *Tabyīn al-ʿajab*, p. 28; al-Jīlānī, I, 205.

as if he fasted one hundred years and spent the nights of a hundred years awake.[64] According to a tradition reported on the authority of ʿAlī b. Abī Ṭālib, the Prophet promised forgiveness of ten years (of sins) to the man who would fast that day and would supplicate at the breaking of the fast (*daʿā ʿinda l-ifṭār*).[65] It is noteworthy that ʿAbdallah b. ʿAbbās — according to a tradition reported on the authority of al-Ḥasan al-Baṣrī — used to practice the *iʿtikāf* on the twenty-seventh day of Rajab, and recite (among other *sūra's* of the Qur'ān) the *sūra* of Laylat al-Qadr.[66] This may, of course, point to the continuity of the Jāhiliyya practice of *iʿtikāf* during Rajab in the period of Islam and support the proposition of Wagtendonk about the link between the *laylat al-qadr* and the twenty-seventh day of Rajab.[67] The link between *laylat al-qadr* and the month of Rajab is indicated in some comments on Sūra XIII, 39. Mujāhid relates this verse to the former, while Qays b. ʿUbād refers it to the tenth of Rajab.[67a]

Of special merit was also fasting on the first day of Rajab. The Prophet, according to a tradition reported by Abū Dharr, said: "He who fasts the first day of Rajab, will get the reward equivalent to the fasting of a month." The seven gates of Hell will remain closed — continues the tradition — for a man who fasts seven days of Rajab; he who fasts eight days — the eight gates of Paradise will be opened for him. God will turn into good deeds the wrong ones of a man who would fast ten days of Rajab. He who fasts eighteen days — a herald will call from Heaven: "God already forgave you (your sins), so start work (scil. of worship) again".[68] Slightly different is the scale of rewards in a Shīʿī tradition. Nūḥ embarked on his ark on the first day of Rajab and ordered the people of the ship to fast this day. The fire of Hell will keep a distance of one year's journey from a man who fasted this day. The seven fires of Hell will be closed to a man who fasted seven days of Rajab. The eight gates of Paradise will be opened in the face of a man who fasted eight days of Rajab. The wishes of a man who fasts ten days of this month will be fulfilled. The sins of a man who fasted twenty five days will be forgiven and he will be told: "start again your (pious) work". He who adds (days of) fasting — his rewards will be augmented.[69] A tradition reported on the

[64] Ibn Ḥajar, *Tabyīn al-ʿajab*, p. 27; al-Suyūṭī, *al-Durr al-manthūr*, III, 235 inf.; al-Jīlānī, I, 205; ʿAlī al-Qāri', *al-Adab*, fol. 65a.

[65] Ibn Ḥajar, *Tabyīn al-ʿajab*, p. 28.

[66] Al-Jīlānī, I, 205.

[67] K. Wagtendonk, pp. 117–118.

[67a] Al-Ṭabarī, *Tafsīr*, ed. Maḥmūd Muḥ. Shākir, XVI, p. 479, No. 20471 and p. 489, No. 20505.

[68] Al-Jīlānī, I, 201.

[69] Al-Baḥrānī, XIII, 381; al-Suyūṭī, *al-La'ālī l-maṣnūʿa fī l-aḥādīthi l-mauḍūʿa* (Cairo n.d.) II, 115; see Ibn Ḥajar, *Tabyīn al-ʿajab*, p. 23.

authority of Ibn ʿUmar records as reward for fasting on the first day of Rajab the equivalent of fasting a year. If the believer would fast seven days, the seven gates of Hell would be closed for him. If we hould fast ten days, a herald would announce from Heaven: "Ask (anything you like) and you will be granted (it)"[70]. A gradually decreasing list of rewards is given in a tradition reported on the authority of Ibn ʿAbbās: God will forgive the sins of three years for fasting on the first day of Rajab, two years for fasting on the second day of Rajab, one year for fasting on the third day of Rajab, then fasting on every following day will be counted with reward of one month.[71] A considerable reward is promised for fasting on the first day of Rajab in another tradition: God will forgive sixty years' sins to the man who fasts on the first day of Rajab; God will bring a mild judgment upon a man (*ḥāsabahu ḥisāban yasīran*) who fasts fifteen days; God will grant His favour to a man (*kataba llāhu lahu riḍwānahu*) who fasts thirty days of Rajab and He will not punish him.[72]

Some versions of the traditions quoted above do not mention the first day of Rajab, but mention only the rewards of fasting "a day of Rajab". Unusual in its generosity is a list of rewards reported on the authority of ʿAlī. The Prophet said:

> "The month of Rajab is a great month; he who fasts one day of this month — God will count for him (the reward of) fasting a thousand years. He who fasts two days — God will count for him (the reward of) fasting two thousand years. He who fasts three days of this month — God will count for him (the reward of) fasting three thousand years. He who fasts seven days — the gates of Hell will be closed for him..."[73]

Among the fourteen nights of the year, which the faithful are urged to spend awake, there are three nights of Rajab: the eves of the first, of the fifteenth and of the twenty seventh of Rajab.[74] The eve of the first day of Rajab is counted among the five nights in the year; if its practices are properly observed by the believer he will enter Paradise.[75] Of special merit is also fasting on the first Thursday of Rajab (connected with the vigils of the eve of Friday and *ṣalāt al-raghā'ib*), the fifteenth and the last day of Rajab.[76]

70 Al-Muttaqī al-Hindī, VIII, 360, No. 2648.

71 *Ibid.*, VIII, 360, No. 2647; al-Suyūṭī, *al-Jāmiʿ al-ṣaghīr*, II, 45; al-ʿAzīzī, II, 391.

72 Al-Jīlānī, I, 201 inf.

73 See Ibn al-Jauzī, *Kit. al-mauḍūʿāt*, ed. ʿAbd al-Raḥmān Muḥ. ʿUthmān (Cairo 1966), II, 206–207.

74 Al-Jīlānī, I, 202; Abū Ṭālib al-Makkī, I, 93; al-Ghazālī, I, 328.

75 Al-Jīlānī, I, 202.

76 *Ibid.*, I, 204.

A current tradition about fasting in Rajab reported on the authority of Saʿīd al-Khudrī gives a detailed account of the rewards of fasting on every day of the month. "Rajab is the month of God, Shaʿbān is my month, Ramaḍān is the month of my people" — says the Prophet. Therefore he who fasts one day[77] of Rajab out of belief and piety (*īmānan wa-ḥtisāban*) deserves God's greatest favour (*istaujaba riḍwāna llāhi l-akbara*) and God will lodge him in the upper part of Paradise. He who fasts two days of Rajab will get a double reward; the weight of every single reward will be like the mountains of the world. He who fasts three days God will put between him and between the fire (of Hell) a ditch extending for a distance of a year's journey.[78] He who fasts four days of Rajab, will be healed from madness, elephantiasis, leprosy, the trial of the false Messias (*fitnat al-masīḥi l-dajjāli*) and the chastisement of the grave (*ʿadhāb al-qabr*). He who fasts five days, will be protected from the chastisement of the grave (*wuqiya ʿadhāba l-qabri*).[79] He who fasts six days, will step out from his grave, his face shining more than the moon at the night of full-moon. He who fasts seven days — God will close for him the seven gates of Hell (closing for every day of fasting one gate). He who fasts eight days of Rajab, God will open for him the eight gates of Paradise (opening for every day of fasting one gate). He who fasts nine days, he will step out from his grave proclaiming *lā ilāha illā llāhu* and his face will not be turned away from Paradise. He who fasts ten days — God will lay for him at every mile of the path to heaven bedding (*farāsh*) on which he might rest. As for him who fasts eleven days — there will be at the Day of Resurrection no believer superior to him except a believer who would fast the same number of days or more. He who fasts twelve days — God will bestow upon him two garments, one of which would be better than the world and all that is in the world. He who fasts thirteen days — a table will be put up for him in the shade of the Throne (of God) and he will eat from it, while other people will remain in distress (*wa-l-nāsu fī shiddatin shadīdatin*). He who fasts fourteen days — God will grant him a reward which no eye has seen, no ear has heard, and which has not occurred to the mind of men (*wa-lā khaṭara ʿalā qalbi basharin*). He who fasts fifteen days — God will raise him on the Day of Resurrection in the stand (*mauqif*) of the believers.[80] He who fasts sixteen days — he will be among the

[77] "*Yauman*" omitted in Ibn al-Jauzī's *Mauḍūʿāt* and in Suyūṭī's *La'ālī*.

[78] Comp. Muḥ. b. al-Ḥasan al-ʿĀmilī, *al-Jawāhir al-saniyya fī l-aḥādīth al-qudsiyya* (Najaf 1964), p. 140.

[79] The reward of five days is not mentioned in Ibn Jauzī's *Mauḍūʿāt* and in Suyūṭī's *La'ālī*.

[80] Here the tradition stops in Ibn al-Jauzī's *Mauḍūʿāt* II, 206, in Ibn Ḥajar's *Tabyīn* p. 12 and in Suyūṭī's *La'ālī* II, 115, line 2 (there is however an additional phrase in Jīlānī's *Ghunya* I, 198: *fa-lā yamurru bihi malakun muqarrabun wa-lā nabiyyun mursalun illā qāla ṭūbā laka anta min al-āminīn*); it is continued in Jīlānī's *Ghunya* with the remark: *wa-fī lafẓin ākhara ziyādatun ʿalā khamsata ʿashara wa-hiya*...; and see Ibn Ḥajar, *Tabyīn al-ʿajab*, p.12 inf.

first who would visit the Merciful, look at Him and hear His speech. He who fasts seventeen days — God will arrange for him at every mile of the path to Heaven a resting place.[81] He who fasts eighteen days — God will build for him a palace opposite the palace of Ibrāhīm and Ādam; they would greet him and he would greet them. He who fasts twenty days — a herald will proclaim for Heaven: "God has forgiven you what passed, begin thus anew your (pious) work."[82]

Some descriptions of the rewards of people who fasted the whole month of Rajab are of the type of stories of the *quṣṣāṣ* and describe the palaces in Paradise, the meals and the *ḥūrīs* awaiting these people in Paradise.[83]

A Shīʿī tradition gives the following vivid description of the Day of Resurrection.

> "At the Day of Resurrection — says the tradition reported on the authority of Jaʿfar al-Ṣādiq — a herald will call from the interior of the Throne: "Where are the *Rajabīs* (people fasting in Rajab)?" Then will stand up people with faces shining for the gathered (crowds), on their heads will be crowns of kingdom inlaid with sapphires and pearls. On the right side of every man of them will be a thousand angels and on the left side a thousand angels. They will say: "O servant of God, mayest thou enjoy the grace of God". Then will follow the call from God, the Exalted: "My servants and My maidens, I swear by My majesty and power: I shall honour your residence and I shall bestow upon you gifts in bounty. I shall introduce you into apartments in Paradise under which rivers will flow and you will be for ever in it. How good is the reward of the pious. You volunteered to fast for Me a month which I sanctified and whose observance I bade. My angels, Introduce My servants and maidens into Paradise". Then Jaʿfar b. Muḥammad said: "That concerns also people who fasted a part of Rajab, even one day at the beginning of the month, in its midst or at its end".[84]

One of the most discussed topics involving the Rajab fast was fasting during the whole month.[85] The opponents of fasting in Rajab based their argument

[81] See above the reward for fasting ten days.

[82] Al-Jīlānī, I, 198–199; al-Suyūṭī, *al-La'ālī*, II, 114–115; Ibn Ḥajar, *Tabyīn al-ʿajab*, pp. 10–12, 29–30; comp. Ibn Bābūyah, pp. 52–57 sup. (continued until the thirtieth of Rajab); Muḥ. b. Fattāl, 396–400 (continued until the thirtieth of Rajab); and see al-Sahmī, pp. 56 inf., 302 inf.

[83] J. Goldziher, *Muh. Studien* (Halle 1890), II, 160; al-Baḥrānī, XIII, 400; al-Zajjājī, *Amālī* (Cairo 1935), p. 134.

[84] Al-Baḥrānī, XIII, 401 (and see *ibid.*, pp. 381, 396 about rewards for fasting of the first and the fifteenth of Rajab).

[85] See K. Wagtendonk, p. 121.

on the well-known *ḥadīth* reported on the authority of Ibn ʿAbbās: "The Prophet forbade fasting in Rajab".[86] Later scholars transmitted this tradition with the addition of the word "whole" (*nahā ʿan ṣaumi rajabin kullihi*).[87] Partisans of fasting in Rajab criticized this tradition, emphasizing that two of its transmitters were "weak". The two weak transmitters were Dā'ūd b. ʿAṭā'[88] and Zayd b. ʿAbd al-Ḥamīd.[89] They argued further that the word "*nahā*" was erroneously inserted into the text, as the tradition referred originally to the actions of the Prophet; it was the transmitter who changed erroneously the word into prohibition (*wa-innamā l-riwāyatu fīhi min fiʿli l-nabiyyi ṣallā llāhu ʿalayhi wa-sallama fa-ḥarrafa l-rāwī l-fiʿla ilā l-nahyi*). If this version (i.e. *nahā*) is correct, the interdiction indicates merely a preventive measure (*thumma in ṣaḥḥa fa-huwa maḥmūlun ʿalā l-tanzīhi*). It has to be interpreted according to the opinion of al-Shāfiʿī. Al-Shāfiʿī stated that he would disapprove of fasting a whole month like the fasting of Ramaḍān, or fasting on a peculiar day. He was afraid that some ignorant person might imitate such practices considering it obligatory.[90] This opinion of al-Shāfiʿī is quoted by al-Subkī (d. 771 AH),[91] (like by Ibn Ḥajar), from al-Bayhaqī's (d. 458 AH) *Faḍā'il al-auqāt*. Al-Bayhaqī records the opinion of al-Shāfiʿī with a remarkable phrase: "*wa-in faʿala fa-ḥasanun*", and comments that as it is common knowledge among the Muslims that the only obligatory fast is Ramaḍān, the idea of reprehensibility (connected with fasting a whole month, in this case Rajab) is accordingly lifted (*fa-'rtafaʿa bi-dhālika maʿnā l-karāhiyyati*).

Consequently it can be deduced from the arguments of al-Bayhaqī that the tradition of Ibn Mājah merely expresses disapproval of fasting the *whole* of Rajab if this fast is put on an equal footing with Ramaḍān as obligatory. As the Muslim community is aware of the fact that the only month of mandatory fasting is Ramaḍān, there is no reprehensibility in fasting a whole month (in this case Rajab); if the believer fasts this month — it is a good deed.

Although al-Subkī could not find the additional phrase *wa-in faʿala fa-ḥasanun* in other sources — he accepts the version recorded by al-Bayhaqī

86 Ibn Mājah, I, 531 (*anna l-nabiyya ṣallā llāhu ʿalayhi wa-sallama nahā ʿan ṣaumi rajabin*); al-Shaukānī, *Nayl*, IV, 210; comp. about the interdiction of fasting of the whole month of Rajab: Aḥmad b. Ḥanbal, I, 231, No. 181; al-Ṭurṭūshī, p. 130; al-Khaṭīb al-Baghdādī, II, 227; K. Wagtendonk, p. 121 (and note 4).

87 Ibn Ḥajar, *Tabyīn al-ʿajab*, p. 33; al-Dhahabī, *Mīzān al-iʿtidāl*, II, 104, No. 3015.

88 See on him Ibn Ḥajar, *Tahdhib*, III, 193, No. 370; al-Dhahabī, *Mīzān*, II, 12, No. 2631.

89 See on him Ibn Ḥajar, *Tahdhīb*, III, 417, No. 764.

90 Ibn Ḥajar, *Tabyīn al-ʿajab*, p. 31 inf.–32 sup.; and see al-Shaukānī, *Nayl*, IV, 210, line 8 from bottom.

91 *Ṭabaqāt al-Shāfiʿiyya al-kubrā*, ed. al-Ḥilw, al-Ṭanāḥī (Cairo 1966), IV, 12–13.

as sound. As the interdiction of fasting of the whole month of Rajab is not a sound one — it has to be considered, states al-Subkī, as *mustaḥabb*, desirable (*wa-idhā lam yakun al-nahyu ʿan takmīli ṣaumīhi ṣaḥīḥan baqiya ʿalā aṣli l-istiḥbāb*); the utterance of al-Shāfiʿī indicates that fasting the whole month of Rajab is good (*hādhā l-naṣṣu lladhī rawāhu l-Bayhaqiyyu ʿan al-Shāfiʿiyyi fīhi dalālatun bayyinatun ʿalā anna ṣauma rajabin bi-kamālihi ḥasanun*). This, al-Subkī states, confirms the opinion of ʿIzz al-Dīn b. ʿAbd al-Salām[92] that he who forbids to fast in Rajab is ignorant of the principles of the Law (*man nahā ʿan ṣaumi rajabin fa-huwa jāhilun bi-maʾkhadhi aḥkāmi l-sharʿi*).

Al-Shaukānī (d. 1250 AH) discusses the problem of fasting in Rajab in connection with fasting the whole month of Shaʿbān and concludes that the traditions enjoining fasting during the holy months (*al-ashhur al-ḥurum*) include the recommendation of fasting of the month in Rajab. There are no traditions stating that fasting in Rajab is reprehensible (*makrūh*).[93]

Al-Qasṭallānī discusses the contradictory traditions about fasting during the whole month of Shaʿbān.[94] The reference to fasting on Shaʿbān is indicated in the *ḥadīth* reported on the authority of Usāma b. Zayd in which the Prophet said: "That (i.e. Shaʿbān) is a month neglected by the people, (a month) between Rajab and Ramaḍān. It is a month in which the deeds are brought before the Lord of the Worlds, and I want therefore that my deeds be brought before Him when I am fasting."[95] Al-Qasṭallānī remarks that many people think that fasting in Rajab is preferable to fasting in Shaʿbān, because Rajab is one of the holy months (*al-ashhur al-ḥurum*); but it is not so (i.e. fasting of Rajab is not preferable to the fasting of Shaʿbān). Al-Zurqānī supports the opinion of al-Qasṭallānī, quoting the *ḥadīth* reported on the authority of ʿĀʾisha, that when people fasting Rajab were mentioned to the Prophet, he said: "How (poor are) they (in their reward compared to those fasting in) Shaʿbān."[96] Nevertheless al-Qasṭallānī admits that some of the Shāfiʿīyya considered fasting of Rajab as more meritorious than fasting of other months. Fasting in Rajab is recommended as Rajab is one of the holy months; the fast of these months is indicated in the tradition recorded by Abū Dāʾūd. ʿAbdallah b.

[92] See below, p. 207.

[93] Al-Shaukānī, *Nayl*, IV, 209–210.

[94] Al-Zurqānī, VIII, 124–125.

[95] *Ibid.*, VIII, 126; and see al-Shaukānī, *Nayl*, IV, 210 sup.; al-Haythamī, *Majmaʿ al-zawāʾid*, III, 192.

[96] Al-Zurqānī, VIII, 126; this tradition is recorded by Ibn Ḥajar, *Tabyīn al-ʿajab*, p. 33 with the following story: "A woman entered the home of ʿĀʾisha and mentioned that she fasted Rajab. ʿĀʾisha said: fast Shaʿbān, as the merit is in (fasting) Shaʿbān." She then quoted the utterance of the Prophet.

ʿUmar stated that the Prophet used to fast in Rajab and honoured this month. Although the *ḥadīth* of Ibn Mājah forbidding the fast of the whole month of Rajab is a weak one — the Ḥanbalis considered it as valid. They concluded on the basis of this tradition, says al-Zurqānī, that it was reprehensible to single out the month of Rajab as a month of fasting (*yukrahu ifrāduhu bi-l-ṣaumi*).[97]

A significant passage quoted from a book of al-Damīrī (d. 808 AH) by ʿAlī b. Aḥmad al-ʿAzīzī (d. 1070 AH)[98] records the favourable opinion of two scholars of the seventh century of the Hijra towards fasting in Rajab. Abū ʿAmr b. al-Ṣalāḥ[99] was asked whether fasting the whole month of Rajab was a sin or whether it was a rewarded practice. He answered that there was no sin in it at all. None of the Muslim scholars, argued Abū ʿAmr b. al-Ṣalāḥ, considered it as sin. It is true that some scholars of *ḥadīth* stated that there were no sound *ḥadīths* about the merits of fasting Rajab; that does not however imply any sin in fast; traditions about fasting in general and about fasting in the holy months in particular indicate that this fasting (i.e. in Rajab) is meritorious. The tradition of Ibn Diḥya claiming that the fire of Hell is kindled every year for the people fasting Rajab is not sound and its transmission is unlawful.[100]

ʿIzz al-Dīn b. ʿAbd al-Salām[101] was asked about the opinion of scholars who denounce the fast of Rajab and its observance and whether fasting the whole month as a vow was lawful. ʿIzz al-Dīn gave permission to vow fasting the whole month arguing that none of the scholars of Islam included Rajab among the reprehensible periods of fasting (*fīma yukrahu ṣaumuhu*); on the contrary: it is a pious deed (*qurba*) as indicated by sound traditions and it is recommended. He who honours Rajab in a different way than the people of the Jāhiliyya, the argument says, does not imitate them. Besides, not everything practised by the people of the Jāhiliyya is forbidden to follow (in Islam), unless it is interdicted by the Law (*wa-laysa kullu mā faʿalathu l-jāhiliyyatu manhiyyan ʿan mulābasatihi illā idhā nahat al-sharīʿatu ʿanhu wa-dallat...*). Truth should not be abandoned on the ground that people of falsehood practised it, says ʿIzz al-Dīn. Furthermore, he gives his statement about the ignorant scholar who forbids fasting on Rajab as quoted above from Subkī's *Ṭabaqāt*.

Al-Damīrī sums up the two *fatwās* in a poem of ten verses, concluding that

97 Al-Zurqānī, VIII, 127.

98 *Al-Sirāj al-munīr*, II, 391–392.

99 See on him al-Dhahabī, *Tadhkirat al-ḥuffāẓ*, IV, 1430, No. 1141.

100 See this *fatwā* in *Fatāwā Ibn al-Ṣalāḥ* (Cairo 1348 AH), p. 21.

101 See on him al-Kutubī, *Fawāt al-wafayāt*, ed. Muḥ. Muhyī l-Dīn ʿAbd al-Hamīd (Cairo 1951), I, 594, No. 234.

fasting the whole month of Rajab is recommended. A vow of fasting in the month is binding (*wa-bi-l-nadhri yajib*). In the opinion of Aḥmad (b. Ḥanbal) singling out the month for fasting is reprehensible, but the opinion that forbids it should be rejected. The prohibition of fasting was reported by Ibn Mājah, but the *ḥadīth* proved to be weak because of its (weak) *isnād*. The shaykh ʿIzz al-Dīn stated that he who forbade fasting in any case is heedless. He strongly rejected the opinion of scholars who forbade fasting, and stated that they should not be consulted for *fatwā*. The transmitters of the Sharīʿa did not reprehend fasting the whole (month). The recommendation of fasting (in this month) is included in the recommendation of fasting in general and there is no sin upon the fasting (person). Ibn al-Ṣalāḥ stated that the *ḥadīth* about punishment for fasting in Rajab was not a sound one, and it was not permissible to attribute it to the Prophet. The merits of fasting in general, as stated in (valid) texts, indicate that it is even desirable (*mustaḥabb*) in particular — this is how al-Damīrī concludes his poem.

Ibn ʿAsākir (Abūl l-Qāsim ʿAlī b. al-Ḥasan)[102] devoted a special chapter in his *Amāli* to the merits of Rajab. He composed some verses in which the river Rajab in Paradise is mentioned:

> O he who wants a drink from Rajab in Paradise,
> If you desire it — fast for God in Rajab
> And pray the prayer of the longing[103] and fast
> Because everyone who exerts himself in (deeds of) obedience will not be disappointed.[104]

Orthodox scholars denied any merit to fasting in Rajab, basing their argument on the tradition reported on the authority of Saʿīd b. Jubayr.[105] When Saʿīd b. Jubayr was asked about the merits of fasting in Rajab, he said: "I was told by Ibn ʿAbbās that the Prophet used to fast (to an extent) that we thought that he would never break his fast, and he used to break his fast (so often) that we thought that he would not (start again to) fast."[106] Al-Qasṭallānī remarks rightly that this tradition indicates that fasting in Rajab is neither forbidden nor recommended (*wa-l-ẓāhiru anna murāda Saʿīdin* — i.e. Saʿīd b. Jubayr — *bi-hādhā l-istidlālu ʿalā annahu lā nahya ʿanhu wa-lā nadba fīhi, bal lahu ḥukmu bāqī l-shuhūri*).[107] The opponents of fasting in Rajab argue that this tradition

102 See on him C. Brockelmann, *GAL*, *S*I, 566.

103 "*Ṣalāt al-rāghibīna*": the *ṣalāt al-raghā'ib* is here, of course, alluded to.

104 Abū Shāma, pp. 55–57.

105 See on him Ibn Khallikān, *Wafayāt al- aʿyān*, ed. Aḥmad Farīd Rifāʿī (Cairo n.d.) VI, 127–136.

106 Al-Ṭurṭūshī, p. 128; Ibn Ḥajar, *Tabyīn al-ʿajab*, p. 32.

107 Al-Zurqānī, VIII, 127; and see al-ʿAzīzī, II, 392, line 23 (the opinion of al-Nawawī).

points clearly to the fact that the Prophet used to fast during different months of the year. It is accordingly evident that the Prophet did not single out any month for fasting, and therefore no special merit can be attached to the fasting of Rajab; the only meritorious month of fasting is Ramaḍān.

There is a version of the tradition of Saʿīd b. Jubayr quoted above, reported on the authority of ʿĀ'isha. "The Prophet used to fast (to an extent) that we thought... etc." This *ḥadīth* has however a significant addition: "And I did not see the Prophet, states ʿĀ'isha, completing the fast of any month at all except Ramaḍān, and I did not see him fasting more (in any month — K) than in Shaʿbān."[108] Two points in this tradition are noteworthy: the one stressing that the Prophet did not complete fasting in any month except Ramaḍān. This implies that it is not permitted to fast a whole month except in Ramaḍān. The other point emphasizes that he used to fast in Shaʿbān more than in any other month. One may not be surprised to find a contradictory tradition, reported on the authority of ʿĀ'isha, stating that the Prophet used to fast the whole month of Shaʿbān (*kāna yaṣūmu shaʿbāna kullahu*).[109] Another tradition, reported on the authority of Abū Hurayra, gives a different version: "The Prophet did not complete the fast of any month besides Ramaḍān except for Rajab and Shaʿbān "(*anna rasūla llāhi ṣallā llāhu ʿalayhi wa-sallama lam yutimma ṣauma shahrin baʿda ramaḍāna illā rajaba wa-shaʿbāna*).[110] Ibn Ḥajar classifies the tradition as "*munkar*",[111] because of the transmitter Yūsuf b. ʿAṭiyya,[112] who is considered as "very weak".[113] It is not surprising, however, that the *ḥadīth* on which opponents of fasting in Rajab based their argument is also reported on the authority of ʿĀ'isha: "The Prophet did not single out any month of the year for fasting" (*inna l-nabiyya ṣallā llāhu ʿalayhi wa-sallama mā kāna yakhuṣṣu shahran min al-sanati bi-ṣaumin*).[114]

Opponents of fasting in Rajab attempted to prove that the Companions, like the Prophet, disapproved of fasting Rajab, did not attach any sanctity to the month and considered fasting during Rajab as adherence to Jāhiliyya observ-

9949), II, 77 ult., No. 711.

108 Muḥ. Fu'ād ʿAbd al-Bāqī, *al-Lu'lu' wa-l-marjān fīmā ttafaqa ʿalayhi l-shaykhān* (Cairo 1949), II, 22 ult., No. 711; Ibn Ḥajar, *Bulūgh al-marām*, ed. Muḥ. Ḥāmid al-Fiqqī (Cairo 1933), p. 137, No. 701.

109 Al-Haythamī, *Majmaʿ al-zawā'id* (Cairo 1352 AH), III, 192; and see *ibid.*: *kāna yaṣūmu shaʿbāna wa-ramaḍāna yaṣiluhumā.*

110 Al-Haythamī, III, 191 penult.; Ibn Ḥajar, *Tabyīn al-ʿajab*, p. 9 inf.

111 See about the definition of "*munkar*" Muḥ. ʿAbd al-Ḥayy al-Luknawī, *al-Rafʿ wa-l-takmīl*, ed. ʿAbd al-Fattāḥ Abū Ghudda (Ḥalab, n.d.), pp. 92–99.

112 See on him al-Dhahabī, *Mīzān al-iʿtidāl*, IV, 488, No. 9877.

113 Ibn Ḥajar, *Tabyīn al-ʿajab*, p. 10, line 1.

114 Al-Ṭurṭūshī, p. 128.

ances. ʿUmar, says the tradition, used to beat the hands of people fasting in Rajab when they lifted them from (dishes of) food and compelled them to put them into it. He used to say: "Eat because Rajab was merely adored by the people of the Jāhiliyya."[115] In another version of this tradition, ʿUmar used to flog people who fasted the whole month of Rajab.[116]

Another tradition states that Ibn ʿUmar disliked to see people prepare for fasting Rajab. He told them: "Fast (some days) of it (i.e. of the month) and break the fasting; it is merely a month which the people of the Jāhiliyya revered".[117] According to these traditions fasting on some days of Rajab, just as fasting some days of other months, is not forbidden; but fasting for the whole month and attaching sanctity to the month itself are not lawful.

The adoration of Rajab might endanger the position of Ramaḍān. This is reflected in a story about Abū Bakr. When he saw his people prepare for fasting Rajab he said: "Do you make (i.e. observe) Rajab like Ramaḍān?" (*a-jaʿaltum rajaban ka-ramaḍāna*).[118] Ibn ʿAbbās insisted that Rajab be not established as an obligatory feast (*ʿīd*) like Ramaḍān. Al-Ṭurṭūshī concludes that these traditions indicate that "the honouring of Rajab by some people is a vestige of the bonds of the Jāhiliyya" (*dallat hādhihi l-āthāru ʿalā anna lladhī fī aydī l-nāsi min taʿẓīmihi innamā hiya ghabarātun min baqāyā ʿuqūdi l-jāhiliyyati*).[119] In summary al-Ṭurṭūshī states that fasting in Rajab is not obligatory, it is not a *sunna* of the Prophet and is not meritorious; it is reprehensible.[120]

A special treatise against fasting in and veneration of Rajab, named *Adāʾu mā wajab min bayāni waḍʿi l-waḍḍāʿīna fī rajab*, was compiled by Ibn Diḥya.[121] From this treatise the following *ḥadīth* is with all probability quoted: "The Prophet said: 'Hell is kindled from year to year for the people fasting in Rajab'."[122]

One of the main arguments of the opponents of the Rajab fast was the tenet

115 Al-Shaukānī, *Nayl*, IV, 210 (here the tradition is quoted from Ibn Abī Shayba's *al-Muṣannaf*. The remark of Wagtendonk, p. 121, note 3 that "these are late traditions" can hardly be accepted.); al-Ṭurṭūshī, p. 129; Ibn Ḥajar, *Tabyīn al-ʿajab*, p. 32; al-Haythamī, *Majmaʿ al-zawāʾid*, III, 191; Jamāl al-Dīn al-Qāsimī, *Iṣlāḥ al-masājid min al bidaʿi wa-l-ʿawāʾid* (Cairo 1341 AH), pp. 76–77; al-Muttaqī al-Hindī, VIII, 409, No. 2966; Abū Shāma, p. 38; al-Manbijī, *Kit. al-samāʿi wa-l-raqṣ* in *Majmūʿat al-rasāʾil al-kubrā li-Ibn Taymiyya* (Cairo 1323 AH), II, 360 inf.

116 Al-Ṭurṭūshī, p. 129.

117 *Ibid.*, p. 129.

118 *Ibid.*, p. 129; al-Qāsimi, p. 77; Abū Shāma, p. 38.

119 Al-Ṭurṭūshī, p. 129 ult.–130 sup.

120 *Ibid.*, pp. 130–131; Ibn Ḥajar, *Tabyīn al-ʿajab*, pp. 34–35; al-Qāsimī, pp. 77–78; Abū Shāma p. 38 (all quoting al-Ṭurṭūshī).

121 See on him al-Dhahabī *Tadhkirat al-ḥuffāẓ* (Hyderabad 1958) IV 1420 No. 1136.

122 Al-ʿAzīzī, II, 391, line 6 from bottom; and see above p. 207.

that the believer is not entitled to establish days or months of religious practices to which particular merits may be attached; this privilege is exclusively reserved for the Lawgiver (*fa-l-ḥāṣilu anna l-mukallafa laysa lahu manṣibu l-takhṣīṣi bal dhālika ilā l-shāriʿi*).[123] As the tradition reported by Saʿīd b. Jubayr (stating that the Prophet used to fast through the whole year) refutes the traditions about fasting in Rajab, as the Companions repremanded this fasting, as the traditions about fasting in Rajab are weak and untrustworthy — the view that the Rajab fast may be included into the category of good deeds has to be rejected. Good deeds necessitate the approval of the Prophet, which the fasting of Rajab did not get. As the traditions about fasting in Rajab are lies, the fast is, of course, unlawful (*fa-in qīla- a-laysa hādhā huwa istiʿmāla khayrin? qīla lahu: istiʿmālu khayrin yanbaghī an yakūna mashrūʿan min al-nabiyyi ṣallā llāhu ʿalayhi wa-sallama; fa-idhā ʿalimnā annahu kadhibun kharaja min al-mashrūʿiyyati*).[124]

Opponents of Rajab tried to show the weakness or the forgery of the pro-Rajab traditions, revealing the weakness of the *isnād*. Abū Shāma (d. 665 AH), who devoted a good deal of his *Bāʿith* to the rebuttal of pro-Rajab *ḥadīths*, and Ibn Ḥajar (d. 852 AH) in his *Tabyīn al-ʿajab*, a treatise with the same aim, both used the same method of scrutinizing *isnāds*. The tradition about the Rajab river in Paradise was rejected by Abū Shāmā[125] on the ground that Mūsā al-Ṭawīl[126] was a liar. The *ḥadīth*: "Rajab is the month of God, Shaʿbān is my month etc." was discarded because the transmitter was al-Naqqāsh al-Mauṣilī,[127] a famous liar and forger of *ḥadīth*. The *ḥadīth*: "*kāna rasūlu llāhi ṣalla llāhu ʿalayhi wa-sallama idhā dakhala rajabun qāla llāhumma bārik lanā fī rajabin wa-shaʿbāna*... etc."[128] was rejected on the ground that Ziyād b. Maymūn[129] was considered as "discarded" (literally: "abandoned", "*matrūk*"). Ma'mūn b. Aḥmad al-Sulamī[130] and Aḥmad b. ʿAbdallah al-Juwaybārī,[131] transmitters of pro-Rajab *ḥadīths*, were known as notorious liars;[132] Ibn al-Jauzī counts both Ma'mūn b. Aḥmad and Aḥmad

123 Abu Shāma, p. 37.

124 *Ibid.*, p. 38.

125 *Ibid.*, p. 55 penult.

126 See on him al-Dhahabī, *Mīzān al-iʿtidāl*, IV, 209, No. 8888.

127 See on him al-Dhahabī, *Mīzān al-iʿtidāl*, III, 520, No. 7404.

128 See Ibn al-Sunnī, *ʿAmal al-yaum wa-l-layla* (Hyderabad 1358 AH), p. 178; al-Suyūṭī, *al-Jāmiʿ al-ṣaghīr*, II, 105; al-Khaṭīb al-Baghdādī, *Mūḍiḥ auhām*, II, 473; al-Jarrāḥī, I, 186, No. 554; ʿAlī al-Qāri', *al-Adab*, fol. 65a, inf.; al-Majlisī, *Biḥār*, XX, 338 (lithogr. edition).

129 See on him al-Dhahabī, *Mīzān al-iʿtidāl*, II, 94, No. 2967.

130 See on him al-Dhahabī, *Mīzān al-iʿtidāl*, III, 429, No. 7036.

131 See on him al-Dhahabī, *Mīzān al-iʿtidāl*, I, 106, No. 421.

132 Abū Shāma, p. 55.

b. ʿAbdallah in the list of "big liars".[133] Both are accused of the transmission of the forged *ḥadīth*, in which the Prophet foretold: "Among my people will be a man called Muḥammad b. Idrīs; he will be more harming for my people than Iblīs"; one of them invented the *ḥadīth*.[134] By Muḥammad b. Idrīs, the imām al-Shāfiʿī is meant. It is quite plausible that al-Shāfiʿī's assessment of the personality of Ma'mūn b. Aḥmad was concise: *Ma'mūn ghayru ma'mūn*.[135] The *ḥadīth*: "He who fasts the twenty seventh day of Rajab, God will write for him a reward of sixty months; it is the first day when the angel Gabriel brought the Prophet the Message" is marked by Abū Khaṭṭāb (i.e. Ibn Diḥya) as a spurious tradition. The tradition that the date of the *Isrā'* was the twenty seventh day of Rajab is marked as "the essence of lie".[136] One of the transmitters of the tradition: "He who fasts three days of Rajab — God will count for him (the reward of) fasting of a month... etc." was Abān (b. abī ʿAyyāsh).[137] Ibn al-Jauzī rejects the tradition as unsound because of Abān. He quotes negative opinions of scholars about Abān, and records the saying of Shuʿba[138] that he prefers adultery to transmission of the traditions reported by Abān.[139]

The scholars opposing the fasting of Rajab faced the hostile attitude of the common people who practised fasting and special devotions in some nights of Rajab. They faced the pressure of the rulers as well. A peculiar case of this kind is reported in connection with the activities of ʿIzz al-Dīn b. ʿAbd al-Salām, whose favourable opinion about Rajab fasting was mentioned above. In the year 637 AH ʿIzz al-Dīn acted as preacher and imām of the mosque of Damascus; he was a very learned and pious man, strictly following the *sunna*. Just before the beginning of Rajab, he preached in the mosque on Friday, and stressed that the *ṣalāt al-raghā'ib* was a *bidʿa* and that the *ḥadīth* enjoining the practice of this prayer was a lie. ʿIzz al-Dīn compiled a treatise in which he expounded his view and warned the people against the practice of this *bidʿa*; he named it "*al-tarhīb ʿan ṣalāti l-raghā'ib*". He was however compelled by the common people and the sultan to change his mind and to compile a treatise which contradicted his former treatise. In his second treatise he issued a favourable judgment about the *ṣalāt al-raghā'ib*.[140]

The orthodox permission of the popular Rajab fast in the tenth century of the Hijra is fairly exposed in the treatise of the Ḥanafī scholar ʿAlī al-Qāri'

133 Al-Shaukānī, *al-Fawā'id*, p. 426.

134 *Ibid*, p. 420; see al-Dhahabī, *Mīzān*, III, 430; al-Suyūṭī, *al-La'ālī*, I, 457.

135 Abū Shāma, p. 55, line 5 from bottom.

136 *Ibid.*, p. 56 sup.

137 See on him al-Dhahabī, *Mīzān* I, 10–15, No. 15.

138 See on him al-Dhahabī, *Tadhkirat al-ḥuffāz*, I, 193, No. 187.

139 Ibn al-Jauzī, *al-Mauḍūʿāt*, II, 206. And see his assessment of *isnāds*, *ibid.*, pp. 207–28

140 Abū Shāma, pp. 32–33.

"*al-Adab fī rajab*". Although he follows strictly the path of orthodox assessment of the *ḥadīth* concerning fasting Rajab, he nevertheless gives his consent to fasting Rajab and regards it rewardable. The interdiction of fasting Rajab in the *ḥadīth* of Ibn Mājah — argues ʿAlī al-Qāri' — has to be considered as an interdiction of its obligatory character, as it was in the period of the Jāhiliyya (*wa-ammā mā rawāhu Ibn Mājah annahu ʿalayhi l-salāmu nahā ʿan ṣiyāmi rajabin fa-maḥmūlun ʿalā ʿtiqādi wujūbihi kamā kāna fī l-jāhiliyyati*).[141] Except that (i.e. this reason for the reprehensibility of fasting) none of the scholars said that fasting in Rajab was reprehensible (*wa-illā fa-lam yaqul aḥadun min al-ʿulamā' bi-karāhati ṣaumihi*).[142] The opinion that every *ḥadīth* about fasting Rajab and prayers in some nights of Rajab is a forged one deserves to be re-examined. It is true that there are some forged traditions, but traditions about fasting in Rajab are numerous and they, although weak, strengthen each other.[143] Scholars agree, argues al-Qāri', that it is permissible to perform pious deeds having recourse to "weak" traditions (*wa-ajmaʿa l-ʿulamā'u bi-jawāzi l-ʿamali bi-l-aḥādīthi l-ḍaʿīfati l-wāridati fī faḍā'ili l-aʿmāli*). The interdiction of fasting Rajab by some scholars and considering it a *bidʿa* is therefore not plausible (*wa-lā maʿnā li-nahyi...*). What is required from the believers is worship and obedience according to their ability. Rajab, as can be deduced from tradition, is a month surpassing other months in merits.[144]

Radical and uncompromising scholars rejected all the traditions about the virtues of Rajab and the merits of its fast. Ibn Taymiyya states that all the traditions about fasting in Rajab, fasting on the first Friday of Rajab and other merits are lies according to the consensus of the scholars. The best *ḥadīth* on this subject is, of course, the *ḥadīth* recorded by Ibn Mājah, stating that the Prophet forbade the fast of Rajab.[145]

IV

Among the distinctive features of Rajab are the special prayers and supplications connected, of course, with the fasting. These special prayers, devotions and supplications were the subject of fervent discussions and were strongly reproved by orthodox scholars.

Rajab is a month of repentance, of refraining from sin and of doing pious

141 ʿAlī al-Qāri', *al-Adab*, fol. 65b.

142 ʿAlī al-Qāri', *al-Aḥādīth al-mauḍūʿa*, fol. 61a.

143 *Ibid.*, fol. 61a.

144 Idem, *al-Adab*, fol. 65b.

145 Al-Manbijī, II, 306; Ibn al-Jauzī, *al-Mauḍūʿāt*, II, 208 (*mā ṣaḥḥa fī faḍli rajabin wa-fī ṣiyāmihi ʿan rasūli llāhi ṣallā llāhu ʿalayhi wa-sallama shay'un*); al-Jarrāḥī, II, 421.

deeds. This idea of Rajab is expounded in a tradition attributed to the Prophet. In a speech delivered a week before Rajab, the Prophet stated that the rewards for good deeds in this month were doubled, supplications responded to by God and distress relieved by Him. The Prophet bade the believers to fast the days of Rajab and to keep vigilance in its nights. He who prays during some days of Rajab fifty prayers, reciting in every *rakʿa* passages from the Qur'ān — God will grant him rewards for his good deeds as much as the number of his hairs. He who fasts one day — God will reward him with the reward of fasting of a year. He who keeps his tongue (from bad speech) — God will tutor him in arguments of his defence when the two angels Munkir and Nakīr would come to question him (in his grave). He who would give some alms — God will save his neck from the fire of Hell. He who does good deeds to his people — God will treat him kindly in this world and in his life to come, and will help him against his enemies during his lifetime. He who visits a sick person — God will order the noble of His angels to visit him and greet him. He who prays in a funeral ceremony during this month, is as one who revives a buried girl-child. He who gives food to a believer — God will lodge him on the Day of Resurrection at a table where Ibrāhīm and Muḥammad will be sitting. He who clothes a believer during this month — God will put on him a thousand of the suits of Paradise. He who bestows a favour upon an orphan and strokes his head — God will forgive him as many of his sins as the number of the hairs (scil. on the head of the orphan) upon which his hand passed. God will grant forgiveness to the believer who asks it. He who praises God once — will be counted in God's presence among the people mentioning God many times. He who completes in this month the reading of the Qur'ān — God will crown him and his parents with crowns inlaid with pearls and he will be assured not to be inflicted with the horrors of the Day of Resurrection.[146]

ʿAbdallah b. al-Zubayr is said to have stated: "He who comforts a believer in his hardship during the month of Rajab, 'the Deaf', the month of God — God will grant him a palace in Paradise as big as his gaze can reach. Therefore, urges the tradition, venerate Rajab and God will bestow upon you a thousand graces."[147] He who gives alms once in Rajab — says a *ḥadīth* attributed to the Prophet — God will keep him away from the fire of Hell, at a distance equivalent to that which a crow flies during its lifetime (literally flight of a crow since flying as a chick until its death in decrepitude — a crow lives five hundred years).[148] A *ḥadīth* reported on the authority of Salmān al-Fārisī records the following utterance of the Prophet:

146 Ibn Ḥajar, *Tabyīn*, pp. 25–26; al-Shaukānī, *al-Fawā'id*, p. 439, lines 9–12 (the beginning of the tradition).

147 ʿAbd al-Qādir al-Jīlānī, I, 200.

148 *Ibid.*, I, 200.

> "He who fasts one day of Rajab is (considered) as if he had fasted a thousand years. He who grants alms (once) is (considered) as if he would give alms of a thousand dinars and God will credit him for every good deed with a number of rewards equal to the number of his hairs. God will raise him a thousand steps, erase a thousand of his sins and credit him for every donation of alms with (the reward of) a thousand pilgrimages and of a thousand *ʿumras* and build for him in Paradise a thousand courts and a thousand palaces and a thousand apartments; in every apartment there will be a thousand enclosures, in every enclosure a thousand *ḥūrīs*, who are a thousand times more beautiful than the sun.[149]

According to a Shīʿī tradition, an angel called al-Dāʿī proclaims every night of Rajab from the seventh Heaven on the order of God: "Blessed are those who remember (Me), blessed are the obedient." God the Exalted says:

> I am the Companion of (the believer) who would sit by Me, I obey him who obeys Me, I forgive (the believer) who asks My forgiveness; the month is Mine, the servant is Mine, the mercy is Mine; he who would call Me — I shall respond to him; he who supplicates Me — I shall give to him, he who will ask my guidance — I shall guide him. I made this month a rope between Me and My servants; he who will hold fast by it — will reach Me.[150]

Al-Shaukānī points out as a reprehensible innovation in Rajab and Shaʿbān, that people use to exert themselves in acts of obedience and adhere to religious prescriptions during these months, but neglect these actions during the rest of the year.[151]

Of interest is an Ismāʿīlī exhortation stressing the sanctity of Rajab (called *al-aṣamm, al-fard, al-aṣabb*) and summoning the faithful to practise fasting, repentance and submission to God. The rewards of good deeds in this month are multiplied.[152]

The main point in the fervent discussion about Rajab devotions is the topic of *ṣalāt al-raghā'ib*, a prayer performed on the eve of the first Friday of Rajab.[153] To this *ṣalāt al-raghā'ib* the Prophet referred in a *ḥadīth* reported on the authority of Anas b. Mālik. The Prophet, when asked why the month of Rajab was nicknamed "the month of God", answered: "It is because it is singled out (*makhṣūṣ*) with (the quality of) forgiveness. In this month blood-

149 *Ibid.*, I, 201.

150 Al-Majlisī, XX, 338 (lithogr. ed.).

151 *Al-Fawā'id*, p. 440.

152 *Al-Majālis al-mustanṣiriyya*, ed. Muḥ. Kāmil Ḥusayn (Cairo, n.d.), p. 112.

153 But *ṣalāt al-raghā'ib* was formerly called the prayer of the midst of Shaʿbān, see Abū Shāma, p. 29, line 8 from bottom.

shed is prevented. God forgave his prophets in this month and rescued his saints (*auliyā'*) from the pains of punishment." The Prophet further counted the rewards of fasting in Rajab and recommended to an old man, who had complained that he would not be able to fast the whole month, that he restrict his fasting to the first day of Rajab, to the middle day of Rajab and to its last day. "Do not be heedless — continued the Prophet — about the eve of the first Friday of Rajab; it is a night called by the angels *al-rahgā'ib*, "the large (desirable) gifts"." This (is so) because after passing of the first third of this night no angel on Earth or in Heaven remains who does not gather in the Ka'ba or around it. God the Exalted has a look (at them) and says: "My angels, ask Me whatever you want", and they answer: "Our need is that Thou mayest forgive the people fasting Rajab". Then God the Exalted says: "I have done it already". The Prophet enjoined the believers to fast the day of the first Thursday of Rajab and to pray in the first third of this night (i.e. the eve of Friday) twelve *rak'as* reciting in every *rak'a* the *fātiḥa* once, the *sūra* "*innā anzalnāhu fī laylati l-qadri*" three times, the *sūra* "*qul huwa llāhu aḥadun*" twelve times; between every *rak'a* a *taslīma* has to be recited. After this prayer the believer has to recite seventy times "*llāhumma ṣalli 'alā l-nabiyyi l-ummiyyi wa-'alā ālihi*". Then he has to perform a prostration during which he has to say seventy times "*sabūḥun, quddūsun, rabbu l-malā'ikati wa-l-rūḥi*". Then he would raise his head and say seventy times "*rabbī ghfir wa-rḥam wa-tajāwaz 'ammā ta'lamu, innaka anta l-'azīzu l-a'ẓamu*". Then he should prostrate a second time repeating the supplication quoted above (in the first *sajda*). Then he pleads for his needs and his plea will be responded to by God. Every servant of God with no exception — says the tradition — praying this prayer, God will forgive him all his sins even if they were (as much) as the foam of the sea and numbering the number of leaves of the trees, and he will intercede for seven hundred of his people at the Day of Resurrection. At the first day of his stay in his grave, he will be visited by the Reward of this prayer. The Reward will greet him with a bright countenance and tell him: "O my beloved, rejoice because you were delivered from every woe". He will then ask: "Who are you, as I have not seen a face finer than yours and I have not smelled a smell more fragrant than yours". Then Reward will reply: "O my beloved, I am the Reward of the prayer, which you prayed that night of that and that month; I came this night to you in order to fulfil the obligation towards you and to cheer you up in your loneliness. When the Horn will be blown, I shall be the shade above your head. Rejoice, because you will receive bounty from your Lord."[154]

[154] Ibn Ḥajar, *Tabyīn*, pp. 19–21; Abū Shāma, pp. 29–32; 'Abd al-Qadir al-Jīlānī, I, 204–205; al-Suyūṭī, *al-La'ālī*, II, 55–56; al-Shaukānī, *al-Fawā'id*, pp. 47 inf.–50; al-Majlisī, XX, 344 (lithogr. ed.); Ibn al-Jauzī, *al-Mauḍū'āt*, II, 124–125.

Al-Nawawī classifies the *ṣalāt al-raghā'ib* as a shameful *bid'a* (*hiya bid'atun qabīḥatun munkaratun*), which has to be abandoned, reprehended and prevented. In his *fatwā* he points out that although many people observe this prayer and that the *ḥadīth* about the merits of the prayer was recorded in Abū Ṭālib al-Makkī's *Qūt al-qulūb* and in al-Ghazālī's *Iḥyā'*[155] — it is nevertheless a futile *bid'a* (*bid'atun bāṭilatun*).[156]

Ibn Ḥajar classifies this *ḥadīth* as forged. 'Alī b. 'Abdallah b. Jahḍam is accused of the forgery of this *ḥadīth.*[157] Al-Ṭurṭūshī mentions as the *ṣalāt al-raghā'ib* the prayer of fifteenth Sha'bān[158] and Rajab. The prayer of Rajab was introduced for the first time in Jerusalem: it happened after 480 AH.[159] Al-'Abdarī refutes in a special chapter,[160] the opinion that the *ṣalāt al-raghā'ib* is meritorious or even lawful. He records the *fatwā* of 'Abd al-Azīz b. 'Abd al-Salām[161] strongly condemning this prayer. It is evident that this *fatwā* is the first *fatwā* of 'Izz al-Dīn mentioned by Abū Shāma. 'Izz al-Dīn was compelled, as quoted above, to compile a *fatwā* with a contradictory opinion about this prayer. Beside the detailed refutation of the lawfulness of this prayer in the special chapter — al-'Abdarī stresses the reprehensible features of the performance of the prayer: men and women mix together in the mosque during the *ṣalāt al-raghā'ib*. If somebody claims that there exists a *ḥadīth* recommending this prayer quoted by al-Ghazālī — then the prayer has to be performed by the believer privately (*fī khāṣṣati nafsihi*), not as a common prayer in the mosque. Further it is reprehensible to turn it into a continuous and obligatory *sunna* (*sunna dā'ima lā budda min fi'lihā*). The traditions about "merits of actions" (*faḍā'il al-a'māl*) have weak *isnāds* — argues al-'Adbarī; although Muslim scholars permitted believers to act according to these *ḥadīths*, they allowed it on the condition that the practice would not be a continuous one. Thus if the believer acts according to such a tradition even once in his life, he would be considered as obeying the (recommendation of)

155 *Iḥyā'* (Cairo 1289 AH), I, 182 (al-Ghazālī remarks that the people of Jerusalem are eager to perform this prayer).

156 Al-Nawawī, *Fatāwā al-imām al-Nawawī* (*al-masā'il al-manthūra*), ed. 'Alā l-Dīn b. al-'Aṭṭār (Cairo 1352 AH), p. 28; al-'Abdarī, IV, 259.

157 See Abū Shāma, pp. 30–31; al-Shaukānī, *al-Fawā'id*, p. 49, n. 1; al-Suyūṭī, La'ālī II, 56 inf., al-Dhahabī, *Mīzān al-i'tidāl*, III, 142, No. 5879; Jamāl al-Dīn al-Qāsimī, pp. 105–106; al-Pattanī, pp. 43 ult.–44; 'Alī al-Qāri', *al-Aḥādīth al-mauḍū'a*, fol. 61 a. Ibn Jahḍam is said to have confessed to the forgery of this tradition before his death; cf. Sibṭ Ibn al-Jauzī, *Mir'āt al-zamān*, Ms. Karacelebi 284, fols. 272b–273b.

158 See above, note 153.

159 Al-Ṭurṭūshī, pp. 121–122; and see *ibid.*, note 4 of the editor, M. Talbi.

160 *Al-Mudkhal* IV, 248–282.

161 *Ibid.*, pp. 277–282 (he is, however, mentioned as Abū Muḥammad b. 'Abd al-'Azīz 'Abd al-Salām b. Abī Qāsim al-Sulamī al-Shāfi'ī).

tradition — if it is indeed a sound one; if, however, the tradition has an *isnād* which is dubious and open to dispute (*wa-in yakun al-ḥadīthu fī sanadihi maṭʿanun yaqdaḥu fīhi*) — his action (performed according to this *ḥadīth*) would not harm (him) as he performed a good deed (*li-annahu faʿala khayran*) and did not turn it into a publicly performed rite (*shaʿīratun ẓāhiratun*), like Ramaḍān or other (obligatory) practices. He finally remarks that according to the *madhhab* of Mālik, the *ṣalāt al-raghā'ib* is reprehensible (*makrūh*).[162]

ʿAlī al-Qāri' differs, as in the case of fasting Rajab, in his opinion about the *ṣalāt al-raghā'ib*. He records the tradition about this prayer in his *Risālat al-aḥādīth al-mauḍūʿa*[163] and in his *al-Adab fi Rajab*.[164] He quotes the opinion of al-Nawawī (d. 676 AH), as recorded in his commentary on Muslim's *Ṣaḥīḥ*, that this prayer is a reprehensible *bidʿa* of error (*bidʿatu ḍalālatin*) and ignorance containing reprehensible actions (*munkarāt*). "May God curse the inventor of this prayer and the man praying it" — says al-Nawawī.

Al-Nawawī based his disproof of the prayer on a tradition forbidding the singling out of the eve of Friday by vigilance and the day of Friday by fasting (*la takhtaṣṣū laylata l-jumuʿati bi-qiyāmin wa-la takhtaṣṣū yauma l-jumuʿati bi-ṣiyāmin*).[165] ʿAlī al-Qāri' disagrees arguing that calling the prayer of the eve of Friday *ḍalāla* is subject to inquiry (*maḥallu baḥthin*), because prayer is the best deed. If this tradition is forged, the sin is upon its inventor, but no harm is on the believer who acts according to it. Besides, the singling out of the eve of Friday by vigils and the day of Friday by fasting are subject to discussion by the scholars: they contradict each other in their opinions on whether it is reprehensible. It seems that it is in fact a reprehensibility of violation of the preventive measure (*al-karāhatu al-tanzīhiyyatu*). The tradition about the prayer recorded only by Razīn is a weak one, but the famous scholar Ibn al-Ṣalāḥ permitted the prayer, the *ḥadīth* is recorded by al-Ghazālī and accepted by scholars and learned men. The argument that the prayer was invented in the fifth century of the Hijra does not justify its designation as *bidʿa sayyi'a*, as the principle of prayer is well based on the Book and the Sunna. In fact, a *bidʿa sayyi'a*, states ʿAlī al-Qāri', is the mixing of sexes during the prayer, dancing, *samāʿ* and wasting money for lighting the mosques on the eve of the prayer.

The practice of the *ṣalāt al-raghā'ib* was formally forbidden by a decree of the sultan al-Kāmil Muḥammad b. ʿAbī Bakr b. Ayyūb (d. 1238 AD).[166] However, it seems that this order of the sultan was not effective for a long

162 *Al-Mudkhal*, I, 293–294.

163 Fol. 61a.

164 Fol. 65a.

165 Al-Nabhānī, *al-Fatḥ al-kabīr* (Cairo 1350 AH), III, 318.

166 Jamāl al-Dīn al-Qāsimī, p. 105.

period: the prayer remained a practice widely observed by common people and ṣūfī fraternities, and gained the approval of some scholars.

V

Rajab continued to be a venerated month in Islam. The tradition that the Prophet performed the *ʿumra* in Rajab was indeed questioned and subjected to discussion,[167] but the people of Mecca used to perform their *ʿumra* in Rajab.[168] ʿAlī al-Qāri' 's attitude towards performing the *ʿumra* in Rajab is a positive one. His arguments in the case of the *ʿumra* are very similar to those which he used in the case of fasting and prayers. He gives in fact his consent to the existing custom, arguing that the *ʿumra*, payment of *zakāt* and other pious deeds performed during Rajab are permissible and rewardable (*wa-kadhā ikhrājuhu l-zakāta min al-dirhami wa-l-dīnāri wa-ghayru dhālika min aʿmāl al-abrāri fa-lā shubhata fī jawāzi dhālika wa-mazīdi l-ajri wa-l-thawābi hunālika*).[169] Although al-Qāri' records the tradition about the *ʿumra* of the Prophet in Rajab and the categorical denial of ʿĀ'isha — he points out that when ʿAbdallah b. al-Zubayr re-built the Kaʿba, he ordered the people of Mecca to perform the *ʿumra* and slaughtered animals, dividing the meat among poor and needy; the celebration was performed on the twenty-seventh day of Rajab.[170] The Companions of the Prophet (in this case ʿAbdallah b. al-Zubayr) — argues al-Qāri' — should be imitated according to the utterance of the Prophet: "My Companions are like the stars: whomever you follow — you will then be following the right path" (*aṣḥābī ka-l-nujūmi bi-ayyihim iqtadaytum ihtadaytum*).[171] Al-Qāri' 's consent to the popular practice of the *ʿumra* is further aided by an utterance attributed to the Prophet: "What the Muslims

167 Aḥmad b. Ḥanbal, VII, 233, 248 (No. 5383, 5416; and see the references given by the editor), IX, 3, 131, 210 (No. 6126, 6295, 6430); al-Zarkashī, *al-Ijāba li-īrādi mā stadrakathu ʿĀ'isha ʿalā l-ṣaḥāba*, ed. Saʿīd al-Afghānī (Damascus 1939), pp. 114–116; al-Bayhaqī, V, 11; M. Gaudefroy-Demombynes, p. 193, note 2.

168 Al-Shaukānī, *al-Fawā'id*, p. 440; al-Pattanī, 117, line 11–12 (read *iʿtimār* not *iʿtimād*). See also al-Fāsī, *Shifā'u l-gharām* (Cairo 1956), I, 98: *wa-ahlu Makkata yaʿtamirūna fī laylati sabʿin wa-ʿishrīna min rajabin fī kulli sanatin wa-yansibūna hādhihi l-ʿumrata ilā bni l-Zubayri.* Comp. C. Snouck-Hurgronje, *Mekka in the Latter Part of the* 19*th Century*, tr. J. H. Monahan (Leyden 1931), p. 66.

169 *Al-Adab*, fol. 65b.

170 See K. Wagtendonk, p. 107.

171 See this tradition in Muḥ. ʿAbd al-Luknawī, *Iqāmat al-ḥujja ʿalā anna l-ikthāra min al-taʿabbudi laysa bi-bidʿa*, ed. ʿAbd al-Fattāḥ Abū Ghudda (Ḥalab 1966), pp. 48–51 (and see the references of the editor, *ibid.*); al-Sulamī, *Ādāb al-ṣuḥba* (Jerusalem 1954), p. 80, note 239.

consider as good is considered as good by God"[172] (*ma ra'āhu l-muslimūna ḥasanan fa-huwa ʿinda llāhi ḥasanun*)[173].

The attendance of large crowds of people in Mecca in Rajab in early times is attested by the report recorded by Ibn Ẓahīra, that Muʿāwiya used to send scents for prayers in the Kaʿba twice each year: in the season (of the pilgrimage) and in Rajab.[174] Khālid b. ʿAbdallah al-Qasrī was the first who ordered to light lamps (on the way) between al-Ṣafā and al-Marwa during the time of the ḥajj and during Rajab; it occurred in the time of Sulaymān b. ʿAbd al-Malik.[175]

The people of Sarw used to perform their *ʿumra* in Rajab; ʿUmar b. al-Khaṭṭāb is said to have guaranteed to them for this *ʿumra* the reward of a pilgrimage.[176]

Snouck Hurgronje gives a vivid description of the Rajab caravans setting out from Mecca to Medina to visit the tomb of the Prophet and graves of saints.[177]

The practice of *iʿtikāf* in Rajab can be traced in early times in the story of a woman who vowed to practise the *iʿtikāf* during Rajab in a mosque (although that year Ziyād ibn Abīhi forbade women to practise this rite); Wakīʿ records the verdict of Shurayḥ (the judge) in this case.[178]

Among the popular practices of Rajab was the payment of the *zakāt* during this month, which was reproved by orthodox scholars.[179]

Orthodox scholars classified the traditions about the observances of the night which falls in the middle of Rajab[180] and of the first day of Rajab[181] as forged. But the common people stuck to these popular celebrations. Al-ʿAbdarī

172 See this tradition in Ibn al-Daybaʿ, p. 179 (and see the references *ibid.*); al-Jarrāḥī, II, 188, No. 2214; Muḥ. ʿAbd al-Ḥayy al-Luknawī, p. 53.

173 ʿAlī al-Qāri', *al-Adab*, fol. 66a.

174 Ibn Ẓahīra, *al-Jāmiʿ al-laṭīf fī faḍli Makkata wa-ahlihā* (Cairo 1921), p. 110 sup.

175 Al-Suyūṭī, *al-Wasā'il ilā musāmarati l-awā'il*, ed. Asʿad Ṭalas (Baghdad 1950), p. 35 (*awwalu man istaṣbaḥa bayna l-Ṣafā wa-l-Marwa Khālidu bnu ʿAbdillāh*); al-Fākihī, *Ta'rīkh Makka*, Ms. Leiden, Or. 463, fol. 443a.

176 Ibn al-Mujāwir, *Descriptio Arabiae Meridionalis*, ed. O. Löfgren (Leiden 1951), I-26 ult. (*wa-ghāyatu ḥajji l-qaumi ʿumratu awwali rajabin wa-qad ḍamana lahum amīru l-mu'minīna ʿUmaru bnu l-Khaṭṭābi tilka l-ʿumrata bi-ḥijjatin maqbūlatin*).

177 *Mekka*, p. 60.

178 Wakīʿ, *Akhbār al-quḍāt*, ed. ʿAbd al- ʿAzīz al-Marāghī (Cairo 1947 II, 325, 360).

179 Al-Shaukānī, *al-Fawā'id*, p. 440, line 6–7; and see ʿAbd al-Qādir al-Jīlānī, I, 196, line 6 from bottom; al-Pattanī, 117 line 10 (and see the differing opinion of ʿAlī al-Qāri', above p. 219).

180 Al-Shaukānī, *al-Fawā'id*, p. 50; Ibn Ḥajar, *Tabyīn*, p. 22; al-Suyūṭī, *al-La'ālī*, II, 57; Ibn al-Jauzī, *al-Mauḍūʿāt*, II, 126.

181 See Ibn al-Jauzī, II, 123; al-Suyūṭī, *al-La'ālī*, II, 55; Ibn Ḥajar, *Tabyīn*, p. 17 (and see ʿAbd al-Qādir al-Jīlānī, I, 202).

records some details about the customs of the celebration of the first day of Rajab. People used to prepare kinds of sweet shaped in different figures. He points out that it is an interdicted practice and states that people looking at these shaped kinds of sweet and not forbidding its usage must not be permitted to act as witnesses in courts. If these shaped sweets would even be broken into pieces — "people of merit" (*ahlu l-faḍli*) would have to avoid to buy them because these sweets were prepared in a way forbidden by the Law. People, and especially young couples and the betrothed, used to send expensive gifts to their relatives. Al-ʿAbdarī draws a line between the pious predecessors (*al-salaf*) and contemporary people in observing Rajab; the pious predecessors used to increase in it their pious deeds and worship and to venerate in a proper way this month, the month of the improvement of actions (*tazkiyat al-aʿmāl*), the month of blessing (*baraka*), the first of the four holy months (*al-ashhur al-ḥurum*). Contemporary people celebrate it by vying in eating and dancing and by spending money on expensive gifts.[182]

The *ṣalāt al-raghā'ib* mentioned above was performed in lavishly lightened mosques; men and women crowded the mosques and the imāms led the prayers.[183]

Similar practices are recorded by al-ʿAbdarī concerning the eve of the twenty-seventh day of Rajab, the honoured night of the *miʿrāj*:[184] people gather in illuminated mosques, carpets are spread out, food is brought and people eat and drink in the mosque. Qur'ān is read in a reprehensible way,[185] the *dhikr* is recited in a way that the words are almost not understandable (*lā yilāh yillāh* instead of the correct *lā ilāha illā llāhu*). Disorder prevails in the mosque, as some people recite poetry, while others recite Qur'ān. Cleanliness is not observed in the mosque and its surroundings, as people used to go out to relieve themselves; some ladies pass water in the mosque itself in vessels, which are collected and emptied by some men paid for this service.[186] E. W. Lane gives a detailed description of the celebration of the twenty-seventh day of Rajab, the *laylat al-miʿrāj*, in Cairo.[187]

182 Al-ʿAbdarī, I, 291–293.

183 *Ibid.*, I, 293.

184 See on these prayers: ʿAbd al-Qādir al-Jīlānī, I, 205; Ibn ʿAsākir, *Ta'rīkh*, VII, 344 (but the twenty-ninth day of Rajab is recorded, not the twenty-seventh); Ibn Ḥajar, *Tabyīn*, pp. 18, 27–28; ʿAlī al-Qāri', *al-Adab*, fol. 65b (quoted from al-Suyūṭī's *al-Jāmiʿ al-kabīr*); Ibn al-Jauzī, II, 124–126.

185 *wa-l-qāri'u yaqra'u l-qur'āna fa-yazīdu fīhi mā laysa minhu wa-yanquṣu minhu mā huwa fīhi bi-ḥasbi tilka l-naghamāt wa-l-tarjīʿāt llatī tushbihu l-ghinā'a wa-l-hunūk* (? – probably: *wa-l-hanāt* — K) *llatī qad iṣṭalaḥū ʿalayhā...* etc.

186 Al-ʿAbdarī, Iʿ 294–298.

187 *The Manners and Customs of the Modern Egyptians* (London 1954), pp. 473–476.

Ṣūfīs and common people believed in a special group of the *abdāl*[188] called *al-rajabiyyūn*.[189]

People of Laḥj and Abyan used in ancient times (*fī sālifi l-dahri*) to set out in Rajab for pilgrimage.[190]

Popular practices of Rajab in ʿIrāq were recorded by Aḥmad Ḥāmid al-Sarrāj.[191] Every Saturday of Rajab is called *sabt al-banāt*. In these Saturdays girls wear their best dresses and go out to visit the holy shrines (*mazārāt*). They use to sit down in the court of the *mazār*, near the shrine (*marqad*) and talk about subjects of interest to them. This custom is especially observed in big cities.

"*Ṣaum al-yatīma*" is a practice of fasting observed by girls in the last Tuesday of Rajab. It is connected with a tale of a girl ill-treated and persecuted by her step-mother. She fasted the last Tuesday of Rajab and vowed to fast on this day of Rajab for ever if God would deliver her from her distress. She cooked a meal of coarsly ground wheat (*jarīsha*) in a hidden place, fasted the day and supplicated God in prayer. After some time the wife of the sultan, who sought a bride for her son, was pleased by the beauty and manners of the poor girl and chose her as wife for him. They married and lived happily. Young girls follow the practice of the *yatīma*, cook in a hidden place the *jarīsha* and break their fast with a meal of it. They fast and supplicate God to fulfil their wishes.

The twenty-seventh day of Rajab is a venerated day in the Jaʿfarī community. On this day amulets and charms are prepared.

The fast of the last Wednesday of Rajab is called Shābiryūn. This fact is connected with a tale of a poor wood-cutter, who became happy fasting this day. Once, says the story, when he was sleeping under a tree in the desert, he saw three birds: Shāhbiryūn, Māh-biryūn and Asmā-biryūn. The birds told him that if he would fast the last Wednesday of Rajab and break his fast by eating barley-bread, sesame and sugar, place before himself a vessel with water and light a candle, praying to God — God would grant him his livelihood in abundance. He did so and indeed his wife who was barren bore a child; she was after some time taken to the palace of the king as a nurse for his child. The wood-cutter became a gardener in the garden of the king. When after a year of pleasant life the couple forgot to fast this day of Rajab, a distress befell them: a bird caught the jewels of the king's daughter when

188 See EI2., *s.v.* "*Abdāl*"; and see al-Jarrāḥi, I, 25, No. 35; al-Suyūṭī, *al-Durr al-manthūr*, I, 320–321.

189 See on them Ibn al-ʿArabī, *Muḥādarat al-abrār* (Cairo 1906), I, 245.

190 Ibn al-Mujāwir, I, 105.

191 *Awābid al-shuhūr* (Les Superstitions attachées aux Mois), Loghat el-ʿArab (1928), VI, 28–32.

she was bathing in the company of the wife of the wood-cutter. The wood-cutter and his wife were accused of having stolen the jewels and were put in prison. In this month of Rajab, when in prison, they remembered the story of the birds and fasted the month. One day (of this month) the wood-cutter saw a man running hastily to rescue a dying man. The wood-cutter asked him to bring him the products needed for the breaking of the fast of Shābiryūn and promised him that the man would recover. In fact when the products were brought the wood-cutter and his wife consumed the products after the fast, put the vessel with water before them and lit the candle. The ill-man recovered and a bird came to the palace and brought in its beak the jewels of the king's daughter. The wood-cutter and his wife were freed and lived happily until the end of their days. Women in Iraq used to fast on the last Wednesday of Rajab until midday; this — they believe — brings the blessing (*baraka*). They buy barley-bread, sugar, sesame, light candles and the family sits down to a midday-meal. The fasting girl tells the story of Shābiryūn.

The first day of Rajab is a local holiday (*rajabiyya*) in Saiwun (Ḥaḍramaut) and various local festivals fall within this month — reports Philby. "The sighting of the new moon of Rajab — attests Philby — was announced by firing an ancient piece of artillery".[192] This is reminiscent of course, of some practices pertaining to Ramaḍān.

The incessant struggle of the orthodox scholars against the practices of Rajab has not been entirely successful. Some of them yielded to the pressure of popular belief and granted their approval to some observances, counting them among the meritorious deeds of the faithful. Even the veneration of Rajab in the period of the Jāhiliyya got its recognition and was described by a contemporary Muslim scholar as "a remainder of the *ḥanīfiyya*".[193] Only a small group of orthodox extremists of the type of Ibn Taymiyya remained stubbornly opposed to the Rajab practices. These survived and form until the present time an essential part of Muslim popular belief and devotion.

192 *Sheba's Daughters* (London 1939), p. 278.

193 Ibn Qutayba, *al-Ma'ānī al-kabīr*, I, 67, note 3 ('Abd al-Raḥmān b. Yaḥyā al-Yamanī)

XIII

« YOU SHALL ONLY SET OUT FOR THREE MOSQUES »
A STUDY OF AN EARLY TRADITION

« You shall only set out for three mosques: The Sacred Mosque (in Mecca), my mosque (in Medina) and al-Aqṣā mosque » (in Jerusalem)[1], this well-known tradition of the Prophet licensed the pil-

[1] Literally: « The saddles (of the riding beasts) shall not be fastened (for setting out for pilgrimage) except for three mosques » ... *lā tushaddu l-riḥālu illā ilā thalāthati masājida : ilā l-masjidi l-ḥarāmi wa-masjidī hādhā wa-l-masjidi l-aqṣā*. Aḥmad b. Ḥanbal: *Musnad*, ed. Aḥmad Muḥ. Shākir, Cairo 1953, XII, 177, no. 7191, 241 no. 7248 with a version *tushaddu l-riḥālu*; and see the references given by the editor ad no. 7191; Muḥ. Fu'ād 'Abd al-Bāqī: *al-Lu'lu'u wa-l-marjān fīmā 'ttafaqa 'alayhi l-Shaykhān*, Cairo 1949, II, 97, no. 882; 'Abd al-Razzāq: *al-Muṣannaf*, Ms. Murad Molla 604, ff. 39b-40a with the following *isnāds*: Ma'mar (died 153 AH)> al-Zuhrī (died 124 AH)> Ibn al-Musayyab (died 94 AH)> Abū Hurayra; Ibn Jurayj (died 150 AH)> 'Amr b. Dīnār (died 126 AH)> Ṭalq b. Ḥabīb (died circa 100 AH)> Ibn 'Umar; Ibn Jurayj> Naḍra b. Abī Naḍra (with the version: *lā tu'malu l-maṭiyyu*); Ibn Ḥajar: *Bulūgh al-marām min adillati l-aḥkām*, ed. Muḥ. Ḥāmid al-Fiqqī, Cairo 1933, p. 287, no. 1408; al-Muttaqī al-Hindī: *Kanz al-'ummāl*, Hyderabad 1965, XIII, 233, no. 1307: *lā tushaddu riḥālu l-maṭiyyi ilā masjidin yudhkaru llāhu fīhi illā...* The combined tradition contains recommendations of the Prophet in connection with the times of prayer, fasting and prohibition concerning women travelling unaccompanied; ib., p. 234, no. 1310: *innamā yusāfaru ilā thalāthati masājida: masjidi l-Ka'bati wa-masjidī wa-masjidī Īliyā*; in an additional utterance the Prophet states that a prayer in his mosque (i.e. in Medina) is more liked by God than a thousand prayers elsewhere except in the mosque of the Ka'ba.; ib., p. 235, no. 1318; p. 170, no. 955; p. 172, no. 966; al-Suyūṭī: *al-Durr al-manthūr*, Cairo 1314 AH, IV, 161; al-Zarkashī: *I'lām al-sājid bi-aḥkām al-masājid*, ed. Muṣṭafā al-Marāghī, Cairo 1358 AH, pp. 208, 268, 288, 388; al-Subkī: *Shifā'u l-saqām fī ziyārati khayri l-anām*, Hyderabad 1952, pp. 117-124, 140; al-Wāsiṭī: *Faḍā'ilu l-bayti l-muqaddas*, Ms. Acre, f. 37b-38a; al-Bayhaqī: *al-Sunan al-kubrā*, Hyderabad 1352 AH, V, 244; al-Suyūṭī: *al-Jāmi' al-ṣaghīr*, Cairo 1330 AH. II, 200, 1.8; al-Shaukānī: *Nayl al-auṭār*, Cairo 1347 AH, VIII, 211; Ibn al-Najjār: *al-Durra al-thamīna fī ta'rīkh al-Madīna*, appended to al-Fāsī's *Shifā' al-gharām*, Cairo 1956, II, 357; al-Samhūdī: *Wafā' al-wafā bi akhbār dār al-muṣṭafā*, Cairo 1326 AH, I, 294; al-Ghazālī: *Iḥyā' 'ulūm al-dīn*, Cairo 1933, I, 219; Ibn Taymiyya: *Majmū'at al-rasā'il al-kubrā* (*fī ziyārati bayti l-maqdisi*, Cairo 1323 AH), II, 53, 55; id.: *Tafsīr sūrati l-ikhlāṣ*, Cairo 1323 AH, pp. 121, 124; id.: *Minhāj al-sunnati l-nabawiyya fī naqḍi kalāmi l-shī'ati l-qadariyya*, ed. Muḥ. Rashād Sālim, Cairo 1964, II, 340; Mujīr al-Dīn: *al-Uns al-jalīl bi-ta'rīkh al-Quds wa-l-Khalīl*, Cairo 1283 AH, I, 205; Aḥmad b. 'Abd al-Ḥamīd al-

grimage to the mosques of Medina and Jerusalem in addition to the obligatory *ḥajj* and *'umra* to Mecca. A vivid controversy arose over the authenticity of this tradition which grants, as it does, an exceptional position to Medina and Jerusalem [2].

This *ḥadīth* is in fact a restricting one and seems to imply the prohibition of pilgrimage and visit to mosques and sacred places other than those indicated. The custom of such pilgrimage apparently had its origin at a very early period and was already in vogue in the second century. In the course of the fierce polemics concerning the permission of journey to visit the tomb of the Prophet, the minor sanctuaries and the graves of prophets and saints, this *ḥadīth* was closely studied and analyzed and became the pivot of the discussion which lasted through many centuries. The crucial point was to establish the meaning and the intention of the initial phrase of the sentence: *lā tushaddu l-riḥālu illā ilā*... « the saddles shall not be fastened (for journey) except for»... As the exception is of the kind of *al-istithnā' al-mufarragh* in which the general term is not expressed — the partisans

'Abbāsī: *'Umdat al-akhbār fī madīnat al-mukhtār*, ed. As'ad al-Ṭarābzūnī, Alexandria, n.d., p. 72; al-Nuwayrī: *Nihāyat al-arab fī funūn al-adab*, Cairo 1925, I, 327; Ch. D. Matthews: *The Kit. Bā'iṯu-n-nufūs of Ibnu-l-Firkāḥ*, JPOS, XV (1935), p. 54 (id.: *Palestine-Mohammedan Holy Land*, New-Haven 1949, p. 10); Shihāb al-Dīn al-Maqdisī: *Muthīr al-gharām fī ziyārati l-Qudsi wa-l-Shām*, Ms. Damascus, Ẓāhiriyya, Ta'rīkh 720, p. 133; Shams al-Dīn al-Suyūṭī: *Itḥāf al-akhiṣṣā bi-faḍā'ili l-masjidi l-aqṣā*, Ms. Hebrew Univ., f. 7a; Abū Ṭālib al-Makkī: *Qūt al-qulūb*, Cairo 1932, III, 182; Taqī al-Dīn 'Abd al-Malik b. Abi l-Munā, 'Ubayd al-Ḍarīr: *Nuzhatu l-nāẓirīn*, Cairo 1308 AH, p. 98 sup.; Ibrāhīm al-Samnūdī al-Manṣūrī: *Sa'ādat al-dārayn fī l-radd 'alā l-firqatayn al-wahhabiyyati wa-l-muqallidati l-ẓāhiriyya*, Cairo 1319 AH, pp. 120-21, id.: *Nuṣratu l-imāmi l-Subkī bi-raddi l-ṣārimi l-munkī*, Cairo, n.d., Maṭba'at al-jumhūr, pp. 36, 161, 182, 191; al-Dārimī: *Sunan*, al-Madīna 1966, I, 271, no. 1428; al-Khaṭṭābī: *Ma'ālim al-sunan*, Ḥalab 1933, II, 222; al-Jarrāḥī: *Kashf al-khafā' wa-muzīl al -ilbās 'ammā 'shtahara min al-aḥādīth 'alā alsinati l-nās*, Cairo 1352 AH, II, 354, no. 3016.; al-Nasā'ī: *Sunan*, Cairo 1930, II, 37; Shihāb al-Dīn al-Khafājī: *Nasīm al-Riyāḍ fī sharḥ shifā' l-qāḍī 'Iyāḍ*, Istanbul, 1315 AH., III, 580; al-Ghayṭī: *Qiṣṣat al-isrā' wa-l-mi'rāj*, Būlāq 1295 AH, p. 18.; al-Qasṭallānī: *Irshād al-sārī*, Cairo 1326 AH, III, 239, 244.

[2] I. Goldziher: *Muhammedanische Studien*, Halle 1890, II, 35-36; S.D. Goitein: *The sanctity of Jerusalem and Palestine in early Islam, Studies in Islamic History and Institutions*, Leiden 1966, pp. 135-148; J. Fück: *Die Rolle des Traditionalismus im Islam*, ZDMG, XCIII (1939), pp. 23-24; Muḥ. Zubayr Ṣiddīqī: *Ḥadīth Literature*, Calcutta University Press, 1961, p. XXVI; W. Caskel: *Der Felsendom und die Wallfahrt nach Jerusalem*, Köln und Opladen 1936, pp. 25-26, notes 36, 38; A.A. Duri: *al-Zuhri*, BSOAS XIX, pp. 10-11; id.: *Baḥth fī nash'ati 'ilmi l-ta'rīkhi 'inda l-'arab*, Beirut 1960, p. 99; Muḥ. 'Ajjāj al-Khaṭīb: *al-Sunna qabla l-tadwīn*, Cairo 1963, pp. 501-514; Muṣṭafā al-Sibā'ī: *al-Sunna wamakānatuhā fī l-tashrī'i l-islamiyyi*, Cairo 1961, pp. 399-402.

of the prohibition of journeys to the grave of the Prophet and to minor sanctuaries maintained that the *ḥadīth* should be interpreted as « do not set out for *any place* except for the three mosques». Those who approved of such pilgrimages argued that the meaning of the phrase was « do not set out for *any mosque* except for the three mosques.» As they considered the general term from which exception is made to be « mosques » they concluded that the faithful should set out — as regards mosques (for the purpose of prayer and devotion) — only for these three mosques; for other sanctuaries there is no reservation [3].

[3] Al-Subkī, *op. cit.*, p. 118 seq... *Fa-ʿlam anna hādhā l-istithnāʾa mufarraghun, taqdīruhu lā tushaddu l-riḥālu ilā masjidin illā ilā l-masājidi l-thalāthati, au lā tushaddu l-riḥālu ilā makānin illā ilā l-masājidi l-thalāthati...*, and see *ib.* p. 121 :... *fa-naqala imāmu l-ḥaramayni ʿan shaykhihi annahu kāna yuftī bi-l-manʿi ʿan shaddi l-riḥāli ilā ghayri hādhihi l-masājidi. qāla : wa-rubbamā kāna yaqūlu « yukrahu », wa-rubbamā kāna yaqūlu « yuḥarramu »...*; al-Ghazālī, *op. cit.*, I, 219 :... *wa-qad dhahaba baʿḍu l-ʿulamāʾi ilā l-istidlāli bi-hādhā l-ḥadīthi fī l-manʿi min al-riḥlati li-ziyārati l-mashāhidi wa qubūri l-ʿulamāʾi wa-l-ṣulaḥāʾi...*; *ib.*, II, 219 :... *wa-yadkhulu fī jumlatihi ziyāratu qubūri l-anbiyāʾi ʿalayhimu l-salāmu wa-ziyāratu qubūri l-ṣaḥābati wa-l-tābiʿīna wa-sāʾiri l-ʿulamāʾi....... wa-yajūzu shaddu l-riḥāli li-hādhā l-gharaḍi wa-lā yamnaʿu min hādhā qauluhu ʿalayhi l-salāmu : lā tushaddu l-riḥālu... li-anna dhālika fī l-masājidi fa-innahā mutamāthilatun baʿda hādhihi l-masājidi... ... wa-ammā l-biqāʿu fa-lā maʿnā li-ziyāratihā siwā l-masājidi l-thalāthati wa-siwā l-thughūri li-l-ribāṭi bihā...*; Aḥmad b. Ḥajar al-Haythamī : *al-Jauhar al-munaẓẓam fī ziyārati l-qabri l-sharīfi l-muʿaẓẓam*, Cairo 1331 AH, pp. 13-14; al-ʿAbdarī, *al-Madkhal*, Cairo, 1929, I, 256; al-Shaukānī *op. cit.*, VIII, 212 : ... *wa-qad tamassaka bi-hādhā l-ḥadīthi man manaʿa l-safara wa-shadda l-raḥli ilā ghayrihā min ghayri farqin bayna jamīʿi l-biqāʿi...* : Abū Bakr al-Ṭurṭūshī : *Kitāb al-ḥawādith wa-l-bidaʿ*, ed. Muḥammad al-Ṭālibī, Tunis 1959, p. 98 :... *wa-lā yuʾtā shayʾun min al-masājidi yuʿtaqadu fīhi l-faḍlu baʿda l-thalāthati masājida illā masjidu Qubāʾa... fa-ammā siwāhu min al-masājidi fa-lam asmaʿ ʿan aḥadin annahu atāhā rākiban wa-lā māshiyan kamā atā Qubāʾa*, and see *ib.*, p. 147-48 :... *thumma raʾā (i.e. ʿUmar) al-nāsa yadhhabūna madhāhiba fa-qāla : ayna yadhhabu hāʾulāʾi, fa-qīla : yā amīra l-muʾminīna, masjidun ṣallā fīhi l-nabiyyu (ṣ) fa-hum yuṣallūna fīhi, fa-qāla : innamā halaka man kāna qablakum bi-mithli hādhā, kānū yattabiʿūna āthāra anbiyāʾihim wa-yattakhidhūnahā masājida wa-biyaʿan...*; and see the preceding tradition : Abū l-Maḥāsin Yūsuf b. Mūsā al-Ḥanafī : *al -Muʿtaṣar min al-mukhtaṣar min mushkil al-āthār*, Hyderabad 1362 AH, I, 26; Ibn Taymiyya : *Minhāj al-sunnati al-nabawiyya*, I, 336 and al-Shāṭibī : *al-Iʿtiṣām*, Cairo, Maṭbaʿat al-saʿāda, n.d., I, 346; Ibn Taymiyya : *Tafsīr sūrati l-ikhlāṣ*, p. 120; id. : *Majmūʿat al-rasāʾil*, II, 55 :... *wa-lau nadhara l-safara ilā qabri l-Khalīli ʿalayhi l-salāmu au qabri l-nabiyyi (ṣ) au ilā l-Ṭūri lladhī kallama llāhu ʿalayhi Mūsā ʿalayhi l-salāmu, au ilā jabali Ḥirāʾa lladhī kāna l-nabiyyu ṣallā llāhu ʿalayhi wa-sallama yataʿabbadu fīhi wa-jāʾahu l-waḥyu fīhi, au al-ghāri l-madhkūri fī l-qurʾāni, au ghayri dhālika min al-maqābiri wa-l-maqāmāti wa-l-mashāhidi l-muḍāfati ilā baʿḍi l-anbiyāʾi wa-l-mashāyikhi au ilā baʿḍi l-maghārāti, au al-jibāli — lam yajibi l-wafāʾu bi-hādhā l-nadhri bi- ʾttifāqi l-aʾimmati l-arbaʿati fa-inna l-safara ilā hādhihi l-mawāḍiʿi manhiyyun ʿanhu li-nahyi

They could in fact quote a *ḥadīth* in which they could find a convincing proof of their argument : *lā tushaddu riḥālu l-maṭiyyi ilā masjidin yudhkaru llāhu fīhi illā ilā thalāthati masājida*...« the saddles of the riding beasts shall not be fastened (for their journey) *to a mosque* in which God is invoked except to the three mosques »...[4] Even more explicit in favour of this view is another *ḥadīth* : *lā yanbaghī li-l-muṣallī an yashudda riḥālahu ilā masjidin yabghī fīhi l-ṣalāta ghayra l-masjidi l-ḥarāmi wa-l-masjidi l-aqṣā wa-masjidī hādhā.* « It is not proper that a man praying set out for a mosque in which he seeks to pray except the mosque of the Ḥarām, the mosque al-Aqṣā and my mosque ».[5] It is evident that these traditions confirm the view that the three mosques are to be preferred in comparison with other mosques; one shall set out for these mosques to gain the benefit of prayer and devotion; but he is permitted, and it is even recommended to him, to set out for other sanctuaries which are not mosques.

The close observation of the *ḥadīth* about the three mosques is illustrated by a curious story reported by al-Wāsiṭī [6] : Sa'īd b. 'Abd al-'Azīz used to visit the Miḥrāb Da'ūd [7] on foot; only on his return he used to ride. When asked about it he answered : I was told that 'Abdallah b. 'Abdallah used to set out for the mosque of Qubā' [8] riding a horse without a saddle; (this he used to do because) he considered that fastening the girth of the saddle of the horse was like fastening the saddles of the riding beasts which is mentioned (scil. as forbidden) according to the tradition : « you shall not fasten the saddles... except for three mosques »...

G. E. von Grunebaum characterizes this *ḥadīth* as an « earlier battle, long since abandoned, which the theologians fought against the cult of those minor sanctuaries » [9]. This battle was in fact an early one.

l-nabiyyi (*ṣ*) : *lā tushaddu*... etc.; al-Samnūdī al-Manṣūrī : *Sa'ādat al-dārayn*, p. 120 seq.; 'Alī Maḥfūẓ : *al-Ibdā' fī maḍārri l-ibtidā'*, Cairo, Maṭba'at al-istiqāma, 4th ed., pp. 194-96.

4 Al-Samnūdī al-Manṣūrī : *Sa'ādat al-dārayn*, p. 121 sup.

5 Ib.; but see the interpretation of this *ḥadīth* given by Ibn Taymiyya in al-Qasṭallānī, *Irshād al-sārī* III, 240 (he forbids the journey to the grave of the Prophet on the ground of this *ḥadīth*).

6 Al-Wāsiṭī, *op. cit.*, f. 47a.

7 On Miḥrāb Dā'ūd see Ibn. Ḥauqal : *Ṣūrat al-arḍ*, ed. J.H. Kramers, Leiden 1938, I, 171; Mujīr al-Dīn, *op. cit.*, pp. 227, 302, 366-67, 407.

8 See on the mosque of Qubā' : al-Samhūdī, *op. cit.*, II, 16-28.

9 G.E. von Grunebaum : *The sacred character of Islamic cities*, *Mélanges Taha Husain*, ed. Adburrahman Badawi, Cairo 1962, p. 27.

Mālik b. Anas records in his *Muwaṭṭa'* [10] a story about a discussion between Abū Hurayra and Ka'b (al-Aḥbār) concerning the question at what hour on Friday God fulfils the wishes of the faithful. This discussion took place when Abū Hurayra met Ka'b on his pilgrimage to al-Ṭūr. In a parenthetical passage Malik reports thāt Abū Hurayra on his return was rebuked by Baṣra b. Abī Baṣra [11] who told him: « Had I met you before you went out (scil. to al-Ṭūr) you would not have set out; I heard the Prophet saying: the riding beasts shall be driven only to three mosques... etc. » [12]. A similar tradition (in which the name of Abū Hurayra is however not mentioned) is recorded by 'Abd al-Razzāq [13] in his *Muṣannaf* [14]: a man who returned from a journey to al-Ṭūr was reproached and reminded of the utterance of the Prophet about the three mosques. Another tradition records a talk between 'Arfaja and Ibn 'Umar. Ibn 'Umar, when consulted by 'Arfaja about a journey to al-Ṭūr, answered: You shall only set out for three mosques, the mosque of Mecca, the mosque of the Prophet (i.e. Medina) and the mosque al-Aqṣā; abandon al-Ṭūr and do not go there [15].

Commentators are agreed that by al-Ṭūr in these traditions Mt. Sīnā is meant [16]. Mt. Sīnā was in fact regarded as a sacred place.

10 Mālik B. Anas: *al-Muwaṭṭa'*, Cairo, Maṭba'at Dār Iḥyā' l-Kutub l-'Arabiyya, n.d., I, 130-133.

11 See on him Ibn Ḥajar: *al-Iṣāba*, Cairo 1323 AH, I, 167, no. 713, 714 and II, 41, no. 1845 (recorded by 'Abd al-Razzaq as Naḍra b. Abī Naḍra; see note 1, above); al-Suyūṭī: *Is'āf al-Mubaṭṭa'* p. 8 (appended to Mālik's *Muwaṭṭa'* with Suyūṭī's *Tanwīr al-ḥawālik*, quoted in the preceding note); al-Zurqānī: *Sharḥ 'alā Muwaṭṭa' Mālik*, Cairo 1936, I, 224; Abū 'Ubayd: *Gharīb al-ḥadīth*, Hyderabad 1966, III, 23, note 6.

12 See this tradition al-Nasā'ī: *Sunan*, Cairo 1930, III, 113-116; al-Zurqāni: *Sharḥ 'alā Muwaṭṭa' Mālik*, I, 222-225 (about al-Ṭūr: « *wa-huwa lladhī kullima fīhi Mūsā wa-huwa lladhī 'anā Abū Hurayra* »; Ibn 'Abd al-Barr: *al-Istī'āb*, ed. Muh. al-Bijāwī, Cairo, n.d., I, 184; 'Abd al-Qādir al-Jīlānī: *al-Ghunya*, Cairo 1322 AH, II, 70: and see Helga Hemgesberg: *Abū Huraira*, Frankfurt am Main 1965, p. 105 (with references given by the author); and see al-Samnūdī: *Nuṣratu al-imām al-Subkī*, p. 1912, discussing the following comment: — *wa-li-hādhā fahima l-ṣaḥābatu min nahyihi an yusāfara ilā ghayri l-masājidi l-thalāthati anna l-safara ilā Ṭūri Sīnā'a dākhilum fī l-nahyi wa-in lam yakun masjidan...*; and see *ib.*, p. 192: — *al-ṣalāt fī l-Ṭūr.*

13 See on him Brockelmann, GAL, S. I, 333; F. Sezgin: *Geschichte des arabischen Schrifttums*, Leiden 1967, I, 99; al-Dhahabī: *Mīzān al-i'tidāl*, II, 609, no. 5044;

14 'Abd al-Razzāq, *op. cit.*, f. 39b.

15 *Ib.*, f. 40a.

16 See e.g. note 12 above; but see al-Harawī: *al-Ishārāt ilā ma'rifati l-ziyārāt*, ed. Janine Sourdel-Thomine, Damas 1953, p. 21, 11. 16-17.

According to Muslim tradition the Prophet was instructed by the angel Jibrīl to pray there during his night journey to Jerusalem[17]. At the « *laylat al-qadr* » the angels will hoist their flags in four mosques: the mosque of Mecca, the mosque of the Prophet, the mosque of Jerusalem and at Ṭūr Sīnā.[18] Ibn Taymiyya stresses that the journey to Mt. Sīnā is forbidden on the ground of the utterance of the Prophet about the exclusiveness of the journey to the three mosques[19].

By the beginning of the second century there seems to have already been a unanimity of the Muslim community about the sanctity of these three mosques and consequently about the sanctity of these three cities; this is later reflected in the rich literature concerning the virtues of these cities.

There appear, however, to have existed earlier trends which aimed at emphasizing the sanctity of Mecca, or the sanctity of both Mecca and Medina, while minimizing that of Jerusalem. These trends are reflected in some early traditions, only partly preserved in the canonical collections of *ḥadīth*. These traditions which probably preceded the Muslim consensus regarding the *ḥadīth* of the three mosques will be viewed in the following pages.

I

A tradition recorded on the authority of ʻĀ'isha, the wife of the Prophet, mentions only two mosques: the mosque of Mecca and the mosque of Medina. The Prophet said according to this tradition: « I am the seal (*khātam*) of the prophets and my mosque is the seal of the mosques of the prophets. The mosques which deserve mostly to be visited and towards which the riding beasts should be driven are the mosque of Mecca and my mosque (i.e. the mosque of Medina). The prayer in my mosque is better than a thousand prayers in any other mosque except that of Mecca »[20].

[17] See e.g. al-Wāsiṭī, *op. cit.*, f. 49b, 1.6 and f. 60a, penult.: ... *ṣallayta bi-Ṭūri Sīnā' ḥaythu kallama llāhu Mūsā ṣallā llāhu ʻalayhi wa-sallama* ...; Ibn. Kathīr: *Tafsīr al-Qur'ān al-ʻaẓīm*, Beirut 1966, IV, 245, 1.7; al-Zarkashī, *op. cit.*, p. 298.

[18] ʻAbd al-Qādir al-Jīlānī, *op. cit.*, II, 14; ʻAbd al-ʻAzīz al-Dīrīnī: *Ṭahārat al-qulūb*, Cairo 1354 AH, 124.

[19] Ibn Taymiyya: *Majmūʻat al-rasā'il* II, 55, 1. 3: — *wa-lau nadhara l-safara ilā... ... au ilā l-Ṭūri lladhī kallama 'llāhu ʻalayhi Mūsā ʻalayhi l-salām.* »

[20] al-Mundhirī: *al-Targhīb wa-l-tarhīb min al-ḥadīth al-sharīf*, ed. Muḥyī al-Dīn ʻAbd al-Ḥamīd, Cairo 1961, III, 50, no. 1732; al-Muttaqī al-Hindī, *op. cit.*, XIII, 233, no. 1306; Ibn al-Najjār, *op. cit.*, II, 357; al-Samhūdī, *op. cit.*, I, 259; Ahmad b. ʻAbd

An almost identical tradition is reported on the authority of Ṭāwūs [21] : « You shall set out for two mosques : the mosque of Mecca and the mosque of Medina » [22]. The initial phrase of this tradition is almost identical with that of the tradition about the three mosques; mention is however made in this tradition of two mosques only, those of Mecca and Medina. A similar tradition is recorded by al-Mundhirī : « The best mosque towards which the riding beasts should be driven is the mosque of Ibrāhīm (i.e. the mosque of Mecca) and my mosque » [23].

A significant tradition reported by Ibn Jurayj sheds some light on the attitude of certain Muslim scholars of the second century towards the pilgrimage to the three mosques. Ibn Jurayj records that Ibn 'Aṭā [24] reported a tradition recommending the pilgrimage to the three mosques and adds : « 'Aṭā' used to exclude (the mention of) the Aqṣā, but he reverted later to counting it with them » (*kāna 'Aṭā'un yunkiru l-Aqṣā thumma 'āda fa-'addahu ma'ahā*) [25].

It is 'Aṭā' who was asked by Ibn Jurayj : « What (is your opinion) about a man who vowed to walk from Baṣra to Jerusalem ». He answered : « You were merely ordered (to pilgrimage to) this House (i.e. the Ka'ba) [26]. Ṭāwūs, on whose authority the tradition about the two mosques was transmitted, bade people who vowed to journey to Jerusalem to set out for Mecca [27].

These traditions bear evidence to the fact that among scholars

al-Ḥamīd al-'Abbāsī : *op. cit.*, p. 73; *Juz' Abī l-Jahm al-'Alā' b. Mūsā*, Ms. Hebrew Univ., Majmū'a, p. 43, l. 3

21 See on him Ibn Ḥajar : *Tahdhīb al-tahdhīb*, V. 8; al-Dhahabī : *Tadhkirat al-ḥuffāẓ* I, 90; al-Damīrī : *Ḥayāt al-ḥayawān*, Cairo 1963, II, 88-90; Ibn Khallikān : *Wafayāt al-a'yān*, ed. A.F. Rifā'ī, Cairo 1936, VI, 303-305; Ibn Sa'd : *Ṭabaqāt*, Beirut 1957, V, 537-42.

22 'Abd al-Razzāq, *op. cit.*, f. 39b : *yurḥalu ilā masjidayni, masjidi Makkata wa-masjidi l-Madīnati.*

23 Al-Mundhirī, *op. cit.*, III, 63, no. 1775 : *Khayru mā rukibat ilayhi l-rawāḥilu masjidu Ibrāhīma* (*ṣ*) *wa-masjidī.* Two variants are recorded : *masjidī hādhā wa-l-baytu l-ma'mūru* and *masjidī hādhā wa-l-baytu l-'atīqu*; and see the note of al-Mundhirī, *ib.*, inf.; al-Suyūṭī : *al-Jāmi' al-ṣaghīr*, II, 10 sup.; al-Samhūdī, *op. cit.*, I. 259; Aḥmad b. Ḥajar al-Haythamī, *op. cit.*, p. 41.

24 See on him : Ibn Ḥajar : *Tahdhīb al-tahdhīb*, VII, 483-84; al-Dhahabī : *Tadhkirat al-ḥuffāẓ*, I, 98 : 'Aṭā' b. Abī Rabāḥ (died 115 AH; Ibn Jurayj transmitted his traditions); Ibn Sa'd : *Ṭabaqāt*, Beirut 1957, V, 467-70.

25 'Abd al-Razzāq, *op. cit.*, f. 39b.

26 Id., *op. cit.*, Murad Molla 606, f. 40b, inf.

27 *Ib.*, f. 41b.

of Islam in the first half of the second century there was some reluctance to give full recognition of sanctity to the third mosque and to grant Jerusalem an equal position with the two holy cities of Islam, Mecca and Medina.

This reluctance is plainly brought out in a series of traditions in which the Prophet is said to have advised the faithful to refrain from the journey to Jerusalem for prayer and to perform the prayer either in Mecca or in Medina. A tradition told on the authority of Jābir b. ʿAbdallah [28] reports: A man [29] approached the Prophet at the day of the conquest of Mecca and said « O Messenger of God, I vowed to pray in Jerusalem if you conquer Mecca». The Prophet then said: «Pray here». The man asked him another time and the Prophet gave the same answer. He asked him a third time and the Prophet said: «Then the matter is at your disposal» (*fa-shaʾnaka idhan*) [30].

A very similar tradition is recorded on the authority of Abū Saʿīd (al-Khudrī) [31]. But whereas the preceding tradition stresses the preference of Mecca, this one puts Medina to the fore. A man came to the Prophet, it is told in the story, in order to take leave from him before setting out for his journey to Jerusalem. The Prophet told him that a prayer in his mosque (i.e. in Medina) would be better than a thousand prayers in another mosque except the mosque of Mecca. Some versions of this tradition mention the name of the man, al-Arqam, but do not record the phrase about the mosque of Mecca [32].

[28] Jābir b. ʿAbdallah (died 78 AH). See on him al-Dhahabī: *Tadhkirat al-ḥuffāẓ*, I, 43; Ibn Ḥajar: *Tahdhīb al-tahdhīb*, II, 42; al-Balādhurī: *Ansāb al-ashrāf*, ed. Muḥ. Ḥamīdullāh, Cairo 1959, I, 248-49; al-Dhahabī: *Siyar aʿlām al-nubalāʾ*, ed. Asʿad Ṭalas, Cairo 1962, III, 126-29.

[29] According to the report of ʿAbd al-Razzāq, *op. cit.*, Murad Molla 604, f. 37b, 41a and Ibn Ḥajar al-Haythamī: *Majmaʿ al-zawāʾid*, Cairo 1353 AH, IV, 192, the name of the man was al-Sharīd. About al-Sharīd see Ibn Saʿd: *Ṭabaqāt* V, 113; Ibn Ḥajar: *al-Iṣāba* III, 204, no. 3887.

[30] Ibn Ḥajar: *Bulūgh al-marām*, p. 287, no. 1407; Abu Dāʾūd: *Ṣaḥīḥ sunan al-muṣṭafā*, Cairo 1348 AH, II, 79 with a variant to pray two *rakʿa*; *ib*, inf. another variant: « if you would pray here it would be counted (*ajzaʾa*) as much as the prayer in Jerusalem »; al-Shaukānī, *op. cit.*, VIII, 210 with a variant: *la-qaḍā ʿanka dhālika kulla ṣalātin fī bayti l-maqdisi*; al-Tibrīzī: *Mishkāt al-maṣābīḥ*, Karachi 1350 AH, p. 298; ʿAbd al-Razzāq *op. cit.*, f. 41a; al-Subkī, *op. cit.*, pp. 94-95; al-Bayhaqī, *op. cit.*, X, 82; ʿAbd al-Ghanī al-Nabulsī: *Dhakhāʾir al-mawārīth*, Cairo 1943, I, 145, no. 1324; Shihāb al-Dīn al-Maqdisī, *op. cit.*, p. 134.

[31] See his biography in Ibn Ḥajar's *Iṣāba*, III, 85, no. 2189; al-Dhahabī: *Tadhkirat al-ḥuffāẓ*, I, 44.

[32] Al-Samhūdī, *op. cit.*, I, 295; Aḥmad b. Ḥajar al-Haythamī, *op. cit.*, p. 41; al-Dhahabī: *Siyar aʿlām al-nubalāʾ*, ed. al-Abyārī, Cairo 1957, II, 342.

To this category of traditions belongs the story told about Maymūna the wife of the Prophet. A woman became ill and vowed to perform a pilgrimage to Jerusalem if she recovered. Having recuperated and prepared provisions for her journey she came to Maymūna to take her leave. Maymūna advised her to stay at Medina, to consume her provisions there and to fulfil her vow by praying in the mosque of the Prophet (in Medina). Maymūna quoted in this connection the utterance of the Prophet that a prayer in his mosque was better than a thousand prayers in any other mosque except that of the Ka'ba [33].

A story closely resembling the preceding tradition is told on the authority of Sa'īd b. al-Musayyab [34]. The story told about 'Umar is however in favour of Mecca, not of Medina. A man came to 'Umar asking permission to travel to Jerusalem. 'Umar ordered him to prepare his provisions. But when these were prepared 'Umar bade him to perform the *'umra* instead of going to Jerusalem [35].

The essential reason for the resistance of a group of Muslim scholars to grant license of pilgrimage to Jerusalem is plainly reflected in another story about 'Umar told on the authority of the same Sa'īd b. al-Musayyab, who transmitted the preceding story; it is recorded by the early scholar of *ḥadīth*, 'Abd al-Razzaq b. Hammām in his *Muṣannaf*. According to this story, when 'Umar was in an enclosure of camels of *ṣadaqa* two men passed by. He asked them wherefrom they came and they answered that they had come from Jerusalem. 'Umar hit them with his whip and said: « (Have you performed) a pilgrimage like the pilgrimage of the Ka'ba »? They said: « No, o Commander of the faithful, we came from such and such a territory, we passed by it (scil. Jerusalem) and prayed there. » Then 'Umar said: « Then it is so », and let then go [36].

33 Al-Bayhaqī, *op. cit.*, X, 83; al-Shaukānī, *op. cit.*, VIII, 210; *Juz' Abī l-Jahm al-'Alā' b. Mūsā*, Ms., p. 42; Shihāb al-Dīn al-Maqdisī, *op. cit.*, Ms. p. 134.

34 See on him Ibn Khallikān, *op. cit.*, VI, 136-143; Ibn Ḥajar: *Tahdhīb al-tahdhīb*, IV, 84-88; Abū Nu'aym al-Iṣfahānī: *Ḥilyat al-auliyā'*, Cairo 1933, II, 161-173.

35 'Abd al-Razzāq, *op. cit.*, f. 39b.

36 'Abd al-Razzāq, *op. cit.*, f. 39b: 'Abd al-Razzāq> Ma'mar b. Rāshid> 'Abd al-Karīm al-Jazarī (died 127 AH; see on him Ibn Ḥajar: *Tahdhīb al-tahdhīb*, VI, 373-75; Ibn 'Abd al-Barr: *Tajrīd al-tamhīd*, Cairo 1350 AH, p. 107)> Ibn al-Musayyab: *Baynā 'Umaru fī na'amin min na'ami l-ṣadaqati marra bihi rajulāni, fa-qāla: min ayna ji'tumā, qālā: min al-bayti l-muqaddasi, fa-'alāhumā ḍarban bi-l-dirrati wa-qālā: ḥajjun ka-ḥajji l-bayti, qālā: yā amīra l-mu'minīna, innā ji'nā min arḍi kadhā wa-kadhā fa-mararnā bihi fa-ṣallaynā fīhi, fa-qāla: kadhālika idhan, fa-tarakahumā.*

The story shows clearly that Muslim scholars feared that Jerusalem might become a place of pilgrimage like Mecca and acquire a sanctity like that of Mecca. The two sanctuaries, that of Mecca and the one of Jerusalem are mentioned jointly in the verse of al-Farazdaq:

Wa-baytāni baytu llāhi naḥnu wulātuhu:
wa-baytun bi-a'lā Īliyā'a musharrafu

(To us belong) two Houses: the House of God, of which we are the governors: and the revered House in the upper (part of) Īliyā'a (i.e. Jerusalem)[37].

This verse testifies to the veneration of these two sanctuaries at the end of the seventh century. It is significant that the two sanctuaries are referred to as being on the same level[38]. This these scholars tried to prevent. Jerusalem could only be considered as a place of devotional prayer, a holy place endowed with special merits for pilgrims to Mecca; but it could not be awarded the rank of Mecca and it never got it.

The reluctance to perform the pilgrimage to Jerusalem found its expression in some utterances reported on the authority of the Companions of the Prophet. ('Abdallah) b. Mas'ūd is stated to have said: « If (the whole distance) between me and Jerusalem were two parasangs I would not go there[39].

Mālik (b. Anas) refrained from coming to Jerusalem for fear that this may become a *sunna*[40].

The justification of this attitude which tried to diminish the importance of the pilgrimage to Jerusalem is found in a remarkable saying of al-Sha'bi[41]: « Muḥammad, may God bless him, was only turned

[37] Al-Farazdaq: *Dīwān*, ed. al-Ṣāwī, Cairo 1936, p. 566; *Naqā'iḍ Jarīr wa-l-Farazdaq*, ed. Bevan, Leiden 1905, p. 571.

[38] Comp. another verse of al-Farazdaq, *Dīwān*, p. 619, composed in the first decade of the eighth century:

wa-bi-l-masjidi l-aqṣā l-imāmu 'lladhī 'htadā: bihi min qulūbi l-mumtarīna ḍalāluhā.

[39] 'Abd al-Razzāq, *op. cit.*, f. 39b, inf.: 'Abd al-Razzāq> al-Thaurī> Jābir> al-Sha'bī> Shaqīq (see on him Ibn Ḥajar: *Iṣāba* III, 225, no. 3977; id.: *Tahdhīb al-tahdhīb*, IV, 361)> ('Abdallah) b. Mas'ūd: *lau kāna baynī wa-bayna bayti l-maqdisi farsakhāni mā ataytuhu.*

[40] Al-Shāṭibī, *op. cit.*, I, 347: *wa-qad kāna Mālikun yakrahu l-majī'a ilā bayti l-maqdisi khīfata an yuttakhadha dhālika sunnatan.*

[41] See on him al-Dhahabī: *Tadhkirat al-huffāẓ*, I, 79-88: Ibn 'Asākir: *Ta'rīkh*, ed. Ibn Badrān, Damascus, n.d., VII, 138-155; Ibn Ḥajar: *Tahdhīb al-tahdhīb*, V, 69-61.

away from Jerusalem (i.e. from his first *qibla*) because of his anger.» A gloss added to this tradition states : « he means (anger with regards to Jerusalem » [42].

The son of Sa'd b. Abī Waqqāṣ, 'Āmir [43] and his daughter 'Ā'isha [44] reported on the authority of their father that he would like much more to pray in the mosque of Qubā' than in Jerusalem. [45]

'Umar is also said to have stated that he preferred one prayer in the mosque of Qubā' than four prayers in Jerusalem [46].

The superiority of the mosque of Medina over al-Aqṣā was expressed by the Prophet himself. According to a tradition reported on the authority of Abū Hurayra, the Prophet was asked whether prayer in al-Aqṣā was better than prayer in his mosque (i.e. in Medina). The Prophet answered : « A prayer in my mosque is better than four prayers in it». (i.e. in al-Aqṣā) [47].

A peculiar tradition attributed to the Prophet recommends to journey to three mosques only, exactly as in the tradition discussed

[42] 'Abd al-Razzāq, *op. cit.*, f. 40a, sup. : 'Abd al-Razzāq> al-Thaurī> Jābir : *sami'tu l-Sha'biyya yuqsimu bi- llāhi mā rudda Muḥammadun* (ṣ) *'an bayti l-maqdisi illā 'an sukhṭihi, ya'nī 'alā bayti l-maqdisi.* See al-Thaurī : *Tafsīr al-Qur'ān al-karīm*, Rampur 1965, ed. Imtiyāz 'Alī 'Arshī, p. 12 : Sufyān> Jābir al-Ju'fī, *qāla* : *aqsama bi- llāhi l-Sha'biyyu* : *mā rudda l-nabiyyu 'alā ahli bayti l-maqdisi illā li-sukhṭihi 'alā ahli bayti l-maqdisi.* The text of this tradition is of course blurred and has to be corrected according to the record of *al-Muṣannaf*. The editor of al-Thaurī's *Tafsīr* remarks that he could not find this utterance in the compilations of *tafsīr* and *ḥadīth.* — comp. Ṭabarī : *Tafsīr*, ed. Maḥmūd Muḥ. Shākir and Aḥmad Muḥ. Shākir, Cairo, ca. 1960, III, 173 : *qāla ba'ḍuhum* : *kariha qiblata bayti l-maqdisi min ajli anna l-yahūda qālū* : *yattabi'u qiblatanā wa-yukhālifu dīnanā...*, al-Nuwayrī, *op. cit.*, I, 329 :- *wa- khtalafū fī l-sababi lladhī kāna 'alayhi l-ṣalātu wa-l-salāmu min ajlihi yakrahu qiblata bayti l-maqdisi wa-yahwā qiblata l-Ka'bati...*

[43] On him see Ibn Ḥajar : *Tahdīb al-tahdhīb*, V, 64

[44] On her see Ibn Ḥajar : *al-Iṣāba*, VIII, 141, no. 703

[45] Al-Bayhaqī, *op. cit.*, V, 249; al-Mundhirī, *op. cit.*, III, 55, no. 1748; al-Samhūdī, *op. cit.*, II, 19; al-Ḥākim : *al-Mustadrak*, Hyderabad, III, 12; Aḥmad b. 'Abd al-Ḥamīd al-'Abbāsī, *op. cit.*, p. 412 sup. (three versions); al-Qasṭallānī, *op. cit.*, III, 242.

[46] 'Abd al-Razzāq, *op. cit.*, f. 37b.

[47] Ibn 'Asākir : *Ta'rīkh madīnat Dimashq*, ed. Ṣalāḥ al-Dīn al-Munajjid, Damascus 1951, I, 163; Mujīr al-Dīn, *op. cit.*, I, 206; al-Wāsiṭī, *op. cit.*, f. 42a; Shihāb al-Dīn al-Maqdisī, *op. cit.*, Ms. pp. 130, 146; al-Suyūṭī : *Al-Durr al-manthūr*, IV, 161; Shams al-Dīn al-Suyūṭī, *op. cit.*, f. 17a; Abū l-Maḥāsin Yūsuf b. Mūsā al-Ḥanafī, *op. cit.*, I, 24 inf.

above. This tradition, however, places the mosque of al-Khayf [48] instead al-Aqṣā as the third mosque [49].

The traditions quoted above can be taken to represent an early stratum of lore in which the opposition displayed by certain circles of Muslim scholars at the beginning of the second century to the ranking of Jerusalem on the level of Mecca and Medina is reflected. They bring out quite clearly the tendency of those who tried to subdue the excessive veneration which was forming with regard to the sanctuary of Jerusalem.

II

Against the records in which an attempt is made to diminish the position of the sanctuary of Jerusalem one can notice quite well in the traditions the existence of a trend going in the opposite direction: it aims at granting Jerusalem the rank of Medina and emphasizes the peculiar features of sanctity of the mosque, of the city and of the region of Jerusalem.

« The assignment of relative ratings of efficacy to prayer in different localities is a common method of ranking towns in terms of their holiness» stated G. von Grunebaum [50]. This was indeed applied to Jerusalem in comparison to Mecca and Medina.

A significant tradition granting the mosque of Jerusalem an unusually high rank is recorded on the authority of Abū Hurayra and ʿĀ'isha. « A prayer in my mosque (i.e. in Medina) — says the Prophet in this *ḥadīth* — is better than a thousand prayers in any other mosque except al-Aqṣā» [51]. It is evident that this tradition contradicts the well-known tradition in which the concluding phrase reads: « except (prayer in) the mosque of Mecca» [52]. The phrase « except (prayer in)

[48] See on al-Khayf: al-Bakrī: *Muʿjam mā 'staʿjam*, ed. Muṣṭafā al-Saqā, Cairo 1945, II, 526; Yāqūt: *Muʿjam al-buldān*, s.v. Khayf; Abū l-Baqā': *al-Manāqib al-mazyadiyya*, Ms. Br. Mus., f. 93a (the grave of Muḍar in the mosque of al-Khayf).

[49] Al-Zarkashī, *op. cit.*, p. 68; al-Fāsī: *Shifā' al-gharām*, I, 263 inf.; al-Dhahabī: *Mīzān al-iʿtidāl*, ed. al-Bijāwī, Cairo 1963, I, 650, no. 2495; Ibn Ẓahīra: *al-Jāmiʿ al-laṭīf fī faḍli Makkata wa-ahlihā wa-binā' i l-bayti l-sharīf*, Cairo 1921, p. 334.

[50] G.E. von Grunebaum, *op. cit.*, p. 31.

[51] al-Mundhirī, *op. cit.*, III, 53, no. 1740: *Ṣalātun fī masjidī khayrun min alfi ṣalātin fīmā siwāhu min al-masājidi illā l-masjidi l-aqṣā*; *al-Samhūdī*: *op. cit.*, I, 296 sup.

[52] Al-Samhūdī, *op. cit.*, I, 296; al-Suyūṭī: *al-Jāmiʿ al-ṣaghīr*, II, 47; ʿAbd al-Razzāq, *op. cit.*, f. 37b; al-Mundhirī, *op. cit.*, III, 50, no. 1731; Aḥmad b. Ḥanbal: *al-Musnad* III, no. 1605, VII, no. 4838, 5153, 5155, 5358, VIII, no. 5778, XII, no. 7252; Muḥ.

the mosque of Mecca» was in this *ḥadīth* replaced by the phrase «except (prayer in) al-Aqṣā ».

Another tradition reported on the authority of Ibn ʿAbbās links the *ḥadīth* about the three mosques with the utterance of the Prophet about the value of the prayer in these mosques granting al-Aqṣā preference over the mosque of Medina. « A prayer in the mosque of Mecca (*al-masjid al-ḥarām*) — says the Prophet — is worth a hundred thousand prayers, a prayer in my mosque (i.e. in Medina) is worth a thousand prayers, and a prayer in al-Aqṣā is worth ten thousand prayers» [53]. This tradition occurs with greater exaggeration in *Muthīr al-gharām* [54] : The Prophet states that a prayer in the mosque of Mecca is worth a hundred thousand prayers, a prayer in the mosque of Medina a thousand prayers and a prayer in Jerusalem twenty thousand prayers.

More restrained are two traditions recorded by Ibn Majāh. One of them states that the Prophet when asked about the mosque of Jerusalem recommended to come to Jerusalem, the land of the Resurrection and the place of assembly for the Final Judgement [55] and to pray there, as a prayer performed in it is worth a thousand prayers

Fu'ād ʿAbd al-Bāqī, *op. cit.*, II, 97, no. 881; Abū Yūsuf al-Anṣārī : *al-Āthār*, ed. Abū l-Wafā, Cairo 1355 AH, p. 65, no. 320; Ibn al-Najjār, *op. cit.*, II, 357; Ibn Ẓahīra, *op. cit.*, p. 193; al-Fāsī, *op. cit.*, I, 79-81; al-Zarkashī, *op. cit.*, 115-119, Ibn Taymiyya : *Majmūʿat al-rasā'il*, II, 54, inf.; Aḥmad b. ʿAbd al-Ḥamīd al-ʿAbbāsī, *op. cit.*, p. 72-73; Abū Ṭālib al-Makkī, *op. cit.*, III, 182; Ibn ʿAbd al-Barr : *Tajrīd al-tamhīd*, p. 99, no. 305; al-Dārimī, *op. cit.*, I, 270, no. 1425; al-Rabīʿ b. Ḥabīb : *al-Jāmiʿ al-ṣaḥīḥ*, Cairo 1349 AH, I, 52; Abū l-Maḥāsin al-Ḥanafī, *op. cit.*, I, 24; al-Nawawī : *al-Īḍāḥ fī l-manāsik*, Cairo 1298 AH, p. 65; al-Jarrāḥī, *op. cit.*, II, 27, no. 1605; Muḥ. b. al-Fattāl : *Rauḍat al-wāʿiẓīn*, al-Najaf 1966, p. 408; al-Qasṭallānī, *op. cit.*, III, 240 inf.; etc...

53 Ch. D. Matthews : *The Kit. Bāʿiṯu-n-nufūs*, JPOS, XV (1935), p. 54; idem : *Palestine*, p. 4.

54 Shihāb al-Dīn al-Maqdisī, *op. cit.*, Ms. p. 129 with the following *isnād* : Hishām b. Sulaymān (see on him al-Dhahabī : *Mīzān al-iʿtidāl* IV, 299)> Ibn Jurayj> ʿAṭā'> Ibn ʿAbbās> the Prophet. The ḥadīth is evaluated as weak (*wāhin*).

55 For *arḍu l-maḥshar wa-l-manshar* see al-Rabaʿī : *Faḍā'il al-Shām wa-Dimashq*, ed. Ṣalāḥ al-Dīn al-Munajjid, Damascus 1950, p. 15, no. 25; and see ib., the introduction of Munajjid, p. 10, note 2; and see ib., Appendix 1, p. 85, ed. no. 25; Shihāb al-Dīn al-Maqdisī, *op. cit.*, pp. 12, 143; and see ʿAbd al-Wahhāb al-Shaʿrānī : *Mukhtaṣar tadhkirat al-Qurṭubī*, Cairo 1935, p. 43; al-Wāsiṭī, *op. cit.*, f. 51b-53b, 57b; and see H. Busse, *Der Islam und die biblischen Kultstätten*, Der Islam, 1966, p. 124; Asad b. Mūsā : *Kit. al-Zuhd*, ed. Rudolf Leszynsky, Kirchhain 1909 (*Mohammedanische Traditionen über das jüngste Gericht*) pp. XXI, 46, 49-50; Ibn Kathīr, *op. cit.*, VI, 411; al-Suyūṭī : *al-Durr al-manthūr* VI, 110; Ch. D. Matthews : *Palestine*, p. 120.

elsewhere [56]. The second tradition records the utterance of the Prophet assigning to the prayer in the mosque of Jerusalem the value of fifty thousand prayers, to the prayer in the mosque of Medina fifty thousand prayers and to the prayer in the mosque of Mecca a hundred thousand prayers [57].

In another tradition, reported on the authority of Ibn ʿAbbās, the Prophet assigned to a prayer in the mosque of Mecca the value of a hundred thousand prayers, to a prayer in the mosque of Medina fifty thousand prayers and to a prayer in the mosque of Jerusalem twenty thousand prayers [58]. In another tradition reported as well on the authority of Ibn ʿAbbās the value of a prayer in the mosque of Jerusalem is considerably reduced. The Prophet — according to this tradition — assigned to a prayer in the mosque of Medina the value of hundred thousand prayers, to a prayer in the mosque of Mecca a hundred thousand prayers and to a prayer in the mosque of Jerusalem a thousand prayers [59]. Another tradition reported on the authority of Abū l-Dardā' states that the Prophet assigned to a prayer in the mosque of Mecca the value of a hundred thousand prayers, to a prayer in the mosque of Medina the value of a thousand prayers and to a prayer in the mosque of Jerusalem the value of five hundred prayers [60]. Ibn Taymiyya records as the number of prayers

[56] Ibn Mājah : *Sunan al-Muṣṭafā*, Cairo 1349 AH, I, 429 (Abū l-Ḥasan Muḥ. b. ʿAbd al-Hādī remarks in his comment *ib.*, that the Prophet was probably asked whether the prayer was permitted in the mosque of Jerusalem after the *Qibla* was diverted from it. He also remarks that only prayers in mosques other that those of Mecca and Medina are meant, as a prayer in the mosque of Jerusalem is like a prayer in Medina) ; al-Zarkashī, *op. cit.*, p. 289; al-Wāsiṭī, *op. cit.*, f. 41b; al-Samhūdī, *op. cit.*, I, 295; Ibn Bābūya : *Thawāb al-aʿmāl*, Tehran 1375 AH, p. 30; Shihāb al-Dīn al-Maqdisī, *op. cit.*, Ms. p. 128; Abū l-Maḥāsin Yūsuf b. Mūsā al-Ḥanafī, *op. cit.*, I, 25.

[57] Ibn Mājah, *op. cit.*, I, 431; al-Zarkashī, *op. cit.*, p. 287, 118; Shihāb al-Dīn al-Maqdisī, *op. cit.*, Ms. p. 219; al-Tibrīzī : *Mishkāt al-maṣābīḥ*, p. 72.

[58] Ch. D. Matthews : *Kit. Bāʿiṯu-n-nufūs*, ib., p. 60 (*Palestine*, p. 11).

[59] Al-Zarkashī, *op. cit.*, p. 118 (quoted from al-Ṭabarānī's *al-Muʿjam al-kabīr*); al-Samhūdī, *op. cit.*, I, 299 (quoted from al-Zarkashī); Abū Ṭālib al-Makkī, *op. cit.*, III, 182.

[60] Al-ʿAbdarī, *op. cit.*, II, 39; al-Samhūdī, *op. cit.*, I, 298 (quoted from al-Ṭabarānī); al-Zarkashī, *op. cit.*, p. 117 (quoted from al-Bazzār's *Musnad*); al-Muttaqī al-Hindī, *op. cit.*, XIII, 168, no. 938 (on the authority of Jābir), no. 939, 941 (on the authority of Abū l-Dardāʿ); Ch. D. Matthews : *Palestine*, p. 10; Shihāb al-Dīn al-Maqdisī, *op. cit.*, Ms., p. 128; Abū l-Maḥāsin Yūsuf b. Mūsā al-Ḥanafi, *op. cit.*, I, 25, 1.3; al-Jarrāḥī, *op. cit.*, II, 27, no. 1605; al-Qasṭallānī, *op. cit.*, III, 241.

corresponding to a prayer in the mosque of Jerusalem five hundred or fifty [61].

It is evident that the traditions which assign values to prayer in the mosque of Jerusalem are contradictory and mutually exclusive. They have to be seen against the background of a controversy concerning the weight to be accorded to prayer in the mosques of Mecca and Medina. These two cities contended for a long time for the superiority of their sanctuaries [62] and their merits [63]. Quite early traditions reflecting this controversy are recorded in ʿAbd al-Razzāq's *Muṣannaf*. When asked by a man whether to journey to Medina ʿAṭāʾ answered :

[61] Ibn Taymiyya : *Majmūʿat al-rasāʾil*, II, 54 inf.

[62] See for instance al-Samhūdī, *op. cit.*, I, 296 (*wa-dhahaba baʿḍuhum ilā anna l-ṣalāta fī masjidi l-Madīnati afḍalu min al-ṣalāti fī masjidi Makkata bi-miʾati ṣalātin*); and see ib. pp. 297-300 the discussion about the value of the prayer in Medina in comparison with the prayer in Mecca; al-Zarkashī, *op. cit.*, pp. 186-190; Shihāb al-Dīn al-Khafājī, *op. cit.*, III, 583.

[63] See for instance al-ʿAbdarī, *op. cit.*, II, 31; al-Samhūdī, *op. cit.*, I, 34, 52; The Prophet was created from the clay of Medina as reported in the tradition that a man is buried in the earth from which he is created. A contradictory tradition was recorded by al-Zubayr b. Bakkār. According to this tradition the Prophet was created from the clay of the Kaʿba. See al-Shaukānī, *op. cit.*, V. 25; Ibn Ẓahīra, *op. cit.*, p. 18; and see G. E. von Grunebaum : *Muhammadan Festivals*, New York 1951, p. 20. Ibn Ḥajar al-Haythamī : *al-Niʿma al-kubrā ʿalā l-ʿālam bi -maulid Sayyid banī Ādam*, Ms. (in my possession) f. 7a. Al-Shaʿbi disliked to stay in Mecca because the Prophet departed from Mecca; he considered Mecca « *dār aʿrābiyya* » (al-Samhūdī, *op. cit.*, I, 35; for the expression « *dār aʿrābiyya* » see Abū l-Maḥāsin Yūsuf b. Mūsā al-Ḥanafī, *op. cit.*, II, 203, l. 8); and see al-Khaṭīb al-Bahgdādī : *Taqyīd al-ʿilm*, ed. Yūsuf al-ʿUshsh, Damascus 1949, p. 72 : Marwān b. al-Ḥakam mentioned in his speech the merits of Mecca, its sanctity and the merits of its people. Rāfiʿ b. Khudayj reminded him of the sanctity of Medina, the merits of its people and mentioned the fact that it was declared as *ḥaram* by the Prophet and that the declaration was kept in Medina, written on a *khaulānī* skin. Marwān answered : « I heard something about it. » (*qad samiʿtu baʿḍa dhālika*); al-ʿAbdarī, *op. cit.*, II, 34; Aḥmad b. ʿAbd al-Ḥamīd al-ʿAbbāsī, *op. cit.*, p. 58 :... *wa-yastadillūna bihi ʿalā afḍaliyyati hādhihi l-baldati ʿalā sāʾiri l-buldāni muṭlaqan, Makkata wa-ghayrihā...*; and see *ib.*, p. 61 about the doubled blessing of the Prophet granted Medina compared with the blessing of Abraham for Mecca.; and see al-Samhūdī, *op. cit.*, I, 26 : *al-Madīnatu khayrun min Makkata*; al-Suyūṭī : *al-Jāmiʿ al-ṣaghīr*, II, 184; al-Fāsī, *op. cit.*, I, 79 seq.; al-Samhūdī, *op. cit.*, I, 24-26; Aḥmad b. ʿAbd al-Ḥamīd al-ʿAbbāsī, *op. cit.*, p. 69 (*muslimu l-Madīnati khayrun min muslimi Makkata*); al-Fāsī, *op. cit.*, pp. 77-79; al-ʿAbdarī, *op. cit.*, I, 257 (— *wa-qad taqaddama annahu ʿalayhi l-ṣalātu wa-l-salāmu afḍalu min al-Kaʿbati wa-ghayrihā...*); and see ib., II, 38; about the partisans of the superiority of Medina and those of Mecca see al-Shaukānī, *op. cit.*, V, 24; Taqī al-Dīn ʿAbd al-Malik b. Abī l-Munā, *op. cit.*, p. 97; al-Zurqānī : *Sharḥ al-Mawāhib al-ladunniyya*, Cairo 1329 AH, VIII, 322; Shihāb al-Dīn al-Khafājī, *op. cit.*, III, 584-587.

« to circumambulate the Ka'ba seven times is better than your journey to Medina » [64]. Al-Thaurī is said to have answered when asked about a journey to Medina : « do not do it » (*lā taf'al*) [65]. 'Aṭā' reported that he heard 'Abdallah b. al-Zubayr stating in his speech on the *minbar* (scil. of Mecca) : « a prayer in the mosque of Mecca is better than a hundred prayers in any other of the mosques. » «It seems to me — added 'Aṭā' — that he intended the mosque of Medina » [66]. Qatāda said it plainly : « A prayer in the mosque of Mecca is better than a hundred prayers in the mosque of Medina » [67]. An identical utterance on the authority of 'Abdallah b. al-Zubayr is reported by Abū l-'Āliya [68].

These traditions, some of which are early ones, shed some light on the rivalry between Mecca and Medina [69]. The idea of the sanctity of Jerusalem grew and developed within the framework of this contest.

III

As against the tendency of restriction and limitation one can notice the opposite one, which aims to extend the number of holy mosques by the addition of one or two mosques to the three mosques, about the pilgrimage to which a consensus of the Muslim community had been reached. « The most distinguished mosques are : the mosque of Mecca, then the mosque of the Prophet (i.e. Medina), then the mosque of Jerusalem, then — it has been said — the mosque of al-Kūfa because of the consent of the Companions of the Prophet about it ; and people said : the mosque of Damascus » [70].

The mosque of Damascus was ranked with the three mosques and the relative value of prayers in it was fixed in a saying attributed

[64] 'Abd al-Razzāq, *op. cit.*, f. 39b : *'Abd al-Razzāq qāla akhbaranī abī qāla qultu li-l-Muthannā : innī urīdu an ātiya l-Madīnata ; qāla : lā taf'al ; sami'tu 'Aṭā'an qāla — wa-sa'alahu rajulun — fa-qāla lahu : ṭawāfun sab'an bi-l-bayti khayrun min safarika ilā l-Madīnati.*

[65] 'Abd al-Razzāq, *op. cit.*, f. 39b.

[66] *Ib.*, f. 37b.

[67] *Ib.*, f. 38a.

[68] *Ib.*, f. 38a.

[69] For the sanctity of Medina see G. E. von Grunebaum : *The sacred character of Islamic cities*, p. 31.

[70] Yūsuf b. 'Abd al-Hādī : *Thimār al-maqāṣid fī dhikri l-masājid*, ed. As'ad Ṭalas, Beirut 1943, p. 183.

to Sufyān al-Thaurī. When asked by a man about the value of a prayer in Mecca Sufyān answered : « the value of a prayer in Mecca is of a hundred thousand prayers, in the mosque of the Prophet fifty thousand prayers, in the mosque of Jerusalem forty thousand prayers and in the mosque of Damascus thirty thousand prayers» [71]. The equality of the mosque of Damascus with the mosque of Jerusalem is stressed in a story of a conversation between Wāthila b. al-Asqaʿ [72] and Kaʿb al-Aḥbār [73]. Wāthila intended to set out for Jerusalem, but Kaʿb showed him a spot in the mosque of Damascus in which the prayer has the same value as the prayer in the mosque of Jerusalem [74].

Shīʿite tradition put the mosque of al-Kūfa in the rank of the three mosques; Ḥudhayfa b. al-Yamān stated that it was the fourth mosque after Mecca, Medina and Jerusalem [75]. The mosque of al-Kūfa is said to have been — like the mosques of Jerusalem and Mecca — the mosque of Adam [76] the place of prayer of prophets [77] and the place where the Prophet (Muḥammad) prayed [78] at the night of his

[71] Al-Rabaʿī, *op. cit.*, p. 36, no. 64 and p. 86 (ad no. 64); Ch. D. Matthews : *The Kit. Bāʿiṯu-n-nufūs*, JPOS, XV, p. 61; Shams al-Dīn al Suyūṭī, *op. cit.*, f. 17b.; al-Manīnī : *al-Iʿlām bi-faḍā'il al-Shām*, ed. Aḥmad Sāmiḥ al-Khālidī, Jerusalem, n.d., pp. 84-85.

[72] See on him Ibn Ḥajar : *Tahdhīb al-tahdhīb*, XI, 101; idem, *al-Iṣāba* VI, 310, no. 9088; al-Dhahabī : *Siyar aʿlām al-nubalā'* III, 257-59.

[73] See S. D. Goitein, *op. cit.*, p. 144; and see on Kaʿb; I. Wolfensohn : *Kaʿb al-Aḥbār und seine Stellung im Ḥadīṯ und in der islamischen Legendenliteratur*, Gelnhausen, 1933.

[74] Al-Rabaʿī, *op. cit.*, p. 37, no. 65.

[75] Al-Majlisī, *Biḥār al-anwār*, lithogr. ed., XXII, 88; al-Burāqī : *Ta'rīkh al-Kūfa*, al-Najaf, 1960, p. 36.

[76] See al-Wāsiṭī, *op. cit.*, f. 53b (the grave of Adam); Ch. D. Matthews : *Palestine*, pp. 32-33; Ibn Ẓahīra, *op. cit.*, p. 143 (the prayer of Adam in Mecca); and see G. E. von Grunebaum; *Muhammadan Festivals*, p. 20 (« *Adam is said to be buried in Mecca* »).

[77] See for instance Shams al-Din al-Suyūṭī, *op. cit.*, ff. 15b, 7b,8b; Shihāb al-Dīn al-Maqdisī, *op. cit.*, Ms. p. 125 seq.; and see about the graves of seventy prophets in the Kaʿba and graves of the prophets in Jerusalem, al-Suyūṭī : *al-Durr al-manthūr* I, 136; about the prayer of seventy prophets in the mosque of al-Khayf (see above note 48) see Ibn Ẓahīra, *op. cit.*, p. 334 etc.

[78] About the prayer of the Prophet in Jerusalem see e.g. Ibn Hishām : *al-Sīra al-nabawiyya*, ed. al-Saqā, al-Abyārī, Shalabī, Cairo 1936, II, 38, 39; Ibn Sayyid al-Nās : *ʿUyūn al-athar*, Cairo 1356 AH, I, 141, 144; Ibn Kathīr : *op. cit.*, IV, 241, 245; but see the tradition stating that the Prophet did not pray in Jerusalem *ib.* pp. 254-255; and see this tradition discussed Abū l-Maḥāsin Yūsuf b. Mūsā al-Ḥanafī, *op. cit.*, II, 176-177.

Isrā' [79]. The value of a thousand prayers was assigned to a prayer in the mosque of al-Kūfa [80].

Some of the Shīʿī traditions bring out a rivalry which existed between al-Kūfa and Jerusalem. A man came to ʿAlī b. Abī Ṭālib — says one of these traditions — when he was in the mosque of al-Kūfa to take his leave; the man was about to set out for Jerusalem. ʿAlī bade him to sell his mount, to consume his provisions and to pray in the mosque of al-Kūfa, as the obliging prayer performed there has the value of a pilgrimage (to Mecca) and the voluntary prayer has the value of an *ʿumra* [81].

Jaʿfar al-Ṣādiq (Abū ʿAbdallah) was asked by a man about mosques of merits. Jaʿfar mentioned the mosques of Mecca and Medina. The man asked about the Aqṣā mosque and Jaʿfar answered: « that is in heaven, there the Prophet was carried at night» (*ilayhi usriya rasūlu llāhi*). The man said : « people say *bayt al-maqdis* » (Jerusalem - K) Jaʿfar said : « al-Kūfa is better than that » [82].

A peculiar utterance attributed to ʿAlī runs as follows : « You shall set out only for three mosques: the mosque of Mecca, the mosque of Medina and the mosque of al-Kūfa» [83]. In this tradition, styled exactly like the discussed tradition about the three mosques, the mosque of Jerusalem was replaced by the mosque of al-Kūfa. To ʿAlī is attributed the following utterance as well : « Four are the palaces of Paradise in this world : the mosque of Mecca, the mosque of Medina, the mosque of Jerusalem and the mosque of al-Kūfa » [84].

A mosque ranked with the three mosques was the mosque of al-Janad in al-Yaman. To the Prophet was attributed an utterance

[79] Al-Barqī : *al-Maḥāsin*, al-Najaf 1964, p. 43, no. 86 (Kit. *Thawāb al-aʿmāl*); al-Burāqī, *op. cit.*, p. 49; al-Majlisī, *op. cit.*, XXII, 85 inf., 89, 90 (lithograph. ed.); Muḥ. Mahdī al-Mūsāwī; *Tuḥfat al-sājid fī aḥkām al-masājid*, Baghdād 1376 AH, p. 447; Muḥ. b. al-Fattāl, *op. cit.*, p. 410.

[80] Ibn Bābūya, *op. cit.*, p. 30; al-Burāqī, *op. cit.*, pp. 31, 32, 49, 50.

[81] Yāqūt : *Muʿjam al-buldān*, s.v. al-Kūfa; al-Majlisī, *op. cit.*, XXII, 90 (lithogr. ed.).

[82] Al-Burāqī, *op. cit.*, p. 29 (quoted from *Tafsīr al-ʿAyyāshī*).

[83] *Ib.*, p. 48.

[84] Abū Jaʿfar Muḥ. b. al-Ḥasan al-Ṭūsī : *al-Amālī*, Najaf 1964, I, 379; comp. the ḥadīth attributed to the Prophet about the four cities of Paradise in this world : Mecca, Medina, Jerusalem and Damascus, al-Suyūṭī : *al-Laʾālī al--maṣnūʿa fī l-aḥādīth al-mauḍūʿa*, Cairo, al-Maktaba al-Tijāriya, n.d., I, 459-60; al-Jarrāḥī, *op. cit.*, I, 450, no. 1466; al-Rabaʿī, *op. cit.*, pp. 28-29; and see *ib.*, p. 28 the utterance of Kaʿb about five cities of Paradise : Ḥimṣ, Damascus, Jerusalem, Bayt Jibrīn and Ẓafār in al-Yaman; and comp. Muḥ b. al-Fattāl, *op. cit.*, p. 409.

bading to set out for the mosques of Mecca, Medina, Jerusalem and al-Janad [85].

* * *

Tradition emphasized the common features of sanctity of these mosques, stressed the special graces bestowed on them or on each of them and pointed out the close relations between these sanctuaries. « The earth was water — reads a tradition attributed to ʿAlī — God sent a wind which wiped away the water and on the earth appeared a foam, which He divided into four pieces; of one of these pieces He created Mecca, from the other He created Medina, from the third one He created Jerusalem and from the fourth He created al-Kūfa [86]. At the Day of Resurrection the Kaʿba will be carried to the Rock in Jerusalem [87]. The mount Qāsiyūn granted his shadow to the mountain of Jerusalem and was granted the grace of God [88]. The Kaʿba was built from the stones of five mountains : Lubnān, Ṭūr Zayta, al-Jūdī, Ṭūr Sīnā and Ḥirāʾ [89]. From the splits of Mt. Sīnā, which splitted at the day when God spoke to Moses, three mountains in Mecca arose (Ḥirāʾ, Thabīr, Thaur) and three in Medina (Uḥud,

85 Ch. D. Matthews : *Palestine*, p. 4, inf. and p. 140, note 13.

86 Al-Wāsiṭī, *op. cit.*, f. 38a, inf.; al-Suyūṭī : *al-Durr al-manthūr*, IV, 158 (quoted from al-Wāsiṭī); Shihāb al-Dīn al-Maqdisī, *op. cit.*, Ms. p. 70; and see about the building of the mosque of Mecca and the mosque of Jerusalem ib., pp. 53-57; and see the discussion about this subject Ibn Ẓahīra, *op. cit.*, p. 20 and Taqī al-Dīn ʿAbd al-Malik b. Abi l-Munā, *op. cit.*, p. 96 and the commentary of al-Suyūṭī on the *Sunan* of al-Nasāʾī, Cairo 1930, III, 2; al-Nawawī, *op. cit.*, p. 72; al-Zarkashī, *op. cit.*, pp. 29-31.

87 Al-Wāsiṭī, *op. cit.*, f. 45a. 58a; al-Nuwayrī, *op. cit.*, I, 335; Shams al-Dīn al-Suyūṭī, *op. cit.*, f. 15b; Shihāb al-Dīn al-Maqdisī, *op. cit.*, Ms., p. 143; al-Suyūṭī : *al-Durr al-manthūr*, I, 136 inf.; (but see *ib*, I, 137 sup. : the Kaʿba will be brought to the grave of the Prophet, scil. in Medina —; the Kaʿba promises to intercede for people who visited her, asking the Prophet to intercede for people who did not visit her). About the intercession of the mosque of al-Kūfa for the people praying in this mosque see al-Majlisī, *op. cit.*, XXII, 86 (lithogr. ed.).

88 Shihāb al-Dīn al-Maqdisī, *op. cit.*, Ms. p. 52; al-Rabaʿī, *op. cit.*, p. 38; al-Manīnī, *op. cit.*, p. 106.

89 ʿAbd al-Razzāq, *op. cit.*, f. 34a, sup.; al-Suyūṭī : *al-Durr al-manthūr*, I, 130, 133, 134; al-Azraqī : *Akhbār Makka*, Mecca 1352 AH, I, 18, 26; al-Fāsī, *op. cit.*, I, 93; al-Bakrī : *Muʿjam mā ʾstaʿjam*, s.v. al-Jūdī; Shihāb al-Dīn al-Maqdisī, *op. cit.*, Ms. p. 17; and see H. Busse : *Der Islam und die biblischen Kultstätten*, « Der Islam », 1966, p. 121; Yāqūt : *Muʿjam al-buldān*, s.v. Thabīr; and see G. E. von Grunebaum : *Muhammadan Festivals*, p. 19 sup.

Wariqān, Raḍwā)[90]. The mountain of al-Khalīl (Ḥebron), Lubnān, al-Ṭūr and al-Jūdī will on the Day of Resurrection be brought to Jerusalem, set at her corners and God will put his throne upon them to judge the people of Paradise and those of the Hell[91]. Al-Ṭā'if was originally a place in Palestine — says a tradition attributed to Ibn 'Abbās; it was removed by God and placed in the spot of al-Ṭā'if of today[92]. Three angels are entrusted with the guard of the three mosques: one is entrusted with the mosque of Mecca, one with that of Medina and one with al-Aqṣā[93].

The shared sanctity of the mosques gave rise to traditions which talk of the merits of performing devotions distributed between them. To the Prophet is attributed the following utterance: « Whoever goes on pilgrimage or on a pious visit from al-Aqṣā to the mosque of Mecca — the faults he has committed and those he may later commit will be covered for him and he shall be granted Paradise ».[94]. On the authority of Ibn 'Abbās the following saying is related: « Whoever makes pilgrimage and prays in the mosques of Medina and al-Aqṣā in the same year, he shall be absolved from his faults as he was on the day his mother bore him »[95]. A group of people — Ibn al-Firkāḥ reports, quoting from the book of Ibn al-Murajjā — used to stay in 'Abbādān[96] during the month of Ramaḍān, then they

[90] Aḥmad b. 'Abd al-Ḥamīd al-'Abbāsī, *op. cit.*, p. 135; al-Majlisī, *op. cit.*, Tehran 1358 AH, XIII, 224; and see ib., p. 217, no. 9.

[91] Asad b. Mūsā, *op. cit.*, p. XXI; Ch. D. Matthews: *Palestine*, p. 120.

[92] Yāqūt: *Mu'jam al-buldān*, s.v. al-Ṭā'if; Ibn al-Mujāwir: *Descriptio Arabiae Meridionalis*, ed. O. Löfgren, Leiden 1951, I, 22.

[93] Shams al-Dīn al-Suyūtī, *op. cit.*, f. 16b; al-Suyūṭī: *al-La'ālī al-maṣnū'a*, I, 92.

[94] Al-Bayhaqī, *op. cit.*, V, 30; Ch. D. Matthews: *Palestine*, p. 13; Abū Ṭālib al-Makkī, *op. cit.*, IV, 103; al-Nuwayrī, *op. cit.*, I, 339; al-Zarkashi, *op. cit.*, p. 289; al-Muttaqī al-Hindī, *op. cit.*, XIII, 250, no. 1380; *ib.*, V, 2, no. 19; *ib.* p. 5, no. 47, 48; comp. *ib.* XIII, 264, no. 1460: the pilgrimage started from 'Umān (for Mecca) is better than two pilgrimages from any other place.

[95] Shihāb al-Dīn al-Maqdisī, *op. cit.*, Ms. p. 126; Ch. D. Matthews; *Palestine*, p. 12; idem, JPOS, XV, 61; al-Zarkashī, *op. cit.*, p. 296.

[96] See on 'Abbadān Yāqūt: *Mu'jam al-buldān*, s.v. 'Abbādān:... *fīhi qaumun munqaṭi'ūna, 'alayhim waqfun fī tilka l-jazīrati yu'ṭauna ba'ḍahu wa-aktharu mawāddihim min al-nudhūr... wa-yaqṣiduhum al-mujāwirūna fī l-mawāsimi li-l-ziyārati, wa-yurwā fī faḍā'ilihā aḥādīthu ghayru thābitatin...*; Muḥ. Ṭāhir b. 'Ali al-Hindi: *Tadhkirat al-mauḍū'āt*, Cairo 1343 AH, p. 120:... two gates open in this world for Paradise are 'Abbādān and Qazwīn; the first place which believed in Muḥammad was 'Abbādān...; and see Abū Ṭālib al-Makkī, *op. cit.*, IV, 103.

would go to Mecca on pilgrimage and come to Jerusalem for prayer [97]. « Whoever performs the pilgrimage to the Ka'ba and does not visit me (i.e. the grave of the Prophet in Medina) treats me harshly» — says a tradition attributed to the Prophet, told on the authority of Ibn 'Umar [98]. A tradition recorded on the authority of 'Abdallah b. Mas'ūd (or 'Abdallah b. 'Umar) contains all the three sanctuaries. The Prophet said: « He who performs the pilgrimage to Mecca and wisits my grave (in Medina) and goes forth to fight (in a holy war — *ghazā ghazwatan*) and prays for me in Jerusalem — God will not ask him about what he (failed to perform of the prescriptions) imposed on him» [99]. A *ḥadīth* attributed to the Prophet states: « He who visits me (i.e. the grave of the Prophet in Medina) and visits the grave of my father (i.e. my ancestor) Ibrāhīm (i.e. in Ḥebron) within one year — shall enter Paradise» [100]. Al-Zarkashī considers the *ḥadīth* as forged and mentions an opinion that it was transmitted only after the conquest of Jerusalem by Ṣalāḥ al-Dīn in 583 AH.

IV

With the general admission by the scholars of the *ḥadīth* about the three mosques the old controversy about the position of Jerusalem fell into oblivion. Traditions aiming at minimizing of the importance of Jerusalem were not recorded in the canonical collections of *ḥadīth*. The main concern of the scholars of Islam came to be to fight objectionable practices of *bid'a* in connection with the pilgrimage to Mecca, Medina, Jerusalem and other sanctuaries.

According to prescriptions visitors should perform the circumambulation of the Rock in the direction opposite to that prescribed for the circumambulation of the Ka'ba. The Rock should be circumambulated being on the right of the visitor [101] The *ṭawāf* around

[97] Ch. D. Matthews: *Palestine*, p. 12.

[98] al-Subkī, *op. cit.*, pp. 27-29; Muḥ. Ṭāhir al-Hindī, *op. cit.*, p. 76, 1. 3.

[99] Al-Subkī, *op. cit.*, p. 34; Muḥ. Ṭāhir al-Hindī, *op. cit.*, p. 73; al-Samnūdī: *Nuṣratu l-imāmi l-Subkī*, p. 163.

[100] al-Zarkashī, *op. cit.*, p. 296; al-Jarrāḥī, *op. cit.*, II, 251, no. 2490; al-Nawawī, *op. cit.*, p. 84; Abū Shāma: *al-Bā'ith 'alā inkār al-bida' wa-l-ḥawādith*, ed. Muh. Fu'ād Minqāra, Cairo 1955, p. 72.

[101] Shams al-Dīn al-Suyūṭī, *op. cit.*, f. 21b; J. W. Hirschberg: *The sources of Moslem traditions concerning Jerusalem*, Rocznik Orientalistyczny, XVII, (1951-52), p. 317; R. Kriss - H. Kriss-Heinrich: *Volksglaube im Bereiche des Islams* Wiesbaden 1960, I, 144.

the Rock is a *bid'a*[102]. Similarly the *ṭawāf* around the grave of the Prophet was forbidden[103]. The visitor in the Dome of the Rock has to put his hand on the Rock, but it is forbidden to kiss the Rock[104]. It is as well forbidden to kiss the grave of the Prophet[105]. It is forbidden to pray behind the Rock towards Mecca in order to combine the *qibla* of the Rock and the *qibla* of Mecca[106]. It is forbidden to kiss the stones of the building or to kiss the stones of the Cave, as only one stone in the world is recommended to touch and to kiss: the stone of the Ka'ba. Forbidden is as well to imitate the *ḥajj*[107].

Al-'Abdarī reports about a curiuos instance of *bid'a* performed by the visitors of the sanctuary of Jerusalem : people, men and women alike, come to a place called « the navel of the earth », expose their navels and press them towards this spot, exhibiting in this fashion their naked bodies[108].

About similar customs in Mecca reports al-Nawawī : « some wicked deceivers claimed that a place in the wall surrounding the Ka'ba, opposite the door of the Ka'ba, was « *al-'urwa al-wuthqā* ». Those people led them fraudently to believe that whoever touched it was in possession of the *'urwa al-wuthqā*. As the spot was a high one the people would climb on the back of each other in order to touch it and it would come about that women ascended on the backs of men, thus mixing together and touching each other. Another *bid'a* was the custom of the touching of the 'navel of the earth' : a nail in the mosque of Mecca was claimed to be « the navel of the earth » and common people would swarm to this spot, uncovering their navels and pressing them towards the « navel of the earth »[109].

Al-Ṭurṭūshī tells about the celebration of the « Day of 'Arafa » in the mosque of Jerusalem. People from Jerusalem and neighbouring

102 Al-'Abdarī, *op. cit.*, IV. 243.

103 Al-Nawawī, *op. cit.*, p. 81.

104 Shams al-Dīn al-Suyūṭī, *op. cit.*, f. 21b.

105 Al-Nawawī, *op. cit.*, p. 81; but see a contradictory opinion Shihāb al-Dīn al-Khafājī, *op. cit.*, III, 577 inf. :... *wa-lā yamassahu bi-shay'in min jasadihi fa-lā yuqabbilhu, fa-yukrahu massuhu wa-taqbīluhu wa-ilṣāqu ṣadrihi li-annahu tarku adabin; wa-kadhā kullu ḍarīḥin yukrahu fīhi dhālika; wa-hādhā amrun ghayru mujma'in 'alayhi, wa-li-dhā qāla Aḥmadu wa-l-Ṭabariyyu : lā ba'sa bi-taqbīlihi wa- ltizāmihi.*

106 Al-'Abdarī, *op. cit.*, IV, 243.

107 L. A. Mayer : *A sequel to Mujīr ad-Dīn's Chronicle*, JPOS 1931, pp. 9-10 (=93-94)

108 Al-'Abdarī, *op. cit.*, IV, 243 inf.

109 Al-Nawawī, *op. cit.*, p. 66; Abū Shāma, *op. cit.*, p. 71.

villages stood in prayer facing Mecca, raising their voices in the *du'ā*, just as if they were attending the *wuqūf* of 'Arafa. The common belief was that the preformance of four *wuqūfs* in Jerusalem was equivalent to the pilgrimage to Mecca [110].

A *bid'a* innovation started in al-Aqṣā in 448 AH. It was introduced by a man from Nablus called Abū l-Ḥamrā'. He prayed the *ṣalāt al-raghā'ib* in the mosque, people joined him and it became a practice, almost a *sunna* [111].

Another *bid'a* reported about was the prayer of *rajab* (*ṣalāt rajab*) introduced in the mosque of Jerusalem in 480 AH [112].

Muslim scholars condemned severely the *bid'a* of songs and dances performed in al-Khalīl (Hebron) after the afternoon-prayer and called « *naubat al-Khalīl* » [113]. Ibn Ḥajar al-Haythamī reports about « shameful actions », *qabā'iḥ*, committed during the *ṭawāf* of the Ka'ba, the kissing of the Black Stone and during the maulid-festivals in Mecca [114].

But the persevering struggle of the orthodox scholars against these innovations failed. *Bid'as* and beliefs about miraculous properties of sanctuaries and graves spread nevertheless widely among the common people.

Ibn Taymiyya waged in vain his campaign againsτ the sanctity of the Rock in Jerusalem, trying to prove that only Jews and some Christians adored the Rock (*wa-kadhālika l-ṣakhratu, innamā yu'aẓẓimuhā l-Yahūdu wa-ba'ḍu l-Naṣārā*); none of the Companions of the Prophet or the *Tābi'ūn* had adored the Rock [115]. Muslim tradition claimed that God ascended the Heaven from the Rock [116] and that it was God's dwelling for forty years [117]. This was strongly refuted

110 Abū Bakr al-Ṭurṭūshī, *op. cit.*, 116-17 (quoted by Abū Shāma, *op. cit.*, p. 22); and see S. D. Goitein, *op. cit.*, p. 137 (about *ta'rīf*); Ibn Taymiyya . *Majmū'at al-rasā'il*, II, 57 : ... *au an yusāfira ilayhā li-yu'arrifa bihā 'ashiyyata 'Arafa...*

111 Abū Bakr al-Ṭurṭūshī, *op. cit.*, p. 121 (quoted by abū Shāma, *op. cit.*, p. 24).

112 Al-Ṭurtūshī, *op. cit.*, p. 122.

113 Al-'Abdarī, *op. cit.*, IV, 245-46; and see the passage against the pilgrimage to al-Khalīl in Ibn Taymiyya's *Minhāj al-sunna* I, 335-36.

114 Ibn Ḥajar al-Haythamī : *al-Ni'ma al-Kubrā*, f. 3a-3b.

115 Ibn Taymiyya : *Majmū'at al-rasā'il*, II, 58 (quoted in Jamāl al-Dīn al-Qāsimī : *Iṣlāḥ al-masājid min al-bida'i wa-l-'awā'id*, Cairo 1341 AH, pp. 214-17.

116 Al-Wāsiṭī, *op. cit.*, f. 51a-b; al-Nuwayrī, *op. cit.*, I, 336-37 (quoting al-Wāsiṭī); and see al-Majlisī, *op. cit.* VIII, 574 (lithogr. ed.).

117 'Ubāda b. al-Ṣāmit swore : *lā, wa-lladhī kānat ṣakhratu bayti l-maqdisi lahu maqāman arba'īna sanatan*, when arguing about something with 'Abdallah b. Mas'ūd, al-Wāsiṭī, *op. cit.*, f. 51a.

by Shīʿī [118] and Ibāḍī traditions alike [119], but this refutation seems to have had no effect.

Ibn Taymiyya tried to explain that there was no *ḥaram* in Jerusalem or in Khalīl and that there did only exist three *ḥarams* : the *ḥaram* of Mecca, the *ḥaram* of Medina and the *ḥaram* of Wajj (recognized only by some Muslim scholars) [120]. This attempt was also set at nought; the sanctuary of Jerusalem is called till the present day *al-Ḥaram al-Sharīf* and that of al-Khalīl is called *al-Ḥaram al-Ibrāhīmī*.

Thus it seems that the tradition about the three mosques, a very early one itself and one whose aim was to exclude the claims for pilgrimage to other shrines, was only granted general recognition following a period of internal struggle at the beginning of the second century. During that period the status of Jerusalem was disputed by certain orthodox circles while other sanctuaries vied for acceptance as places of pilgrimage.

The tradition about the three mosques was granted the consensus of the orthodox scholars, while at the same time elements of popular belief left their indelible mark on the rituals of pilgrimage to these sanctuaries.

Jerusalem,
The Hebrew University,
Institute of Asian and African Studies.

118 See Warrām b. Abī Firās al-Mālikī al-Ashtarī : *Tanbīh al-Khawāṭir*, al-Najaf 1964, pp. 260-61.

119 Al-Rabīʿ b. Ḥabīb : *al-Jāmiʿ al-ṣaḥīḥ*, III, 39.

120 Ibn Taymiyya : *Majmūʿat al-rasāʾil*, II, 60.

ADDITIONAL NOTES

Note 1:

Ibn Abī Shayba, *al-Muṣannaf*, Hyderabad 1390/1970, IV, 65-7; Amin Maḥmūd Khaṭṭāb, *Fatḥ al-malik al-maʿbūd, takmilat al-manhal al-ʿadhb al-maurūd, sharḥ sunan abī dāwūd*, Cairo 1394/1974, II, 234; Aḥmad b. ʿAbdallah, Muḥibbu l-Dīn al-Ṭabarī, *al-Qirā li-qāṣidi ummi l-qurā*, ed. Muṣtafā l-Saqā, Cairo 1390/1970, p.655; al-Fākihī, *Taʾrīkh Makka*, Ms. Leiden Or. 463, fols.353a-b, 354a; al-Khuwārizmī, *Mukhtaṣar ithārati l-targhīb wa-l-tashwīq ilā l-masājidi l-thalātha wa-ilā l-bayti l-ʿatīq*, Ms. Br. Mus. Or. 4584, fol.22a; al-Isfarāʾīnī, *Zubdat al-aʿmāl*, Ms. Br. Mus. Or. 3034, fol.73b, 113a; Ibn al-Athīr, *Usd al-ghāba*, Cairo 1280, II, 55; al-Dhahabī, *Tadhkirat al-ḥuffāẓ*, Hyderabad 1958, I, 319; al-ʿAzīzī, *al-Sirāj al-munīr, sharḥ ʿalā l-jāmiʿ al-ṣaghīr*, Cairo 1957, III, 462; al-Azraqī, *Akhbār Makka* (ed. Wüstenfeld, Leipzig 1858) p.302.

Note 12:

And see al-Fasawī, *al-Maʿrifa wa-l-taʾrīkh*, Esad Ef. 2391, fol.88b: *...ʿan abī hurayrata qāla: ataytu l-Ṭūra fa-laqiyanī Ḥumayd b. Naḍra...;* Al-Ṭayālisī, *al-Musnad*, Hyderabad 1321, p.192, no. 1348; Ibn ʿAbd al-Barr, *al-Istīʿāb*, ed. al-Bijāwī, I, 405; Ibn al-Athīr, *Usd al-ghāba*, I, 201.

Note 15:

Ibn Abī Shayba, *op.cit.*, II, 374-5, IV, 65.

note 16:

Cf. Ibn Qutayba, *Tafsīr gharīb al-Qur'ān*, ed. Aḥmad Ṣaqr, Cairo 1958, p.424: *al-Ṭūru jabalun bi-Madyana kullima ʿindahu Mūsā ʿalayhi l-salāmu.*

note 20:

al-Suyūṭī, *al-Durr al-manthūr*, II, 54.

note 30:

Al-Isfarāʾīnī, *op.cit.*, fol.73b; al-Bukhārī, *al-Taʾrīkh al-kabīr*, Hyderabad 1380, III, II, no. 2066; al-Azraqī, *op.cit.*, p.302.

note 35:

al-Azraqī, *op.cit.*, p.302.

note 36:

al-Fākihī, *Taʾrīkh Makka*, Ms. Leiden Or. 463, f. 353b; al-Azraqī, *op.cit.*, p.302.

note 39:

A similar saying is attributed to the Companion of the Prophet, Ḥudhayfa: *lau sirtu ḥattā lā yakūna baynī wa-bayna bayti l-maqdisi illā farsakhan au farsakhayni mā ataytuhu wa-mā aḥbabtu an ātiyahu.* (Ibn Abī Shayba, *op.cit.*, II, 374). More explicit is the utterance traced back to Abū Dharr: *la-an uṣalliya ʿalā ramlatin ḥamrāʾa aḥabbu ilayya min an uṣalliya fī bayti l-maqdisi* (ib.) Kaʿb stated that an *ʿumra* is preferrable to a journey to Jerusalem (al-Fākihī, *op.cit.*, f. 327b, 1.17).

note 48:

See Ibn Ḥajar al-Haythamī, *op.cit.*, III, 297 (new ed.); Ibn Ẓahīra, *op. cit.*, p.334.

note 50:

Comp. al-Zamakhsharī, *Rabī' al-abrār*, Ms. Br. Mus., Or. 6511, f.77b: *al-biqā'u tusharrafu wa-tufaḍḍalu bi-muqāmi l-ṣāliḥīna l-akhyāri; wa-laqad sharrafa llāhu bayta l-maqdisi bi-muqāmi l-anbiyā'i, wa-l-madīnata bi-hijrati rasūli llāhi ṣallā llāhu 'alayhi wa-sallama wa-aṣḥābihi raḍiya llāhu 'anhum.*

note 52:

al-Baḥrānī, *al-Ḥadā'iq al-nāḍira*, ed. Muḥ. Taqī al-Ayrawānī, Najaf 1389, VII, 315-317; al-Suyūṭī, *al-Durr al-manthūr*, II, 53-54.

note 59:

An Ismā'īlī tradition records the reward of hundred thousand prayers for a prayer in the mosque of Mecca, ten thousand prayers for a prayer in that of Medina and thousand prayers for a prayer in Jerusalem. (*al-Majālis al-mustanṣiriyya*, ed. Muḥ. Kāmil Ḥusayn, Cairo, n.d., p.52).

note 60:

al-Suyūṭī, *al-Durr al-manthūr*, II, 53 inf., Al-Khuwārizmī, *op.cit.*, fol. 23a.

Note 63:

See the utterance of the Prophet as recorded in al-Daylamī's *Firdaus*, Ms. Chester-Beatty, 3037, fol.173a, 1.3: *al-madīnatu afḍalu min makkata;* and see al-Khuwārizmī, *op.cit.*, fols. 30b-31a: *thumma khtalafū fī anna makkata afḍalu au al-madīnatu, fa-dhahaba ba'ḍu l-ṣaḥābati (r) ilā tafḍīli l-madīnati 'alā makkata wa-huwa qaulu mālikin wa-akthari l-madaniyyin (r); wa-dhahaba abū ḥanīfata wa-l-shāfi'ī wa-aḥmadu (r) ilā tafḍīli makkata 'alā l-madīnati; ammā ḥujjatu l-ṭā'ifati l-ūlā fa-mā ruwiya anna l-nabiyya (ṣ) lammā kharaja min makkata wa-tawajjaha ilā l-madīnati qāla: ilāhī, inna ahla makkata akhrajūnī min aḥabbi l-biqāʿi ilayya fa-anzilnī ilā aḥabbi l-biqāʿi ilayka, fa-anzalahu bi-l-madīna; wa-lā shakka anna maḥbūba llāhi (taʿālā) afḍalu min maḥbūbi l-nabiyyi (ṣ), wa-li-hādhā khtāra l-muqāma fīhā ilā an māta wa-dufina bihā (ṣ); wa-ammā ḥujjatu l-ṭāʾifati l-thāniyati fa-qauluhu (ṣ) ṣalātun fī masjidi l-madīnati bi-ʿasharati ālāf ṣalātin, wa-ṣalātun fī l-masjidi l-aqṣā bi-alfi ṣalātin, wa-ṣalātun fī l-masjidi l-ḥarāmi bi-miʾati alfi ṣalātin; fa-lau anna ma-kkata afḍalu la-mā juʿilat al-ṣalātu bi-l-madīnati bi-ʿasharati ālāf ṣalātin wa-bi-makkata bi-miʾati alfi ṣalāt; wa-qad taqaddamat al-aḥādīthu l-dāllatu ʿalā taḍʿīfi l-ajri fī l-masājidi l-thalātha*...etc.; and see al-Fākihī, *op.cit.*, fol. 383b, inf,: (ʿUmar asking ʿAbdallāh b. ʿAyyāsh): ... *fa-qāla: anta l-qāʾilu la-makkatu khayrun min al-madīnati, fa-qāla ʿabdu llāhi: hiya ḥaramu llāhi wa-amnuhu wa-fīhā baytuhu; fa-qāla ʿumaru (r) lā aqūlu fī bayti llāhi wa-lā fī ḥaramihi shayʾan; thumma nṣarafa ʿabdu llāhi;* and see Ibn al-Nadīm, *al-Fihrist*, Cairo 1348, p.283 (a compilation by al-Abharī *Kitāb faḍl al-madīna ʿalā makka*), p.188, 1.11 (= p.202). See the tradition in which the obligation is restricted to the mosque of Mecca: Ibn Saʿd, *al-Ṭabaqāt*, VI, 115 inf.: *samiʿa ʿumara ya-qūlu: lā tushaddu l-riḥālu illā ilā l-bayti l-ʿatīqi* (on the authority of ʿAbdallah b. abī l-Hudhayl); Ibn Abī Shayba, *op.cit.*, II, 375; al-Bukhārī, *al-Taʾrīkh al-kabīr*, III, I, No.727 (=V, 222-3):... ʿabd allāh b. abī l-hudhayl: *samiʿtu ʿumara bna l-khaṭṭābi khaṭīban bi-l-rauḥāʾi: lā tashuddū l-riḥāla illā ilā l-bayti l-ʿatīqi; wa-qāla l-nabiyyu (ṣ) illā ilā thalāthatin; wa-ḥadīthu l-nabiyyi (ṣ) aulā;* al-Fākihī, *op.cit.*, fol. 354a; and see the story of the speech of Marwān: al-Haythamī, *Majmaʿ al-zawāʾid*, III, 298-299 (new ed.) And see *ib.* the utterance of the Prophet reported by Rāfiʿ: *al-madīnatu khayrun min makkata.*

note 78:

See al-Qushayrī, *al-Mi'rāj*, ed. Abū Ḥasan ʿAbd al-Qādir, Cairo 1964, p.103: Jerusalem was chosen by God as the place of the *Mi'rāj* because He wanted that the Prophet might see the graves of the prophets. Jerusalem is the abode of the prophets; God wanted that the Prophet might follow their path. And see al-Shaukānī, *al-Fawāʾid al-majmūʿa*, p.441 about the prayer of the Prophet in Hebron and Betlehem (a forged tradition).

note 79:

al-ʿAyyāshī, *Tafsīr*, Ms. India office, f.166a-b, 208a-b; al-Baḥrānī, *op. cit.*, VII, 315 inf., 321.

note 80:

About the virtues of the mosque of Kūfa see al-Baḥrānī, *op.cit.*, VII, 316-326.

note 81:

al-Tauḥīdī, *al-Baṣāʾir wa-l-dhakhāʾir*, ed. Ibrāhīm al-Kaylānī, Damascus 1964, III, 613-614; Ibn Abī Shayba, *op.cit.*, f.241b.

note 82:

al-ʿAyyāshī, *op.cit.*, f.209a.

note 83:

Ibn Bābūyah al-Qummī, *al-Khiṣāl*, ed. ʿAlī Akbar al-Ghaffārī, Tehran 1389, I, 143, no.166; al-Majlisī, *Biḥār al-anwār*, XCIX, 240.

note 84:

See Ibn al-Jauzī, *al-Mauḍūʿāt*, ed. ʿAbd al-Raḥmān Muḥ. ʿUthmān, Cairo 1966, II, 51; cf. al-Khuwārizmī, *op.cit.*, fol.26a: *arbaʿu madāʾina fī l-dunyā min al-jannati: makkatu wa-l-madīnatu wa-baytu l-maqdisi wa-dimashq.*

note 86:

See *Durar al-Kalām*, p.26: ... *fa-min ayna rakibahā nūḥun. qāla: min al-ʿirāqi. qāla: wa-ayna balaghat. qāla: ṭāfat bi-l-ʿatīq usbūʿan wa-bi-l-bayti al-muqaddasi usbūʿan fa-stawat ʿalā l-jūdī,* al-Majlisī, *op.cit.*, LX, 251 ; Al-Khuwārizmī, *op.cit.*, fol.26a.

note 87:

See al-Fākihī, *op.cit.*, f.328, inf.: ... *tuḥsharu l-Kaʿbatu ilā bayti l-maqdisi mutaʿalliqan bi-astāriha man ḥajja wa-ʿtamara.*

note 89:

Al-Shiblī, *Maḥāsin al-wasāʾil fī maʿrifati l-awāʾil,* Ms. Br. Mus., Or. 1530, fol.25b, 32b; al-Isfarāʾīnī, *op.cit.*, fol.65b (and see *ib.* other versions); Abū Isḥāq al-Ḥarbī, *Kitāb al-manāsik,* ed. Ḥamad al-Jāsir, al-Riyāḍ 1389/1969, p.481; al-Ṣāliḥī, *Subul al-hudā wa-l-rashād fī sīrat khayri l-ʿibād,* ed. Muṣṭafā ʿAbd al-Wāḥid, Cairo 1392/1972, I, 183; Ibn Ṭāwūs, *Saʿd al-suʿūd,* Najaf 1950, p.37.

note 90:

Al-Shaukānī, *al-Fawāʾid,* p.445, no.9; Ibn al-Jauzī, *al-Mauḍūʿāt,* I, 120-121; al-Fākihī, *op.cit.*, f.483b.

note 92:

Al-Ṭabarī, *Tafsīr*, ed. Shākir, III, 52; al-ʿAyyāshī, *op.cit.*, f.14b (=I, 60 of the printed ed.); al-Majlisī, *op.cit.*, XII, 109, nos. 30-31; Ibn Bābūyah, *ʿIlal al-sharāʾiʿ*, Najaf 1966, p.442; comp. Baḥshal, *Taʾrīkh Wāsiṭ,* ed. G. ʿAwwād, Baghdād 1967, p.36: *lammā kāna yaumu l-ṭūfāni nqaṭaʿat arḍun min al-arḍi l-muqaddasati fa-ṣārat ilā mā hāhunā...;* and comp. al-Majlisī, *op.cit.*, LX, 213: ... *wa-huwa* (i.e. Qumm) *qiṭʿatun min bayti l-maqdisi;* and comp. the tradition recorded by al-Fākihī, *op.cit.*, f.477b according to which the *rukn* was hidden in the time of the Deluge in the mountain of Abū Qubays (and see this tradition in Ibn Ẓahīra, *op.cit.*, 340-341); and see al-Majlisī, *op.cit.*, LX, 251: the mountain of Abū Qubays sheltered during the Deluge the Temple of Jerusalem and the Rock. And comp. Baḥshal, *op.cit.*, p.35: when the Temple of Jerusalem was destroyed by Bukhtanaṣṣar all the places on the earth wept, but Kaskar wept more than any other place; God promised to reward it by establishing of a mosque in it; it is said to be the mosque of Wāsiṭ; and see al-Masʿūdī, *Ithbāt al-waṣiyya*, al-Najaf 1374/1955, p.39 (al-Ṭāʾif removed by God to the Arabic peninsula); al-Suyūṭī, *al-Durr al-manthūr*, I, 124 (the tradition on al-Ṭāʾif); Abū Isḥāq al-Ḥarbì, *op.cit.*, pp.482-3 (the *rukn* hidden in Abū Qubays); al-Quḍāʿī, *Taʾrīkh*, Ms. Bodley, Pococke 270, fol.6b (Shīth buried in the cave of Abū Qubays); Anonymous, *The history of the prophets*, Ms. Br. Mus., Or. 1510, fol.3a (the first mountain created on earth: Abū Qubays); and see Abū l-Ḥasan al-Iṣfahānī al-Gharawī, *Muqaddimat tafsīr mirʾāt al-anwār*, Qumm 1393, pp.222-3 (al-Najaf is a part of Mt. Sīnā); al-Ṣāliḥī, *op.cit.*, I, 213 (on the night of the fifteenth of Shaʿbān the well of Sulwān joins Zamzam).

note 93:

See al-Shaukānī, *al-Fawāʾid*, p.465; Ibn al-Jauzī, *al-Mauḍūʿāt*, I, 147.

note 94:

Al-Fākihī, *op.cit.*, fol.324a, inf.; al-Muḥibb al-Ṭabarī, *al-Qirā*, pp.104-5; see Nāṣir al-Dīn al-Albānī, *Silsilat al-aḥādīth al-ḍaʿīfa wa-l-mauḍūʿa*, Damascus 1384, I, III, no.211.

note 96:

And see al-Rāfiʿī, *al-Tadwīn bi-dhikri ahli l-ʿilmi bi-qazwīn*, Ms. LALELI 2010, f.3a): *qāla rasūlu llāhi ṣallā llāhu ʿalayhi wa-sallama: bābāni maftūḥāni fī l-jannati: ʿabbādān wa-qazwīn; qulnā ʿabbādān muḥdathun, qāla: wa-lakinnahā awwalu buqʿatin āmanat biʿīsa bni maryama.* (See f.7a: Qazwīn and ʿAsqalān are from the cities of Paradise; and see al-Majlisī, *op.cit.*, LX, 229 the utterance of the Prophet, stating that Qazwīn is one of the doors of Paradise; and comp. the saying of Jaʿfar al-Ṣādiq that Rayy, Qazwīn and Sāwa are cursed cities, al-Majlisī, *ib.* And see the traditions about the sanctity of Qazwīn and its virtues in Rāfiʿī, *op.cit.*; and see the opinion of Yāqūt about these traditions in his *Muʿjam al-buldān*, s.v. Qazwīn).

note 99:

Al-Shaukānī, *al-Fawāʾid*, p.109, no.18.

note 100:

See al-Khuwārizmī, *op.cit.*, fol.22b, sup.: ... *wa-fī ḥadīthin ākhara ʿan rasūli llāhi (ṣ) qāla: lā tushaddu l-riḥālu illā ilā arbaʿati masājida: masjidi l-ḥarāmi wa-masjidī hādhā wa-l-masjidi l-aqṣā wa-masjidi l-khalīl ʿalayhi l-salām.* The mosque of Hebron, attached in this ḥadīth to the three most venerated mosques, got the highest rank of sanctity; Ibn Taymiyya, *Majmūʿa*, II, 339; al-Nawawī, *Fatāwā*, Cairo 1352 , p.125.

note 101:

Al-Khuwārizmī, *op.cit.*, fol.25a.

XIV

Ḥaddithū 'an banī isrā'īla wa-lā ḥaraja

A Study of an early tradition

This widely current tradition was variously interpreted by Muslim scholars. They differed in their opinions about the significance of the words of this *ḥadīth*, its intent and its implications. The core of the discussion lay in fact in the problem whether it was lawful to turn to Jewish and Christian sources for guidance, to study Jewish and Christian compilations and to incorporate certain aspects from them into the Muslim cultural tradition and belief. Scrutiny of some of these discussions may help to elucidate the tendencies of the various religious groups in Islam and assist us in gaining a deeper insight into the attitudes of Muslim scholars.

I

The tradition *Ḥaddithū 'an banī isrā'īl* was considered by Goldziher as one which is opposed to the trend of Muslim orthodox scholars who watched with reluctance the influence of Jewish Aggada and of Christian legends on Muslim tradition.[1] The transmission of this *ḥadīth*, says Goldziher, serves as evidence of the controversy among the scholars of the second century about the transmission of Jewish lore. The earliest source in which this tradition is recorded is the *Risāla* of al-Shāfi'ī (d. 204).[2]

This tradition is also reported in the *Jāmi'* of Ma'mar b. Rāshid (d. 154),[3] and in 'Abd al-Razzāq's *Muṣannaf* with the following *isnād*: 'Abd al-Razzāq > al-Auzā'ī[4] > Ḥassān b. 'Aṭiyya[5] > Abū Kabsha[6] > 'Abdallah b. 'Amr b. al-'Āṣ. The Prophet said: "Transmit on my authority, be it even one verse (from the Qur'ān), narrate (traditions) concerning the Children of Israel and there

1 *Muhammedanische Studien* (Halle, 1890), II, 137, note 3; and see G. Vajda, "Juifs et Musulmans selon le *Ḥadīṯ*", *JA* CLXXIX (1937), 115–120; S. D. Goitein, *Banū Isrā'īl*, *EI*2.

2 *Mélanges Judéo-Arabes*, IX, "Isrā'īliyyāt", *REJ* XLIV (1902) 64, note 2.

3 Ms. Feyzullah 541, fol. 59b, inf. (See F. Sezgin, *GAS*, I, 291).

4 See on him F. Sezgin, *GAS*, I, 516.

5 See on him Ibn Ḥajar, *Tahdhīb al-tahdhīb* (Hyderabad, 1327), II, 251, no. 460; al-Dhahabī, *Mīzān al-i'tidāl*, ed. 'Ali Muḥammad al-Bijāwī (Cairo, 1382/1963), I, 479, no. 1809.

6 See on him Ibn Ḥajar, *Tahdhīb*, XII, 210, no. 974.

is nothing objectionable (in that); he who tells a lie on my authority — let him take his place in Hell."[7]

In the *Musnad* of Aḥmad b. Ḥanbal[8] this tradition is recorded with the same chain of transmitters; it contains however a slight variant: *wa-man kadhaba 'alayya muta'ammidan*, "intentionally".[9]

[7] Ms. Murad Molla 604, fol. 113b: *ballighū 'annī wa-lau āyatan wa-ḥaddithū 'an banī isrā'īla wa-lā ḥaraja fa-man kadhaba 'alayya kadhibatan fa-l-yatabawwa' maq'adahu min al-nāri*. And see this tradition: al-Ṭabarānī, *al-Mu'jam al-ṣaghīr*, ed. 'Abd al-Raḥmān Muḥammad 'Uthmān (Cairo, 1388/1968), I, 166; al-Fasawī, *al-Ma'rifa wa-l-ta'rikh*, Ms. Esad Ef. 2391, fol. 162b; al-Nuwayri, *Nihāyat al-arab* (Cairo [reprint] 1964), XIV, 182; Abū Nu'aym, *Ḥilyat al-auliyā'* (Cairo, 1351/1932), VI, 78.

[8] Ed. Aḥmad Muḥammad Shākir (Cairo, 1953), XI, 127, no. 6888; cf. al-Bayhaqī, *Ma'rifat al-sunan wa-l-āthār*, ed. Aḥmad Ṣaqr (Cairo, 1389/1968), I, 48–51.

[9] See about the tradition *man kadhaba 'alayya*: Ibn al-Jauzī, *Kitāb al-mauḍū'āt*, ed. 'Abd al-Raḥmān Muḥammad 'Uthman (Cairo, 1386/1966), I, 55–98; and see *ibid.*, p. 63 the remark of Wahb b. Jarīr: *wa-llāhi, mā qāla "muta'ammidan", wa-antum taqūlūna "muta'ammidan"*; cf. al-Khaṭīb al-Baghdādī, *Taqyīd al-'ilm*, ed. Youssef Eche (Damascus, 1949), p. 29: *wa-man kadhaba 'alayya; qāla hammāmun: aḥsibuhu qāla "muta'ammidan"... fa-l-yatabawwa'...*; cf. J. Goldziher, *Muh. St.*, II, 132 (see notes 3–4); and see Aḥmad b. Ḥanbal, *op. cit.*, IV, nos. 2675, 2976; V, nos. 3694, 3801, 3814, 3847; II, nos. 584, 629, 630, 903, 1000–1001, 1075, 1291; I, nos. 326, 469, 507; VI, nos. 4338, 4742; VII, nos. 5232, 5291; IX, nos. 6309, 6478; X, nos. 6592, 6593. And see an interesting setting of this utterance *ibid.*, VI, no. 4156: *jama'anā rasūlu llāhi (s) wa-naḥnu arba'ūna, fa-kuntu fī ākhiri man atāhu, qāla: innakum manṣūrūna wa-muṣībuna wa-maftūḥun lakum, fa-man adraka dhālika fa-l-yattaqi llāha wa-l-ya'mur bi-l-ma'rūfi, wa-l-yanha an al-munkari, wa-man kadhaba 'alayya muta'ammidan...*; and see a remarkable version *ibid.*, V, no. 3025: *ittaqū l-ḥadītha 'annī illā mā 'alimtum; qāla: wa-man kadhaba 'alā l-qur'āni bi-ghayri 'ilmin fa-l-yatabawwa'...*; cf. al-Daylamī, *al-Firdaus*, Ms. Chester Beatty 3037, fol. 27a: *ittaqū l-ḥadītha 'annī illā mā 'alimtum, fa-innahu man kadhaba 'alayya muta'ammidan...*; cf. Aḥmad b. Ḥanbal, *op. cit.*, IV, no. 2976: *...man kadhaba 'alayya... wa-man kadhaba fī l-qur'āni...*; and see *ibid.*, III, no. 2069: *...man qāla fī l-qur'āni bi-ghayri 'ilmin...*; and see Ibn Sa'd, *Ṭabaqāt* (Beirut, 1957), II, 337: *...man qāla 'alayya mā lam aqul fa-qad tabawwa'a...*; cf. al-Jarrāḥī, *Kashf al-khafā' wa-muzīl al-ilbās* (Cairo, 1352), II, 275, no. 2593; Ibn al-Athīr, *al-Nihāya*, ed. al-Zāwī-al-Ṭanāḥī (Cairo, 1963), I, 159; al-Tirmidhī, *Ṣaḥīḥ* (Cairo, 1934), XIII, 167 where this utterance is connected with the story of *khāṣif al-na'l*; al-Qundūzī, *Yanābī' al-mawadda* (Kāẓimiyya, 1385), pp. 59, 209; al-Khaṭīb al-Baghdādī, *Ta'rīkh Baghdād* (Cairo, 1349/1931), I, 265; al-Safārīnī, *Ghidhā' al-albāb* (Cairo, 1324), I, 118; Yūsuf b. Mūsā al-Ḥanafī, *al-Mu'taṣar min al- mukhtaṣar* (Hyderabad, 1362), II, 261–262; al-Ṭabarānī, *op. cit.*, II, 55; al-Fasawī *op. cit.*, fol. 158a; al-Ḥākim, *al-Mustadrak* (Hyderabad, 1342), II, 401; al-Dhahabī, *Mīzān*, IV, 393 sup.; Abū Nu'aym, *op. cit.*, II, 369; cf. Abū 'Ubayd, *Faḍā'il al-qur'ān*, Ms. Leiden, Or. 3056, fol. 3b: *...anna rasūla llāhi (ṣ) 'ahida ilaynā fī ḥajjati l-wadā'i fa-qāla: 'alaykum bi-l-qur'āni fa-innakum sa-tarji'ūna ilā qaumin yashtahūna l-ḥadītha 'annī fa-man 'aqila shay'an fa-l-yuḥaddith 'annī bihi, wa-man qāla 'alayya mā lam aqul fa-l-yatabawwa' baytan au maq'adan fī jahannam*; and see al-Suyūṭī, *al-Jāmi' al-kabīr*, Ms. al-Jazzār, Acre, I, 351: *ḥaddithū 'annī kamā sami'tum wa-lā ḥaraja, illā man akhbara 'alā llāhi kadhiban muta'ammidan li-yuḍilla bihi l-nāsa bi-ghayri 'ilmin fa-l-yatabawwa' maq'adahu min al-nāri*; Ibn 'Abd al-Ḥakam, *Futūḥ Miṣr*, ed.

Ḥaddithū ʿan banī isrāʾīla

The tradition *ḥaddithū ʿan banī isrāʾīl* forms, as we see, a part of a combined *ḥadīth* in which the Prophet bids the faithful to transmit verses (of the Qurʾān), urges them to narrate (traditions) concerning the Children of Israel and warns them not to lie while transmitting traditions on his authority. In some versions only two parts of the combined tradition are recorded: "Transmit on my authority be it even one verse and narrate concerning the Children of Israel and there is nothing objectionable (in that)."[10]

The same version as given in the *Jāmiʿ* of Maʿmar b. Rāshid, consisting of three parts, is recorded by al-Muʿāfā b. Zakariyya (d. 390) in his *al-Jalīs al-ṣāliḥ al-kāfī wa-l-anīs al-nāṣiḥ al-shāfī*,[11] and is accompanied by a comprehensive comment by the author. The Children of Israel, al-Muʿāfā argues, were specified in this tradition because of the miraculous events which had happened to them, just as the sea was specified because of the miraculous features which are in it; the permission was granted to narrate about (the wonders of) the sea with keeping away from sin of lie.[12]

The tendency apparent in this tradition to emphasize the miraculous and wonderful aspect of the stories about the Children of Israel is reflected in an enlarged version of this saying: *ḥaddithū ʿan banī isrāʾīla fa-innahu kānat fīhim aʿājību.*[13]

Al-Muʿāfā records two views about the syntax of *wa-lā ḥaraja*. These views give two quite different interpretations of the expression. According to one opinion *lā ḥaraja* is a *khabar*, a predicate; the meaning of the expression is thus: there is nothing objectionable in telling these stories. As many people, argues Muʿāfā, are reluctant to listen to these stories, this *ḥadīth* grants permission to transmit them, for refraining from transmitting them might bring about the disappearance of wisdom and might cause the roads of thought to be closed up, the means of knowledge to be interrupted, the doors of consideration and exhortation to be shut. The other view considers the phrase *wa-lā ḥaraj* as denoting a prohibition. It is equivalent with *wa-lā taḥrujū*, do not commit sin by telling stories which you know are lies deceiving people by telling these stories.[14]

C. Torrey (New Haven, 1922), 273 inf.-274: *man kadhaba ʿalayya kadhibatan mutaʿammidan...* associated with: *alā, wa-man shariba l-khamra...*

10 Ibn ʿAbd al-Barr, *Jāmiʿ bayān al-ʿilm wa-faḍlihi* (Cairo, 1346), II, 40; al-Quḍāʿī, *Shihāb al-akhbār*, Ms. Br. Mus., Or. 6496, fol. 39a.

11 Ms. Topkapi Saray, Ahmet III, 2321, fols. 3a–4a.

12 Fol. 4a: *...wa-khaṣṣa banī isrāʾīla bi-hādhā li-mā maḍā fīhim min al-aʿājībi kamā khaṣṣa l-baḥra bimā fīhi min al-aʿājībi...* (the allusion refers apparently to the well known utterance, or proverb: *ḥaddith ʿan al-baḥri wa-lā ḥaraj*; see al-Jarrāḥī, *op. cit.*, I, 352, no. 117).

13 Al-Daylamī, *op. cit.*, fol. 72a; *L ʿA*, s.v. *ḥ r j.*

14 Al-Muʿāfā, *op. cit.*, fol. 4a: *...wa-lā ḥaraja yattajihu fīhi taʾwīlāni, aḥaduhumā an yakūna khabaran maḥḍan fī maʿnāhu wa-lafẓihi, ka-annahu dhakara banī isrāʾīla wa-kānat fīhim*

The two grammatical constructions reflect in fact two conflicting interpretations of the tradition. Taking *lā ḥaraja* as *khabar* implies that there is no objection whatsoever to tell the stories about the Children of Israel whether true or invented. The motivation adduced for this permission is of interest: refraining from transmitting these stories would bring to a stop the transmission of the *ḥikma*, the wisdom, and of thoughtful scrutiny of stories concerning past people and prophets. Further it brings to light the fact that some orthodox circles disliked stories about the Children of Israel, which must have been widely current. On the other hand *lā ḥaraja*, taken as prohibition, implies an interdiction to transmit popular stories similar to those of the *quṣṣāṣ*.

Al-Khaṭīb al-Baghdādī records the same *ḥadīth* in a different context altogether. "Do not write anything on my authority except the Qur'ān" — says the Prophet. "Let one who writes anything else efface it. Narrate (traditions) concerning the Children of Israel and there is nothing objectionable (in that). He who tells lies on my behalf shall take his place in Hell."[15] In this version of the *ḥadīth* the permission to narrate stories about the Children of Israel is coupled with the interdiction to record in writing the utterances of the Prophet.

A certain difference is noticeable in the intent of a tradition recorded on the authority of Abū Hurayra. The Prophet, the tradition says, saw people writing his utterances. He rebuked them and forbade to write his *ḥadīth*. "Do you desire a book besides the book cf God"? — the Prophet asked. "The only thing that led astray the peoples preceding you was the fact that they put down in writing (things) from books beside the Book of God." Then people asked the Prophet: "Shall we transmit (traditions) on your authority?" "Transmit on my authority, said the Prophet, and there is nothing objectionable (in that); and he who lies about me intentionally let him take his seat in Hell." Those present asked: "Shall we tell the stories about the Children of Israel"? The Prophet answered: "Narrate concerning them and there is nothing objectionable (in that). Whatever you tell about them, there are always

a'ājibu, wa-kāna kathīrun min al-nāsi yanbū sam'uhum 'anhā, fa-yakūnu hādhā maqṭa'atan li-man 'indahu 'ilmun minhā an yuhadditha l-nāsa bihā; fa-rubbamā addā hādhā ilā durūsi l-ḥikmati wa-nqiṭā'i mawāddi l-fā'idati wa-nsidādi ṭarīqi i'māli l-fikrati wa-ighlāqi abwābi l-itti'āẓi wa-l-'ibrati, fa-ka-annahu qāla: laysa fī taḥadduthikum bi-mā 'alimtumūhu min dhālika ḥarajun; wa-l-ta'wīlu l-thānī an yakūna l-ma'nā fī hādhā l-nahya; fa-ka-annahu qāla: wa-lā taḥrajū bi-an tataḥaddathū bi-mā qad tabayyana lakum l-kadhibu fīhi, muḥaqqiqīna lahu au ghārrīna aḥadan bihi.

[15] *Taqyīd al-'ilm*, pp. 30–31: *lā taktubū 'annī shay'an illā l-qur'āna, fa-man kataba ghayrahu fa-l-yamḥuhu, wa-ḥaddithū 'an banī isrā'īla wa-la ḥaraja, wa-man kadhaba 'alayya fa-l-yatabawwa' maq'adahu min al-nāri.*

things which are more wonderful."[16] The permission to narrate stories about the Children of Israel is here put in opposition to the prohibition to record the traditions of the Prophet in a written form. It is however established as being on a par with the oral transmission of Prophetic traditions. Even the wording is identical: *ḥaddithū 'annī wa-lā ḥaraja* and *ḥaddithū 'an banī isrā'īla wa-lā ḥaraja*.

Of quite a different content is the tradition reported by Zayd b. Aslam and recorded in Ma'mar b. Rāshid's *Jāmi'*.[17] The Prophet said: "Do not ask the people of the Book about anything, because they will not show you the right path having already led themselves astray." We asked: "O Messenger of God, may we not narrate (stories) concerning the Children of Israel"? The Prophet answered: "Narrate, there is nothing objectionable (in that)." In this tradition the setting and the circumstances of the utterance are quite different. Here a clear line is drawn between the problem whether to consult the people of the Book in religious matters and the question whether to narrate stories from their history. It is forbidden to ask the people of the Book about problems of religion and belief; they cannot guide anyone because they themselves went astray. But it is permitted to narrate stories about them.

Ibn al-Athīr records[18] some of the interpretations already mentioned, in which the miraculous character of the stories is stressed, and he further mentions some additional ones. *Ḥaraj* denotes narrowness[19] and is applied to denote "sin" and "forbidden deeds." *Lā ḥaraja* has to be glossed: *lā ithma, lā ba'sa.*[20] The expression indicates that there is no sin, there is nothing objectionable in narrating the wonderful events which happened to the Children of Israel, even if these events might not happen to the Muslims; this does not mean, however, that one is permitted to tell lies.

Slightly different is another interpretation quoted by Ibn al-Athīr that there is no sin or objection to narrate about the Children of Israel stories as they

16 *Ibid.*, p. 34: *kharaja 'alaynā rasūlu llāhi (ṣ) wa-naḥnu naktubu l-aḥādītha, fa-qāla: mā hādhā lladhī taktubūna? qulnā: aḥādīthu nasma'uhā minka. qāla: kitābun ghayru kitābi llāhi?, atadrūna mā [a] ḍalla l-umama qablakum? alā bi-mā ktatabū min al-kutubi ma'a kitābi llāhi ta'ālā? qulnā: a-nuḥaddithu 'anka yā rasūla llāhi? qāla: ḥaddithū 'annī wa-lā ḥaraja, wa-man kadhaba 'alayya muta'ammidan fa-l-yatabawwa' maq'adahu min al-nāri. qulnā: fa-nataḥaddathu 'an banī isrā'īla? qāla: ḥaddithū wa-lā ḥaraja, fa-innakum lam tuḥaddithū 'anhum bi-shay'in illā wa-qad kāna fīhim a'jabu minhu...*

17 Fol. 59b; 'Abd al-Razzāq, *al-Muṣannaf*, Ms. fol. 113b: *bāb hal yus'alu ahlu l-kitābi 'an shay'in... 'an zaydi bni aslama anna l-nabiyya (ṣ) qāla: lā tas'alū ahla l-kitābi 'an shay'in fa-innahum lan yahdūkum, qad aḍallū anfusahum. qīla: yā rasūla llāhi, alā nuḥaddithu 'an banī isrā'īla? qāla: ḥaddithū wa-lā ḥaraja.*

18 *Al-Nihāya*, I, 361.

19 See Rāghib al-Iṣfahānī, *al-Mufradāt fī gharīb al-qur'ān* (Cairo, 1324), p. 111, s.v. *ḥ r j*.

20 See al-Majlisī, *Biḥār*, IV, 495 (new ed.).

were told, whether these stories are true or not; the remoteness of time (i.e. between the period of the Children of Israel and the time of Islam — K) makes it impossible to verify the story and the transmitter cannot be responsible for its reliability. This is set in opposition to the traditions about the Prophet: a *ḥadīth* should only be transmitted after one has made sure about the soundness of the transmission and the righteousness of the transmitters.[21]

This interpretation was adopted by al-ʿAzīzī (d. 1070) who is even more explicit in his comment. "Narrate concerning the Children of Israel" glosses al-ʿAzīzī by "tell about them the stories and exhortations" (*ballighū ʿanhum al-qiṣaṣa wa-l-mawāʿiẓa*). *Lā ḥaraja* is explained by the statement that there is no sin incumbent upon a transmitter who records these stories without *isnād*. Because of the remoteness of time it is enough to make an assumption that the tradition concerns them (*fa-yakfī ghalabatu l-ẓanni bi-annahu ʿanhum*). This tradition is followed by a *ḥadīth*, which urges people to transmit traditions about the Prophet and warns against invention and lie in such traditions.[22] Here the expression *ḥaddithū ʿannī bimā tasmaʿūna* is explained by the recommendation to observe sound *isnāds* and to refrain from the transmission of *ḥadīths* with faulty *isnāds*.

The reasons for the permission to narrate stories about the Children of Israel as opposed to consulting them concerning their religious tenets is expounded by al-Munāwī (d. 1031). There is no contradiction between the *ḥadīth* which allows the transmission of stories and the one which interdicts the transmission of tenets and rules, al-Munāwī argues. The transmission of their religious law is in fact forbidden because their rules were abrogated.[23]

Al-ʿAlqamī (d. 969) considers the permission to narrate stories in the light of the changes which took place in the Muslim community. The Prophet, al-ʿAlqamī argues, disapproved of studying the books of the Children of Israel and deriving knowledge from them. Later the situation improved and the prohibition was lifted. The prohibition was issued when the prescriptions of Muslim law and the foundations of the Islamic religion had not been firmly established, out of fear of a *fitna* (allurement). When that which was apprehended ceased, permission to narrate was granted, because listening to accounts of past events

[21] *Al-Nihāya*, I, 361; and see al-Jazarī, *Qiṣaṣ al-anbiyā'* (al-Najaf, 1964), p. 522 (quoting Ibn Athīr); and see *ibid.*, p. 522 supra, a Shīʿī permission to transmit the stories of the Children of Israel.

[22] *Al-Sirāj al-munīr* (Cairo, 1957), II, 223: *ḥaddithū ʿannī bimā tasmaʿūna wa-lā taqūlū illā ḥaqqan, wa-man kadhaba ʿalayya buniya lahu baytun fī jahannama yartaʿu fīhi.*

[23] Al-ʿAzīzī, *op. cit.*, II, 145: ...*wa-idhnuhu lā yunafī nahyahu fī khabarin ākhara li-anna l-maʾdhūna fīhi l-taḥdīthu bi-qiṣaṣihim wa-l-manhiyyu ʿanhu l-ʿamalu bi-aḥkāmihim li-naskhihā.*

entails edification.[24] Al-'Alqamī seems thus to consider the saying *ḥaddithū 'an banī isrā'īla* as an utterance abrogating an earlier prohibiting utterance.

Al-Jarrāḥī (d. 1162) quotes this interpretation among other interpretations recorded by him. As proof of the prohibition to narrate stories concerning the Children of Israel al-Jarrāḥī mentions the story of 'Umar who was forbidden by the Prophet to copy from the Torah. Later, says al-Jarrāḥī, the permission to narrate such stories was granted, and this is why the utterance was issued.[25]

Some of the interpretations reflect a tendency to limit this permission or even to cancel it. The *lā ḥaraja*, "there is nothing objectionable", may be complemented by a phrase: "if you do not narrate".[26] The *ḥadīth* thus stresses the obligatory character of the transmission of a tradition of the Prophet, but leaves it to the discretion of the faithful whether to narrate about the Children of Israel.

A restricting interpretation asserts that the term Banū Isrā'īl refers to the sons of Jacob; the *ḥadīth* urges their story to be narrated together with that of Joseph. This interpretation is rejected by al-'Azīzī with the remark: *wa-hādhā ab'adu l-aujuhi.*[27] A peculiar interpretation explains the reason for this permission by stating that the stories about the Children of Israel contain some distasteful expressions and therefore it was necessary to stress that their transmission was not objectionable.[28]

But these restricting interpretations were not effective. The saying *ḥaddithū 'an banī isrā'īla wa-lā ḥaraja*, attached to various other traditions, became widely current among Muslims in the first half of the second century. This permission to narrate stories about the Children of Israel caused the door to be opened widely to Jewish lore and traditions transmitted by Muslim scholars.

II

The themes covered by the stories about the Children of Israel are very extensive. They include stories about prophets and their warnings, about sins committed by the Children of Israel and the punishment inflicted on them,

24 *Ibid.*,: *...wa-qāla l-'alqamiyyu: ay lā ḍīqa 'alaykum fī l-taḥdīthi 'anhum li-annahu kāna taqaddama minhu (ṣ) al-zajru 'an al-akhdhi 'anhum wa-l-naẓari fī kutubihim thumma ḥaṣala l-tawassu'u fī dhālika; wa-kāna l-nahyu waqa'a qabla istiqrāri l-aḥkāmi l-islāmiyyati wa-l-qawā'idi l-dīniyyati khashyata l-fitnati; thumma lammā zāla l-maḥdhūru waqa'a l-idhnu fī dhālika limā fī simā'i l-akhbāri llatī kānat fī zamanihim min al-i'tibāri.*

25 Al-Jarrāḥī, *op. cit.*, I, 353.

26 Ibn al-Athīr, *op. cit.*, I, 361: *...wa-ḥaddithū 'an banī isrā'īla wa-lā ḥaraja, ay: lā ḥaraja 'alaykum in lam tuḥaddithū 'anhum*; and see al-Jarrāḥī, *op. cit.*, I, 353, ll. 11–12; al-'Azīzī, *op. cit.*, II, 145.

27 *Al-Sirāj al-munīr*, II, 145.

28 *Ibid.*

about the sufferings of the righteous and pious and the reward granted to them by God, about utterances and sayings of sages and wise men, about supplications of prophets and pious men, about speeches and wills of nobles, saints and martyrs. These stories usually called "*Isrā'īliyyāt*" included predictions of the early prophets about the appearance of the Prophet and descriptions of the Muslim community, about Caliphs and rebels, about decline of dynasties, about the Mahdī and the signs heralding the Day of Judgement. This lore was transmitted by Jews and Christians or by members of these two religions who studied their Scriptures and embraced the faith of Islam.

In the widely current tradition about the supplications of Moses,[29] he implored the Lord to grant his people, the Children of Israel, the excellent qualities and merits which were enumerated in the Torah; God preferred however to choose the Muslim community and to grant them these qualities and merits.[30] The Torah also contains the description of the Prophet.[31] God revealed to Moses that the Prophet would be sent and bade him inform the Children of Israel to obey him and embrace his faith.[32] God also disclosed in the Psalms to David the appearance of the Prophet and recorded the qualities of his people.[33] Isaiah predicted in his prophecy the appearance of Jesus and Muḥammad.[34] God bade Jesus urge his people to embrace the faith of Muḥammad and told him about the latter's personality.[35] Accordingly, it is evident that Muḥammad is the heir of the preceding prophets and that the Muslim community inherited the rank and position of the Chosen People.

A Shī'ī tradition tells a story about a talk of the Prophet with a Jew in which the Prophet said that the first passage in the Torah stated: Muḥammad is the Messenger of God; in Hebrew it is *Ṭāb* (Ṭov — K); the Prophet then quoted other passages in which the *waṣiyy* 'Alī, his children Ḥasan and Ḥusayn (*Shubbar* and *Shubbayr*) and Fāṭima were explicitly mentioned.[36] It may be

29 See Miskawayh, *al-Ḥikmatu l-khālidatu*, ed. 'Abd al-Raḥmān Badawī (Cairo, 1952), p. 133 (*munājāt mūsā*).

30 Abū Nu'aym, *op. cit.*, V, 385–386; Ibn Ẓafar, *Khayru l-bishar bi-khayri l-bashar* ([n.p.], 1280), pp. 25–34; Ibn al-Jauzī, *al-Wafā bi-aḥwāl al-muṣṭafā*, ed. Muṣṭafā 'Abd al-Wāḥid (Cairo, 1386/1966), I, 38–42; al-Tha'labī, *Qiṣaṣ al-anbiyā'* (Cairo [n.d.]), p. 27; al-Suyūṭī, *al-Ḥāwī li-l-fatāwī*, ed. Muḥammad Muḥyi l-Dīn 'Abd al-Ḥamīd (Cairo, 1387/1959), II, 281, 282 ult.-283; Ibn Kathīr, *Shamā'il al-rasūl*, ed. Muṣṭafā 'Abd al-Wāḥid (Cairo, 1386/1967), 114–115; al-Bayhaqī, *Dalā'il al-nubuwwa*, Ms. Br. Mus., Or. 3013, fol. 64b.

31 See Abū Nu'aym, *op. cit.*, V, 387; Ibn Kathīr, *Shamā'il*, pp. 111–115; al-Suyūṭī, *al-Ḥāwī*, II, 282–283.

32 Abū Nu'aym, *op. cit.*, VI, 33–35; al-Majlisī, *Biḥār*, XIII, 332–333, 340–341 (new ed.).

33 Al-Suyūṭī, *al-Ḥāwī*, II, 281 inf.-282; Ibn Kathīr, *Shamā'il*, p. 115.

34 Ibn Kathīr, *al-Bidāya wa-l-nihāya*, II, 32.

35 Al-Suyūṭī, *al-Ḥāwī*, II, 114; Ibn al-Jauzī, *al-Wafā*, I, 60.

36 Al-Majlisī, *op. cit.*, XIII, 331–332 (new ed.).

mentioned that the names of the two sons of 'Alī, Ḥasan and Ḥusayn, were given by the Prophet himself. The angel Gabriel revealed to the Prophet the names of the two sons of Aharon, Shubbar and Shubbayr, which are written in the Torah and ordered him to give these names to the two children of 'Alī. The rendering of these names is al-Ḥasan and al-Ḥusayn[37] (probably Hebrew: Shefer and Shafīr — K). Taking into account the fact that at first the name intended to be given to the children was *Ḥarb* and that the Prophet stated in the well known *ḥadīth* that 'Alī was in relation to the Prophet like Aharon to Moses, one can assess the political implication of the story.

Scholars of the Holy Scriptures, Jews and Christians, were supposed to have the ability to foretell future events: they were thought to derive their knowledge from the Torah or other Holy Books. Ka'b standing at Ṣiffīn put his leg on a stone and said: "Woe to you Ṣiffīn! The Children of Israel fought here with each other and left on the battle-field seventy thousand killed; so it will be with the Muslims." It really happened at the battle of Ṣiffīn between 'Alī and Mu'āwiya. "There is no space on earth the events of which were not recorded in the Torah" — said Ka'b.[38] In a talk with 'Umar, Ka'b is stated to have said: "Were it not for a sentence in the Qur'ān (Sūra xiii, 39), I would foretell to you everything which will happen until the Day of Judgement."[39] Ka'b was accordingly able to tell 'Umar that the description of his personality is given in the Torah as *qarn min ḥadīd*, and he could further predict that 'Umar would be killed; then the following Caliph will be killed by an unjust faction; afterwards disasters will prevail.[40] A bishop consulted by 'Umar could assert that he found 'Umar's description in his Scriptures as *qarn min ḥadīd* (glossed

37 Al-Dhahabī, *Siyar a'lām al-nubalā'*, ed. As'ad Ṭalas (Cairo, 1962), III, 165; *Yawāqīlt al-siyar*, Ms. Br. Mus., Or. 3771, fol. 141a; al-Ṭabarī, *Dalā'il al-imāma* (al-Najaf, 1383/1963), pp. 63, 73; Ibn Mākūlā, *al-Ikmāl*, (Hyderabad, 1381/1962), IV, 378; al-Ṭūsī, *Amālī* (al-Najaf, 1384/1964), I, 377; *Rijāl al-Kashshī* (al-Najaf [n.d.]), p. 26; al-Majlisī, *op. cit.*, XII, 113; XXXIX, 63; XLIII, 237–242 (new ed.).

38 Ibn Abī l-Dunyā, *al-Ishrāf fī manāzil al-ashrāf*, Ms. Chester Beatty 4427, fol. 69a; Ibn 'Abd al-Barr, *al-Istī'āb*, ed. 'Alī Muḥ. al-Bijāwī (Cairo [n.d.]), III, 1287; al-Suyūṭī, *al-Ḥāwī*, II, 283–284; al-Qurṭubī, *al-Tadhkira*, ed. Aḥmad Muḥ. Mursī (Cairo [n.d.]), p. 543; Ibn Ḥajar, *al-Iṣāba* (Cairo, 1325/1907), V, 250, no. 7157; al-Suyūṭī, *al-Khaṣā'iṣ al-kubrā*, ed. Muḥammad Khalīl Harās (Cairo, 1386/1967), I, 80.

39 Al-Ṭabarī, *Tafsīr*, ed. Maḥmūd Muḥ. Shākir (Cairo, 1969), XVI, 484, no. 20485; al-Qurṭubī, *Tafsīr*, ed. Ibrāhīm Itfīsh (Cairo, 1387/1967), IX, 330; a Shī'ī source (al-'Ayyāshī, *Tafsīr*, II, 215, no. 54) attributes this saying to 'Alī b. al-Ḥusayn.

40 Al-Haythamī, *Majma' al-zawā'id* (Beirut, 1967), IX, 65 infra.-66; cf. Abū Nu'aym, *op. cit.*, V, 387 ult.-388 supra.; Muḥ. b. Yaḥyā al-Ash'arī al-Mālaqī, *al-Tamhīd wa-l-bayān fī maqtal al-shahīd 'uthmān*, ed. Maḥmūd Yūsuf Zāyid (Beirut, 1964), p. 21; Ibn Ra's Ghanama, *Manāqil al-Durar*, Ms. Chester Beatty 4254, fol. 23a; Nu'aym b. Ḥammād, *Kit. al-fitan*, Ms. Br. Mus., Or. 9449, fol. 22a–b; al-Suyūṭī, *al-Khaṣā'iṣ*, I, 77.

by him as *qawiyyun*, *shadīdun*) and predict that he will be followed by a man, who has nothing objectionable in him (*lā ba'sa bihi*), but he will prefer his relatives; 'Umar recognized forthwith that it would be 'Uthmān. Afterwards, said the bishop, there will be "a crack in the rock" which he explained as "a sword drawn and blood shed." Later there will be a united congregation (*jamā'atun*).[41] 'Abdallah b. Salām reported that the description of 'Uthmān in the Book of God was: "the Commander of those who forsake and kill,"[42] and foretold that he would be murdered.[43] Ka'b foretells the rule of Mu'āwiya.[44] 'Abdallah b. al-Zubayr stated that everything foretold by Ka'b about his rule really happened to him.[45] It is a Jew who foretells the just rule of 'Umar b. 'Abd al-'Azīz;[46] and it is from the Torah that the prediction that heaven and earth will bewail the death of 'Umar b. 'Abd al-'Azīz is quoted.[47] Ka'b foretells the appearance of the black banners of the 'Abbasids,[48] gives the names of the descendants of 'Abbās who will rule the Muslim community[49] and emphasizes in a separate statement: *al-manṣūru manṣūru banī hāshimin.*[50] It is, of course, an utterance with important political implications. Who was the person the Yemenīs believed to be *al-Manṣūr*, can be gauged from the refutation of 'Abdallah b. 'Amr (b. al-'Āṣ): *yā ma'shara l-yamani, taqūlūna inna l-manṣūra minkum, fa-lā; wa-lladhī nafsī bi-yadihi, innahu la-qurashiyyun abūhu, wa-lau ashā'u an ansibahu ilā aqṣā jaddin huwa lahu fa'altu.*[51] Tubay', the stepson of Ka'b, quoted from the Torah the name of Saffāḥ and predicted that he would live forty years.[52] 'Abdallah b. 'Amr b. al-'Āṣ quoted from the Books which he found after the battle of Yarmūk the names of the 'Abbasid Caliphs who would rule the Muslim community: Saffāḥ, Manṣūr, al-Amīn etc.[53] Ka'b

41 Nu'aym b. Ḥammād, *op. cit.*, fol. 28a; al-Suyūṭī, *al-Khaṣā'iṣ*, I, 78–79.

42 Nu'aym b. Ḥammād, *op. cit.*, fol. 41b; but al-Mālaqī, *al-Tamhīd*, p. 113 has instead of "*amīrun 'alā l-khādhil wa-l-qātil*" "amīrun 'alā l-qātil al-āmir" (erroneous) and "*amīrun 'alā l-qātil wa-l-āmir*" (correct); al-Suyūṭī, *al-Khaṣā'iṣ*, I, 78–79.

43 Al-Mālaqī, *op. cit.*, p. 113, 135–136, 176–177; al-Qurṭubī, *Tadhkira*, p. 534; al-Haythamī, *op. cit.*, IX, 92–93.

44 Nu'aym b. Ḥammād, *op. cit.*, fol. 28b.

45 Nu'aym b. Ḥammād, *op. cit.*, Ms. Atif Ef. 602, fol. 4a, l. 5 from bottom; al-Suyūṭī, *al-Khaṣā'iṣ*, I, 80 ult.-81.

46 Nu'aym b. Ḥammād, *op. cit.*, Ms. Br. Mus., Or. 9449, fol. 28a; al-Suyūṭī, *al-Khaṣā'iṣ*, I, 81.

47 Al-Suyūṭī, *al-Ḥāwī*, II, 284.

48 Nu'aym b. Ḥammād, *op. cit.*, Ms. Br. Mus., fol. 53a.

49 *Ibid.*, fol. 27b: ...*'an ka'bin qāla*: *yamliku thalāthatun min wuldi l-'abbāsi al-manṣūru wa-l-mahdiyyu wa-l-saffāḥu.*

50 *Ibid.*, fol. 27a.

51 *Ibid.*, fol. 27a. 52 *Ibid.*, fol. 27a.

53 *Ibid.*, fol. 25b; and see about the books and these traditions Ibn Kathīr, *al-Bidāya*, II, 298 infra.- 299 supra.

predicts the signs which will announce the end of the 'Abbasid rule,[54] gives details about civil wars which will occur in the different provinces of the Muslim Empire,[55] and foretells the appearance of the Sufyānī.[56] Farqad al-Sabakhī predicts from the Holy Scriptures cruel battles in Judda.[57]

Jews and Christians predicted the appearance of the Prophet[58] and it was Jews and Christians who knew the exact date of his death: two Jewish scholars from Yemen informed Jarīr b. 'Abdallah al-Bajalī on the day of the death of the Prophet about the sad event.[59] A monk could fix precisely the date of the death of the Prophet for Ka'b b. 'Adiyy according to what he found in his Book.[60] A Jew from 'Umān informed 'Amr b. al-'Āṣ on the day of the death of the Prophet about this; 'Amr recorded the date, checked it later and found it accurate.[61]

The opinion that the Holy Books of Jews and Christians include information about the life and actions of prophets of the period preceding Islam, about the Prophet and the fate of his community and the events which will occur became widely accepted.[62] It was further a common belief that the contents of the Qur'ān are included in the Books of the prophets preceding Muḥammad.[63] The Qur'ān, on the other hand, includes the contents of the Books revealed to the earlier prophets. "What is contained in the Qur'ān is contained in the earlier Books", formulates it al-Suyūṭī.[64]

[54] Nu'aym b. Ḥammād, *op. cit.*, fol. 56a–b, 57a–b, 58b, 60b, 61b.

[55] *Ibid.*, fols. 34b, 61b, 62a, 63a–b, 65a–b, 69b, 71a–b, 72a–b.

[56] *Ibid.*, fols. 74a–b, 81a.

[57] Al-Fākihī, *Ta'rīkh Makka*, Leiden, Or. 463, fol. 414a.

[58] See e.g. al-Nuwayrī, *op. cit.*, XVI, 136, 143, 149–153; al-Haythamī, *al-Ni'ma l-kubra* (Ḥalab [n.d.]), pp. 28–29, 52–53, 62.

[59] Ibn Kathīr, *al-Bidāya wa-l-nihāya*, V, 278.

[60] *Ibid.*, V, 278–279.

[61] Ibn Ḥubaysh, *al-Maghāzī*, Ms. Leiden, Or. 343, p. 24.

[62] See al-Suyūṭī, *al-Ḥāwī*, II, 283: *...wa-waradat al-āthāru ayḍan bi-anna llāha bayyana li-anbiyā'ihi fī kutubihim jamī'a mā huwa wāqi'un fī hādhihi l-ummati min aḥdāthin wa-fitanin wa-akhbāri khulafā'ihā wa-mulūkihā...* And see 'Abd al-Jabbār, *Tathbīt dalā'ili l-nubuwwa*, ed. 'Abd al-Karīm 'Uthmān (Beirut, 1966–68), II, 413: *innamā lam yatammanau l-mauta li-anna l-yahūda wa-l-naṣārā kānū yu'minūna bi-mūsā wa-ghayrihi mimman kāna yadda'ī l-nubuwwata, wa-qad akhbara hā'ulā'i fī kutubihim bi-nubuwwati muḥammadin (ṣ) fa-lam yuqdimū 'alā l-tamannī li-hādhā...*

[63] Al-Suyūṭī, *al-Ḥāwī*, II, 284: *...wa-qad u'turiḍa 'alayya fī hādhā l-ṭarīqi bi-annahu yalzamu 'alayhi an yakūna kullu mā fī l-qur'āni muḍammanan fī jamī'i l-kutubi l-sābiqati; wa-aqūlu: la māni'a min dhālika, bal dallat al-adillatu 'alā thubūti hādhā l-lāzimi...*

[64] *Ibid.*, II, 285: *...wa-qad naṣṣa 'alā hādhā bi-'aynihi l-imāmu abū ḥanīfata ḥaythu stadalla bi-hādhihi l-āyāti 'alā jawāzi qirā'ati l-qur'āni bi-ghayri l-lisāni l-'arabiyyi, wa-qāla: inna l-qur'āna muḍammanun fī l-kutubi l-sābiqati, wa-hiya bi-ghayri l-lisāni l-'arabī, akhdhan bi-hadhihi l-āyati* (i.e. Sūra xxvi, 197–98), *wa-mimmā yashhadu bi-dhālika waṣfuhu ta'ālā li-l-*

The idea of identity of contents led consequently to the identification of some passages of the Holy Books with those of the Qur'ān. The beginning of the Torah is identical with the beginning of *Sūrat al-An'ām*, the end of the Torah is identical with the end of *Sūrat Hūd.*[65] The *Sūrat Yā Sīn* is called in the Torah *al-Mu'amma.*[66] God urged Moses to read the verse of the Throne (Sūra ii 256) after every prayer and mentioned the reward for this reading.[67] Muḥammad b. Ka'b al-Quraẓī could identify a quotation from some Holy Books mentioned by Abū Sa'īd al-Maqburī with Sūra ii 204.[68] The first sentence in the Torah was Sūra vi 152: "Say: Come, I will recite what your Lord has forbidden you... etc.[69] "*Hādhā*" in Sūra lxxxvii, 18: *inna hādhā lafī l-ṣuḥufi l-ūlā, ṣuḥufi ibrāhīma wa-mūsā* was interpreted as referring to the whole *sūra*; the whole *sūra*, the commentators maintained, was included in the Holy Books of the earlier prophets.[70] Another tradition states explicitly that the *sūra* was copied from the Books of Moses and Abraham.[71] Some commentators tried to limit the extent of *inna hādhā...* to some verses (*āyāt*) of the *sūra.*[72] The Prophet is said to have given an utterance about the *ṣuḥuf* of Ibrāhīm and Mūsā: the *ṣuḥuf* of Ibrāhīm were proverbs, the *ṣuḥuf* of Mūsā were exempla (*'ibar*).[73] Quotations from these *ṣuḥuf* are in fact uttered by the Prophet.[74]

A very early compilation containing wise sayings, stories and exhortations of Ibrāhīm, Mūsā, Ayyūb, Dāwūd, Sulaymān, 'Isā, Yaḥyā b. Zakariyya and Luqmān is the *Kitāb al-mawā'iẓ* of Abū 'Ubayd al-Qāsim b. Sallām (d. 224).[75] The numerous traditions, sayings and stories, provided with chains of *isnād* and recorded by one of the greatest scholars of the second century of the Hijra, attest that in this period knowledge of Jewish and Christian tradition

qur'āni fī 'iddati mawāḍi'a bi-annahu muṣaddiqun (text vowelled: *musaddaqun*) *li-mā bayna yadayhi min al-kutubi*; *fa-lau-lā anna mā fīhi maujūdun fīhā lam yasiḥḥa hādhā l-waṣfu...*

65 Abū Nu'aym, *op. cit.*, V, 378.

66 Al-Suyūṭī, *al-La'ālī al-maṣnū'a*, I, 234.

67 Al-Suyūṭī, *al-La'ālī al-maṣnū'a*, I, 232–233; *idem*, *al-Durr al-manthūr*, I, 325; Ibn Kathīr, *Tafsīr*, I, 546.

68 Al-Ṭabarī, *Tafsīr*, IV, 231–232, nos. 3964–65; al-Suyūṭī, *al-Durr*, I, 238.

69 Al-Mauṣilī, *Ghāyat al-wasā'il ilā ma'rifati l-awā'il*, Ms. Cambridge Qq. 33, fol. 41a; al-Ṭabarī, *Tafsīr*, XII, 227, no. 14157 (and see nos. 14158–59); Abū Nu'aym, *op. cit.*, V, 383.

70 Al-Shaukānī, *Fatḥ al-qadīr* (Cairo, 1383/1964), V, 427; al-Suyūṭī, *al-Durr*, VI, 341.

71 Al-Suyūṭī, *al-Durr*, VI, 341; al-Shaukānī, *Fatḥ al-qadīr*, V, 427: *nusikhat hādhihi l-sūratu min ṣuḥufi ibrāhīma wa-mūsā*; Cf. al-Suyūṭī, *al-Ḥāwī*, II, 285: *hādhihi l-sūratu fī ṣuḥufi ibrāhīma wa-mūsā*; al-Qurṭubī, *Tafsīr*, XX, 24: *inna hādha... qāla*: *hādhihi l-sūratu.*

72 Al-Suyūṭī, *al-Durr*, VI, 341; al-Qurṭubī, *Tafsīr*, XX, 24: *min qaulihi qad aflaḥa ilā ākhiri l-sūrati*; Ibn Kathīr, *Tafsīr*, VII, 273.

73 Al-Suyūṭī, *al-Durr*, VI, 341.

74 *Ibid.*

75 Ms. Hebrew University, Collection Yahuda, Ar. 95.

was widely current and was without serious opposition incorporated into the Muslim religious tradition. "It is written in the Torah", says Khaythama b. 'Abd al-Raḥmān, "O man, exert yourself in My service and I shall fill up your heart with sufficiency and I shall supply your want; but if you do not do it, I shall make your heart busy and shall not supply your wants."[76] "God revealed to Ibrāhīm," Wahb b. Munabbih reports, "O king who undergoes trials, I did not send you in order to collect the goods of this world, nor to erect buildings; I sent you in order to answer on My behalf the call of the oppressed, because I shall not drive it back, even if it comes from an unbeliever."[77] This utterance is recorded by al-Suyūṭī as a *ḥadīth*.[78] Ka'b quotes from the Torah, according to the early *Jāmi'* of Ibn Wahb, a commandment to obey one's parents.[79] A saying about the disobedience of sons to their fathers is transmitted by Ka'b from the "Book of God."[80] Ka'b asserts that the invocation of 'Abdallah b. 'Amr in connection with augury is found in the Torah.[81] From the Torah Ka'b also quotes a saying about the contemptous attitude towards the wise on the part of his own people.[82] The final sentence in the Torah, says Ka'b, is: *al-ḥamdu li-llāhi lladhī lam yattakhidh waladan wa-lam yakun lahu sharīkun fī l-mulki*.[83] Maymūn b. Mihrān states that on the Tablets of Moses was written: "Do not covet the possessions of your neighbour, nor his wife."[84] The Chidren of Israel asked Moses to choose for them a sentence of the Torah, which they could learn by heart. He said: "In the same way you would like people to treat you, treat them." Al-Zamakhsharī remarks: "This phrase is the one chosen best from the Torah."[85] Sa'īd b. abī Hilāl[86] records two commandments in the Tablets of Moses written by God on the tablets "with His own hand" and His injunction: "Like for the people what you like for yourself and dislike for them what you dislike for yourself."[87] In the first tablets given to Moses by God there was written: "Thank Me and thank your parents, then I shall keep you from danger of decay and I shall

76 Abū 'Ubayd, *op. cit.*, f. 9b; al-Majlisī, *op. cit.*, XIII, 357, l. 1 (new ed.); al-'Āmilī, *al-Jawāhir al-saniyya*, al-Najaf 1384/1964, p. 48.

77 Abū 'Ubayd, *op. cit.*, fol. 6b; Ibn Qutayba, *'Uyūn al-akhbār* (Cairo, 1346/1928), II, 263.

78 *Al-Durr*, VI, 341.

79 Ibn Wahb, *Jāmi'*, ed. J. David Weill (Cairo, 1939), p. 12, l. 11.

80 *Ibid.*, page 11, l. 10.

81 *Ibid.*, page 98, l. 4.

82 'Abd al-Jabbār al-Khaulānī, *Ta'rīkh Dārayyā*, ed. Sa'īd al-Afghānī (Damascus, 1369/1950), p. 107.

83 Abū Nu'aym, *op. cit.*, VI, 30.

84 Abū 'Ubayd, *op. cit.*, fol. 9b, l. 9.

85 Al-Zamakhsharī, *Rabī' al-abrār*, Ms. Br. Mus., Or. 6511, fol. 132b, infra.

86 See on him Ibn Ḥajar, *Tahdhīb al-tahdhīb*, IV, 94, no. 159.

87 Ibn Wahb, *op. cit.*, page 20, l. 18.

lengthen your life and I shall give you a good life and transfer you into a better one."[88] Tha'laba b. abī Mālik[89] says that 'Umar invited Jewish scholars and asked them to discuss (religious subjects — K). With them came Tha'laba's father, Abū Mālik, who was a Jewish convert to Islam.[90] He came with a book, opened it and put his hand on a passage of it. When he lifted his hand and the Jewish scholars read: "he who shows filial piety to his father, God will lengthen his life" they admitted that it was revealed by God. People did not know it until that day.[91] Al-Tha'labī records the Ten Commandments revealed to Moses.[92] Al-Nuwayrī quotes al-Tha'labī; he remarks that God revealed to the Prophet the contents of the Ten Commandments in eighteen verses of the Qur'ān, which he records.[93] The maxim that as a part of filial piety one has to be beneficient to the friends of one's father after his death is quoted from the Torah.[94] A *faqīh* quoted from the Torah: "Woe to the man who sins, then asks forgiveness from Me..."[95] "In the Torah it is written", a Shī'ī tradition says, "O man, remember Me when you are angry, then I shall remember you when I am angry and I shall not annihilate you among those whom I shall annihilate; if you are unjustly treated be satisfied with My help to you, as My help is better for you than your help for yourself."[96] "In the Torah it is written: he who sells landed property or (rights on) water not investing the sum gained in land or water (rights), the money (gained) will be squandered."[97] It may be remarked that a similar tradition is reported on the authority of the Prophet: *lā bāraka llāhu fī thamani arḍin au dārin lā yuj'alu fī arḍin au dārin.*[98] Some quotations from the Gospel and "other Books" are transmitted by Thaur b. Yazīd.[99] He read in the *taurāt* that Jesus said to the Apostles: Converse much with God, converse with people a little". They asked: "How should we converse with God"? He said: "Be in solitude with Him in your invocations and supplications".[100] Ka'b states that the well

[88] Al-Majlisī, *op. cit.*, XIII, 358, no. 63.

[89] See on him Ibn Ḥajar, *al-Iṣāba*, I, 209, no. 948; Ibn 'Abd al-Barr, *op. cit.*, I, 212, no. 277

[90] Ibn Ḥajar, *al-Iṣāba*, VI, 169, no. 998.

[91] Ibn Wahb, *op. cit.*, page 15, ll. 9–14.

[92] *Qiṣaṣ al-anbiyā'*, p. 270.

[93] *Nihāyat al-arab*, XIII, 215–217.

[94] Ibn Wahb, *op. cit.*, page 14, ll. 14–15; cf. al-Sulamī, *Ādāb al-ṣuḥba* (Jerusalem, 1954), p. 83, nos. 248–249 (and see *ibid.*, the references of the editor).

[95] Ibn Abī l-Dunyā, *Kit. al-tauba*, Ms. Chester Beatty, 3863, fol. 20b.

[96] Al-Majlisī, *op. cit.*, XIII, 358, no. 66.

[97] Al-Majlisī, *op. cit.*, XIII, 360, 73.

[98] Mughulṭāy, *al-Zahr al-bāsim*, Leiden Or. 370, fol. 120b; al-Ṭabarī, *al-Muntakhab min dhayli l-mudhayyal* (Cairo, 1358/1939), p. 59.

[99] See on him Ibn Ḥajar, *Tahdhīb al-tahdhīb*, II, 33, no. 57.

[100] Abū Nu'aym, *op. cit.*, VI, 94.

of Zamzam is mentioned in "some Books."[101] "I found in the Torah", states Ka'b, that he who prays the five prayers in the mosque of Mecca (*al-masjid al-ḥarām*) God will record for him (the reward of) twelve million and five hundred thousand prayers.[102] Even the verse of al-Ḥuṭay'a

man yaf'al al-khayra lā ya'dam jawāziyahu:
lā yadhhabu l-'urfu bayna llāhi wa-l-nāsi

was stated by Ka'b to be a sentence from the Torah.[103]

Additional quotations "from the Torah" could easily be multiplied.[104] Only few of these quotations are in fact derived from that source.[105] The majority of the flow of these quotations was derived from popular Jewish and Christian stories, legends, wise sayings and traditions which were introduced by Jewish and Christian converts to Islam and gained wide popularity. The Muslim scholars were however aware of the fact that the expressions "I found in the Torah", "it is written in the Torah", "it is recorded in the Torah" do not necessarily refer to the Pentateuch, or even to the Bible. Al-Jāḥiẓ remarks that the expression "*maktūbun fī l-taurāti*" as told on the authority of Ka'b refers in fact to things found in the Scriptures of the Jews like the books of the prophets and the books of Salomon.[106] In a report given by Abū l-Aswad[107] the *Ra's al-Jālūt* explains thst Ka'b lied when he said that his predictions were derived from the Torah; the Torah is a Book like the Qur'ān; Ka'b was in fact quoting from the books of the prophets and their companions, exactly as the Muslims narrate stories of the Prophet and his Companions.[108]

The sources are often referred to in a vague manner: "*maktūbun fī l-kutubi*", "*qara'tu fī ba'ḍi l-kutubi*", "*fī kitābi llāhi*";[109] often the sources are not mentioned at all.

101 Al-Fākihī, *op. cit.*, fol. 342a.

102 *Ibid.*, fol. 453a.

103 Usāma b. Munqidh, *Lubāb al-ādāb*, ed. Aḥmad Muḥ. Shākir (Cairo, 1353/1935), p. 424 ult.; and see al-Ḥuṭay'a, *Dīwān*, ed. Nu'mān Amīn Ṭāhā (Cairo, 1378/1958), pp. 291–292.

104 See e.g. al-Dhahabī, *al-'Uluww li-l-'aliyy l-ghaffār*, ed. 'Abd al-Raḥmān Muḥ. 'Uthmān (Cairo, 1388/1968), p. 95; Abū Nu'aym, *op. cit.*, IV, 48, 38, 58; al-Suyūṭī, *al-Durr*, IV, 182; Ibn Abī l-Dunyā, *al-Ishrāf*, fol. 76a–b; al-Majlisī, *op. cit.*, XIII, 331, 342, 348, 357, 340; al-Ṭūsī, *Amālī* (al-Najaf, 1384/1964), I, 233; al-'Āmilī, *al-Kashkūl*, ed. Ṭāhir Aḥmad al-Zāwī (Cairo, 1380/1961), II, 132, 153.

105 See J. Goldziher, "Über Bibelcitate in muhammedanischen Schriften," *ZATW* XIII (1893), pp. 315–316.

106 *Al Ḥayawān*, ed. 'Abd al-Salām Hārūn (Cairo, 1385/1966), IV, 202–203.

107 See on him Ibn Ḥajar, *Tahdhīb al-tahdhīb*, IX, 307, no. 506.

108 Ibn Ḥajar, *al Iṣāba*, V, 324.

109 See e.g. Abū 'Ubayd, *op. cit.*, fol. 16b; Abū Nu'aym, *op. cit.*, IV, 27, 32, 33, 57; VI 16, 55.

From "*Ḥikmat āl Dāwūd*" Abū 'Ubayd quotes the following passage: "It is incumbent upon a wise man not to be neglectful about four hours: an hour in which he exerts himself for his God, an hour in which "he makes accounts for his soul", an hour in which he talks with his friends who speak to him frankly about his vices and bad behaviour and an hour devoted to his lawful pleasures; this (latter) hour is a recreation for his heart and should help him to carry out the obligations of the three (former) hours. It is incumbent upon a wise man to know his time and to set about his matters. It is incumbent upon a wise man to set out on his journey with provision taken only for his life to come, approving the means of life and lawful pleasure".[110] In some other sources these utterances are quoted from the *Ṣuḥuf Ibrāhīm*.[111]

From the *Ḥikmat āl Dāwūd* the following saying is quoted: "Good health is a hidden good".[112] Some quotations from *Ḥikmat āl Dāwūd* are given by al-'Āmilī[113] and al-Majlisī.[114] Abū Nu'aym records some quotations from "*Mas'alat Dāwūd*".[115] Al-'Āmilī quotes "*Akhbār Dāwūd*" twice.[116]

The Psalms of David seem to have been in wide circulation. Qatāda and Rabī' b. Anas state that the *Zabūr* contains only invocations and praises of God; there are no commandments, no rules of penal-law, no statements about what is lawful or forbidden.[117] The first verses of the Psalms are often quoted. Two translations of these verses are recorded by al-Suyūṭī,[118] a third one by Ibn Abī l-Dunyā.[119] Ibn Ṭāwūs copies from the *zabūr* the following *suwar*:

110 *Al-Mawā'iẓ*, fol. 10b; cf. al-Suyūṭī, *al-Durr*, IV, 189, l. 10; al-Khaṭīb al-Baghdādī-*Mūḍiḥ auhām*, I, 457 (*fī ḥikmati āl dāwūda*); Ibn Kathīr, *al-Bidāya wa-l-nihāya*, II, 15 (*fī ḥikmati āl-dā'ūda*).

111 Al-Majlisī, *op. cit.*, XII, 71; al-Qurṭubī, *Tafsīr*, XX, 25; al-Suyūṭī, *al-Durr*, VI, 341.

112 Ibn Abī l-Dunyā, *al-Ishrāf*, fol. 93a (*al-'āfiyatu l-mulku l-khafiyyu*).

113 *Al-Jawāhir al-saniyya*, p. 90, l. 3 from bottom, p. 95.

114 *Biḥār*, XIV, 36, 41 (new ed.).

115 *Al-Ḥilya*, VI, 56–57; and see Ibn Kathīr, *al-Bidāya wa-l-nihāya*, II, 14 inf.

116 *Al-Jawāhir al-saniyya*, p. 94.

117 Al-Suyūṭī, *al-Durr*, IV, 188.

118 *Ibid.*, IV, 188: *a …ṭūbā li-rajulin lā yasluku ṭarīqa l-khaṭṭā'īna wa-lam yujālis al-baṭṭālīna wa yastaqīmu 'alā 'ibādati rabbihi 'azza wa jalla, fa mathaluhu ka mathali shajaratin nābitatin 'alā sāqiyatin lā tazālu fīhā l-mā'u yafḍulu thamaruhā fī zamāni l-thimāri wa lā tazālu khaḍrā'a fī ghayri zamāni l-thimāri*; (cf. Abū Nu'aym, *op. cit.*, IV, 62 penult.), p. 189: *b …ṭūbā li-man lam yasluk sabīla l-athamati wa-lam yujālis al-khaṭṭā'īna wa-lam yafi' fī hammi l-mustahzi'īna wa-lakinna hammahu sunnatu llahi wa-iyyāhā yata'allamu bi-l-layli wa-l-nahāri, mathaluhu mathalu shajaratin tanbutu 'alā shaṭṭin tu'tā thamaratahā fī ḥīnihā wa-lā yatanātharu min waraqihā shay'un, wa-kullu 'amalihi bi-amrī, laysa dhālika mithla 'amali l-munāfiqīn…*

119 *Kitāb al-tauba*, Chester Beatty, 3863, fol. 15b: *sallām b. miskīn*: *sa'altu naṣrāniyyan mā awwalu l-zabūri, qāla*: *ṭūbā li-'abdin lam yasluk sabīla l-athamati wa-lam yujālis l-mustahzi'īna wa-l-khāṭi'īna*; *fa-dhakartu dhālika li-māliki bni dīnarin fa-qāla*: *ṣadaqa.*

2, 10, 17, 23, 30, 36, 46, 47, 65, 67, 68, 71, 84, 100.[120] The last thirty lines of the *zabūr*[121] and a short passage from this source are given by Wahb.[122] These translations are however not accurate; sometimes no similarity with the text can be detected.

The wise sayings attributed to Salomon[123] can be traced to Ecclesiastes and Proverbs.[124]

Al-Muḥāsibī quotes from *Ḥikmat 'Īsā* a saying about the love for worldly goods[125] and a saying from *Risālāt 'Īsā*.[126] Lengthy chapters from *Ṣaḥā'if Idrīs* and *Sunan Idrīs* are recorded by Ibn Ṭāwūs.[127]

It would be needless to add quotations from the prophets like Isaiah, Jeremiah, Habaquq or from the *Injīl* of Jesus. The compilation of Abū 'Ubayd may serve as the best proof for the flow of Jewish and Christian traditions which poured into Muslim circles and were gladly taken up by Muslim scholars.

Reading the Torah was made lawful by the Prophet's permission. 'Abdallah b. 'Amr b. al-'Āṣ told the Prophet about his dream. He saw that he had on one of his fingers honey and on the other one butter. The Prophet explained the dream and said: "You will read the two Books: the Torah and the Furqān (i.e. the Qur'ān — K)". He read in fact both these Books.[128] This tradition, transmitted by Ibn Lahī'a,[129] was vehemently attacked by al-Dhahabī in the eighth century AH: nobody was allowed to read the Torah after the Qur'ān had been revealed. The Torah, argues al-Dhahabī, had been changed and tampered with; truth and falsehood are mixed in this book. It is permissible to read this book for one purpose only: to answer the Jews.[130] But opinions about the study of the Torah were quite different in the first century. Ibn

120 *Sa'd al-su'ūd* (al-Najaf, 1369/1950), pp. 47–63; a great part of the quotations of Ibn Ṭāwūs were copied by al-Majlisī, *op. cit.*, XIV, 43–48; and see *ibid.*, pp. 36–37.

121 Abū Nu'aym, *op. cit.*, IV, 46–47.

122 *Ibid.*, IV, 67 inf.

123 Usāma b. Munqidh, *op. cit.*, p. 444: "*wa-min kalāmi sulaymāna bni dāwūda 'alayhi l-salām*".

124 Proverbs xxvii 1, 2, 10; xxix 19; Ecclesiastes xi 1.

125 *A'māl al-qulūb wa-l-jawāriḥ*, ed. 'Abd al-Qādir Aḥmad 'Aṭā (Cairo, 1969), p. 45.

126 *Ibid.*, p. 82.

127 *Sa'd al-su'ūd*, pp. 32–40; cf. al-Majlisī, *op. cit.*, XI, 120–121, 151–152, 269, 282–283 (new ed.).

128 Al-Dhahabī, *Ta'rīkh al-islām* (Cairo, 1367), III, 38; Abū l-Maḥāsin Yūsuf b. Mūsā al-Ḥanafī, *al-Mu'taṣar min al-mukhtaṣar* (Hyderabad, 1362), II, 265; cf. al-Mauṣilī, *Ghāyat al-wasā'il*, Ms. Cambridge Qq 33 (10) fol. 42 inf.

129 See on him Ibn Kathīr, *al-Bidāya*, VI, 242 ult. (*ḍa'ī*); al-Tibrizī, *Mishkāt al-maṣābīḥ* (Karachi, 1350), p. 160, l. 5 (*ḍa'īf*); al-Dhahabī, *Mīzān al-i'tidāl*, I, 479, ult.; *ibid.*, III, 267 (*wa-bnu lahī'ata mimman qad tabarra'nā min 'uhdatihi*); *ibid.*, II, 475–483, no. 4530; al-Fasawī. *op. cit.*, fol. 84a, inf.; Mughulṭāy, *al-Zahr al-bāsim*, Ms. Leiden, Or. 370, fol. 116a.

130 *Siyar a'lām al-nubalā'*, ed. As'ad Ṭalas (Cairo, 1962), III, 57.

Sa'd records a story about 'Āmir b. 'Abd Qays and Ka'b sitting in a mosque: Ka'b read the Torah and explained some interesting passages to 'Āmir.[131] Abū l-Jald al-Jaunī used to read the Qur'ān and the Torah. He used to celebrate each conclusion of reading of the Torah (he read it during six days) summoning people (for this purpose) and used to quote a saying that Mercy descends at each conclusion of the reading of the Torah.[132]

Shī'ī tradition explicitly stressed the link between the Torah and the true knowledge of the Prophet, 'Alī and the succeeding Imāms. The Tablets of Moses reached the Prophet and he handed them over to 'Alī.[133] The Tablets of Moses, the Gospel, the *Ṣuḥuf Ibrāhīm* and the *Zabūr* are in the possession of the Shī'ī Imāms.[134] The *White Jafr* contains the Torah, the Gospel, the *Zabūr* and the first Books of God.[135]

The idea that there was identity of contents between Jewish revelation and Islam was followed by the idea which established identity of fate between these two peoples. Ibn 'Abbās stated that everything which happened among the Children of Israel will happen to the Muslim community.[136] The Children of Israel were righteous until the sons of their captive women grew up. They championed *ra'y*[137] and therefore went astray and led other people astray, said the Prophet.[138] This tradition is recorded by al-Fasawī and after it comes the following remark: "Sufyān said: 'We examined it and found that the first person to champion *ra'y* in Medīna was Rabī'a, in Kūfa Abū Ḥanīfa, in Baṣra al-Battī; they were the sons of captive women'."[139] The Prophet predicted that the Muslim community would follow a path identical with that of the Children of Israel and of the Christians.[140]

These points of resemblance refer, of course, to pejorative aspects of Jewish history; they are used to point out dangers which the Muslim community is facing. Sometimes, however, the identification is done in a laudatory spirit.

131 *Ṭabaqāt*, VII, 110.

132 *Ibid.*, VII, 222.

133 Al-Majlisī, *op. cit.*, XIII, 225 (new ed.); and see al-Ṣaffār al-Qummī, *Baṣā'ir al-darajāt*, ([n.p.], 1285), pp. 37–38 sup.; al-'Ayyāshī, *op. cit.*, Ms. India Office 4153, fol. 127b.

134 Al-Majlisī, *op. cit.*, XXVI, 180–189 (new ed.).

135 *Ibid.*, XXVI, 18.

136 Nu'aym b. Ḥammād, *op. cit.*, fol. 4b: *lam yakun fī banī isrā'īla shay'un illā wa-huwa fīkum kā'inun.*

137 Cf. "Aṣḥāb al-Ra'y", *EI*² (Schacht).

138 Ibn Mājah, *Sunan* (Cairo, 1349), I, 28; al-Bayhaqī, *Ma'rifat al-sunan*, I, 110 (and see the references of the editor).

139 *Al-Ma'rifa wa-l-ta'rīkh*, fol. 271a.

140 Al-Muttaqī l-Hindī, *Kanz*, XI, 123, nos. 555–556; Ibn al-Athīr, *al-Nihāya*, IV, 28; Ibn Ṭāwūs, *Sa'd*, pp. 64, 65, 116, l. 3; al-'Ayyashī, *op. cit.*, Ms. fol. 93a–b; and see M. Talbi, "Les Bida", *Studia Islamica*, XII, 50.

Ḥaddithū 'an banī isrā'īla

The Aus and the Khazraj, says a tradition recorded by Ibn Isḥāq, are descendents of four hundred scholars from among the Children of Israel, left by *Tubba'* in Medīna. Abū Ayyūb was the descendant of the scholar whom *Tubba'* entrusted with the keeping of the letter for the Prophet; Abū Ayyūb indeed handed it over to the Prophet.[141] A late compilation recording the story remarks that this genealogy of the Anṣār is a Jewish plot.[142]

The Prophet states, according to a Shī'ī tradition, that his name is Aḥmad and Isrā'īl and that the obligations laid by God upon Isrā'īl are incumbent on him as well.[143] By Children of Israel the ('Alid — K) *Āl Muḥammad* are meant.[144] The 'Alids in the Umayyad period complained that they were "like the *Āl Mūsā* in the time of *Āl Fir'aun*".[145] Ibn Ṭāwūs records many passages from the Torah about Aaron[146] in order to stress the importance of the utterance of the Prophet, that 'Alī is in relation to the Prophet in the position of Aaron in relation to Moses.[147] The role of 'Alī as *waṣiyy* in relation to the Prophet corresponds to the role of Joshua b. Nūn in relation to Moses.[148]

But the feeling of affinity or identity which Muslims experienced with regard to the righteous from among the Children of Israel did not detract from the latter's faults, sins and vices. The *sunna* of the Children of Israel should not be followed. In many traditions the Faithful are warned of these *sunan* and ordered to act contrary to them.[149]

Even their strictness in observing religious rites was criticized. "Do not be like the Children of Israel; having been strict with themselves, God imposed strictness on them."[150]

141 Al-Samhūdī, *Wafā' al-wafā*, ed. Muḥ. Muḥyī l-Dīn 'Abd al-Ḥamīd (Cairo, 1374/1955), I, 188–189; Mughulṭāy, *op. cit.*, fol. 194a; Ibn Ẓuhayra, *al-Jāmi' al-laṭif*, (Cairo, 1357/1958), pp. 51–54; al-Ṣāliḥī, *al-Sīra al-shāmiya*, Ms. Atif 1753, fol. 69a.

142 'Abd al-Ḥāfiz b. 'Uthmān al-Qāri' al-Ṭā'ifī, *Jalā' al-qulūb wa-kashf al-kurūb bi-manāqib abī ayyūb*, (Istanbul, 1298), pp. 14–15.

143 Al-'Ayyāshī, *op. cit.*, I, 44, no. 45 (and see *ibid.*, note 6).

144 *Ibid.*, I, 44, nos. 43, 44 (refers to Sūra ii 48).

145 Furāt, *Tafsīr* (al-Najaf [n.d.]), p. 47, l. 1.

146 *Sa'd al-su'ūd*, pp. 43–46; Ex. xxix 5, 27, 31, 44, 13; Num. xvii 17.

147 *Sa'd al-su'ūd*, pp. 43–46 (and see p. 43: *i'lam anna qaula l-nabiyyi* (*ṣ*) *li-maulānā 'aliyyi bni abī ṭālibin* (*'a*) *anta minnī bi-manzilati hārūna min mūsā yashtamilu 'alā khaṣā'iṣa 'aẓīmatin naḥwi l-khilāfati*; *wa-qad wajadtu fī l-taurāti min manāzili hārūna min mūsā mā yaḍīqu mā qaṣadnāhu bi-fuṣūli hādhā l-kitābi mimmā yantafi'u bi-ma'rifatihā dhawū* (text: *dhawī*) *l-albābi.*

148 Furāt, *op. cit.*, pp. 65–68.

149 Furāt, *op. cit.*, p. 42: *wa-lā ta'khudhū sunnata banī isrā'īla kadhdhabū anbiyā'ahum wa-qatalū ahla baytihim.*

150 Al-'Āmilī, *al-Kashkūl*, I, 221: *inna llāha yuḥibbu an yu'khadha bi-rukhaṣihi kamā yuḥibbu an yu'khadha bi-'azā'imihi, fa- qbalū rukhaṣa llāhi wa-lā takūnū ka-banī isrā'īl ḥīna shaddadū 'alā anfusihim fa-shaddada llāhu 'alayhim*; and see Ibn Kathīr, *Tafsīr*, I, 193–194; cf. Samau'al la-Maghribī, *Ifḥām al-yahūd*, ed. M. Perlmann (New York, 1964), pp. 71–85.

III

Contrary to the permission to transmit traditions about the Children of Israel concerning their history or stories about their prophets and saints, the early sources point clearly to the tendency of the orthodox circles to prevent the Faithful from learning or copying the Holy Scriptures of the People of the Book, and especially of legal chapters or chapters concerning the tenets of faith. 'Umar, says a tradition, walked past a Jew from Qurayẓa and asked him to copy for him summary chapters from the Torah. When he came to the Prophet and begged his permission to read these chapters, the face of the Prophet became changed (scil. with anger — K). 'Umar was frightened by this and exclaimed: "I am satisfied by Allāh as God, by Islām as religion and by Muḥammad as Prophet." When the rage of the Prophet had gone, he remarked: "I swear by Him Who keeps in His hand the soul of Muḥammad: were Moses among you and if you followed him, leaving me, you would have gone astray; you are my lot among the peoples and I am your lot among the prophets".[151]

It is interesting to note that the Jew in the story is referred to in a favourable manner: *marartu bi-akhin lī min qurayẓata.*[152] It is also of interest that the Prophet emphasizes the adherence of Moses to his faith. According to a tradition on the authority of Anas, the Prophet met Jesus[153] and al-Dhahabī considered Jesus as one of the Companions of the Prophet.[154] An utterance of the Prophet similar to the one about Moses is recorded in the story of Ḥafṣa. She brought to the Prophet a shoulder-bone on which was written the story of Joseph. The Prophet became angry, the colour of his face changed and he said: "Were Joseph to come while I am amongst you and were you to follow him, you would have gone astray".[155]

Slightly different is the utterance of the Prophet as recorded in another tradition. 'Umar asked the Prophet whether he would be permitted to write down traditions (*aḥādīth*) heard from Jews, by which he was pleased. The

151 *Al-Jāmi'*, fol. 60a; 'Abd al-Razzāq, *al-Muṣannaf*, fol. 114a; al-Suyūṭī, *al-Durr*, II, 48; cf. another version of this tradition 'Abd al-Razzāq, *op. cit.*, fol. 114a with the utterance: *innamā bu'ithtu fātiḥan wa-khātaman wa-u'ṭītu jawāmi'a l-kalimi wa-fawātiḥahu wa-khtuṣira lī l-ḥadīthu ikhtiṣāran.* And see Abū Dā'ūd, *Marāsīl* (Cairo, 1310), p. 48; al-Khaṭīb al-Baghdādī, *Taqyīd*, p. 52.

152 See another version of this tradition in Muttaqī al-Hindī's *Kanz*, I, 334, no. 1629: 'Umar visited Khaybar and was pleased by some sayings of a Jew. The Jew dictated the sayings to 'Umar upon his request and 'Umar wrote them down on a skin which he brought to the Prophet. When 'Umar read it to the Prophet, he became angry and erased the writing. He said: "Do not follow these people because they got confused".

153 Al-Suyūṭī, *al-Ḥāwī*, II, 288.

154 *Ibid.*, p. 289, sup.

155 Ma'mar b. Rāshid, *al-Jāmi'*, fol. 133b; 'Abd al-Razzāq, *al-Muṣannaf*, fol. 114a.

Prophet said: "Are you following the Jews and Christians in their confusion? I brought it (i.e. the religion, or the Qur'ān — K) white and pure; if Moses were alive he would have to follow me".[156]

A special *āya* was revealed in connection with this problem. Some Muslims, the tradition asserts, brought to the Prophet certain books which they had copied from the Jews. The Prophet said: "It is an error grave enough when people prefer a thing brought by someone else to another people over that which their own Prophet brought to them". Then *āya* 51 of *Sūra* 29 was revealed: *a-wa-lam yakfihim annā anzalnā 'alayka l-kitāba yutlā 'alayhim...* etc.[157] The Prophet finally gave his decisive utterance when asked by 'Umar about studying the Torah: "Do not learn the Torah, you have to learn what has been revealed to you (i.e. the Qur'ān — K) and believe in it".[158]

In fact 'Umar forbade copying or reading the Books of Jews and Christians. According to a tradition a man came to 'Umar and informed him about a wonderful book which he had found in Madā'in when the Muslims had conquered the city. "Is it from the Book of Allāh"? (i.e. the Qur'ān — K) 'Umar asked. "No", said the man. 'Umar began to beat him with his whip, reciting the first four *āyas* from *Sūrat Yūsuf* and said: "What caused the peoples who lived before you to perish was that they devoted themselves to the study of books of their scholars and bishops and abandoned the Torah and the Gospel until those two Books became effaced and knowledge of them disappeared".[159] In another story a similar case is told. 'Alqama and al-Aswad came to Ibn Mas'ūd and showed him a scroll (*ṣaḥīfa*) containing a story which they found pleasing. 'Abdallah b. Mas'ūd ordered to efface the script. "These hearts are vessels (of knowledge — K); engage them with the Qur'ān, not with anything else", he said.[160]

'Umar seems to have been especially concerned about the *Book of Daniel*. The book is said to have been found in a grave in Tustar when the Muslims conquered the city. It is said to have been Daniel's grave.[161] The book was brought to 'Umar and he sent it to Ka'b who rendered it into Arabic. It is

156 Al-Zamakhsharī, *al-Fā'iq*, ed. 'Alī Muḥ. al-Bijāwī – Muḥ. Abū l-Faḍl Ibrāhīm (Cairo, 1367/1948), III, 218; Abū 'Ubayd, *Gharīb al-ḥadīth* (Hyderabad, 1385/1966), III, 28–29; cf. Ibn al-Athīr, *al-Nihāya*, s.v. *h w k*; al-Majlisī, *op. cit.*, VIII, 211 (lithogr. ed.).

157 Al-Suyūṭī, *Lubāb al-nuqūl* (Cairo, 1373/1954), p. 170; al-Qurṭubī, *Tafsīr*, XIII, 355; Ibn Shahrāshūb, *Manāqib āl abī ṭālib* (al-Najaf, 1376/1956), I, 48; Ibn 'Abd al-Barr, *Jāmi' bayān al-'ilm*, II, 40–41.

158 Al-Muttaqī l-Hindī, *op. cit.*, I, 333, no. 1627.

159 *Ibid.*, I, 335, no. 1632.

160 Abū 'Ubayd, *Faḍā'il al-Qur'ān*, Ms. Leiden, Or. 3056, fol. 4a–b. Abū 'Ubayd remarks: "We think that this scroll was taken from a man who belonged to the People of the Book, therefore 'Abdallah b. Mas'ūd disliked it".

161 See *EI*², s.v. "Dāniyāl" (G. Vajda).

said to have contained information about strifes (*fitan*) which will happen.[162] Abū l-ʿĀliya[163] says about the book: "I was the first Arab to read this book the way I read the Qur'ān." It contained, says Abū l-ʿĀliya, information about your history (*sīratukum*) and your matters, your religion and the ways of your speech (*luḥūn kalāmikum*) and what will happen in the future.[164] When ʿUmar was informed about a man who copied (or read) the Book of Daniel, he ordered that man to be brought into his presence, beat him with his whip until he promised to burn books of this kind and not to read them.[165]

A saying from *Kitāb Dāniyāl* is recorded by Ḥamd b. Muḥammad al-Khaṭṭābī.[166] A lengthy passage about the campaigns of the Sufyānī is quoted from *Kitāb Dāniyāl* by Abū l-Ḥusayn Aḥmad b. Jaʿfar b. al-Munādī in his *Kitāb al-malāḥim* and recorded by al-Qurṭubī.[167] A significant passage from *Kitāb Dāniyāl* is recorded by al-Majlisī. It contains predictions about weather during the year, crops, plagues and wars established according to the date of the first day of Muḥarram (Saturday, Sunday, Monday... etc.) and the month in which the eclipse of the sun or the moon will occur. Al-Rāwandī marks this material as stories of the type of *malāḥim*.[168] The Book of Daniel seems to have been read by Kaʿb and the twenty Jewish scholars in their discourse in Jerusalem. Kaʿb gave orders to throw this book, which he described as being "the Torah as revealed by God to Moses, unchanged and unaltered", into the sea of Tiberias. Kaʿb feared that people might rely on it (*khashītu an yuttakala ʿalā mā fīhā*). When the man sent by Kaʿb arrived at the middle of the sea, the waters parted so that he could see the bottom of the sea, and he threw the Book into the sea.[169]

There was, of course, the danger of the intentional changes and alterations of the Scriptures carried out by the People of the Book. This is reflected in a tradition about Kaʿb. He brought a book, whose leaves were torn out, to ʿUmar stating that it contained (chapters of) the Torah, and asked permission to

162 Nuʿaym b. Ḥammād, *op. cit.*, fol. 4b (= Ms. Atif, fol. 3a).

163 See on him Ibn Saʿd, *op. cit.*, VII, 112–117.

164 Al-Bayhaqī, *Kit. dalā'il al-nubuwwa*, Ms. Br. Mus., Or. 3013, fol. 65a; Ibn Kathīr, *al-Bidāya wa-l-nihāya*, II, 40–41.

165 Al-Khaṭīb al-Baghdādī, *Taqyīd*, p. 51; al-Muttaqī al-Hindī, *op. cit.*, I, 332–333, no. 1626; *ibid.*, 335–336, no. 1633; ʿAbd al-Razzāq, *op. cit.*, fol. 114a.

166 *Kitāb al-ʿuzla* (Cairo, 1352), p. 80.

167 *Al-Tadhkira*, ed. Aḥmad Muḥ. Mursī (Cairo [n.d.]), pp. 610–611.

168 *Biḥār al-anwār*, LVIII, 346–350 (new ed.).

169 Al-Dhahabī, *Siyar aʿlām al-nubalā'*, III, 323–325; and see *idem.*, *Ta'rīkh al-islām*, III, 99–101, on the bottom of the sea of Tiberias are buried the Ark of the Covenant and the Staff of Moses; they will be raised on the Day of Judgement. See al-Nuwayrī, *op. cit.*, XVI, 43.

read it. ʻUmar said: "If you know that the book contains the Torah revealed by God to Moses on Mount Sinai, read it day and night."[170]

Ibn Kathīr, quoting the traditions which forbid the consultation of scholars from among the People of the Book remarks: "These traditions serve as evidence that they made changes in the Holy Scriptures which they possess (*...baddalū mā bi-aydīhim min al-kutubi l-samāwiyati*), altered them and interpreted them in an improper way." They did not possess comprehensive knowledge of their Scriptures; in their translations into Arabic they made many errors and mistakes. Furthermore, they had bad intentions and erroneous views. One part of the Torah is manifest, publicly revealed, but a great part of it is hidden. The manifest parts of the Torah contain changes, alterations, erroneous expressions and elusive ideas. Ibn Kathīr accuses Kaʻb of transmitting traditions many of which are not worth the ink with which they are written, and some of which are false.[171] "Some of the *Isrāʼīliyyāt* were invented by some of their *zanādiqa*; some of them may be sound, but we do not need them: what is written in the Book of God (i.e. the Qur'ān — K) is sufficient for us and we do not need to look for it in the remaining books (revealed) before it; neither God nor His Messenger caused us to lack their knowledge."[172] The same accusations of lies, alterations, changes and intentional misinterpretations are repeated by Ibn Kathīr in the course of a section in which he records the traditions which forbid consultation of scholars from among the People of the Book.[173]

Ibn al-Jauzī, the prolific author of the sixth century AH, expresses similar views. The stories concerning the early peoples and especially the Children of Israel rarely contain authentic accounts. The Muslim religious law (*sharʻ*), Ibn al-Jauzī says, is sufficient and the Prophet ordered ʻUmar to discard certain passages from the Torah which he brought to him. Some stories of the Isrāʼīliyyāt are absurd, like the story about David who sent Uriyah to be killed in order to marry his wife.[174]

The early sources mentioned in this paper bear evidence of the close contacts between Muslims, Jews and Christians at the end of the first century of the Hijra. The traditions recorded by Maʻmar b. Rāshid in his *Jāmiʻ* can be estimated as going back to original sources of the end of the first century. The material of Abū ʻUbayd in his *Mawāʻiẓ* seems to stem from the same

170 Abū ʻUbayd, *Gharīb al-ḥadīth*, IV, 262; al-Zamakhsharī, *al-Fāʼiq*, I, 651; Ibn al-Athīr, *al-Nihāya*, II, 468, s.v. *sh r m*; J. Goldziher, "Über Muh. Polemik gegen *Ahl al-Kitāb*", *ZDMG* XXXII, 345 (read correctly: *fa-qraʼhā ānāʼa l-layli*).

171 Ibn Kathīr, *al-Bidāya wa-l-nihāya*, II, 132–134.

172 Ibn Kathīr, *Tafsīr*, IV, 282.

173 *Ibid.*, V, 329–330.

174 Ibn al-Jauzī, *Kit. al-quṣṣāṣ*, Ms. Leiden, Or. 988, fol. 20a.

period. The assumption of W. Montgomery Watt[175] that the material of the Bible discussed above was directed in the first phase towards illiterate people with no knowledge of the Bible, can hardly be accepted. W. M. Watt takes it that the passage in Ibn 'Abd al-Barr's *Jāmi' bayān al-'ilm*, II, 40–43 about "Avoidance of information from Jews and Christians" suggests "that it belongs to the first phase" because "it envisages Muslims conversing with Jews and Christians, but not reading their books";[176] but this argument is in fact untenable. The tradition recorded by al-Bukhārī[177] reports explicitly that "the Jews used to read the Torah in Hebrew and to interpret it to the people of Islam in Arabic." Al-Suddī reports that some Jews used to compile books, claiming that they are books revealed by God, and used to sell them at cheap prices to the Arabs.[178] The stories about books of *Ahl al-Kitāb* being copied by Muslims, quoted above and mentioned in the chapter of Ibn 'Abd al-Barr bear evidence that the contacts between Muslims and the People of the Book were not confined to mere consultation. Lastly it may be remarked that the title of the chapter is: *Bāb mukhtaṣar fī muṭāla'ati kutubi ahli l-kitābi wa-l-riwāyati 'anhum.* It is plainly stated that the subject discussed in the chapter is the reading of books of the *Ahl al-Kitāb* and transmission of traditions on their authority, not merely conversing. W. M. Watt's doubts, as to "whether any of it (i.e. the traditions recorded by Ibn 'Abd al-Barr) had its present form at a still earlier period" are unfounded; as far as the "*Jāmi'*" of Ma'mar and the "*Muṣannaf*" of 'Abd al-Razzāq are concerned, the traditions and their *isnāds* are copied by Ibn 'Abd al-Barr with accuracy; this can be ascertained by comparing the material of Ibn 'Abd al-Barr with the Mss. quoted in this paper.

As already mentioned there was no serious opposition to the Jewish and Christian traditions transmitted by Jewish and Christians converts, in so far as they concorded with the views of orthodox Islam. Opposition seems to have appeared in connection with those aspects of the Jewish and Christian tradition which may have some bearing on Muslim belief or practice. In such cases the motives are clear; the stories about the prohibition to copy the Scriptures of *Ahl al-Kitāb* seem to be connected with cases of this kind. This can be gauged from the tradition about a group of Jews who embraced Islam, but asked the Prophet's permission to observe the Sabbath and to study the Torah at night. They were, of course, denied this permission. A verse of the Qur'an (Sura ii 208) was revealed about it.[179]

175 *The Early Development of the Muslim Attitude to the Bible* (Glasgow Univ. Oriental Society Transactions, XVI, 1955–1956, pp. 50–62.

176 *Ibid.*, pp. 60–62. 177 *Al-Ṣaḥīḥ* (Cairo [n.d.]), VI, 25; Ibn Kathīr, *Tafsīr*, I, 329.

178 Al-Suyūṭī, *al-Durr al-manthūr*, I, 83.

179 Al-Ṭabarī, *Tafsīr*, IV, 255–256, no. 4016; Ibn Kathīr, *Tafsīr*, I, 439–440; al-Suyūṭī, *al-Durr*, I, 271; al-Rāzī, *Tafsīr*, V, 226.

The orthodox solution was that a Muslim had to believe in the Torah and the Gospel, but not to observe the practices enjoined in these Books. The Prophet said: "Believe in the Torah, the *Zabūr* and the Evangel, but the Qur'ān should suffice you."[180]

This formula, which breathes an air of compromise, enabled indeed the transmission of Jewish and Christian tradition. This tradition, licensed by the utterance *ḥaddithū ʿan banī isrāʾīl* became part and parcel of Muslim literature as is abundantly reflected in the literature of the *tafsīr*, *zuhd* and *adab*.[181]

180 Ibn Kathīr, *Tafsīr*, I, 329–330: *qāla rasūlu llāhi: āminū bi-l-taurāti wa-l-zabūri wa-l-injīli wa-l-yasaʿkumu l-qurʾānu*, and comp. *ibid.*: *innamā umirnā an nuʾmina bi-l-taurāti wa-l-injīli wa-lā naʿmala bi-mā fīhimā*; and see al-Suyūṭī, *al-Durr*, II, 225–226: *lā dīna illā l-islāmu, wa-kitābunā nasakha kulla kitābin, wa-nabiyyunā khātamu l-nabiyyīna, wa-umirnā an naʿmala bi-kitābinā wa-nuʾmina bi-kitābikum.*

181 I wish to thank Dr. M. Nadav and Mr. E. Wust of the National and University Library, Jerusalem; Dr. A. Sj. Koningsveld of the University Library of Leiden; the keepers and staff of the British Museum; Cambridge University Library; Chester Beatty Collection, Dublin; and the Süleymaniye, Istanbul, for granting me permission to peruse manuscripts and providing me with microfilms.

ADDITIONAL NOTES

ad p.216, note 7: al-Ṭaḥāwī, *Mushkil al-āthār*. Hyderabad 1333, I, 40-42, 168 inf. - 169 sup. (from ʿAbd al-Razzāq); al-Muttaqī l-Hindī, *Kanz al-ʿummāl*, X, 129, no. 1094.

ad p.216, note 8: cf. al-Ḥumaydī, *al-Musnad*, ed. Ḥabīb al-Raḥmān al-Aʿẓamī, Beirut-Cairo 1382, II, 492, no. 1165; and see the combined tradition recorded in Suyūṭī's *Taḥdhīr al-khawāṣṣ min akādhībi l-quṣṣāṣ*, p.14, no. 13; *la-taktubū ʿannī shay'an siwā l-qur'āni, fa-man kataba ʿannī shay'an ghayra l-qur'āni fa-l-yamḥuhu, wa-ḥaddithū ʿan banī isrā'īla wa-lā ḥaraja, wa-ḥaddithū ʿannī wa-lā ta kdhibū alayya, fa-man kadhaba ʿalayya fa-l-yatabawwa maqʿadahu min al-nār;* ʿAlī al-Qārī, *al-Asrār al-marfūʿa fī l-akhbāri l-mauḍūʿa*, ed. Muḥammad al-Ṣabbāgh, Beirut 1391/1971, p.9; al-Munāwī, *Fayḍ al-qadīr*, Beirut 1391/1972, III, 377, no. 3691; al-Muttaqī l-Hindī, *op.cit.*, X, 129, no. 1096.

ad p.216, note 9: See al-Bayhaqī, *Maʿrifat al-sunan*, I, 45-47 (different versions are recorded: *man qāla ʿalayya ma lam aqul...,...inna lladhī yakdhibu ʿalayya yubnā lahu baytun fī l-nār..., man kadhaba ʿalayya falyaltamis li-janbihi malja'an min al-nār;* and see the references provided by the editor): Abū Yūsuf, *Kitāb al-āthār*, ed. Abū l-Wafā, Cairo 1355, p.207, no. 922; al-Suyūṭī, *Taḥdhīr al-khawāṣṣ min akādhībi l-quṣṣāṣ*, pp. 8-65 (and see the references of the editor); al-Ṭaḥāwī, *Mushkil al-āthār*, I, 164-175; Aḥmad b. ʿAlī al-Marwazī, *Musnad Abī Bakr*, ed. Shuʿayb al-Arnāʾūṭ, Beirut 1390/1970, pp. 132-133, no. 69; al-Muttaqī l-Hindī, *op.cit.*, X, nos. 1401, 1408-1409, 1415-1418; Ibn Ḥajar al-Haytamī, *al-Zawājir ʿan iqtirāf al-kabāʾir*, Cairo 1390/1970, I, 97-98.

ad p.216, note 9: Abū Yaʿlā, *Musnad*, Ms. Fātiḥ 1149 fol. 19b; al-Ḥumaydī, *op.cit.*, II, 492, no. 1166; Ibn Ḥazm al-*Iḥkām fī uṣūli l-aḥkām*, ed. Muḥamad Aḥmad ʿAbd al-ʿAzīz, Cairo 1398/1978, I, 249, 255, II, 1065.

ad p.222, note 30: Cf. Ibn ʿArabī, *Muḥāḍarat al-abrār*, 1388/1968, II, 141-144; al-Suyūṭī, *al-Durr al-manthūr*, III, 120-126; Abū Nuʿaym, *Ḥilya*, III, 375-376; al-Majlisī, *Biḥār al-anwār*, XCIV, 6-7, 10-19, 185-187.

ad p.223, note 37: Cf. Anonymous, *al-Taʾrīkh al-muḥkam*, Ms. Br. Mus., Or. 8653, fols. 23a, 41a-b; Ibn Bābūyah, *ʿIlal al-sharāʾiʿ*, Najaf 1385/1966, pp. 137-139, nos. 5-9; al-Faḍl b. al-Ḥasan al-Ṭabarsī, *Iʿlām al-warā bi-aʿlam al-hudā*, ed. ʿAlī Akbar al-Ghaffārī, Tehran 1338, p. 217; al-Ganjī, *Kifāyat al-ṭālib fī manāqib ʿalī b. abī ṭālib ʿalayhi l-salām*, ed. Muḥammad Hādī l-Amīnī, Najaf 1390/1970, p. 352(and see the references supplied by the editor); cf. al-Sayyid al-Ḥimyarī, *Dīwān*, ed. Shākir Hādī Shakar, Beirut n.d., pp.201, 249.

ad p.223, note 38: See Ibn Kathīr, *al-Bidāya*, VI, 235; al-Suyūṭī, *al-Durr al-manthūr*, III, 125.

ad p.223, note 40: Cf. Ibn Nāṣir al-Dīn al-Dimashqī, *Jāmiʿ al-āthār fī maulidi l-nabiyyi l-mukhtār*, Ms. Cambridge Or. 913, fols. 16a, 47a, inf.

ad p.223, note 40: See Ibn Asākir, *Taʾrīkh (tahdhīb)*, I, 438.

ad p.228, note 92: See ʿAbd al-Malik b. Ḥabīb, *Taʾrīkh*, Ms. Bodl. Marsh, 228, pp. 61inf. -63; Abū Nuʿaym, *Ḥilya*, III, 265-266; al-Suyūṭī *al-Durr al-manthūr*, III, 122.

ad p.229, note 106: Cf. Ibn Nāṣir al-Dīn al-Dimashqī, *Jāmiʿ al-āthār* fol. 8a, inf. -8b sup. The author discusses the meaning of the word "Torah" in the prediction of the Prophet that ʿAbdallah b. ʿAmr b. al-ʿĀṣ would read the Torah and the Qurʾān stressing that Torah may denote a wider meaning than the Torah of Moses: *wa-janaḥa baʿḍu l-mutaʾakhkhirīn, wa-tābaʿahu baʿḍu aṣḥābihi ilā anna hādhā l-waṣfa l-madhkūra fī ḥadīthi ʿabdi llāhi bni ʿamri bni l-ʿāṣi (r) ʿan al-taurāti lā yurīdu bihi l-taurāta l-muʿayyanata llatī hiya kitābu mūsā (ʿa.s) fa-inna lafẓa l-taurāti wa-l-injīli wa-l-qurʾāni wa-l-zabūri yurādu bihi l-kutubu l-muʿayyanatu tāratan wa-yurādu bihi l-jinsu tāratan; fa-qauluhu : akhbirnī bi-ṣifati rasūli llāhi (s) fī l-taurāti immā an yurīdu bihi jinsa l-kutubi l-mutaqaddimati wa-kulluhā tusammā taurātan wa-yakūnu hādhā l-waṣfu fī baʿḍihā, au yurīdu bihi l-taurāta l-muʿayyanata: kitāba mūsā (ʿa.s)...*

ad p.230, note 110: See Ibn Qayyim al-Jauziyya, *Ighāthat al-lahfān min maṣāyid al-shayṭān*, Cairo 1358/1939, I, 79; Ibn Abī l-Dunyā, *al-ʿAql wa-faḍluhu*, ed. Muḥammad Zāhid al-Kautharī, Cairo 1365/1946, p. 15.

ad p. 231, note 128: See al-Khargūshī, *al-Bishāra wa-l-nidhāra fī taʿbīr al-ruʾyā*, Ms. Br. Mus. Or. 6262, fol. 121a; Ibn Nāṣir al-Dīn, *Jāmiʿ al-āthār*, fol. 8a; al-Fāsī, *al-Iqd al-thamīn*, V, 224; Ibn ʿAbd al-Ḥakam, *Futūḥ miṣr*, p. 254, ll. 12-15.

ad p.232, note 131: Another *tābiʿ* who used to read the Torah and the Gospel was Aus b. Bishr; he is said to have been equal in knowledge with ʿAbdallah b. ʿUmar. It is noteworthy that he was the *ʿarīf* of the Maʿāfir (Ibn ʿAsākir, *Taʾrīkh* [*tahdhīb*] III, 158).

ad p.233, note 141: Cf. Ibn Nāṣir al-Dīn, *op.cit.*, fol. 52a-b.

ad p.233, note 145: Cf. Ibn Saʿd, *Ṭabaqāt*, V. 95, 219 ult. -220.

ad p.234, note 151: See Nūr al-Dīn al-Haythamī, *Majmaʿ al-zawāʾid*, II, 182.

ad p.234, note 152: Cf. al-Suyūṭī, *al-Durr al-manthūr* IV, 3 (different versions of the story).

ad p.235, note 156: See Abū Nuʿaym, *Ḥilya*, V, 136.

ad p.236, note 165: Cf. Nūr al-Dīn al-Haythamī, *Majmaʿ al-zawāʾid*, II, 182.

ad p.237, note 170: See Ibn al-Athīr, *Jāmiʿ al-uṣūl min aḥādīthi l-rasūl (ṣ)*, Cairo 1374/1955, XII, 372, no. 9469. Cf. ʿAbd al-Razzāq, *al-Muṣannaf*, VIII, 111, no. 14518 (and see the references given by the editor).

XV

THE BATTLE OF THE ḤARRA

Some Socio-Economic Aspects

The numerous reports of the revolt against Yazīd b. Muʿāwiya b. abī Sufyān in Medina and the bloody battle of the Ḥarra (27 Dhū l-Ḥijja, 63 AH = 26 August, AD 683) contain many details on the preparations for the battle, letters sent by the Caliph to the leaders of the rebels, speeches of the leaders and the battle itself, as well as about rebels killed on the battlefield or executed at the order of Muslim b. ʿUqba, the commander of the army sent by Yazīd to quell the rebellion.[1] The various accounts, some

1 See Khalīfa b. Khayyāṭ, *Ta'rīkh* (ed. Ḍiyā' al-Dīn al-ʿUmarī) (Baghdād, 1386/1967) I, 224–225; Ibn Saʿd, *Ṭabaqāt* (Beirut, 1377/1957) V, 38–39, 144–147, 170–172, 177, 215, 225–226, 255–256, 259–260, 263–267, 270, 274–275, 277–280, 295–296, 298; al-Balādhurī, *Ansāb al-ashrāf* (ed. M. Schloessinger) (Jerusalem, 1938) IVb, 19–46; al-Yaʿqūbī, *Ta'rīkh* (al-Najaf, 1384/1964) II, 237–238; al-Dīnawarī, *al-Akhbār al-ṭiwāl* (ed. ʿAbd al-Munʿim ʿĀmir — Jamāl al-Dīn al-Shayyāl) (Cairo, 1960), 264–267; al-Fākihī, *Ta'rīkh Makka*, Ms. Leiden Or. 463, fol. 400a; Muṣʿab b. ʿAbdallah al-Zubayrī, *Nasab Quraysh* (ed. Levi-Provençal) (Cairo, 1953), 133, 215, 222, 228, 256, 282, 361, 371, 384; al-Ṭabarī, *Ta'rīkh* (Cairo, 1358/1939) IV, 366–381; Ibn Qutayba, *ʿUyūn al-akhbār* (Cairo, 1343/1924) I, 202; Ibn ʿAbd Rabbihi, *al-ʿIqd al-farīd* (ed. Aḥmad Amīn, Aḥmad al-Zayn, Ibrāhīm al-Abyārī) (Cairo, 1381/1962) IV, 387–390; al-Masʿūdī, *Murūj al-dhahab* (ed. Muḥammad Muḥyī l-Dīn ʿAbd al-Ḥamīd) (Cairo, 1357/1938) III, 17–18; idem, *al-Tanbīh wa-l-ishrāf* (ed. de Goeje) (Leiden, 1894), 304–306; Ibn Qutayba, *al-Maʿārif* (ed. al-Ṣāwī) (Cairo, 1390/1970; reprint), 153, 172; Ps. Ibn Qutayba, *al-Imāma wa-l-siyāsa* (Cairo, 1331) I, 168–190; Abū l-Faraj, *al-Aghānī* (Cairo, 1285) I, 12–16; Ibn Ra's Ghanama, *Manāqil al-durar fī manābit al-zahar*, Ms. Chester Beatty 4254, fols. 73b–81a; Ibn ʿAsākir, *Ta'rīkh* (*tahdhīb*) (ed. Ibn Badrān) (Damascus, 1351) VII, 372–374, 407–413; Sibṭ Ibn al-Jauzī, *Tadhkirat al-khawāṣṣ* (al-Najaf, 1383/1964), 287–292; al-Dhahabī, *Ta'rīkh al-Islām* (Cairo, 1368) II, 354–359; idem, *Siyar aʿlām al-nubalā'* (ed. Asʿad Ṭalas) (Cairo, 1962) III, 217–220; Ibn Kathīr, *al-Bidāya wa-l-nihāya* (Beirut — al-Riyāḍ, 1966) VI, 233–235; VIII, 211–212, 215–224; al-Qurṭubī, *al-Tadhkira* (ed. Aḥmad Muḥammad Mursī) (Cairo, n.d.), 605–606; al-Damīrī, *Ḥayāt al-ḥayawān* (Cairo, 1383/1963) I, 60–61; al-Bayhaqī, *al-Maḥāsin wa-l-masāwī* (ed. Muḥammad Abū l-Faḍl Ibrāhīm) (Cairo, 1380/1961) I, 99–104; Muṭahhar b. Ṭāhir al-Maqdisī, *al-Bad' wa-l-ta'rīkh* (ed. C. Huart) (Paris, 1919) VII, 13–14; al-Suyūṭī, *Ta'rīkh al-khulafā'* (ed. Muḥammad Muḥyī l-Dīn ʿAbd al-Ḥamīd) (Cairo,

of which contain divergent details or contradictions, help us nevertheless to gain an insight into the consecutive stages of the conflict, the attitudes of different tribal groups and their leaders and the particulars of the military operation.

The reports on the factors of the conflict between the Caliph and the people of Medina and the causes of the revolt are, however, meagre and give almost unanimous emphasis to the religious motives of the clash. Some scattered details, occurring in fragmentary accounts outside the generally known sources, may shed new light on the roots of the conflict and the factors which were responsible for the battle of the Ḥarra.

I

Some details of the relations between Yazīd and Medina may be surveyed in the following lines. In the short period beginning with the investiture of Yazīd as Caliph and ending with the battle of the Ḥarra, there were frequent changes of governors in Medina. The governor appointed by Muʿāwiya, al-Walīd b. ʿUtba, was deposed shortly after Yazīd ascended the throne because he failed to prevent the escape of the two Qurashī leaders, al-Ḥusayn and ʿAbdallah b. al-Zubayr.[2] His successor, ʿAmr b. Saʿīd al-Ashdaq,[3] also failed to get an oath of allegiance from ʿAbdallah b. al-Zubayr or to seize him. He was then ordered by the Caliph to send against him a troop levied from among the people listed in the payment-roll.[4] A supplementary passage records the composition of the force sent by ʿAmr b. Saʿīd: four hundred soldiers, groups of the *mawālī banī umayya* and groups not listed in the payment list.[5] The people enrolled in the *dīwān* were reluctant to set out for Mecca in order to fight ʿAbdallah b. al-Zubayr.[6] Abū Mikhnaf stresses in his report that the majority of

1371/1952), 209–210; al-Diyārbakrī, *Taʾrīkh al-khamīs* (Cairo, 1283) II, 302–303; al-Samhūdī, *Wafāʾ al-wafā bi-akhbār dār al-Muṣṭafā* (ed. Muḥammad Muḥyī l-Dīn ʿAbd al-Ḥamīd) (Cairo, 1374/1955) I, 125–138; Ibn al-ʿImād, *Shadharāt al-dhabab* (Beirut, n.d.; reprint) I, 71; Khalīl b. Aybak al-Ṣafadī, *Tamām al-mutūn fī sharḥ risālat Ibn Zaydūn* (ed. Muḥammad Abū l-Faḍl Ibrāhīm) (Cairo, 1389/1969), 208–212; al-ʿIṣāmī, *Simṭ al-nujūm al-ʿawālī* (Cairo, 1380) III, 88–94; and see *EI*², s. v. al-Ḥarra (L. Veccia Vaglieri).

2 J. Wellhausen, *Das arabische Reich und sein Sturz* (Berlin, 1902; reprint), 92.

3 Al-Balādhurī, *op. cit.* IVb, 23, lines 9–10.

4 See al-Balādhurī, *op. cit.* IVb, 23, lines 18–19: *... kataba ilā ʿamri bni saʿīdin al-ashdaqi yaʾmuruhu an yuwajjiha ilā ʿabdi llāhi bni l-zubayri jayshan min ahli l-ʿaṭāʾi wa-l-dīwāni ...* (al-Balādhurī records it from the report of al-Wāqidī).

5 Al-Balādhurī, *op. cit.* IVb, 25, lines 15–21. 6 Ps. Ibn Qutayba, *op. cit.* I, 184: *... fa-ḍaraba ʿalā ahli l-dīwāni l-baʿtha ilā makkata wa-hum kārihūna li-l-khurūji.*

the recruited force preferred not to join the force and sent instead hired men, who ought to fight in their place. Most of the force sympathized with ʿAbdallah b. al-Zubayr. ʿAbdallah b. al-Zubayr sent against them troops recruited from among the people of al-Ḥijāz who were imbued with a fighting spirit and religious zeal and convinced that they were fighting for a just cause.[7] It was no wonder that the force sent by the governor of Medina under the command of ʿAmr b. al-Zubayr (the brother of ʿAbdallah b. al-Zubayr) was defeated; ʿAmr b. al-Zubayr was captured and treacherously and cruelly executed.

The sympathy of wide circles of the Muslim community was indeed with ʿAbdallah b. al-Zubayr. There were some doubts about the stability and duration of the Umayyad rule and an apprehension that ʿAbdallah b. al-Zubayr may succeed in grasping the power from the Umayyads. This feeling of uncertainty was rife even among some Umayyad officials. The governor of Medina, ʿAmr b. Saʿīd, according to one tradition, sent a messenger to ʿAbdallah b. ʿAmr b. al-ʿĀṣ (who stayed in Egypt) inquiring about it. ʿAbdallah b. ʿAmr b. al-ʿĀṣ, well known for his knowledge, piety and his ability to foretell future events because he was acquainted with the "Book of Daniel", answered that the rule would continue to be in the hands of the Umayyad Caliph and that ʿAbdallah b. al-Zubayr would not succeed in his effort to seize authority in the Muslim Empire. This led ʿAmr b. Saʿīd to take several measures so as to get hold of ʿAbdallah b. al-Zubayr by stratagem and deceit.[8] ʿAbdallah b. al-ʿAbbās proved to have had a sound evaluation of the situation after the death of Muʿāwiya: He assured the people in his presence that the Umayyad rule would endure and summoned them to give the oath of allegiance to Yazīd.[9] These stories may be spurious, but they help us to gauge the trends in some influential circles of the Muslim community.

ʿAmr b. Saʿīd failed to seize ʿAbdallah b. al-Zubayr, or to compel him to give the oath of allegiance to Yazīd. He was deposed (in Dhū l-Ḥijja, 61 AH) and explained to the Caliph the causes of his failure: He did not have at his disposal regular troops by which he could have subdued ʿAbdallah b. al-Zubayr. Yazīd rightly reprimanded him, asking why

7 See al-Balādhurī, *op. cit.* IVb, 24, lines 14–16: ... *wa-kāna aktharu l-jayshi budalāʾa min al-ʿaṭāʾi wa-julluhum yahwauna bna l-zubayri ʿabda llāhi, fa-sārū ḥattā ntahau ilā makkata, fa-akhraja ilayhim ʿabdu llāhi bnu l-zubayri rijālan min ahli l-ḥijāzi, dhawī dīnin wa-faḍlin wa-raʾyin wa-thabātin wa-baṣāʾira* ...; cf. Ps. Ibn Qutayba, *op. cit.* I, 184 inf.

8 Al-Ṭabarī, *op. cit.* IV, 365–366; Ibn Ra's Ghanama, *op. cit.*, fol. 72b.

9 Ps. Ibn Qutayba, *op. cit.* I, 166 inf.–167 sup.

he did not ask for a military force to be despatched from Syria.[10] Al-Walīd b. ʿUtba was reinstated as governor of Medina in 61 AH and was the official leader of the *ḥajj* in that year.[11]

ʿAbdallah b. al-Zubayr feigning loyalty to Yazīd, and hinting that he would be ready to undertake some acts of reconciliation, complained to the Caliph of the rudeness of al-Walīd b. ʿUtba and asked to replace him by a milder governor. Yazīd responded, deposed al-Walīd b. ʿUtba and appointed ʿUthmān b. Muḥammad b. abī Sufyān. The pilgrimage ceremony was still officially led by al-Walīd b. ʿUtba in 62 AH.[12]

ʿUthmān b. Muḥammad, an inexperienced and lenient young man, remained in the office of the governor only eight months.[13] He tried to start a new policy of appeasement with the malcontent Medinans, who openly manifested their sympathy for ʿAbdallah b. al-Zubayr. He despatched, at the Caliph's order, a representative deputation of the nobles (*ashrāf*) of the city to Damascus, the capital of the Empire. They were welcomed by the Caliph and granted munificent gifts. However, when they returned to Medina they circulated shocking stories about the licentious behaviour of the profligate and corrupt Caliph, stirred the people against him and threw off his allegiance.[14] The leaders of the rebellion, ʿAbdallah b. Ḥanẓala,[15] ʿAbdallah b. al-Muṭīʿ,[16] Maʿqil b. Sinān[17] and others, were heedless to the warnings and advice of the

10 Cf. al-Ṭabarī, *op. cit.* IV, 367; al-Balādhurī, *op. cit.* IVb, 29, lines 12–18.

11 Khalīfa, *op. cit.* I, 225 penult.–226, ll. 2–5; al-Ṭabarī, *op. cit.* IV, 366.

12 Al-Balādhurī, *op. cit.* IVb, 29 penult.–30 sup. (and see p. 19, lines 15–16); al-Ṭabarī, *op. cit.* IV, 368 sup., 369, line 3 from bottom; according to Khalīfa, *op. cit.* I, 227, line 7 the *ḥajj* was led in 62 AH by ʿUthmān b. Muḥammad b. abī Sufyān.

13 Wakīʿ, *Akhbār al-quḍāt* (ed. ʿAbd al-ʿAzīz Muṣṭafā al-Marāghī) (Cairo, 1366/1947) I, 123.

14 See Khalīfa, *op. cit.* I, 227–228; Ibn Ra's Ghanama, *op. cit.*, fol. 74a (quoted from Khalīfa); al-Ṭabarī, *op. cit.* IV, 368; al-Balādhurī, *op. cit.* IVb, 31; Ibn ʿAsākir, *op. cit.* VII, 372; Ibn Ḥajar, *al-Iṣāba* (Cairo, 1328) II, 299, No. 4637 (quoted from Khalīfa); Ibn ʿAbd Rabbihi, *op. cit.* IV, 387 inf.–388; al-Dhahabī, *Taʾrīkh* II, 354.

15 See on him *EI*2, s.v. ʿAbd Allah b. Ḥanẓala (Zettersteen–Pellat).

16 See on him *EI*2, s.v. ʿAbd Allah b. Muṭīʿ (Zettersteen–Pellat); and see al-Fāsī, *al-ʿIqd al-thamīn* (ed. Fu'ād Sayyid) (Cario, 1385/1966) V, 287/288 (and see the references given by the editor).

17 See on him Ibn Qutayba, *al-Maʿārif*, 129; Ibn ʿAbd al-Barr, *al-Istīʿāb* (ed. ʿAlī Muḥammad al-Bijāwī) (Cairo, 1380/1960), 1431, No. 2460 (and see the list of the Qurashites killed when in bonds on the order of Muslim b. ʿUqba after the defeat at al-Ḥarra; the list is given according to the accounts of Ibn Isḥāq, al-Wāqidī and Wathīma); Ibn Ḥajar, *al-Iṣāba* III, 446, No. 8136.

messengers sent to Medina or friendly persons writing to them from Damascus.[18] They tried to dissuade them from getting involved in a clash with the force which the Caliph prepared against them. But the Medinan malcontents felt that they were united in their resistance to the licentious Caliph and that his messengers merely attempted to undermine this unity.[19] It may be pointed out that this so-called unity was not total: The ʿAlids remained neutral and did not join the rebels.[20] ʿAbdallah b. ʿUmar stressed the legitimacy of the oath of allegiance to Yazīd.[21] Persons like ʿAbdallah b. al-ʿAbbās, Abū Barza, and ʿAbdallah b. ʿUmar denied that the struggle between ʿAbdallah b. al-Zubayr and the Umayyads was for the cause of God: Both parties fought, in their opinion, to gain their lot in this world.[22] When ʿAbdallah b. al-Zubayr asked the wife of ʿAbdallah b. ʿUmar to prevail upon her husband that he should join him and grant him the oath of allegiance, he argued that his decision to come out in revolt against the impious Muʿāwiya, his son and his family was due to the fact that the latter appropriated for themselves the revenues (*fay*', belonging, of course, by right to the believers — K.); he did it for the cause of God, His Prophet, the Muhājirūn and the Anṣār. When the wife brought ʿAbdallah b. al-Zubayr's message to Ibn ʿUmar, the latter remarked that ʿAbdallah b. al-Zubayr desired no more than the grey mules on which Muʿāwiya performed his pilgrimage.[23] There was almost no *Ṣaḥābī* who took an active part in the revolt of Medina.[24] The opinions of the pious about the two parties struggling in order to gain authority, power and a share of this world is in full agreement with Wellhausen's conclusion that the religious formulation given to the rebels' arguments against the Umayyads was used as a cover for their

18 Of special interest is the role played by ʿAbdallah b. Jaʿfar, who interceded with Yazīd for the Medinans (see e.g. Ps. Ibn Qutayba, *op. cit.*, 169 inf.–170; these details were omitted in Zettersteen's entry on ʿAbdallah b. Jaʿfar in *EI*2).

19 See e.g. al-Balādhurī, *op. cit.* IVb, 32: . . . *yā nuʿmānu qad jiʾtanā bi-amrin turīdu bihi tafrīqa jamāʿatinā wa-ifsāda mā aṣlaḥa llāhu min amrinā* . . .; Ibn Saʿd, *op. cit.* V, 145; al-Ṭabarī, *op. cit.* IV, 369; Ps. Ibn Qutayba, *op. cit.* I, 170.

20 Ibn Saʿd, *op. cit.* V, 215; cf. Ibn Kathīr, *op. cit.* VIII, 218.

21 Ibn Saʿd, *op. cit.* V, 144; al-Dhahabī, *Taʾrīkh* II, 355, sup.; Ibn Raʾs Ghanama, *op. cit.*, fol. 72a; al-ʿIṣāmī, *op. cit.* III, 90 inf.

22 Al-Fākihī, *op. cit.*, fol. 402a, inf.–402 sup.; cf. al-Balādhurī, *op. cit.* V, 195–196 (ed. S.D. Goitein); Ibn Raʾs Ghanama, *op. cit.*, fol. 72a; al-Ḥākim, *al-Mustadrak* (Hyderabad, 1342) IV, 470.

23 Abū l-Faraj, *op. cit.* I, 12.

24 See al-ʿIṣāmī, *op. cit.* III, 91: . . . *wa-lam yuwāfiq ahla l-madīnati ʿalā hādhā l-khalʿi aḥadun min akābiri aṣḥābi rasūli llāhi(ṣ)*.

desire to gain political authority and power.[25] There seems, however, to have been a considerable difference in aims and objectives between the rebels of Medina and those who resisted the Umayyad authority and prepared their rebellion under the leadership of ʿAbdallah b. al-Zubayr in Mecca.

II

The widely current report, as recorded in the sources, is that the cause of the revolt in Medina was the fact that the Medinan leaders were reluctant to give the oath of allegiance to Yazīd after they had seen his licentious behaviour when they paid a visit to his court.

A quite different account of the causes of the revolt in Medina is given in al-Yaʿqūbī's (d. 292 AH) *Taʾrīkh*,[26] where it is related that Yazīd appointed ʿUthmān b. Muḥammad b. Abī Sufyān as governor over Medina. Ibn Mīnā, who was in charge of the estates of Muʿāwiya (*ṣawāfī muʿāwiyata*), came to ʿUthmān and informed him that the people of Medina did not let him collect the crops of wheat and dates and carry them (scil. to the Caliph — K.) as he had been in the habit of doing every year. The governor, ʿUthmān b. Muḥammad, summoned a group of people from Medina and rebuked them harshly for their deed. They rose in revolt against him and against the Banū Umayya in Medina and expelled them from the city; on their way out the expelled Umayyads had stones thrown at them.

A similar report is recorded by al-Samhūdī (d. 911 AH) in his *Wafāʾ al-wafā*.[27] It is, as al-Samhūdī remarks, a summary (*mulakhkhaṣ*) of an account of al-Wāqidī, as given in his "*Kitāb al-Ḥarra*". Ibn Mīnā in this report carries the title "*ʿāmil ʿalā ṣawāfī l-madīna*", "the official in charge of the estates of al-Madīna". "There were at that time many *ṣawāfī* in Medina," the report says. Muʿāwiya yielded from the estates of Medina and its environs (*aʿrāḍuhā*) crops amounting to a hundred fifty thousand *wasq* of dates and a hundred thousand *wasq* wheat. After the appointment of ʿUthmān b. Muḥammad by Yazīd, Ibn Mīnā came with a party (of labourers — K.) from the Ḥarra, betaking himself to the lands (*amwāl*) of Muʿāwiya. He led the party unhindered until he reached the area of the Balḥārith b. al-Khazraj and proceeded to till (*naqaba*) the fields in their territory. The Balḥārith came out and had an argument with Ibn

[25] Wellhausen, *op. cit.*, 102–103.

[26] Ed. Muḥammad Ṣādiq Baḥr al-ʿulūm (al-Najaf, 1384/1964) II, 237.

[27] I, 127–128.

Mīnā, stating that he had no right to carry out his work and that his action was an unlawful innovation (*ḥadath*) and (constituted — K.) an injury (*ḍarar*) for them. The governor, having been informed by Ibn Mīnā about the conflict, asked three men of the Balḥārith to grant Ibn Mīnā a permit to pass their territory. They gave their consent, but when he came with his party to work, the Balḥārith barred him from the estates. When he complained to the governor, the latter ordered him to "gather those he could" against them (i.e. against the Balḥārith — K.) and attached to this troop some of (his) soldiers (*baʿḍa jundin*). He ordered him to cross their lands "even if they had to do it on their bellies" (*wa-lau ʿalā buṭūnihim*; scil. on the bellies of the Balḥārith — K.), as the wording of the account puts it. When Ibn Mīnā proceeded next day with his party to the estates of Muʿāwiya, he was confronted by a party of Anṣār who came aided by a group of Qurashites and prevented him from carrying out his work. The situation became serious and Ibn Mīnā returned to the governor, reporting the events. The governor communicated with the Caliph and urged him to take steps against the people of Medina. The Caliph decided to dispatch a military force against Medina.

Al-Wāqidī's brief report, as given by al-Samhūdī at the end of the ninth century (AH) can be supplemented by additional details from a combined account recorded by Abū l-ʿArab (d. 333 AH) at the end of the third century and based mainly on the authority of al-Wāqidī.[28] The first sentences of the account are almost identical;[29] the account differs, however, on some important particulars of the story. The clashes of Ibn Mīnā and his labourers with the Balḥārith, says the account, continued for a month. They sometimes allowed him to carry out some work; sometimes they gathered against him and no work could be done at all.[30] After Ibn Mīnā complained to the governor, the latter summoned three men from the Balḥārith: Muḥammad b. ʿAbdallah b. Zayd, Zuhayr b. abī Masʿūd and Muḥammad b. al-Nuʿmān b. al-Bashīr. They gave their consent and Ibn Mīnā came with his labourers and did some work. A group of people of Medina: al-Miswar b. Makhrama,[31] ʿAbd al-Raḥmān

[28] Abū l-ʿArab, *Kitāb al-miḥan*, Ms. Cambridge Qq. 235, fols. 51a–65a; see on the author: Sezgin, *GAS* I, 356–357.

[29] The difference in the quantities of the crops recorded here (51,000 *wasq* dates and 100,000 *wasq* wheat) may probably be traced back to a clerical error.

[30] See *al-Miḥan*, fol. 51b: . . . *wa-ḍararun ʿalaynā, fa-makathū ʿalā dhālika shahran, yaghdū bnu mīnā wa-yarūḥu bi-ʿummālihi fa-marratan yaʾbauna ʿalayhi* . . .

[31] See on him Muṣʿab b. ʿAbdallah, *op. cit.*, 262–263; Anonymous, *al-Taʾrīkh al-muḥkam*, Ms.Br.Mus., Or. 8653, fol. 111b; Ibn Ḥajar, *al-Iṣāba* III, 419, No. 7993;

b. ʿAbd al-Qārī,[32] ʿAbd al-Raḥmān b. al-Aswad b. ʿAbd Yaghūth,[33] ʿAbdallah b. Muṭīʿ and ʿAbdallah b. abī Rabīʿa,[34] went to "these people" (apparently the Balḥārith who gave their consent to resume the work of Ibn Mīnā — K.), incited them[35] and asked them not to permit Ibn Mīnā to till in their estates[36] except by their consent and willingness. The rest of the story agrees with al-Samhūdī:[37] The force of Ibn Mīnā, aided by soldiers supplied by the governor, was barred from work by a Qurashī-Anṣārī troop. Some divergence can be noticed in an additional passage recorded by Abū l-ʿArab, on the authority of al-Wāqidī:[38] A delegation composed of ten Qurashites and a group of Anṣār called on the governor, ʿUthmān b. Muḥammad, and complained about the actions of Ibn Mīnā and the fact that he had gathered a force against them. They were disappointed to find that the governor himself was behind Ibn Mīnā and his actions. The conversation between the governor and the delegation became harsh and the governor decided to write to the Caliph on the hostile attitude of the Medinans towards the Caliph. The Caliph despatched to the Medinans a sharp letter warning them of the consequences of their actions and threatening that he would use force against them.

The account recorded by Abū l-ʿArab gives us a better insight into the attitudes of the land-owners in Medina, and the contacts between the Anṣār and the Qurashites in Medina in order to make a common cause against what they regarded as the unlawful claims of the Umayyad ruler and his unjust appropriation of their estates.

Ibn ʿAbd al-Barr, *al-Istīʿāb,* 1399, No. 2405; al-Balādhurī, *Ansāb al-ashrāf* IVa (ed. M. Schloessinger), index.

32 See on him Ibn Ḥajar, *al-Iṣāba* III, 71, No. 6223; Ibn ʿAbd al-Barr, *op. cit.*, 839, No. 1433.

33 See on him al-Fāsī, *op. cit.* V, 342, No. 1712; Ibn Ḥajar, *op. cit.* II, 390, No. 5081; Muṣʿab b. ʿAbdallah, *op. cit.*, 262.

34 See on him Muṣʿab b. ʿAbdallah, *op. cit.*, 318.

35 In text مسردوهم ; I could not find a suitable interpretation of this word in this context.

36 The term in this passage is: ... *wa-qālū lā tadaʿūhu yanqub fī ḥaqqikum illā bi-ṭībi nafsin minkum* . . .

37 It may be remarked that here, in this version, the phrase "and gather against them whom you can" has an additional word: "*min mawālīkum*" "from among your mawālī".

38 Fol. 52a, line 6: *qāla l-wāqidī: fa-ḥaddathanī usāma bnu zaydin al-laythī ʿan muḥammadi bni qaysin* . . .

III

Some of the words or terms recorded in the account of al-Wāqidī are obscure and vague. An attempt should be made to elucidate the meanings of these words in order to enable a more accurate understanding of the text.

The account says that Ibn Mīnā was in charge of the *ṣawāfī* of Medina and adds that there were at that time many *ṣawāfī* in Medina. The word *ṣawāfī* usually denotes "a public land", "state domains".[39] Saleh A. el-Ali, referring to the passage discussed here, remarks that al-Wāqidī "probably included in these *ṣawāfī* the public lands and the seven endowments which had belonged to the Prophet. Nevertheless they did not exploit them for their own personal purposes, otherwise they would have aroused opposition and the sources would have mentioned that the Prophet granted several Muslims some of the uncultivated lands either for dwelling, or for cultivation, or for other purposes."[40]

But *ṣawāfī* in this account, and generally in this period, does not only denote state domains or public land. *Iṣṭafā* implies in fact confiscation of land and property.[41] The confiscated property could be transferred or given as gift. So, for instance, ʿAbdallah b. al-Zubayr confiscated the property of Muʿāwiya in Mecca; one of the courts confiscated was given by him as a gift to his son Ḥamza.[42] It is implausible to assume that there were "state domains" in Mecca and Medina, as Medina was not conquered by force, and the land of Medina was divided by the Prophet himself and alotted to the people of the *ṣaḥāba*. The clue for the understanding of the term is given by al-Yaʿqūbī. Muʿāwiya, al-Yaʿqūbī reports,

39 See Løkkegaard, *Islamic Taxation in the Classical Period* (Copenhagen, 1950), 49–51.

40 Saleh A. el-Ali, Muslim Estates in Hidjaz in the First Century AH., *JESHO* 2 (1959), 251. The explanation of Muḥammad Muḥyī l-Dīn ʿAbd al-Ḥamīd, the editor of al-Samhūdī's *Wafāʾ al-wafā*, of the word "*ṣawāfī*" as palm trees (I, 127, n. 1) is erroneous and it is useless to discuss it. H. Lammens (*Le Califat de Yazīd 1er* [Beirut, 1921], 219) translates *ṣawāfī*: "domaines de Moʿāwia".

41 See al-Ṭabarī, *op. cit.*, Glossarium, s.v. *ṣafā*: *ṣāfiyatun* id quod confiscatum est, *al-ṣawāfī* = praedia confiscata.

42 Al-Azraqī. *Akhbār Makka* (ed. F. Wüstenfeld) (Leipzig, 1858; reprint), 460: ... *iṣṭafāhā fī amwāli muʿāwiyata fa-wahabahā li-bnihi ḥamzata*; and see *ibid.*, 452. *Ṣawāfī* as recorded by al-Azraqī and al-Samhūdī denote lands and property belonging to and administered by the Caliph. The term usually refers to the property of the Umayyads confiscated by the ʿAbbasids. See e.g. al-Azraqī, *op. cit.*, 461 penult.: ... *ḥattā uṣṭufiyat ḥīna kharajat al-khilāfatu min banī marwāna* ...; 467: ... *iṣṭafāhu amīru l-muʾminīna abū jaʿfar, wa-kāna fīhi ḥaqqun qad kāna baʿḍu banī umayyata shtarāhu fa-ṣṭufiya minhum* ...; and see 453: ... *fa-lam tazal fī l-ṣawāfī ḥattā raddahā*

confiscated the property of people and appropriated it for himself.[43] The true character of Muʿāwiya's *ṣawāfī* in Medina is explicitly exposed in another passage of al-Yaʿqūbī. Stressing the appropriation of state-estates in the conquered territories by Muʿāwiya, al-Yaʿqūbī says: "He was the first to own *ṣawāfī* in the whole world, even in Mecca and Medina and an amount (of crops — K.) of dates and wheat was carried to him every year."[44] The *ṣawāfī* were thus identical with the *amwāl muʿāwiya*, the private possessions of Muʿāwiya in Medina. Ps. Ibn Qutayba in his *al-Imāma* says that Ibn Mīnā[45] came with a party[46] of men from the Ḥarra proceeding towards the estates of Muʿāwiya (*yurīdu l-amwāla llatī kānat li-muʿāwiyata*). The true character of these *ṣawāfī*, or *amwāl*, is indicated in an explanatory sentence added by the author: "These were estates acquired by Muʿāwiya and orchards of date-palms, which yielded hundred sixty thousand *wasqs*."[47] It is indeed the way of acquisition (*iktisāb*) which brought about the conflict between the Medinans and the Caliph.

The reports about Muʿāwiya's *ṣawāfī* are corroborated by numerous reports concerning his purchase of courts, palaces,[48] estates and lands

l-muʿtaṣimu bi-ilāhi...; and see 449, 460, 463, 464, 467: ...*fa-hiya l-yauma fī l-ṣawāfī*. Comp. al-Samhūdī, *op. cit.* II, 699, lines 11–12: *fa-ṣārat baʿdu fī l-ṣawāfī, wa-kānat al-dawāwīnu fīhā wa-baytu l-māli*...; *ibid.* II, 721: ... *anna dāra marwāna ṣarat fī l-ṣawāfī, ay li-bayti l-māli*...; and see *ibid.* II, 729–730. About the "*ṣawāfī daulati banī umayya*" in Egypt see al-Muḥasibī, *Aʿmāl al-qulūb wa-l-jawāriḥ* (ed. ʿAbd al-Qādir Aḥmad ʿAṭā) (Cairo, 1969), 230–231.

43 Al-Yaʿqūbī, *op. cit.* II, 221, lines 1–2: ... *wa-staṣfā amwāla l-nāsi fa-akhadhahā li-nafsihi*; comp. *ibid.*, lines 18–20: ... *baʿda an akhraja muʿāwiyatu min kulli baladin mā kānat mulūku fārisa tastaṣfīhi li-anfusihā min al-ḍiyāʿi l-ʿāmirati wa-jaʿalahu ṣāfiyatan li-nafsihi fa-aqṭaʿahu jamāʿatan min ahli baytihi.* And see about an attempt at confiscation of the property of ʿAbdallah b. ʿĀmir b. Kurayz: Muṣʿab b. ʿAbdallah, *op. cit.*, 148 inf.; al-Fāsī, *op. cit.* V, 189.

44 Al-Yaʿqūbī, *op. cit.* II, 222, lines 9–13: ... *wa-faʿala muʿāwiyatu bi-l-shaʾmi wa-l-jazīrati wa-l-yamani mithla mā faʿala bi-l-ʿirāqi min istiṣfāʾi mā kāna li-l-mulūki min al-ḍiyāʿi wa-taṣyīrihā li-nafsihi khāliṣatan wa-aqṭaʿahā ahla baytihi wa-khāṣṣatahu; wa-kāna awwala man kānat lahu l-ṣawāfī fī jamīʿi l-dunyā ḥattā bi-makkata wa-l-madīnati, fa-innahu kāna fīhimā shayʾun yuḥmalu fī kulli sanatin min ausāqi l-tamri wa-l-ḥinṭati*; and see D.C. Dennet Jr., *Conversion and the Poll Tax in Early Islam* (transl. by Fauzī Fahūm Jādallah; revised by Iḥsān ʿAbbās) (Beirut, 1960), 65, No. 76 (and see the note of the editor, *ibid.*).

45 Ps. Ibn Qutayba, *op. cit.* I, 169 (in text: *Ibn Mīthā*, a clerical error).

46 In text erroneously: *bi-sirāḥin.*

47 I, 169: ... *wa-kānat amwālan iktasabahā muʿāwiyatu wa-nakhīlan yajuddu minhā miʾata alfi wasqin wa-sittīna alfan.*

48 See al-Samhūdī, *op. cit.* III, 962: ... *wa-ammā qaṣr banī jadīlata fa-inna mu-*

in Medina[49] and his activities of cultivation and irrigation.[50] Muʿāwiya's business transactions were carefully planned and thoughtfully worked out.[51]

*   *   *

ʿāwiyata bna abī sufyāna banāhu li-yakūna ḥiṣnan, wa-lahu bābāni: bābun shāriʿun ʿalā khaṭṭi banī jadīlata...wa-kāna lladhī waliya bināʾahu li-muʿāwiyata l-ṭufaylu bnu abī kaʿbin l-anṣāriyyu wa-fī wasaṭihi biʾr ḥāʾ .... See the story about the purchase of a part of the orchard of Biʾr Ḥāʾ by Muʿāwiya, *ibid.* III, 962, sup., 963 inf. And see *ibid.* II, 741: ... *wa-kānat hādhihi l-dāru* (i.e. *dār al-rabīʿ*, named *dār ḥafṣa* — K.) *qaṭīʿatan min rasūli llahi ṣallā llāhu ʿalahyi wa-sallam li-ʿuthmāna bni abī l-ʿāṣi l-thaqafiyyi fa-btāʿahā min wuldihi muʿāwiyatu bnu abī sufyāna* .... (See on ʿUthmān b. abī l-ʿĀṣ: Ibn Saʿd, *op. cit.* VII, 40; I, 313; VIII, 51). Saʿīd b. al-ʿĀṣ enjoins his son ʿAmr to sell only his palace in al-Arṣa after his death to Muʿāwiya, arguing that it is merely a leisure resort, not an agricultural farm (Abū l-Faraj, *op. cit.* I, 17: ... *innamā ttakhadhtuhu nuzhatan wa-laysa bi-mālin*); and see the story of the acquisition of Arṣa by Muʿāwiya: al-Samhūdī, *op. cit.* III, 1056–1057; Yāqūt, *Muʿjam al-buldān*, s.v. Arṣa (see the report about the building of the palace by Saʿīd b. al-ʿĀṣ, the digging of a well, the planting of orchards and the qualities of these orchards). And see about the building of the fortress Qaṣr Khall by Muʿāwiya: al-Samhūdī, *op. cit.* IV, 1289–90; and see *ibid.* II, 699 (cf. *ibid.*, 701) about the purchase of the court of ʿUmar (or the court of ʿAbd al-Raḥmān b. ʿAuf) by Muʿāwiya. About a court of Muʿāwiya in Medina see Ibn ʿAsākir, *op. cit.*, Ms. Ẓāhiriyya, *op. cit.* IX, fol. 109b (... *wa-lahu dārun bi-l-madīnati tashraʿu ʿalā balāṭi l-fākihati* ...). About two courts, *dār al-nuqṣān* and *dār al-qaṭirān*, built by Muʿāwiya see al-Samhūdī, *op. cit.* II, 750. About the purchase of the court of Sufyān b. al-Ḥārith b. ʿAbd al-Muṭṭalib by Muʿāwiya see al-Samhūdī, *op. cit.* II, 758 (he attached it to the *muṣallā* of the Prophet); comp. al-Fākihī, *op. cit.*, fol. 458a (Muʿāwiya proposes Khālid b. al-ʿĀṣ to sell him his property. The answer of Khālid is significant: "Do you think that a man would sell the place where his father is buried?").

49 See about the purchase of the lands of al-Zubayr as recorded in al-Fasawī's *al-Maʿrifa wa-l-taʾrīkh*, Ms. Esad Ef. 2391, fol. 129a; and see about an estate bought by Muʿāwiya from Qays b. Saʿd b. ʿUbāda: al-Dhahabī, *Siyar aʿlām al-nubalāʾ* III, 70 (*bāʿa qaysu bnu saʿdin mālan min muʿāwiyata bi-tisʿīna alfan*). About the purchase of Thaniyat al-Sharīd see al-Samhūdī, *op. cit.*, 1066–1067; cf. Saleh A. el-Ali, *op. cit.*, 256. About the purchase of Bughaybigha see: al-Samhūdī, *op. cit.* IV, 1150–1152.

50 See al-Samhūdī, *op. cit.* III, 937–938; *ibid.*, IV, 1232 (*saddu muʿāwiya*); III, 985, 987 (*ʿaynu l-azraq*); and see Majd al-Dīn al-Fayrūzābādī, *al-Maghānim al-muṭāba fī maʿālim Ṭāba* (ed. Ḥamad al-Jāsir) (al-Riyāḍ, 1389/1969), 295–296. About the irrigation of *rauḍat banī umayya* and *amwāl bani umayya* see al-Samhūdī, *op. cit.* III, 1075. It may be stressed that Muʿāwiya employed a special agent in charge of his estates; in this passage the estates are called "*al-ḍiyāʿ*" (al-Samhūdī, *op. cit.* IV, 1276 sup.: *qāla muʿāwiyatu bnu abī sufyāna li-ʿabdi l-raḥmāni bni abī aḥmada bni jaḥshin, wa-kāna wakīlahu bi-ḍiyāʿihi bi-l-madīnati, yaʿnī audiyatan shtarāhā wa-ʿtamalahā* ...); cf. al-Balādhurī, *op. cit.* IVa, 110 inf.–111 sup. (ed. M. Schloessinger) (Jerusalem, 1971).

51 See al-Jahshiyārī, *Kitāb al-wuzarāʾ wa-l-kuttāb* (ed. al-Saqā, al-Abyārī, al-Shalabī (Cairo, 1357/1938), 26: ... *ittakhidh lī ḍiyāʿan wa-lā takun bi-l-dārūm*

It is evident that these palaces, fortresses, courts and estates needed manpower for maintenance and cultivation. This was provided by captives taken in the wars of conquest and by slaves.[52] Groups of skilled labourers were brought from the conquered provinces to Mecca and Medina.[53] Muʿāwiya is said to have been the first Caliph to use forced labour.[54] The *mawālī* were entrusted with various duties and carried out different kinds of work, as imposed on them by their patrons. Consequently the *mawālī* society was not based on egalitarian principles; among a group of *mawālī*, attached to a certain family or clan, there were great differences of rank and position. They were considered loyal and reliable. When Muʿāwiya complained to Ziyād of the attitude of his relatives, Ziyād advised him to rely upon *mawālī*, because they were more apt to provide aid, more prone to forgive and more grateful (than others — K.).[55] Possessing a multitude of *mawālī* was considered a sign of strength; families and clans vied among themselves in acquiring *mawālī*. Some of these *mawālī* were absorbed into the clans who strived to gain a firm and strong position.[56] Referring to the contest between the Sufyānids and the Merwānids, each attempting to outnumber the other, ʿAbd al-Raḥmān b. al-Ḥakam argues against Muʿāwiya: "If you found none but negroes, you would strive to outnumber us by (adopting and attaching — K.) them" (scil. to your clan — K.).[57]

In the battle of the Ḥarra the *mawālī* fought as a special military formation under the command of Yazīd b. Hurmuz,[58] under their own ban-

al-mijdāb, wa-lā bi-qaysariyyata l-mighrāq, wa-ttakhidhhā bi-majārī l-saḥāb; fa-ttakhadha lahu l-buṭnān min kūrati ʿasqalān .... As for his policy of purchasing property in Mecca see *JESHO* 15 (1972), 84–85; and see Ibn Ḥajar, *al-Iṣāba* II, 291, No. 4597. Cf. for Syria: al-Balādhurī, *op. cit.* IVa, 50, lines 5–7; 52, lines 7–12.

52 See Saleh A. el-Ali, *op. cit.*, 252; and see *JESHO* 3 (1960) 334. About "the black and the red" (*al-ḥumrān wa-l-sūdān*) servants (*ghilmān*) of Muʿāwiya working in his estates see: al-Balādhurī, *op. cit.* IVa, 42 inf.–43 sup.

53 See about labourers who made baked bricks for the houses of Muʿāwiya in Mecca: al-Azraqī, *op. cit.*, 496 ult.–497, lines 1–2; al-Fākihī, *op. cit.*, fol. 503a: *kāna yaʿmalu fīhā nabaṭun baʿatha bihim muʿāwiyatu bnu abī sufyāna (r) yaʿmalūna l-ajurra li-dūrihi bi-makkata* ...

54 See al-Yaʿqūbī, *op. cit.* II, 221, line 1: ... *wa-banā wa-shayyada l-bināʾa wa-sakhkhara l-nāsa fī bināʾihi wa-lam yusakhkhir aḥadun qablahu.*

55 Al-Balādhurī, *op. cit.* IVa, 23, lines 17–18.

56 See e.g. al-Balādhurī, *op. cit.* V, 163, lines 7–8: ... *wa-hum yaḍummūna man taʾashshaba ilayhim li-yataʿazzazū bihi.*

57 Al-Balādhurī, *op. cit.* IVa, 53, lines 12–13: ... *lau lam tajid illā l-zanja la-takaththarta bihim ʿalaynā.*

58 See on him Khalīfa b. Khayyāṭ, *Ṭabaqāt* (ed. Akram Ḍiyāʾ al-ʿUmarī) (Baghdād,

ner;[59] they were entrusted with the defence of the section of the ditch, dug by the Medinans against the approaching Syrian army, stretching from Rātij[60] until the quarter of the Banū ʿAbd al-Ashhal.[61] Their force was divided into squadrons (*karādīs*) positioned behind each other.[62] They were assaulted by a unit of the Syrian army and called upon to surrender; the commander, Yazīd b. Hurmuz, refused and decided to continue the fight.[63] It is remarkable that the *mawālī* fought in such a steadfast and courageous manner, while the Banū Ḥāritha, who were freemen, forsook their quarter and opened it treacherously, permitting the Syrians to attack their brethren in Medina.[64] Some commentators of the Qur'ān stated indeed that verse 14 of *Sūrat al-aḥzāb*: "If the enemy had entered from all sides and they had been exhorted to treachery, they would have committed it, and would have hesitated thereupon but little," referred to the shameful deed of the Banū Ḥāritha.[65]

The number of the Umayyad *mawālī*, the *mawālī banī umayya*, or *mawālī muʿāwiya*, seems to have been considerable. This can be gauged from a unique report recorded by Ibn Ra'S Ghanama. The direct cause of the expulsion of the Umayyads from Medina and the throwing off of the allegiance of Yazīd, says the report, was a clash between the people of Medina and the *mawālī muʿāwiya*. A powerful flow of water poured one day into Medina and the people hurried to direct the water into their fields (*ilā amwālihim*). The *mawālī muʿāwiya* went out (apparently in order to divert the water into the estates of Muʿāwiya — K.) and the people started to fight them (apparently preventing them from carrying out their work — K.) and a clash ensued between them (*wa-kharaja mawālī muʿāwiyata fa-qātalahum ahlu l-madīnati*). The event took place at the time when Yazīd was denigrated (by the opposition — K.) and Ibn al-Zubayr already had thrown off his allegiance to him, the report remarks. The people of the market hoisted a banner (*fa-ʿaqada ahlu*

1387/1967), 249 (. . . *kāna ra'sa l-mawālī yauma l-ḥarra* . . .), 255; al-Balādhurī, *op, cit.* IVb, 35, line 5.

59 Abū l-ʿArab, *op. cit.*, fol. 53a, ult.

60 See about Rātij: al-Samhūdī, *op. cit.* IV, 1215.

61 See Abū l-ʿArab, *op. cit.*, fol. 53a (from Dhubāb until Mirbad al-Naʿam, the market of the cattle); al-Samhūdī, *op. cit.* I, 129; IV, 1206, line 1.

62 Abū l-ʿArab, *op. cit.*, 53a ult.–53b, line 1: . . . *qad ṣaffa aṣḥābahu karādīsa, baʿḍahum khalfa baʿḍin, ilā ra'si l-thaniyyati* . . .

63 Abū l-ʿArab, *op. cit.*, fol. 53b.

64 Al-Samhūdī, *op. cit.* I, 130, penult; Abū l-ʿArab, *op. cit.*, fol. 53b, inf.

65 Al-Suyūṭī, *al-Durr al-manthūr* (Cairo, 1314) v, 188,; al-Samhūdī, *op. cit.* I, 131; al-Dīnawarī, *op. cit.*, 265.

l-sūqi rāyatan), fought the *mawālī muʿāwiya* and killed (probably some of — K.) them. This caused an upsurge among the people of Medina and they expelled the governor.[66]

Whatever the historical value of this report, it helps us to gain an insight into the character and the duties of a special group established by the ruler, the *mawālī muʿāwiya*. Some of these *mawālī muʿāwiya* took part in the expedition against ʿAbdallah b. al-Zubayr, as mentioned above. The Umayyads expelled from Medina left the city accompanied by their *mawālī*.

Important details about the formation of some groups of *mawālī* can be deduced from the story about the dismissal of the governor of Medina, ʿAmr b. Saʿīd. When al-Walīd b. ʿUtba was reinstalled as governor of Medina (in 62 AH) he arrested some three hundred *mawālī* and servants (*ghilmān*) of the deposed governor. ʿAmr secretly sent a messenger to those arrested, and promised to provide them with camels which would halt in the market of Medina; on a given sign the arrested would break the door of the jail, mount the camels and join him in Syria. The plan was indeed carried out successfully.[67] These *mawālī* thus had personal loyalty and attachment; they were not the official guard of the governor, they were the personal property of ʿAmr b. Saʿīd. The opinion of the new governor, al-Walīd b. ʿUtba, seems to have been different: He considered them as property of the state, which had consequently to be transferred to the successive governor. For ʿAmr b. Saʿīd had fraudulently appropriated to himself the payments sent by the Caliph to the people of Medina and had used these sums for the acquisition of servants and slaves. This was one of the causes for the fact that relations between the people of Medina and the rulers deteriorated and that they felt bitterly about their governor.[68]

Further instances of Umayyad *mawālī*, who identified themselves with their masters and fought bravely for their cause, are recorded. A *maulā* of ʿUtba b. abī Sufyān fortified himself with a group of fifty men in

66 Ibn Ra's Ghanama, *op. cit.*, fol. 74b.

67 Al-Ṭabarī, *op. cit.* IV, 366–367; Ibn Ra's Ghanama, *op. cit.*, fol. 72b. There is however a remarkable report recorded by Ibn Junghul, in his *Taʾrīkh* (Ms. BM Or 5912, I, 162b), according to which the rebelling Medinans under the command of ʿAbdallah b. Ḥanẓala arrested the slaves (*ʿabīd*) of ʿAmr b. Saʿīd and got hold of property, possessions and produce in Medina after the return of the deputation from Damascus in 62 AH. The 300 slaves managed to escape according to a plan devised by ʿAmr b. Saʿīd and succeeded in joining him.

68 Ps. Ibn Qutayba, *op. cit.* I, 189, lines 17–18.

al-Ṭā'if; he later surrendered and was executed by ʿAbdallah b. al-Zubayr in Mecca.[69]

The role of the *mawālī* in the struggle between ʿAbdallah b. al-Zubayr and the Umayyads can be deduced from the story of al-Miswar b. Makhrama. He transferred weapons and coats of mail from Medina to Mecca and distributed them among his trained and steadfast *mawālī* in order to fight the Syrian troops sent by Yazīd. They surrounded him during the fight, trying to defend him; later they abandoned him, but they succeeded in killing several Syrian soldiers.[70]

The reports quoted above help us to elucidate to some extent the meaning of the two key expressions: "*ṣawāfī muʿāwiya*" and "*mawālī muʿāwiya*". The battle of the Ḥarra with its sad result is closely linked to the *ṣawāfī* and the *mawālī* of the Umayyads.

IV

The Medinans, Anṣāris and Qurashites, barring Ibn Mīnā from access to the estates of Muʿāwiya (i.e. the estates of Yazīd — K.), argued that his action constitutes *ḥadath* and *ḍarar*. This would indicate that in their opinion the rights of Muʿāwiya to these estates were unfounded and his ownership caused damage to their rights. This argument was explicitly formulated in the talk of the deputation of Anṣāris and Qurashites who called on the governor of Medina. "You know, they said, that all these estates belong to us and that Muʿāwiya preferred others in the granting of payments and did not give us even a *dirhem*, let alone more.[70a] This was so until the time when we were pressed by hard time and oppressed by hunger, that Muʿāwiya (by exploiting our distress — K.) bought it (i.e. our land — K.) by a hundredth of its (real — K.) value".[71] It is evident that the former landowners considered the acquisition of their property in such a way as an iniquitous transaction by which they were afflicted; they referred to it by the expressions "*ḥadath*" and "*ḍarar*" and considered it void. In their opinion Muʿāwiya's ownership was not lawful and they apparently demanded the restitution of their rights.

In a talk with ʿAbdallah b. Jaʿfar, who interceded for the people of Medina, Yazīd responded partly to the demands of the Medinans by promising to grant them as an exceptional favour two payments every

69 Al-Balādhurī, *op. cit.* IVb, 30, lines 12–15.

70 Al-Dhahabī, *Siyar aʿlām al-nubalāʾ* III, 263.

70a On the delay of payments to the Ansar, see Ibn ʿAsākir, *op. cit.* III, 369; Ibn Ḥajar, *al-Iṣāba* I, 194, No. 902.

71 Ps. Ibn Qutayba, *op. cit.* I, 169.

year (in summer and in winter) and to fix the price of wheat in Medina at a rate equal to that in Syria.[72] Yazīd also undertook to repay fully the amounts withheld by Muʿāwiya.[73] In a slightly different version, in which the terms of Muslim b. ʿUqba were formulated, the two former promises, that of making the price of wheat the same as in Syria and that of giving them two payments a year, are supplemented by a promise to repay the amounts dishonestly taken by ʿAmr b. Saʿīd.[74] The Medinans rejected the terms of the Caliph as conveyed by Muslim b. ʿUqba.

The rebelling Medinans had, however, no political programme, nor a plan of action. ʿAbdallah b. al-Zubayr claimed sagaciously and shrewdly that he demanded only to adhere to the idea of the *shūrā*.[75] It is remarkable that it was a courageous *maulā*, Abū Ḥurra, who dared accuse ʿAbdallah b. al-Zubayr of striving to declare himself caliph, not caring to act according to the principle of *shūrā* which he advocated; he consequently parted company with Ibn al-Zubayr.[76] The Medinans, in contradistinction, proclaimed that they would not swear the oath of allegiance to Yazīd, as reported in the current sources.[77] They were overconfident of their victory. They thought that if Syrian troops faced them even for a month they would kill not even one of the Medinans.[78] They exerted themselves in imitating the Prophet in their military tactics and strategy and dug ditches in Medina, basing their defence on this device,[79] as did the Prophet in the Battle of the Ditch. They were asked by their leaders to swear the oath of fighting until death,[80] as did the Companions of the Prophet at al-Ḥudaybiyya. They heedlessly let the Umayyads and their *mawālī* leave Medina, credulously convinced that

72 Lammens, *op. cit.*, p. 242 reads according to the version of al-Bayhaqī's *al-Maḥāsin wa-l-masāwī* (I, 101) الخبط and translates: "Le calife s'engage a faire vendre chez vous le froment, au prix du fourrage." The text in Ps. Ibn Qutayba, *op. cit.* I, 170: *an ajʿala l-ḥinṭata ʿindahum ka-siʿri l-ḥinṭati ʿindanā; wa-l-ḥinṭatu ʿindahum . . .* and I, 189: *an ajʿala siʿra l-ḥinṭati ʿindakum ka-siʿri l-ḥinṭati ʿindanā . . .* seems to be preferable.

73 Ps. Ibn Qutayba, *op. cit.* I, 170.

74 *Ibid.* I, 189.

75 See al-Balādhurī, *op. cit.* IVb, 16, line 9; 17, line 6; comp. *ibid.*, 29, line 15; 27, lines 11–12; and see *ibid.* V, 195, lines 9–13; Ibn Ra's Ghanama, *op. cit.*, fol. 73a.

76 Al-Balādhurī, *op. cit.* IVb, 27; V, 188.

77 See Ibn Saʿd, *op. cit.* V, 144, line 18; al-Ṭabarī, *op. cit.* IV, 370.

78 Ibn Saʿd, *op. cit.* V, 146: *kunnā naqūlu: lau aqāmū shahran mā qatalū minnā shay'an.*

79 Ps. Ibn Qutayba, *op. cit.* I, 173; Abū l-ʿArab, *op. cit.*, fol. 53a; al-Samhūdī, *op. cit.* IV, 1205.

80 Ps. Ibn Qutayba, *op. cit.* I, 173; Abū l-ʿArab, *op. cit.*, fol. 53a.

they would fulfil their solemn oath not to help the Syrian force if it proceeded against Medina, and that they would even try to persuade the Syrian force not to attack Medina.[81] They could have successfully used the Umayyads as hostages when they faced the attack of the Syrian force against Medina, as Marwān himself rightly estimated.[82]

The Medinan leaders who succeeded in escaping the massacre of the Ḥarra were deeply shocked, disappointed and embittered. They compared their defeat after a short battle, lasting less than a day, with the resistance of ʿAbdallah b. al-Zubayr which lasted six months; the fighting force in Medina numbered two thousand zealous fighters, while ʿAbdallah b. al-Zubayr fought with a small force and a troop of Khawārij.[83] It was again Marwān who soundly assessed the fighting forces in his talk with Muslim b. ʿUqba. He explained that the common people in Medina had no fighting spirit and that only few of them would fight with resolution and conviction; they also lacked weapons and riding beasts, he remarked.[84]

The battle of the Ḥarra is thus seen to be the result of a conflict between the owners of estates and property in Medina and the unjust Umayyad rulers who robbed them of their property.

81 See al-Ṭabarī, *op. cit.* IV, 373, lines 5–6; Ps. Ibn Qutayba, *op. cit.* I, 171.

82 *Ibid.*

83 See Ibn Saʿd, *op. cit.* V, 146, inf.; Ps. Ibn Qutayba, *op. cit.* I, 178, 181.

84 Ps. Ibn Qutayba, *op. cit.* I, 172.

XVI

THE SEVEN ODES

SOME NOTES ON THE COMPILATION OF THE *Mu'allaqāt*

The meaning of the word *mu'allaqāt* by which the Seven Jāhilī Odes were entitled by some transmitters and commentators has been discussed at length by scholars and several suggestions have been put forward for the interpretation of the word [1]. The story that the Odes were suspended in the Ka'ba has been rejected by the majority of the scholars, but they have almost unanimously agreed, although with some reservations, that " the man responsible in the first instance for selecting the seven poems and making them into a separate anthology was a certain Ḥammād, called al-Rāwiya (the Transmitter) " [2]. This statement is indeed based on reports of early authorities who describe the literary activity of Ḥammād under Yazīd b. 'Abd al-Malik and Hishām b. 'Abd al-Malik [3] and record the tradition told on the authority

---

[1] T. NÖLDEKE: *Beiträge zur Kenntniss der Poesie der alten Araber*, Hannover 1864, XVII–XXIII; R. A. NICHOLSON: *A Literary History of the Arabs*, Cambridge 1956, 101–103; C. BERNHEIMER: *L'Arabia Antica e la sua poesia*, Napoli 1960, 85–86; *Bulletin des Études Arabes*, Alger 1946, 152–158; CH. PELLAT: *Langue et Littérature Arabes*, Paris 1952, 68; H. A. R. GIBB: *Arabic Literature*, Oxford 1963, 22–24; CH. J. LYALL: *Translations of Ancient Arabian Poetry*, London 1930, XLIV; Nāṣir al-Dīn al-Asad: *Maṣādir al-shi'r al-jāhilī*, Cairo 1962, 169–171; 'Abd al-Salām Hārūn in his *Introduction* to al-Anbārī's *Sharḥu l-qaṣā'idi l-sab'i l-ṭiwāli*, Cairo 1963, 11–13; J. M. 'Abd al-Jalīl: *Brève Histoire de la Littérature Arabe*, Paris 1946, 37; Sibā'ī Bayyūmī: *Ta'rīkh al-adab al-'arabī*, Cairo, n.d., I, 153–155; Aḥmad Muḥ. al-Ḥaufī: *Al-ḥayāt al-'arabiyya min al-shi'r al-jāhilī*, Cairo 1962, 200–212; 'Umar Farrūkh; *Ta'rīkh al-adab al-'arabī*, Beirut 1965, 75; Najīb Muḥ. al-Bahbītī: *Ta'rīkh al-shi'r al-'arabī*, Cairo 1961, 194–195; Shauqī Ḍayf: *Ta'rīkh al-adab al-'arabī, al-'aṣr al-jāhilī*, Cairo 1965, 140–141; Ḥannā al-Fākhūrī: *Ta'rīkh al-adab al-'arabī*, Beirut 1960, 65–66; R. BLACHÈRE: *Histoire de la Littérature Arabe*, Paris 1952, I, 143–147; G. WIET: *Introduction à la Littérature Arabe*, Paris 1966, 29–31; F. GABRIELI: *La Letteratura Araba*, Firenze 1967, 24, 34–44; A. J. ARBERRY: *The Seven Odes*, London 1957, 16–24, 232, 244–254.

[2] A. J. ARBERRY, *op. cit.*, 16.

[3] Yāqūt: *Mu'jam al-udabā'*, ed. Aḥmad Farīd Rifā'ī, Cairo 1938, X, 258–266; Ibn Khallikān: *Wafayāt al-a'yān*, ed. Aḥmad Farīd Rifā'ī, Cairo 1936, V,

of al-Naḥḥās (d. 337 H) [1] according to which Ḥammād collected (*jama'a*) the Seven Long Odes [2]. Al-Jumaḥī (d. 231 H) states that Ḥammād was the first who collected the poems of the Arabs and recorded the stories of these poems (*wa-kāna awwala man jama'a ash'āra l-'arabi wa-sāqa aḥādīthahā Ḥammādun al-rāwiyatu*). He adds, however, that he was not trustworthy (*wa-kāna ghayra mauthūqin bihi*) [3].

The records about the collection of the Seven Long Odes [4] by Ḥammād al-Rāwiya are contradicted by an account of 'Abd al-Qādir al-Baghdādī (d. 1093 H), that 'Abd al-Malik b. Marwān (d. 86 H) " discarded the poems of four of them and established in their place four (other poets) " (*wa-qad ṭaraḥa 'Abdu l-Maliki bnu Marwāna shi'ra arba'atin minhum wa-athbata makānahum arba'atan*) [5]. If this report were true there must have existed a collection of the Seven Odes in the times of 'Abd al-Malik. This fact was pointed out by Nāṣir al-Dīn al-Asad, who quotes as well a saying of Mu'āwiya, reported by 'Abd al-Qādir al-Baghdādī [6] that " the *qaṣīda* of 'Amr b. Kulthūm and the *qaṣīda* of al-Ḥārith b. Ḥilliza are among the prideworthy creations

---

119–129; al-'Iṣāmī: *Simṭ al-nujūm al-'awālī*, Cairo 1380 H, III, 216–217; *al-Aghānī*, index; al-Marzubānī: *Nūr al-qabas*, ed. R. Sellheim, Wiesbaden 1964, index; Abū l-Ṭayyib al-Lughawī: *Marātib al-naḥwiyyīn*, ed. Muḥ. Abū l-Faḍl Ibrāhīm, Cairo 1955, 72–73; Ḥamza al-Iṣfahānī: *al-Tanbīh 'alā ḥudūth al-taṣḥīf*, ed. Muḥ. Ḥasan Āl Yāsīn, Baghdad 1967, 38, 125, 186; al-'Askarī: *Sharḥ mā yaqa'u fīhi l-taṣḥīf*, ed. 'Abd al-'Azīz Aḥmad, Cairo 1963, 141–143.

[1] See on him Yāqūt, *op. cit.*, IV, 224–230; Ibn Khallikān, *op. cit.*, I, 209–211; al-Qifṭī: *Inbāh al-ruwāh*, ed. Muḥ. Abū l-Faḍl Ibrāhīm, Cairo 1950, I, 101–104 (and see the references of the editor).

[2] Yāqūt, *op. cit.*, X, 266; Ibn Khallikān, *op. cit.*, V, 120; J. W. FÜCK, *E.I.*[2] s.v. Ḥammād al-Rāwiya.

[3] Muḥ. b. Sallām al-Jumaḥī: *Ṭabaqāt fuḥūl al-shu'arā'*, ed. Maḥmūd Muḥ. Shākir, Cairo 1952, 40–41; al-Marzubānī, *op. cit.*, 185.

[4] The early sources mention the Seven Odes as *al-sab'u l-mashhūrāt* (M. SCHLÖSSINGER: *Ibn Kaisān's Commentar zur Mo'allaqa des 'Amr ibn Kulṯūm nach einer Berliner Handschrift*, *ZA*, XXVI, 19, note 1); *al-sab'u l-ṭiwāl al-jāhiliyyāt* (ib., 18), *al-sumūṭ* (Abū Zayd al-Qurashī: *Jamharat ash'ār al-'arab*, Beirut 1963, 80); *al-mudhahhabāt* (Ibn 'Abd Rabbihi: *al-'Iqd al-farīd*, ed. Aḥmad Amīn, Aḥmad al-Zayn, Ibrāhīm al-Abyārī, Cairo 1965, V, 269); *al-mu'allaqāt* (ib., *wa-qad yuqālu lahā l-mu'allaqāt*). A poem from the collection of the Seven Odes was referred to as *al-wāḥida* (see al-Jumaḥī, *op. cit.*, 115); the poets of the Odes were called *aṣḥāb al-wāḥida* (ib., 128), as rightly explained by the Editor (ib., note 3). See the discussion of this problem al-Ḥaufī, *op. cit.*, 202–206.

[5] *Khizānat al-adab*, ed. 'Abd al-Salām Hārūn, Cairo 1967, I, 127.

[6] *Khizānat al-adab*, Cairo 1299 H, I, 519.

of the Arabs (*min mafākhiri l–'arabi*); they were suspended for a long time in the Ka'ba " and concludes that " people knew about the *mu'allaqāt* and their being suspended in the Ka'ba a long time before Ḥammād " [1].

A new light on the time of the compilation of the Seven Odes, the identity of their collectors, the purpose of the compilation and the changes it underwent, is shed in a significant passage of Aḥmad b. Abī Ṭāhir Ṭayfūr's (d. 280 H) *Kitāb al–manthūr wa–l–manẓūm* [2].

According to a tradition told on the authority of al–Ḥirmāzī [3] Mu'āwiya ordered the transmitters of poetry [4] to choose for him poems (*qaṣā'id*) which he would teach his son to recite; they chose for him twelve poems (*qaṣā'id*):

1. *Qifā nabki min dhikrā ḥabībin wa–manzilī* (Imru l–Qays)
2. *Li–Khaulata aṭlālun bi–burqati Thahmadī* (Ṭarafa)
3. *A–min Ummi Aufā dimnatun lam takallamī* (Zuhayr)
4. *Ādhanatnā bi–baynihā Asmā'ū* (al–Ḥārith b. Ḥilliza)
5. *'Afati l–diyāru maḥalluhā fa–muqāmuhā* (Labīd)
6. *Alā hubbī bi–ṣaḥniki fa–ṣbaḥīnā* ('Amr b. Kulthūm)
7. *In buddilat* [5] *min ahlihā wuḥūshan* ('Abīd b. al– Abraṣ)
8. *Basaṭat* [6] *Rābi'atu l–ḥabla lanā* (Suwayd b. Abī Kāhil)
9. *Yā dāra Mayyata bi–l– 'Alyā'i fa–l–Sanadī* (al–Nābigha)
10. *Yā dāra 'Ablata bi–l–Jiwā'i (takallamī)* ('Antara)

Al–Ḥirmāzī remarks that he thinks (*wa–aẓunnu*) that the two additional poems were:

11. *Waddi' Hurayrata inna l–rakba murtaḥilū* by al–A'shā
12. *(A–)sa'alta rasma l–dāri am lam tas'alī* by Ḥassān b. Thābit [7]

---

[1] *Maṣādir al–shi'r al–jāhilī*, 170–171; comp. Abū l–Baqā' Hibatu llāh: *al–Manāqib al–mazyadiyya*, Ms. Br. Mus. f. 38b: *wa–qālū: mafākhiru l–'arabi thalāthatun: qaṣīdatu l–Ḥārithi bni Ḥillizata l–Yashkuriyyi... wa–qaṣīdatu 'Amri bni Kulthūmin l–Taghlibiyyi... wa–qaṣīdatu Ṭarafata bni l–'Abdi...*

[2] Ms. Br. Mus., Add. 18532, ff. 49a–50a; on Aḥmad b. Abī Ṭāhir see FUAT SEZGIN: *Geschichte des Arabischen Schrifttums*, Leiden 1967 I, 348–349.

[3] Al–Ḥasan b. 'Alī al–Ḥirmāzī. See on him al–Marzubānī, *op. cit.*, 208–210; Yāqūt, *op. cit.*, IX, 24–27.

[4] In the text: *qāla l–Ḥirmāziyyu: wa–qad ruwiya anna Mu'āwiyata min al–ruwāti an yantakhibū lahu qaṣā'ida yurawwīhā bnahu*; I read: *amara l–ruwāta...*

[5] In the text: *in tubuddilat.*

[6] In the text: *nashaṭat.*

[7] Aḥmad b. Abī Ṭāhir Ṭayfūr, *op. cit.*, f. 50 a.

Another tradition told on the authority of al–Ḥirmāzī traced back to some scholars (... *annahu qāla: dhakara lī ghayru wāḥidin min al–'ulamā'i* ...) gives a valuable report about the selection of the Seven Odes carried out by 'Abd al–Malik. "The number of seven odes", states al–Ḥirmāzī, "was fixed by 'Abd al–Malik and he collected them" (*anna l–sab'a l–qaṣā'ida llatī sabba'ahā 'Abdu l–Maliki bnu Marwāna wa–jama'ahā*). No one in the Jāhiliyya ever collected them (*wa–lam yakun fī l–jāhiliyyati man jama'ahā qaṭṭu*). People consider, says al–Ḥirmāzī, that in the Jāhiliyya period they were made use of in prayer (*wa–l–nāsu yarauna annahu kāna yuṣallā bihā fī l–jāhiliyyati*)[1]. Al–Ḥirmāzī records six odes chosen by 'Abd al–Malik in the following order:

1. *Alā hubbī bi–ṣaḥniki fa–ṣbaḥīnā*	by 'Amr b. Kulthūm
2. *Ādhanatnā bi–baynihā Asmā'ū*	by al–Ḥārith b. Ḥilliza
3. *Basaṭat Rābi'atu l–ḥabla lanā*	by Suwayd b. Abī Kāhil
4. *A–min al–manūni (wa–)raybihā tatawajja'ū*	by Abū Dhu'ayb al–Hudhalī
5. *In buddilat min ahlihā wuḥūshan*	by 'Abīd b. al–Abraṣ
6. *Yā dāra 'Ablata bi–l–Jiwā'i*[2] *takallamī*	by 'Antara

Al–Ḥirmāzī continues: "Then 'Abd al–Malik stumbled and came to a halt in the choice of the seventh ode (*qāla: thumma urtija 'alā 'Abdi l–Maliki l–sābi 'atu*). At that moment his son, Sulaymān, then a young boy, entered into his presence and recited the poem of Aus b. Maghrā' in which the poet says:

Muḥammadun[3] *khayru man yamshī 'alā qadamin*
wa–ṣāḥibāhū wa–'Uthmānu bnu 'Affānā[4].
Muhammad is the best of those who walk on feet
and his two Companions and 'Uthmān b. 'Affān.

---

[1] This expression is not clear; it may probably denote that they were venerated, esteemed and respected by the people of the Jāhiliyya.

[2] In Ms. *bi–Liwā'in*.

[3] In Ms. *Muḥammadun ṣallā llāhu 'alayhi wa–ālihi*.

[4] Al–Jumaḥī, *op. cit.*, 410 records some verses of this poem. But the verse quoted by Ibn Abī Ṭāhir consists of the first hemistich of verse four and the second hemistich of verse two, as recorded by al–Jumaḥī. The verses of Aus

'Abd al-Malik became impassioned in favour of the poem (*wa-ta'aṣṣaba lahā*) and said *maghghirūhā* i.e. include the poem of Ibn Maghrā' in with them (i.e. with the six afore-mentioned ones – *fa-qāla 'Abdu l-Maliki, wa-ta'aṣṣaba lahā, maghghirūhā ay adkhilū qaṣīdata bni Maghrā'a fīhā*) [1].

There is no reason to cast a doubt about the authenticity of these two accounts of al-Ḥirmāzī. The deep interest of Mu'āwiya in poetry, his close contacts with contemporary poets and the high esteem in which he held them are well attested [2]. 'Abd al-Malik's familiarity with poetry was not less than that of Mu'āwiya [3]. The circumstances mentioned for the composition of the collection by Mu'āwiya for the prince (it was probably Yazīd) are quite plausible: Mu'āwiya wanted to give him a literary education in the manner of Arab society, to teach him the poems which were considered the best and probably most widely discussed and recited in the circles of chiefs and governors[4] whom he had

---

b. Maghrā' are mentioned by al-Jumaḥī in connection with the story of a contest between al-Akhṭal and Jarīr in the presence of al-Walīd b. 'Abd al-Malik. When al-Akhṭal recited the poem of 'Amp b. Kulthūm - al-Walīd urged Jarīr to recite the poem of Aus b. Maghrā' saying, exactly as in the text of Ibn Abī Ṭāhir, *maghghir yā Jarīr*. *L'A*, s.v. *m gh r* mentions that 'Abd al-Malik bade Jarīr to recite the verses of Ibn Maghrā' saying *maghghir* (but the verses are not quoted). Comp. al-Zamakhsharī: *al-Fā'iq*, ed. al-Bijāwī-Muḥ. Abū l-Faḍl Ibrāhīm, Cairo 1948, III, 40 ('Abd al-Malik: *maghghir yā Jarīr*). Ibn Ḥajar al-'Asqalānī in his *Iṣāba*, Cairo 1323 H, I, 118, n. 495 records the verse as quoted in the Ms. and mentions the opinion of Ibn Abī Ṭāhir about the poem of Aus b. Maghrā': " nobody composed a poem nicer than this ".

On Aus b. Maghrā' see: al-Aṣma'ī: *Fuḥūlat al-shu'arā'*, ed. Khafājī-Zaynī, Cairo 1953, 44; al-Balādhurī: *Ansāb al-ashrāf*, Ms., f. 1046b; Ibn Qutayba: *al-shi'r wa-l-shu'arā'*, ed. M. J. de Goeje, Leiden 1904, 432; al-Bakrī: *Simṭ al-la' ālī*, ed. al-Maymanī, Cairo 1936, 795; *al-Aghānī*, index; Shauqī Ḍayf: *al-Taṭawwur wa-l-tajdīd fī l-shi'r al-umawī*, Cairo 1965, 20.

On the daughter of Aus b. Maghrā', Zaynab, see al-Balādhurī, *op. cit.*, Ms. f. 397a.

On the son of Aus b. Maghrā', Wabr, see *Naqā'iḍ*, ed. A. A. Bevan, Leiden 1909, 717–718; M. Nallino: *An-Nābiġah al-Ġa'dī e le sue poesie*, *RSO*, 1934, 393–399; idem: *Le poesie di an-Nābiġah al-Ġa'dī*, Roma 1953, 135–136.

[1] Ibn Abī Ṭāhir, *op. cit.*, f. 50a.

[2] See e.g. *Aghānī*, index; al-Suyūṭī: *Ta'rīkh al-khulafā'*, ed. Muḥ. Muḥyi l-Dīn 'Abd al-Ḥamīd, Cairo 1952, 202–203; Ibn Abī l-Ḥadīd: *Sharḥ nahj al-balāgha*, ed. Muḥ. Abū l-Faḍl Ibrāhīm, Cairo 1964, XX, 156; al-Balādhurī, *op. cit.*, Ms. ff. 348b, 349a, 350a, 352a, 354b, 355a, 357b, 359a, 361a–363b, 364b–365b, 367b, 370a–b, etc.

[3] See e.g. *Aghānī*, index; al-Suyūṭī, *op. cit.*, 220–221; Ibn Abī l-Ḥadīd, *op. cit.*, XX, 161–165; Kuthayyir 'Azza: *Dīwān*, ed. H. Pérès, Alger 1930, index.

[4] See J. Obermann: *Early Islam* (in R. C. Dentan's -ed.- *The Idea of History in the Ancient Near East*, Yale University Press 1966, 289): " ... genealogy and poetry

to meet. It was the heritage of Arabism which he had to absorb and display. It was probably the same aim that 'Abd al-Malik pursued when he decided to compile his anthology: to educate the crown prince within the Arabic tradition of poetry. It was evidently the same reason which caused al-Manṣūr to employ al-Mufaḍḍal al-Ḍabbī and to engage him to compile the anthology of the *Mufaḍḍaliyyāt* [1].

Ibn Abī Ṭāhir furnishes us with important details about the Seven Long Odes (*al-qaṣā'idu l-sab'u l-ṭuwalu*), current in his period, in the third century of the Hijra. He records two lists. In the first list he enumerates eight poems in the following order:

1. Imru l-Qays: *Qifā nabki min dhikrā ḥabībin wa-manzili*
2. Ṭarafa: *Li-Khaulata aṭlālun bi-burqati Thahmadi*
3. 'Abīd b. al-Abraṣ: *Aqfara min ahlihi Malḥūbu*
4. Zuhayr b. Abī Sulmā [2]
5. 'Antara [2]
6. Labīd [2]
7. 'Amr b. Kulthūm [2]
8. Al-Ḥārith b. Ḥilliza [2]

Ibn Abī Ṭāhir attempts an assessment of the merits of the odes. He mentions the opinion of scholars that the Seven Odes surpassed all other poems because of the many themes which they contained; they had no match.

The *qaṣīda* of Imru l-Qays contained themes superior to those of other (poets); other poets derived theirs from him and based their poems on his poetry.

The *qaṣīda* of Ṭarafa is one of the best odes written by one of the *Aṣḥāb al-wāḥida* [3]. He closed it with the most eloquent proverb: *sa-tubdī laka l-ayyāmu mā kunta jāhilan: wa-ya'tīka bi-l-akhbāri man lam tuzawwidi*. Some poets of the period of the Jāhiliyya tried to compose a poem like this, but without success.

---

must be seen to enjoy far greater popularity in the early Islamic era than Koran and Ḥadīṯ"; and see Shauqī Ḍayf, *op. cit.*, 145–146.

[1] See R. SELLHEIM: *Prophet, Chalif und Geschichte*, Oriens, 18–19, 1967, 41: "Natürlich musste der junge Prinz als künftiger Regent des islamischen Reiches, als höchster Vertreter der muslimischen Gemeinde, als Verwandter des Propheten mit der Kultur und Geschichte der arabischen Ahnen vertraut sein".

[2] The poem is not mentioned.

[3] See note 4, p. 28, above.

No one in the Jāhiliyya, except Dhū l–Iṣba' al–'Adwānī, composed a poem in the metre and *'arūḍ* of the poem of 'Abīd b. al–Abraṣ: *aqfara min ahlihi Malḥūbu* [1]; this poem of Dhū l–Iṣba' is more likely to be an eloquent speech than a *qaṣīda*.

The *qaṣīda* of Zuhayr has no match in its description of the war, in what he says about peace, in the manner he made reproaches and in the proverbs he used.

The *qaṣīda* of 'Antara surpassed other poems by the use of descriptive passages and by expressions of bravery. Every poet borrowed from it.

The *qaṣīda* of Labīd is the best of his poems (*'aynu shi'rihi*) and contains beautiful themes. It was therefore incorporated into the collection of the odes though Labīd is not like them (i.e. he is inferior to the poets of the odes).

The *qaṣīdas* of 'Amr b. Kulthūm and al–Ḥārith b. Ḥilliza are concerned with approximately the same theme, they produced fine poems, but they are not like the preceding ones (i.e. they are inferior to them).

Some people, continues Aḥmad b. Abī Ṭāhir, added to the Seven Odes the *qaṣīda* of al–Nābigha concerning the subject of apology; it is unique in this matter. As this *qaṣīda* is the best of al–Nābigha's poetry, some people incorporated this poem: *Yā dāra Mayyata bi–l–'Alyā'i wa–l–Sanadi* into the (collection of) Seven Odes. The author quotes a saying of Abū 'Amr b. al–'Alā' stating that Zuhayr does not deserve to be a hireling of al–Nābigha, remarks however that, in his opinion, Abū 'Amr erred [2].

The *qaṣīda* of al–A'shā: *Waddi' Hurayrata inna l–rakba murtaḥilu* is excellently done but it stands in no relation to the afore–mentioned odes.

" General consent ", concludes Ibn Abī Ṭāhir, " is in accordance with what we have said " (i.e. about the eight odes, without the additional ones) [3].

In another passage Ibn Abī Ṭāhir records the second list of the Seven Odes. Here only seven poems are mentioned. The order of the poems is different.

" We found the transmitters agreed upon the Seven Long Jāhilī Odes ", says Ibn Abī Ṭāhir (*wa–lladhī wajadnā 'alayhi l–ruwāta mujtami-'īna fī qaṣā'ida l–sab'u l–ṭuwalu l–jāhiliyyātu*):

---

[1] See on the metre of this *qaṣīda* the note of Lyall in his edition of the *Dīwān* of 'Abīd, Leyden 1913, 5, note I.

[2] See this saying quoted: Ibn Abī l–Ḥadīd, *op. cit.*, XX, 161.

[3] Ibn Abī Ṭāhir, *op. cit.*, f. 49a–49b.

1. Imru l–Qays: *Qifā nabki*
2. Zuhayr: *A–min Ummi Aufā*
3. Ṭarafa: *Li–Khaulata aṭlālun*
4. 'Amr b. Kulthūm: *Alā hubbī*
5. 'Antara: *Hal ghādara l–shu'arā'u*
6. Labīd: *'Afati l–diyāru*
7. Al–Ḥārith b. Ḥilliza: *Ādhanatnā bi–baynihā Asmā'u*

Some people, says Ibn Abī Ṭāhir, incorporated (*wa–minhum man adkhala*) into the collection:

1. 'Abīd: *Aqfara min ahlihi Malḥūbu*
2. Al–A'shā: *Waddi' Hurayrata inna l–rakba murtaḥilu*
3. Al–Nābigha: *Yā dāra Mayyata bi–l–'Alyā'i wa–l–Sanadi*

" We have not found them ", concludes Ibn Abī Ṭāhir, " mentioning other poems except these, composed by these first class poets in accordance with what we have mentioned about their selection " (*wa–lam najidhum dhakarū ghayra hādhihi l–qaṣā'idi li–hā'ulā'i l–mutaqaddimīna li–mā dhakarnā min ikhtiyārihim*) [1].

The ten poets of these Jāhiliyya Odes are considered by Abū 'Ubayda the excelling poets of the Jāhiliyya (*wa–qāla Abū 'Ubaydata: ash'aru shu'arā'i l–jāhiliyyati 'asharatun, awwaluhum Imru l–Qaysi*...etc.) [2].

The account of Ibn Abī Ṭāhir shows clearly that the collectors of the odes started almost immediately with the establishment of the Umayyad rule. The collection of Mu'āwiya contained twelve odes and was intended as an anthology for the education of his son (apparently the crown prince). The expression *yurawwihā bnahu* does not make it possible to decide whether these odes were written down or not. The anthology of Mu'āwiya contained indeed the ten poems which form te collection of the *mu'allaqāt*. The two additional poems were of two contemporaries: Suwayd b. Abī Kāhil and Ḥassān b. Thābit. Suwayd b. Abī Kāhil was a famous poet [3] and his *qaṣīda* was known

---

[1] Ib., f. 50a; for the variants of *al–mutaqaddimīn* see e.g. Ibn Qutayba, *op. cit.*, 141, " a " (*al–ma'dūdīn* and *al–muqaddamīn*).

[2] Al–'Abbās b. 'Alī al–Ḥusaynī al–Mūsawī: *Nuzhatu l–jalīs wa–munyatu l–adīb l–anīs*, Najaf 1968, II, 182; and comp. Ibn Sharaf al–Qayrawānī: *Rasā'il al–intiqād* (in Kurd 'Alī's *Rasā'il al–bulaghā'*, Cairo 1946, 314–316).

[3] See on him: Ibn Qutayba, *op. cit.*, 92, 141, 250–251; *Aghānī*, XI, 165–167; al–Bakrī: *Simṭ al–la'ālī*, 313; Ibn Ḥajar: *al–Iṣāba*, III, 172, no.

as *al-yatīma* in the time of the Jāhiliyya; it contained many *ḥikam* and was probably therefore incorporated into the collection [1]. Ḥassān b. Thābit was an adherent of 'Uthmān and favoured Mu'āwiya. The poem itself is a Jāhilī one and is therefore considered a fine one [2].

'Abd al-Malik reduced the number of the odes from twelve to seven. He included however among these seven odes two odes which were not contained in the selection of Mu'āwiya: the *qaṣīda* of Abū Dhu'ayb and the *qaṣīda* of Aus b. Maghrā', both poets who composed their poems in the period of Islam. The tendency of 'Abd al-Malik in his incorporation of the *qaṣīda* of Aus is obvious and can be gauged from the verse recited by his son Sulaymān: the Prophet is mentioned with his two Companions (i.e. Abū Bakr and 'Umar) and 'Uthmān b. 'Affān. 'Alī is not mentioned. This was in perfect harmony with the Umayyad idea of the legitimacy of the Muslim government. The *qaṣīda* of Abū Dhu'ayb was included in the anthology of 'Abd al-Malik because of its popularity: already Mu'āwiya, according to tradition, recited verses of this *qaṣīda* before his death [3].

The tradition about the compilation of the anthology of the Seven Odes, begun by Mu'āwiya and concluded by 'Abd al-Malik, fell into oblivion probably due to the fall of the Umayyad dynasty and the victory of the Abbasids. Scholars of a later period apparently were not satisfied with the selection of 'Abd al-Malik and returned to the

---

3716; IBN DURAYD: *al-Ishtiqāq*, ed. 'Abd al-Ṣalām Hārūn, Cairo 1958, 340–341; *al-Mufaḍḍaliyyāt*, ed. Lyall, Introduction, p. XIV; Ṣadr al-Dīn al-Baṣrī, *al-Ḥamāsa al-baṣriyya*, ed. Mukhtār al-Dīn Aḥmad, Hyderabad 1964, I, 94; IBN QUTAYBA: *'Uyūn al-akhbār*, Cairo 1928, II, 10; al-Baghdādī: *Khizānat al-adab*, Cairo 1299 H, II, 546–548; Abū Ḥanīfa al-Dīnawarī: *al-Akhbār al-ṭiwāl*, ed. 'Abd al-Mun'im 'Āmir—Jamāl al-Dīn al-Shayyāl, Cairo 1960, 308; Muḥ. 'Alyān al-Marzūqī: *Mashāhid al-inṣāf 'alā shawāhid al-kashshāf*, Cairo 1354 H, 72 (appended to al-Zamakhsharī's *Kashshāf*); Muḥ. Bāqir al-Sharīf: *al-Jāmi' al-shawāhid*, Iṣbahān 1380 H, II, 25; al-Anṣārī: *Mughnī l-labīb 'an kutub al-a'ārīb*, ed. Muḥ. Muḥyi l-Dīn 'Abd al-Ḥamīd, Cairo, al-Maktaba al-tijāriyya, n.d., I, 328, n. 533; idem: *Shudhūr al-dhahab fī ma'rifati kalām al-'arab*, ed. Muḥ. Muḥyi l-Dīn 'Abd al-Ḥamīd, Cairo 1942, 138, no. 63.

[1] See the contradictory opinions of OMAR A. FARRUKH: *Das Bild des Frühislam in der Arabischen Dichtung – von der Hiğra bis zum Tode 'Umar's*, Leipzig 1937, 22: 50, 98, 110 and Shauqī Ḍayf: *al-Taṭawwur wa-l-tajdīd fī l-shi'r al-umawī*, p. 20 about whether this qaṣīda is a Jāhilī one or it is influenced by the teachings of Islam.

[2] See the opinion of al-Aṣma'ī: *hādhā Ḥassānu bnu Thābitin faḥlun min fuḥūli l-jāhiliyyati fa-lammā jā'a l-islāmu saqaṭa shi'ruhu* (Ibn Qutayba: *al-Shi'r wa-l-shu'arā'*, 170).

[3] See al-Balādhurī, *op. cit.*, f. 380a.

anthology of Mu'āwiya. They confined themselves to the Seven Jāhilī Odes upon which " the scholars unanimously agreed " and which form the popular anthology of the seven *mu'allaqāt* to the present day. The odes of Suwayd b. Abī Kāhil and Ḥassān b. Thābit were eliminated. The three additional odes of the collection of Mu'āwiya ('Abīd, al-Nābigha, al-A'shā) were in fact incorporated in a wider anthology already in the third century of the Hijra, as attested by Ibn Abī Ṭāhir; this was the collection of the Ten Odes which is in fact transmitted even today.

The merit of Ḥammād seems to have been that he transmitted the Seven Jāhilī Odes derived from the collection of Mu'āwiya and that he discarded the collection of 'Abd al-Malik. Later literary tradition attributed the selection to Ḥammād.

In the third century these Odes gained wide acclaim and children were taught them in the *kuttāb* [1].

---

[1] Ibn Abī Ṭāhir, *op. cit.*, f. 49b.

INDEX